Studies in Church History

48

THE CHURCH AND LITERATURE

THE CHURCH AND LITERATURE

EDITED BY

PETER CLARKE

and

CHARLOTTE METHUEN

PUBLISHED FOR
THE ECCLESIASTICAL HISTORY SOCIETY
BY
THE BOYDELL PRESS
2012

First published 2012

A publication of the Ecclesiastical History Society
in association with The Boydell Press
an imprint of Boydell & Brewer Ltd
PO Box 9, Woodbridge, Suffolk IP12 3DF, UK
and of Boydell & Brewer Inc.
668 Mt Hope Avenue, Rochester, NY 14620-2731, USA
website: www.boydellandbrewer.com

ISBN 978-0-95468-099-2

ISSN 0424-2084

A CIP catalogue record for this book is available
from the British Library

The publisher has no responsibility for the continued existence or accuracy
of URLs for external or third-party internet websites referred to in this
book, and does not guarantee that any content on such websites is, or will
remain, accurate or appropriate.

Details of previous volumes are available from Boydell & Brewer Ltd

Produced by Toynbee Editorial Services Ltd
Typeset in Bembo Std

Papers used by Boydell & Brewer Ltd are natural, recyclable products
made from wood grown in sustainable forests

Printed in Great Britain by
CPI Antony Rowe, Chippenham and Eastbourne

CONTENTS

PREFACE

When 'The Church and Literature' was proposed by Dr Sheridan Gilley as the theme for his presidency of the Ecclesiastical History Society in 2010–11, it prompted strong approval but also much debate within the society's committee. Some considered the theme too broad, but Dr Gilley wished to keep the theme as broad as possible so that it would attract a wide response and result in a volume of wide interest. The editors of SCH certainly received offers of a wide range of communications in relation to the theme, and in order to keep the Summer Meeting and the year's volume to manageable proportions, we had to make a rigorous selection among them. Two main interpretations of the theme have emerged: the representation of the Church and its teachings in literature; and the influence of different literary genres on Christian writing. Not all the literary works discussed here might be seen as 'canonical' but they all address Christian themes and sometimes reached extensive Christian readerships, particularly in the nineteenth and twentieth centuries. The contributions edited here comprise seven plenary papers given at the Summer Meeting in 2010 and Winter Meeting in 2011, and a selection of the communications delivered at the Summer Meeting.

The editors are grateful to those who chaired communication sessions at the Summer Meeting and peer-reviewed with such thoughtful expertise and efficiency the communications offered for publication. We are also grateful to the authors of all papers in the volume for their timely and cooperative responses to our requests for revisions, and we and the society remain much indebted to the assistant editor, Dr Tim Grass, for his sterling copy-editorial work. We further thank the society for continuing to fund his essential post.

The society wishes to thank the University of St Andrews for hosting the Summer Meeting and Dr Williams's Library, London, for accommodating the Winter Meeting. It is also grateful to the conference secretary, Professor Michael Walsh, for organizing both meetings, and to Stephen Holmes for arranging the excursion which concluded the Summer Meeting. Finally, the society is grateful to Professor Tony Claydon, outgoing co-editor of SCH, for leading the Round Table together with Peter Clarke in its customary exploration of the president's theme across all periods of church history and in the light of the papers presented at the Summer Meeting, the academic proceedings of which it concluded.

Peter Clarke
University of Southampton

Charlotte Methuen
University of Glasgow

ILLUSTRATIONS

CONTRIBUTORS

Daniel ANLEZARK
> Senior Lecturer and Associate Dean (Undergraduate),
> Department of English, University of Sydney

Clyde BINFIELD
> Professor Emeritus in History, University of Sheffield

John BONEHAM
> Assistant to the Sub-Administrator, Westminster Cathedral

Philip BROADHEAD
> Pro-Warden (Students and Learning Development),
> Goldsmiths, University of London

David BROOKS
> Lecturer in History, Queen Mary, University of London

Renie CHOY (*EHS postgraduate bursary*)
> Postgraduate Student, University of Oxford

Thomas N. CORNS
> Professor of English, Bangor University

Eamon DUFFY
> Professor of the History of Christianity, University of
> Cambridge

David N. DUMVILLE
> Sixth-Century Professor in History, Palaeography and
> Celtic, University of Aberdeen

Jessica Lee EHINGER
> Postgraduate Student, University of Oxford

Benjamin L. FISCHER
> Assistant Professor of English, Northwest Nazarene
> University, Nampa, Idaho

Sarah FOOT
> Regius Professor of Ecclesiastical History, University of
> Oxford

Sheridan GILLEY
> Emeritus Reader in Theology, Durham University

Crawford GRIBBEN
>Long Room Hub Associate Professor in Early Modern
>Print Culture, School of English, Trinity College Dublin

Bernard HAMILTON
>Professor Emeritus of Crusading History, University of
>Nottingham

Colin HAYDON
>Reader in Early Modern History, University of
>Winchester

George HERRING
>Part-time Tutor, Centre for Lifelong Learning, York
>University

Kathleen JAEGER
>Inglis Professor, University of King's College, Halifax, Nova
>Scotia

Oliver LOGAN
>Lecturer in European History, University of East Anglia
>(retired)

Judith MALTBY
>Chaplain and Fellow, Corpus Christi College, and Reader
>in Church History, University of Oxford

Stuart MEWS
>Reader Emeritus in Religious Studies, University of
>Gloucestershire

Katharine K. OLSON
>Lecturer in Medieval and Early Modern History, Bangor
>University; Postdoctoral Fellow in Celtic Studies, Harvard
>University

George OPPITZ-TROTMAN (*EHS postgraduate bursary*; *Michael
J. Kennedy Postgraduate Prize*)
>British Academy Postdoctoral Fellow, University of Cambridge

W. B. PATTERSON
>Professor of History Emeritus, University of the South,
>Sewanee, Tennessee

Salvador RYAN
>Professor of Ecclesiastical History, St Patrick's College,
>Maynooth

Andrew SANDERS
>   Emeritus Professor of English Literature, Durham
>   University

Mark SMITH
>   University Lecturer in English Local and Social History,
>   University of Oxford

Martin SPENCE
>   Lecturer in the History of Christianity, International
>   Christian College, Glasgow

John TOOK
>   Professor of Dante Studies, University College, London

Caroline WATKINSON (*EHS postgraduate bursary*)
>   Postgraduate Student, Queen Mary, University of London

Peter WEBSTER
>   Editorial Controller, British History Online, Institute of
>   Historical Research

Martin WELLINGS
>   Methodist minister, Oxford

John WOLFFE
>   Professor of Religious History, Open University

ABBREVIATIONS

ACW	Ancient Christian Writers, ed. J. Quasten and J. C. Plumpe (New York etc, 1946–)
Add. MS	Additional Manuscript
AHR	*American Historical Review* (New York, 1895–)
AThR	*Anglican Theological Review* (New York / Evanston. IL, 1918–)
BL	British Library
Bodl.	Bodleian Library
CChr	Corpus Christianorum (Turnhout, 1953–)
CChr.SL	Corpus Christianorum, series Latina (1953–)
CHC	*Cambridge History of Christianity*, 9 vols (Cambridge, 2005–9)
ChH	*Church History* (New York / Chicago, 1932–)
CSEL	Corpus Scriptorum Ecclesiasticorum Latinorum (Vienna, 1866–)
DBI	*Dizionario biografico degli Italiani* (Rome, 1960–)
DWL	Dr. Williams's Library
EHR	*English Historical Review* (London, 1886–)
Ep.	*Epistulae / Epistolae*
ET	English translation
HistJ	*Historical Journal* (Cambridge, 1958–)
HThR	*Harvard Theological Review* (New York / Cambridge, MA, 1908–)
JBS	*Journal of British Studies* (Hartford, CT, 1961–)
JCS	*Journal of Celtic Studies* (Baltimore, MD, 1949–82; Aberdeen, 2004–)
JEH	*Journal of Ecclesiastical History* (Cambridge, 1950–)
JHI	*Journal of the History of Ideas* (London, 1940–)
JMH	*Journal of Modern History* (Chicago, IL, 1929–)
JRH	*Journal of Religious History* (Sydney / Oxford, 1960–)
LCL	Loeb Classical Library (London and Cambridge, MA, 1912–)
LPL	Lambeth Palace Library

MGH	Monumenta Germaniae Historica inde ab a. c. 500 usque ad a. 1500, ed. G. H. Pertz et al. (Hanover / Berlin etc., 1826–)
MGH AA	Monumenta Germaniae Historica, Auctores antiquissimi, 15 vols (1877–1919)
MGH Epp.	Monumenta Germaniae Historica, Epistolae (1887–)
MGH Epp. Sel.	Monumenta Germaniae Historica, Epistolae Selectae (1916–)
MGH SRL	Monumenta Germaniae Historica, Scriptores rerum Langobardicarum et Italicarum (1878)
MGH SRM	Monumenta Germaniae Historica, Scriptores rerum Merovingicarum (1884–1951)
MGH SS	Monumenta Germaniae Historica, Scriptores (in folio) (1826–)
NPNF I	A Select Library of the Nicene and Post-Nicene Fathers of the Christian Church, ed. P. Schaff, 14 vols (New York and Edinburgh etc., 1887–92 and subsequent edns)
NPNF II	A Select Library of the Nicene and Post-Nicene Fathers of the Christian Church: Second Series, ed. P. Schaff and H. Wace, 14 vols (New York and Oxford etc., 1890–1900 and subsequent edns)
NLW	National Library of Wales
ODNB	Oxford Dictionary of National Biography, ed. H. C. G. Matthew and Brian Harrison, 60 vols + index vol. (Oxford, 2004)
OED	Oxford English Dictionary
OMT	Oxford Medieval Texts (Oxford, 1971–)
P&P	Past and Present: A Journal of Scientific History (London / Oxford, 1952–)
PG	Patrologia Graeca, ed. J.-P. Migne, 161 vols (Paris, 1857–66)
PL	Patrologia Latina, ed. J.-P. Migne, 217 vols + 4 index vols (Paris, 1844–64)
RIA	Royal Irish Academy
s.a.	sub anno (under the year)
SC	Sources chrétiennes (Paris, 1941–)
SCH	Studies in Church History (London / Oxford / Woodbridge, 1964–)
SCJ	Sixteenth Century Journal (Kirksville, MO, 1970–2006)

s.n.	*sub nomine* (under the name)
Speculum	*Speculum: A Journal of Medieval Studies* (Cambridge, MA, 1925–)
s.v.	*sub verbo* (under the word)
TNA	The National Archives
TRHS	*Transactions of the Royal Historical Society* (London / Cambridge, 1871–)

INTRODUCTION

Christianity is the religion of a Book, the Bible, but the translation of its message into the culture of any era has vastly expanded the literature produced by Christianity. John Wesley called himself 'a man of one book', but his own prodigious literary output shows that he did not consider other books superfluous. The Bible has spawned millions of books, not only commentaries on its text, but also works which draw upon the manifold traditions which have come to surround it, some of them deriving from the Church's classical inheritance, some of them condemnatory of any rival form of secular literature, some of them the product of major literary movements, as of Romanticism in the nineteenth century. Any reader of this volume will be struck by the variety of literary genres and types that it addresses: letters, homilies, apologetic, apocalyptic, poetry, drama and novels. As the Ecclesiastical History Society passes its fiftieth year, the range of material studied in this volume with both criticism and understanding is testimony to the long-enduring breadth of spirit and catholicity of interests of the society itself.

There is a vast range of historical themes and problems which can be explored from literary material: practical behaviour and morality; attitudes to class and social order; Church–state relations; and secular and ecclesiastical politics. One recurring theme is the tension between Christianity and culture, as to whether literature is the ally or enemy of Christianity, reflecting a wider division within the tradition between holy worldliness and other-worldliness, between loving the world in order to convert it and rejecting the world and withdrawing from it. This volume gives particular attention to one form of interaction between religion and literature, the nineteenth-century novel, both as field of conflict between Protestants and Catholics and as evidence of a more tolerant religious atmosphere. The understanding of literature invoked here is a catholic one, with the aspirations to universality of Christianity itself.

It should also be obvious that this volume is the work of historians, and not primarily of literary critics interested in questions of style, unless this can be shown to be of wider historical significance. Thus Renie Choy shows how the clichéd formulas of the requests of ancient and early medieval letter-writers for the prayers of their correspondents were richly significant in bonding friendship and personal union between author and recipient, while seeking to effect urgent change across spiritual and geographical space. Daniel Anlezark enunciates the stress in the writings of Gregory the Great on Scripture rather than on pagan learning as the proper subject matter of a Christian's reading, and the distinction between Gregory's desire for monastic ascetic seclusion and contemplation and his response to the practical administrative demands of a Christian polity on earth, despite his belief in the approaching end of the world. This double emphasis on piety and practice passed to Gregory's English admirers and expositors, the Venerable Bede and King Alfred the Great, whose programme of cultural renewal included the translation of Gregory's *Pastoral Rule* and *Dialogues* into English.

The historical function of a literary text is significant. Jessica Lee Ehinger persuasively argues that the anti-Islamic Christian apologetic in surviving debates and letters in the eighth and ninth centuries is more a literary record of Christian arguments for Christians in a period of mass conversion to Islam than direct historical evidence of actual exchanges between Christians and Muslims. Underlying the Irish literature of chronicle and correspondence between 1066 and 1166 explored by David Dumville is the then-European movement for ecclesiastical reform, but this was linked to issues of apocalyptic, morality and the Scriptures, including catechetical *quaestiones* expressing a hair-splitting sense of humour, even diverging to explain a board game with seventy-two pieces. The indictment of ecclesiastical corruption and the need to separate the true papal spiritual authority from its abuse and from its secular political counterpart are among Dante's themes explored by John Took's study of *The Divine Comedy*, which describes the ever-deepening transformation of the soul and self through the horrors of hell, with its wealth of contemporary reference, through purgatory, under the sublime guidance of the pagan Virgil, and into heaven and the new life of Christ already present in believers through his sacramental Church, and so to the vision of the love which moves the sun and the other stars. As one of the greatest (perhaps the greatest) of Christian poets, Dante might also be regarded as the supreme Christian theologian.

In a study which ranges over Irish bardic poetry as well as preaching, hagiography and even travel literature, Salvador Ryan shows that there is a much greater variety and richness to the role of Christ's cross than is always recognized in the common account of the transition from an early medieval understanding of the cross as the instrument of Christ's triumph over sin and death to the later medieval depiction of the cross as a symbol of empathetic suffering. The two ideas coexisted, while the cross bore a poetically elaborated range of meanings: the cosmic light-giver; the intercessory means of salvation and consolation and of condemnation and damnation, of victory over demons and in battle and bringer of peace; and mother and refuge, there being a kind of *communicatio idiomatum* between Christ's body and the blood-soaked wood of the cross itself.

For the end of the Middle Ages, Katharine Olson explores the rich mauscript culture and Welsh literary tradition of 'The Great Century' in Wales, especially as a repository of religious devotion, and discusses the degree to which this can be said to have survived the Reformation. Here again, one is struck by the international content of late medieval religious life.

Philip Broadhead describes the manner in which Hans Sachs, the celebrated shoemaker, composer, poet and Mastersinger of Nuremberg, propagated the Reformation by casting portions of Luther's Bible into verse for public performance. His early compositions laid a heavy stress on the individual's duty to translate the Christian faith into charitable works; the later ones emphasized the need for such a translation to take an ordered and disciplined spiritual and communal form in a society ideally at unity with itself. On the other side, Eamon Duffy argues that Sir Thomas More's *Confutation* of William Tyndale's *Answer* to More's *Dialogue* is not evidence of personal loss of control in its literary form, with its copious quotations from his opponent, but is a matter of successful literary choice, later widely imitated. In its commitment to the punishment of the heresy of the Protestant martyrs and its ridicule of the marriage of monks and nuns in defiance of their vows of chastity, the *Confutation* affords evidence, not of More's guilty sexuality or hysteria and interior disintegration, but of the views of mainstream medieval Christendom. Here modern literary judgements have been influenced by continuing religious controversy.

George Oppitz-Trotman surveys the ambiguous yet powerful figure of Vice in Tudor drama, with its obscure origins and its associations with the themes of the actor as vagabond, of Catholicism and social disorder; its status as a figure of revenge in conflict with conscience and of moral weakness; and its connection with an anti-theatrical tradition in the theatre itself. Here again is evidence of the anti-literary strand in Christianity which did so much to make many Christians suspicious of the theatre.

W. B. Patterson shows that the puritan preacher William Perkins, in his *Arte of Prophecying*, advocated a direct and simple method of preaching which had a lasting importance for English prose and which took into account the varying levels of understanding of different categories of hearer, with an overall rhetorical concern for clear communication, in contrast to more flamboyant types of Tudor and Stuart pulpit style. Thomas Corns charts the evolution of John Milton's thought about the English Church from an initial rejection of both Calvinism and Prelacy and an aspiration to see the Church unite with foreign Protestants, with a subsequent progressive rejection of Presbyterian and Independent clerical ministries in favour of a Church requiring only the ministry of uneducated laymen. Milton's commitments to religious toleration and to freedom of expression were associated with his interest in legislation in favour of divorce, proceeding from an understanding of Christianity, usually tolerant and undogmatic (though anti-Catholic), with marked affinities to the views of many lay Anglicans today. In Sachs, Perkins and Milton we see Protestantism creating its own new literary culture.

There is also a contemporary reference to the modern preoccupation with priestly paedophilia in Colin Haydon's study of eighteenth-century English anti-Catholic pornography, especially the publications about the scandal of the Jesuit Jean-Baptiste Girard and his ecstatic penitent Marie-Catherine Cadière. The essay relates the genre of anti-Catholicism to the unpopularity of the 'out-group', from the early Christians to the modern Methodists, as well as to the enduring British Protestant repugnance at the confessional and at sacerdotal and conventual celibacy, alleged to be the origin of every sexual perversion, a preoccupation popular in the nineteenth century and today.

A quite different view from that of the convent as an object of sexual fantasy occurs in Caroline Watkinson's account of the eighteenth-century literature recording visits to English convents on the Continent. English travellers tended to judge them well as English institutions abroad. In some cases, these tourists wanted to convince their readers of their own tolerance, but they also sympathetically recorded 'an image of nuns as sociable and engaged', cheerful and agreeable, in a more mixed depiction of conventualism than one might expect from the conception of Britain as a bastion of anti-Catholic Protestant nationalism. The theme of the alien recurs in Benjamin Fischer's argument that because the fast expanding world of British Protestant Evangelicalism in the late eighteenth and early nineteenth century was opposed to the increasing popularity of novels and of secular periodicals, it found a counterweight to the excitements of fiction in the exotic factuality of the travelogues and biographies of missionaries.

Where Evangelicals at first tended to oppose the new Romantic culture even while drawing upon it, the Oxford Movement tried to make it Catholic. John Boneham demonstrates the literary importance of the movement's principle of reserve, of faith as the appropriation of the Christian mystery by the religious mind and heart, with the concomitant idea that the mystery was better conveyed in poetry than in prose. In his three poems, *The Cathedral*, *The Baptistery* and *The Altar*, the Tractarian poet Isaac Williams draws on imagery from ecclesiastical architecture and art as well as from nature as the work of its creator, to expound the doctrines of the eucharistic sacrifice, apostolic succession through episcopal and priestly ministry, and tradition. George Herring shows how another Tractarian cleric, W. E. Heygate, attempted in his novel *William Blake* to depict an idealized reforming English country parson and his conversion to high churchmanship of a young farmer. This had its social dimension in the aspiration to reduce class barriers through social paternalism, though this was not very effective in society at large. The difficult relationship between religion and culture recurs in Kathleen Jaeger's account of the Roman Catholic convert and novelist Lady Georgiana Fullerton, who experienced a deep division within herself, exacerbated by her confessor Fr Frederick Faber, between her ' "personality" as an artist and her "character" as a religious', discouraging to her literary activity and suggesting no easy resolution of the problem of Christian and worldly modes of life.

The huge increase in the volume of nineteenth-century popular fiction was exploited by a host of Christian writers. Martin Spence shows how an evangelical competition open to working men, on the value of the Sabbath, drew on Romantic and democratic arguments as well as explicitly scriptural ones. The Protestant adoption of the once suspect genre of the novel appears in Mark Smith's sketch of the nineteenth-century English fiction about the 'aboriginal Protestant' Waldensians of the Savoy, which depicted them as poor but godly and industrious peasant mountaineers, the victims of Catholic persecution. Anti-Jesuitism was also common among Catholics, and John Wolffe's analysis of anti-Jesuit novels discerns a frequent distinction between evil Jesuits and other, innocent, Catholics. Described by David Brooks as in a class of its own is Benjamin Disraeli's imaginative blend of Anglo-Catholicism, philo-Judaism and nationalist Tory paternalism in his celebrated 'Young England' trilogy of novels urging the moral renewal of English society in the 1840s.

The reader returns to the literary heights with the religion of Charles Dickens. Here Andrew Sanders rejects the idea of a purely secular or humanitarian Dickens, instancing his reverence for the person of Christ and for the New Testament, his profession of Christianity to his children, and his preoccupation, most obviously in *A Tale of Two Cities*, with the theme of the Resurrection, both here and in the hereafter. There is an affinity here with Milton's lay Christianity reaching across the centuries.

The softening of denominational differences appears in Clyde Binfield's account, in the mingling of political radicalism, Anglicanism and Nonconformity in the novels, based upon different generations of one family, by Ada Ellen Bayly under her pen name of Edna Lyall. Martin Wellings shows how the best-selling novels of the enormously prolific Cornish brothers Silas and Joseph Hocking, both sometime ministers of the United Methodist Free Churches, preached an increasingly nondenominational practical and undogmatic Christianity representing the place of the fast expanding body of Nonconformist readers in the wider British culture.

Bernard Hamilton suggests that the lack of polemic in literary references to the papacy, a very mixed bag which includes the works of Frederick Rolfe and Ronald Firbank, might have to do with the diminished importance of the popes after the loss of papal temporal power in 1870. On the other hand, in Oliver Logan's exposition, the militantly ultramontane Fr Antonio Bresciani's novels, originally serialized in the Roman Jesuit gazette *La Civiltà Cattolica*, attacked the *Risorgimento* and Freemasonry through novels of conversion to Catholicism, with youthful heroes and heroines whose passions are tamed by Jesuit pastoral sensitivity. Particularly striking is Fr Bresciani's depiction of women as both tender and tough, and readers may be tempted to learn more about Olga the Croat 'who has managed to join the Austrian army' and Ermine the Eskimo maiden, 'sensitive and compassionate, who can gut a bear and fell a maddened bison with a single pistol-shot'. One imagines Pio Nono putting up his feet in the evening for a good fictional read.

My own essay on the Catholic novelist Canon Patrick Augustine Sheehan attempts to show how through the plots of his novels he comments on many aspects of his faith and his country; 'on the strengths and weaknesses of Irish clerical training and of the Irish Catholic clergy, on the Church's role in Irish life, on the central role of women, on the Irish nationalist tradition in both its constitutional and revolutionary forms, on Irish poverty, capitalism, strikes and emigration to America, on the need for the regeneration of Irish culture through a Catholic literature, and on English landlordism and colonialism and their effects on Irish life'.

Judith Maltby draws attention to the highly literary foundation and character of the novelist Rose Macaulay's commitment to Anglicanism. While dissenting from the destruction wrought by the Reformation, subscribing to a High Anglican view of English church history and professing a strong sacramentalism, she was repelled by the realistic symbolism and doctrinal sharpness of both Anglican papalism and Roman Catholicism. Peter Webster underlines the continuing moral consensus between Church and state in England in the convention under which the Lord Chamberlain, as licenser of the theatre, sometimes consulted the archbishop of Canterbury about plays with a moral or religious theme. The loss of this moral consensus and the gap between the Victorians and their successors within the Church as well as in society at large underlie Stuart Mews's account of the controversy surrounding Bishop John Robinson's testimony in court in 1960 on behalf of

D. H. Lawrence's novel *Lady Chatterley's Lover*. Sarah Foot suggests that the modern detective story with a monastic detective depicts the medieval monastery without much realism as a vaguely semi-Anglican pseudo-medieval pre-modern Eden of peace, which is unspecific about monastic observance itself, a refuge from modern secular sin and chaos: when it is disturbed by a murder, there is an Eden to be restored.

If the medieval monastic novel is clearly a reflection of modern culture, despite its setting, another popular form clearly stands in opposition to modernity in general. Crawford Gribben analyses another best-selling form of literature, the 'Left Behind' novels of the Rapture, drawing on the evangelical pre-millennial dispensational theory of the imminent return of Christ to sweep believers to heaven while leaving the rest in a period of tribulation and conflict with Antichrist on earth. More especially, Gribben shows the prevalence of an activist individualism in this literature, its neglect of prayer and other departures from the pre-existing evangelical tradition, and its counter-cultural anxiety about its own possible marginalization and failure.

With Dr Gribben, the reader may feel that much of the literature surveyed here is of no very great literary quality, embodying the paradox of an anti-literary literature, but all is grist to the mill of the historian, and popular taste may be more revealing of matters of great historical moment than the high literature of a cultivated elite. From Gregory the Great to Dante, from Milton to Dickens, the subject has its peaks as well as its troughs, but the troughs can be as interesting as the peaks. The Word was made flesh in Christ, and is also transmitted through the material in sacraments and sacramentals and in visual art. But the transition from the religion of the Word into other words has an importance which historians cannot neglect if they wish to understand Christian culture and its relationship to ecclesiastical history.

Sheridan Gilley
Durham University

SEEKING MEANING BEHIND EPISTOLARY CLICHÉS: INTERCESSORY PRAYER CLAUSES IN CHRISTIAN LETTERS

by RENIE CHOY

The letter, as the format of twenty-one of the twenty-seven documents in the canonical New Testament, is arguably the literary form which has played the most significant role in the history of Christianity. But scholars have often been troubled by how to treat the conventions framing Christian letters: since little of Christian literature from its earliest time to the medieval period escapes the influence of classical traditions of rhetoric, can constant epistolary formulas be taken as expressions of genuine sentiment?[1] In fact, it is precisely because the lines between classical influence and Christian innovation are so difficult to make out that E. R. Curtius was able to argue that the humility formula of medieval charters, for so long assumed to have originated in Paul, was in fact a pagan Hellenistic prototype like scores of other rhetorical conventions. His study of the formula serves, Curtius writes, to 'furnish a warning against making the Middle Ages more Christian or more pious than it was', and to demonstrate that 'a constant literary formula must not be regarded as the expression of spontaneous sentiment'.[2] So the entrenchment of rhetoric in letter-writing is often set in opposition to genuine Christian feeling, commonplace utterance against living expression, empty verbiage against religious sincerity.

But if the historian's interest lies in the social aspects of intellectual and literary culture, the question of first importance does not concern the sincerity of an epistolary cliché. For even the most formulaic of phrases served an important relational function in the writing and reading of letters.[3] The task is rather to

---

[1] F. Young, 'Classical Genres in Christian Guise; Christian Genres in Classical Guise', in F. Young, L. Ayres and A. Louth, eds, *Cambridge History of Early Christian Literature* (Cambridge, 2004), 251–8.

[2] E. R. Curtius, *Europäische Literatur und lateinisches Mittelalter* (Bern, 1948); ET by W. Trask, *European Literature and the Latin Middle Ages* (London, 1979; first publ. 1953), 'Excursus II: Devotional Formula and Humility', 407–13, at 412.

[3] Proclaiming the author's *paideia* (his education and his cultural and intellectual

discern precisely what a cliché communicates, what is operative socially and dialogically in a commonplace formula for two correspondents bound to the 'epistolary situation' (the temporal and physical separation of writer and recipient).[4] In this essay, I shall take one epistolary convention – the intercessory prayer formula (requests for and assurances of prayer) – and search for the motives at work in its inclusion in the Latin Christian letter-writing tradition from late antiquity to the early Middle Ages.[5] In doing this, I am dissecting an epistolary trope and seeking its social intention: what does '*ora pro me*' (and all its related variants) say apart from 'pray for me'? For my sources, I take as obligatory some sort of word for praying (*orare, intercedere, interpellare, supplicare* etc.), while noting the optional syntactical and stylistic variations of the phrases. For example, a request for prayer may be made with a verb in the imperative or with a prepositional phrase, or with the intercessory aspect being signalled by an ablative of means or agency or by an ablative absolute; further, a prayer phrase may appear in the opening, closing or body of a letter. This generous definition of the cliché allows us to observe the continuity of prayer phrases across Christian history. For, unlike other details of the letter body which are dependent on time, place and individual circumstance, and unlike more particular motifs and expressions which vary according to personal writing style, there was a fixed tradition of asking for prayer through the centuries of Christian letter-writing which permits us to treat our material with little attention to chronology, culture or personal style.[6] In approaching such an unchanging epistolary custom, it is indeed

sophistication), for example; see R. Miles, 'Epistolography', in G. W. Bowersock, R. L. Brown, and O. Grabar, eds, *Late Antiquity: A Guide to the Postclassical World* (Cambridge, MA, 1999), 428–49.

4   G. Constable, *Letters and Letter-Collections* (Turnhout, 1976).

5   The central question posed by Gordon Wiles, in *Paul's Intercessory Prayers: The Significance of the Intercessory Prayer Passages in the Letters of St Paul*, Society for New Testament Studies Monograph Series 24 (Cambridge, 1974), is whether Paul's prayer phrases were merely polite expressions or sincere and serious. He concludes in favour of the latter. On the representations of the 'holy man' as intercessor in Eastern letter-writing between the fourth and sixth centuries, see C. Rapp, '"For next to God, you are my salvation": Reflections on the Rise of the Holy Man in Late Antiquity', in J. Howard-Johnston and P. A. Hayward, eds, *The Cult of Saints in Late Antiquity and the Middle Ages* (Oxford, 1991), 63–81.

6   On the persistence of epistolary formulas and conventional topics in Latin letters over centuries, see C. Lanham, 'Freshman Composition in the Early Middle

difficult to judge sincerity; we may more easily study how the prayer formula was constructed and to what ends it was employed via stylistic markers and usages, in order to appreciate its social meaning among Christians.

The first Christian use of the intercessory prayer formula is found, of course, with that first corpus of Christian letters ascribed to Paul.[7] New Testament scholars have long recognized that Paul's practice of assuring his recipients of his prayers is closely related to the complex prescripts (the formal opening portion) of the Hellenistic style of letter-writing common from the first to fourth centuries AD.[8] The prayer formula was tied primarily to phrases of concern for the other's health, expressed by the phrase 'above all, I pray that you are well' or (most often) in the form of making obeisance to the god(s) on the recipient's behalf, the so-called *proskynēma* formula.[9] The Christianized version of this same formula in fourth-century papyri is identifiable only by a reference to the Lord, Christ or God, instead of the gods.[10] But the rather

---

Ages: Epistolography and Rhetoric before the "Ars dictaminis"', *Viator* 23 (1992), 115–34.

7   Wiles, *Paul's Intercessory Prayers*; R. N. Longenecker, *Studies in Paul, Exegetical and Theological*, New Testament Monographs 2 (Sheffield, 2004), ch. 2, 'Prayer in the Pauline Letters'.

8   Wiles, *Paul's Intercessory Prayers*, 158. These assurances of prayer are found in the 'thanksgiving' (*eucharistō*) segment of Paul's letters, e.g. Rom. 1: 8–10; Phil. 1: 3–5; 1 Cor. 1: 4–9; 2 Cor. 1: 10b–11; 1 Thess. 1: 2–10; 2 Thess. 1: 3–12. For Paul's linking of intercession with thanksgiving, see P. Schubert, *Form and Function of the Pauline Thanksgivings*, Beihefte zur Zeitschrift für die neutestamentliche Wissenschaft 20 (Berlin, 1939).

9   D. Aune, 'Epistolography', in idem, ed., *The Westminster Dictionary of New Testament and Early Christian Literature and Rhetoric* (Louisville, KY, 2003), 166–7. For an extended analysis of the *proskynēma* prayer, see H. Koskenniemi, *Studien zur Idee und Phraseologie des griechischen Briefes bis 400 n. Chr.* (Helsinki, 1956), 139–45. See also J. A. D. Weima, *Neglected Endings: The Significance of the Pauline Letter Closings*, Journal for the Study of the New Testament Supplement Series 101 (Sheffield, 1994), ch. 2, for the development of this form. For examples of the *proskynēma* formula in first- to fourth-century papyri, see S. Stowers, *Letter Writing in Greco-Roman Antiquity*, Library of Early Christianity 5 (Philadelphia, PA, 1986); M. Trapp, *Greek and Latin Letters: An Anthology, with Translation*, Cambridge Greek and Latin Classics (Cambridge, 2003). This convention is also found in ancient Babylonian and Assyrian letters: M. Jastrow, *Die Religion Babyloniens und Assyriens*, 2 vols in 3 (Giessen, 1905–12), 2: 521; F. Hesse, *Die Fürbitte im Alten Testament* (Hamburg, 1951), 84.

10   For example: 'We pray for those who are with us. Greet our brothers with you. We pray for your health in the Lord, beloved Papa' (from the Oxyrhynchus papyri, manuscript P.Oxy. 2785) and 'I pray for your health in the Lord God. Emmanuel is my witness. Amen!' (P.Oxy. 1162); quoted in Stowers, *Letter Writing*, 157.

homogeneous and predictable *proskynēma* formula is quite different from the heterogeneity of intercessory prayer passages appearing in letters written by elite and rhetorically trained monks and bishops from the 'golden age of Christian letter-writing' of the fourth and fifth centuries.[11] These churchmen valued literary versatility and, following Paul's example, adapted existing epistolary conventions to express the interests and concerns of the Christian community.[12] While Sidonius (d.489) indicated the formulaic nature of the prayer request ('For a message of greeting is necessarily short ... Whence with the greeting having been said, I soon say "Farewell, pray for me"'),[13] Paulinus of Nola (d.431) demonstrated the extremes to which the convention can be taken: after having explained his need for Florentius's prayers for his salvation, he realized that he had been too loquacious, and ended his letter by begging Florentius to pray for him because he had sinned in using too many words to make his request for prayer.[14] That Christian letter-writers regularly expanded the stock phrase inherited from classical antiquity is an indication that we may inquire more deeply about its social significance.

For Christian letter-writing in late antiquity and the early Middle Ages, the answer to our question may seem obvious. The main function of personal letter-writing was to maintain friendship: reciprocity, trust, assistance, remembrance and loyalty were all motifs common to the Christian friendly letter, of which prayer for the other was just one expression.[15] But if the words with

[11] Stowers, *Letter Writing*, 45.
[12] J. White, *Light from Ancient Letters* (Philadelphia, PA, 1986), 19.
[13] 'nam salutatio ... succincta est; ... unde ave dicto mox vale dicimus. orate pro nobis': Sidonius Apollinaris, *Ep.* 9.9, ed. and French transl. A. Loyen, *Sidoine Apollinaire*, Collection des Universités de France, 3 vols (Paris, 1960), 1: 147.
[14] Paulinus of Nola, *Ep.* 42 (CSEL 29, 361–3).
[15] The literature on letter-writing in relation to friendship is extensive. On classical and late antiquity, see, e.g., Stowers, *Letter Writing*; C. White, 'Friendship in Absence – Some Patristic Views', in J. Haseldine, ed., *Friendship in Medieval Europe* (Stroud, 1999), 68–88; C. Conybeare, *Paulinus Noster: Self and Symbols in the Letters of Paulinus of Nola* (Oxford, 2000). On the medieval period, see G. Knight, *The Correspondence between Peter the Venerable and Bernard of Clairvaux: A Semantic and Structural Analysis* (Aldershot, 2002), ch. 1, 'Letter-Writing and Friendship Reconsidered'; J. Leclerq, 'L'Amitié dans les lettres au moyen âge', *Revue du Moyen Âge latin* 1 (1945), 391–410; idem, *The Love of Learning and the Desire for God: A Study of Monastic Culture*, transl. C. Misrahi (ET 1961; repr. New York, 1985; French original first publ. 1957), esp. 176–9 on monastic letter-writing; H.-W. Goetz, '"Beatus homo qui invenit amicum": The Concept of

which writers chose to compose prayer phrases are any indication, then there is something more cogent at work than the straight-forward corroboration of friendship. While invoking prayer as a surrogate for the physical presence of a friend, letter-writers chose highly energetic words to describe their prayer. Ambrose (d.397), for example, told Gratian that by his prayers, he rushed (*occur-rere*) to him in spirit, followed (*sequor*) him with his entire affec-tion, clung (*inhaerere*) to him in thought and heart, studied (*legere*) his route by day, was transported (*locatus sum*) into his camp by night, and shielded (*praetendere*) it from danger.[16] Ambrose's use of verbs of action gave his assurance of prayer a distinct physicality. In another string of active verbs, Alcuin (d.804) wrote to Arch-bishop Arnonus: 'But I especially follow your holiness's devotion with tears (*vestrae pietatis devotionem lacrimis prosequor*), pursue you with prayers (*orationibus adsequor*), and join you with the support of letters (*litterarum suffragiis consequor*).'[17] Prayer here was not just a static testament to friendship, but an engaged actor in its own right.

Seen as an activity of consequence, Christian letter-writers could invoke prayer to counter the state of physical separation rather than simply accepting it and making do with an imagined, non-corporeal presence. This is a twist on the *parousia* motif: while classical letters commonly spoke of a longed-for but hypothetical reunion after a period of separation, in Christian letters we find statements expressing the idea that a reunion need not be hypo-thetical but was actually achievable through prayer. Letter-writers placed the responsibility of asking God for a physical reunion on his addressee: 'I trust, however, that, assisted by your prayers, I may be permitted when the present hindrance has been removed with all speed to come to you', wrote Augustine (d.430).[18] Ruricius (d.6th century) asked Bishop Aprunculus to 'deign to pray for me and to ask this in particular from our common Lord, that we now, at last, deserve to meet for a while and see each other'.[19] The

---

Friendship in Early Medieval Letters of the Anglo-Saxon Tradition on the Continent (Boniface, Alcuin)', in Haseldine, ed., *Friendship*, 207–15.

[16] Ambrose, *Ep.* 1 (PL 16, col. 877).

[17] Alcuin, *Ep.* 179 (MGH Epp. 4, 297).

[18] Augustine, *Ep.* 124 (CSEL 44, 2); transl. J. G. Cunningham, *The Letters of St. Augustin*, NPNF I 1, 452.

[19] 'ut pro nobis orare dignemini et id a communi domino peculiarius postulare,

prayer phrase was employed to deal directly with the problem of separation. Here, again, we see the intercessory prayer device used not as a static expression of friendship, but as an active vehicle in the service of friendship.

Requests for prayer were not usually general and unspecified statements, but were often attached to particular accounts concerning specific needs which would be met through the addressee's prayer. Regularly the prayer request was made using verbs of accomplishment such as *exorare, impetrare, effectare* and *praebere*, so that prayer was seen 'to obtain what is sought'.[20] Paulinus begged Florentius to 'pray, until you gain your prayer [*ora, donec exores*]'[21] that he would not fall into temptation, and Jerome (d.420) wrote to Theodosius and the anchorites:

> I adjure you (and I know that you can do it [*quia vos impetrare posse non ambigo*]) by your prayers to deliver (*liberetis oratu*) me from the darkness of this world … It rests with you to give effect to my resolve (*nunc vestrum est, ut voluntatem sequatur effectus*). I have the will but not the power; this last can only come in answer to your prayers (*meum est, ut velim; obsecrationum vestrarum est, ut et velim et possim*).[22]

Gregory the Great (d.604) wrote to Eulogius that he needed spiritual respite from bodily pain, a bitter heart and the problem of the barbarians: 'I am confident that I shall obtain it through the intercession of your Beatitude'.[23] Desiderius of Cahors (d.655) wrote to Bishop Dado that he was confident he would 'be able to

---

ut iam tandem aliquando in unum venire et nos videre mereamur': Ruricius, *Ep.* 2.55 (CSEL 21, 436); transl. R. Mathisen, *Ruricius of Limoges and Friends: A Collection of Letters from Visigothic Gaul*, Translated Texts for Historians 30 (Liverpool, 1999), 226–7.

[20] 'plane quia nunc vobis in precibus efficacior sermo est et ad inpetrandum quod in pressuris petitur facilior oratio est' ('since your word is more efficacious in prayer and since prayer is more efficient for obtaining what is sought through suffering'): Cyprian, *Ep.* 76 (CSEL 3/2, 833). Observe the similar phrase frequently used by Boniface, as here in *Ep.* 46 (MGH Epp. Sel. 1, 74): 'praecibus pietatis vestrae impetrare' ('obtain by your holy prayers').

[21] Paulinus of Nola, *Ep.* 42 (CSEL 29, 362); transl. P. G. Walsh, *Letters of Paulinus of Nola 2*, ACW 36 (New York, 1966), 225.

[22] Jerome, *Ep.* 2 (CSEL 54, 11); transl. W. H. Fremantle, G. Lewis and W. G. Martley, *Letters and Select Works*, NPNF II 6, 4.

[23] 'quam per me impetrare non valeo, sed intercessione vestrae beatitudinis hanc me optinere confido': Gregory I, *Ep.* 13.45 (MGH Epp. 1, 408); transl. J. Martyn, *The Letters of Gregory the Great*, 3 vols (Toronto, ON, 2004), 3: 858.

attain' what he wanted 'more by your prayers than by my power'.[24] Avitus (d.517) asked Contumeliosus for his prayers because 'there is nothing that you cannot ... set straight through your prayers (*orando componere*)'.[25] All these phrases emphasize the capacity of a friend's prayer to achieve what is needed. Ultimately, one expected that a prayer request would result in some sort of prayer report: 'indicate to me through some words of your affability what your brotherhood is able to accomplish as regards to those prayers', wrote Boniface (d.754).[26]

Notably, the apparatus which gave definition to the request for prayer was not a theology of God to whom prayer was addressed, but the fact of the two individuals who made up a praying relationship. Here, we benefit from Altman's influential study on epistolary fiction, in which she speaks of the 'pronominal relativity' of epistolary discourse that distinguishes it from all other literary genres: 'The most distinctive aspect of epistolary language is the extent to which it is colored by not one but two persons and by the specific relationship existing between them. ... [T]he interpersonal bond basic to the very language of the letter (I–You) necessarily structures meaning in letter narrative.'[27]

The epistolary mode thereby lent itself perfectly to the entire enterprise of intercessory prayer, an activity necessarily involving two persons. This was encapsulated in that distinct and frequently employed benediction by which the letter-writer essentially prayed to God that his addressee would pray for him. Examples abound; consider that of Desiderius: 'May the power of our Lord Jesus Christ deign to keep you praying for us'.[28] Prayer phrases were thus formulated in such a way as to emphasize relationship, a special interdependency of prayer between letter-writer and letter-recipient by which lives were mutually shaped and each was seen

[24] 'plus me vestris orationibus quam meis viribus adtingere posse confido': Desiderius of Cahors, *Ep.* 1.11, in *Epistulae S. Desiderii Cardurcensis*, ed. D. Norberg, Studia Latina Stockholmiensia 6 (Stockholm, 1961), 30.

[25] Avitus, *Ep.* 15 (MGH AA 6/2, 48); transl. D. Shanzer and I. Wood, *Avitus of Vienne: Selected Letters and Prose*, Translated Texts for Historians 38 (Liverpool, 2002), 265.

[26] 'mihi per aliqua verba tuae affabilitatis indica, quid de istis valeat precibus tua fraternitas perficere': Boniface, *Ep.* 71 (MGH Epp. Sel. 1, 144).

[27] J. Altman, *Epistolarity: Approaches to a Form* (Columbus, OH, 1982), 118.

[28] 'Orantem te pro nobis potentia Domini nostri Iesu Christi conservare dignetur': Desiderius, *Ep.* 1.12 (*Epistulae*, ed. Norberg, 32).

to achieve change in the other's life. The operative force in the prayer formula was its articulation of the potential for creative activity between two persons.[29]

Recognizing this intention in the use of the prayer formula helps us make most sense of two striking pairs of parallelisms by which it was frequently constructed. In the first, a friend's prayer was made syntactically and semantically equal with the act of letter-writing itself. This seems to have been a convention popular among the Greek fathers. Cyril of Alexandria (d.444) asked Succensus, bishop of Diocaesarea, to 'be of aid to us both by writing and by praying for us',[30] and Theodoret (d.457) begged Ibas to 'give me both the prop of your prayers and the comfort of a letter from you'.[31] Latin correspondents also made passionate use of this parallelism. Paulinus, complaining of his literary dullness, told Alethius: 'your prayers and letters (*quem utinam orationes et litterae*), bestowed upon me more frequently, may cause that fount to bubble forth and grow sweet through the wood of your faith and the sweetness of your eloquence (*fidei tuae ligno et eloquii suavitate*)'.[32]

For his spiritual malaise, Ruricius asked Bishop Faustus to 'pray for me ceaselessly (*pro me indesinenter oretis*)' and to 'deign to drench the dryness of my soil with the showers of your eloquence (*dignati fueritis ariditatem terrae meae eloquentiae vestrae imbre perfundere*)'.[33] Prayer – like a letter – was taken to be a sign of active involvement in a friend's life, and the eloquence of a good letter which could emotionally and spiritually awaken a recipient became an accurate descriptor of the effect of a friend's prayer: 'But I beg you in the love of Christ', wrote Alcuin to Adalhard, 'that you may never neglect to restore me by consolatory letters or by prayers'.[34]

---

[29] I use the term 'creative activity' specifically to refer to the causal effect which intercessory prayer between two individuals was believed to achieve. But see also R. L. Simpson's comments about prayer and the 'creative activity at the human level' in *The Interpretation of Prayer in the Early Church* (Philadelphia, PA, 1965), 161–2.

[30] Cyril of Alexandria, *Letter* 45 (PG 77, col. 258); transl. J. McEnerney, *St. Cyril of Alexandria: Letters*, Fathers of the Church 76 (Washington, DC, 1987), 197.

[31] Theodoret, *Letter* 133 (SC 40, 126); transl. B. Jackson, in *Theodoret, Jerome, Gennadius, Rufinus*, NPNF II 3, 304. See also *Letter* 142 (SC 40, 156; transl. Jackson, *Theodoret*, 309): 'I beg you in the first place to support me with your prayers, and further to cheer me by a letter, for by God's grace I have been attacked for the Gospel's sake'.

[32] Paulinus, *Ep.* 33 (CSEL 29, 302); transl. Walsh, *Letters of Paulinus of Nola 2*, 161.

[33] Ruricius, *Ep.* 1.1 (CSEL 21, 352); transl. Mathisen, *Ruricius*, 89.

[34] 'Tamen obsecro in caritate Christi, ne me umquam consolatoriis vel oratoriis dimittas reficere litteris': Alcuin, *Ep.* 9 (MGH Epp. 4, 35).

Requests for prayer were not incidental afterthoughts or secondary to the act of letter-writing, but were held to be at least as important as the writing and reception of the letter itself. Dungalus Scottus (d.9th century) stated that writing a letter to Theodrada, Charlemagne's daughter, was the only fitting proof of his faithfulness in praying for her.[35] The classical connection between friendship and letter-writing in its Christianized form became, more properly and precisely, a connection between *prayer* and letter-writing.

In the second parallelism, equal grammatical weight was afforded to the grace of God and to the prayer of the addressee. The qualifier *dei gratia* and all its variants occur so commonly in Christian literature of all kinds that they hardly need mention, but we must not fail to observe that, in epistolary literature specifically, it is usually just one in a pair, accompanied by another qualifier, *tuis orationibus*. Jerome wrote of his illness 'from which I have only been saved by God's mercy and your prayers (*domini misericordia et tuis orationibus*)'.[36] Boniface wrote to Pope Zacharias that his missionary activity was 'upheld by your prayers and led by God's grace (*vestris orationibus commitante gratia Dei*)'.[37] Lul wrote to Boniface that he would be refreshed 'through the favoring grace of Christ and the intercession of your prayers (*larga Christi clementia preeunte et vestris orationibus intercedentibus*)'.[38] And Hrabanus Maurus (d.856) wrote to Bishop Humbert: 'I especially need your prayer and the mercy of the omnipotent God (*vestra oratione atque omnipotentis Dei misericordia*)' for protection against trial and temptation.[39] The pronominal *I–You* emphasis in epistolary discourse made the writer reluctant simply to attribute things to God without reference to the addressee. Attempts to harmonize the prayers of fallible humans with the will of a sovereign God have preoccupied many a theologian in Christian history, but here in letters, the two parties

---

[35] 'Sed cum recordatus sim domini mei, vestri genitoris, beatae memoriae Karoli ... , quorum memoriam in orationibus cotidianam facio, prout oportet – revocans animum hacque fretus fiducia, istas vobis direxi litterulas': Dungalus Scottus, *Ep.* 7 (MGH Epp. 4, 582).

[36] Jerome, *Ep.* 114 (CSEL 55, 395); transl. Fremantle et al., NPNF II 6, 215.

[37] Boniface, *Ep.* 86 (MGH Epp. Sel. 1, 194); transl. E. Emerton, *The Letters of Saint Boniface* (1940; rev. edn, New York, 2000), 159.

[38] Boniface, *Ep.* 103 (MGH Epp. Sel. 1, 226); transl. Emerton, *Letters*, 153.

[39] 'Ac ideo vestra oratione atque omnipotentis Dei misericordia maxime indigeo, ne deficiam in tribulationibus, in necessitatibus, in periculis et in temptationibus diversis': Hrabanus Maurus, *Ep.* 27 (MGH Epp. 5, 441–2).

were set side by side, unproblematically and without dilemma.[40] The prayer of a friend was placed alongside the powerful activity of God, and if God acted, it was due as much to the prayer uttered by a friend as to his own grace and kind will.

It may be careless to declare the prayer formula all hyperbole, and equally naïve to call it entirely sincere; these conclusions are not of the order which most benefit the historian in any case. In our attention to the affective aspects of the device through a study of its formal qualities, we have been concerned only with appreciating the strong impression which it was meant to convey, how individuals used and formulated an epistolary trope to externalize ideas and establish images of themselves in relation to others.[41] Epistolary tropes had clear spiritual aims and were powerful building blocks of the Christian worldview. The spiritual language embodied in common epistolary clichés contributed to the spiritual expectations and experiences of those who used it. Such language also invites us to investigate why it found particular favour, and here we are reminded of Gabrielle Spiegel's response to the 'linguistic turn' in historical studies, a postmodern movement which encouraged scholars to approach textual documents not as sources objectively reflecting the past, but rather as constituting and actively structuring it. In desiring to restore the connection between language (textual sources) and external referents (historical reality) which post-structuralist theories had severed, Spiegel urged historians to pursue the 'social logic of the text'. Textual language, she argued, could be analyzed within the context of the historically grounded social systems which 'account for its particular semantic inflections and thus aid in the recovery of its full meaning'.[42] Elizabeth Clark's modification – 'socio-theological logic' – to suit the study of specifically Christian texts similarly beckons us to seek the theological rationale and interests which can explain the language of Christian texts.[43] Therefore I offer a

[40]   J. Pelikan, *The Christian Tradition: A History of the Development of Doctrine*, 1: *The Emergence of the Catholic Tradition (100–600)* (Chicago, IL, 1971), 133–9. See Origen, *De Oratione* 5 (PG 11, col. 429–434); Tertullian, *De Oratione* 29 (PL 1, cols 1195–6).

[41]   See Miriam Dobson's comments in 'Letters', in eadem and B. Ziemann, eds, *Reading Primary Sources: The Interpretation of Texts from Nineteenth- and Twentieth-Century History* (London, 2009), 57–73, at 62–4.

[42]   G. Spiegel, 'History, Historicism and the Social Logic of the Text in the Middle Ages', *Speculum* 65 (1990), 59–86, at 77.

[43]   E. Clark, *History, Theory, Text: Historians and the Linguistic Turn* (Cambridge, MA, 2004), esp. 178–81.

brief comment regarding the socio-theological logic of the intercessory prayer cliché by way of concluding. The prayer trope rested on the axiom of spiritual presence despite physical absence, and in this regard was little different from classical usage. But what was distinctive about its social intention in the Christian tradition was the belief that a person could, from one physical place, effect real and actual change in another physical place. Thus, Gregory I's letter to Eulogius about the baptism of ten thousand Englishmen was accompanied by an explanatory statement: 'I described this so that you would know … what you achieve through your prayer, at the edge of the world. For your prayers are in a place where you are not present, and their holy operations are revealed in a place without you.'[44]

Indeed, in the late antique and medieval mind, geographical space existed to reflect spiritual realities. Most vividly, for example, both pilgrimage to holy places and the use of cartography for contemplative prayer were activities directed at transforming earthly terrain into a testimony to the holy. Within this socio-theological culture, the earth could be scoured for evidence of the 'holy operations' of friends: positive change in one corner of the world (such as recovery from an illness, safe travel, the baptism of converts or the suppression of a heresy) could always be attributed to the spiritual action of a trusty friend located in another corner. Geographical space existed to be mined for evidence of the spiritual activity of God and of his servants. Recognizing this socio-theological logic behind the intercessory prayer cliché helps us appreciate why its most crucial function was not simply to affirm friendship (contrary to its usage in classical letter-writing), but to communicate the idea that one friend could achieve change in the life of another, even across the span of the world. Christian epistolary clichés, as consistently employed linguistic symbols signifying spiritual expectations or realities which are mutually and easily recognized by sender and recipient, are rich in social meaning which invites the historian's investigation.

Pembroke College, Oxford

---

[44] Gregory I, *Ep.* 8.29 (MGH Epp. 1, 30); transl. Martyn, 2: 524.

GREGORY THE GREAT: READER, WRITER AND READ

by DANIEL ANLEZARK

An episode unique to the late ninth-century *Life* of Gregory the Great by John the Deacon reports a famine that occurred in the year of Gregory's death; a hostile party blamed the lavish generosity of the late pope for Rome's suffering. The fury of the people was roused and they set out to burn Gregory's books. However, the deacon Peter, Gregory's *familiarissimus*, intervened to dissuade them, telling the people that Gregory's works were directly inspired by God. As proof he asked God to take his life, and promptly dropped dead.[1] This episode is not found in the earlier accounts of Gregory's life: the brief account in the mid seventh-century *Liber pontificalis*, the early eighth-century *Life* by an anonymous monk of Whitby, and the mid eighth-century account by Paul the Deacon.[2] Doubtful as John the Deacon's account of the exchange between Peter and the mob may be, it does tell us something about the status of Gregory and his works in the mid 870s, when Pope John VIII commissioned the new hagiography.[3] Gregory the Great became one of the most widely read authors of the Middle Ages, and even in his lifetime some of his works were eagerly sought after. With his popularity and influence Gregory not only added to the body of Christian literature, but also made a lasting contribution to the debate over what kinds of works it was appropriate for Christians to read. This essay will survey his works and discuss his ideas on reading and literature, and on the estab-

---

[1]   *Vita Gregorii Magni* 4.69 (PL 75, 59–242, at 222); Jeffrey Richards, *Consul of God: The Life and Times of Gregory the Great* (London, 1980), 72–3. See Beryl Smalley, *The Study of the Bible in the Middle Ages* (Oxford, 1952), 12, on the inspired nature of Gregory's works.

[2]   *Liber pontificalis*, ed. L. Duchesne, 2nd edn, 3 vols (Paris, 1955–7), 2: 312; *The Earliest Life of Gregory the Great by an Anonymous Monk of Whitby*, ed. Bertram Colgrave (Lawrence, KA, 1968); Paul the Deacon, *Historia Langobardorum* 3.21–5, 4.1–19 (MGH SRL, 45–187, at 103–5, 114–22); accounts of Gregory's life are also found in Bede, *Ecclesiastical History of the English People* 1.23–30, 2.1; ed. Bertram Colgrave and R. A. B. Mynors (Oxford, 1969), 68–109, 122–35; some (unreliable) detail is found in Gregory of Tours, *Historia Francorum* 9.20, 10.1 (MGH SRM 1/1, 437, 475–81); see also n. 19 below.

[3]   Richards, *Consul*, 2.

lishment of a Christian literary canon. The influence of Gregory's works and ideas will be examined in relation to one particular medieval nation – Anglo-Saxon England. As the instigator of the Anglo-Saxon mission, Gregory enjoyed a great reputation as an author in Anglo-Saxon England, where his ideas on literature and society had a lasting impact.

Gregory was born around 540, elected pope in September 590, and died in March 604. The sixth century was disastrous for the city of Rome. It had been buffeted by Barbarian attacks since the beginning of the fifth century, but the events of the sixth left the city depopulated and falling into decay.[4] The Emperor Justinian launched his campaigns to reconquer lost territories in the West, and the Lombards later invaded Italy from the north. The crumbling city of Gregory's papacy would have borne a shattered resemblance to that of his early childhood. It is no surprise that his works are peppered with references to transience. He writes in his *Moralia in Iob*: 'But a man, who is thoroughly subject to God, knows how to remain fixed among transient things, knows how to plant firmly the footsteps of his mind, amid the lapses of passing years'.[5]

Years of war and plague contributed to drastic economic, social and demographic changes. The Italian economy began to revert to rural subsistence, while cities became depopulated and their defences were neglected. Many of the old aristocracy fled Italy for Constantinople; their position in the government of Italy was eroded. For art and letters this meant a much diminished leisured class to patronize such pursuits. By the end of the century the Roman Senate had ceased to function. The old ruling class was gradually displaced by the military and the Church. Gregory was born into one of these old families, but one which was already known for its piety and service to the Church. He became Prefect

---

4   R. A. Markus, *Gregory the Great and his World* (Cambridge, 1997), 1.
5   'Vir autem bene Deo subditus scit inter transeuntia stare, scit inter lapsus decurrentium temporum mentis gressum figere': Gregory, *Moralia in Iob* 31.28.55 (CChr.SL 143–143B, 1590); ET *Morals on the Book of Job* 18, 21, 23, 31, Library of Fathers of the Holy Catholic Church, 3 vols in 4 (Oxford, 1844–50), 3: 468; see Markus, *Gregory*, 3. On Gregory's integration of Stoicism, see below. In this essay Gregory's works are quoted in translation, with the original in the notes; works by other authors in Latin (and Old English) are given only in translation, unless a textual relationship is being discussed.

of Rome in 573 but adopted the monastic life not long after.[6] However, his desire to leave the secular world was not fulfilled for long, as either Pope Benedict I or Pelagius II made him a deacon of the Roman Church. Soon he was papal representative at the imperial court in Constantinople. It was there he came to know Leander of Seville and gave the talks which were later published in a revised form as his *Moralia in Iob*. Gregory was recalled to Rome in 585/6, and returned to his monastery. War with the Lombards resumed in 587, and when Pope Pelagius II died of the plague in 590 Gregory was elected to succeed him.

A number of works by Gregory survive; some are known to have been lost; and some are disputed.[7] By Gregory's time the papal *scrinium* was keeping a record of papal correspondence in a 'register'. Various extracts from his register survive as eight hundred and fifty letters, written to a range of correspondents on matters sublime and mundane. Letters from the *Registrum* were excerpted by John the Deacon during the papacy of Hadrian I (772–95).[8] The *Moralia in Iob* is a vast historical, allegorical and mostly moral exposition of the Book of Job based on talks Gregory gave to the monastic brethren who accompanied him when he was *apocrisiarios* in Constantinople. This was revised and published soon after his accession to the papacy; its great length, density and interest meant that it was a work for monastic readers in following centuries. The *Liber regulae pastoralis* ('Pastoral Rule' or 'Pastoral Care') was written during the first year of Gregory's pontificate (590–1).[9] It was addressed to bishops, but was later widely held to be useful for kings and other rulers, all of whom were *rectores*.[10] The *Dialogi* ('Dialogues', composed in 593–4) celebrated the holiness of sixth-century Italian saints.[11] The work's authenticity has been questioned but not disproved.[12] In any case, the fact that it

---

[6] Markus, *Gregory*, 8, notes that there is no record of the family's bearing secular office until Gregory himself.

[7] Ibid. 14–16.

[8] Gregory, *Registrum epistolarum libri* (CChr.SL 140, 140A) [hereafter: *Epist.*]; see John R. C. Martyn, transl., *The Letters of Gregory the Great*, 3 vols (Toronto, ON, 2004).

[9] Gregory, *Règle pastorale*, ed. and French transl. B. Judic, 2 vols (Paris, 1992); ET *Pastoral Care*, transl. H. Davis, ACW 11 (Westminster, MD, 1950).

[10] Markus, *Gregory*, 86.

[11] Gregory, *Dialogues*, 3 vols (SC 251, 260, 265); ET *Dialogues*, transl. O. J. Zimmerman (New York, 1959).

[12] See Markus, *Gregory*, 15–16, who accepts the *Dialogues* as genuinely Gregorian;

was indubitably regarded as Gregory's work for more than a thousand years after it was written means he has been the author for most of its readers. It appears to have been designed for as wide an audience as possible. Gregory's *Homiliae in Euangelia* had been delivered publicly in Rome in 590–2.[13] Some were preached by Gregory and recorded by notaries, others were written beforehand and delivered for him when he was too ill to speak; they were revised for publication. Gregory's *Homiliae in Hiezechihelem* were preached between 592 and 593 at the height of the wars with the Lombards, while Rome was under siege.[14] As in all of Gregory's works there is a strong apocalyptic flavour, though here the taste is intense. They were revised eight years later when requested by the brethren.[15] Gregory's *Expositio in Cantica canticorum* survives as two fragmentary homilies.[16] A commentary *In librum primum Regum expositio*, once attributed to him, is now seriously doubted to be authentically Gregorian.[17]

Gregory's attitude to learning in general, and secular learning in particular, has been a matter of debate. In his *Dialogues* he employed a paradox developed by St Paul, comparing a simple saint's 'learned ignorance (*illius doctam ignorantiam*)' with 'our ignorant knowledge (*nostra indocta scientia*)'.[18] The recurrence of this attitude across his works – that holiness knows more than taught knowledge – has fed into a perception of Gregory as one suspicious of an emphasis on book learning, especially secular letters. Gregory himself belonged to a social elite, and his Latinity and

Francis Clark, *The Pseudo-Gregorian Dialogues*, 2 vols (Leiden, 1987); Paul Meyvaert, 'The Enigma of Gregory the Great's *Dialogues*: A Response to Francis Clark', *JEH* 39 (1988), 335–81.
    [13]   Gregory, *Homiliae in Euangelia* (CChr.SL 141) [hereafter: *Hom. Euang.*]; ET *Forty Gospel Homilies*, transl. D. Hurst, Cistercian Studies 123 (Kalamazoo, MI, 1990).
    [14]   Gregory, *Homiliae in Hiezechihelem* [hereafter: *Hom. Hiezech.*] (CChr.SL 142); ET *Homilies on the Book of the Prophet Ezekiel*, transl. T. Tomkinson (Etna, CA, 2008).
    [15]   St Columbanus requested a copy of the work: F. Homes Dudden, *Gregory the Great: his Place in History and Thought*, 2 vols (London, 1905), 2: 92.
    [16]   Gregory, *Expositiones in Canticum canticorum, in librum primum Regum* (CChr.SL 144); see Paul Meyvaert, 'The Date of Gregory the Great's Commentaries on Canticles and on I Kings', *Sacris Erudiri* 23 (1978–9), 191–216.
    [17]   See Adalbert de Vogüé, 'L'auteur du Commentaire des Rois attribué à saint Grégoire: Un moine de Cava?', *Revue bénédictine* 106 (1996), 319–31. Some works have been lost; see Markus, *Gregory*, xiv, 16.
    [18]   Markus, *Gregory*, 34; Gregory, *Dialogues* 3.37.20 (on 1 Cor. 1:18–25); Carole Straw, *Gregory the Great: Perfection in Imperfection* (Berkeley, CA, 1988), 6.

learning reveal a man educated according to the best traditions available in a turbulent time. Unlike Boethius, who died some fifteen years before Gregory was born, he did not know Greek, and knew philosophy only at second or third hand.[19] His works show that Gregory was trained in grammar and rhetoric, with a Latinity remarkably good for its time, a mark of his patrician culture; his letters reveal knowledge of Roman law. Indeed, Justinian sought to guarantee the basics of such an education in the West to maintain the apparatus of the state.[20]

Following the statement of his exegetical principles and procedure in the letter to Leander of Seville which accompanies his *Moralia*, Gregory disdains the laws of rhetoric and grammar, and claims he has happily breached all the 'rules of Donatus' (a noted grammarian), because, as he says, the authors of Scripture ignored them.[21] There is some irony when this rejection of the noted grammarian is delivered in Latin excellent for its time and also represents a trope borrowed from Cassiodorus.[22] Markus has downplayed the significance of Gregory's statement, and points to a much more enlightened view of the role of secular learning – especially grammar and rhetoric – for the Christian reader outlined in the commentary on 1 Kings: 'Almighty God has provided this secular learning plainly as a step for our ascent by which we might reach the height of understanding the Holy Scriptures'.[23] However, this defence is no longer regarded as Gregory's.[24] The significance of Gregory's letter to Desiderius of Vienne, then, returns with its force undiminished:

> But something came to our attention afterwards that we cannot remember without embarrassment, namely that your fraternity

---

[19] G. J. M. Bartelink, 'Pope Gregory the Great's Knowledge of Greek', transl. Paul Meyvaert, in John C. Cadavini, ed., *Gregory the Great: A Symposium* (Notre Dame, IN, 1995), 117–36; Markus, *Gregory*, 34–5. Glowing praise of his learning from his contemporary Gregory of Tours must be treated cautiously (see n. 2 above).

[20] See James Bowen, *A History of Western Education. The Ancient World: Orient and Mediterranean* (London, 1972), 297.

[21] Markus, *Gregory*, 36.

[22] Ibid.

[23] 'Hanc quippe saecularum scientiam omnipotens deus in plano anteposuit, ut nobis ascendendi gradum faceret, qui nos ad diuinae scripturae altitudinem leuare debuisset': Gregory, *In I librum Regum* 5.84 (CChr.SL 144, 472). See Markus, *Gregory*, 38–9.

[24] See n. 17 above.

was teaching grammar to some people. We were so disturbed by this matter and rejected it so strongly that we turned what you had said before into sighs and sadness, because in one mouth praises of Christ do not harmonize with the praises of Jupiter. And consider how serious and wicked it is for a bishop to recite poetry that is not even suitable for a religious layman.[25]

This is more than a reiteration of canonical prohibitions on bishops teaching grammar or reading profane texts: such poetry, for Gregory, is not really appropriate for any Christian. And it is probably no coincidence that this was written in the same month that Gregory heard of the baptism of the pagan king Ethelbert of Kent and ten thousand others; when winning the war on paganism on one front, Gregory would have been unwilling to give ground on another.[26] The attitude outlined in the pseudo-Gregorian commentary has noble antecedents in Cassiodorus and Augustine's *De doctrina Christiana*, in which secular study is acceptable as an aid to the understanding of divine letters.[27] However, as Markus notes, Augustine and Gregory belong to different times: in Augustine's day secular education was a given, and even Cassiodorus could take it for granted. But on the whole, and very much more so without the caveat of the commentary, Gregory's anti-secularism reveals the spirit of a new age. Gregory distances himself from the knowledge of this world (*scientia doctrinae saecularis*) from the point of view of an ascetic monastic culture.[28] In Gregory's more radically apocalyptic worldview, the knowledge of the dying age had much less value, and he is simply dismissive of the *uanas poetarum*

---

[25] 'Sed post hoc peruenit ad nos quod sine uerecundia memorare non possumus, fraternitatem tuam grammaticam quibusdam exponere. Quam rem ita moleste suscepimus ac sumus uehementius aspernati, ut ea quae prius dicta fuerant in gemitu et tristitia uerteremus, quia in uno se ora cum Iouis laudibus Christi laudes non capiunt. Et quam graue nefandumque sit episcopo canere, quod nec laico religioso conueniat, ipse considera': Gregory, *Epist.* 11.34 (June 601; Martyn, transl., *Letters*, 3: 777); cf. Markus, *Gregory*, 37.

[26] The letter dates from June 601. Compare three other letters dated 22 June 601: Gregory, *Epist.* 11.35, to Queen Bertha; ibid. 11.36, to Augustine; ibid. 11.37, to King Ethelbert. All three emphasize the fight against paganism. *Epist.* 11.38 (22 June 601), to Virgil of Arles, mentions the English mission, and warns Virgil on avarice, a form of idolatry.

[27] See Markus, *Gregory*, 36–9.

[28] Gregory, *Moralia* 33.10.19; see Straw, *Perfection*, 128–46.

fabulas ('vain fictions of the poets').[29] By the time of the grammatical works of Isidore of Seville, Leander's younger brother, the two cultures had separated.[30]

In Gregory's world there was really only one book that needed to be read: the Bible. In his *Moralia* Gregory does much to cement a way of reading Scripture which he inherited from earlier commentators, and which would become the norm in the Middle Ages; the system would be further refined and defined by his literary heir, Bede the Venerable.[31] Gregory sees Scripture as a door, a light and nourishment; it is more food than drink because it must be chewed up before being swallowed.[32] His *Letter to Leander* explains how Gregory reads:

> Let it be known, that we run through some passages with a historical exposition, some we trace out allegorically for their typical meaning; others again we discuss by means of allegory only for their moral bearing; some, finally, we investigate thoroughly in all ways by a threefold method. First we lay the historical sense as a foundation; then by following the typical sense, we erect a mental edifice as a stronghold of faith; as the last step, by the grace of the moral sense we, as it were, cover the building by a coat of paint.[33]

This great edifice catered for a range of readers, and was based on the adaptability of the Scripture itself: 'For as the word of God through its mysteries exercises the understanding of the wise, so generally by its surface meaning it nurses the simple-minded.'[34] For

---

29 Gregory, *Moralia, Ad Leandrum* 3.
30 See Markus, *Gregory*, 36–7.
31 See Henri de Lubac, *Medieval Exegesis: The Four Senses of Scripture*, transl. M. Sebanc and E. M. Macierowski, 2 vols (Grand Rapids, MI, 1998), 2: 24–5, 37–8; Smalley, *Study of the Bible*, 32–5.
32 See Grover A. Zinn Jr, 'Exegesis and Spirituality in the Writings of Gregory the Great', in Cadavini, ed., *Symposium*, 168–80; Markus, *Gregory*, 42; cf. *Hom. Hiezech.* 1.10.3–4.
33 'Sciendum uero est, quod quaedam historica expositione transcurrimus et per allegoriam quaedam typica inuestigatione perscrutamur, quaedam per sola allegoricae moralitatis instrumenta discutimus, nonnulla autem per cuncta simul sollicitus exquirentes tripliciter indagamus. Nam primum quidem fundamenta historiae ponimus; deinde per significationem typicam in arcem fidei fabricam mentis erigimus; ad extremum quoque per moralitatis gratiam, quasi superducto aedificium colore uestimus': Gregory, *Moralia, Ad Leandrum* 3.
34 'Diuinus etenim sermo sicut mysteriis prudentes exerciet, sic plerumque

Gregory signs were not as complex as they had been for Augustine.[35] This is true in the real world of events, whose signs may be read in eschatological terms 'as we read in books (*quam in codicibus legimus*)'.[36] Reading the world for Gregory is 'like the pages of our scriptures'.[37] As the world can be read, so can pictures, as Gregory pointed out to Gallic iconoclasts: 'For a picture is provided in churches for the reason that those who are illiterate may at least read by seeing on the walls what they cannot read in books'.[38] Meanings – which are taken to be easily intelligible – have priority over words.

In a letter to Innocent, a praetorian prefect in Africa, Gregory recommends that he should read the works of his countryman Augustine, which are fine flour (*siligo*) and not Gregory's bran (*furfur*).[39] In his preface to his homilies on Ezekiel, addressed to Bishop Martinian, Gregory suggests better reading is available:

> I believe it highly inappropriate that you partake of this poor water, you who are known assiduously to drink the profound and astute streams that flow from the blessed fathers Ambrose and Augustine. But again, as I ponder that amid daily delights simple food also often tastes sweet, I have delivered the least to the one who reads the better, so that when you consume cruder food, you may, as if through aversion, the more eagerly return to subtler feasts.[40]

Gregory's pun on Ambrose's name – his works are a new ambrosia – suggests he was not completely unfamiliar with the *uanas fabulas*

---

superficie simplices refouet': ibid. 4.

[35] For a full discussion of Gregory's adaptation of Augustine's complex ideas on signification, see R. A. Markus, *Signs and Meanings: World and Text in Ancient Christianity* (Liverpool, 1996), 45–70; idem, *Gregory*, 49.

[36] Gregory, *Hom. Euang.* 1.1.1.

[37] Gregory, *Epist.* 3.29 (Martyn, transl., *Letters*, 1: 255); cf. Markus, *Gregory*, 53.

[38] 'Id circo enim pictura in ecclesia adhibetur, ut hi qui litteras nesciunt saltem in parietibus uidendo legant, quae legere in codicibus non ualent': Gregory, *Epist.* 9.209 (Martyn, transl., *Letters*, 2: 674). See Markus, *Gregory*, 175; Celia Chazelle, 'Memory, Instruction, Worship: "Gregory's" Influence on Early Medieval Doctrines of the Artistic Image', in Cadavini, ed., *Symposium*, 181–215.

[39] Gregory, *Epist.* 10.16 (Martyn, transl., *Letters*, 3: 727); Straw, *Perfection*, 6.

[40] 'sed ualde incongruum credidi ut aquam despicabilem hauriret quem constat de beatorum patrum Ambrosii atque Augustini torrentibus profunda ac perspicua fluenta assidue bibere. Sed rursum dum cogito quod saepe inter cotidianas delicias etiam uiliores cibi suauiter sapiunt, transmisi minima legenti potiora, ut, dum cibus grossior uelut pro fastidio sumitur, ad subtiliores epulas auidius redeatur': Gregory, *Hom. Hiezech.* Praefatio.

concerning Olympian gods, but the (recurrent) metaphor of eating sacred knowledge comes directly from Ezekiel 3: 1–3.

Gregory owed his intellectual vocabulary to Cassian, Augustine and Ambrose.[41] Augustine's work served as a reference library for Gregory, though he was often closer to Eastern traditions and he read Augustine in their light.[42] He doubtless knew sections of the *Vitae patrum*, particularly those translated by the deacon who became Pope Pelagius I (556–61) and the subdeacon who became Pope John III (561–74). Carole Straw comments: 'This spirit of asceticism from the desert is always a silent partner in his work, leading Gregory in new directions away from Augustine … The monastic sensibility, the restless vision of the athlete's battle with the devil, left a deep impression.'[43] Gregory encountered eschatological themes across his reading, but his own apocalypticism was more sharply defined, and not relegated to an unknown future moment. While he used the 'end times' as a rhetorical device, Gregory's reading of the history of his age at times led him to see the end quite close at hand. This is particularly so in his Ezekiel homilies, though his attention to administrative matters in his letters also suggests a practical attitude to the affairs of the last age. It would be surprising if Gregory had not had some direct encounter with the writings of Cicero and Seneca, and he certainly encountered Stoic ideas in Ambrose and Augustine.[44] His understanding of balance and self-discipline (*consideratio* and *discretio* are favourite terms) points to a stream of influence incorporating Cassian, the Desert Fathers and the Stoics.[45] Gregory's understanding of the human condition echoes the ideal of the Stoics and Christians who incorporated Stoic thought, in the belief that the soul should achieve a balance (or *constantia mentis*) through self-control and moderation.[46] The problem of the human condition, for Gregory, is that it is beset by instability. In this way the microcosm reflects

---

[41]   See Straw, *Perfection*, 61, 75.
[42]   Ibid. 14–15.
[43]   Ibid. 15.
[44]   See Bartelink, 'Knowledge of Greek', 119; Straw, *Perfection*, 15.
[45]   See G. R. Evans, *The Thought of Gregory the Great* (Cambridge, 1986), 19–25. Straw, *Perfection*, 16, notes other influences.
[46]   Straw, *Perfection*, 76.

the macrocosm; there is an inner likeness shared by the ageing world and man, as both become prone to sickness and disaster.[47]

A constant source of tension in Gregory's life, which is clearly delineated across his works, lies between the active and contemplative life. Gregory's desire for a quiet life of prayer, reflection and sacred reading was ultimately frustrated by the demands of the Roman Church. The prefaces to his works set out these competing demands in clear terms. This sense of burden is found in Gregory's Preface to his *Regula Pastoralis*, a book on how best to incorporate the moral and contemplative life into an active life of service:

> Most dear brother, you reprove me with kind and humble regard for having wished to escape by concealment from the burdens of the pastoral care. Now, lest these burdens might appear light to some, I am explaining, by writing this book, how onerous I regard them, so that he who is free from them may not imprudently seek to have them, and he who has been so imprudent as to seek them may feel apprehension in having them.[48]

Gregory's preferred mode of life, however, is clear.[49] It is only the necessity of work which calls him away from contemplation; there is no joy in earthly office. The same tension is found in the Preface to his *Dialogues*, which begin with Gregory retreating from doing business with worldly men (*saecularium tumultibus*) to a secret place:

> I sat there for a long time in silence and was still deeply dejected when my dearest son, the deacon Peter, came in. ... Seeing me so sick at heart, he asked me 'Have you met with some new misfortune? You seem unusually sad.' 'Peter,' I replied, 'this daily sadness of mine is always old and always new: old by its constant presence, new by its continual increase. With my unhappy soul languishing under a burden of distractions, I

---

[47] Ibid. 50.

[48] 'Pastoralis curae me pondera fugere delitescendo uoluisse, benigna, frater carissime, atque humillima intentione reprehendis; quae ne quibusdam leuia esse uideantur, praesentis libri stilo exprimo de eorum grauedine omne quod penso, ut et haec qui uacat, incaute non expetat; et qui incaute expetiit, adeptum se esse pertimescat': Gregory, *Règle pastorale*, Praefatio.

[49] See Bernard McGinn, 'Contemplation in Gregory the Great', in Cadavini, ed., *Symposium*, 146–67.

recall those earlier days in the monastery where all the fleeting things of time were in a world below me.'[50]

There is undoubtedly humour in Gregory's self-representation here: he parodies his own miserable disposition, with an emphasis on his *new* misfortune, his *unusual* sadness. However, the preferred mode of living is again clear. His letter to Leander of Seville at the head of his *Moralia* makes the same point regarding his refuge among his brethren in Constantinople:

> To their society I fled as to the bosom of the safest port from the rolling swell, and from the waves of earthly occupation; and though that office which withdrew me from the monastery had stabbed to death in me the life of former tranquillity with the point of its employments, yet in their society, by appeals of diligent reading, I was animated with the yearnings of compunction.[51]

Gregory's maritime metaphor (another favourite) runs throughout the letter; he goes on to confess that he sank under the burden of producing his commentary on Job. The desired ideal inscribed by the monastic Gregory in these introductions is far from practical, and in fact stands in contrast to Gregory the practical administrator found across his letters. But it is also noteworthy that his idea of retreat and contemplation necessarily includes reflective reading.

Gregory's sense that the age of the world is coming to an end – a primary motivation to contemplative withdrawal – does not preclude political tussles.[52] Not all of his followers, even those closest to him, necessarily caught the distinction or appreciated the required balance. Gregory's exasperation is tangible in his dealings

---

[50] 'Ibi itaque cum adflictus ualde et diu tacitus sederem, dilectissimus filius meus Petrus diaconus adfuit, … Qui graui excoqui cordis languore me intuens, ait: numquidnam noui aliquid accidit, quod plus te solito moeror tenet? Cui inquam: moerorem, Petre, quem cotidie patior et semper mihi per usum uetus est et semper per augmentum nouus. Infelix quippe animus meus occupationis suae pulsatus uulnere meminit qualis aliquando in monasterio fuit, quomodo ei labentia cuncta subter errant': Gregory, *Dialogues* 12.

[51] 'Ad illorum quippe consortium uelut ad tutissimi portus sinum terreni actus uolumina fluctusque fugiebam, et licet illud me ministerium ex monasterio abstractum, a pristinae quietis uita mucrone suae occupationis exstinxerat, inter eos tamen per studiosae lectionis alloquium, cotidianae me aspiratio cumpunctionis animabat': Gregory, *Moralia, Ad Leandrum* 1.

[52] See Jeffreys, *Consul,* 174–7.

with Marinianus, archbishop of Ravenna. Gregory had success-fully installed Marinianus, one of his monks, as archbishop after the pope's long dispute with the town and see. Gregory's political victory was frustrated by Marinianus's lack of political skill and his monkish habits. Gregory wrote to the deacon Secundinus, another protégé, urging him to urge the new archbishop to action:

> Tell him therefore to change his mind with his place. He should not believe that reading and praying are sufficient for him on their own, so as to be keen to sit apart from others, and not bear fruit with his hand at all. ... But I did admonish him through a letter of mine over some matters concerning his soul, but he has not replied to me at all. This leads me to believe that he did not even deign to read it. For this reason, it was no longer necessary that I should give him any warn-ings through my letter, but I only wrote what an adviser could dictate in worldly matters. For I should not tire myself out in dictating a letter to a man who does not read it.[53]

There is no self-deprecating suggestion of bran here: Gregory thinks his words are worth reading, and he is very much the master of style and tone. However, others were happy to read Gregory and follow his advice, and his reputation as a spiritual writer was estab-lished already in his lifetime. Having sent his *Moralia* to Leander, Gregory was asked for copies of the *Pastoral Rule* and *Moralia* by Bishop Licinianus of Cartagena; he joked in his letter of thanks that if Gregory's advice were followed – that ignorant men not be ordained – there would be no bishops in Spain.[54] By the ninth century Gregory was celebrated as a saint in the East, and his *Dialogues* had been translated into Greek by Pope Zacharias (741–52); the work became popular especially among monastic readers, earning him the surname *Dialogos*. The *Pastoral Rule* was trans-

---

[53] 'Dic ergo ut cum loco mutet mentem. Non sibi credat solam lectionem et orationem sufficere, ut remotus studeat sedere et de manu minime fructificare. ... Quaedam uero eum per epistulam meam de anima sua admonui, sed nil mihi omnino respondit; unde credo quia ea neque legere dignatus est. Pro qua re iam necessarium non fuit debuissem, sed tantum illa scripsi quae in causis terrenis consiliarius dictare potuit. Nam ego ad hominem non legentem fatigari in dictatu non debui': Gregory, *Epist.* 6.33 (Martyn, transl., *Letters*, 2: 427–8); see also ibid. 6.24, 28, 33; 7.39, 40; cf. Richards, *Consul*, 175.
[54] Richards, *Consul*, 210.

lated into Greek in his own lifetime by Anastasius of Antioch.[55] Gregory's international reputation had clearly consolidated by the eighth century, in the East mainly as an author for ascetics, while in the West this was augmented by his reputation in governance. In no place, however, was his reputation stronger or more enduring than in Anglo-Saxon England, where his close involvement in the creation of the English Church gave direction to its developing canon law and theology, an influence witnessed from Bede to Alfred the Great.[56]

BEDE AND GREGORY

The story of the Gregorian mission to England, led by Augustine, one-time prior of the monastery of Sant'Andrea in Rome, is well known and need not be rehearsed here.[57] The origins of the mission and Gregory's motivation for initiating it have been lost in folklore about Angles, angels and alleluias. Gregory's legendary slave-market punning probably is related to his own comments added to the revised version of his *Moralia*: 'For the almighty Lord had covered with his lightning cloud the ends of the sea ... Behold the tongue of Britain which only knew how to utter barbarous sounds has long since begun to sound the divine praises with the Hebrew Alleluia!'[58] Gregory's standing in Anglo-Saxon England was unassailable. For the anonymous monk of Whitby who authored the earliest life of Gregory (704 x 14), Gregory is 'our master' and 'our teacher' and 'our Apostle'.[59] In his *De virginitate*, Aldhelm of Malmesbury calls him 'Gregory, our teacher and instructor ... our teacher – ours, I say, who took away from our parents the foul error of heathendom and handed to them the norm of regenerating grace'.[60] In Bede's *History*, which interweaves the story of

---

[55] Ibid. 259.

[56] See Rolf H. Bremmer Jr, Kees Dekker and David F. Johnson, eds, *Rome and the North: The Early Reception of Gregory the Great in Germanic Europe* (Leuven, 2001).

[57] The story is told in Bede, *Ecclesiastical History* 2.1.

[58] 'Omnipotens enim Dominus coruscantibus nubibus cardines maris operuit ... Ecce lingua Britanniae, quae nihil aliud nouerat, quam barbarum frendere, iam dudum in diuinis laudibus Hebraeum coepit Alleluia resonare': Gregory, *Moralia* 27.11.21; cf. Bede, *Ecclesiastical History* 2.1; Colgrave, ed., *Earliest Life*, 90, 94 (ch. 9).

[59] Paul Meyvaert, *Bede and Gregory the Great* (Jarrow, 1964), 115. See also Kate Rambridge, '*Doctor Noster Sanctus*: The Northumbrians and Pope Gregory', in Bremmer et al., eds, *Rome and the North*, 1–26.

[60] Cited in Meyvaert, *Bede and Gregory*, 115.

Britain with that of Rome, Gregory is in many ways the hero of the tale: 'by his zeal he converted our nation, that is, the nation of the English, from the power of Satan to the faith of Christ, and we can rightly, and should, call him our apostle'.[61] The Anglo-Saxon scholar had an extra reason to be grateful to Gregory: by converting them to Christianity, he had also taught them how to read. Bede tells us that among the equipment brought to England by the Augustinian mission were 'many books'.[62] Bede's scriptural commentaries follow closely the format articulated and developed in Gregory's *Moralia*, and in imitation of Gregory he produced his own collection of Gospel homilies.[63] Gregory's preferred allegorical and moral way of reading Scripture was of direct practical importance in the mission field. When Augustine wrote from Kent asking for advice on marriage and sexual matters, Gregory wrote back dismissing the literal importance of many Old Testament sexual taboos, and instead offered a more spiritual interpretation.[64]

Bede not only read Gregory, but recommended him to others. In his letter of November 734, he recommended the *Pastoral Care* to his pupil, Archbishop Egbert of York, as a work:

> in which he described in the clearest terms the kind of men who should be chosen to rule the Church, how they should live, with what discretion they ought to instruct the great variety of persons they address, and with what care they should daily bear in mind their own weaknesses.[65]

In recommending Gregory, he was following Pope Honorius I (625–38), whose letter to Edwin of Northumbria Bede included in his *History*. Honorius wrote to the newly converted king, exhorting him in the faith: 'So employ yourself in frequent readings from the works of Gregory, your apostle and my lord, and keep before your eyes the love of that teaching which he gladly gave you for the

---

[61] Bede, *Ecclesiastical History* 2.1 (Meyvaert, *Bede and Gregory*, 1). Cf. Bede, *In Cantica Canticorum*, Book 6 (CChr.SL 119B, 359, lines 5–6): 'Gregory, that man beloved of God and men, who is also our father'; Meyvaert, *Bede and Gregory*, 115.

[62] Bede, *Ecclesiastical History* 1.29; Markus, *Gregory*, 179–80.

[63] Bede's homilies often borrow directly from Gregory's; see *Opera homiletica*, ed. D. Hurst (CChr.SL 122), vii.

[64] Bede, *Ecclesiastical History* 1.27; see Markus, *Gregory*, 184.

[65] Cited in Meyvaert, *Bede and Gregory*, 111.

sake of your souls.'[66] The question of what was appropriate reading matter for churchmen (and laypeople) is one that we have seen exercised Gregory's mind in his correspondence with Desiderius of Vienne. This concern is also found in Alcuin's letter to Speratus in 797. The traditional identification of Speratus with Higbald of Lindisfarne has been disputed, but the letter is certainly a response to, and reflection on, the recent raids of Vikings: 'Let God's word be read at the priestly banquet. There it is fitting for the reader to be heard, not the harper: sermons of the fathers, not the songs of heathens. What has Ingeld to do with Christ? The house is narrow: it will not be able to hold them both.'[67] Whether or not Alcuin is deliberately recalling Gregory is hard to say, but there is no doubt that he has inherited a thoroughly Gregorian attitude on the propriety of reading pagan literature.[68] Gregory's habit of reading the events of history in simple terms as divine communications has been thoroughly absorbed, as has his attitude to the wider significance of reading, or indeed singing, pagan poetry. Praise of pagans, let alone their gods, cedes ground in the fight against the devil. The point shared by Alcuin with Gregory is not so much the potential moral harm of pagan literature, but rather its danger in the spiritual war played out in the history of the last age.

If bishops and rulers were not to read about wicked pagans, what should they read? Alcuin suggests patristic sermons. Bede suggests that his *Ecclesiastical History* will make good reading for King Ceolwulf of Northumbria, incorporating the king's desire to know of the deeds and wisdom of the famous men of his race (*nostrae gentis uirorum inlustriam*). Bede does not mean pagan heroes like Ingeld; for him, the illustrious men of the race are warrior

---

[66] Bede, *Ecclesiastical History* 2.17 (ed. Colgrave and Mynors, 94); see Richards, *Consul*, 73.

[67] 'Verba Dei legantur in sacerdotali convivio. Ibi decet lectorem audiri, non citharistam; sermones patrum, non carmina gentilium. Quid Hinieldus cum Christo? Angusta est domus: utrosque tenere non poterit': MGH Epp. 4, 183; see Richard North, *The Origins of Beowulf: From Virgil to Wiglaf* (Oxford, 2006), 132–56. Ingeld is a hero of Germanic legend, referred to in the Old English epic *Beowulf*; see *Klaeber's Beowulf*, ed. R. D. Fulk, Robert E. Bjork and John D. Niles (Toronto, ON, 2008), 68–9, lines 2020–5. Anglo-Saxon aristocratic taste for heroic legend is demonstrated by *Beowulf* itself.

[68] It would be surprising if Alcuin did not know the *Registrum*; see *Registrum*, ed. Norberg, v–xii, esp. vii.

saints such as St Edwin and St Oswald.[69] An important influence on Bede is signalled by the phrasing of his letter to Ceolwulf:

> Now, in order to remove all occasions of doubt about those things that I have written, either in your mind or in the minds of any others who listen to or read this history, I will make it my business to state briefly from what sources I have gained my information.[70]

This statement has long been taken to establish Bede's credentials as a careful historian, though the marvellous nature of some of the events he describes is not generally accepted as contributing to this reputation. Why Bede says what he says is explained by his source here, the preface to Gregory's *Dialogues*. Gregory explains to Peter:

> I shall not hesitate to narrate what I have learned from worthy men. In this I am following the consecrated practice of the Scriptures, where it is perfectly clear that Mark and Luke composed their Gospels, not as eyewitnesses, but on the word of others. Nevertheless, to remove any grounds for doubt on the part of my readers, I am going to indicate on whose authority each account is based.[71]

This is more than the recollection of a felicitous turn of phrase, and Bede's borrowing points to his own attitude to the miracles he has included in the *History*. This also tells us something about why he has included marvellous material in the first place. Bede, imitating Gregory, thought miracles usually belonged to the Church's first age.[72] Gregory's *Dialogues* seem to have been written in response to a demand in Rome for hagiographical stories outside the martyrological genre. When Gregory was a young man, two Roman deacons, Pelagius and John, translated into Latin sayings of Eastern monastic fathers; both men went

---

[69] Bede, *Ecclesiastical History*, Preface, 2.

[70] 'Vt autem in his quae scripsi uel tibi uel ceteris auditoribus siue lectoribus huius historiae occasionem dubitandi subtraham, quibus haec maxime auctoribus didicerim, breuiter intimare curabo': ibid. 2–3 (ed. Colgrave and Mynors, 2).

[71] 'Ea quae mihi sunt uirorum uenerabilium narratione conperta incunctanter narro sacrae auctoritatis exemplo, cum mihi luce clarius constet quia Marcus et Lucas euangelium quod scripserunt, non uisu sed auditu didicerunt. Sed ut dubitationis occasionem legentibus subtraham, per singula quae describo, quibus mihi haec auctoribus sint conperta manifesto': Gregory, *Dialogues* 16–17.

[72] Markus, *Gregory*, 62.

on to become popes. Gregory's *Dialogues* must have fed the same sort of demand, but in a new way. They show this monastic spirit flourishing in sixth-century Italy, producing holiness and miracles. Bede's stories of English saints like Cuthbert and Chad, but also of the early Italian missionaries, do the same in yet another new landscape. There is, in this way of telling, a direct connection between Bede's seventh-century English saints and Gregory's sixth-century Italian ones. Bede not only marks the continuity, but also signals the literary debt to Gregory in his Preface. The *Dialogues* update sanctity, showing that holiness is possible in familiar surroundings. Within the wider context of the great history he is telling, Bede does the same thing: he presents seventh-century English sanctity, something close to home.

Like Gregory, Bede is interested in ascetical, often coenobitic, sanctity. This is unsurprising given Bede's retrospect on the first age of the Anglo-Saxon Church, which saw a remarkable growth of monasticism, of which Bede himself was a product. The monastic ideal is held up in another of Bede's direct borrowings from the *Dialogues'* Preface, in the account of Gregory's life included in the *History*:

> his soul was then above all transitory things, so that he rose superior to all things subject to change. He used to think nothing but thoughts of heaven, so that, even though still imprisoned in the body, he was able to pass in contemplation beyond the barriers of the flesh ...[73]

Bede's written corpus is more resolutely other-worldly than Gregory's, however. Reading can be dangerous, especially if readers take writers at their word. Honorius's recommendation of Gregory's works (included in Bede's *History*) has already been noted. Anyone who took Gregory's prefaces seriously might shun public life altogether. Marinianus of Ravenna made this choice; he had read enough of Gregory, it seems. And indeed this is what King Ceolwulf, Bede's reader, did too. Having become king in 729, Ceolwulf was deposed and tonsured in 731; he then returned to his throne.[74] Bede dedicated the *History* to him in 734; failure

---

[73] Bede, *Ecclesiastical History* 2.1 (ed. Colgrave and Mynors, 124).
[74] See Peter Hunter Blair, *Northumbria in the Days of Bede* (London, 1977), 59; D. P. Kirby, 'Northumbria in the Time of Wilfrid', in idem, ed., *Saint Wilfrid at Hexham*

in dynastic politics led Ceolwulf to retire (perhaps forcibly) to Lindisfarne in 737, where he continued as a monk for thirty years. The tensions within the Gregorian ideal found expression in the political crisis engulfing eighth-century Northumbria, a kingdom which had seen its power, prestige and territorial extent decline since the death of King Ecgfrith in 685.[75] With a monastic detachment, Ceolwulf could easily have contemplated the further decline of the kingdom he once had ruled. A century later another English king, Alfred the Great, was able to achieve a more careful balance between the responsibilities of public life and the desire for reflective retirement. A key to this balance was his close reading of Gregory the Great.

ALFRED AND GREGORY

When Alfred was a boy, he accompanied his father King Æthelwulf of Wessex on a journey to Rome in 851/2. Alfred would have been about ten years old and may have spent up to a year in the city. Still extant at the time was a portrait of Gregory, beside other members of his family, painted on a wall of their old family villa; it is more than likely that Alfred saw this portrait.[76] What we know with certainty, however, is that Alfred was a close reader of Gregory. Alfred, the fourth son of Æthelwulf, came to the throne in 871, having survived his older brothers.[77] At the time the Vikings controlled much of the territory of the English kingdoms; their first raids on Northumbria in the late eighth century had led into a century of warfare and destruction. Indeed, not long after his accession Alfred lost control of Wessex to Viking raiders and was forced to retreat to the marshes of Athelney. Alfred's eventual triumph over the Vikings and consolidation of his rule over Wessex and large parts of Mercia was accompanied by a programme of

(Newcastle upon Tyne, 1974), 1–34, at 20–1; John Blair, *The Church in Anglo-Saxon Society* (Oxford, 2005), 109, 111.

75 See Blair, *Northumbria in the Days of Bede*, 36–61.

76 Meyvaert, *Bede and Gregory*, 109–10, has argued that the unique decorated initial in the mid eighth-century manuscript known as the Leningrad Bede begins the section which is the life of Gregory, and probably contains his portrait. This may well have been based on observation of this portrait of Gregory; it still survived in the mid 870s, when John the Deacon described it in his *Life* of Gregory.

77 See Richard Abels, *Alfred the Great: War, Kingship and Culture in Anglo-Saxon England* (Edinburgh, 1998), 136–68.

cultural and institutional renewal,[78] which included the translation of a number of Latin works into Old English. The first of these was Gregory's *Pastoral Rule*, which is prefaced by a letter from Alfred to his bishops:

> King Alfred sends words of greeting lovingly and amicably to Werferth ... I would have it known that very often it has come into my mind what men of learning there were formerly throughout England, both in religious and secular orders; and how there were happy times throughout England; and how the kings, who had authority over this people, obeyed God and his messengers; and how they not only maintained their peace, morality and authority at home but also extended their territory outside; and how they succeeded both in warfare and in wisdom.[79]

The portrayal of this happy time by Alfred suggests that he has been reading Bede's *Ecclesiastical History*. This golden age, however, gave way to decline as 'everything was ransacked and burned', especially books. These lost books, however, were in a Latin nobody now could read. Consequently, Alfred proposes a programme of translation:

> Therefore it seems better to me ... that we too should turn into the language that we can all understand certain books which are the most necessary for all men to know ... so that all the free-born young men now in England who have the means to apply themselves to it, may be set to learning.[80]

Alfred will lead this programme by example. The example is not only literary, however, as his choice of the first text draws on an important historical example:

> When I recalled how knowledge of Latin had previously decayed throughout England, and yet many could still read

---

[78] See Barbara Yorke, *Wessex in the Early Middle Ages* (London, 1995), 192–239.

[79] Michael Lapidge and Simon Keynes, transl., *Alfred the Great: Asser's Life of King Alfred and other Contemporary Sources* (Harmondsworth, 1983), 124–5; *King Alfred's West-Saxon Version of Gregory's Pastoral Care*, ed. Henry Sweet, 2 vols (Oxford, 1871). See Jennifer Morrish, 'King Alfred's Letter as a Source on Learning in England', in Paul E. Szarmach, ed., *Studies in Earlier Old English Prose* (New York, 1986), 87–108.

[80] Lapidge and Keynes, transl., *Alfred the Great*, 124–5.

things written in English, I then began, amidst the various and multifarious afflictions of this kingdom, to translate into English the book which in Latin is called *Pastoralis*, in English, Shepherd-book, sometimes word for word, sometimes sense for sense, as I learnt it from Plegmund my archbishop, and Asser my bishop, and from Grimbald my mass-priest and John my mass-priest.[81]

Exactly which part of the translation (or even the Preface) is Alfred's is a contentious matter,[82] though there can be no doubt that the work was produced at his court and instituted one of the king's most important policies. His plan for an educational renewal led to the creation of a ruling class with some literacy in English, and to the translation of a number of Latin works for them to read. However, the inclusion of the *Pastoral Rule* comes as a surprise: how could it be considered so necessary for all men to know? The king tells us that copies are to be sent to all his bishops, though we also have his indication that this work, before all others, was to be read by young English noblemen. By the ninth century, the *Pastoral Rule* was certainly required reading for all bishops in Francia and was placed in their hands when they were consecrated.[83] This explains Alfred's desire that there should be a copy for each of his bishops, including Werferth of Worcester, whose copy survives.[84] It seems beyond doubt that Alfred's advisors saw the king's role very much as one of Gregory's *rectores*, making the work suitable for his own reading and for those who shared in his government of the refounded English kingdom.

Gregory's influence on the development of Anglo-Saxon culture and society was far-reaching, most obviously in his decision to send missionaries to England, but also through his works and the ideas they contained. The translation of some of his works into English only extended this.[85] Asser, the king's Welsh advisor,

---

[81] Ibid. 126.

[82] See Richard W. Clement, 'The Production of the *Pastoral Care*: King Alfred and his Helpers', in Szarmach, ed., *Earlier Old English Prose*, 129–52; Malcolm Godden, 'Did King Alfred Write Anything?', *Medium Ævum* 76 (2007), 1–23.

[83] Allen Frantzen, *King Alfred* (Boston, MA, 1986), 25; see Rosamond McKitterick, *The Frankish Church and the Carolingian Reforms, 789–895* (London, 1977), 88–90.

[84] Oxford, Bodl., MS Hatton 20; see N. R. Ker, *Catalogue of Manuscripts containing Anglo-Saxon* (Oxford, 1957), 384–6 (no. 324).

[85] See, e.g., Kees Dekker, 'King Alfred's Translation of Gregory's *Dialogi*: Tales for

tells us in his biography of Alfred that Werferth was commissioned by the king to translate Gregory's *Dialogues*.[86] This must have been soon after the Old English *Pastoral Care* was completed. Alfred provides a preface here too:

> I, Alfred, honoured by the dignity of kingship through Christ's gift, have clearly perceived and frequently heard from statements in holy books that for us, to whom God has granted such a lofty station of worldly office, there is the most urgent necessity *occasionally* to calm our minds amidst these earthly anxieties and direct them to divine and spiritual law. And therefore I sought and petitioned my true friends that they should write down for me from God's books the following teaching concerning the virtues and miracles of holy men, so that, strengthened through the exhortations and love they contain, I might *occasionally* reflect in my mind on heavenly things amidst these earthly tribulations.[87]

It is significant that Gregory's own prefaces are not included by the Anglo-Saxon translators: new times present new contexts, even if these echo the old. The transience of this world and its glories would not have to be explained to a man like Alfred. Gregory had found himself in much the same situation in the Italy of the Lombards, whose destructive violence is closely described in the *Dialogues*. Reflection on the emptiness of this world's glories, however, does not necessarily lead to flight. An alternative, for a ruler of the kind described in the *Pastoral Rule*, is to establish good government on a sound Christian polity. Such an approach requires a balanced reading of Gregory – he is not just the monkishly reluctant pope, longing for his cloister, but also a powerful and capable administrator who understands the rapid change of the political order of his time and creates a new system. Alfred reads both the *Pastoral Rule* and the *Dialogues*, but the *Dialogues* are read only 'occasionally' (a word he

---

the Unlearned?', in Bremmer et al., eds, *Rome and the North*, 27–50; Nicole Guenther Discenza, 'The Influence of Gregory the Great on the Alfredian Social Imaginary', in ibid. 67–82.

[86] *Asser's Life of King Alfred*, ed. W. H. Stevenson (repr. Oxford, 1959), 62.

[87] Lapidge and Keynes, transl., *Alfred the Great*, 96 (italics mine); *Bischof Wærferths von Worcester Übersetzung der Dialoge Gregors des Grossen*, ed. Hans Hecht (Leipzig, 1907), 1.

uses twice in his Preface; Old English *hwilum*), when he has the chance to retreat from the cares of office.

Other works and translations are associated with Alfred's programme – Boethius's *Consolation of Philosophy*, Augustine's *Soliloquies*, Orosius's *World History*, and Bede's *Ecclesiastical History* itself – all of which are treated with a high degree of freedom by their translators.[88] Only Gregory's works are translated with close accuracy and without major omission or interpolation.[89] John the Deacon's *Life* of Gregory was commissioned by John VIII in the 870s, coinciding with the early crisis years of Alfred's faraway kingdom. It has been suggested that the pope was responding to the surprising devotion in the Germanic North to a saint who had become neglected in his own home in the city holding his relics.[90] John the Deacon's claim, in the mouth of his predecessor Peter, that Gregory's works were divinely inspired, is manifest in their careful translation into Old English. This is unlikely to be a coincidence. Alfred, uniquely among English kings, had spent a whole year of his childhood in Rome, Gregory's own city. There can be no doubt that like all Englishmen, he knew that Gregory was the apostle of the English, and that from Rome Augustine had come. But the grown-up Alfred also would have remembered a city in ruins, and as king recognized the similarities between his own precarious situation and Gregory's. Alfred, we know from Asser, suffered a serious and periodically debilitating illness, as had Gregory for much of his reign.[91] In response to pagan

---

[88] Malcolm Godden and Susan Irvine, eds, *The Old English Boethius: An Edition of the Old English Versions of Boethius's* De consolatione philosophiae (Oxford, 2009); *The Old English Orosius*, ed. Janet Bately (London, 1980); *König Alfreds des Grossen Bearbeitung der Soliloquien des Augustinus*, ed. W. Endter (Hamburg, 1922); *The Old English Version of Bede's Ecclesiastical History of the English People*, ed. Thomas Miller (London, 1890).

[89] See Dorothy M. Horgan, 'The Old English *Pastoral Care*: The Scribal Contribution', in Szarmach, ed., *Earlier Old English Prose*, 109–28; David Yerkes, 'The Translation of Gregory's *Dialogues* and its Revision: Textual History, Provenance, Authorship', in ibid. 335–44.

[90] Jeffreys, *Consul*, 260. John was archdeacon of Rome by 853, and may well even have met King Æthelwulf (and Alfred) during their Roman stay. Three surviving pieces of correspondence from John VIII to England each refer to Gregory and the Gregorian mission: to Burgred, king of Mercia (874); to the archbishops of York and Canterbury (873 x 875), which mentions Englishmen keeping St Gregory's Vigil in Rome; and to Ethelred, archbishop of Canterbury (877 x 78); see D. Whitelock, transl., *English Historical Documents, c.500–1042* (London, 1968), 810–13.

[91] See David Pratt, 'The Illnesses of Alfred the Great', *Anglo-Saxon England* 30

Barbarian invasions, Gregory sent out missionaries; Alfred made efforts to convert the Vikings.[92] We know very little about how this proceeded, but do know that Alfred sponsored the Viking king Guthrum at baptism. One of the things which made Alfred 'great' like Gregory was that he was able to achieve the balance between the demands made on the ruler with those made on the human soul, the ruler properly understanding the emptiness of worldly glory while nevertheless working to build Christian society. This ideal, with all its inherent tensions, is one which is found across the Gregorian corpus, even if individual works point in opposite directions. Gregory's contribution to literature, however, lies not just in his works and their universal popularity, but also in the idea of literature he passed on to medieval readers. Christians should read Christian literature by Christian authors, and their reading should focus their minds on the things of heaven. This does not take away from the need to build on earth a society which mirrors the values and order of heaven, which Christian literature should also encourage. In Alfred the Great, Gregory the Great had found an ideal reader.

University of Sydney

(2002), 39–90.
[92] Lapidge and Keynes, transl., *Alfred the Great*, 121.

WAS ANYONE LISTENING?
CHRISTIAN APOLOGETICS AGAINST ISLAM AS A LITERARY GENRE

by JESSICA LEE EHINGER

B y the middle of the eighth century, a new genre of Christian writing had developed among those Christians living within the Islamic empire, that of apologetics intended to defend Christianity against attacks from Muslims. Although the Islamic empire had come into existence a century earlier, a series of changes took place in the mid eighth century, including the rise of the Abbasid caliphal dynasty and the stabilization of the empire's border with Byzantium, which led to more stable internal politics. In this new atmosphere, Christian authors began to consider, for the first time, the theological ramifications of an empire that was ruled by Muslims, but which still had a majority Christian population. The purpose of this essay is to enter into the ongoing scholarly discourse surrounding the genre of Christian apologetics produced under Islam in the eighth and ninth centuries. There are two competing perspectives on studying these works. One argues for them as historical sources authentically representing an ongoing dialogue between Christians and Muslims during a period commonly known as the Golden Age of Islam. The other argues that these texts are literary creations; at its most extreme, this school of thought asserts that these texts are purely fictional, creating a world of Christian rhetorical superiority in the face of mass conversion from Christianity to Islam.[1]

---

[1] The historicizing school is the older of the two, as most of the nineteenth-century scholars who first edited and translated these works in the West accepted them as authentic. Thus Alphonse Mingana in his edition of *The Dialogue of the Patriarch Timothy* argues for it as a basically accurate translation (from Arabic to Syriac) of a real exchange between a religious head and a political head: A. Mingana, ed., *Woodbrooke Studies: Christian Documents in Syriac, Arabic, and Garshūni, Edited and Translated with a Critical Apparatus*, 2 (Cambridge, 1928), 11–13. In the same work, he also argued for the authenticity of *The Apology of al-Kindi*, as did both Sir William Muir and Anton Tien in their 1882 edition. See William Muir, 'The Apology of al-Kindi: An Essay on its Age and Authorship, Read Before the Royal Asiatic Society', in N. A. Newman, ed., *The Early Christian-Muslim Dialogue: A Collection of Documents from the First Three Islamic Centuries (632–900 AD)* (Hatfield, PA, 1993), 376–9. By contrast, Newman, who

This study intends to show how these works, when considered as literary creations, demonstrate the late eighth- and ninth-century understanding of the nature of the Church as expressed by those church leaders who first experienced the mass conversion of their flock to Islam. There is no intention here to 'prove' the validity of this viewpoint over that which argues for the historicity of these texts. Indeed, a great deal of useful work has been done to show that, at the very least, there is a firm historical basis for considering the Islamic Golden Age one of dialogue and intellectual exchange, encouraged by the Abbasid caliphs and fuelled by the developing schools of Arabic literature, science and law. Nevertheless, when these texts are considered as literary creations, they offer a useful source of information about contemporary forms of Christianity, and about how Christian religious leaders and religious thinkers aimed to protect their faith against the encroachment of Islam. Apologetic works, when treated as a literary genre, show how Christian thinkers framed and understood their faith, carefully selecting the best elements and most convincing arguments to highlight, while minimizing those aspects that they considered problematic or weak in the face of Islamic theological claims. In this way, these texts provide evidence for how Christian leaders attempted to create a new image of the Church, in order to fight the gradual mass conversion of their flock from Christianity to Islam.

However, before looking at the texts themselves, it is worth considering a few of the arguments of the historicizing school of thought, in order to understand the genre itself better. Apologetic works were written by all three of the major Christian sects of the Near East in this period: the Chalcedonians or Melkites; the Monophysites or Jacobites; and the Church of the East or Nestorians.[2] However, the corpus of extant complete Christian

---

brought together many of these apologies in his work, generally argued for them as literary creations, citing the same irregularities and problems discussed in the current essay as sufficient evidence against the nineteenth-century consensus.

[2]   The three sects were divided primarily by issues of Christology, in particular the question of the relation between the divine and human natures of Christ. The Chalcedonian interpretation was supported by the Byzantine Empire, and even after the rise of Islam it continued to survive among the urban populations of the Levant and Syria, with most of its proponents writing in Greek well into the ninth century. The Monophysite community was anti-Chalcedonian, and in particular after the rise of Islam it wrote in the vernacular languages, most importantly Armenian, Syriac in

apologetic includes fewer than a dozen texts, with the majority appearing to arise out of the Nestorian community, although many are anonymous and attempt to deny any particular confessional allegiance. The prevalence of Nestorian works is no doubt due to their strength, in the population as well as within the court of the Abbasid caliphate, which had its capital and centre in the former Persian territory of Mesopotamia, the centre of Nestorian Christianity for more than three centuries. The works also span the linguistic variations of the Near East, being produced in Syriac, Arabic and Greek. In general, the corpus is remarkably uniform, with similar themes and motifs used across these confessional and linguistic distinctions, creating a definitively 'Christian' genre. The works within this genre generally take one of two forms. One is that of the public debate, an exchange of ideas between leaders of each community, in which the Christian leader talks rhetorical circles around the Islamic leader, successfully showing both the clarity of Christian doctrine and the incompleteness of Islamic doctrine. The other is that of the letter, or more often a series of letters. The claim is that these are letters exchanged between friends or acquaintances, in which both correspondents, one Christian and one Muslim, ask questions about the other's faith. It is in the course of these questions and answers that the correctness of Christian faith becomes apparent.

Unfortunately it is somewhat difficult to calculate the full number of texts which should be included in this corpus, as several of the extant texts reuse the same premise and basic structure, in particular that of a dialogue between a Muslim political leader and a Christian religious leader, at least three versions of which survive.[3] Therefore it is often difficult to discern whether later citations refer to distinct texts or merely to variations of known works, complicating the issue of the size of the original corpus. As they

---

the Levant and Syria, and Coptic in Egypt. The Nestorian community had established itself in the Persian Empire by the late fifth century, with a large population in Mesopotamia, writing in Syriac. There was also a small but active Monophysite community in Mesopotamia, and both the Monophysites and Nestorians established and supported monasteries throughout the formerly Persian territories.

3   Among extant apologetics, two Monophysite and one Nestorian version of this model survive: the dialogue of an anonymous monk and the amir in Jerusalem and that between the governor of Damascus and the Monophysite Patriarch Joseph in the case of the former, and the dialogue of the caliph and the Nestorian Patriarch Timothy in the case of the latter.

represent the majority of works, in this essay two Nestorian texts will be discussed, one from each of the two apologetic styles – the dialogue of the Patriarch Timothy and the Caliph al-Mahdī and the letters of the Muslim al-Hashāmī and the Christian al-Kindī. In addition, a few works have survived without a clear confessional identity, due to their transmission through several different communities. One example from this sub-corpus will be referred to, the alleged correspondence of the Byzantine Emperor Leo III and the Caliph 'Umar II. Two versions of these letters survive, one in Latin and one in Armenian, but scholars have generally presumed a common Greek source for both. A Greek root source would suggest (although by no means guarantee) a Chalcedonian confession, but it is also generally presumed that the Armenian letters, which are the more complete of the two versions, have undergone some degree of Monophysite redaction, which may have altered the emperor's position on issues of Christology.[4] However, in general, aside from a reference to iconophilia, to be discussed later, the letters bear little evidence for any particular confessional identity.

The historicizing school of thought has been correct to stress that there is nothing historically implausible about either type of work. The use of letters to persuade or convert is not unheard of for this period, particularly among the growing intellectual elite; the letter-type apologetic rarely ends with a clear conversion, but more often with a general sense of superiority for one argument over the other, lending them a sense of authenticity. These letters are generally attached to figures of well-known academic and rhetorical ability; again, there is nothing implausible in the idea that these figures would write to recently apostate friends to try to remind them of the truth of Christianity. Apologetic works in the dialogue style have an even greater wealth of evidence to support their historical relevance. During the period of the Abbasid caliphate, the second of the Muslim ruling dynasties, which lasted from the last half of the eighth until the early eleventh century, the caliphs, as part of their ongoing attempts to nurture the new capital of Baghdad as the intellectual and cultural centre of the world, regularly convened the *majliss* (literally 'a place to sit or

---

[4]   See Arthur Jeffery's introduction, 'Ghevond's Text of the Correspondence between 'Umar II and Leo III', in Newman, ed., *Dialogue*, 57–9.

recline'), a kind of public forum debate in which great thinkers were brought to the court to extemporize and debate over scholarly topics.[5]

According to both Muslim and Christian sources, the caliphs enforced a strict policy of protection for speakers at the *majliss*, and religious belief was often put forward as a topic for debate, not only between Christians and Muslims, but often between the sects of Islam as well.[6] In the *majliss*, it was expected that the speakers would defend their position and their faith to their utmost ability, with only a few limitations placed upon those speaking against Islam: they could not curse the religion, its Prophet or the Qur'ān – regulations which these debate-style apologetic works follow consistently. All of these historical circumstances support the argument that something like the apologetic public debates and letters to be considered here truly existed in the period of the Abbasid caliphate.

The weakness of the historicizing school, however, lies in the difficulty of showing that these apologetics as they have survived were ever part of public life in the Abbasid period. Again, it is worth stressing that only a handful of texts survive and it is difficult to say what percentage of the original corpus these works represent. As has been said, the historicizing school is correct to stress that there is ample evidence to suggest that letters were written and debates staged to defend Christianity, but a close reading of the texts themselves suggest that they are literary creations, relying on historical circumstance for relevance and context, but not aimed at the accurate preservation of historical events.

Several aspects of the texts highlight their redacted or created nature. Firstly, and perhaps most importantly, the Christian and Muslim participants are rarely equal partners. This is especially true of the debate-style apologetic, in which the Muslim figures are often reduced to one-line or even single-word replies. One of the most noticeable cases of this phenomenon comes from a supposed dialogue between the Muslim Caliph al-Mahdī and the Nestorian

---

5 W. Madelung et al., 'Madjlis', in P. Bearman et al., eds, *Encyclopaedia of Islam*, 2nd edn (2010), online at <http://www.brillonline.nl/subscriber/entry?entry=islam_COM-0606>, accessed 12 July 2010.

6 For a discussion on these claims of protection and their historicity, see Sidney H. Griffith, 'The Monk in the Emir's *Majlis*', in Hava Lazarus-Yafeh et al., eds, *The Majlis: Interreligious Encounters in Medieval Islam* (Wiesbaden, 1999), 13–65.

Patriarch Timothy. The dialogue is cast as a *majliss*-style discussion, with the caliph questioning the patriarch about his faith. But the questions are peculiarly brief, and well designed to lead into long monologues by the patriarch, expanding upon the nature of Christianity and the Christian God. For example, in response to the patriarch's introductory statements about Christ as the Son of God, the caliph replies with the succinct question, 'How?',[7] which leads to another monologue from the patriarch about the nature of the incarnation. The caliph's questions subsequently lead to further monologues, first on Mary, then on the nature of Christ's humanity, and finally on the nature of the Trinity.[8] The story quickly becomes one of the patriarch leading the caliph's questions, as opposed to the other way around (which was the correct structure for the *majliss*).

In addition, these works often lack historical grounding, again suggesting that they are in fact literary creations. The letters supposedly exchanged between the Byzantine Emperor Leo III and the Caliph 'Umar II have already been mentioned briefly. The two rulers are natural choices for a literary work; contemporaries, they were both known for their interest in rhetoric and for their fierce defence of orthodox thought within their respective empires. Yet several elements of the letters stand out to those familiar with the period. Firstly, the siege of Constantinople in 718, which had just ended with the Muslims' utter failure and their withdrawal, is given no mention by either leader. Furthermore, the issue of the worship of icons is introduced by the caliph, and the theology is defended by the emperor, who says:

> ... we have always felt a desire to conserve [the disciples'] images, which have come down to us from their times as their living representation. Their presence charms us, and we glorify God who has saved us by the intermediary of His only-begotten Son, who appeared in the world in a similar figure, and we glorify the saints.[9]

This is rather odd, as Leo would be the first of the iconoclast emperors, spending most of his term in office arguing against the

---

7   Mingana, ed., *Woodbrooke*, 2: 17.
8   Ibid. 17–23.
9   Ibid. 92.

theological validity of this very claim, that the worship of the icons was beneficial because it taught Christians to glorify God.

The lack of historical grounding for these texts and the unbalanced nature of the exchanges between the Christian and Muslim characters suggest rather strongly that these texts, at least as they have survived, are not the historical accounts they purport to be, but rather literary inventions. However, as literary inventions they offer a unique source of information about how Christian theology evolved and adapted in the face of the Muslim incursion. The second half of this paper will focus on one aspect of this theology in particular: how Christian authors of the eighth and ninth century understood the nature of the Church, and how they chose to express this doctrine. Inherent in this consideration is also the question of audience, and specifically that of whether these works were directed at converting Muslims and bringing them into the Christian community or at Christians in order to maintain the community that already existed. Based on the theological construction of the Church offered in these works, it seems far more plausible that they were written to bolster Christian belief rather than to convert Muslims, using the Muslims' victory and success as worldly leaders to argue for the continued spiritual importance of the Church.

There are three main points about the nature of the Church in these apologetic works. Two of these are discussed explicitly, the unity of the Church despite the schisms of the fourth and fifth centuries, and the belief that the Islamic expansion was in fact a benefit to the Church because it offered it protection and ended paganism in the Near East. The third is not explicitly developed in the texts but rather grows out of the structure of the works themselves: the apologists' understanding that the authority to expound Christian doctrine was not confined to the hierarchy of the Church but was also disseminated to the wider Christian community, as exemplified by the supposed participants of these works. In some cases, the Christian writers and preachers of these works held high church offices, as with the aforementioned dialogue between the caliph and Patriarch Timothy. Timothy was the head of the Nestorian Church, the largest of the Christian communities in Mesopotamia, and thus the obvious choice to speak with authority to the caliph. But often the Christian speakers hold no such apparent official authority. In the letters between Leo and

'Umar, the emperor does not claim to be speaking as an authority for Christianity but simply as 'the Servant of Jesus Christ and the sovereign of those who know Him', answering 'Umar's questions because 'it is God Himself who commands us to instruct our adversaries with kindliness'.[10]

Indeed, one of the best known of the letter-genre apologetic works is attributed to characters with no official authority whatsoever. The apology of al-Kindī consists of correspondence between two friends in the 'Abbasid court, the Muslim al-Hāshimī and the Christian al-Kindī, both intimates of the Caliph Ma'mun, neither of whom held any official role in their respective religious community. Al-Hāshimī writes to al-Kindī to ask questions about Christianity in order 'to counsel you in all sincerity and with perfect frankness, placing before you those great religious verities which we hold by the grace of God',[11] and al-Kindī responds, considering it a requirement of the pair's close friendship, though he considers himself 'least of the servants of Christ'[12] and 'not sufficient of anything of [himself]'.[13] It appears from contemporary sources that much of the Church's hierarchy had continued under Muslim rule, yet these texts do not appear to argue for an authoritative voice which stems from church office. Instead, Christian apologists appear to argue for the right, and even duty, of individual Christians to answer Muslim attacks against Christian doctrine.

This image of the life of the Church as preserved by individual Christians, as well as by the established hierarchy, is further developed by the two claims made explicitly in these texts. Firstly, there is the apologists' continued belief in the essential unity of the Church, despite the schisms of the previous centuries. This repeated motif appears most often in response to a Muslim claim, which has its roots in the *hadīth*, the sayings of the Prophet, that Christianity had splintered into seventy-two sects. Thus, in response to this accusation, the Emperor Leo tells the Caliph 'Umar:

> it is now eight hundred years since Jesus Christ appeared, and His Gospel has been spread from one end of the earth to the

---

[10] Ibid. 63.
[11] 'The Apology of al-Kindi', ed. Anton Tien, in Newman, ed., *Dialogue*, 381–545, at 383.
[12] Ibid. 411.
[13] Ibid. 412.

other, amongst all people and all languages, from the civilized countries of Greece and Rome to the further countries of the barbarians, and if there is found some divergence among Christians it is because of the differences of language. I have said divergence, because there has never been among us that bitter hostility such as one sees deeply rooted among you. It would appear that under this number seventy-two you must include all the voluptuous, impure, filthy, impious people who conduct themselves like pagans, and among whose number you count us.[14]

He goes on to argue that these 'impious people' should be considered pagans, as they require rebaptism to rejoin 'the Holy Church'. The reference to rebaptism is most likely intended to imply that the emperor is not speaking of the distinctions between Melkite, Monophysite and Nestorian, as it was generally accepted by all three that rebaptism was not necessary for conversion from one to another. But, the author concludes, even mentioning these 'impious people' is perhaps unnecessary, as 'God has long since caused them to disappear completely, so that one no longer sees them.'[15]

This is a remarkable claim, and one that bears almost no resemblance to the world of eighth-century Christianity as it survives in contemporary sources. Instead, the Christian world of Leo's time was rife with schism. Precursors of the eventual schism of Rome and the 'further barbarian countries' (that is, Western Europe) from Eastern Christianity were already being felt. In the Eastern world, the division between Melkite, Jacobite and Nestorian Christians was so engrained as to even appear in Muslim writing as the basic division of Christianity. And, as previously mentioned, Leo himself would shortly institute yet another wave of imperial repression, further dividing Byzantine Chalcedonianism through his policy of imperial iconoclasm. There can be little doubt, then, that the unity of which this author speaks is an imagined one. It is developed in contrast to the Muslims, who, in just over a century, had already splintered into the groups which would come to define

---

[14] Jeffery, 'Ghevond's Text', 73.
[15] Ibid.

43

the competing views of Muslim doctrine, most importantly the Shī'a and the Khawārij.

The final aspect of the Church as developed in Christian apologetics is the belief that the Islamic expansion had benefited the Church. This defence generally relies on one of two arguments, either that the expansion was beneficial because the rise of Islam ended paganism in the Near East, or that it was beneficial because the Muslim authority offered protection to the Eastern churches, in particular the Monophysite and Nestorian Churches, who had suffered repression under Byzantine rule. In his dialogue with the caliph, the character of the Patriarch Timothy gives both of these reasons for the expansion, as well as going so far as to imply that by God's will the Muslims were victorious against Christian heretics as well as against pagans. When asked by the caliph what he thought of Muhammad, the patriarch explained that he was worthy of praise and honour, for:

> … who will not praise, honour and exalt the one who not only fought for God with words, but showed also his zeal for Him in the sword? … He turned his face from idols and their worshippers, whether those idols were those of his own kinsmen or of strangers, and he honoured and worshipped the one God.

It is for this reason that Islam was successful:

> … because of this God honoured him exceedingly and brought low before his feet two powerful kingdoms which roared in the world like a lion and made the voice of their authority heard in all the earth that is below heaven, like thunder, viz. the kingdom of Persia and that of the Romans.[16] The former kingdom, that is to say, the kingdom of the Persians, worshipped the creatures instead of the Creator, and the latter, that is to say the kingdom of the Romans, attributed suffering and death in the flesh to one who can not [sic] suffer and die in any way through any process.[17]

The Patriarch goes on to explain that this same blessing from

---

[16] That is, the Byzantines; the Syriac term *ruhmoiyo* can mean Latin-speaking, Byzantine or Melkite, depending on the context.
[17] Mingana, ed., *Woodbrooke*, 2: 62.

God has been passed on the caliph, the inheritor of Muhammad's rule, but that this is not reason enough for Christians to abandon Christianity and follow Islam. And it is here that the audience for these works becomes clear. The character of the patriarch is presumably no longer speaking to the caliph in these passages, who was never a Christian and probably harboured no interest in converting to Christianity. However, for Christians living under Muslim rule, conversion offered important opportunities: social advancement, geographical mobility and financial benefits. Moreover, that the Muslims had been so fantastically successful – militarily and politically – was taken by both Muslims and Christians as evidence of God's blessing upon Islam. Indeed, Muslim authors regularly interpreted the Islamic expansion as divine validation of Muhammad's message. The character of the patriarch is offering an alternative version, one which explains the Muslims' success without encouraging conversion: the Muslims were rewarded by God for their victory over paganism and Christian heresies. True Christians, though, had been protected by the Muslims, as shown by the patriarch himself and his obviously close relationship to the caliph.

All in all, Christian apologetics create an image of the Church almost completely opposed to the reality of their situation – unified, strong under Muslim rule and defended by individual Christians, as well as by the church hierarchy. In reality, the late eighth and early ninth century saw the first mass conversions away from Christianity to Islam, as the social and political system stabilized and Christians began to seek social and political advancement. But, when addressed to a potentially waning Christian audience, this imagined Church emphasized the importance of their continued faith. This was a universal Church – although they were cut off from Christendom farther west, they were still a part of it. It was a protected Church – protected from paganism and heresy by the rule of Muslims, whom God had made guardians of the true doctrine. And it was an individual's Church – it was required that each Christian protect and defend their own faith against the accusations and false claims of Islam. Again, in a climate of slow conversion, in which the possibility for social advancement began to overshadow questions of faith, the Christian apologists created for their audience a Church which required allegiance, a call edged with both urgency and cosmic significance. It was a literary creation, but an important and relevant one. Ultimately, it was also a failed one, but one that would survive among the small remaining communities of Christians as they continued to shape their own understanding of the nature of their faith.

St Peter's College, Oxford

FRIVOLITY AND REFORM IN THE CHURCH:
THE IRISH EXPERIENCE, 1066–1166

by DAVID N. DUMVILLE

In mid November 1064, what was perhaps the most important pre-Crusade pilgrimage to Jerusalem left Bavaria under
the leadership of Günther, bishop of Bamberg.[1] The number
of pilgrims, all unarmed, is stated as some seven thousand in the
least incredible source text. The leading ecclesiastics came from all
over the northern half of the Empire, from Utrecht to Regens-
burg. A substantial contingent hailed from the province of Mainz,
led by Archbishop Siegfried. Only some two thousand are said to
have returned the following year. Our earliest source is the chronicle kept at Mainz by the Gaelic *inclusus*, Moelbrigte / Marianus
Scottus (d.1082/3), who had lived at Mainz since 1069 and was
certainly writing his chronicle by 1073/4.[2]

The pilgrimage is alleged to have been motivated by a belief,
reported already by Abbo of Fleury in the late tenth century, that
the world would end when a particular kalendarial conjunction
occurred, namely the Annunciation (25 March) and Good Friday
falling on the same day.[3] In the tenth century these criteria were
met four times – in 908, 970, 981 and 992 – without the anticipated result. The next occurrence, after a two-generation gap,
was in 1065. We might also note that 1064 marked the end of
the second Great Paschal Cycle of Dionysius Exiguus. At Easter
1064, something of a crisis seems to have been provoked in the

---

[1] For a very clear introduction to this, see E. Joranson, 'The Great German
Pilgrimage of 1064–1065', in *The Crusades and Other Historical Essays presented to Dana
C. Munro by his Former Students*, ed. Louis J. Paetow (New York, 1928), 3–43.

[2] For brief introductions to Marianus and his work, see James F. Kenney, *The
Sources for the Early History of Ireland: Ecclesiastical. An Introduction and Guide*, ed. L. Bieler
(New York, 1966), 614–16 (no. 443); Michael Lapidge and R. Sharpe, *A Bibliography
of Celtic-Latin Literature, 400–1200* (Dublin, 1985), 196 (no. 728). Further to the literature cited therein, see B. Ó Cuív, 'The Irish Marginalia in Codex Palatino-Vaticano
No. 830', *Éigse* 24 (1990), 45–67; P. Verbist, 'Reconstructing the Past: The Chronicle
of Marianus Scottus', *Peritia* 16 (2002), 284–334. For notice of the quasi-autograph
manuscript, see Elizabeth Duncan, *Catalogue of Latin and Vernacular Manuscripts written
by Gaelic Scribes, A.D. 1000–1200* (Aberdeen, forthcoming), no. 43.

[3] Joranson, 'Great German Pilgrimage', 12–13.

German empire by recognizing the next Easter's potential. What better place could there be than Jerusalem in which to experience the second coming? To apocalypticism and judgement as a theme in Irish history of this period we shall return – at the end, appropriately.

Marianus's account is not without humour, drawing attention to the pomp and circumstance affected by the pilgrim bishops, to the danger which this display occasioned them and their comrades (as well as to its aggravation by their failing to hand over more than a part of their wealth to robbers), and to the cunning (holy guile, perhaps) which they displayed when in peril.[4] Complaints about prelates and wealth were not new to Irish writing, or to Gaelic chronicling in particular.[5]

The later tenth and eleventh centuries had seen reactions in Latin Christendom to three principal types of abuse in and of Christian society. One involved clear violations of gospel precepts by ecclesiastics and required the Church to put its own house in order, perhaps necessarily with the aid of secular authority. A second saw the laity too heavily involved in ecclesiastical matters, corrupting both the working of the Church's institutions and many ecclesiastical personnel. The third found the laity posing a severe threat – through physical violence and unprincipled, single-minded pursuit of material and political self-interest – to the very existence of a Christian society. This interlocking series of problems provoked very various reactions over the course of a turbulent century. Radical tendencies emerged within the Western Church, whether at local or at regional level, in the monastic life, or in the central institutions of the Church. When a party with this outlook

4   MGH SS 5: 558–9 (s.aa. 1064–5). Cf. Joranson, 'Great German Pilgrimage', 5–6 (esp. n. 12), 16.
5   A remarkable example is found in Gaelic literature of around 1100 in a long text – of Goliardic spirit, one might almost say – known as 'The Vision of Mac Conglinne', to which we shall briefly return below: Aislinge Meic Conglinne – The Vision of MacConglinne, A Middle-Irish Wonder Tale, ed. and transl. Kuno Meyer and W. Wollner (London, 1892). For a more recent edition, without translation, see Aislinge Meic Con Glinne, ed. Kenneth Hurlstone Jackson (Dublin, 1990). For the best literary discussion of this text, see S. J. Gwara, 'Gluttony, Lust and Penance in the B-text of Aislinge Meic Conglinne', Celtica 20 (1988), 53–72. On the general Irish context of the abuses satirized, see Kathleen Hughes, 'Sanctity and Secularity in the Early Irish Church', in Derek Baker, ed., Sanctity and Secularity: The Church and the World, SCH 10 (London, 1973), 21–37, repr. in her Church and Society in Ireland, A.D. 400–1200 (London, 1987), essay IX.

gained control of the papacy, in the person of Leo IX (1049–54), an essential condition was met for more vigorous dissemination of reformist views and for the pope himself to press for significant remedial action by ecclesiastical hierarchies.[6]

In England, a monastic reformist tendency – having, indeed, a decidedly revolutionary agenda – had captured the heights of the episcopate in the course of the 960s, enjoying at that point significant royal support. By the 1020s, however, it was clear that this movement had run out of steam in turbulent years marked by Scandinavian invasions and conquest.[7] While the reform ideal was never extinguished in England, the events of 1049–51 must nevertheless have evoked considerable surprise, when (for example) at the Councils of Rheims and Vercelli English ecclesiastics were placed under searching scrutiny with some dramatic results.[8] After the Norman conquest, a good many reform-minded francophone ecclesiastics found themselves in the English Church, a process almost coincident with the emergence of Archdeacon Hildebrand (an active supporter of William's invasion) as Pope Gregory VII (1073–85), who gave his name to a radical outlook on (and movement of) reform in the Western Church, to the eventual point

[6]   On the overarching context of reform, see the life-changing book by Gerhart B. Ladner, *The Idea of Reform*, 2nd edn (New York, 1967). For two helpful and impressively cogent introductions, see Uta-Renate Blumenthal, *The Investiture Controversy. Church and Monarchy from the Ninth to the Twelfth Century* (Philadelphia, PA, 1991); I. S. Robinson, *The Papacy, 1073–1198, Continuity and Innovation* (Cambridge, 1990).

[7]   For accounts of this process from various angles, see David Parsons, ed., *Tenth-Century Studies: Essays in Commemoration of the Millennium of the Council of Winchester and Regularis Concordia* (Chichester, 1975); Mechthild Gretsch, *The Intellectual Foundations of the English Benedictine Reform* (Cambridge, 1999); John Blair, *The Church in Anglo-Saxon Society* (Oxford, 2005); Donald Scragg, ed., *Edgar, King of the English 959–975, New Interpretations* (Woodbridge, 2008). To my mind, the picture left by such writing is itself in need of radical reform: the most penetrating insights of Eric John, *Land Tenure in Early England: A Discussion of Some Problems* (Leicester, 1960; rev. imp. 1964) and *Orbis Britanniae and Other Studies* (Leicester, 1966), remain to be absorbed; and numerous overtly revolutionary agenda of radical parties in the tenth-century English Church need to be acknowledged. I began such an approach from the evidence of books and script: David N. Dumville, *English Caroline Script and Monastic History: Studies in Benedictinism, A.D. 950–1030* (Woodbridge, 1993).

[8]   Frank Barlow, *The English Church, 1000–1066*, 2nd edn (London, 1979; first publ. 1963), ch. 7. For the oblique treatment of these events in the principal English narrative record of the period, see *The Anglo-Saxon Chronicle, according to the Several Original Authorities*, ed. and transl. Benjamin Thorpe, 2 vols (London, 1861), I: 305–13 (text, *s.aa.* 1046–52), and *The Anglo-Saxon Chronicle: A Revised Translation*, transl. Dorothy Whitelock (London, 1961; rev. imp. 1965), 111–17 (annals 1049–51).

of provoking significant conflict with some secular rulers about matters deemed essential to the cause of ecclesiastical self-government.[9]

The first archbishop of Canterbury appointed after the Norman conquest was Lanfranc of Bec (1070–89):[10] his letters reveal a chain of correspondence beginning in 1073 with Pope Gregory VII, urging that abuses in Gaelic society be addressed by Lanfranc.[11] Using pre-Conquest channels of communication with the Celtic world, the post-Conquest archbishops became active in transmitting and amplifying these views, particularly to Irish bishops and kings, urging the convocation of reform councils as fora for corrective action.[12]

In 1080 or 1081 Archbishop Lanfranc received from Domnall Ua hÉnna, bishop in Munster (the southern provincial overkingdom), and his colleagues, a letter (which seems not to have survived) requesting guidance about the relationship of the baptism of infants and their salvation.[13] It is clear that this was not the only content of Bishop Domnall's letter. Lanfranc's reply ends thus:

> You also sent problems *of profane learning* for us to elucidate; but it does not befit a bishop's manner of life to be concerned with studies of that kind. Long ago in our youth we did devote our time to these matters, but when we came to pastoral responsibility we decided to give them up altogether.[14]

---

[9] Robinson, *Papacy*, esp. 398–441; Barlow, *English Church*, 48–9; H. E. J. Cowdrey, *Pope Gregory VII, 1073–1085* (Oxford, 1998).

[10] For biographies, see A. J. Macdonald, *Lanfranc: A Study of his Life, Work & Writing* (London, 1926; 2nd edn 1944); Margaret Gibson, *Lanfranc of Bec* (Oxford, 1978); H. E. J. Cowdrey, *Lanfranc. Scholar, Monk, and Archbishop* (Oxford, 2003).

[11] *The Letters of Lanfranc, Archbishop of Canterbury*, ed. and transl. Helen Clover and M. Gibson (Oxford, 1979), 64–7 (no. 8), where *Scotti* should be translated 'Gaels', not the prejudicially specific 'Irish' or 'Scots'.

[12] For recent discussion, see David N. Dumville, *Councils and Synods of the Gaelic Early and Central Middle Ages* (Cambridge, 1997), 35–46, 50–5; M. Philpott, 'Some Interactions between the English and Irish Churches', *Anglo-Norman Studies* 20 (1997), 187–204; C. Downham, 'England and the Irish-Sea Zone in the Eleventh Century', *Anglo-Norman Studies* 26 (2003), 55–73; M. Brett, 'Canterbury's Perspective on Church Reform and Ireland, 1070–1115', in Damian Bracken and D. Ó Riain-Raedel, eds, *Ireland and Europe in the Twelfth Century. Reform and Renewal* (Dublin, 2006), 13–35.

[13] *Letters*, ed. and transl. Clover and Gibson, 154–61 (no. 49). Whether the identification of the addressee ('D.' or 'Donatus' in different witnesses), and therefore the dating, can be sustained is a moot point: I must confess to some scepticism.

[14] 'Quaestiones *secularium litterarum* nobis soluendas misistis, sed episcopale propositum non decet operam dare huiusmodi studiis. Olim quidem iuuenilem aetatem in

This withering put-down told Bishop Domnall and his colleagues that they were immature and profane-minded, as well as insufficiently focused on their pastoral duties. Whether or not 'profane' or even 'secular' is the right translation of the text's *secularium*,[15] Lanfranc's remarks in 1073/4 in a letter to the king of Dublin about Patrick, newly consecrated bishop of Dublin, make the point of contrast clear: Patrick 'has been nurtured in the monastic life since his youth; he is deeply versed *in sacred learning*; and ... he has an exceptional distinction in good works'.[16] He was not frivolous. Nor of course was Archbishop Lanfranc.

What, then, might these *quaestiones secularium litterarum* have been? We might boggle at the thought of Lanfranc receiving questions about characters from 'The Cattle-raid of Cooley',[17] but perhaps less so if they concerned Virgil – Dido and Aeneas, perhaps, or issues of Latin language and metrics.

The object and the mode of this episcopal discussion were literary, but the issues emerge as essentially moral in character. If we were to turn to other episcopal correspondence of the eleventh and twelfth centuries, different possibilities arise. Abuses identified among ecclesiastics included betting games involving biblical text. An obvious context is the practice of what has been described as 'the age-old custom of [*reuolutio foliorum*,] seeking an oracular response from a sacred text opened at random' – *sortes biblicae* as they have been called. There is much, if scattered, evidence for private testing of Scripture thus. But the practice seems to have had an official role in episcopal consecration, for which likewise there is scattered evidence but also a list of forty-two such prognostics for English prelates from 1070 until about 1123.[18]

---

his detriuimus, sed accedentes ad pastoralem curam abrenuntiandum eis decreuimus': ibid. 158–61 (italics mine).

[15] Cf. P. Dronke, 'Profane Elements in Literature', in Robert L. Benson et al., eds, *Renaissance and Renewal in the Twelfth Century* (Cambridge, MA, 1982), 569–92.

[16] 'monasticis institutionibus a pueritia enutritum, *scientia diuinarum litterarum strenuissime eruditum*, bonorum operum ornamentis ... decentissime adornatum': *Letters*, ed. and transl. Clover and Gibson, 66–9 (no. 9).

[17] For an eleventh-century version, see *Táin Bó Cúailnge, Recension I*, ed. and transl. Cecile O'Rahilly (Dublin, 1976).

[18] G. Henderson, '*Sortes biblicae* in Twelfth-Century England: The List of Episcopal Prognostics in Cambridge, Trinity College MS R.7.5', in Daniel Williams, ed., *England in the Twelfth Century: Proceedings of the 1988 Harlaxton Symposium* (Woodbridge, 1990), 113–35 (quotation at 114).

Again, however, it is not clear how such matters might be raised as *quaestiones* in a letter or whether they would count – given the close relationship with biblical text – as *seculares litterae*. Another tack worth trying is provoked by a different twelfth-century Anglo-Norman codex. British Library MS Additional 37785 contains the *Sententiae* of Isidore of Seville and Alcuin's *De uirtutibus*, in 84 folios of twelfth-century English script and in a perhaps contemporary binding. The provenance and presumed origin are Haughmond Abbey in Shropshire, which belonged to the Augustinians.[19] Part of the binding materials (now folios ii–v) was provided by four leaves in twelfth-century Gaelic minuscule script (albeit under marked influence from late Caroline minuscule): these contain an incomplete and unpublished text of biblical questions in two sequences, beginning *Quot?* and *Quare?* (1) *Quot sunt pondera hominis?* ('How many are the elements of man?') *Sunt octo de quibus factus est hominis* ('There are eight elements of which man was constituted'). (2) *Quare Christus natus est ex uirgine?* ('Why was Christ brought forth from a virgin?')[20] Texts of this sort are quite widespread in the Gaelic literary tradition, both in prose and in verse. Two Middle Gaelic poems, 'The poem of forty questions' and 'The poem of fifty questions', are representative of the same type, as is the prose *Cesta gréga* ('Greek problems').[21] The new (post-Conquest) abbeys of the Anglo-Welsh border developed dependent institutions in colonial Ireland, and one can imagine the Gaelic book in question coming thence and being broken up at Haughmond.[22] However,

---

[19]   *British Museum Catalogue of Additions to the Manuscripts, 1906–10*, ed. Julius P. Gilson (London, 1912), 138–9; cf. Seymour de Ricci, *A Hand-list of a Collection of Books and Manuscripts belonging to The Right Hon. Lord Amherst of Hackney at Didlington Hall, Norfolk* (Cambridge, 1906), 209 (MS 34). See also *Medieval Libraries of Great Britain: A List of Surviving Books*, ed. N. R. Ker (London, 1941), 53 (2nd edn, 1964, 96), where it is dated about 1200.

[20]   For an intelligible answer to this question, the manuscript's text needs emendation. For (scattered) discussion of the text found in London, BL, MS Add. 37785 and its literary congeners, see Robin Flower, *Catalogue of Irish Manuscripts in the British Museum, Volume II* (London, 1926), 433, 520–4.

[21]   R. Thurneysen, 'Das Gedicht der vierzig Fragen von Eochaid ua Cérin', *Zeitschrift für celtische Philologie* 13 (1919–21), 130–6 (*Apraid a éolchu Elga*); K. Meyer, 'Mitteilungen aus irischen Handschriften. Dúan in chóicat cest. Aus Egerton 1782 fo. 49*b*.', *Zeitschrift für celtische Philologie* 4 (1902–3), 234–6 (*Iarfaigid lib cóecait cest*); for these two poems, cf. Flower, *Catalogue II*, 282 (item 36), 280–1 (item 29). For the prose *Cesta gréga*, see W. Stokes, 'Irish Riddles', *Celtic Review* 1 (1904–5), 132–5; cf. Flower, *Catalogue II*, 520–2 (item 3), 107 (item 39).

[22]   For parallel examples, see: (1) London, LPL, MS 1229, fols 7–8 (previously MS

a credible palaeographical argument has been made for a Scottish origin of these leaves.[23]

These questions turn on biblical text but may be held to be of a somewhat secular-minded character, even though they often rest on theological issues. Some of the sections indeed carry source indicators of the type characteristic of earlier medieval exegesis of arguably Gaelic (or Insular Celtic) origin: *hir* (Jerome), *ag* (Augustine), *gg* (Gregory). The whole extended tradition of such biblical question-and-answer literature seems to have at least an Insular dimension to its early history.[24]

These catechetical or dialogue texts have come to be known collectively by the title (attested by about 800) *Ioca monachorum* ('Monks' jokes'), or (as recently suggested by Charles D. Wright) 'Bible-quiz for monks', although in fact there are many variant types with their own titles.[25] This genre and form bit deeply into medieval European literature in both Latin and vernacular traditions.[26]

The circulation of such texts is in part liturgical (attested first in the Bobbio Missal) and in part with creeds and other catechetical texts. This has generated hypotheses of original function

119, fols 1–2), datable *c*.850 × *c*.1000, provenance Lanthony Secunda (Augustinians), in the second half of the twelfth century (Ker, *Medieval Libraries*, 61; 2nd edn, 109), publ. by L. Bieler and J. Carney, 'The Lambeth Commentary', *Ériu* 23 (1972), 1–55; (2) London, BL, MS Harley 2253, written in Herefordshire about 1340, has Anglo-Irish documentary flyleaves from Ardmulghan (Co. Meath), datable to 1312, and overwritten by the scribe of the main manuscript, as shown by P. O'Neill, 'On the Date of the Harley Lyrics Manuscript', *JCS* 3 (1981–2), 132–5. On Lanthony and Ireland, see Arlene Hogan, *The Priory of Llanthony Prima and Secunda in Ireland, 1172–1541: Lands, Patronage and Politics* (Dublin, 2008). On the larger Augustinian context, see Geraldine Carville, *The Occupation of Celtic Sites in Medieval Ireland by the Canons Regular of St Augustine and the Cistercians* (Kalamazoo, MI, 1982); cf. Aubrey Gwynn and R. N. Hadcock, *Medieval Religious Houses, Ireland* (London, 1970).

23 Duncan, *Catalogue*, no. 24.

24 C. D. Wright and R. Wright, 'Additions to "The Bobbio Missal": *De dies malus* and *Joca monachorum* (fols. 6r–8v)', in Yitzhak Hen and R. Meens, eds, *The Bobbio Missal: Liturgy and Religious Culture in Merovingian Gaul* (Cambridge, 2004), 79–139.

25 Ibid. 80 (Latin title), 123 (Bible-quiz).

26 Walther Suchier, *L'Enfant sage: Das Gespräch des Kaisers Hadrian mit dem klugen Kinde Epitus* (Dresden, 1910); idem, *Die mittellateinische Gespräch Adrian und Epictitus nebst verwandten Texten (Joca Monachorum)* (Tübingen, 1955); Lloyd William Daly and W. Suchier, *Altercatio Hadriani Augusti et Epicteti Philosophi* (Urbana, IL, 1939). For editions of Anglo-Saxon texts considered in this wide context, see *The* Prose Solomon and Saturn *and* Adrian and Ritheus, ed. and transl. James E. Cross and T. D. Hill (Toronto, ON, 1982).

as pre-baptismal catechesis or as paraliturgical matter for Lenten catechetical instruction.[27]

Such catechetical *quaestiones* can be more or less sober in presentation. Let me offer an item which may be held to make more than one serious religious point yet which may equally be thought to have an air of humour in its ingenuity. It concerns the nails in Noah's Ark. It is in Middle Gaelic (10th–12th centuries) but retrieved from an early modern Irish copy.

> [What was the best and the worst nail in the Ark?] The wright who built the Ark left one nail-hole empty, for he was sure that he himself would not be taken in the Ark. When Noah with his children went into the Ark, as the angel had told him, Noah shut the windows of the Ark and raised his hand to bless it.
>
> Now the Devil had gone into the Ark beside him as he entered; and when Noah blessed the Ark, the Devil found no other place but the empty hole which the wright had left unclosed, and he went into it in the form of a snake; but so tight was the hole that he could neither go out nor come back. And he was thus until the Flood ebbed. And that was the best and the worst nail in the Ark.[28]

Ingenuity and humour are certainly important strains of Gaelic ecclesiastical culture in the Old and Middle Gaelic linguistic periods (600–1200), whether in the vernacular or in Latin. These are features of the literary culture which have attracted or repelled modern readers, depending on their temperament and taste and

---

[27] Wright and Wright, 'Additions', 123. Text of this type is found also in a twelfth-century Irish gospel book, perhaps from Armagh: London, BL, MS Harley 1023, fol. 63[r] (Flower, *Catalogue II*, 432–3, 521); cf. Duncan, *Catalogue*, no. 28.

[28] 'Do fhácaib sáer na háircci inadh tarrnge fás innti, air ba derb lais nach bértha é féin inni. In tan dochuaid Nái cona chlainn isin áircc amail isbert in t-aingel fris, do druid Nái sinistre na háirci 7 do tócaib a láim dia bennachad. Dodechaid immorro in diabal ria cois isin áirc ac dul dó innti, 7 an tan do bennaich Nái in áircc, ní uair in diabal conair n-aili acht in poll fás ro fácaibh in sáer gan drud, 7 dochuaid a richt naithrech ann, 7 ar cumga in puill nír féd dul amach iná techt ar cul, 7 do bí mar sin no gur tráigh in díli, 7 is é sin tairrnge is dech 7 is mesa do bí isin áirc': O. J. Bergin, 'The Best and Worst Nail in the Ark', *Ériu* 5 (1911), 49, edited and translated from a largely medical book, Dublin, RIA, MS Stowe C.iv.2 (466), fol. 14[r]; see T. F. O'Rahilly et al., *Catalogue of Irish Manuscripts in The Royal Irish Academy*, 28 fascicules (Dublin, 1926–70), 10: 1217–20; I have altered Bergin's translation here and there. Cf. Flower, *Catalogue II*, 280–1 (item 29).

their religious standpoint. What foreign observers of medieval Gaelic ecclesiastics frequently noted was a formidable knowledge of the Bible and great ingenuity (not to say hair-splitting) in its interpretation. What we might add to this characterization is the evident sheer delight in Scripture and its unlimited creative possibilities, as well as its overflowing supply of human interest stories.[29] All this lent itself to a rich vein of anti-Gaelic satirical poetry composed in Carolingian Francia and indeed in early eleventh-century Normandy.[30]

Let me add one further item to this collection of types of *quaestiones* before turning to larger issues. This is drawn from a Gaelic, probably north-eastern Irish, gospel book of the twelfth century, produced in a reforming context (now Oxford, Corpus Christi College, MS 122),[31] in which, following the Eusebian canons, we meet on folio 5ᵛ a table of a board game, *Alea Euangelii* ('Gospel dice'), which Dubinsi, bishop of Bangor (d.953), took away from the court of Æthelstan, King of the English from 927 to 939 (this is an inaccurate copy made some two centuries later). Folio 6 is occupied by a lengthy explanation of the game, played with seventy-two pieces. First published and discussed in 1923,[32] this has been the subject of a series of articles over the last couple of decades, in which authorship (or co-authorship) has been attributed to a famous Briton (Breton, indeed), Israel the Grammarian, whose connections with Æthelstan's court have been demonstrated.[33] (It

---

[29] For a fine thumbnail sketch of this, see Vivien Law, *The Insular Latin Grammarians* (Woodbridge, 1982), 6–7.

[30] Bernhard Bischoff, *Mittelalterliche Studien. Ausgewählte Aufsätze zur Schriftkunde und Literaturgeschichte*, 3 vols (Stuttgart, 1966–81), 2: 19–25; cf. idem, 'Anecdota carolina', in *Studien zur lateinischen Dichtung des Mittelalters: Ehrengabe für Karl Strecker*, ed. W. Stach and H. Walther (Dresden, 1931), 1–11; D. Schaller, 'Poetic Rivalries at the Court of Charlemagne', in R. R. Bolgar, ed., *Classical Influences on European Culture, A.D. 500–1500* (Cambridge, 1971), 151–7; idem, 'Vortrags- und Zirkulardichtung am Hof Karls des Grossen', *Mittellateinisches Jahrbuch* 6 (1970), 14–36. For Normandy, see *Warner of Rouen, Moriuht: A Norman Latin Poem from the Early Eleventh Century*, ed. and transl. Christopher J. McDonough (Toronto, ON, 1995), with further discussion by David N. Dumville, *Celtic Essays, 2001–2007*, 2 vols (Aberdeen, 2007), 1: 123–35, at 131–4.

[31] Duncan, *Catalogue*, no. 37.

[32] J. Armitage Robinson, *The Times of Saint Dunstan* (Oxford, 1923), frontispiece, 69–71, 171–81.

[33] The decisive contribution was that of Michael Lapidge, 'Israel the Grammarian in Anglo-Saxon England', in *From Athens to Chartres: Neoplatonism and Medieval Thought. Studies in Honour of Édouard Jeauneau*, ed. Haijo Jan Westra (Leiden, 1992),

bears signs of being an elaborate relative of an old Celtic game known as *gwyddbwyll* in Welsh, *fidchell* in Old Gaelic, 'wood-sense', where it seems to be an attribute of royalty.)[34] Perhaps *Alea Euangelii* was played by displaying knowledge of the Gospels, with the winner capturing the central position, marked 'I', representing the indivisible substance of the Trinity.

This is by no means a merely Celtic issue. Clerical addiction to the pleasures of the dice is a recurrent medieval theme: Dicing with the Virtues was a game invented by Wibold, bishop of Cambrai, in 965, in an attempt to retrieve his clergy from the gaming tables.[35] Reform of clerical behaviour in general is of course an ever-present issue in ecclesiastical discourse.

We entered these islands in the context of the efforts of a reforming papacy, and of Norman-appointed archbishops of Canterbury, to carry reform throughout the several Churches of Britain and Ireland. It was a process which led to the planting of Benedictine and then more modern monastic orders in Scotland, encouraged from Canterbury, and of the far from happy employment of English monks – Turgot from Durham and Eadmer from Canterbury – as bishops at St Andrews.[36] The reforming prelates we see – especially where we have their correspondence[37] – as

---

97–114, repr. in idem, *Anglo-Latin Literature, 900–1066* (London, 1993), 87–104; cf. idem, 'Schools, Learning and Literature in Tenth-Century England', *Settimane di studio del Centro italiano di studi sull'alto medioevo* 38 (1991), 951–1005, at 968–71. Cf. David N. Dumville, 'Mael Brigte mac Tornáin, Pluralist Coarb († 927)', *JCS* 4 (2004), 97–116, repr. in idem, *Celtic Essays*, 1: 137–58. See further D. Howlett, 'Alea Euangelii', in *Mélanges François Dolbeau* (forthcoming).

34 For an early discussion of these words, see Whitley Stokes, ed., *Three Irish Glossaries* (London, 1862), liii–liv, 21–2. See further *Táin bó Fraích*, ed. Wolfgang Meid (Dublin 1967; 2nd edn, 1974), 28–9 (ad 81). Cf. E. MacWhite, 'Early Irish Boardgames', *Éigse* 5 (1946–7), 25–35.

35 Robinson, *Dunstan*, 181.

36 On the links, both royal and episcopal, between Anglo-Norman England and Scotland, there is now a substantial literature. See esp. R. Gameson, 'The Gospels of Margaret of Scotland and the Literacy of an Eleventh-Century Queen', in Jane Taylor and L. Smith, eds, *Women and the Book. Assessing the Visual Evidence* (London, 1997), 148–71; Lois L. Huneycutt, *Matilda of Scotland: A Study in Medieval Queenship* (Woodbridge, 2003). For the next generations' wider interest in monasticism, see Christopher N. L. Brooke, *Churches and Churchmen in Medieval Europe* (London, 1999), 159–73; G. W. S. Barrow, *The Kingdom of the Scots: Government, Church and Society from the Eleventh to the Fourteenth Century*, 2nd edn (Edinburgh, 2003), 151–86.

37 For Lanfranc's correspondence, see n. 11 above. For the very much larger surviving corpus of Anselm's letters, see *S. Anselmi Cantuariensis Archiepiscopi Opera Omnia*, ed. Franciscus Salesius Schmitt, 6 vols (Seckau, etc., 1938–61), III–V; *The Letters*

solemn, upright, pious and determined men, inspired no doubt by the model of St Paul, by no means necessarily endowed with or cultivating a sense of humour or an enjoyment of the lighter sides of life, while presumably seeing much of that at the royal courts in which they had to spend significant amounts of time. The advice dispensed by Archbishops Lanfranc and Anselm – men with much similar history yet temperamentally quite different[38] – was firm and determined, though by no means harsh, uncivil or inhumane. Yet we have seen how easy it was for Lanfranc's Irish correspondents to irritate him by inviting him to participate in some literary question-and-answer which was perhaps with them merely a matter of convention.[39]

We might indeed turn here to such an example, which, apart from displaying an anticipated exchange of clerics' views on literary matters, reveals in its manuscript context some of the tensions then current in ecclesiastical Gaeldom. The great vernacular codex known since the late nineteenth century as the Book of Leinster was put together towards the end of the twelfth century from two or more manuscripts perhaps written not long after the middle of the century.[40] On a lower margin (above which the main text – in the same hand – is a pseudohistory of the province of Munster) is

of Saint Anselm of Canterbury, transl. Walter Fröhlich, 3 vols, Cistercian Studies 96, 97, 142 (Kalamazoo, MI, 1990).

38   For Anselm, in addition to his letters we have a hagiography written by Eadmer of Canterbury who served the archbishop and wrote an intimate portrait: *The Life of St Anselm, Archbishop of Canterbury, by Eadmer*, ed. and transl. R. W. Southern, OMT (Oxford, 1972; first publ. 1962); for commentary, see R. W. Southern, *Saint Anselm and his Biographer: A Study of Monastic Life and Thought, 1059 – c.1130* (Cambridge, 1963); idem, *Saint Anselm, a Portrait in a Landscape* (Cambridge, 1990). For examination of Anglo-Celtic interaction and mutual perception in the second half of the Middle Ages through a Celtic prism, see D. N. Dumville, '"Celtic"Visions of England', in Andrew Galloway, ed., *The Cambridge Companion to Medieval English Culture* (Cambridge, 2011), 107–28.

39   See Hughes, *Church and Society in Ireland*, essay XII, 86, for characterization of such an occurrence – in the only Gaelic vernacular letter of the period. For a full discussion, see S. L. Forste-Grupp, 'The Earliest Irish Personal Letter', *Proceedings of the Harvard Celtic Colloquium* 15 (1995), 1–11 (it is not, of course, the first [surviving] Irish personal letter, but the first in the Irish language).

40   For an edition of the whole, see *The Book of Leinster, formerly Lebar na Núachongbála*, ed. R. I. Best et al., 6 vols (Dublin, 1954–83). The fundamental study of the palaeography and codicology of this codex is W. O'Sullivan, 'Notes on the Scripts and Make-up of The Book of Leinster', *Celtica* 7 (1966), 1–31; until recently the only indication that anyone had understood the force of O'Sullivan's analysis was provided by D. Ó Corráin, 'The Education of Diarmait Mac Murchada', *Ériu* 28 (1977), 71–81.

a glossed copy of a vernacular letter addressed by a bishop to an abbot and ecclesiastical scholar (*fer léginn*, a master of a school at a 'monastic' house).

> Life and health from Finn, bishop `viz, of Kildare´, to Aed Mac Crimthainn, *fer léginn* of the overking of Leth Moga `viz, Nuadat´ and heir of [St] Colum mac Crimthainn and principal *senchaid* of Leinster in wisdom and knowledge and book-lore and science and learning. And let the conclusion of this little tale be written for me
> > accurately by you, O acute Aed,
> > O man of stately form.
> > Whether I be a long or short while away from you,
> > my desire is that you should be with me.
>
> Let the poem-book of Mac Lonáin be brought to me so that we may discover the meanings of the poems which are in it. *Et uale in Christo.*[41]

Two poets of this name are known: Flann, who was killed in 896, was a secular;[42] Loingsech, who died in 1012, was abbot of Roscrea (Co. Tipperary) and therefore the heir of a saint.[43] The Aed named here recurs in the codex in a rubricated marginale: 'Aed Mac Crimthaind wrote this book and collected it from many

---

[41] 'Betha 7 slainte o Fhind epscop `.i. Cilli Dara´ do Aed mac Crimthainn do fhir leigind ardrig Leithi Moga `i. Nuadat´ 7 do chomarbu Choluim meic Crimthaind 7 do phrimsenchaid Laigen ar gaes 7 eolas 7 trebaire lebur 7 fessa 7 foglomma 7 scribthar dam deired in sceoil bicse
    cu cinte duit a Aed amnais.
    a fhir cosinn aeb ollmais.
    cian gar dom beith it hingnais.
    mían dam do bith im comgnais.
Tuctar dam duanaire Meic Lonain co faiccmis a cialla na nduan filet ann. Et uale in Christo.' On fol. ccvi^v (page 288) in Hand F, see *Book of Leinster*, ed. Best et al., 1: xv–xvi. The very odd idea that this marginale is the original of Bishop Finn's letter remains current. On the name and status of Aed Mac Crimthainn, see T. Ó Concheanainn, 'LL and the Date of the Reviser of LU', *Éigse* 20 (1984), 212–25, at 212–14.

[42] For his death, see *The Annals of Ulster (to A.D. 1131)*, 1, ed. and transl. Seán Mac Airt and G. Mac Niocaill (Dublin, 1983), 350–1 (*s.a.* 896.10). For a lengthy poem attributed to him, a lament for a king who died in 906(!), see M. E. Dobbs, 'A Poem ascribed to Flann mac Lonáin', *Ériu* 17 (1955), 16–34.

[43] *The Annals of Inisfallen (MS. Rawlinson B.503)*, ed. and transl. Seán Mac Airt (Dublin, 1951), 182–3 (*s.a.* 1012.2); *Annals of Ulster*, 1, ed. and transl. Mac Airt and Mac Niocaill, 444–5 (*s.a.* 1012.5 b). Cf. C. O Lochlainn, 'Poets on the Battle of Clontarf', *Éigse* 3 (1941–2), 208–18; 4 (1943–4), 33–47, at 42–6.

books'.[44] The 'book' in question may have been the collection of royal genealogies which this note accompanies. Aed was abbot of Terryglass (Co. Tipperary), another saint's heir, and one of the men whose manuscripts became part of the Book of Leinster.[45]

In the present context, it should be noted that this manuscript contains, at the end of the copy of a new recension of the Ulster-cycle prose epic *Táin bó Cuailnge*, 'The Cattle-raid of Cooley', a bilingual colophonic statement which has considerably engaged modern literary critics and historians of the twelfth century:

> A blessing on everyone who shall faithfully memorise the *Táin* as it is written here and shall not add any other form to it.
>
> But I who have written this story, or rather this fable, give no credence to the various incidents related in it. For some things in it are the deceptions of demons, others poetic figments; some are probable, others improbable; while still others are intended for the delectation of foolish men.[46]

The same scribe (T) copied both paragraphs, as well as the whole of the long text which they conclude. The first paragraph is in the vernacular. The second is in Latin. And the writing which once occupied the rest of the page (at the end of a quire) has been erased. There is much to ponder in the contrast of attitudes expressed successively in the two languages.

There are questions here aplenty about the relationship of humour, indeed frivolity, and ecclesiastical reform. I do not know to what

---

[44] 'Aed mac meic Crimthaind ro-scríb in lebor so ocus ra-thinóil a llebraib imdaib'; see *Book of Leinster*, ed. Best et al., 1: xv; 6: 1337, n. * (fol. 32ʳ / page 313, lower margin): this note has allowed the siglum 'A' to be given to this hand. Cf. O'Sullivan, 'Notes'.

[45] I have discussed elsewhere the status, use and transmission of verse among the Gaels: 'What is Mediaeval Gaelic Poetry?', in *Explorations in Cultural History: Essays for Peter Gabriel McCaffery*, ed. David F. Smith and Hushang Philsooph (Aberdeen, 2010), 81–153.

[46] 'Bendacht ar cech óen mebraigfes go hindraic Táin amlaidseo 7 na tuillfe cruth aile furri. Sed ego qui scripsi hanc historiam aut uerius fabulam quibusdam fidem in hac historia aut fabula `non´ accommodo. Quaedam enim ibi sunt praest `I´ gia demonum, quaedam autem figmenta poetica; quaedam similia uero, quaedam non; quaedam ad delectationem stultorum': *Táin bó Cúalnge from The Book of Leinster*, ed. and transl. Cecile O'Rahilly (Dublin, 1967), 136 (text), 272 (translation), from folio 68ᵛb (page 104b); cf. *Book of Leinster*, ed. Best et al., 2: 399. For the most extended and thoughtful treatment, see P. Ó Néill, 'The Latin Colophon to the "Táin Bó Cúailnge" in The Book of Leinster: a Critical View of Old Irish Literature', *Celtica* 23 (1999), 269–75.

extent students of the Protestant Reformation have directly addressed this matter. But it certainly does surface in medieval discourse, in various ways and used by various types of players to various ends. What is perhaps lacking is an overall sense of whether the driven and the professional reformers in the Middle Ages employed humour (as an aid or a weapon) and whether they regarded what they perceived to be others' frivolity as a marker of such persons' inability to grasp the central message or messages of reform.

Medieval Gaelic literature is renowned for its exuberance, something which has not always redounded to its credit in modern times.[47] Appreciation of its strong vein of humour has been longer in coming but has developed since the 1960s,[48] aided by Vivian Mercier's book on humour in Irish literature of all periods and languages.[49] While there is an entirely respectable argument that all Gaelic literature before 1200 is ecclesiastical,[50] given that it was transmitted – often bilingually – in ecclesiastical manuscripts (and provenance may in this matter be held to indicate origin), nevertheless I leave the literature of secular persons and themes aside here for the sake of clarity of exposition.

Pointed humour in matters of personal moral reform one can find already in the mid eighth century in the brief poem (of two quatrains), preserved in Irish chronicles, which celebrates the career of the ascetic sage and jurist of Iona, Cú Chuimne (d.747), and has gained its own celebrity in the translation of John V. Kelleher:[51]

---

47 For an infamous instance, see D. Greene, 'Robert Atkinson and Irish Studies', *Hermathena* 102 (1966), 6–15. For mitigating comment, see *Liadain and Curithir. An Irish Love-Story of the Ninth Century*, ed. and transl. Kuno Meyer (London, 1902), 7; Seán Ó Lúing, *Kuno Meyer, 1858–1919: A Biography* (Dublin, 1991), 8.

48 As in other areas of medieval literature: cf. Peter Dronke, *Medieval Latin and the Rise of the European Love-Lyric*, 2 vols (Oxford, 1965–6; 2nd edn, 1968).

49 Vivian Mercier, *The Irish Comic Tradition* (Oxford, 1962). There is much to be found in Patrick Crotty, ed., *The Penguin Book of Irish Verse* (London, 2010).

50 For the end of that state of affairs, see R. I. Best, 'The Graves of the Kings at Clonmacnoise', *Ériu* 2 (1905), 163–71, at 169–71; cf. P. Mac Cana, 'The Rise of the Later Schools of *Filidheacht*', *Ériu* 25 (1974), 126–46.

51   Cu Chuimne
   Ro legh suithi co druimne,
   A lleth n-aill hiaratha
   Ro leici ar chaillecha.

   Ando Coin Cuimne ro-mboi,
   Im-rualaid de conid soi,
   ro leic caillecha ha faill,
   ro leig al-aill arith-mboi.

   `Muime Chon Cuimne cecinit´.

Cú Chuimne in youth
read his way through half the Truth.
He let the other half lie
While he gave women a try.

Well for him in old age.
He became a holy sage.
He gave women the laugh.
He read the other half.

This poem is, rather cheerfully (if also conventionally), attributed to Cú Chuimne's foster-mother![52]

The later eighth century brought a sterner, more obviously self-righteous, type of ascetic, *céle Dé*, 'the client of God', caught for us in a vividly fascinating consuetudinal literature focused on Mael Ruain, abbot and bishop of Tallaght (Co. Dublin), who died in 792.[53] Any humour found in that context is decidedly accidental and either the militant ascetic's humour of the gallows or that of the frivolous non-ascetic.

Extreme asceticism might, however, be parodied in a saint's Life – in this case, a probably twelfth-century vernacular text from Munster celebrating St Finnchú of Brí Gobann (Brigown, Co. Cork):[54] I can testify that this is a work which might change a teenager's life. It seems to be a classic case of a hagiographer

---

For a literal translation, see *Annals of Ulster*, 1, ed. and transl. Mac Airt and Mac Niocaill, 200–1; cf. Thomas Owen Clancy, ed., *The Triumph Tree: Scotland's Earliest Poetry, 550–1350* (Edinburgh, 1998), 117. There is a very interestingly different version in *Annala Rioghachta Eireann, Annals of the Kingdom of Ireland, by The Four Masters*, ed. and transl. John O'Donovan, 2nd edn, 7 vols (Dublin, 1856), 1: 342–5. Kelleher's translation was first published in *Teangadóir* 2 (1954–5), 39, and reissued in his book *Too Small for Stove Wood, Too Big for Kindling: Collected Verse and Translations* (Dublin, 1979), 12; it is also in John Montague, ed., *The Faber Book of Irish Verse* (London, 1974), 89. For commentary and approbation, see Hughes, *Church and Society in Ireland*, essay VIII, 109–10; and cf. James Carney, ed. and transl., *Medieval Irish Lyrics* (Dublin, 1967), xxi.

52 For another example, see K. Meyer, 'Stories and Songs from Irish Manuscripts', *Otia Merseiana* 1 (1899), 113–28; 2 (1900–1), 75–105; 3 (1903), 46–54, at 84–92.

53 For that literature, see especially *The Rule of Tallaght*, ed. and transl. Edward [J.] Gwynn (Dublin, 1927), to be reissued in idem and D. N. Dumville, ed. and transl., *Ireland's Desert-Fathers, the Culdees* (Aberdeen, forthcoming). For recent discussion, see Westley Follett, *Céli Dé in Ireland: Monastic Writing and Identity in the Early Middle Ages* (Woodbridge, 2006).

54 See *Lives of Saints from The Book of Lismore*, ed. and transl. Whitley Stokes (Oxford, 1890), 84–98 (text), 231–46 (translation), 347–8 (notes); cf. Charles Plummer, *Miscellanea Hagiographica Hibernica* (Bruxelles, 1925), 189–90 (Catalogue, no. 36).

drawing deeply on native secular saga to provide, albeit in apparent parody, crucial attributes for the saint. The style is extremely wordy and I forbear to quote it here, but the highlight of the saint's asceticism must be recorded: the saint had had fashioned for himself seven sickles on which he impaled himself for seven years, 'in order that he might gain heaven'; in that time he came off them for but a single day in which he allowed himself the duty of going on a military campaign (on which he did very hound-like heroic deeds – albeit presented in what seems a parodistic mode).[55] We may seem to have humorous parody here – but, given that this is a Life of the saint, a work which should be expected to be in the interests of his cult and his institutional heirs, the question '*cui bono?*' is a deeply troublesome one.

I move towards closure, with a glance towards biting satire, parody and censure in a remarkable text, first published by Kuno Meyer, to which the adjective 'goliardic' has often been applied as an indication of its tone. In no strict sense is this accurate. The work, 'The Vision of Mac Conglinne',[56] does not have the sharp, biting, profane, contemptuous wit – directed at the sacred texts and central institutions of Christianity – which we find in goliardic poetry and, if produced around 1100, this text is in any case too early to be of that ilk.[57] But its attack on ecclesiastical, and especially monastic, privilege, corruption and complacent arbitrariness in everything is part of that literary movement (of reaction to patent ecclesiastical immorality) which produced the goliards.[58] It is also remarkable for its dense parody of just about every convention of the inherited Gaelic literary tradition. We

---

[55] *Lives*, ed. and transl. Stokes, 88–9, 235–7. It is a pity that such a work was not discussed by Paul Lehmann, *Die Parodie in Mittelalter*, 2nd edn (Stuttgart, 1963; first publ. 1922). For the relationship of Gaelic saga and hagiography, see F. Ó Briain, 'Saga Themes in Irish Hagiography', in *Essays and Studies presented to Professor Tadhg Ua Donnchadha (Tórna)*, ed. Séamus Pender (Cork, 1947), 33–42; Joseph Falaky Nagy, *Conversing with Angels and Ancients: Literary Myths of Medieval Ireland* (Ithaca, NY, 1997).

[56] *Aislinge Meic Conglinne*, ed. and transl. Meyer and Wollner.

[57] For discussion of dating, see *Aislinge*, ed. Jackson, xx–xxvi (cf. 73–140); cf. M. Ní Mhaonaigh, 'Pagans and Holy Men: Literary Manifestations of Twelfth-Century Reform', in Bracken and Ó Riain-Raedel, eds, *Ireland and Europe*, 143–61, at 159–61.

[58] Cf. *Les Poésies des goliards*, ed. and transl. Olga Dobiache-Rojdestvensky (Paris, 1931). For discussion of a different Insular connection, see J. Mann, 'Giraldus Cambrensis and the Goliards', *JCS* 3 (1981–2), 31–9. For one enduring motivation, see Josef Benzinger, *Invectiva in Romam: Romkritik im Mittelalter vom 9. bis zum 12. Jahrhundert* (Lübeck, 1968).

have to allow here, I think, that Gaelic ecclesiastics got by their own route to a similar end point, but in the vernacular. In that text frivolity was king. However, amid a literary *tour de force* of parody lie serious messages of reform, but by no means necessarily the same as those offered by continental bishops writing from stand-points in England.[59]

A short prose tale in Middle Irish, perhaps of the twelfth century, which 'explains' why 'the abbots of Drimnagh and Crumlin (Co. Dublin) parted from each other', was first published (by the ubiquitous Kuno Meyer) in the inaugural volume of the solemnly named *Anecdota from Irish Manuscripts* in 1907, as the 'Story of the Abbot of Druimenaig, who was changed into a woman';[60] its first translation into English, however, by John Montague and Donncha Ó Corráin in 1980, was as 'The Sex Change of the Abbot of Drimnagh' in a volume of erotic prose.[61] The story is an Irish reflex of an international tale-type.[62] It presents two married sword-bearing young abbots — we meet a parallel Welsh type in the work of Giraldus Kambrensis[63] — whose churches were in union with one another. The problems are to understand how an original audience would have reacted to such a presentation of the relationship and its termination and whether there is an implied call to reform. For the intended audience, which was the more shocking (if indeed either was) — the presentation of the notably secular life and behaviour of the participants or the use of such a story to describe the relationship (indeed the divorce) of two churches?

Let us end, however, where we began. The power of arithmetically determined prophecy would return to bite Ireland a generation later than the Jerusalem pilgrimage of 1064/5. 1095/6 was

---

59 Cf. M. Holland, 'Were Early Irish Church Establishments under Lay Control?', in Bracken and Ó Riain-Raedel, eds, *Ireland and Europe*, 128–42.

60 O. J. Bergin et al., eds, *Anecdota from Irish Manuscripts*, 5 vols (Halle an der Saale, 1907–13), 1: 76–9.

61 Alan Bold, ed., *Mounts of Venus: The Picador Book of Erotic Prose* (London, 1980), 57–8. It was, however, translated into French immediately after publication: H. Gaidoz, 'Du changement de sexe dans les contes celtiques', *Revue de l'histoire des religions* 57 (1908), 317–32, at 320–3.

62 For this (and the identification of a total of four manuscript copies of the text), see Flower, *Catalogue II*, 542 (item 25); cf. 475 (item 4).

63 *Itinerarium Kambriae* 2.5 (*Giraldi Cambrensis Opera*, ed. J. S. Brewer et al., 8 vols (London, 1861–91), 6: 122–3); *Gerald of Wales, The Journey through Wales and The Description of Wales*, transl. Lewis Thorpe (Harmondsworth, 1978), 180–1.

a year of terrible weather, disease and famine in north-western Europe, which provoked a variety of responses. In Ireland, which suffered an epidemic from the beginning of August 1095 to the beginning of May 1096,[64] a very peculiar and vigorous reaction was provoked both by the severity of these phenomena and by a remarkable local twist. It was prophesied – we have the details from a bilingual text published as 'The Second Vision of Adomnán' – that, when the Feast of the Decollation of St John the Baptist (29 August) fell on a Friday in a leap year, Ireland would be destroyed. 1096 was that year and the beginning of a reform movement.[65]

University of Aberdeen

[64] *Annals of Ulster*, 1, ed. and transl. Mac Airt and Mac Niocaill, 528–31 (*s.aa.* 1095.8, 1096.3); *The Annals of Tigernach*, ed. and transl. Whitley Stokes, 2nd edn, 2 vols (Felinfach, 1993), 2: 322 (*s.a.* 1096.1); *Annals of Inisfallen*, ed. and transl. Mac Airt, 250–3 (*s.a.* 1095.13); *The Annals of Loch Cé*, ed. and transl. William M. Hennessy, 2 vols (London, 1871), 1: 80–3 (*s.aa.* 1095.5, 1096.4); *Chronicum Scotorum*, ed. and transl. William M. Hennessy (London, 1866), 304–5 (*s.a.* 1096.1); *The Annals of Clonmacnoise ... translated into English A.D. 1627 by Conell Mageoghagan*, ed. Denis Murphy (Dublin, 1896), 186–7 (*s.a.* 1094.6); *Annala rioghachta Eireann*, ed. and transl. O'Donovan, 2: 948–53 (*s.aa.* 1095.3, 1096.6).

[65] W. Stokes, 'Adamnan's Second Vision', *Revue celtique* 12 (1891), 420–43. For discussion of this connexion, see Dumville, *Councils*, 35–42. Cf. Kenney, *Sources*, 749–53; Martin McNamara, *The Apocrypha in the Irish Church* (Dublin, 1975), 64–7 (nos 55–7). See now A. M. O'Leary, 'Mog Ruith and Apocalypticism in Eleventh-Century Ireland', *Celtic Studies Association of North America* [*CSANA*] *Yearbook* 1 (2001), 51–60.

ECCLESIOLOGY ON THE EDGE:
DANTE AND THE CHURCH

by JOHN TOOK

Dante is probably famous above all for three things: for his encounter at the age of nine with Beatrice, for his exile in 1301 from Florence (to which he never returned), and for his nothing if not graphic account of sin and suffering in hell.[1] Each of these things, had we time and space, would benefit from an essay of its own, for each alike points on beyond itself to the still centre of Dante's spirituality as a Christian poet, the anecdotal and the occasional everywhere being taken up in the analytical and the ontological, in an account of what it might mean for man as man fully and unambiguously *to be* as a creature of moral and eschatological self-determination. Thus his early encounter with Beatrice, far from being exhausted by its merely historical interest, provides the basis for a fresh enquiry into the nature of love precisely as such, as a matter by turns of acquisition and of disposition, of self-ingratiation and of self-transcendence, the historical thus shading off, as it always does in Dante, into the reflective and the philosophical. In the same way, the experience of exile furnishes in all its grim historicity the basis for an account of human experience generally as a matter of far-wandering and of homecoming in respect of the call to be in, through and for God, while the *Inferno*, for all its animated account of suffering in the next life, contains within itself, as, in fact, its point of arrival, an

---

[1] Readable, reliable, and in English, for those coming afresh to Dante are J. A. Scott, *Understanding Dante* (Notre Dame, IN, 2004); S. Bemrose, *A New Life of Dante*, revised and updated edn (Exeter, 2009). On Dantean ecclesiology (inasmuch as this is distinguishable from his political theology generally), see J. Scott, 'The Rock of Peter and *Inferno* XIX', *Romance Philology* 23 (1970), 462–79; S. Botterill, 'Not of This World: Spiritual and Temporal Powers in Dante and Bernard of Clairvaux', *Lectura Dantis* 10 (1992), 8–21; idem, 'Ideals of the Institutional Church in Dante and Bernard of Clairvaux', *Italica* 78 (2001), 297–313, repr. in R. Lansing, ed., *Dante: The Critical Complex*, 8 vols (New York, 2003), 4: 405–21; P. Acquaviva and J. Petrie, eds, *Dante and the Church: Literary and Historical Essays* (Dublin, 2007); P. Nasti, 'Of This World and the Other: *Caritas*-Ecclesiology in Dante's *Paradiso*', *The Italianist* 27 (2007), 206–32. In Italian, see R. Manselli, 'Dante e l'*ecclesia spiritualis*', in *Dante e Roma. Atti del Convegno di studi, Roma, 8–10 aprile 1965* (Florence, 1965), 115–35; L. Stefani, *Dante e la sua Chiesa* (Florence, 1979).

invitation to consider the no less tortured state of the soul in this life, the eschatological thus constituting (again as it always does in Dante) but a mode of the existential, the abiding truth of what *is* under the aspect of time and space. Everywhere, then, the pattern is the same. Everywhere the iconic moment points beyond itself to a more spacious meditation, in terms of which it stands ultimately to be interpreted.

But for those who have lived for any length of time with the *Commedia* there is a further feature of the text quite as striking as any of these, namely its thoroughgoing indictment of the contemporary Church in its worldliness, in the sorry spectacle of its greed and self-seeking. It all begins with the avaricious and the prodigal in hell, Dante, as protagonist in his own poem and witness, therefore, to the opprobrium of it all, being unable to make out whether it is a question here of laity or of clergy:

> And I, heart-wrung at this, said: 'Master, now declare to me who are these people, and if all these tonsured ones on our left were clerics.' And he [Virgil] to me: 'Each and all of these were so asquint of mind in the first life that they followed there no right measure in their spending; most clearly do they bark this out when they come to the two points of the circle where opposite faults divide them. These who have no covering of hair on their head were clerics and popes and cardinals, in whom avarice wreaks its excess.'[2]

But that is only the beginning, for deeper down in the pit are the simonists or traders in ecclesiastical office, souls including, or about to include, a series of popes from Nicholas III through to Clement V, each alike suffering the indignity of being thrust upside down in a fissure of rock with something parodying the flame of the Holy Spirit playing upon his feet. The image, as always, is eloquent, the

---

[2] 'E io, ch'avea lo cor quasi compunto, | dissi: "Maestro mio, or mi dimostra | che gente è questa, e se tutti fuor cherci | questi chercuti a la sinistra nostra". | Ed elli a me: "Tutti quanti fuor guerci | sì de la mente in la vita primaia, | che con misura nullo spendio ferci. | Assai la voce lor chiaro l'abbaia, | quando vegnono a' due punti del cerchio | dove colpa contraria li dispaia. | Questi fuor cherci, che non han coperchio | piloso al capo, e papi e cardinali, | in cui usa avarizia il suo soperchio"': *Inferno* 7.36–48; text from G. Petrocchi, *Dante Alighieri. La Commedia secondo l'antica vulgata* (Milan, 1966–7); ET slightly modified from C. S. Singleton, *The Divine Comedy* (Princeton, NJ, 1973–80).

topsy-turvyness of it all testifying to the completeness of Christ's betrayal here, to the reversal of everything he stood for by way of compassion and of self-sacrifice. Taking his courage in both hands, therefore, and softening for the moment his reverence for the keys, Dante the pilgrim sets about denouncing the blasphemy of clerical greed, and, with it, the politicking of priests, the prostitution of the Church as the bride of Christ, the worship of gold and silver as a way of life in the Church, and the whole programme of decay and degeneration inaugurated by Constantine's endowment (an endowment, incidentally, which he was no more entitled to make than the Church was to receive):

> I do not know if here I was overbold, in answering him in just this strain: 'Pray now tell me how much treasure did our Lord require of Saint Peter before he put the keys in his keeping? Surely he asked nothing save: "Follow me". Nor did Peter or the others take gold or silver of Matthias when he was chosen for the office which the guilty soul had lost. Therefore stay right here, for you are justly punished; and guard well the ill-gotten gain that made you bold against Charles. And were it not that reverence for the great keys which you held in the glad life even now forbids it to me, I would use yet harder words, for your avarice afflicts the world, trampling down the good and exalting the bad. It was shepherds such as you that the evangelist had in mind when she that sitteth upon the waters was seen by him committing fornication with the kings: she that was born with the seven heads, and from the ten horns had her strength, so long as virtue pleased her spouse. You have made you a god of gold and silver; and wherein do you differ from idolators, save that they worship one, and you a hundred? Ah, Constantine, of how much ill was the mother, not your conversion, but the dowry which the first rich father took from you!'[3]

---

[3] 'Io non so s'i' mi fui qui troppo folle, | ch'i' pur rispuosi lui a questo metro: | "Deh, or mi dì: quanto tesoro volle | Nostro Segnore in prima da san Pietro | ch'ei ponesse le chiavi in sua balìa? | Certo non chiese se non 'Viemmi retro'. | Né Pier né li altri tolsero a Matia | oro od argento, quando fu sortito | al loco che perdé l'anima ria. | Però ti sta, ché tu se' ben punito; | e guarda ben la mal tolta moneta | ch'esser ti fece contra Carlo ardito. | E se non fosse ch'ancor lo mi vieta | la reverenza de le somme chiavi | che tu tenesti ne la vita lieta, | io userei parole ancor più gravi; | ché la vostra avarizia il mondo attrista, | calcando i buoni e sollevando i pravi. | Di

But even that is not all, for passing over for the moment any number of similarly spirited moments in the text relative to those responsible in Dante's generation for steering the ship of the Church – including, therefore, his reference towards the end of *Paradiso* 21 to the modern Cephas so richly arrayed and splendidly mounted that it is a matter here of two beasts under but a single cloak[4] – we come to Peter's pronouncement on the contemporary Church in *Paradiso* 27, the high point of Dante's outrage hereabouts. True, the *incipit* is euphoric and the pilgrim's sense of resting at last in the *pax* and the *gaudium* of paradise – the static and the ecstatic conditions respectively of being in its ultimate emergence – complete:

> 'Glory be to the Father, to the Son, and to the Holy Spirit!' all paradise began, so that the sweet song held me rapt. What I saw seemed to me a smile of the universe, so that my rapture entered both by hearing and by sight. O joy! O ineffable gladness! O life entire of love and of peace! Oh wealth secure without longing![5]

But heaven at once falls silent as Peter embarks on his litany of indictment, an indictment which, proceeding by way both of the self-giving of those who spilled their blood for the Church (Sixtus, Pius, Calixtus and Urban) and of the self-seeking of those who in more recent times ravage the Church by way of their endless greed, reaches its climax in a declaration of usurpation and of

---

voi pastor s'accorse il Vangelista, | quando colei che siede sopra l'acque | puttaneggiar coi regi a lui fu vista; | quella che con le sette teste nacque, | e da le diece corna ebbe argomento, | fin che virtute al suo marito piacque. | Fatto v'avete dio d'oro e d'argento; | e che altro è da voi a l'idolatre, | se non ch'elli uno, e voi ne orate cento? | Ahi, Costantin, di quanto mal fu matre, | non la tua conversion, ma quella dote | che da te prese il primo ricco patre!': *Inferno* 19.88–117. On the illegitimacy of Constantine's donation, both in the making and in the receiving of it, see *Monarchia* 3.10; text and translation, P. Shaw, *Dante: Monarchia* (Cambridge, 1995).

4   'Cuopron d'i manti loro i palafreni, | sì che due bestie van sott' una pelle': *Paradiso* 21.133–4.

5   'Al Padre, al Figlio, a lo Spirito Santo", | cominciò, "gloria!", tutto 'l paradiso, | sì che m'inebrïava il dolce canto. | Ciò ch'io vedeva mi sembiava un riso | de l'universo; per che mia ebbrezza | intrava per l'udire e per lo viso. | Oh gioia! oh ineffabile allegrezza! | oh vita intègra d'amore e di pace! | oh sanza brama sicura ricchezza!': *Paradiso* 27.1–9.

vacancy, of Peter's place as at present unoccupied in the sight of God:

> The providence which there assigns turn and office had imposed silence on the blessed choir on every side, when I heard, 'If I change colour, marvel not, for, as I speak, you shall see these change colour. He who on earth usurps my place, my place, my place, which in the sight of the Son of God is vacant, has made my burial-ground a sewer of blood and of stench, so that the perverse one who fell from here above takes comfort there below.'[6]

Dante's, then, is a nothing if not ferocious condemnation of those responsible in his day for administering the precious merits of the Christ, theirs at every stage being a scandalous appropriation both of power and of property in the interests of self-aggrandizement. But – and this now is the point – what of the underlying principles of all this, the basic ecclesiology or conception of the Church tending from out of the depths to authorize this expression of anger? Properly understood, then, the Church, Dante thinks, is nothing other than Christ's continuing presence to us under the conditions of time and space.[7] Committed to the care of Peter and to those standing in the line of apostolic descent, it is committed to one whose authority is not that, however, of Christ himself, but of Christ's vicar,[8] whose responsibility it is to bring home the faithful to the happiness of the next life under the guidance of the Spirit and on the basis of God's word as revealed in Scripture.[9] Proceeding, then, by way of the keys his in consequence of the Matthean commission (by way, that is to say, of the power of absolution represented by the golden key and the power of discernment represented by the silver key), his task is to further God's work in Christ by – provided only that those before him are

---

[6] 'La provedenza, che quivi comparte | vice e officio, nel beato coro | silenzio posto avea da ogne parte, | quand' ïo udi': "Se io mi trascoloro, | non ti maravigliar, ché, dicend' io, | vedrai trascolorar tutti costoro. | Quelli ch'usurpa in terra il luogo mio, | il luogo mio, il luogo mio, che vaca | ne la presenza del Figliuol di Dio, | fatt' ha del cimitero mio cloaca | del sangue e de la puzza; onde 'l perverso | che cadde di qua sù, là giù si placa"': *Paradiso* 27.16–27.

[7] *Monarchia* 3.15.3.

[8] Ibid. 3.3.7; 3.6.2–6.

[9] Ibid. 3.16.9–10.

properly penitent – unlocking the gate of heaven and letting them in. This, at any rate, is the burden of the 'Whenever one of these keys fails' passage placed by Dante upon the lips of the guardian of purgatory proper in the second canticle of the poem, a passage confirming the ideal transparency of everything the priest says and does to God's restorative purposes, to his forever holding out the possibility of new life to those seeking it in earnest:

> Ashes or earth that is dug out dry, would be of one colour with his vesture, and from beneath it he drew two keys, the one of gold and the other of silver. First with the white and then with the yellow he did so to the gate that I was content. 'Whenever one of these keys fails so that it does not turn rightly in the lock', he said to us, 'the passage does not open. The one is more precious; but the other requires great skill and wisdom before it will unlock; for this is the one that disentangles the knot. From Peter I hold them, and he told me to err rather in opening than in keeping shut, if but the people prostrate themselves at my feet.'[10]

The pope's authority is in this sense pre-eminently, indeed exclusively, spiritual in kind, his, ideally, being the kind of piety and compassion always and everywhere proper to those busy about Christ's work, anything other than this constituting an affront both to the substance and to the significance of his suffering on the cross. And it is this – this sense of the Church's forever betraying its proper calling by way of a blasphemous combination of effrontery and forgetfulness – that determines the shape of Dante's political theology, his sense of the parallel nature of imperial and eccle-

---

[10] 'Cenere o terra che secca si cavi | d'un color fora col suo vestimento; | e di sotto da quel trasse due chiavi. | L'una era d'oro e l'altra era d'argento: | pria con la bianca e poscia con la gialla | fece a la porta sì, ch'i' fu' contento. | "Quandunque l'una d'este chiavi falla, | che non si volga dritta per la toppa", | diss' elli a noi, "non s'apre questa calla. | Più cara è l'una; ma l'altra vuol troppa | d'arte e d'ingegno avanti che diserri, | perch' ella è quella che 'l nodo digroppa. | Da Pier le tegno; e dissemi ch'i' erri | anzi ad aprir ch'a tenerla serrata, | pur che la gente a' piedi mi s'atterri"': *Purgatorio* 9.115–29. Cf. Thomas Aquinas: 'Et secundum hoc distinguuntur duae claves; quarum una pertinet ad judicium de idoneitate ejus qui absolvendus est; et alia ad ipsam absolutionem' ('Accordingly we may distinguish two keys, the first of which regards judgement about the worthiness of the person to be absolved, while the other regards absolution itself'): *Summa Theologiae*, III (suppl.).17.3; see also P. Armour, *The Door of Purgatory: A Study of Multiple Symbolism in Dante's* Purgatorio (Oxford, 1983).

siastical authority as a matter, that is to say, of divine willing. In response, then, to the patterns of papal hierocracy familiar to him from a long tradition of polemical literature leading up to and surrounding the bull *Unam sanctam ecclesiam* of 1302, his was a sense of the way in which all authority in Christendom flows from God himself as its first and final cause, and this in such a way as to encourage as far as this life is concerned complementary but mutually exclusive orders of jurisdiction.[11]

Thus while it belongs to the emperor, as assisted by the philosopher and proceeding on the basis of specifically philosophical wisdom, to lead man to his proper happiness here and now, it belongs to the pope, authorized by Scripture and proceeding on the basis of the theological virtues, to see him through to his proper happiness hereafter. The pope's, therefore, is a strictly pastoral (as distinct from political) order of oversight, compassionate rather than in any sense coercive. The key passage here, lengthy but worth quoting in full for its special brand of political dualism, runs as follows:

> Ineffable providence has thus set before us two goals to aim at: happiness in this life, which consists in the exercise of our own powers and is figured in the earthly paradise, and happiness in the eternal life, which consists in the enjoyment of the vision of God (to which our own powers cannot raise us except with the help of God's light) and which is signified by the heavenly paradise. Now these two kinds of happiness must be reached by different means, as representing different ends. For we attain the first through the teachings of philosophy, provided that we follow them putting into practice the moral and intellectual virtues; whereas we attain the second through spiritual teachings which transcend human reason, provided that we follow them putting into practice the theological virtues, i.e. faith, hope and charity. These ends and the means to attain

[11] In general on papal hierocracy and the publicistic tradition in the late Middle Ages, see W. Ullmann, *Medieval Papalism* (London, 1949); J. A. Watt, *The Theory of Papal Monarchy in the Thirteenth Century* (London, 1965); J. H. Burns, ed., *The Cambridge History of Medieval Political Thought* (Cambridge, 1988); A. Black, *Political Thought in Europe 1250–1450* (Cambridge, 1992); J. Canning, *A History of Medieval Political Thought 300–1450* (London and New York, 1996). As regards Dante, see G. Holmes, 'Dante and the Popes', in C. Grayson, ed., *The World of Dante: Essays on Dante and his Times* (Oxford, 1980), 18–43.

them have been shown to us on the one hand by human reason, which has been entirely revealed to us by the philosophers, and on the other by the Holy Spirit, who through the prophets and sacred writers, through Jesus Christ the Son of God, coeternal with him, and through his disciples, has revealed to us the transcendent truth we cannot do without; yet human greed would cast these ends and means aside if men, like horses, prompted to wander by their animal natures, were not held in check 'with bit and bridle' on their journey. It is for this reason that man had need of two guides corresponding to his twofold goal: that is to say the supreme Pontiff, to lead mankind to eternal life in conformity with revealed truth, and the Emperor, to guide mankind to temporal happiness in conformity with the teachings of philosophy.[12]

In fact, there is in this same chapter of the *Monarchia* evidence to the effect that, though never in doubt about his conclusion in this passage, about the mutual independence, that is to say, of imperial and ecclesiastical authority this side of death, Dante nevertheless had some doubts about the viability of the distinctions upon which that conclusion rests, about the propriety, and indeed about the feasibility, of separating out so completely the moral-philosophical and the theological as areas of human spirituality; for in well-nigh the same breath he allows that there may after all

---

[12] 'Duos igitur fines providentia illa inenarrabilis homini proposuit intendendos: beatitudinem scilicet huius vite, que in operatione proprie virtutis consistit et per terrestrem paradisum figuratur; et beatitudinem vite ecterne, que consistit in fruitione divini aspectus ad quam propria virtus ascendere non potest, nisi lumine divino adiuta, que per paradisum celestem intelligi datur. Ad has quidem beatitudines, velut ad diversas conclusiones, per diversa media venire oportet. Nam ad primam per phylosophica documenta venimus, dummodo illa sequamur secundum virtutes morales et intellectuales operando; ad secundam vero per documenta spiritualia que humanam rationem transcendunt, dummodo illa sequamur secundum virtutes theologicas operando, fidem spem scilicet et karitatem. Has igitur conclusiones et media, licet ostensa sint nobis hec ab humana ratione que per phyltosophos tota nobis innotuit, hec a Spiritu Sancto qui per prophetas et agiographos, qui per coecternum sibi Dei filium Iesum Cristum et per eius discipulos supernaturalem veritatem ac nobis necessariam revelavit, humana cupiditas postergaret nisi homines, tanquam equi, sua bestialitate vagantes "in camo et freno" compescerentur in via. Propter quod opus fuit homini duplici directivo secundum duplicem finem: scilicet summo Pontifice, qui secundum revelata humanum genus perduceret ad vitam ecternam, et Imperatore, qui secundum phylosophica documenta genus humanum ad temporalem felicitatem dirigeret': *Monarchia* 3.16.7–10.

be a sense in which imperial authority is, in fact, subordinate to papal authority, the latter irradiating the former with the light of paternal grace, at which point the difficulties implicit in seeing and setting up the political issue in quite this way rise up to trouble him in conscience:

> But the truth concerning this last question should not be taken so literally as to mean that the Roman Prince is not in some sense subject to the Roman Pontiff, since this earthly happiness is in some sense ordered towards immortal happiness. Let Caesar therefore show that reverence towards Peter which a firstborn son should show his father, so that, illumined by the light of paternal grace, he may the more effectively light up the world, over which he has been placed by Him alone who is ruler over all things spiritual and temporal.[13]

But however that may be, the conclusion itself survives intact, Dante's, here as throughout, being a thoroughgoing commitment to the mutual demarcation of ecclesiastical and imperial jurisdiction this side of death, anything other than this – any confusion, that is to say, of the sword and crozier[14] – making for an affront, not only to God's self-evident purposes in the universe, but to the purity and simplicity of the gospel message.

Given, however, what amounts – at any rate in its sacerdotal and sacramental aspect – to a largely unexceptional ecclesiology, the argument needs now to be developed in terms of a number of counter-considerations tending, not only to qualify that ecclesiology, but to call ultimately for its reconfiguration; for if Dante's was indeed a sense of the religious life as a matter of *belonging*, of living within (and thus of living out) the sacramental structures of the Church as but the continuing presence of the Christ to us,

---

[13] 'Que quidem veritas ultime questionis non sic stricte recipienda est, ut romanus Princeps in aliquo romano Pontifici non subiaceat, cum mortalis ista felicitas quodammodo ad inmortalem felicitatem ordinetur. Illa igitur reverentia Cesar utatur ad Petrum qua primogenitus illius debet uti ad patrem: ut luce paterne gratie illustratus virtuosius orbem terre irradiet, cui ab Illo solo prefectus est, qui est omnium spiritualium et temporalium gubernator': ibid. 3.16.17–18.

[14] 'L'un l'altro ha spento; ed è giunta la spada | col pasturale, e l'un con l'altro insieme | per viva forza mal convien che vada; | però che, giunti, l'un l'altro non teme' ('The one has quenched the other, and the sword is joined to the crook; and the one together with the other must perforce go ill, since, joined, the one does not fear the other'): *Purgatorio* 16.109–12.

then it was also a sense of the religious life as a matter of *being*, of the emergence of self into the fullness of its proper humanity, at which point episcopacy becomes a matter of *self*-episcopacy, of self-oversight on the plane of properly human knowing and loving. And if by the same token his is a commitment to the indispensability of the ecclesiastical encounter in particular as a condition of ultimate homecoming, then it is at the same time a commitment to the indispensability of the cultural encounter in general as a principle of new life, as having about it, in its own proper sacramentality, its own power to spiritual renewal. And if, finally, his is a sense of the indispensability of the Christ as the means of entering fully and finally into God's presence (for no one comes to the Father but by way of the Son), it is at the same time a sense of the love-susceptibility of the Godhead apt precisely in its open-endedness to bring home at last all those – Christian and pagan alike – living out in good faith the substance of their proper humanity. Dante's, then, although an ecclesiology obedient in every formal respect to the patterns of thought to which he was heir, is at the same time, and at a deeper level of conscious-ness and commitment, an ecclesiology 'on the edge', on the point of deconstruction and of reconstruction in response to its at once ontological and affective substance.

To take, then, the first of these things, the notion of episcopacy as a matter of *self*-episcopacy, of self as presiding over self in the forum of conscience, we may begin by saying that the *Commedia*, as an account of the soul's journey into God, is at the same time a journey of the soul into self, into the fullness of its own humanity, there to discover the power of self both to self-annihilation and to self-affirmation on the plane of properly human being. Following, then, on the moment of descent represented by the *Inferno*, the moment of self-confrontation in the forum of consciousness, comes the moment of ascent represented by the *Purgatorio* and by the *Paradiso*, the purgatorial phase in particular of the journey culminating in a fresh sense of spiritual self-possession, in a sense both of kingship as a matter of *self*-kingship and of episcopacy as a matter of *self*-episcopacy, of *self*-superintendence on the plane of properly human being and doing:

> When all the stair was sped beneath us and we were on the topmost step, Virgil fixed his eyes on me and said: 'The

temporal fire and the eternal you have seen, my son, and are come to a part where I of myself discern no farther onward. I have brought you here with understanding and with art. Take henceforth your own pleasure for your guide. Forth are you from the steep ways, forth from the narrow. See the sun that shines on your brow, see the tender grass, the flowers, the shrubs, which here the earth of itself alone produces; till the beautiful eyes come rejoicing which weeping made me come to you, you may go and sit among them. No longer expect any word or sign from me. Free, upright and whole is your will, and it would be wrong not to act according to its pleasure; wherefore I crown and miter you over yourself.'[15]

Now the issue here requires careful statement, for never at any stage can there be any question in Dante of his setting aside or of his sitting lightly to the notion of the pope as pastor, as one, that is to say, entrusted by Christ with the feeding of his sheep. And neither can there be any question of his setting aside or of his sitting lightly to being and becoming in man as a matter of grace both in its operative and in its cooperative aspect, of grace, that is to say, as a matter both of original and of continuing spiritual empowerment.[16] But neither − and this now is the point − can there be any question of the soul's remaining a babe in the faith or of its feeding upon milk rather than upon meat. On the contrary, and as part of what it means to speak of man as made in the image of God, it is a question now of his emergence from adolescence into adulthood, into the kind of maturity proper to one called as

---

[15] 'Come la scala tutta sotto noi | fu corsa e fummo in su 'l grado superno, | in me ficcò Virgilio li occhi suoi, | e disse: "Il temporal foco e l'etterno | veduto hai, figlio; e se' venuto in parte | dov' io per me più oltre non discerno. | Tratto t'ho qui con ingegno e con arte; | lo tuo piacere omai prendi per duce; | fuor se' de l'erte vie, fuor se' de l'arte. | Vedi lo sol che 'n fronte ti riluce; | vedi l'erbette, i fiori e li arbuscelli | che qui la terra sol da sé produce. | Mentre che vegnan lieti li occhi belli | che, lagrimando, a te venir mi fenno, | seder ti puoi e puoi andar tra elli. | Non aspettar mio dir più né mio cenno; | libero, dritto e sano è tuo arbitrio, | e fallo fora non fare a suo senno: | per ch'io te sovra te corono e mitrio"': *Purgatorio* 27.124–42.

[16] On the question of grace and of the theology of grace in Dante, see especially, in English, J. T. Chiampi, 'The Role of Freely Bestowed Grace in Dante's Journey of Legitimation', *Rivista di Studi Italiani* 17 (1999), 89–111; A. Mastrobuono, *Dante's Journey of Sancification* (Washington, DC, 1990); in Italian, B. Panvini, 'La concezione tomistica della grazia nella *Divina Commedia*', *Letture classensi* 17 (1988), 69–85; P. Cherchi, 'Da me stesso non vegno (*Inf.* X, 61)', *Rassegna europea di letteratura italiana* 18 (2001), 103–6.

of the essence to cooperate in the working out of his historical and eschatological destiny – at which point the ecclesiological is taken up in the ontological, in the rhythm of existence itself as the whereabouts of its proper contemplation.

But there is more, for this taking up of the ecclesiological in the ontological, in the rhythm of existence itself in its moment-by-moment unfolding, is at every point accompanied in Dante by a sense of the sacramental status, not simply of the ecclesiastical encounter in particular, but of the cultural encounter in general, the ecclesiological thus being taken up also in what today we would call a theology of culture. Here again the text is perfectly explicit, perfectly forthcoming in its sense of the ordinary (as distinct from the extraordinary) encounter as a channel of grace, as that whereby God looks to implement his purposes for this or that man or woman as a creature of moral and eschatological accountability; so, for example, in respect of the Virgilian phase of the soul's journey into God, the 'Virgil sweetest father' passage towards the end of the *Purgatorio*, perfectly secure in its sense of the salvific substance of the encounter, of its power to new life:

> As soon as on my sight the lofty virtue smote that had already pierced me before I was out of my boyhood, I turned to the left with the confidence of a little child that runs to his mother when he is frightened or in distress, to say to Virgil: 'Not a drop of blood is left in me that does not tremble for I recognize the signs of the ancient flame.' But Virgil had left us bereft of himself, Virgil sweetest father, Virgil to whom I gave myself for my salvation; nor did all that our ancient mother lost keep my dew-washed cheeks from turning dark again with tears.[17]

– while in respect of the Beatrician phase the 'O lady, in whom my hope is strong' passage towards the end of the *Paradiso*, where, again in the context of leave-taking, Dante is anxious to acknowledge

---

[17] 'Tosto che ne la vista mi percosse | l'alta virtù che già m'avea trafitto | prima ch'io fuor di püerizia fosse, | volsimi a la sinistra col respitto | col quale il fantolin corre a la mamma | quando ha paura o quando elli è afflitto, | per dicere a Virgilio: "Men che dramma | di sangue m'è rimaso che non tremi: | conosco i segni de l'antica fiamma." | Ma Virgilio n'avea lasciati scemi | di sé, Virgilio dolcissimo patre, | Virgilio a cui per mia salute die'mi; | né quantunque perdeo l'antica matre, | valse a le guance nette di rugiada, | che, lagrimando, non tornasser atre': *Purgatorio* 30.40–54.

the presence of Beatrice to him both as a condition and as a coefficient of his coming at last into the fullness of his proper humanity:

'O lady, in whom my hope is strong, and who for my salvation did endure to leave in hell your footprints, of all those things which I have seen I acknowledge the grace and the virtue to be from your power and your excellence. It is you who have drawn me from bondage into liberty by all those paths, by all those means by which you had the power so to do. Preserve in me your great munificence, so that my soul, which you have made whole, may be loosed from the body, pleasing unto you.' So did I pray; and she, so distant as she seemed, smiled and looked on me, then turned again to the eternal fountain.[18]

Everywhere, then, the pattern is the same, those closest to the individual in the course of his or her *itinerarium in Deum* functioning as a principle of renewal and of redemption, as that whereby they know themselves in their gradual movement into God.

But even this is not all, for bearing also on the ecclesiological question and again offering an invitation to its rethinking, is that of election, the question of whom God chooses and why. It is impossible to overstate the difficulty of this issue for Dante, his, by virtue of what amounts not only to the bilingualism but also to the biculturalism of his circumstances, being a commitment both to the Graeco-Roman and to the Judeo-Christian component of his spirituality, both to its pagan – above all in the form of its Aristotelian – and to its Christian elements.[19] The question straightaway

---

[18] '''O donna in cui la mia speranza vige, | e che soffristi per la mia salute | in inferno lasciar le tue vestige, | di tante cose quant' i' ho vedute, | dal tuo podere e da la tua bontate | riconosco la grazia e la virtute. | Tu m'hai di servo tratto a libertate | per tutte quelle vie, per tutt' i modi | che di ciò fare avei la potestate. | La tua magnificenza in me custodi, | sì che l'anima mia, che fatt' hai sana, | piacente a te dal corpo si disnodi.'' | Così orai; e quella, sì lontana | come parea, sorrise e riguardommi; | poi si tornò a l'etterna fontana': *Paradiso* 31.79–93.

[19] Kenelm Foster, on the threshold of what amounts to his final meditation on the complexity of Dantean spirituality even into the *Commedia*, puts it thus: 'Dante was attached, simultaneously, to Christianity and to paganism. This was not a half-way position, nor a wavering between two conceptions of life according to mood or circumstance. The attachment to paganism was more like that which a man may feel to his youth, except that paganism was a stage in the history of Dante's race, not of himself individually. Yet there is a sense in which the pagan "object" of his attachment was not something past and done with, existing only in history or legend or works of art; rather it was a permanent part of himself, an *alter ego;* it was that second self which his imagination took into the Other World in the form of Virgil and which,

arises, then, as to what we are to say about those living according to their lights but unfortunate enough to be born either before or beyond the Christian dispensation. Are they ever to be brought home, or must we, like them, resign ourselves to their fate as forever lost to their maker? The *Inferno*, it is true, with its location of the virtuous pagans of antiquity in a place less of suffering than of sighing, offers a solution of sorts, the best, perhaps, that can be done in the circumstances. But in the *Paradiso*, where it is a question precisely of divine justice and the intelligibility thereof, the whole thing surfaces once more in all its combination of intractability and inescapability. Dante, then, comes straight to the point. If a man dies unbaptized through no fault of his own, where is the justice which condemns him:

> For you said: 'A man is born on the banks of the Indus, and none is there to speak, or read, or write, of Christ, and all his wishes and acts are good, so far as human reason sees, without sin in life or in speech. He dies unbaptized, and without faith. Where is this justice which condemns him? Where is his sin if he does not believe?'[20]

once it had assumed this form, was allowed to take charge of, to guide and govern the Christian protagonist of the resulting poem. Because the hero of the *Divine Comedy* is a Christian the poem is Christian, but through two-thirds of it the hero is guided by a pagan. And even "guided" is too weak a term; Virgil in the poem is the hero's "leader", "master", "teacher", "lord". Above all he is Dante's "father" – "my sweet father", "sweet and dear father", "my more than father". Seldom in literature has the filial sentiment, blending reverence and affection, been so finely expressed as in this relationship which carries the central narrative line through so much of the great poem. And it is of its essence that the father here is a pagan, the son a Christian; simultaneously so close and so separated': K. Foster, *The Two Dantes* (London, 1977), 156.

[20] 'ché tu dicevi: "Un uom nasce a la riva | de l'Indo, e quivi non è chi ragioni | di Cristo né chi legga né chi scriva; | e tutti suoi voleri e atti buoni | sono, quanto ragione umana vede, | sanza peccato in vita o in sermoni. | Muore non battezzato e sanza fede: | ov' è questa giustizia che 'l condanna? | ov' è la colpa sua, se ei non crede?": *Paradiso* 19.70–8. On Dante, Virgil and the noble pagans of antiquity, see G. Rizzo, 'Dante and the Virtuous Pagans', in *A Dante Symposium in Commemoration of the 700th Anniversary of the Poet's Birth (1265–1321)*, ed. W. De Sua and G. Rizzo (Chapel Hill, NC, 1965), 15–40; E. TeSelle, 'Dante's Virtuous Romans', *Dante Studies* 96 (1978), 145–62; A. A. Iannucci, 'Limbo: The Emptiness of Time', *Studi danteschi* 52 (1979–80), 69–128; N. Iliescu, 'Will Virgil be saved?', *Mediaevalia* 12 (1986), 93–114, repr. as 'Sarà salvo Virgilio?' in *Dante: Summa medievalis. Proceedings of the Symposium of the Center for Italian Studies, SUNY Stony Brook*, ed. C. Franco and L. Morgan (Stony Brook, NY, 1995), 112–33; M. Allan, 'Does Dante Hope for Vergil's Salvation?', *Modern Language Notes* 104 (1989), 193–205; T. Barolini, 'Q: Does Dante Hope for Vergil's Salvation?', *Modern Language Notes* 105 (1990), 138–49; M. L. Colish, 'The Virtuous Pagan: Dante

Nothing if not courageous, then, in putting the question, Dante begins step by step to develop a reply, contenting himself as far as Canto 19 of the *Paradiso* is concerned with a restatement of the gospel sense of Christ being the way, the truth and the life and the sole means of access to the kingdom,[21] and with a warning against any attempt to fathom the divine mind at this point.[22] Aware, however, that this, far from resolving the issue, merely intensifies it (for what, still, of those who through no fault of their own are innocent both of Christ and of clergy?), Dante begins straightaway to experiment with an alternative and altogether more exhilarating line of thought. Seeing before him, then, the pagan figures of Trajan and Rhipeus encrusted like jewels within the brow of the eagle of divine righteousness, he proceeds by way of one of the more difficult of Christ's sayings in the gospel (the 'from the days of John the Baptist until now the kingdom of heaven suffers violence, and the violent take it by force' passage of Matthew 11, with a parallel passage in Luke 16),[23] he fashions from it an essay in the love-vulnerability of God, in God's always reaching out, that is to say, to honour those who live and love according to their lights, his forever being vanquished by love, however, merely confirming his victory as a lover, the completeness of his triumph over lovelessness: '*Regnum celorum* suffers violence from fervent love which vanquishes the divine will; not as man overcomes man, but vanquishes it because it wills to be vanquished, and, vanquished, vanquishes with its own benignity.'[24]

---

and Christian Tradition', in *The Unbounded Community: Papers in Christian Ecumenism in Honor of Jaraslov Pelikan*, ed. W. Caferro and D. G. Fisher (London, 1996), 43–92. More generally, see R. V. Turner, '"Descendit ad Inferos". Medieval Views on Christ's Descent into Hell and the Salvation of the Ancient Just', *JHI* 27 (1966), 173–94.

[21] 'A questo regno | non salì mai chi non credette 'n Cristo, | né pria né poi ch'el si chiavasse al legno' ('To this kingdom none ever rose who believed not in Christ, either before or after he was nailed to the tree'): *Paradiso* 19.103–5; cf. John 14: 6.

[22] 'Oh terreni animali! oh menti grosse! | La prima volontà, ch'è da sé buona, | da sé, ch'è sommo ben, mai non si mosse' ('O earthly animals! O gross minds! The primal will, which of itself is good has never moved from itself'): *Paradiso* 19.85–7.

[23] Matt. 11: 12: 'A diebus autem Iohannis Baptistae usque nunc regnum caelorum vim patitur, et violenti rapiunt'; cf. 'Lex et prophetae usque ad Johannem ex eo regnum Dei evangelizatur et omnis in illud vim facit': Luke 16: 16.

[24] '*Regnum celorum* vïolenza pate | da caldo amore e da viva speranza, | che vince la divina volontate: | non a guisa che l'omo a l'om sobranza, | ma vince lei perché vuole esser vinta, | e, vinta, vince con sua beninanza': *Paradiso* 20.94–9. But see already *Purgatorio* 15.67–72 on the love-eagerness of God, his eagerness – somewhat after the

True, Dante at once beats a retreat, his account in what follows of the miraculous conversion of Trajan and Rhipeus to Christianity chiming with the particularism of Canto 19, with the notion of explicit belief as a condition of salvation. But by that stage it is too late, for by that stage he has unleashed a set of intuitions tending not so much to confirm as to call into question the particularist habit of mind, to refer the ecclesiological question to its innermost reasons – to (in short) the love which moves the sun and the other stars.

What, then, are we to say about Dante and the Church? First, that for all its subsisting 'on the edge', its forever inviting from deep within itself the most far-reaching kind of reconstruction, Dante's even so is an ecclesiology obedient in every formal respect to the patterns of thought to which he was heir. The Church, then, properly speaking, must be seen and understood as, again, nothing but the continuing presence of Christ to us, as founded by Christ,[25] as commissioned by Christ,[26] and, by way of the pope as the servant of Christ's servants, as shedding abroad the light of his grace[27] – to all of which we should for the sake of completeness add a more recognizably mystical sense of the Church as the bride of Christ, as bound to him, and he to her, by way of a special kind of nuptial intensity; so, for example, the 'bride of God rising to sing her matins' passage of *Paradiso* 10:

> Then, like a clock which calls us at the hour when the Bride of God rises to sing her matins to her Bridegroom, that he may love her, in which one part draws or drives the other,

manner of the father in the parable of the prodigal son – to see from afar, to hasten to meet and to embrace the lover and penitent spirit: 'Quello infinito e ineffabil bene | che là sù è, così corre ad amore | com' a lucido corpo raggio vene. | Tanto si dà quanto trova d'ardore; | sì che, quantunque carità si stende, | cresce sovr' essa l'etterno valore' ('That infinite and ineffable good that is there above speeds to love as a ray of light comes to a bright body. So much it gives of itself as it finds of ardour, so that how far soever love extends, the more does the eternal goodness increase upon it'). Cf. M. Picone, 'La "viva speranza" di Dante e il problema della salvezza dei pagani virtuosi. Una lettura di *Paradiso* 20', *Quaderni di Italianistica* 10 (1989), 1–2, 251–68; G. Cannavò, ed., *Regnum celorum vïolenza pate. Dante e la salvezza dell'umanità. Letture Dantesche Giubilari, Vicenza, Ottobre 1999 – Giugno 2000* (Montella (Avellino), 2002); also B. D. Schildgen, 'Dante and the Indus', *Dante Studies* 111 (1993), 177–93.

[25] *Monarchia* 3.10.7; 3.14.3.

[26] Ibid. 3.15.3.

[27] Ibid. 3.4.20; 3.16.17–18. For the 'servant of Christ's servants', see *Inferno* 15.112 ('servo de' servi').

sounding *ting! ting!* with notes so sweet that the well-disposed spirit swells with love, so did I see the glorious wheel move and render voice to voice with harmony and sweetness that cannot be known except there where joy is everlasting.[28]

or the 'bride of him who with loud cries espoused her with his blessed blood' passage of *Paradiso* 11 (part of Aquinas's hymn to Francis of Assisi):

The providence that governs the world with that counsel in which every created vision is vanquished before it reaches the bottom, in order that the bride of him who, with loud cries, espoused her with the blessed blood, might go to her delight, secure within herself and also more faithful towards him, ordained on her behalf two princes, who on this side and that might be her guides.[29]

or the 'succoured his bride with two champions' passage of *Paradiso* 12 (part of Bonaventure's hymn to Dominic):

Christ's army, which cost so dear to rearm, was moving behind the standard, slow, mistrustful and scanty, when the emperor who reigns eternally took thought for his soldiery that was in peril, of his grace only, not that it was worthy, and, as has been said, succoured his bride with two champions by whose deeds, by whose words, the scattered people were rallied.[30]

Throughout, then, the pattern is the same: Dante, in his sense both of the *what* and of the *how* of the Church as a community of men

---

[28] 'Indi, come orologio che ne chiami | ne l'ora che la sposa di Dio surge | a mattinar lo sposo perché l'ami, | che l'una parte e l'altra tira e urge, | tin tin sonando con sì dolce nota, | che 'l ben disposto spirto d'amor turge; | così vid' ïo la gloriosa rota | muoversi e render voce a voce in tempra | e in dolcezza ch'esser non pò nota | se non colà dove gioir s'insempra': *Paradiso* 10.139–48.

[29] 'La provedenza, che governa il mondo | con quel consiglio nel quale ogne aspetto | creato è vinto pria che vada al fondo, | però che andasse ver' lo suo diletto | la sposa di colui ch'ad alte grida | disposò lei col sangue benedetto, | in sé sicura e anche a lui più fida, | due principi ordinò in suo favore, | che quinci e quindi le fosser per guida. | L'un fu tutto serafico in ardore; | l'altro per sapïenza in terra fue | di cherubica luce uno splendore': *Paradiso* 11.28–36.

[30] 'L'essercito di Cristo, che sì caro | costò a rïarmar, dietro a la 'nsegna | si movea tardo, sospeccioso e raro, | quando lo 'mperador che sempre regna | provide a la milizia, ch'era in forse, | per sola grazia, non per esser degna; | e, come è detto, a sua sposa soccorse | con due campioni, al cui fare, al cui dire | lo popol disvïato si raccorse': *Paradiso* 12.37–45.

and women professing the name of Christ both here and hereafter, is reflecting the substance both of high scholastic and of Cistercian consciousness hereabouts. But by the same token there can be no understating the implications in the area of ecclesiology of what amounts in the *Commedia* to an essay in the inwardness of the moral and religious life in man, in the nature of that life as a matter less of observance than of emergence, of the soul's issuing at last into the fullness of its humanity by way of a first-person encounter with self in the recesses of self (the *Inferno*), by way of a nothing if not painful reconfiguration of self on the plane of properly human loving (the *Purgatorio*), and, as the ecstatic outcome of these things, by way of an actualization of self in its proper capacity for God (the *Paradiso*). This, at any rate, is where Dante begins and ends in his poem. He begins with an account of the soul as lost to itself and to the reasons of its humanity, and concludes with an account of its finding itself in and through communion with the One who *is* as of the essence, all of which serves, if not, certainly, to liquidate the substance of specifically ecclesiological consciousness, then immeasurably to deepen it, and, in deepening it, to confirm it in its accountability to something infinitely more sublime than itself, to − again − the rhythm of existence itself in the moment-by-moment unfolding of existence.

University College London

'NO MILKLESS COW': THE CROSS OF CHRIST IN MEDIEVAL IRISH LITERATURE

by SALVADOR RYAN

The cross of Christ in the Middle Ages was the most powerful symbol of God's victory over sin, death and the forces of evil, while also representing the most abject suffering and degradation of Jesus Christ, the God-Man. A simplistic reading of the evolution of the theology of the cross during this period posits a transition from the early medieval victorious and heroic Christ figure, reigning and triumphant upon the cross, to a late medieval emaciated and tortured object of pity whose ignominious death was supposed to elicit heartfelt compassion for his plight and sincere sorrow for the sin which placed him on the beams of the tree of crucifixion. Of course, there is a great deal of value in this argument, and much evidence might be brought forward to support its central thesis. However, it should not be pushed too far; it might also be remembered that the essential paradox of Christ the victor-victim is a constant theme in Christian theology, expressed in the sixth-century *Vexilla regis* in its identification of the cross as 'victim of the passion's glory, by which life brought death to an end, and, by death, gave life again' and in the hymn *Victimae paschali laudes* from the central medieval period: 'Death with life contended, combat strangely ended, life's own champion slain yet lives to reign'.[1] The image of the victorious cross of Christ, conceived of as simultaneously an instrument of triumph and of torture, would persist right through the late medieval period, despite the development of a greater emphasis on the physical sufferings of Christ in his passion and their ever more graphic depictions. This essay, which examines the way in which the cross of Christ is presented in medieval Irish literature, provides sufficient examples to make this point clear; these are drawn from a variety of sources including religious verse, saints' lives, medieval travel accounts and sermon material. Of course, these examples are

---

[1] Cited in Richard Viladesau, *The Beauty of the Cross: The Passion of Christ in Theology and the Arts − From the Catacombs to the Eve of the Renaissance* (Oxford, 2006), 39.

best viewed within the context of a broader medieval European devotional culture from which Ireland was certainly not immune.[2]

BLATHMAC AND ERIUGENA

The eighth-century Irish poet Blathmac manages to capture in verse the horror of Christ's experience on Calvary while also emphasizing his ultimate victory.[3] In a long poem addressed to Mary, the mother of Jesus, he recalls:

> Your people seized your Son; Mary, they flogged him ...
> It was a hideous deed ... that was done to him: that his very mother-kin should crucify the man who had come to save them.[4]

Blathmac proceeds to recount how 'when every outrage was committed against him, when capture was completed, he took his cross upon his back – he did not cease being beaten'.[5] Upon the cross, Christ is pierced by a lance and wine is spilled from his 'gleaming sides' upon the pathway.[6] Yet this flowing blood accomplishes two feats in succession: firstly, according to Blathmac, 'the flowing blood ... baptised the head of Adam, for the shaft of the cross of Christ had [been] aimed at his mouth'. Here Blathmac draws from legends concerning the prehistory of the tree of crucifixion in which its wood grows from seeds given to Seth in paradise which are placed in the mouth of the dead Adam. This legend appears in full in later medieval bardic poems on the cross of Christ.[7] The second feat is the cure of Longinus from blindness (he is known in Irish literature as 'An Dall' – the blind man) by means of the blood of Christ which runs down the shaft of his

[2] The influence of English and Continental devotional cultures on medieval Irish piety and the manuscript transmission of much of the following literature are discussed in Salvador Ryan, 'The Devotional Landscape of Medieval Irish Cultural Catholicism *inter hibernicos et inter anglicos*, c.1200 – c.1550', in Oliver Rafferty, ed., *Irish Catholic Identities* (Manchester, forthcoming).
[3] For the connections between Blathmac's work and the Culdee movement, see Brian Lambkin, 'Blathmac and the Céilí Dé: A Reappraisal', *Celtica* 23 (1999), 132-54.
[4] *The Poems of Blathmac, son of Cú Brettan*, ed. James Carney (Dublin, 1964), 17, stanzas 46–7.
[5] Ibid. 19, stanza 49.
[6] Ibid. 21, stanza 55–6.
[7] See the poem *Marthain duit a chroch an Choimhdhe*: Lambert McKenna, ed., 'To a Crucifix', *Irish Monthly* 50 (1922), 117–19, 154–6, 209–10. This poem is discussed further below.

lance and with which Longinus then rubs his eyes. In Blathmac's poem, the cataclysmic events following Christ's crucifixion include an explosion of blood upon the surrounding landscape: 'A stream of blood gushed forth (severe excess) so that the bark of every tree was red; there was blood on the breasts of the world, in the tree-tops of every great forest.'[8] While Blathmac admits that 'Jesus, darling son of the pure Virgin, achieved a deed of pure victory',[9] yet in condemning the Jews for their kin-slaying he does not fail to note how 'his wretchedness was greater than that of any noble captive',[10] exclaiming: 'alas, for anyone who has seen the son of the living God stretched fast on the cross! Alas, the body possessing wisest dignity, that has plunged into gore!'[11] Yet that same body, some verses later, is said to have 'saved a prey with stout victory'[12] and would return at the end of time to exact justice from all those who were not prepared to lament his death: Blathmac speaks to Mary of the 'angry coming of your son with his cross on his reddened back'.[13]

Christ's death on the cross is conceived by Blathmac in the familiar patristic imagery of a battle against the devil in which Christ emerges 'victorious from fighting' and the devil's strength is crushed and 'a great prey taken from him'.[14] Some verses later he notes that 'his crucified body was his victory';[15] yet in order for the battle imagery to be truly effective and the drama heightened, Christ is said to have 'suffered a shameful affliction and battle in hell' and to have received 'good nursing' when he eventually reached heaven.[16] However, as Celia Chazelle reminds us for the same period, we should be careful not to regard references to Christ's hardship as simply a means to underscore his victory; rather, contemplation of Christ's sufferings was also conceived of as having a value in its own right.[17] The transformative power of

---

8   *Blathmac*, ed. Carney, 23, stanza 64.
9   Ibid. 37, stanza 105.
10   Ibid. 41, stanza 120.
11   Ibid. 43, stanza 121.
12   Ibid. 47, stanza 137.
13   Ibid. 49, stanza 142.
14   Ibid. 61, stanza 175.
15   Ibid., stanza 178.
16   Ibid., stanzas 178–9.
17   Celia Chazelle, *The Crucified God in the Carolingian Era: Theology and Art of Christ's Passion* (Cambridge, 2007), 23.

Christ's shedding of blood on the cross is expressed by Blathmac in an image echoing Revelation 7: 14 when he states that it is 'in his blood that every saint washes his bright garment', and is continued in his graphic statement that 'the blood of the Son of the King reddens a body of clay in the brightness of gore' rendering it resplendent anew.[18] In this poem, then, a delicate balance is maintained between the glory and horror of the crucifixion on Calvary, a creative tension that is at the heart of the Christian mystery; this paradox can also be identified in the famous Anglo-Saxon poem *The Dream of the Rood*, in which the cross is portrayed both as drenched in jewels and soaked in blood.[19]

In a different context, several decades after Blathmac's poems were most likely written, the Irish scholar John Scotus Eriugena departed Ireland for a career on the Continent at the court of Charles the Bald where, aside from being commissioned to make translations of important Greek works, he was patronized as a court poet. In his Latin poems written around 859, Eriugena emphasizes in particular the triumph of the cross of Christ:

Now let us see the high triumphs of Christ
And the stars shining bright in our mind.
See the wood of the cross that embraces the four-cornered world:
Of his own accord did Our Lord hang upon it.
And the Word of the Father deigned to receive the flesh,
In which for our sake he became a victim who pleased.
Behold the pierced palms, the shoulders and feet,
The temples girt with the cruel wreath of thorns.
From the midst of his side, the unlocked fount of salvation,
Flow living draughts of water and blood.
The water washes the whole world clean of its sin of old;
The blood makes us mortals divine ...[20]

---

[18] *Blathmac*, ed. Carney, 71, stanza 205.

[19] 'A Vision of a Rood', in J. A. W. Bennett, ed., *Poetry of the Passion: Studies in Twelve Centuries of English Verse* (Oxford, 1982), 26–31, lines 7, 16, 23, 48.

[20] *Ioannis Scotti Eriugenae: Carmina*, ed. Michael Herren (Dublin, 1993), 59 (poem 1). See especially Richard Hawtree, 'Christ on the Cross in Eriugena's *Carmina* for Charles the Bald', in Richard Hawtree, Juliet Mullins and Jenifer Ní Grádaigh, eds, *Envisioning Christ on the Cross in the Early Medieval West: c.500–1200* (Turnhout, forthcoming).

Here, while emphasizing Christ's victory on the cross, Eriugena's audience are nevertheless invited to behold the 'wood of the cross', reflecting the emergence of the unveiling of the cross in the Frankish liturgy of Good Friday.[21] However, Eriugena goes further still, zooming in, if you like, on Christ's pierced palms, his shoulders and feet and his temples surrounded by thorns, in what might be termed an affective manner.[22] The reference to the cosmic significance of the cross – embracing 'the four-cornered world' – brings to mind the representation on the ninth-century high cross of St Muiredach at Monasterboice in County Louth, in which the crucified figure of Christ is joined by what may possibly be Gaia, the personification of the earth, and Tellus or Ocean, the personification of water, in addition to the Sun and Moon, as pointed out by Peter Harbison.[23]

In another poem dedicated to the cross itself, John Scotus Eriugena speaks of the cross with an orb spreading light like the rays of the sun and which commands the worship of 'all that is being, non-being and beyond-being'.[24] Michael Herren suggests that Eriugena is here being influenced by the great Irish high crosses with which he would have been familiar before leaving Ireland.[25] Eriugena depicts the cross as having been prefigured by Moses's staff, recounting how 'clothed in the skin of the snake you astonished Pharaoh, as you devoured the others the Sorcerer furnished through cunning', which recalls Exodus 7: 12, in which there is a stand-off between Moses and Aaron and Pharaoh's magicians. He recalls how 'you [the cross] divide the Red Sea's marble waves; you proceed victorious and make a path for your people'.[26] The cross as bronze serpent 'hisses as it hangs aloft; its poison quenched'.[27] Here, the work of Eriugena resembles that of Alcuin of York in

[21] See Louis van Tongeren, *Exaltation of the Cross: Toward the Origins of the Feast of the Cross and the Meaning of the Cross in Early Medieval Liturgy* (Leuven, 2000).

[22] Cf., e.g., the fourteenth-century Anglo-Irish poem 'Christ on the cross' in BL, Harley MS 913: 'Look at His nails, in hand and also in foot, and how the streams of His precious blood flow. Begin at His head and look all the way to His toes. You will find in His body only excruciating suffering and affliction': Angela Lucas, ed., *Anglo-Irish Poems of the Middle Ages* (Dublin, 1995), 122–4, at 123.

[23] Peter Harbison, *The Crucifixion in Irish Art* (Dublin, 2000), 4.

[24] *Ioannis Scotti Eriugenae*, ed. Herren, 65, poem 2.

[25] Ibid. 136.

[26] Ibid. 65.

[27] Ibid. 67.

his *Carmen figuratum* completed for Charlemagne some decades earlier (some time between 780 and 800), which makes use of similar parallels.[28] More importantly, Eriugena's earlier compatriot Blathmac also drew upon the brazen serpent as a figure of Christ in his poetry: 'your son is the blessed serpent by whom the perverse old serpent was smitten'.[29] Eriugena goes on to exclaim 'O Christ, Word of God, Power, Wisdom of the Father, the wave of your blood, in which the altar of the cross is bathed, purges, redeems, releases, leads us back to life'.[30] In this poem in particular Christ and the cross can be identified with each other: for instance, early in the poem it is the cross which 'summons the wretched race from the depths of Hell, it pierces the Tartarean Styx with its point'.[31] The piercing of the devil or hell with the use of Christ's cross as a weapon would become a familiar feature of medieval iconography.

THE SIGN OF THE CROSS

As noted above, it is commonly argued that the early Middle Ages conceived of the cross as primarily a sign of victory rather than an instrument of torture, and that it symbolized Christ's conquest of death, the devil and the underworld. One particularly useful way of examining how that victory was understood to be actualized in the lives of the saints is to explore the efficacy of the sign of the cross itself in medieval literature. Here, there are many examples of its usefulness in preserving people from the influence of the devil. In an Irish bardic religious poem *Marthain duit a chroch an Choimhdheadh* ('Hail, O Cross of the Lord'), dating from the thirteenth century, the poet addresses the cross in the following way:

> Thou art our shield and sword, O Cross wherein Christ shed his blood;
> I cease to hear that flood (of Christ's blood) when I make not thy sign upon me.[32]

Tracing the sign of the cross upon oneself was understood to

---

[28] Chazelle, *Crucified God*, 17.
[29] *Blathmac*, ed. Carney, 71, stanza 209.
[30] *Ioannis Scotti Eriugenae*, ed. Herren, 67.
[31] Ibid. 65.
[32] McKenna, ed., 'To a Crucifix', 156, stanza 38.

claim the victory of the cross over the power of evil. Muirchú's late seventh-century life of St Patrick, which presents the saint as a great wonder-worker, attests to the importance which was accorded the use of this sign and its efficacy as a symbol of victory: 'He also signed himself with the victorious sign of the cross a hundred times at every hour of the day and night and wherever he saw a cross he would descend from his chariot and go out of his way to pray before it.'[33]

The power of the sign of the cross is also highlighted in Adamnán's life of St Columcille, written at Iona near the end of the seventh century. Here the saint is asked by a young man to bless a pail of new milk which, upon Columcille making the sign of the cross over it, shakes violently and falls to the earth, spilling the greater part of its contents. The saint explains to the boy that a demon had lurked in the bottom of the vessel and being 'unable to bear the power of that sign, he has quickly fled in terror'.[34] It is in this saint's life, too, that we find what is reputed to be the first mention in literature of the Loch Ness monster, which was despatched in similar manner by Columcille. Having encouraged one of his companions to swim across the lake as bait, which immediately set the monster in pursuit, the saint

> ... raised his holy hand, while all the rest, brethren as well as strangers, were stupefied with terror, and, invoking the name of God, formed the saving sign of the cross in the air, and commanded the ferocious monster, saying, 'Thou shalt go no further, nor touch the man; go back with all speed.' Then at the voice of the saint, the monster was terrified, and fled more quickly than if it had been pulled back with ropes.[35]

The sign of the cross played a prominent role in medieval sermon *exempla*, enabling many a would-be saint to get out of a sticky situation. The sixteenth-century Irish bardic poet Aonghus Fionn Ó Dálaigh, in the poem *Iomdha sgéal maith ar Mhuire* ('Many the good tale of Mary'), tells the familiar story of a young hermit

---

33 Muirchú, *Vita S. Patricii* 2.1, in Ludwig Bieler, ed. and transl., *The Patrician Texts in the Book of Armagh* (Dublin, 1979), 114–15.

34 Adomnán, *The Life of Columba*, ch. 15, CELT: Corpus of Electronic Texts edition, <http://www.ucc.ie/celt/published/L201040/index.html>, accessed 16 July 2010.

35 Ibid., ch. 28.

who loved only the Virgin Mary. Hearing a knock on the door of his dwelling in the middle of the desert, he finds a woman asking for admittance in Mary's name. He complies and, being so struck by her beauty, he falls in love with her, forgetting his vow of love for the Virgin. Soon after, another woman's voice calls to him from outside, seeking shelter. Being a sensible man, he is reluctant to allow the second woman in, instead advising her to put God's cross between her and harm. The second woman asks how she might do this and the hermit gives her the words. On pronouncing the words of the sign of the cross, the woman he admitted vanishes, the Virgin having preserved the hermit from sin.[36] A Middle Irish tale recounts how the sign of the cross could be even more efficacious for a heathen who invoked it out of great fear when his house was attacked by demons, who were instantly prevented from laying a hand upon the man. The tale ends with the observation that 'Three things were hung on the cross, i.e. Christ's body, the devil and the sin of Adam. The devil fears the cross of Christ for it is on [the cross] that the devil and the sin of Adam were wasted and destroyed'.[37] In the Passion of Longinus found in the early fifteenth-century *Leabhar Breac* ('Speckled Book'), Longinus interrogates a host of demons as to why they have chosen to inhabit pagan idols and receives the following response: 'We found the stone images ... without the Sign of the Cross on them and without being named in the name of God ... for where Christ is not honoured nor the sign of the cross, there is our dwelling forever.'[38] A number of tales relating the wonders of the cross are included in a late thirteenth-century Irish Franciscan preaching collection entitled *Liber Exemplorum*. These include the tale of a nun who was assailed by the devil after biting into a lettuce without first blessing herself (a borrowing from Gregory the Great's *Dialogues*) and an incident from the *Book of the Deeds of Barlaam and Josaphat*.[39] In the latter tale, the young

---

[36] Lambert McKenna, ed., *Dánta do chum Aonghus Fionn Ó Dálaigh* (Dublin, 1919), poem 48.

[37] P. A. B., 'Story of the Heathen Saved by the Sign of the Cross', *Éigse* 31 (1999), 102.

[38] *The Passions and Homilies from the Leabhar Breac*, ed. Robert Atkinson (Dublin, 1887), 302.

[39] David Jones, ed., *Friars' Tales: Thirteenth-Century Exempla From the British Isles* (Manchester, 2011), 41–3.

Christian son of the 'king of India' is sent a bevy of beautiful girls in an effort to cause his chastity to totter, all to no avail. The demons who report their failure to their master, a magician, speak of the boy's defences in the following way:

> We were not able to resist nor indeed to look upon the strength of Christ and the banner of His Passion, which they call the Cross. At that sign we turned, weakened and consumed, and the princes and rulers of darkness fled. For before the young man was strengthened with the sign of the Cross, we rushed upon him and attacked him strongly, but as he called on Christ for help and armed himself with the sign of the Cross, he angrily chased after us and built for himself the most impregnable fortress ...[40]

The sign of the cross could, of course, be employed for other uses: in a Middle Irish life of Patrick found in the early fifteenth-century 'Book of Lismore', the saint uses it to heal a head-wound,[41] while in a tale of St Brigid included in Robert Rochford's life of the saint published in 1625, the sign of the cross is employed to inflict damage to the head of a slanderer during an interrogation scene.

> A woman, who falsely and deliberately accused one of Patrick's bishops, namely Broon, of fathering her child, was questioned by Brigid. When she refused to retract her claim, Brigid signed her mouth with the Sign of the Cross at which her head swelled up with a great tumour. Turning to the child, she then enquired of him who his father was, at which time the truth came out.[42]

Moreover, the Irish would also have been very familiar with one of the most noteworthy uses of the sign of the cross in medieval hagiography: that is, as a device for extracting oneself from the belly of

[40] Ibid. 43.

[41] Whitley Stokes, ed., *Betha Patraic: On the Life of Saint Patrick, Three Middle-Irish Homilies* (Calcutta, 1877), CELT: Corpus of Electronic Texts edition, <http://www.ucc.ie/celt/published/T201009/index.html>, accessed 16 July 2010.

[42] Robert Rochford, *The life of the glorious bishop S.Patricke apostle and primate togeather with the lives of the holy virgin Bridgit and of the glorious abbot S.Columbe patrons of Ireland* (St Omer, 1625), facsimile repr. in D. M. Rogers, ed., *English Recusant Literature 1558–1640*, 210 (London, 1974), 132.

a dragon, exemplified in the case of St Margaret of Antioch, who managed to explode herself out to safety, later earning the celestial post of patroness of women in childbirth.

THE FINDING OF THE CROSS

By the central and later Middle Ages in Ireland, there was increasing interest in the discovery of passion relics and particularly those of the cross of Christ itself. This is evidenced in the popularity of the story of the *Inventio Sanctae Crucis* and its frequent appearance in manuscript collections commissioned by the native Irish nobility. In the *Leabhar Breac* we find a short account of the finding of the true cross, the greater part of which is concerned with the victory of the emperor Constantine in battle. The tale, which is more fully told with some variations in the *Golden Legend*, recounts how Constantine is repeatedly defeated in battle by the barbarians of the East until he is visited by St Michael the archangel, who diagnoses the problem: 'It is quite clear', Michael states, 'that the power of Christ is not assisting thee'. He then introduces Constantine to the cross:

> Behold now … that which we call the cross; for this is the shape and semblance of the tree on which Christ was cruci-fied. Tomorrow make thou its likeness out of a large rod and bear it on thy back to the battle. And if thou art victorious, then do thou, with all those over whom thou hast power, believe in my Lord.[43]

Constantine takes the archangel's advice and is duly victorious on the following day. When he tells the story to his mother Helena, however, she advises that Constantine not settle for anything but 'the real thing', commenting that 'it would be a great help to thee if the true cross of Christ were at thy back'. Thus is precipitated Helena's famous expedition to Jerusalem where, in this version of the tale, she demands the cross from the Jews who are hiding it, threatening to make a great onslaught on the city if it is not handed over. The story ends with Helena seizing three of the city's elders, whom she has tortured to extract the information as to the cross's whereabouts. A fifteenth-century bardic poem entitled *Cairt*

---

[43] Vernam E. Hull, 'Two Middle Irish Religious Anecdotes', *Speculum* 3 (1928), 98–103, at 101.

a siothchana ag siol Adhaimh ('The peace charter of Adam's race'), by Tadhg Óg Ó hUiginn (d.1448), recounts how Helena eventually unearths three crosses, not knowing which one is that of Christ. She then has a vision in which she is told to unearth three corpses and to apply one of the crosses to each of them; of course, the one which encounters the true cross of Christ is summarily brought back to life.[44] The friar-poet Philip Bocht Ó hUiginn (d.1487) tells much the same story in his poem *Ceithre croinn croch Dé* ('Four trees from God's cross') but adds the fascinating detail that the Jews kept the cross hidden 'so as to get power'.[45]

The positioning of the story of the finding of the true cross in some late medieval Irish manuscripts is interesting, as in at least three cases it serves as a preface to the chivalric romance known in Middle English as the legend of 'Sir Firumbras' and in Middle Irish as 'Stair Fortibrais' or the 'history of Fortibras'. This tale begins with the murder of the pope by the Saracens and the theft of important passion relics, including the crown of thorns and the nails of the true cross, which then have to be recovered by Charlemagne and his knights Roland and Oliver. In British Library MS Egerton 1781, written in Cavan between 1484 and 1487, the *Historia Caroli Magni* or 'Chronicle of Pseudo-Turpin', which was ascribed to Charlemagne's contemporary, Archbishop Turpin of Reims, is placed directly following the Fortibras text. It also appears in the late fifteenth-century Irish manuscript known as the 'Book of Lismore'. In this tale of Charlemagne's alleged conquest of Spain, we find an example of the sign of the cross functioning not as an omen of victory in earthly battle, but as the seal of martyrdom, which was conceived of as a victory of a different order. The night before going into battle against Furre, one of the chiefs of the Navarri, at the mountain of Gasrem, Charlemagne asks God to show him 'who of his people would die in the battle on the morrow':

> And there was revealed to him a red sign in the shape of a cross of crucifixion on the shoulders of the people who were to fall. And when Charles saw that sign on those people he

---

44   Lambert McKenna, ed., *Dán Dé* (Dublin, 1922), poem 3, stanzas 29–30.
45   Lambert McKenna, ed., *Philip Bocht Ó hUiginn* (Dublin, 1931), poem 5, stanza 37.

locked them up in his chapel to avoid death for them in the battle. Inscrutable is the judgment of God and unknowable are his ways. And on finishing the battle and slaying the prince whose name was Furre, together with three thousand Saracens, the people whom Charles had left shut up he found lifeless, and the number who were there was thrice fifty. O most holy victors, although no sword of your adversary touched you, ye did not put from you the martyr's crown ...[46]

The historian Philip O'Sullivan Beare in his *Historiae Catholicae Iberniae*, published in Lisbon in 1621, describes how, moments before the execution of the archbishop of Cashel, Dermot O'Hurley, in 1584, a dear friend seized the prelate's hand and in so doing impressed upon his palm the sign of the cross in an indelible red colour.[47] To be signed by a red cross, then, could be interpreted as a brand of martyrdom. It was certainly interpreted as a 'passport to paradise'; in a version of the Gospel of Nicodemus appearing in the late fourteenth-century Irish manuscript known as the 'Yellow Book of Lecan', Christ sets the sign of his cross on Adam and his children when visiting hell to release them. As Adam is escorting the others to paradise, 'a horrible and ugly shape' comes towards the company with the sign of the cross on his shoulder. The figure, who is Dismas, the good thief on the cross, states that Christ

> placed the sign of the cross on my shoulder saying 'Go forth to paradise and if the angel guarding paradise will not let you enter, show him the sign of the cross and say to him that it was Jesus Christ, Son of the Living God, whom the Jews crucified, that sent you on ahead'.[48]

Preoccupation with the discovery of the cross of Christ by Helena was matched by the interest shown in the legend of the cross's more ancient history going back to the death of Adam.

---

[46] *The Conquests of Charlemagne: Edited from the Book of Lismore and three other Vellum MSS*, ed. Douglas Hyde (London, 1917), 47–9.

[47] *Ireland under Elizabeth: Chapters towards a History of Ireland in the Reign of Elizabeth, being a Portion of the History of Catholic Ireland by Don Philip O'Sullivan Bear*, ed. Matthew J. Byrne (Dublin 1903; repr. New York, 1970), 36, CELT: Corpus of Electronic Texts edition, <http://www.ucc.ie/celt/published/T100060/index.html>, accessed 16 July 2010.

[48] *Stair Nicoméid: the Irish Gospel of Nicodemus*, ed. and transl. Ian Hughes (London, 1991), 45.

Marthain duit a chroch an Choimhdheadh recounts how Adam and Eve's son, Seth, on a visit to paradise, saw the withered stock of the tree of knowledge which brought about his parents' expulsion from the garden. Suddenly a comely youth appeared on the tree after which it bloomed once more. Three seeds from the apple tree fell upon Seth and he brought them to his father, asking the meaning of what he had seen. Adam admitted that it was they who had withered the tree and that God's son, the comely youth, saved them, reviving the tree in the process. Adam died soon after and Seth placed the three seeds from the tree into his mouth, out of which three plants grew: one of these would become the cross of crucifixion.[49] In this poem, the poet claims that 'in no place ever saw I shrine as thy woven shrine, or church like thy church, O bright, round-beamed cross',[50] suggesting perhaps that he or his patron may have actually made a trip to the Church of the Holy Sepulchre in Jerusalem. Certainly the Anglo-Irish friar Simon Fitzsimon, in his account of a visit to the Holy Land in 1324, mentioned seeing on Mount Calvary 'a round hole in which the cross of Christ was fixed' and, south of the hole, the spot 'where the head of Adam was found'.[51] A variation on the story of the three seeds can be found in an Irish version of the travels of Sir John Maundeville, who supposedly departed on his journey to Jerusalem in 1322; it also appears in some fifteenth-century Irish manuscripts, including British Library MS Egerton 1781, which also contains the Finding of the Cross, the legend of Fortibras and the Pseudo-Turpin chronicle.[52] In the Irish Maundeville, Seth is given four seeds by an angel in paradise and is instructed to place them on the tongue of the dead Adam. One of these seeds would grow into the tree which would become the cross of Christ. The Irish Maundeville account also relates how, after the flood had

---

[49] See McKenna, ed., 'To a Crucifix'.

[50] Ibid., stanza 44.

[51] *Itinerarium Symonis Semeonis ab Hybernia ad Terram Sanctam*, ed. Mario Esposito (Dublin, 1960), 109. The tenth-century Irish collection of religious verse known as *Saltair na Rann*, in its account of the death of Adam, recounted how the waves of the deluge carried Adam's head to Jerusalem, where it remained at the gate of Jerusalem, and that later the cross of Christ was fixed in the body of Adam; see Máire Herbert and Martin McNamara, eds, *Irish Biblical Apocrypha* (Edinburgh, 1989), 16.

[52] Whitley Stokes, 'The Gaelic Maundeville', *Zeitschrift für Celtische Philologie*, 2 (1899), 1–63, CELT: Corpus of Electronic Texts edition, <http://www.ucc.ie/celt/published/G305000/index.html>, accessed 16 July 2010.

subsided, Adam's head was found on the site of Calvary 'as a token that his sin should be redeemed therein'.[53]

FOUR TREES OF THE CROSS OF CHRIST

The Irish Maundeville also contains an excursus on the four trees which comprised the cross of Christ. While this was a relatively common theme in late medieval Irish religious literature, it is worth noting the symbolism attached to each of the four woods (cedar, cypress, palm and olive),[54] according to this source: cedar was used on account of its durability, for it was believed that the body of Christ would be left on the cross as long as the cross itself held together (cedar, therefore, was the beam which went into the ground); the upper beam upon which his body was stretched was cypress on account of its sweet odour which would prevent the smell of decay from affecting passers-by; the horizontal beams were made of palm because of its association with victory in battle (which the Jews believed to have achieved over Christ); the titulus board made of olive signified the peace they thought would reign after putting Christ to death.[55] The bardic poem *Droichead na bpeacthach páis Dé* ('The sinner's bridge is God's passion') depicts Christ as builder of a bridge to save humanity. Beneath each end of the bridge, which becomes a highway out of hell, he places stone blocks and then a layer of stones beneath the wood of the bridge (Christ collects these stones on Passion Sunday when, as the poet states, by allowing himself to be stoned he redeemed the world).[56] In this poem it is the cypress which supports the cross and which bears noble fruit. The transverse beams are made of palm, as in the Maundeville account; the poet notes how 'our sins' cure was effected on it; it shows forth its power'. The olive is associated with God's peace-offering to Adam's race.[57] For Philip Bocht Ó hUiginn in his fifteenth-century poem *Ceithre croinn croch*

---

[53]   Ibid. 45.

[54]   An earlier form of the tradition, perhaps based on the *Collectanea* of Pseudo-Bede, identifies the trees as cedar, cypress, pine and beech; see Martin McNamara, *The Apocrypha in the Irish Church* (Dublin, 1984), 76–7.

[55]   Stokes, 'Gaelic Maundeville', 11.

[56]   Lambert McKenna, ed., 'The Bridge of Salvation', *Irish Monthly* 58 (1930), 51–4, at 51, stanza 9. This is a curious verse. There are two references in the Gospel of John to instances in which the Jews attempt to stone Jesus (John 8: 59; 10: 31–3). In the second, his opponents claim that they are stoning him on account of his blasphemy.

[57]   Ibid., stanzas 16–19.

Dé ('Four trees from God's cross'), however, the four trees of the cross are 'battle-weapons' fighting for his salvation as intercessors in the manner of the five wounds of Christ or, indeed, the *arma Christi*, of which, of course, they constitute the most important example.[58]

Having surveyed examples of the importance of the cross of Christ in medieval Irish literature, let us now sharpen our focus by examining more closely the vertiginous array of images associated with the cross in Irish bardic poetry, for it is here, in this very rich resource, that we perhaps come closest to understanding the deep significance of this symbol for medieval Irish Christians.

IMAGERY ASSOCIATED WITH CHRIST'S CROSS IN IRISH BARDIC POETRY

Our discussion of imagery associated with the cross of Christ should begin with an examination of some bardic poems specifically dedicated to the cross. The poem *Sbéacláir na cruinne an chroch naomh* ('The world's beacon is the Holy Cross') makes its earliest appearance in a seventeenth-century poem-book commissioned by an Irish privateer and veteran of the battle of Bila Gora of the Thirty Years War, Captain Somhairle MacDomhnaill, in Ostend in 1631.[59] Although attributed to a renowned thirteenth-century poet, Donnchadh Mór Ó Dálaigh, it is almost certainly a later composition. Just as Eriugena spoke of the cross with an orb spreading light like the rays of the sun, this poem begins with the cross identified as the 'world's beacon … bright-shining', while in the same stanza it speaks of 'this tree of the five wounds [which] points to a path most clear to see',[60] as if the light which the cross emits is filtered through its gaping wounds (it might be noted here that the wounds are associated with the cross and not with Christ's body per se; this was not an uncommon feature of Irish bardic religious poetry, Christ's body and the cross itself being in many instances interchangeable). The wounds of Christ are not only a light but also a text: 'When the Lord's wound-marks are beheld, his passion is read therefrom; thou seest on it our salvation'.[61]

---

[58] McKenna, ed., *Philip Bocht*, poem 5, stanza 7.
[59] McKenna, ed., 'To a Crucifix', 250–3.
[60] Ibid., stanza 1.
[61] Ibid., stanza 3.

The juxtaposition of the bright cross and its status as an instrument of torture is further emphasized in the lines:' 'tis justly called a light, Christ's holy torture-cross, tree of sacred blood-stained branches which dispelled the world's darkness'.[62] The power of the cross to crush sin is implicitly linked to the fact that it was soaked in the Lord's blood: 'on it were shed copious floods of God's wine-blood − dread[ful] story! This empurpled beacon-tree utterly destroyed men's sins'.[63] The dramatic effect which the flow of Christ's blood has on the cross is highlighted in other poems, such as the fifteenth-century *Ceithre croinn croch Dé* by the friar-poet Philip Bocht Ó hUiginn, who suggests that Christ's blood transforms the cross, glorifying it: 'Glory was given the cross by the blood of his dying limbs, the bluntness and the hardness of the nail − could torture be greater? − burning his white hand which unlocked his grace'.[64] Later in the poem Ó hUiginn makes his point more explicitly still, stating that on the cross the Lord warmed justice with his love (and, by implication, his warm blood) so that justice is transformed, making it possible now for mankind to approach God with confidence.[65] Thus it was the red cross of Christ which was so often regarded as efficacious in the later Middle Ages, on account of its contact with the blood of Christ. This allows to some extent a *communicatio idiomatum* of sorts between the cross of Christ and Christ's body.

A good example of this is the Irish adaptation of the medieval English 'Charter of Christ' allegory, which represents Christ as granting mankind a charter on Calvary in which Christ's body is the parchment, the lance and nails the pens by which it is drawn up, his blood the ink, his heart-wound the inkwell, his wounds the letters, and so on. This allegory appears in Ireland before the middle of the fifteenth century. In the poem *Cairt a síodhchána ag Síol Ádhaimh* ('The peace charter of Adam's race'), Tadhg Óg Ó hUiginn addresses the cross and not Christ's body as the charter: 'Thou art the sealed charter, O Cross of God, O payment of the tribute: O Charter of the world, put me 'neath the protection of thy rider'.[66] Here, too, Ó hUiginn mixes his metaphors, alluding to the common

[62] Ibid., stanza 5.
[63] Ibid., stanza 6.
[64] McKenna, ed., *Philip Bocht*, poem 5, stanza 9.
[65] Ibid., stanza 19.
[66] McKenna, ed., *Dán Dé*, poem 3, stanza 10.

depiction of Christ riding into battle against demonic forces on his steed, the cross; Ó hUiginn makes this reference on account of his allusion to Christ winning the 'war of the apple tree' elsewhere in the same poem.[67] In *Sbéacláir na cruinne an chroch naomh*, there is also a reference to the tree of crucifixion as 'a peace-charter, a cross of salvation, a noble beacon bright-gleaming with its fair strong beams'.[68] It continues by noting 'many its dread mark of wounding, trace of mangling, place of piercing', proceeding in the succeeding verse to state how 'to see the marks on its reddened wood stirs pity, promises salvation, helps to ward off (sin's) wounding and saves our soul'.[69] Thus does the bloodied cross function in much the same way as the performance of the sign of the cross in the examples discussed above. To see the image and to contemplate its meaning is regarded as particularly important. In later verses the poet elaborates on this point: 'My friend who lookest at the cross, if thou think of its burden thou canst not delay to bow down to that noble sacred image'.[70] The poet then leads his audience in an extended meditation on the cross image: 'Think first how that image, its form hacked and rough and thick, sad and piteous picture, is a sign of the world's salvation.'[71] Here the cross itself becomes a kind of *imago pietatis*, the state of the cross mirroring the state of Christ's body.

We find examples of this elsewhere, most notably, perhaps, in a thirteenth-century poem entitled *Lóchrann soilse ag síol Adhaimh* ('Adam's race has a torch of flame') in which the poet, addressing the cross, cries out: 'Lay not on me the blame for thy wounds O hacked cross of the Lord!'[72] In the poem *Sbéacláir na cruinne an chroch naomh* the meditation on the cross continues:

> The reason why God's son was bound on that tree – divine suffering! – prophets were those who foretold it – was that man might be freed from his bonds.

---

[67] Ibid., stanza 13.

[68] McKenna, ed., 'To a Crucifix', 250–3, stanza 8.

[69] Ibid., stanzas 9–10.

[70] Ibid., stanza 16. One of the fourteen *merita missae* ('benefits of the mass') found in the early fifteenth-century Irish manuscript *Liber Flavus Fergusiorum* (Dublin, RIA, MS 476) states that 'if you go to Mass out of love and pray before the cross of crucifixion the doors of heaven will open to you and the doors of hell will close and all the demons will not be able to attack you': Gearóid Mac Niocaill, 'Disiecta Membra', *Éigse* 8 (1955–7), 74–7, at 74–5.

[71] McKenna, ed., 'To a Crucifix', 250–3, stanza 17.

[72] McKenna, ed., *Dán Dé*, poem 28, stanza 21.

The reason why the Lamb of God, our sister's child, extended his arms was that excessive love urged him to save all men on that tree …

The reason why the Lord bent his head serving us – sad story! – was that, in sore strait for our sake, he was humiliated utterly.

The reason why a tree caused the torture of this majestic hero in saving us was that (in Eden) we could have been of his folk and that through a tree came the loss of this (privilege).[73]

However, the image of the cross was not a sign of salvation for all; the distinction between the saving and condemnatory cross was very much in the eye of the beholder, and this is why the reddened cross of Christ, battle weapon that it was conceived to be, was always going to be double-edged.

Late medieval religious literature is replete with tales of those who invoke or reject the intercessory power of the most prominent symbols of passion devotion, whether they be the five wounds of Christ, his holy blood, the *arma Christi* or 'instruments of Christ's passion' or, indeed, the symbol par excellence, the cross itself. For those who placed their confidence in these, salvation was possible; for those who rejected them, damnation was assured. The expectation that a red cross would appear in the sky at the judgement is attested in Irish literature as early as the eighth-century poetry of Blathmac. The late medieval bardic poets generally express fear at this sign, associating it with Christ's wrath as the red cross, in Tadhg Óg Ó hUiginn's words, 'points me out to him', the poet asking Christ in another poem to 'hide from us thy red cross so that thy wrath be not seen, close thy gaping side'.[74] The thirteenth-century poet Donnchadh Mór Ó Dálaigh, in the poem *Dia dom fheitheamh ar fheirg Dhé* ('May God guard me from God's wrath'), spoke of how 'the red cross on his white shoulder shall make the stars in heaven tremble, and displace the earth; it puts unbearable anger on him'.[75] In his tract on penance, *Scáthán Shacramunite na hAithridhe* (1618), the Irish Franciscan friar Aodh Mac Aingil, drawing his inspiration from medieval *exempla*, warned that

---

[73] McKenna, ed., 'To a Crucifix', 250–3, stanzas 19, 20, 23, 24.
[74] McKenna, ed., *Dán Dé* poem 3, stanza 18; poem 16, stanza 17.
[75] Ibid., poem 27, stanza 3.

if you do not [honour the cross] … your eyes will see, on the Day of Judgement, the cross of crucifixion in the air, casting your evil and your sin in your face, and especially the insult that you paid to the holy cross itself and the holy blood that flowed from it [by] refusing to heal yourself with it. Should you be in sin while seeing the cross, Christ says, you will be perpetually crying and weeping [on account of] your sin … however, if you repent in time, you will see the same cross as a standard of victory and courage, delighting you and making you joyful, you who will be beginning eternal glory.[76]

And yet it is this same blood of Christ and this same open heart-wound which are also frequently invoked as a shelter for sinful humanity, frequently in the same poem, just as the flow of Christ's blood transforms the cross from simple beams of wood to an instrument of salvation through which God's grace is unlocked. Tadhg Óg Ó hUiginn, in the fifteenth-century poem *Slán ar n-a mharbhadh mac Dé* ('Alive again after death is God's Son'), states that 'ye have surely seen before your eyes the image of Christ; ye remember not the tortured body; but in its bright (cured) state it watches you',[77] to which he quickly juxtaposes the glory of the cross: 'so sublime was the Son of God's death that it has caused the wood of the cross to be distributed (over the world) to inspire your prayer; alas for all against whom it stands as witness'.[78] Not all, however, were considered to be immediately worthy of approaching the cross for intercession, as is evidenced in an Irish retelling of the story of Mary of Egypt (found in the seventeenth-century manuscript, Brussels, Bibliothèque Royale, MS 20978–9), in which a woman is prevented from going into the temple in Jerusalem to beseech the holy cross (by some kind of force on account of her sin); she then goes to a church where there was a statue of the Virgin Mary (whom she is allowed to approach) and asks for help.[79] Here Mary functions, as she so often does, as the most reliable 'back door' to Christ's grace.

---

[76] Aodh Mac Aingil, *Scáthán Shacramuinte na hAithridhe*, ed. Cainneach Ó Maonaigh (Dublin, 1952), 40.

[77] Lambert McKenna, ed., *Aithdioghluim Dána*, 2 vols (Dublin, 1939–40), vol. 2, poem 78, stanza 33.

[78] Ibid., stanza 34.

[79] Íde Ní Uallacháin, *Exempla Gaeilge* (Maynooth, 2004), 122–3.

The late medieval bardic poets employed a wide variety of metaphors when speaking of the cross, embracing many of the classic models of redemption from the patristic and central medieval periods.[80] Christ overcame the powers of darkness by riding his cross into battle. For the sixteenth-century poet Maolmhuire, son of Cairbre Ó hUiginn, Christ was the ultimate warrior because he rode into battle, suffered a heart-wound and yet continued to fight (for his people):

> The cross was his steed when he was wounded; there would be nothing strange in a wounded man riding a steed were it not for the fact that he was wounded in the heart …
>
> No man wounded in the heart could have recovered as Christ did; scarce anyone survives a heart-wound; it was always dreaded.[81]

Ó hUiginn also notes how Christ, furious at his wounds, drove his horse (the cross) recklessly up to the gates of hell 'on the Sunday morning raid' and emptied its dungeon.[82] In the anonymous poem *Crann toruidh croch an Choimhdhe* ('A fruitful tree is the Lord's cross'), most likely composed to honour the shrine of the true cross at Holy Cross Abbey in County Tipperary, there is a description of Christ breaking down the doors of hell with his cross and snatching souls away as his booty.[83] And yet, side by side with this martial imagery are found allusions to the cross as 'our saving herb, our flower of blessing, our bond of perfect peace'.[84]

This poem is particularly interesting in that, at one point, it personifies the cross as a woman, addressing it as 'lady-leech' and 'lady so famous who reachest out thy hand to cure me'.[85] It speaks of the cross being anointed by the blood of Christ's hands and feet, and of its being washed in the Lord's blood.[86] Then, still addressing the cross, it states that: ' 'till thou didst drink of the King's blood

---

[80] See Salvador Ryan, 'Reaping a Rich Harvest of Humanity: Images of Redemption in Irish Bardic Religious Poetry', in Brendan Leahy and Seamus O'Connell, eds, *Having Life in his Name: Living, Thinking and Communicating the Christian Life of Faith* (Dublin, 2011), 239–52.

[81] McKenna, ed., *Aithdioghluim Dána*, poem 77, stanzas 35, 37.

[82] Ibid., stanza 27.

[83] Ibid., poem 88, stanza 6.

[84] Ibid., stanza 9.

[85] Ibid., stanza 17.

[86] Ibid., stanza 19.

thou couldst not cure his race with any herb; now find in the blood which thou didst drink a sweet draught to cure me'.[87] The blood-drinking cross also appears in the fifteenth-century poem *Ceithre croinn croch Dé* when, addressing the cross, the poet states that God's grace was in bonds until 'thou didst drink, while it was warm, the blood of his feet'.[88] He continues: 'owing to love ruling him at his death no drop of his body's blood tarried on thee, but thou didst slake thy thirst with it'.[89] There may well be an allusion in these blood-drinking verses to the Irish topos of keening women drinking the blood of their deceased husbands or sons, which often appears in native Irish literary works.[90] Indeed, in a fifteenth-century Irish translation of a text entitled *Liber de Passione Christi*, attributed to St Bernard of Clairvaux, Mary relates how, after Christ's death, 'I clasped his head and his hands to my bosom and my heart and I set about kissing and drinking the blood of the Saviour, and Joseph and Nicodemus took the body from me and they did not allow me my fill or the satisfaction of my desire'.[91] It is tempting to see a eucharistic allusion in the Virgin's craving of Christ's blood. However, if Mary was here being held up as a model to be imitated, her desire for the reception of the blood of Christ could not but have raised difficulties for those advocating the continued withholding of the chalice from the laity.

In a poem by the sixteenth-century bardic poet Tadhg, son of Dáire Ó Bruaideadha, the cross is also depicted as a woman; in this case, however, it is as a nursing mother.[92] This was not a uniquely Irish phenomenon, however; the Anglo-Saxon *Dream of the Rood*,

---

[87] Ibid., stanza 20.

[88] McKenna, ed., *Philip Bocht*, poem 5, stanza 21.

[89] Ibid., stanza 22.

[90] See, e.g., the story of Eibhlín Dubh Ní Chonaill, in Seán Ó Tuama, ed., *Caoineadh Airt Uí Laoghaire* (Dublin, 1961), 35; also a fifteenth-century account of the actions of Deirdre lamenting the death of her husband Naoise with the words '"Let me kiss my husband". And she took to kissing Naoise and drinking his blood, and she uttered this lay': Rachel Bromwich, 'The Keen for Art O'Leary', *Éigse* 5 (1945–7), 236–52, at 249. For an extended discussion of this motif, see Salvador Ryan, 'Popular Religion in Gaelic Ireland, 1445–1645', 2 vols (Ph.D. thesis, National University of Ireland, Maynooth, 2002), 2: 172–9.

[91] R. A. Q. Skerrett, 'Two Irish Translations of the *Liber de Passione Christi*', *Celtica* 6 (1963), 82–117, at 109.

[92] *Dioghluim Dána*, ed. Láimhbheartach Mac Cionnaith (Dublin, 1938), poem 2, stanza 3.

for example, has its speaking cross liken itself to Mary in its selection from the trees of the forest.[93]

The cross and the associated instruments of Christ's passion are often presented as places of refuge in bardic verse. In the poem *Mairg nach taithigh go teagh ríogh* ('Woe to all who frequent not the Lord's house'), the sixteenth-century poet Diarmuid Ó Cobhthaigh depicts Christ hunting for his race while it attempts to flee from him. He states how 'the hunt continued till that youth of our race was driven by us to the wood'.[94] This wood ('the cross') then begins to shelter humanity from Christ's wrath and covers over humanity's sins. Ó Cobhthaigh continues: 'Well for all men that the wood which gives them refuge is so dense; may that wood of thy grace get ever denser and hide our growing sins'.[95] For Ó Cobhthaigh, the cross is 'the great sheltering tree whereon was shed thy blood; hanging on that deep-pierced tree thou didst shelter thy race from thy own anger'.[96] In this way the cross acts much as the Virgin Mary is depicted as doing elsewhere; for instance, in the anonymous poem *Éasga ar nglanadh grás Muire* ('Mary's grace easily cleanses us') the Virgin is described as a fragrant branch of choice foliage which hides Christ's wrath.[97] Elsewhere, in the fifteenth-century poetry of Philip Bocht Ó hUiginn, the cross is expected to perform an intercessory gesture in much the same way as the Virgin Mary might. In the poem *Ceithre croinn croch Dé*, Ó hUiginn implores the cross on judgement day to 'take ... hold of his grace which will soften his wrath against me; that I may keep away my sins, show him thy four woods', thereby inviting the cross to imitate the actions of Christ and Mary before the Father in the medieval double intercession theme, he displaying his wounds, she her exposed breast.[98]

When attempting to express the saving effects wrought by Christ's death on Calvary, bardic poets often employ images which

---

93 Miri Rubin, *Mother of God: A History of the Virgin Mary* (New Haven, CT, 2009) 105–6.

94 McKenna, ed., *Aithdhioghluim Dána*, poem 67, stanza 8.

95 Ibid., stanza 18.

96 Ibid., stanza 25.

97 Ibid., poem 93, stanza 6. This is reminiscent, of course, of the Virgin's sheltering of sinners beneath her cloak, a favourite late medieval image.

98 McKenna, ed., *Philip Bocht*, poem 5, stanza 52; see Salvador Ryan, 'The Persuasive Power of a Mother's Breast: The Most Desperate Act of the Virgin Mary's Advocacy', *Studia Hibernica* 32 (2002–3), 59–74.

present the cross as a fruit-bearing tree which, in the words of the poem *Crann toruidh croch an Choimhdhe*, 'recompensed for the tree of the debt'.[99] In the anonymous poem *Olc an connradh a chlann Ádhaimh* ('Harsh the contract, O children of Adam'), the poet speaks of the whole world as a heap of withered wood before the blood of Christ sinks into it, transforming it utterly.[100] Other poets such as Diarmuid Ó Cobhthaigh speak of the blood-rain from Christ's wounds as 'the shower that made our seed grow; ... the heavier the rain, the brighter the sunshine after it'.[101] For his contemporary Maolmhuire, son of Cairbre Ó hUiginn, in the poem *Do-ní éanmhac ionad cloinne* ('One son takes the place of all'), Christ's heart-blood yielded a heavy harvest of grace for Adam's race.[102] In the same poem this fruit-harvest is identified as Adam's race itself: 'Weighty the fruit of the cross, great the fruit-gathering from the tree of the wounds; it gathered Adam's race on itself and caused them to cluster thick on it'.[103] Elsewhere Diarmuid Ó Cobhthaigh speaks of the ground (Christ's flesh) being prepared for this harvest, the world's weight (of sin) pressing on him like a plough which tilled the field of his body.[104] In a variation on this image, the spear of Longinus is also likened to a plough by which a rich harvest of humanity is yielded.[105] Ó Cobhthaigh remarks that 'heavy [was] the fruit of the tree which saved the Six generations; our wood contained not a single fruitful tree till thou didst droop thy head on the cross'.[106]

Because of Christ's death on the cross, the reversal of fortune which was Eden had now been overturned: in the words of Donnchadh Mór Ó Dálaigh in the poem *Dia dom fheitheamh ar fheirg Dhé* ('May God guard me from God's wrath'), 'the perfume of that tree saved us; God's garden has become ours'.[107] Little wonder, then, that Simon Fitzsimon on his journey to Jerusalem in the 1320s made a special note of an unusual fruit he encountered

99 McKenna, ed., *Aithdioghluim Dána*, poem 88, stanza 3.
100 Ibid., poem 98, stanza 20.
101 Ibid., poem 63, stanza 29.
102 Ibid., poem 77, stanza 4.
103 Ibid., stanza 11.
104 Ibid., poem 63, stanza 2; also poem 65, stanza 29.
105 Ibid., poem 65, stanza 30.
106 Ibid., stanza 21. The 'Six generations' refers to the six ages of the world's history and the people who had lived in them.
107 McKenna, ed., *Dán Dé*, poem 27, stanza 24.

in the town of Fouah, near Alexandria in Egypt. Calling them 'apples of paradise' (most likely plantains), the friar explained that these oblong fruits 'when cut traversely ... exhibit most clearly the image of Christ extended on the cross'.[108]

The cross is a multi-faceted presence throughout medieval Irish literature: at once a sign of victory and an object of shame; a symbol to evoke pity and a standard with which one might invoke the power of Christ over the demonic forces of hell; it condemns, yet saves, exposes humanity's sins, yet its branches also hide incriminating evidence from God's wrath; it intercedes for humanity, while at the same time holding it to account; it is a keening mother, yet also a warhorse, a battle standard and a torch to light a path for humanity; it is both a stark sign of torture and also a blossom-laden tree. These images do not simply supersede each other from the early through to the later Middle Ages; rather, they coexist, and are to be found employed separately or (at times) together across the medieval period, in an effort to make some sense of the mystery of the cross. This mystery of Christ, for the thirteenth-century poet Donnchadh Mór Ó Dálaigh, was the gift that kept on giving: he states that 'a cow runs not dry for her owners by what she gives of her milk',[109] echoing the words by which his eighth-century predecessor Blathmac described the cross: 'to the men of the world', Blathmac noted, 'it was no milkless cow'.[110]

St Patrick's College, Maynooth

---

[108] *Itinerarium Symonis Semeonis*, ed. Esposito, 65.
[109] McKenna, ed., *Dán Dé*, poem 27, stanza 36.
[110] *Blathmac*, ed. Carney, poem 21, stanza 13.

'Y GANRIF FAWR'? PIETY, LITERATURE AND PATRONAGE IN FIFTEENTH- AND SIXTEENTH-CENTURY WALES

by KATHARINE K. OLSON

This essay offers a reconsideration of the idea of 'The Great Century' of Welsh literature (1435–1535) and related assumptions of periodization for understanding the development of lay piety and literature in fifteenth- and sixteenth-century Wales.[1] It focuses on the origins of these ideas in (and their debt to) modern Welsh nationalist and Protestant and Catholic confessional thought, and their significance for the interpretation of Welsh literature and history. In addition, it questions their accuracy and usefulness in the light of contemporary patterns of manuscript production, patronage and devotional content of Welsh books of poetry and prose produced by the laity during and after this 'golden age' of literature. Despite the existence of over a hundred printed works in Welsh by 1660, the vernacular manuscript tradition remained robust; indeed, 'native culture for the most part continued to be transmitted as it had been transmitted for centuries, orally or in manuscript' until the eighteenth century.[2] Bardic poetry's value as a fundamental source for the history of medieval Ireland and Wales has been rightly acknowledged.[3] However, more generally, Welsh manuscripts of both poetry and prose must be seen as a crucial historical source. They tell us much about contemporary views, interests and priorities, and offer a significant window onto the devotional world of medieval and early modern Welsh men and women. Drawing on recent work on Welsh literature, this paper explores the production and patronage of such books and the dynamics of cultural and religious change. Utilizing National Library of Wales Llanstephan MS 117D as a

---

[1] I am grateful to Professor Huw Pryce and Dr Diana Luft for their comments on a draft of this paper.

[2] E. Rees, *The Welsh Book Trade Before 1820* (Aberystwyth, 1988), vi.

[3] Cf. Katharine Olson, '*Ar ffordd Pedr a Phawl:* Welsh Pilgrimage and Travel to Rome, c.1200–1530', *Welsh History Review* 24/2 (December 2008), 1–40; Salvador Ryan, 'A Slighted Source: Rehabilitating Irish Bardic Religious Poetry in Historical Discourse', *Cambrian Medieval Celtic Studies* 48 (2004), 75–99.

case study, it also examines their significance and implications for broader trends in lay piety and the nature of religious change in Wales.

The period from 1282 to 1536 has been characterized as 'a crucial and distinctive period in the development of a literate mentality in Wales'.[4] This essay suggests that neither this medieval mentality nor the triumphs of the Welsh literary tradition came to an end as a result of Tudor political and religious policies as represented by the first Act of Union (1536) and the Henrician Reformation, particularly the dissolution of the monasteries. The stark periodization between medieval and early modern, as developed in the early Welsh nationalist thought of the distinguished dramatist, nationalist and literary critic Saunders Lewis (1893–1985) and others, and inherent in his later influential idea of 'The Great Century',[5] overstates and oversimplifies the immediate impact of Tudor policies in the growth of 'nationalism'. Change was much longer in duration, as Goronwy Edwards has argued,[6] and more complex. Indeed, to a degree, the act 'simply recognised existing trends and gave statutory recognition to changes that had already taken place',[7] whilst others were happening gradually or had yet to occur. The Act of Union did, however, in Glanmor Williams's word, represent a 're-orientation' which redefined both jurisdictional and administrative boundaries, thereby establishing a more unified system of justice, law and administration, as well as providing the Welsh with a new and improved legal status.[8]

Likewise, other related changes sprang to an extent from processes of much longer duration and complexity, amongst them religious, cultural, social and economic developments. 'The Great Century' itself did not comprise one cohesive era in the Welsh literary tradition. Nor, as already argued variously in an English context, did the 1530s signal an absolute cultural or religious divide

---

4   L. B. Smith, 'Inkhorn and Spectacles: The Impact of Literacy in Late Medieval Wales', in H. Pryce, ed., *Literacy in Medieval Celtic Societies* (Cambridge, 1998), 202–22, at 203.

5   Saunders Lewis, *Braslun o Hanes Llenyddiaeth Gymraeg* (Cardiff, 1932), ch. 7.

6   J. G. Edwards, *The Principality of Wales, 1267–1967* (Caernarfon, 1969), 35–9.

7   W. S. K. Thomas, *Tudor Wales* (Llandysul, 1983), 58.

8   Glanmor Williams, *Renewal and Reformation: Wales, c.1415–1642* (Oxford, 1993), 274–5.

between the medieval and the early modern.[9] Neither popular piety nor the Welsh literary tradition remained static or moribund after 1535. But alongside various longer-term shifts, some continuities remained in the patronage, writing, reading and contents of Welsh manuscripts, underscoring more generally Welsh cultural and religious conservatism into the mid Tudor period (and indeed beyond) and the duration and complexity of change. Indeed, the medieval prose tradition continued into the seventeenth century in some areas of Wales, while various later poets were certainly able and in demand. The later seventeenth century witnessed the last days of the bardic order and rise of amateur poets in their stead.[10] To a degree, then, this influential periodization of medieval Welsh literature and its *terminus ad quem* have been shaped by modern attempts to facilitate nation-building through the selective invocation of Wales's sovereign past as a golden age characterized by the triumphs and patriotism of its medieval poetry and civilization prior to the advent of Tudor political and religious policies from 1536 and their destructive legacy for Welsh identity and culture.

Y GANRIF FAWR, WELSH LITERATURE AND NATIONALISM

By 1415, the ill-fated revolt of Owain Glyndŵr was ending, but this was cold comfort to many in Wales. Economic hardship and hunger would loom large in the years to come; many had suffered the wholesale destruction of villages, farms, crops, livestock and churches. It was remembered as a desolate time: 'the whole country then was but a forest … [a] waste of inhabitants and overgrown with woods'.[11] Even a century later, some areas remained affected by the revolt's destruction, unoccupied or in ruin;[12] the Welsh Church took decades to recover. Yet it is generally accepted that by the mid fifteenth century Wales had experienced a signifi-

---

[9]   See, e.g., G. MacMullan and David Matthews, eds, *Reading the Medieval in Early Modern England* (Cambridge, 2007).

[10]   G. Thomas, 'Golwg ar Gyfundrefn y Beirdd yn yr Ail Ganrif ar Bymtheg,' in R. G. Gruffydd, ed., *Bardos: Penodau ar y Traddodiad Barddol Cymreig a Cheltaidd* (Cardiff, 1982), 76–94, at 94.

[11]   John Wynn, *History of the Gwydir Family and Memoirs*, ed. J. G. Jones (Llandysul, 1990), 51.

[12]   L. T. Smith, ed. *The Itinerary of John Leland in or about the years 1535–1543* (Carbondale, AZ, 1906), vi, 10, 41, 52.

cant recovery and revival. The later fifteenth century witnessed an upsurge in church building, furnishing and adornment, much of it due to lay patronage, as well as the increased popularity of pilgrimages, including those to Rome and Santiago de Compostela. Lay initiative and participation were significant components of this; whether in devotions to the saints, domestic and international pilgrimages, or fraternities, many contemporary records reveal the breadth and vigour of late medieval lay piety, though the institutional Church also clearly betrayed some vulnerabilities.

Part and parcel of this renewal, it has been suggested, was a spectacular literary renaissance of Welsh bardic poetry from 1435 to 1535. This was what Saunders Lewis first termed *Y Ganrif Fawr* (The Great Century) in his survey of medieval Welsh literature which appeared in 1932,[13] singling out this period as the 'finest flowering' of an unbroken Welsh literary tradition stretching back a thousand years. The era of poets such as Lewis Glyn Cothi, Gutun Owain, Dafydd Nanmor, Guto'r Glyn and Tudur Aled represented a 'golden age' of Welsh literature, suffused with a 'spirit of confidence and faith in Wales' and 'concrete' patriotism, before the final loss of Welsh independence.[14] Lewis regarded the poetry of the *Beirdd yr Uchelwyr* (Poets of the Gentry) between 1435 and 1535 as 'the core of the literary canon' and its high point; indeed, terming it 'The Great Century' may be seen as 'an innovative way of emphasizing its status'.[15]

Lewis best articulated his rationale for the conclusion of this literary 'golden age' and his related periodization in his early nationalist writings, particularly his pamphlet of 1926, *Egwyddorion Cenedlaetholdeb* (*Principles of Nationalism*). He argued that 'The Great Century' was brought to an untimely end by destructive Tudor policies after 1535. For Lewis, '[w]hen Wales was conquered in the Middle Ages by England, no great harm came … it went on as before, living its own life and developing its culture.' It was 'when Wales was freed and made part of England under the Tudors, [that] it was dealt a mortal blow', and entered a new, grim age in which

---

[13] Lewis, *Braslun o Hanes Llenyddiaeth Gymraeg*, ch. 7; cf. Glanmor Williams, *The Welsh Church from Conquest to Reformation*, 2nd edn (Cardiff, 1976), 247–68, 414–60.

[14] Ibid. 123.

[15] Tudur Hallam, *Canon Ein Llên* (Cardiff, 2007), 148.

'the civilization of Wales wasted away and declined'.[16] This saw the destruction of 'the order of the old Welsh life ... the old religion of the Welsh people was supplanted also, and instead of order and civilisation there came upon Wales darkness and anarchy'.[17] If Welsh gentry patrons and an Aristotelian, aristocratic society were the 'backbone' of Welsh civilization for Lewis, it depended for its heart and inspiration on Catholicism, and on the protection given by the medieval Catholic Church to Welsh civilization and culture. These made 'The Great Century' possible, and Tudor policies and the growth of Protestantism signalled its destruction. The 'moral unity' of the Catholic Church was replaced by the state authority of nationalism, which instead embraced oppression, enforced violence, tyranny and uniformity (of language, government, law, culture and religion).[18]

Indeed, in Lewis's view, the 'mortal blow' to Welsh civilization was not dealt by secondary factors such as the decline of the native gentry, the emergence of a middle class which embraced English culture rather than its own, the end of the bardic order, or 'betrayal' by the Tudors.[19] Rather, the rise of nationalism under the Tudors led to the destruction of Welsh civilization through its errant policies, especially the destruction of the Catholic Church. 'Sixteenth-century nationalism was nothing but the triumph of materialism over spirituality, of paganism over Christianity. It was materialistic and pagan triumph that destroyed our Wales.'[20] Instead, Lewis urged the Welsh to embrace 'our nationalism', which was 'a return to medieval principle; a denial of the benefits of political uniformity ... Not a fight for Wales' independence but for Wales' civilisation.'[21] Whilst written in 1926, his *Principles of Nationalism* has held a place as 'the cornerstone of Welsh nationalist thinking'; indeed, the idea that the act itself actively undermined the Welsh language, culture and identity has remained particularly influen-

[16] Saunders Lewis, *Egwyddorion Cenedlaetholdeb: Principles of Nationalism*, transl. B. Griffiths (Cardiff, 1975; first publ. 1926), 2–3.
[17] Dafydd Glyn Jones, 'His Politics', in A. R. Jones and G. Thomas, eds, *Presenting Saunders Lewis* (Cardiff, 1973), 23–79, at 49.
[18] Lewis, *Braslun*, 116; idem, *Williams Pantycelyn* (London, 1927), 18; idem, *Egwyddorion Cenedlaetholdeb*, 4–7.
[19] Lewis, *Egwyddorion*, 2–3.
[20] Ibid. 8–9.
[21] Ibid.

tial in subsequent efforts to build a sense of Welsh nationhood and in language activism.[22] By the early 1930s similar rhetoric was being echoed in the Catholic press; in 1932 one article declared that the Protestant Reformation 'destroyed the soul of the Welsh nation'.[23] These views were in turn countered by contemporary Welsh Liberal nationalists such as J. E. Lloyd and O. M. Edwards, who embraced a 'progressionist' or teleological perspective on Welsh history.[24]

Yet while it has been acknowledged that 'his sense of history … made of pre-Protestant Reformation, medieval Wales a vibrant force',[25] the validity of Lewis's 'Great Century', the periodization of Welsh literature, and related assumptions bear further scrutiny. Indeed, these may have been shaped by his personal political, religious and social perspective. Perhaps best known for his renowned political and language activism, including his founding role in *Plaid Genedlaethol Cymru* (the Welsh Nationalist Party), Lewis himself was a Catholic convert, and sprang from esteemed Nonconformist stock; both his father and grandfather were Calvinistic Methodist ministers. While he officially converted only after the death of his father in 1932, by 1922 (if not earlier) he was already a Catholic 'as far as intellectual assent goes'.[26] The inherent sacramentalism and 'aesthetic appeal of Catholicism' were significant in its appeal for him, as was his relationship with his wife, who had converted in 1923.[27] Likewise, the medieval civilization and modern Catholic culture of Western Europe fascinated Lewis, and he was 'deeply influenced' by French Catholic writers such as Claudel, Dawson and Gilson.[28]

His views were also in part a response to other contemporary Welsh perspectives on the Act of Union and the advent of Prot-

---

[22] Jones, 'His Politics', 27; cf., e.g., Saunders Lewis, 'Tynged yr Iaith' (BBC radio broadcast, 13 February 1962).
[23] Trystan Owain Hughes, 'An Uneasy Alliance? Welsh Nationalism and Roman Catholicism', *North American Journal of Welsh Studies* 2/2 (Summer 2002), 1–6, at 4, citing *Welsh Catholic Times,* 15 July 1932, ii.
[24] Huw Pryce, *J. E. Lloyd and the Creation of Welsh History* (Cardiff, 2011), 81, 206; cf. R. W. Jones, *Rhoi Cymru'n Gyntaf: Syniadaeth Plaid Cymru,* 1 (Cardiff, 2007), 66–76.
[25] Branwen Jarvis, 'Saunders Lewis: A Welsh Catholic View of Women?', *Journal of Welsh Religious History* 7 (1999), 119–35, at 127.
[26] Ibid. 119, 122.
[27] Jarvis, 'Saunders Lewis', 123–5.
[28] Ibid. 122; cf. D. Smith, ed., *A People and the Proletariat* (London, 1980).

estantism. These included Williams's portrayal of Tudor policies in Wales as heralding the positive growth of enlightened modernity, and older nationalist thought rooted in teleological Protestant Nonconformist historiography, as epitomized in the writings of Emrys ap Iwan and O. M. Edwards.[29] Likewise, Lewis opposed the conclusions of W.S. Gruffydd that the period from the Protestant Reformation to William Williams Pantycelyn (1717–91) was the golden age of poetry and especially prose, which 'led the mind of the nation'.[30] Equally, Lewis's own confessional bias is apparent to some extent in his periodization: what was finest and most alive in Welsh literature and life was 'despoiled' with the loss of the Catholic 'sacramental view of life' and its innate gaiety.[31] In this, he was seemingly influenced both by European writers and by Welsh contemporaries such as Hirsch-Davies, who argued in 1916 that 'Catholicism stood for more than the old religion; it also stood for Welsh nationality. All that was best and noblest in the Welsh story was intertwined with the history of the [now] roofless abbeys.'[32] For Lewis, then, 'Christianity and Nationalism were clearly intertwined.'[33]

Lewis's particular perspective has not escaped the notice of literary critics either. Some contemporary reviewers of his survey of medieval Welsh literature questioned his approach, use of facts and personal biases.[34] Tudur Hallam urged caution 'before accusing Saunders Lewis of concealing his Catholic beliefs', but conceded that Lewis's religious views meant that he interpreted literature from a 'special perspective'.[35] On the other hand, D.G. Jones questioned Lewis's social biases, suggesting that his dark picture of the 'Tudor revolution' and its effects on an idealized Welsh civilization was a 'Myth of a Golden Age' distinguished by its unbroken tradition of Welsh poets, shared European philosophy, culture, lessons for the present, and its version of the nameable boojum. Its rationale

---

[29] W. Llywelyn Williams, *The Making of Modern Wales* (London, 1919); Jones, 'His Politics', 52–7.

[30] W. J. Gruffydd, *Llenyddiaeth Cymru, o 1450 hyd 1600* (Liverpool, 1922), 71–2.

[31] M. Dafydd, ed., *Ati Wŷr Ifanc: Ysgrifau gan Saunders Lewis* (Cardiff, 1986), 8–13.

[32] J. E. Hirsch-Davies, *Catholicism in Mediaeval Wales* (London, 1916), 146–7.

[33] Hughes, 'Uneasy Alliance', 4.

[34] Hallam, *Canon*, 77, 83, 107–10, citing Iorwerth C. Peate, *Sylfeini* (Wrexham, 1938),151–2; W. J. Gruffydd, 'Adolygiad o Braslun o Hanes Llenyddiaeth Gymraeg', *Y Llenor* 11 (1932), 249–56, at 253.

[35] Hallam, *Canon*, 79, 81.

was primarily social: like other contemporary members of the educated bourgeoisie, Lewis attacked the middle class to which he belonged, extolling instead the 'order, hierarchy, and authority' of aristocratic society and its trappings.[36] However, despite these criticisms Lewis's lasting influence in the critical interpretation of the Welsh literary tradition and formation of the idea of a single corpus of Welsh literature has continued to be acknowledged.[37]

Subsequent scholarship on Welsh literature has also tended to confirm many of Lewis's conclusions, while suggesting some grounds for further nuance and revision. Indeed, whilst detailed consideration is beyond the scope of this study, the idea of a single cohesive literary era from 1435 to 1535 is in itself an oversimplification; it has been suggested that the year 1480 may be seen as a *terminus ad quem* for the *cywyddwyr* of Morgannwg, heralding a new literary generation, for example.[38] Yet the idea of 'The Great Century' and Lewis's related perspective on periodization remain influential, though not slavishly followed, as demonstrated by the superb editions of Welsh poetry (1282 – c.1525) produced by the Centre for Advanced Welsh and Celtic Studies. Likewise, Dafydd Johnston concluded his brilliant literary survey of medieval Welsh literature with the death of the great Tudur Aled in about 1525 (on the basis that no subsequent poets equalled him), while noting the rapidly approaching changes to be wrought by the dissolution of the monasteries (1536–40) and the Anglicization of the gentry. At the same time, however, he recognized William Llŷn (1534/5–80) as 'the last of the master poets of the middle ages', and saw the prose of Elis Gruffudd (c.1490–1552?) as having 'one foot steadfastly in the middle ages'.[39] Others have indirectly questioned the immediate effects of the Act of Union and the chronology of bardic decline. Parry viewed the act as the main catalyst for change – the 'curse of the acts and the general policy of the Tudors' – but saw this as a gradual process, occurring after *circa* 1550.[40] Similarly, it has been suggested that the golden age' of Welsh poetry came to

---

[36] Jones, 'His Politics', 47–9.
[37] Hallam, *Canon*, 77, 83, 107–10.
[38] Ceri W. Lewis, 'The Literary Tradition of Morgannwg', in G. Williams, ed., *Glamorgan County History*, 3: *Early Modern Glamorgan* (Cardiff, 1971), 449–577, at 509.
[39] Dafydd Johnston, *Llên yr Uchelwyr* (Cardiff, 2005), 401, 420, 435.
[40] Thomas Parry, *Hanes Llenyddiaeth Gymraeg hyd 1900* (Cardiff, 1944), 125–6.

an end by *circa* 1550, with the years from 1550 to 1700 witnessing a new 'period' of manuscript poetry.[41]

'The Great Century' and related ideas of periodization have also been prominently coupled by Glanmor Williams in Welsh historiography with a teleological narrative of late medieval decline and the inevitability of change.[42] Williams recognized the potential of Welsh literature as a source for the writing of ecclesiastical history, and adopted an interdisciplinary approach, utilizing Welsh literature (particularly poetry) extensively. He embraced the idea of 'The Great Century', remarking on the 'astonishing renaissance' of Welsh literature, particularly religious works, which he saw as symptomatic of the remarkable larger mid fifteenth-century recovery which followed the revolt of Glyndŵr.[43] Yet he expressed unease about the laicization of late medieval religion and deviation from earlier ideals, which led to 'an incredible mix of sincere devotion and blatant superstition, of rarefied mysticism and gross credulity, of Christian piety and semi-pagan mumbo-jumbo'.[44] The idea of the renewal, recovery and vitality of late medieval piety as seen particularly in Welsh religious literature in the century prior to the Reformation thus rests incongruously beside both his picture of the decay, decline and vulnerability of the pre-Reformation Church and religious life and his own insistence that the act's immediate political significance had been overstated and that it was rather the Industrial Revolution which constituted the great historical divide.[45] Yet as an interdisciplinary approach to the writing of pre-modern Welsh history remains essential today, it is clear that the idea of 'The Great Century' and related conclusions about the nature of cultural and religious change, periodization and the Welsh literary tradition require reassessment in light of more recent scholarship. While many potential grounds for this exist, the necessary brevity of this study means that it will

[41] Daniel Huws, *Medieval Welsh Manuscripts* (Cardiff, 2000), 20; idem, *Cynnull y Farddoniaeth* (Aberystwyth, 2004), 11.

[42] Katharine Olson and Huw Pryce, 'The Reluctant Medievalist?', in *Degrees of Influence: A Memorial Volume for Glanmor Williams*, ed. G. H. Jenkins and G. E. Jones (Cardiff, 2008), 30–57.

[43] Glanmor Williams, *Wales and the Reformation* (Cardiff, 1997), 17.

[44] Williams, *Welsh Church*, 464.

[45] Olson and Pryce, 'Reluctant Medievalist?', 31–2; Williams, *Renewal and Reformation*, 253–78.

focus on select aspects of the production, patronage and contents of fifteenth- and sixteenth-century Welsh books, and their wider implications for the Welsh literary tradition and popular piety.

MANUSCRIPTS, CULTURAL REORIENTATION AND THE LAITY

The portrait of an idealized, unchanging golden age ignores a number of longer-term developments and shifts, including those in Welsh literary tradition and religious life which saw the laity take on an increased role after 1400. At the turn of the fifteenth century, the fine library of the layman and literary patron Hopcyn ap Tomas held copies of the *Elucidarium*, *Seint Greal* and *Annales*, according to Dafydd y Coed.[46] Indeed, some one hundred and sixty Welsh-language books survive from the mid thirteenth century to 1539, most of them post-1400.[47] The earliest extent vernacular *llyfr llys* or court book – the Welsh equivalent of the Irish *dunaire* collection made for an individual person or family – dates to *circa* 1250, and by *circa* 1350 vernacular manuscripts of devotional content made for lay patrons were also extant.[48] In line with wider European trends, thirteenth-century Wales witnessed a decline in manuscript production at monastic and cathedral *scriptoria* such as Margam and Neath, as the superb work of Huws has demonstrated. During the following century, Cistercian houses remained central to manuscript production and bardic patronage while monasteries were gradually secularized and a burgeoning market for independent scribes emerged.[49] Some Cistercian abbots, such as Siôn ap Rhisiart of Valle Crucis and Thomas Pennant of Basingwerk, certainly continued to act as enthusiastic bardic patrons, though overall the popularity of monastic foundations and their role in lay piety and manuscript production had waned somewhat prior to 1535.

Indeed, by 1400 if not earlier the laity played an augmented role in religious life and patronage, and manuscript production was increasingly in the hands of independent lay scribes working for lay patrons, suggesting a dedicated literate lay audience in the period from 1400 to 1550. By 1450 the writing of manuscripts

---

[46] G. J. Williams, *Traddodiad Llenyddol Morgannwg* (Cardiff, 1948), 12–13.

[47] Huws, *Welsh Manuscripts*, 36.

[48] Ibid. 13.

[49] Cf. Huws, *Welsh Manuscripts*, 12, 52–3.

was often undertaken by Welsh poets too.[50] Indeed, a longer-term trend towards poets recording their own work in manuscript first occurs in this period, with autograph manuscripts surviving for poets such as Lewys Glyn Cothi, Gwilym Tew and Hywel Dafi.[51] Primarily laymen themselves, they were highly educated and trained at the bardic schools. Likewise, the later fifteenth century and subsequent years saw literate laymen such as John Edwards of Chirk – neither professional scribes nor poets, who did not necessarily possess a patron, but sometimes patrons themselves – pen personal compilations of religious and secular material; such compilations are discussed further below. Surviving Welsh manuscripts between about 1400 and 1550 are mostly poor cousins to contemporary English ones, and have been described as a 'largely a do-it-yourself activity' due to declining standards of production.[52] Yet despite their shortcomings they suggest a variety of significant long-term religious and cultural shifts before 1535, including the secularization of manuscript production and patronage and the use of books in household and individual devotions.

Read together with other contemporary evidence, they indicate that the eventual decline of the Welsh literary tradition and bardic patronage was due not to Tudor policies of the 1530s but to a variety of longer-term problems and processes of social, economic, political, religious and cultural change, as well as local and regional dynamics. In 1535 many notable poets were just emerging and others had yet to be born, Gruffudd Hiraethog, Lewys Morgannwg, Wiliam Cynwal, Siôn Tudur, Wiliam Llŷn and Simwnt Fychan amongst them. While the laity, particularly the gentry, had taken on a greater role in literary patronage, this was not lightly abandoned. The cultural betrayal of Welsh gentry patrons, creating men who, as soon as they saw 'the river Severn, or the steeples of Shrewsbury, and hear the English but once say "Good Morrow", ... begin to put their Welsh out of mind',[53] oversimplifies.

After 1535 many important patrons remained amongst the Welsh clergy and gentry; indeed, some thirty court books between 1550 and 1650 have been identified to date, made for families

---

50 Ibid. 16; Owen, 'Prose', 318.
51 Huws, *Welsh Manuscripts*, 16, 20; idem, *Cynnull,* 10; Owen, 'Prose', 318.
52 Huws, *Welsh Manuscripts*, 16.
53 T. Herbert and G. E. Jones, eds, *Tudor Wales* (Cardiff, 1988), 30.

all over Wales, including the Mostyns, the Wynns of Gwydir and the Lloyds of Rhiwedog.[54] Newer patrons also emerged, lacking ancient pedigrees and renowned ancestors, but craving honour, status and legitimacy. Free-metre verse flourished, including carols and *cwndidau,* many on religious themes, while interest in and demand for traditional strict metre elegies, eulogies and religious poetry for saints' days, holidays and other time-honoured themes remained, as the books of the period from 1550 to 1700 and the poet Rhys Cain's bardic circuit (*circa* 1600) through North Wales and the Marches attest.[55] While poetic standards and patronage did decline over time, as late as 1600 Welsh poetry was still very much alive and in demand among gentry and other patrons in many areas. The seventeenth century witnessed a general decline – though the remarkable Phylip family of Ardudwy produced poets until 1677 – and after 1695 no poet made a living solely through his craft.[56] Thus the eventual decline of the bardic order, its poetry and its patronage is best understood as the product of a variety of significant longer-term shifts and problems as well as local and regional contexts of change.

Likewise, Welsh prose in the medieval tradition was being interpreted, imaginatively copied, translated, written and actively read[57] into the seventeenth century, preserved and developed by notable writers and copyists such as Llywelyn Siôn, Robert Gwyn and William Dafydd Llywelyn. Some embraced the antiquarian impulse inherent in Welsh humanism and collected, interpreted and preserved older manuscripts, as did others, notably Sir Thomas Mostyn in his famed library.[58] Ultimately, then, 'The Great Century' and related ideas of periodization fail to do justice to the duration of cultural reorientiation or its complexities.

LAY PIETY AND THE MEDIEVAL LITERARY TRADITION

In order to bring the religious implications of Tudor policies into further focus, it remains to consider a brief case study illustrating the perils of drawing too strict a periodization between medieval

---

[54] Huws, *Cynnull,* 12, 35–6.
[55] NLW, Peniarth MS 178, ii, 56–72; Huws, *Cynnull,* 11.
[56] Huws, *Cynnull,* 6, 11.
[57] Owen, 'Prose', 315.
[58] Thomas, 'From Manuscript to Print', 244.

and the early modern in terms of the medieval Welsh literary tradition and mentality and the nature of lay piety in sixteenth-century Wales. National Library of Wales MS Llanstephan 117D (1542–1554/5) is a personal compilation known as the 'Book of Ieuan ap William ap Dafydd ap Einws', after its writer, a layman and constable of Ruabon (Denbighshire) in 1554.[59] His book has been called 'a remarkable collection of late medieval devotional literature and *Fachliteratur*'.[60] Its prose is distinguished by its colloquial nature and its use of Middle Welsh literary forms and structure. Primarily a collection intended for devotional use, it was meant for wider circulation, and achieved this by the 1580s. It features Welsh versions of a variety of popular devotional material, including the lives of Saints Catherine, Margaret and Mary Magdalene, prayers, biblical stories, apocryphal gospels, liturgical material, the *Elucidarium*, the *Spiritus Guidonis,* the *Visio Sancti Pauli* and charms. It also includes a wealth of Welsh religious poetry on popular themes: *cywyddau* (poems) on Mary, the passion of Christ and the mass; in contemplation of Christ's body and wounds; on the Veronica (or *Sudarium,* the veil with which St Veronica wiped Christ's sweating face on the way to Calvary, which afterwards bore an image of his face) and its miraculous qualities; and a meditation on death, for example. Taken together, these poems demonstrate a familiarity with the prevailing devotional trends of late medieval piety in Wales and Europe. Indeed, its contents are broadly typical of other Welsh devotional manuscripts written by and compiled for Welsh laymen from the turn of the fifteenth century onwards, such as the *Llyfr Coch Talgarth* (*c.*1400), largely the work of the prolific lay scribe Hywel Fychan ap Hywel Goch of Buellt for his patron, the gentleman Rhys ap Tomas ab Einawn.[61]

Ieuan's book also speaks to his daily life, concerns and devotional world. It records the births of his children and memoranda about rents, events of local, regional and wider interest, and Henri-

[59] NLW, Llanstephan MS 117D, 45; cf. Katharine Olson, 'Religion, Politics, and the Parish in Tudor England and Wales: A View from the Marches of Wales, 1534–1553,' *Recusant History* 30 (2011), 527–36, reading 'county, shire, county court, lordship, hundred, administrative unit' for 'shire' at 531–3; eadem *Popular Religion, Culture, and Reformation in Wales and the Marches, c.1415–1603* (Oxford, forthcoming).
[60] Aberystwyth, Centre for Advanced Welsh and Celtic Studies, Daniel Huws, 'Repertory of Welsh Manuscripts and Scribes' (2010 draft). I am grateful to Mr Huws for encouraging me to work on this MS.
[61] Llanstephan MS 27.

cian and Edwardian ecclesiastical and liturgical changes. Likewise, while books of hours, so plentiful in late medieval England, rarely survived in Wales, his book and other late medieval devotional compilations intended as guides for the religious life of the layman suggest a similar devotional world. Ieuan copied a calendar of the Sarum use and containing substantial local and regional content 'for those who love learning and art and calendars' in addition to the lives of the native saints Beuno and Collen.[62] Indeed, Ieuan's book is very much in keeping with other late medieval books associated with north-east Wales which point, for example, to the popularity of 'complex, coloured calendars'[63] and of local and regional saints in popular devotions alongside material in wider circulation reflecting wider devotional trends in Wales and Europe. One of these, National Library of Wales MS 3026C, which reflects the religious and secular interests of 'a literate layman of the upper stratum of Welsh society',[64] was penned for the gentleman John Edwards of Chirk (d.1498) by the poet Gutun Owain (fl. c.1451–98). In addition to personal annotations, it contains material of a local and regional devotional nature, including a calendar of the Sarum use noting the feasts of native saints such as Dyfnog, Derfel Gadarn, Collen and Sannan.[65] Also included is the *Buchedd Martin*, based on Sulpicius Severus's life of St Martin of Tours, patron saint of the nearby parish of Llanfarthin – a stone's throw from the Edwards family's parish of Chirk.[66] Similar themes also find rich expression in medieval Welsh religious poetry, underscoring, for example, the import of *gwyliau mabsant* (feasts of patronal saints) and devotions to the saints, from the roasting of piglets in the guise of rabbits during the festivities of St Brigit's *mabsant* in St Bride's Major,[67] to sober praise of St Gwenfrewi for her miraculous cures.[68]

Ieuan himself expressed a variety of reasons for his writing and choice of religious texts: clearly this was no arbitrary compilation.

---

[62] Llanstephan MS 117D, 77.

[63] M. Owen, 'Prolegomena i Astudiaeth Lawn o Lawysgrif NLW 3026', in Iestyn Daniel et al., eds, *Cyfoeth y Testun* (Cardiff, 2003), 349–84, at 374.

[64] Smith, 'Grammar and Commonplace Books', 175.

[65] NLW, MS 3026C, 13–24; Owen, 'Prolegomena', 351–2.

[66] NLW, MS 3026C, 37–62; Owen, 'Prolegomena', 352.

[67] *Gwaith Iorwerth Fynglwyd*, ed. Howell Jones and E. I. Rowlands (Cardiff, 1975), 91–2.

[68] *Gwaith Ieuan Brydydd Hir*, ed. M. P. Bryant Quinn (Aberystwyth, 2000), 57–8.

He wished to provide good examples for 'those who desire to read fine Welsh', as only Latin and English books were available.[69] Likewise, he laboured 'in order to teach those who take [to] learning and bring his own soul to remembrance by those to whom this book comes and anyone who possesses it'.[70] In this he echoed the plea of earlier Welsh scribes such as Hywel Fychan that all readers pray 'to God for them [himself and his patron]. And the forgiveness of their sins. And to grant [them] true limitless and unending happiness.'[71] This formula and others like it were meant to ensure the devout prayers of future readers and the welfare of the souls of its writer and/or patron. Ieuan also instructed that those reading of Christ's passion must do so in a sorrowful and contemplative manner, mindful of his suffering: 'bring your sins to mind and meditate on … how grievous it was for him to go to his crucifixion'.[72] Likewise, the stories of the saints and their lives were copied to 'to show an example to the people to better their lives'.[73] Ieuan's book, like many others before it, therefore supplied the layman with models for good conduct and materials for active devotional use: it was a guide for leading a pious life, dying a good death and achieving salvation.

His book offers an exceptional window onto the private devotional world, tastes and priorities of a Welsh layman and sometime local official of comparatively modest economic status during a time of religious upheaval. Its content is certainly not static. A new humanist impulse is present in his wish to provide Welsh translations of devotional texts and his collection of material, for example. Yet in many ways the contents of his book also powerfully reflect traditional late medieval piety and Welsh literature. Its contents indicate the continued appetite for and import of Christocentric devotion (found in evangelical piety also), the Virgin Mary, relics, pilgrimage and saints' lives and feasts, as well as belief in the efficacy of customary charms and prayers. More broadly, in its purpose and intent it suggests a substantial degree of Welsh conservatism and continuity in the reading and writing of popular devotional

---

[69] Llanstephan MS 117D, 134.
[70] Ibid. 298.
[71] Williams, 'Rhyddiaith', 339–41.
[72] Llanstephan MS 117D, 120–1, 153.
[73] Ibid. 153.

literature in Welsh manuscripts during the religious upheavals of the 1540s and 1550s.

It is perhaps unsurprising that the devotions, beliefs and practices of the laity remained largely unrestrained by changing church doctrine given the very limited success of the Henrician and Edwardian Reformations in Wales, the problems of language and the continuing popular appeal of the native saints and pilgrimages to destinations such as Holywell and Clynnog Fawr, despite the admonitions of Elizabethan bishops such as Richard Davies and Nicholas Robinson. More broadly, the devotional world reflected in Ieuan's book and other contemporary Welsh manuscripts, such as the commonplace book of the Welsh humanist Sir John Prise (1501/2–55)[74] indicates that confessional divisions for many of the Welsh laity remained fluid, neither clearly defined or articulated, into the 1540s and 1550s, and beyond for some. It is clear that the matter of religious identities in sixteenth-century Wales and beyond requires further scrutiny.

This brief study has suggested that the concept of 'The Great Century' and related ideas of periodization do not provide a satisfactory model for understanding the nature and development of literature and religion in fifteenth- and sixteenth-century Wales. Neither the Henrician Reformation nor the Act of Union can be seen to constitute a decisive religious or cultural divide between medieval and modern Wales. Such periodization fails to take into account the nature, complexity and duration of change, its local and regional contexts, or the effects of longer-term shifts and developments and various continuities. Generalizations about the destructive nature of Tudor policies on Welsh identity, culture, religion and society on the one hand and Tudor progress towards an enlightened modern Church and state on the other remain selective and perilous. They serve to obscure rather than illuminate, and must be treated with caution. Moreover, for all their many great contributions, for scholars such as Lewis, Lloyd and Edwards the medieval past was worth reclaiming precisely because they saw it as a crucial tool for nation-building and the future of modern Welsh culture, politics and identity. Further scrutiny is needed of the influence and legacy of both nationalist and confessional histo-

---

[74] Oxford, Balliol MS 353.

riography in the selection, definition and articulation of the Welsh literary canon.

The evidence considered suggests that our understanding of the nature and development of religious identities, popular culture and piety in sixteenth-century Wales needs to be significantly broadened and refined. Indeed, Wales as a case study has much to contribute to wider British and European dialogues on these issues. One important way forward lies in the rich interdisciplinary evidence offered by its vernacular literary tradition. While many contemporary Welsh manuscripts remain unmined, they offer much potential for understanding, re-evaluating and illuminating contemporary piety, religious identity, popular culture and vernacular literature, not only in Wales but also in a broader British, Irish and European context. Indeed, while Wales shared in many wider trends, it also offers a rich and varied perspective on the complex development and negotiation of native culture, society, religion and identity in fifteenth- and sixteenth-century Europe.

Bangor University / Harvard University

THE BIBLICAL VERSE OF HANS SACHS: THE POPULARIZATION OF SCRIPTURE IN THE LUTHERAN REFORMATION

by PHILIP BROADHEAD

The Protestant Reformation was a movement based on Scripture and its leaders believed that it was important for all clergy and laity to know and understand the word of God. In 1522 Luther published his translation of the New Testament into German and, although it was not the first translation available, it made an enormous impact, selling in large numbers despite being a relatively expensive book for ordinary readers.[1] In recent years the impression of laypeople readily accepting the Reformation as a result of individual reading of the Bible and evangelical preaching has been challenged, but there is evidence that gradually ordinary people did become aware of Protestant beliefs and the biblical basis for those teachings.[2] Familiarity with the Bible has been shown to have been spread in a variety of ways, including attendance at regular worship, the production of children's Bibles and the publication of extracts from Scripture, including the Psalms and Gospels.[3] Another medium was the mastersingers, guilds of artisans found in several south German cities, who wrote and performed their own verses (*Meisterlieder*) that followed strict musical and poetic rules. This paper will consider how they used their literary traditions to popularize evangelical teaching and to spread knowledge and awareness of the Bible in ways that were readily comprehensible to ordinary people. The focus is on the work of the Nuremberg shoemaker and poet Hans Sachs, who

---

[1] Mark U. Edwards Jr, *Printing, Propaganda, and Martin Luther* (Berkeley, CA, 1994), 123.

[2] Gerald Strauss, *Luther's House of Learning: Indoctrination of the Young in Reformation Germany* (Baltimore, MD, 1978); idem, 'The Reformation and Its Public in an Age of Orthodoxy', in R. Po-Chia Hsia, ed., *The German People and the Reformation* (Ithaca, NY, 1988), 194–214. There is evidence that popular religious beliefs and practices did change in Protestant areas over the course of the sixteenth century; see, e.g., Philip Broadhead, 'Public Worship, Liturgy and the Introduction of the Lutheran Reformation into the Territorial Lands of Nuremberg', *EHR* 120 (2005), 277–302.

[3] Ruth B. Bottigheimer, 'Bible Reading, "Bibles" and the Bible for Children in Early Modern Germany', *P&P*, no.139 (1993), 66–89, at 67–8.

achieved national fame, both for his works of the early 1520s in support of religious reform and for his creativity as a playwright and mastersinger. It will show too how changing perceptions of the role of the individual in Christian society in the Reformation period were embedded within the messages found in Sachs's poems.

Hans Sachs was a prolific and successful author and composer whose output included amongst other things, around 4,400 *Meisterlieder*, of which over 2,000 were on spiritual or biblical themes.[4] Amongst these is a large body of compositions in which Sachs transcribed into verse form substantial parts of the Old and New Testaments. These verses were written for public performance, and here I shall examine both how they reflected the changing outlook of Sachs and their potential impact on religious attitudes in Nuremberg. The eighty-five Shrovetide plays and the early polemical religious works of Sachs have been studied in detail, but his biblical verses are passed over by scholars with little comment or analysis.[5] They were clearly of significance to Sachs, who composed them in considerable numbers over several decades, indicating that he found the biblical texts a great source of personal inspiration and that he wished to share the messages he took from the Bible with his audience. These texts, in being biblical transcriptions, differed from his more widely known hymns and religious songs.[6] They usually followed a format in which the Bible texts were rendered into verse which closely echoed the words used in the original. This was followed by a conclusion, in which Sachs provided an explanation of the text and its significance for the listener and, in some cases, included other biblical texts in verse that served to reinforce his interpretation. Sachs used Luther's translation of the Bible, with which he was clearly very familiar. His transcriptions tend to simplify the original version by pulling out the salient points for emphasis, in ways which may have appealed to a less formally educated audience or those unfamiliar with the texts. Luther believed that music and verse could increase the impact of

---

4   Barbara Könneker, *Hans Sachs* (Stuttgart, 1971), 31.
5   Ibid. 17.
6   E.g. the collection: Hans Sachs, *Schöne Geistliche / inn der schrifft gegrundte lieder / für die Layen zu singen* (n.pl., 1550).

words and had himself set texts from the Psalms to verse in 1524.[7] Sachs was following this lead with his talent and vast experience as a poet who wrote for a lay and largely unlearned audience. His skilful identification of the main narrative lines, taken with the incorporation of rhyme and rhythm, make the Sachs versions of biblical events both memorable and comprehensible.

Unlike other artisans who had written pamphlets in support of religious reform in the early 1520s, Sachs continued to write and publish on religious themes over the following decades.[8] Much of Sachs's prolific output was published during his lifetime, sometimes in several editions, but only some of these transcriptions appear to have been published. He kept a record of all his writings throughout his life and in a summary of his work, written in verse in 1567, Sachs devoted a section to his biblical verse transcriptions.[9] He said that he had set books from all parts of the Bible as *Meisterlieder* which included glosses and explanations. Sachs's account also makes it clear that these verses were widely known by young and old in Germany and had prompted many to sing to the honour and praise of God.[10] Whether published or not, the works had been performed and may have existed as manuscripts and copies for the use of mastersingers in Nuremberg and elsewhere.

Sachs was a master shoemaker and, as such, a member of the artisan elite of Nuremberg. He had established his own household and workshop in 1519, by which stage he was also active as a mastersinger.[11] Between 1520 and 1523 he seems to have written nothing, and it may have been that during that period he was studying the Bible and the works of Luther, as he emerged as a strong exponent of the Reformation with a detailed knowledge of Scripture. Sachs's own records show that by 1522 he owned forty

---

[7]   Gerhard Hahn, *Evangelium als literarische Anweisung: Zu Luthers Stellung in der Geschichte des deutschen kirchlichen Lieder* (Munich, 1981), 246–7.

[8]   Martin Arnold, *Handwerker als theologische Schriftsteller: Studien zu Flugschriften der frühen Reformation 1523–1525* (Göttingen, 1990), 57.

[9]   Adelbert von Keller and Edmund Goetze, eds, *Hans Sachs, Werke*, 26 vols (Tübingen, 1870–1908) [hereafter: KG], 21: 340.

[10]   Ibid.: 'Auß den ich allen vil gedicht | In meistergsang hab zugericht | Mit kurtzer glos und ir außlegung | Auß guter christlicher bewegung, | Einfeltig nach meinem verstand, | Mit gottes hülff nun weit erkandt | In teutschem land, bey jung und alten, | Darmit vil singschul werdn gehalten'.

[11]   Berndt Hamm, *Bürgertum und Glaube: Konturen der städtischen Reformation* (Göttingen, 1996), 187–8.

published works by Luther.[12] In 1523 he published his most famous
work, *Die Wittenbergisch Nachtigall* ('The Wittenberg Nightingale'),
in which he likened Luther's teaching to birdsong that announced
the end of spiritual night and the dawning of a new day.[13] Sachs
condemned the opponents of Luther for their attempts to silence
him and included a wide-ranging account of the campaign against
Luther and an attack on the clergy, papacy and the institutions and
teaching of the Church. He emphasized that the belief of Luther,
that individuals were saved by their faith, was based on Scripture, and that none of Luther's opponents had been able to refute
this teaching from the Bible. In the introduction to the work,
Sachs said that his aim was to explain the religious disputes to
the common man, to encourage those who had heard the gospel
to spread it further, and to persuade those who had rejected the
gospel to think again.[14]

In 1524 Sachs published four prose dialogues in which he examined the consequences of evangelical teaching from a number of
lay perspectives.[15] Many significant themes emerged that made it
clear that major concerns for Sachs were those of how the gospel
related to the conduct of the individual Christian and the role of
the Christian in society. Sachs believed that salvation was obtained
through faith, but he placed heavy emphasis on the belief that
Christians would want to perform charitable works that benefited
their neighbours who were in need. He attached great significance
to the gospel account in which Christ described the saved and
the damned being separated at the last judgement on the basis
of whether they had responded to the needs of the hungry, the
thirsty and the stranger, tended the sick, given clothing to the

---

[12] Franz Otten, '*Mit hilff gottes zw tichten …got zw lob vnd zw auspreittung seines heilsamen wort*': *Untersuchungen zur Reformationsdichtung des Hans Sachs* (Göppingen, 1993), 2.

[13] Gerald Seufert, ed., *Die Wittenbergisch Nachtigall: Spruchgedicht, vier Reformationsdialoge und das Meisterlied 'Das Walt got'* (Stuttgart, 1974), 16.

[14] Ibid. 15.

[15] KG, 22: 6–84: 'Disputation zwischen einem chorherren und schuchmacher, darinn das wort gottes vnnd ein recht Christlich wesen verfochten wirt', 6–33; 'Eyn gesprech von den scheinwercken der gaystlichen und iren gelübdten, damit sy zu verlesterung des bluts Christi vermaynen selig zu werden', 34–50; 'Ein dialogus des inhalt ein argument der Römischen wider das christlich heüflein, den geytz, auch ander offenlich laster u.s.w. betreffend', 51–68; 'Eyn gesprech eynes evangelischen Christen mit einem Lutherischen, darin der ergerlich wandel etlicher, die sich lutherisch nennen, angezaigt und brüderlich gestrafft wirt', 69–84.

naked and visited the prisoner.[16] For Sachs, the performance of
these charitable works was an absolute requirement for salvation
and he placed no limit on the duty of the Christian to help the
needy.[17] The deep concern of Sachs for those in need is apparent,
and he rejected too any notion that the poor were responsible
for their circumstances, as he pointed out that they were victims
of the greed and exploitation of the wealthy traders, forestallers,
moneylenders and the Church. A key concern for Sachs was that
there should not be compulsion in matters of religion, but that
laypeople should be familiar with the gospel, so that they were in
a position to freely make their own decisions over matters of faith.
This point was critical, as Sachs believed that the main failing of
society was the pursuit of self-love and self-interest over the needs
of the common good of the whole community. His hope was that
awareness of the gospel would counteract what he saw as the sinful
urge to follow self-interest and would stimulate instead the desire
to serve one's neighbour.

The verse transcriptions of biblical texts studied here were
composed later. In the intervening period significant changes had
taken place in the religious situation in Nuremberg and in that of
Sachs himself. In 1525 Nuremberg had legislated in favour of the
Lutheran Reformation and brought an end to Catholic worship
and preaching. Subsequently, in 1526, Sachs was accused by the city
council of having sympathies and contacts with religious radicals
in Nuremberg and as a result was forbidden to publish his poems
and other writings, until the ban was lifted in 1530.[18] These events
point to some contradictions in Sachs that are apparent in his
writing, including his biblical verse transcriptions. He seems by
nature to have been conservative and much of his indignation
against greed, self-love and the neglect of the poor was inspired
by the changes that were occurring,[o], to the economy and society
of Nuremberg as a consequence of the growth in the number
of piece-workers employed by entrepreneurs. At a time of rising
prices, many amongst the labouring inhabitants of the city strug-

---

[16]   Matt. 25: 31–46.
[17]   Philip Broadhead, 'The Contribution of Hans Sachs to the Debate on the
Reformation in Nuremberg: A Study of the Religious Dialogues of 1524', in R.
Aylett and P. Skrine, eds, *Hans Sachs and Folk Theatre in the Late Middle Ages* (Lewiston,
ME, 1995), 43–62, at 52–3.
[18]   Hamm, *Bürgertum und Glaube*, 227–8.

gled to support themselves, and in the early years of the sixteenth century up to a third of the population were paupers.[19] Sachs believed that the effect of the gospel would be to make people behave in a Christian way towards their neighbour, which would lead to a peaceful revolution, not in the social order but in social relationships.

Within a brief survey it is not possible to analyse systematically the entire output of biblical transcriptions by Sachs; what follows draws on a sample, mostly from the New Testament and with examples from the 1530s and the 1560s. According to Hamm, throughout his subsequent career Sachs remained true to the social message he had expounded in the dialogues of 1524 but, as society resisted the changes he had expected, Sachs looked more to intervention by God and the imminent prospect of the day of judgement. The biblical extracts and the explanations given to them by Sachs provide an opportunity to test and perhaps refine these theories.[20] It is not clear how Sachs selected his biblical texts, but they do not necessarily correspond to the liturgical cycles of the year. They may have reflected particular concerns that he had at certain times or which were topical, for example when, in July 1550, he transcribed the Old Testament account of 'Krieg und sieg des frummen künigs Assa' ('War and victory of the pious King Asa').[21] He described how the king, who had put down idolatry in his land, was protected from the mighty armies of his opponents by the intervention of God, which was a timely rallying call for the Protestant powers of Germany in the wake of the defeat of the forces of the Smalkaldic League by Charles V. In his conclusion Sachs said it was an example to Christian authorities in his own time to root out false worship and keep their subjects from idolatry, for God would then give his help for miraculous victories against all tyrants.[22] It was also apparent that Sachs frequently selected passages that supported Lutheran teachings and used his conclusions to draw attention to the biblical basis of Lutheran theology. This was the case, for example, in the transcription of

---

[19] Günther Vogler, *Nürnberg 1524/25: Studien zur Geschichte der reformatorischen und sozialen Bewegung in der Reichsstadt* (Berlin, 1982), 25.

[20] Hamm, *Bürgertum und Glaube*, 211, 220–30.

[21] 2 Chr. 14: 1–15; KG, I: 234–6.

[22] Ibid. 236.

'Der gleyßner und offen sünder' ('The hypocrite and the sincere sinner') of 1562, in which a Pharisee and a tax collector pray in the Temple.[23] While the Pharisee congratulated himself on his piety and good works, the tax collector acknowledged his sin and threw himself on God's mercy. Sachs points out that it was the tax gatherer, not the Pharisee, who had his sins forgiven by God, for the Pharisee's works of piety were rooted in self-love and were of no avail.

Sachs repeatedly made use of biblical texts to reinforce concerns over the dangers of self-love and selfishness, and the neglect of the common good of the Christian community. For him this meant that Christians had a duty of charity to the poor, weak and vulnerable, and to any needy neighbour. These themes emerged strongly in verses written in the 1530s, and can be found, for example, in 'Von dem reichen mann und armen Lazaro' ('Of the rich man and poor Lazarus') of 1531 and 'Der Samaritter mit dem wunden' ('The Samaritan with the wounded man') of 1535.[24] In both of these Sachs stressed the importance of individual Christians engaging directly with their neighbours through acts of personal charity. He showed that in this way the situation of the needy was improved, as was the spiritual well-being of those who acted charitably. In his telling of the parable of the rich man and Lazarus, Sachs recounted how, when poor Lazarus died, he went to heaven where he joined Abraham, but the rich man, who enjoyed all good things on earth, when he died went to hell. The rich man, who had ignored Lazarus on earth, now called to Abraham to send Lazarus to him with water and, when that plea was refused, requested that he should go to earth to warn his family of what awaited them. The message for Sachs was clear, that people must care for the poor. He added that in the current expensive times there were many poor and sick across the land. In every street, he said, the poor could be found, and Lazarus was lying outside every door.[25] To drive the message home, Sachs ended with thirteen other texts from the Bible which emphasized the duty to give to

---

[23] Luke 18: 10–14; KG, 15: 355–8.
[24] 'Von dem reichen mann und armen Lazaro': Luke 16: 19–31; KG, 1: 269–72; 'Der Samaritter mit dem wunden': Luke 10: 25–37; ibid. 273–6.
[25] Ibid. 270: 'Darbey wir sollen klar verstan, | Der armen uns zu nemen an, | Der wir in dieser thewren zeyt | Haben sehr vil im lande weyt'.

the poor. These included two quotations from St Matthew giving instructions to perform acts of mercy, the same teaching that had been singled out by him in the dialogues of 1524.[26]

The importance of personal acts of charity and their part in obtaining salvation was again made clear in his account of the parable of the Good Samaritan. Sachs recounted the parable along with the preceding verses, in which Jesus was asked to explain how one's neighbour could be identified.[27] The story was told simply by Sachs, but with his own emphasis, for when he described the priest and the Levite who ignored the plight of the wounded man, he described them as showing the victim no charity, rather than as crossing over the road, as in the biblical version. In his conclusion Sachs said that the main message to be gained from the passage occurred in the final section when the questioner, having identified the Samaritan as the true neighbour of the wounded man, is instructed by Jesus to go and do the same. In this passage too Sachs alluded to the importance of performing acts of mercy for those in need, for those without mercy, he warned, did not have God's Spirit within them.[28]

In these early biblical transcriptions there were many resonances with the messages contained within the dialogues of 1524, but by the 1560s, although Sachs did not waver in his belief that Christians should help their neighbour, there were changes in the conclusions he drew from the texts. Like the Lutheran movement in general, he increasingly used his transcriptions and explanations of the Bible to draw out the importance of order and discipline for the Christian community, and he emphasized the importance of spiritual well-being above material considerations. The belief that people could not please God by human acts but only by setting their minds on spiritual things came out strongly in his verses of 1563 on chapter eight of the Epistle to the Romans, 'Das VIII. Capitel zun Römern. Von der urstend' ('The VIIIth chapter of Romans. Of the Resurrection').[29] He made it clear that those who were guilty of self-love were damned and lost to God, but those who lived

---

[26] Ibid. 271–2.
[27] Ibid. 273–6.
[28] Ibid. 275–6.
[29] KG, 15: 402–4.

with Christian discipline were God's children.[30] In the course of further transcriptions composed in 1563 and based on the Epistles, Sachs drew on the experience of the Early Church to describe how members of Christian communities should behave towards each other. For example, he recounted how Christians should give up their old lives of greed, usury, swearing and drunkenness and should not oppress others. Instead he said that they should renounce frivolous habits, avoid anger and bitterness, and forgive as Christ forgives, in order to live in a friendly and brotherly way with their neighbour.[31] Sachs stressed the need for unity, which came from living a disciplined Christian life, and while he remained concerned about attending to the needs of one's neighbour he was interested more in their spiritual needs than their material welfare.

When Sachs transcribed parts of the First Epistle of John, he emphasized the call for brotherly love between Christians.[32] In contrast to his earlier works, Sachs did not specify how brotherly love should be shown (by acts of mercy, for example), but wrote only of the need to have a pure heart and spirit. These ideas were developed using texts from the Epistle to the Romans. Sachs said that pious Christians should be prepared to sacrifice their own interests for the good of the Christian community in which all had a share. To support this Sachs stressed the biblical teaching that all members of the Christian community were important to each other, just as all parts of the human body have their own essential role to play for the good of the whole.

The change of emphasis in Sachs's writing on the Bible was made clear in his second transcription of the parable of the Good Samaritan, 'Der Samariter. Allegoria' ('The Samaritan. Allegory') written in 1562.[33] In this account Sachs omitted the early section, in which Jesus was asked to define one's neighbour, and the final section in which he gave the instruction to go and do the same

---

[30] 'Das ieder mensch das seinig sucht, | In eigner lieb steckt gar verrucht, | Und lebet unter gottes zorn | Verflucht, verdammet und verlorn': ibid. 403.

[31] 'Sonder sollen sein allesander | Freundlich und hertzlich mit einander, | Gantz brüderlich und christlich leben | Und einer dem andren vergeben': Eph. 4: 18–32; KG, 15: 409–12.

[32] 'Ir lieben, last uns allesander| Brüderlich lieben an einander, | Wann die liebe ist von gott worn, | Wer lieb hat, ist von gott geborn | Und erkennet gott in dem liecht; | Wer nicht lieb hat, der kennt gott nicht': 1 Jn 4: 1–21; KG, 15: 424–7.

[33] KG, 15: 351–4.

as the Samaritan. Only the words of the story are set to verse, and Sachs then explains them in an allegorical sense. The man left to die by thieves represented fallen humankind, which had been wounded in spirit and stripped of its innocence. The priest represented Moses, but the law he brought could not help humankind that was mired in self-love. The Levite represented the prophets, who foretold Christ but did not offer comfort to the people. The Samaritan was Christ, who had mercy on humankind and who poured into his wounds both wine, representing the law, and oil, representing the comforting gospel. Christ took man from the desert of sin to the inn of the Christian community, where he was nourished with the word and sacraments. The emphasis here was on the saving power of Christ and on spiritual nourishment within the community, rather than on individual acts of charity.

There was a change in the messages found in Sachs's later biblical verse transcriptions from those he had written in the 1530s. The call to love one's neighbour remained prominent but what this meant to Sachs was transformed. He no longer saw this as being made up of individual acts by Christians, which served only the material requirements of the needy. Instead it involved a change of ethos within the community, based on unity, peace, discipline and brotherly love, while a focus on spiritual needs had become his main concern. This indicated that Sachs recognized that the Reformation in Nuremberg had moved to a new stage, in which it was evident that the spiritual changes to the community that he and other supporters of reform desired would come only through a long-term corporate process based on religious order and discipline. Sachs never lost faith in the power of Scripture to change the lives of ordinary people, nor in the effectiveness of his verses to transmit the meaning of the Bible to his audiences. The different emphasis within his poems that was apparent over the course of years indicates not only how the views of Sachs had altered, but also how the notion of the Christian community in Nuremberg had changed as a result of the religious and political upheavals of the Reformation.[34]

Goldsmiths', University of London

---

[34] For more detailed accounts of the Reformation in Nuremberg, see Vogler, *Nürnberg 1524/25*; Hamm, *Bürgertum und Glaube*; Harold J. Grimm, *Lazarus Spengler: A Lay Leader of the Reformation* (Columbus, OH, 1978).

THOMAS MORE'S *CONFUTATION*: A LITERARY FAILURE?

by EAMON DUFFY

etween June 1529 and December 1533 Thomas More
published no fewer than seven books comprising more
than a million words against the Reformation. The young
More had achieved European fame as the author of *Utopia*, and
the friend and defender of the greatest scholar, satirist and literary
innovator of the age, Desiderius Erasmus. *Utopia* remains one
of the handful of books which would have to be included in
any representative library of Western civilization. More himself,
however, came to place a far higher value on the remarkable
stream of English works which gushed from his pen in the four
years leading up to his arrest and imprisonment in the Tower,
which, however, are nowadays read, if at all, mainly as evidence
that More was losing his grip. They form a remarkable series: the
Dialogue Concerning Heresies and the *Supplication of Souls*, in June
and September 1529 respectively; the *Confutation of Tyndale's Answer*
(Part I, the Preface and Books I–III, published in January 1532, and
Part II, Books IV–VIII, more than a year later, after his resignation
as Chancellor). That same year, 1533, saw the last four in this astonishing polemical outpouring, the *Apology of Sir Thomas More*, the
Debellation of Salem and Byzance, the *Answer to a Poisoned Book* and
the *Letter Against Frith*.[1] Though these books were directed against
a variety of authors, More's main target, implicit even in writings ostensibly directed against others, was the Bible translator and
controversialist William Tyndale. More viewed Tyndale as the most

[1]   In all cases More's writings are cited from the Yale edition of *The Complete Works
of St Thomas More. A Dialogue Concerning Heresies* is vol. 6, ed. Thomas M. C. Lawlor,
Germain Marc'hadour and Richard C. Marius (New Haven, CT, 1981). The *Supplication of Souls* and the *Letter Against Frith* are both in vol. 7, ed. Frank Manley, Germain
Marc'hadour and Clarence H. Miller (New Haven, CT, 1990). *The Confutation of
Tyndale's Answer* is vol. 8, ed. Louis A. Schuster, Richard C. Marius, James P. Lusardi
and Richard J. Schoeck (New Haven, CT, 1973). The *Apology of Sir Thomas More* is vol.
9, ed. J. B. Trapp (New Haven, CT, 1979). The *Debellation of Salem and Byzance* is vol.
10, ed. John Gut, Ralph Keen, Clarence H. Miller and Ruth McGugan (New Haven,
CT, 1987). The *Answer to a Poisoned Book* is vol. 11, ed. Stephen Merriam Foley and
Clarence H. Miller (New Haven, CT, 1985).

important conduit for Lutheran ideas into England, and he saw in Tyndale's version of the New Testament the fountainhead from which lesser heresiarchs drew lethal draughts of error with which to poison the souls of unsuspecting English men and women.

Notoriously, More's anti-heretical English writings were the literary aspect of a struggle which he vigorously pursued by other means. Between 1521 and 1529 Henry VIII and Cardinal Wolsey had orchestrated a theological campaign against the Reformation, of which Henry's own *Assertio Septem Sacramentorum* was the first and most famous outcome.[2] More was one of those who vetted the *Assertio* in draft, and he himself contributed to the campaign pseudonymously in a long and vitriolic Latin diatribe against Luther in 1523.[3] From the end of 1525 this specifically theological opposition to the new ideas took on a heightened urgency, directed now against the apparently unstoppable expansion of the trade in imported Protestant books and, from the spring of 1526, especially against Tyndale's English New Testament.[4] As a trusted royal councillor, and a close associate of the circle of humanist clergy who formed the spearhead of the Henrician defence of Catholic orthodoxy (notably Bishops Fisher of Rochester, Tunstall of London and Nicholas West of Ely), More was deeply involved in this campaign. In December 1525, in his dual capacity as a member of Wolsey's heresy commission and Chancellor of the Duchy of Lancaster, he led a series of nocturnal raids on the houses of the German merchants of the London Steelyard, the prelude to a series of high-profile arrests and public recantations. He took a lawyer's close interest in the arrests, interrogations and legatine trials directed by Wolsey and by Bishop Tunstall from 1526 onwards, designed to stem the spread of evangelical ideas in the diocese of London, the universities and the kingdom more generally. More was to make powerful use of his insider knowledge of these proceedings in the *Dialogue* and the books that followed. In March 1528 Tunstall sought to harness the specifically *literary* talents of More 'who can equal Demosthenes ... in our native tongue', by formally commis-

[2] For which see Richard Rex, 'The English Campaign against Luther in the 1520s', *TRHS* ser. 5, 39 (1989), 85–106.

[3] *Complete Works of Thomas More*, 5: *Responsio ad Lutherum*, ed. John Headley (New Haven, CT, 1969).

[4] On the shifting of gears in the campaign against heresy, see Craig D'Alton, 'The Suppression of Lutheran Heretics in England, 1526–1529', *JEH* 54 (2003), 228–53.

sioning him 'to reveal to the unlettered and simple people the cunning malice of the heretics', sending him a parcel of Protestant books and licensing him to read them.[5]

All More's English writings against the Reformation stemmed from this commission, and its first-fruits in 1529 were two polemical masterpieces, the *Dialogue* and the *Supplication of Souls*. But his personal involvement in the campaign against heresy took on a new (and to modern eyes sinister) intensity with his elevation to the Lord Chancellorship in late October 1529. As Chancellor, More considered that he had a special responsibility for the defence of Catholic orthodoxy, despite his lay status, since heresy undermined ancient law, custom and morality and threatened 'the final subversion and desolation of this noble realm'.[6] A proclamation of 1530, which More certainly helped draft, underlined the king's detestation of the 'malicious and wicked sects of heretics and Lollards' who by perverting Scripture and inducing error, sow 'sedition among Christian people, and ... do disturb the peace and tranquillity of Christian realms, as late happened in some parts of Germany, where by the procurement and sedition of Martin Luther and other heretics were slain an infinite number of Christian people'. In the name of the king the proclamation called on civil officials, from the Chancellor himself down to the justices of the peace, and 'other officers having governance of the people', to 'give their whole power and diligence to put away and to make utterly to cease and destroy all manner of heresies and errors'.[7] More acted vigorously on this mandate. With his assumption of the chancellorship, the pace of the London campaign against the underground book trade intensified, and More pushed his legal powers as Chancellor to the limit in pursuing heresy and its fomentors, cutting jurisdictional corners by calling cases into Star Chamber. Several suspects were imprisoned and examined by him in his own house at Chelsea, and evidence collected by him in

---

[5] E. F. Rogers, ed., *The Correspondence of Sir Thomas More* (Princeton, NJ, 1947), 386–8 (letter 160).

[6] P. L. Hughes and J. F. Larkin, eds, *Tudor Royal Proclamations*, 3 vols (New Haven, CT, 1964), 1: 194 [hereafter: *TRP*].

[7] *TRP*, 1: 181–6; the proclamation condemns books first published in 1530, making the date suggested by the editors (March 1529) impossible.

this way was instrumental in securing the condemnation of three of the six heretics burned while he was Chancellor.[8]

Inevitably, the rumour mill got to work on all this: allegations of maltreatment and torture began to circulate. More categorically and convincingly denied all such allegations in the *Apology*,[9] but, elaborated by the Protestant martyrologist John Foxe, they persisted, reiterated in our time by popular historians from Jasper Ridley to Brian Moynahan. Most recently they form the basis of Hilary Mantel's brilliantly hostile portrayal of More, 'our friend in Chelsea', in her Booker Prize-winning historical novel, *Wolf Hall*. It all seems a long way from the wise and genial saint of Catholic hagiography, or the martyr for liberal individualism celebrated in Robert Bolt's superbly misleading play.

Admirers of More, not least his first major twentieth-century biographer, R. W. Chambers, have variously tried to minimize, explain or ameliorate More's implacable pursuit of heresy and heretics.[10] For the last thirty years or so, however, such exculpation has been out of fashion. Instead, it has become customary to emphasize the alleged harshness and imbalance of More's attitudes to heresy and heretics, and the morbid vehemence of his language against them in his polemical writings. This hostile take on More on heresy has been underpinned by elaborate psychosexual speculation about More himself. In a famous character sketch of More in a letter of 1519 to Ulrich von Hutten, Erasmus remarked that More had seriously considered a vocation to the priesthood or monastic life.[11] Discovering in himself however a strong attraction to women, he had opted instead for marriage, considering it better to be a good husband than a bad priest. Pious Elizabethan and Stuart recusant biographers elaborated this single sentence, and on this flimsy base, modern biographers and interpreters of More have erected – the word is emphatically the *mot juste* – a theory that

---

[8]   For summaries of More's activities against heresy, see John Guy, *The Public Career of Thomas More* (Brighton, 1980), 97–174; idem, *Thomas More* (London, 2000), 106–25. For a sane and judicious overview of More's anti-heretical activities and attitudes, see Richard Rex, 'Thomas More and the Heretics: Statesman or Fanatic?', in George Logan, ed., *The Cambridge Companion to Thomas More* (Cambridge, 2010), 93–115.

[9]   More, *Apology*, 116–20.

[10]   R. W. Chambers, *Thomas More*, Bedford Historical Series 2 (London, 1938), 274–82.

[11]   Erasmus's letter to Hutton is in *Opus Epistolarum Des. Erasmi Roterodami*, ed. P. S. Allen, H. M. Allen et al., 12 vols (repr. Oxford, 1992), 4: 17 (no. 999).

More's dealings with heresy were dogged by his own unresolved sexual problems, and that his writings about heresy are therefore obsessive, hysterical and increasingly uncontrolled.

The late Sir Geoffrey Elton set the pattern with a series of debunking essays spread over thirty years, in which he argued that the young More had spent four 'idiot years'[12] trying to be a monk of the Charterhouse, and, having opted instead for marriage, spent the rest of his life struggling with a sense of 'failure in the face of the monastic challenge'. On this account, the man for all seasons was a repressed 'sex-maniac', unable to shake off the conviction 'that he had failed to live up to what he regarded as God's ultimate demand on man', namely, celibacy. As a consequence, More was 'preoccupied with the problems of sexuality', and in his anti-heretical writings returned to the alleged sexual misdemeanours of Luther and the other reformers with 'obsessional frequency'.[13] This, for Elton, was the explanation not only of what he considered More's morbid self-flagellation and hair shirt, but also of the tone of More's writings against Tyndale, 'endless, nearly always tedious, passionate, devoid of humour and markedly obsessive'. The *Confutation* in particular was for Elton one 'interminable high-pitched scream of rage and disgust which at times borders on hysteria', a display of 'helpless fury' rooted in More's own misanthropic pessimism, and above all in his unresolved and morbid sexuality.[14]

This picture received further influential endorsement in 1982 from a highly charged reading of More's entire literary output by the literary historian Alistair Fox. Fox deployed this psychosexual account of More, the guilt-ridden failed monk, as the interpretative key to all the writings up to his arrest and imprisonment in the Tower, and above all as the explanation for what Fox took to be the *literary* failure of More's vernacular writings against heresy. For Fox, the combination of a deep Augustinian pessimism about

---

[12] G. R. Elton, *Studies in Tudor and Stuart Politics and Government*, 4 vols (Cambridge, 2003), 4: 148–9.

[13] Ibid. 3: 352–5.

[14] More's most influential modern biographer, Richard Marius, similarly saw in More a man 'cruelly divided' by his decision to marry on the one hand and his longing for the cloister on the other. These unresolved sexual and psychological problems gave a 'terrible intensity' to his anti-heretical writings, and in Marius's view account for the 'grim pleasure' he took in the burning of heretics: *Thomas More* (London, 1993; first publ. 1974), 35, 37, 42, 320–1, 331, 391, 396, 403, 450.

human moral endeavour and a disordered sexuality underlie and explain More's negative reaction to the Reformation. His controversial writings thus conceal an inner experience 'which ... threatened to destroy his sense of providence and ... eventually brought him close to despair'. In them we find 'a pattern of progressive deterioration: dialogue gives way to debellation, self-control yields to loss of proportion and perspective, candour is replaced by dishonesty'. More's 'snarling invective' and 'polemical ferocity' display 'an almost demoniac emotional violence towards his opponents', a 'vileness of sentiment', which went far beyond sixteenth-century convention. This 'descent into subjective involvement' and the evident accelerating 'deterioration of his self-composure' were rooted in an 'interior psychological conflict arising from a continuing preoccupation with problems of sexuality'. More's astonishing stream of books against the Reformation was therefore a sustained act of morbid compensation, the attempt to assuage his own guilt at not being a monk: 'by continuing to write one book after another he was seeking to prove a central private conviction: that human imperfection was no cause for despair'.[15]

Two related charges, of moral and of literary failure, are embodied in this now very widespread perception of More's writing and legal action against heresy and heretics. It is widely held both that More's dealings with heretics reveal him, in Brian Moynahan's words, as a 'strange, tortured and cruel man'[16] and that, in writing against heretics, More became verbose, repetitive, boring and incoherent. The picture of More as a relentless sadist is of course itself a literary construction, invented by John Foxe in the 1560s, drawing on evangelical testimony which More explicitly and categorically repudiated. But the fiction has persisted, given new and brilliant currency in Hilary Mantel's *Wolf Hall*, in which More is portrayed as a master torturer, deploying rack, scourge and the vile machine known as 'Skeffington's Daughter' in 'the twin arts of stretching and compressing the servants of God'.[17]

As will be evident, most scholarly writing on this subject since Elton has depended on a highly suspect cod psychology, and the

[15] Alistair Fox, *Thomas More: History and Providence* (Oxford, 1982), 111, 119–20, 123, 125, 143, 145.
[16] Brian Moynahan, *William Tyndale: If God Spare My Life* (London, 2003), 349.
[17] Hilary Mantel, *Wolf Hall* (London, 2009), 298–9.

mistaken notion that ascetical practices accepted as routine by medieval Christians, like the hair shirt More wore under his robes of office, constitute evidence of a morbid sexuality. But these negative perceptions also rest to a large extent on the simple and undeniable fact that More unblinkingly endorsed the use of the death penalty against unrepentant or relapsed heretics, and as chief law officer of the Crown acted on this conviction. There is a complex and perhaps ultimately unresolvable issue here about what we are to make of the acceptance by otherwise admirable people in the past of moral axioms and actions which we now find repellent.

But these are all issues for another occasion. My specific concern here is with the widespread perception that More's vernacular writings against heresy fail, individually and cumulatively, as *literary* constructs, and that the *Confutation of Tyndale's Answer* in particular is a shapeless, repetitious and boring work whose immense bulk and inflamed rhetoric reflects the collapse of More's control over his material, and hence his failure as artist, persuader and polemicist. In this general chorus of condemnation, the *Dialogue Concerning Heresies* has fared rather better than the books that followed it. The young Lutheran spark who is More's interlocutor in the book is of course ultimately convinced of the Catholic truth, but along the way he is given many of the *Dialogue's* wittiest lines and all the best jokes, so that C. S. Lewis put the *Dialogue* in an altogether different class from the rest of More's polemical works: written when 'the iron ... [had] not yet entered into More's soul', it was, Lewis claimed, a 'great Platonic dialogue: perhaps the best specimen of that form ever produced in English'.[18]

By contrast, the *Dialogue's* far lengthier sequel, the *Confutation of Tyndale's Answer*, has found few sympathetic readers, and no advocates for its literary merits. Treated as a shapeless mountain of abuse at odds with More's earlier humanism, it has been quarried for

---

[18] R. S. Sylvester and G. Marc'hadour, eds, *Essential Articles for the Study of Sir Thomas More* (Hamden, CT, 1977), 392–3. See also the positive view of the *Dialogue* in Brian Cummings, 'Reformed Literature and Literature Reformed', in David Wallace, ed., *The Cambridge History of Medieval English Literature* (Cambridge, 1999), 834–5. For a recent positive discussion of the *Dialogue* which sees it as the signal for a new and sterner phase in the anti-heresy campaign, see Craig D'Alton, 'Charity or Fire? The Argument of Thomas More's 1529 Dyaloge', *SCJ* 33 (2002), 51–70. I have discussed the *Dialogue* at greater length in '"The comen knowen multytude of crysten men": *A Dialogue Concerning Heresies* and the Defence of Christendom', in Logan, ed., *Cambridge Companion to More*, 191–215.

nuggets of lurid rhetoric. Notoriously, these include More's deliberately shocking dismissal of Tyndale's disciple Thomas Hitton,
burned at Maidstone in February 1530, as 'the devil's stinking
martyr', and what Elton called his 'relentless harping' on Luther's
marriage and the marriages of other leading reformers, as men
'runne oute of relygyon and fallen to fleshe and caryn and lyve
in lechery with a none under the name of wedloke, and all the
chyfe heddys of them, late monkys and freres, and now apostates
and lyvynge with harlots under the name of wyves'.[19] This allegedly 'tedious and hysterical' invective has been variously treated
as symptomatic of More's secret envy of the reformers' sex-lives,
of a 'frankly vicious self-confidence' and heartlessness, and of a
'fanatical, frenzied loathing' of the victims of the Henrician heresy
hunt.[20]

The *Confutation*, especially Part I, published in the spring of
1532, is indeed a ferocious book, which deploys all More's formidable resources of invective and an unrelenting battery of argument against Tyndale and his fellow reformers. But it is neither
hysterical nor shapeless, nor is it evidence of failing emotional or
artistic control. It is indeed a very different kind of book from the
Dialogue, but the difference is not a matter of loss of grip, but of
considered literary choice. In More's judgement the religious situation in England had worsened dramatically since the publication of
the *Dialogue*: the need to alert the literate public to the true nature
and threat of heresy and the heretical books now flooding into the
country, and to expose the speciousness of their arguments, had
become ever more urgent. More therefore dropped the leisurely
fictional framework of the *Dialogue* as inadequate to this changed
situation. There is indeed still a dialogue in progress in the *Confutation*, but now More brought all his legal skills to bear on Protestant
teaching, not as in the *Dialogue* through the ironical fiction of a
discussion with a wavering Cambridge scholar, but in a detailed
forensic deconstruction of Tyndale's own words, quoted at length
and scrutinized minutely for every negative nuance and insinua-
tion. In the process More deployed a literary form, new in English,

[19] More, *Confutation*, 17, 41–2.
[20] Elton, *Studies*, 3: 347, 349, 352, 446; Fox, *History and Providence*, 23; James Simpson, *Burning to Read: English Fundamentalism and its Reformation Opponents* (Cambridge, MA, 2007), 263; David Daniell, *William Tyndale: A Biography* (New Haven, CT, 1994), 185.

though already in use in Latin polemic against Luther by Fisher, Latomus and others,[21] in which long passages from an opponent are given verbatim and then answered sentence by sentence, clause by clause. More was well aware of the dangers implicit in such a form – excessive length, redundancy and repetition, boredom, not to mention the fact that it unavoidably gave added circulation to forbidden heretical opinions. He addressed those formal issues and explained his strategy in risking them explicitly in the *Confutation* itself, and then in more detail in 1533, in the *Apology*. Once that strategy is understood, the *Confutation* takes on an altogether more formidable appearance. And, as we shall see, the form More devised for the *Confutation* was far from being considered self-defeating by More's contemporaries. It was in fact to exercise a direct and decisive influence on confessional debate in the reign of Elizabeth and beyond.

To understand what More was about in the *Confutation* and its sequels, we first need to register the context in which it was published. The two previous years, an anxious time of famine and epidemic disease, had also seen a steady escalation both in the spread of heresy, and in the campaign to halt that spread. In May 1530 Henry had established an Ecclesiastical Commission of court clergy and theologians from both universities to consider the problem of heresy. Presided over by Warham (archbishop of Canterbury) and Tunstall, the Commission had only one lay member, More himself. Despite the inclusion of closet reformers like Edward Crome and Hugh Latimer, the Commission produced an immense list of condemned propositions, culled mainly from Tyndale's writings. It also issued a homily to be read from the pulpit by all preachers, denouncing heretical books, and explaining why at this juncture the king had decreed that it was neither necessary nor desirable to have the New Testament in English translation.[22]

---

[21]   A point I owe to my colleague Richard Rex.

[22]   Proceedings of the Commission in Daniel Wilkins, *Concilia Magnae Britanniae et Hiberniae*, 4 vols (London, 1737), 3: 727–37. These measures were reiterated in a proclamation of 22 June 1530, which More almost certainly drafted, so it has been assumed that he endorsed and perhaps even initiated this ban on an English Bible. In fact the ban probably originated with the more conservative clerical members of the Commission, and More probably disagreed with it. He had argued at length for a Catholic translation of the New Testament in the *Dialogue*. Despite the official

Despite the increased vigilance of the authorities, however, the trade in forbidden books continued unabated. Three thousand copies of Tyndale's venomous anti-Divorce tract, the *Practice of Prelates*, were in circulation by the summer of 1530. Henry was determined to halt this flood of contraband literature. The return of the new and fiery bishop of London, John Stokesly, from diplomatic service overseas the same month was reflected in an immediate intensification of the campaign against heresy in London, as More and Stokesly joined forces to increase the pressure on city evangelicals.[23] More was active in a number of arrests and trials that year. His interrogation of George Constantine proved particularly devastating to the evangelical cause, for Constantine turned king's evidence, and his circumstantial revelations about book smuggling and distribution networks led to a series of arrests and confiscations. In August 1531 Thomas Bilney was burned as a relapsed heretic in Norwich, and December 1531 saw the executions of Richard Bayfield and John Tewkesbury, both of whom had been arrested and interrogated by More at Chelsea.[24]

But this royally endorsed campaign against heresy was complicated by Henry's growing impatience over the Divorce question, and by the consequent escalating campaign of intimidation against the clergy, designed to bully the Church into line over the King's Great Matter. The exigencies of the Divorce even led Henry to authorize friendly overtures to hitherto hunted Protestant activists, who might be useful in mustering international support behind the king's cause. Tyndale himself, whom Henry loathed, was approached by royal agents in the early months of 1531, and the runaway friar, abjured heretic and wanted book-smuggler Robert Barnes, who had taken refuge in Wittenberg, was recruited to bring Luther on side. By November 1531 Barnes was back in London under royal safe-conduct, appearing openly

---

moratorium on such a translation till the populace 'do utterly abandon and forsake all perverse, erroneous and seditious opinions', More retained his arguments for an official Bible translation in the revised edition of the *Dialogue* published in 1531. As Chancellor he was obliged to defend the ban in justifying royal measures against heresy in the *Confutation*, but he reiterated his personal support for an English New Testament in the *Apology* a year later.

[23] For a (slightly overheated) account of the 1530–1 campaign and More's part in it, see Susan Brigden, *London and the Reformation* (Oxford, 1989), 179–98.

[24] Guy, *Public Career*, 165–74.

in lay dress and consorting with known dissidents. On 13 January 1532 the third session of the Reformation Parliament opened, and it became clear at once that lay grievance against clerical jurisdiction generally, and the ex officio powers used in heresy proceedings in particular, was to be a major focus of Commons attack. These rumblings, orchestrated by Cromwell, were to culminate in March with the presentation of the *Commons Supplication against the Ordinaries*. Despite ritual protestations of horror at the spread of 'new, fantastical and erroneous opinions', the *Supplication* struck at the very roots of the episcopal campaign against heresy, portraying the suspects as innocent victims of the bishops and their agents.[25]

It was against this background that the first part of the *Confutation of Tyndale's Answer* appeared. More has been widely perceived as a desperate man at this stage, aware that power was slipping from him as his known disaffection over the Divorce brought a showdown with Henry ever closer, and conscious that he and the bishops were losing the battle with the heretics. His modern editors endorsed this perception by heading their account of the year 1531 'More's Gethsemane'.[26] But there is too much hindsight here. More was well aware of the danger in which he stood, but in January 1532 there was still everything to play for. For all his flirting with Tyndale and Barnes, Henry remained a determined opponent of sacramental heresy: the Protestant sympathies of many of Cromwell's protégés were as dangerous to them as More's opposition to the Divorce was to him. The *Confutation* is therefore not the long despairing cry of a doomed loser, but a considered and powerful play in a battle which might yet be won.

The first point to be made about the 1532 *Confutation of Tyndale's Answer* is that, though it would ultimately form just under half of the completed work, in fact it stands alone and works well as a self-contained book. It is slightly shorter than the *Dialogue Concerning Heresies*, and like the *Dialogue* it is carefully structured in four discrete parts. A forty-page 'Preface to the crysten reader' sets out More's reasons for writing the book, emphasizing the seditious and destructive character of heresy and the urgency of the

[25] Stanford E. Lehmberg, The *Reformation Parliament 1529–1536* (Cambridge, 1970), 138–9.
[26] So, e.g., Brigden, *London and the Reformation*, 181: 'This Chancellor's campaign against heresy was desperate because he knew that time was short'. For 'More's Gethsemane', see *Confutation*, 1229.

fight against it, stressing Henry VIII's leadership in the campaign which More and the bishops had been waging for the last three years, and deploying More's unrivalled knowledge of evangelical personnel and networks in England to discredit the claims of the reformers to superior Christian insight or holiness. The rest of the 1532 book tackles successively three distinct aspects of Tyndale's teaching. Book One examines Tyndale's polemic against the Church's sacraments, ceremonies and pious observances, including the institution of vowed celibacy. Book Two focuses on Tyndale's translation of the New Testament, and the third and final book (by far the longest) examines the related questions of whether the Church existed before the gospel or the gospel before the Church, and the authority of God's word, written and unwritten.

Tyndale had begun his *Answer* to More's *Dialogue* with an extended preface which his modern editors describe as a 'foundational essay', setting out all the main planks of his teaching.[27] Throughout the *Confutation*, More focused his fire on this essay, exploiting the clarity and focus of Tyndale's preface to give a uniting theme to successive sections of his own reply. There is no space here to examine each of the component parts of the *Confutation* of 1532. So I want to focus instead on just three of the issues which have most often been taken to demonstrate the failure of the *Confutation* as a literary construct — More's invective against the executed Protestants Thomas Hitton, John Tewkesbury and Richard Bayfield; his repeated references to the marriages of the reformers; and the repetitive nature of the form he devised for the *Confutation*. In fact, most writing about the *Confutation* has ignored the work's formal structure, on the assumption that it has none, only hysterical incoherence. Yet shape and purpose are very much in evidence, and despite the harshness of tone, there is no hysteria. More is perfectly in control of his material, which he marshals into a vehement but carefully crafted piece of advocacy.

For all its monumentality, the *Confutation* of 1532 was an occasional piece, directed to very specific circumstances. The mounting and managed anti-clericalism which was soon to culminate in the *Commons Supplication against the Ordinaries* presented the London campaign against heresy as arbitrary clerical oppression of inno-

[27] *An Answere Unto Sir Thomas More's Dialoge*, ed. Anne M. O'Donnell and Jared Wickes, The Independent Works of William Tyndale 3 (Washington, DC, 2000), xxxv.

cent victims. More was concerned to vindicate that campaign by demonstrating the poisonous nature of heresy itself, the forbearance of the bishops and their officials in dealing with it, and the duplicity and guilt of the heretics. His own encounters with heretics over the previous seven years, and the ambiguities, evasions and downright deceit which they had understandably deployed to escape detection, had given him a low opinion of their honesty and integrity. 'But and yf they were ones founde out and examined | we se them alwaye first redy to lye and forswere them selfe yf that wyll serve', he had declared in the *Dialogue*. 'And whan that wyll not helpe but theyr falshed and periury proved in theyr faces | than redy be they to abiure and forsake it | as longe as that may save theyr lyves.'[28]

More made that claim before the executions had begun: the burning of six Protestant martyrs since then seemed to give him the lie. In his *Answer* to More's *Dialogue*, therefore, Tyndale claimed that those burned were glorious martyrs for the gospel truth, and he named especially the priest Thomas Hitton, executed at Maidstone in February 1530.[29] That is why More devotes the bulk of the Preface of the *Confutation* to showing that heresy could never make saints, and that these victims in particular had been dupes of the devil and were themselves incorrigible deceivers. The nuggets of abuse which have so scandalized modern commentators are part of that sustained argument, in which More drew on his own detailed knowledge of individual cases to establish a wider point.

England had for several years been in the grip of famine and epidemic disease. More's opening sentence links the failure of the crops directly to God's hatred of heresy: '[May] Our lorde sende us nowe some yeres as plenteouse of good corne, as we have hadde some yeres of late plenteous of evyll bokes'. God punishes sin with the scourge of disease and death, especially 'that odyouse and hatefull synne of the soule, that spyleth the frute from all manner of virtues, I meane unbelyefe, false fayth and infydelyte, and to tell you all at ones in playne englyshe heresye'.[30] England, therefore, stands under God's judgement so long as she tolerates heresy. Books full of 'pestylent poisoned heresyes' had 'in other

[28] More, *Dialogue*, 201, 422.
[29] Tyndale, *Answer*, 112; for the six victims, ibid. 424–6.
[30] More, *Confutation*, 3.

realms all redy kylled by scysmes and warre many thousande bodyes ... and many mo thousand soules'. Now a few 'malycyouse myschevouse persones', in defiance of the king's proclamations, were flooding England with such books, 'to corrupte and infecte all good and vertuouse people'.[31] Naming some of these propagators of error – Tyndale himself, John Frith, George Joye, George Constantine, Robert Barnes – More put the best face he could on official connivance at the open presence in London of Barnes, 'at thys daye comen to the realme by saufe conducte'. This was by the 'blessyd disposycyon' of the king, who hated heresy, yet who indulged heretics like Barnes 'to thende that yf there might yet any sparke of grace be founden in hym, yt myghte be kepte, kyndeled and encreaced, rather than the man be caste away'. But More recalled ominously that the king had been ill requited for the similar indulgence granted to Richard Bayfield and George Constantine, who had both returned to Tyndales heresies, 'lyke a dogge returnynge to his vomyte'.[32]

All this is the prelude to More's central concern in the preface, his repudiation of the claim that executed heretics like Bayfield and Hitton were Christian martyrs. For Tyndale, More insisted, such deaths were a cause of obscene and unholy triumph: 'the grete feste and glory of Tyndales develysh prowde dyspytouse harte, to delyte and reioyce in the effusyon of such people's blode as hys poisoned bokes have miserably bewyched, and from trew crysten folke, turned into false wycked wreches'.[33]

More's accusation, that Tyndale had no pity for the spilled blood of these victims, may baffle and even repel. More, as we shall see, insisted that most of those burned had gone straight to the eternal fires of hell, and that they were therefore the devil's martyrs. This insistence has struck even well-disposed modern readers as 'heartless mockery' of their deaths.[34] But we need to grasp the precise terms of More's argument here. For him, as for St Augustine and the whole of mainstream medieval Christian theology, heresy was always a culpable choice, and damnation never a cause for pity. The stubborn or relapsed heretic was emphatically not the victim

---

[31]   Ibid. 11–12.
[32]   Ibid. 17.
[33]   Ibid. 16–17, 34.
[34]   Simpson, *Burning to Read*, 265.

of some unfortunate mistake. The heretic had been shown the saving truth, and God always gave souls the grace to embrace that truth. Through pride and perversity, therefore, they had rejected that truth, and in the process, turned away from God. To die in that state of refusal was to be damned, and the damned were, in a perfectly literal sense, hate-ful. They had deliberately turned their back forever on love, and were therefore themselves impossible to love. As fellow mortals we can lament their tragedy, we can pity the waste, we can grieve at the ruin of one of God's creatures, but we can never forget that they have of their own free will renounced truth, light and love, and placed themselves forever beyond the reach of charity, outside the common life of the redeemed.

The damned have chosen their own destruction, for human will is free. Each had had 'myche favour shewed hym, & myche labour charytablye taken for the saving of hym': the legal process against heresy and the clergy who administered it were both just and merciful. But in the end for their obstinacy each victim had been delivered to the secular arm and 'burned uppe in hys false fayth and heresyes, whereof he lerned the great parte of Tyndales holy bokes', and the spirit of lies 'hath taken his wreched soule with hym from the shorte fyre to the fyre everlastyng'.[35]

But they had been propelled towards that ruin by the influence of others, and More points again and again to Tyndale as the murderer of these men's souls. Hitton, Bayfield and Tewkesbury were indeed damned, since they had died 'of hard herte and malycyouse mynde incurable'.[36] But in hell their damnation would deepen and increase the misery of the one who had perverted them. More dwelt on these double deaths of body and soul not to gloat, or because he rejoiced in suffering, but to bring out the full horror of Tyndale's responsibility for the ruin of these immortal souls. Tewkesbury, he insisted, would never have fallen from grace 'yf Tyndales ungracious bokes had never come in hys handes'. Because of Tyndale, 'the pore wreche lyeth now in hell and cryeth out on hym | and Tyndale yf he do not amende in tyme, he is lyke to fynd hym when they come togyther an hote fyrebronde burnynge at hys bakke, that all the water in the worlde wyll not

---

[35] More, *Confutation*, 16.
[36] Ibid. 18.

be able to quenche'.[37] That horrifying vision would not be out of place in Dante's *Inferno*, but like Dante's poem it sprang not from the writer's psychic disorders but from More's imaginative assimilation of the mainstream eschatology of medieval Christendom.

To offset these appalling images of souls doomed to a shared damnation by their own pride and stubbornness and the malign influence of Tyndale's teaching, More offered a portrait of a heretic saved at the very last by the grace of repentance. More had discussed the first trial and abjuration of Thomas Bilney at length in the *Dialogue*, though, since Bilney *had* abjured, More refrained from naming him there. In the *Dialogue*, More had nevertheless been unimpressed by Bilney's protestations of good intent and he had predicted his eventual relapse. So it is all the more striking that in the *Confutation* More returned to Bilney for a portrait of a repentant heretic. Bilney had once been every bit as proud and deceitful as Hitton, Bayfield and Tewkesbury; like them had lied and dissembled to escape detection; had abjured like them; and then, like them, had relapsed though pride and had sought to pervert others from the truth. Yet, according to More, by God's grace at the very last, Bilney had renounced his errors and died repentant, an orthodox Catholic lamenting especially his sacramental errors and the contempt for 'Crystes catholyke knowen chyrche' which was the root of all heresy. During his examination, Bilney had 'waxed styffe and stoburne in hys opynyons'. But by the grace and goodness of God, 'he was finally so fully converted unto Cryste and hys trewe catholyke fayth that not onely at the fyre, as well in wordes as wrytynge, but also man[y] dayes before | he had revoked, abhorred and detested such heresyes as he before had holden'.[38] The legal penalty for a relapsed heretic could not be set aside, and Bilney had been burned. But the man himself had been saved: God 'hath forthwith from the fyre taken hys blessed soule to heven'. Bilney, though no martyr, *was* a saint. Though every unrepentant heretic was doomed to eternal torment, God would accept the repentant Bilney's suffering in the fire as his purgatory, 'and settynge the merytes of hys owne paynefull passion therunto, hath forthwith from the fyre taken hys blessed soule to heven, where he now prayeth incessauntly for the repentaunce

37 Ibid. 22.
38 Ibid. 23.

and amendement of all suche as have ben by hys meanes whyle he
lyved, into any suche errours induced or confyrmed'.[39]

The reliability of More's claim that Bilney died a devout and
penitent Catholic has been much debated.[40] As a consequence,
the literary purpose of his portrait of Bilney, as a deliberate foil
to those of the 'devils stinking martyrs', has been largely ignored.
Whatever the facts about Bilney's end, More's skilful handling of
the episode is designed to balance and contrast with his portraits of
the unrepentant heretics Hitton, Bayfield and Tewkesbury, acqui-
escent victims of Tyndale's false teaching. We are dealing here not
with random abuse and relish in burnings, but with a careful if
daunting polemical construction.

I have been arguing that a psychological interpretation of
More's invective against heresy has blinded readers to the literary
and argumentative function of that invective, which is to be found
mainly in the opening section of the *Confutation*. The same is true
of his much more widespread attacks on the marriages of the
reformers. The frequency and vehemence of More's language
about the 'bestely bychery' of monks and nuns in bed together
has been taken as a reflection of his own sexual preoccupations.
In fact, any reader of More's account in the *Dialogue* of the shrine
of St Walery in Picardy, famed for its cures of sexual ailments and
impotence, hung about with *ex voto* replicas of 'men's gear and
women's gear in wax', and ablaze with candles measured to the
dimensions of the male pilgrim's genitalia, will realise that More
had a robust and unprurient sense of humour about sex. And in
the *Confutation* he displays no interest whatever in the details of
what these former monks and nuns are actually *doing* to each other
in bed. For him, the simple fact that they have not only abandoned
vowed chastity but have sanctimoniously disguised that abandonment of their solemn vows with a pretence of positive Christian
virtue is the outrage. More importantly, it pulls the rug from under
any Protestant claims to truth or holiness. More returned to the
marriages of the reformers again and again because he saw in them

---

[39] Ibid. 23–5.
[40] Starting, classically, with Foxe: John Foxe, *The Unabridged Acts and Monuments
Online*, 1185ff (1570 edn, republ. Sheffield, 2011), online at <http//www.johnfoxe.
org >; unpersuaded modern discussions in Gordon Rupp, *Studies in the Making of the
English Protestant Tradition* (Cambridge, 1966), 29–31; Guy, *Public Career*, 167–71; Marius,
Thomas More, 396–401.

a devastating common-sense disproof of their claims to the moral high ground. He knew, too, that his conservative Tudor audience was likely to share his take on the credibility of a preaching friar who bedded down every night with a nun. For a millennium and a half monks and nuns had taken solemn vows to God to live in chastity, and the whole Christian people had recognized clerical unchastity as an abomination. Medieval literature, from the pulpit invective of the Gregorian reformers to the dirty jokes of the *Decameron*, was full of contempt for the squalors of unchaste monks and nuns. But, however laughable, it was also shocking, and so, More pointed out, people 'have always iested that Antecryste sholde be borne between a frere and a none'.

Even as More wrote, the Protestant presses of Germany were pouring out propaganda prints satirizing the sexual misbehaviour of Catholic priests and religious. Within three years of his writing, Cromwell's monastic visitors would use just such alleged misbehaviour to close down religious houses. More, therefore, was playing a very strong card by reiterating that the leading reformers, monks and friars who had renounced chastity and taken women into their beds, had turned a sick medieval joke into sober modern reality. In defiance of

> the hole consent of crystendome so many hundred yeres … foure or five fond freres runne out of relygon and lyvynge in lechery, take upon themselfe to preche and saye to the people of theym selfe, we be the spyrytuales, we serche the botome of God's secrets … and all that have been called holy doctors and interpretours before our dayes, were eyther false or folyes and … brought all crysten nacyons oute of the right fayth / tyll now that god of hys high goodness sent us and our wyves to preche fayth, and teche heresy, and show lechery to torne the worlde to grace.[41]

More's references to the reformers and their wives always carry this polemical point, because he was confident that even the most unlettered lay man or woman who reflected on this single fact about the reformers would thereby see through them, 'syth ye se Tyndale now teche and allowe theyr lechery and avowe it solempnely for good and laufull matrimony: I nothing fere your iudge-

---

ment in this matter'.[42] In confronting the *Confutation's* constant
jibes against the reformers' marriages, we are dealing not with the
obsessive scratching of a sexual itch, but the strategic reiteration
of what its author felt to be an unanswerable populist argument.

I turn finally to the literary form in which the *Confutation* is
cast. I have suggested that Part I of the *Confutation* can be treated
as an integral work in its own right, and its Preface and successive
books focus effectively on distinct aspects of Tyndale's teaching
and the Protestant challenge. But the technique of learned literary
debate which More was adapting here for a vernacular readership,
citing extended extracts from Tyndale and then refuting them at
length, inevitably makes for repetitiveness. He was accused of both
tedium and redundancy by his evangelical opponents, as he has
been by critics ever since. It has also been suggested that the form
is doubly self-defeating, because in order to refute it gives wider
circulation to the works being refuted.

More was well aware of all these criticisms, and offered a
robust defence in the *Apology*. He quoted Tyndale at such length,
he wrote, so that no-one should accuse him of distortion: 'lothe
would I be to miss reherse any mannys reason against whome I
wryte, or to reherse hym slenderly'. More claimed that Tyndale's
book could be reconstructed simply by omitting More's refutation,
a claim conceded by the far from friendly Victorian editors of the
Parker Society edition of Tyndale's works. In this More certainly
differed from Tyndale, who, he claimed, distorted by selective or
tendentious quotation and 'rehersyth myne in every place faintly
and falsely to / and leveth out the pyth and strength'.[43] As for
its length, that was unavoidable. The most ignorant heretic could
spread a heresy in a single page of eye-catching aphorisms: to
unpick the errors in that single page might take the wisest man in
the world forty times as long. For all the charge of tedium, nonetheless, More insisted that he knew of good men who had read
his book three times over as a comprehensive source of orthodox
arguments, making 'tables thereof for their own remembraunce'.[44]

As that suggests, More insisted that his book was not *meant*
to be read consecutively or as a whole. The *Confutation* was a

---

[42] Ibid. 141.
[43] More, *Apology*, 6.
[44] Ibid. 8.

compendium, a manual of controversies, which could be randomly browsed, or searched for specific issues.

> I sometyme take the payne to reherse some one thynge in diverse fashions in mo places than one, bycause I wolde that the reder sholde in every place where he fortuneth to fall in redynge, have at hys hande without remyttynge ellys where or labour of ferther sekynge for it, as myche as shall seme requysite for that mater that he there hathe in hande.[45]

Readers were prone to 'wexe wery to rede over a long boke': he had designed this book so that 'they shal not need to rede over any chapyter but one, and that yt shall not force greatly whych one thorow all the boke'.[46] So whether some 'yndyfferent' reader picked up the *Confutation* at random, or 'the beste evangelyste of all this evangelycall bretherhed' searched to see what More had to say about 'some chosen piece in whyche hym selfe had went that hys evangelycall father Tyndale sayed wonderfull well', he would find a complete refutation.[47]

Nor did More fear that his book gave fresh currency to forbidden ideas. He knew better than anyone the reach of the trade in evangelical books, and in the preface to the *Confutation* argued that heretics even gave their books away free, 'so greate a pestilent pleasure have some develysh people caught, with the labour, travayle, coste, charge, parell, harme and hurte of them selfe, to seke the destruccyone of other'.[48] Heretical books were already everywhere, to say nothing of the 'bold erroneous talkynge that is now allmoste in every lewde laddys mouth'.[49]

More had declared in the *Confutation* that he would far prefer it if nobody read either his book or the evangelical writings which had elicited it. 'The very tryacle were well loste, so that all venome and poison were utterly loste therwyth'. But where there was heresy, there must be refutation, and the defenders of orthodoxy must not sleep while Judas went about his work. 'Evyl and ungracyouse folke shall ever fynde the meanys that suche bookes shall never in some corners lakke, wherby good people may be

45 Ibid.
46 Ibid. 10.
47 Ibid.
48 Ibid. 12.
49 Ibid. 11.

deceived and corrupted: yt ys more thenne necessary that men have agayne suche bookes as may well arme them, to resyste and confute theym'.[50] But it is clear that in adapting a learned Latin argumentative form to provide that necessary vernacular antidote to heresy, More was conscious of creating a different kind of work, combative, baggy, encyclopaedic, cyclical, a form which should be judged by the targeting and effectiveness of its individual parts, rather than its correspondence to some modern notions of what makes a good read.

Judged in this way, the *Confutation* stands up far better to scrutiny than has been allowed. Entire books can stand alone, especially Book VIII, a sustained polemic against Robert Barnes which returns brilliantly to the comic mode of the *Dialogue* in a series of extended conversations in which Barnes is bested in debate by women, most devastatingly his landlady, 'the good wife of the botell of Botolph's wharf'.[51] But the rest of the *Confutation*, read in short bursts as More envisaged it would be, is full of good things, as in the passages where More deploys common usage or his humanist training in Greek to challenge Tyndale's translation of contested terms,[52] or as in this passage, in which he picks on one of Tyndale's stylistic habits to score a debating point:

> Tyndale is a great marker | there is nothynge with hym now but marke, marke, marke. It is pitye the man were not made a marker of chases in some tenys playe. For in good fayth he sholde be therin mych better occupied than he is in this | when he sytteth and marketh all other mennis fautes and leveth hys owne unmarked | which every other man marketh well inough.[53]

One test of the value of any literary innovation is whether or not the form is adopted by other serious writers. The vernacular debating form More had introduced into English was indeed to have a decisive influence on the shape of the religious debates of the Elizabethan era. In Queen Mary's reign, the *Confutation* was included in William Rastell's superb folio edition of More's English

---

50 More, *Confutation*, 36–9.
51 Ibid. 883–905.
52 Ibid. 169–73.
53 Ibid. 139.

works, a collection designed to provide the Marian Church with a major polemical resource.[54] Eight years later, in 1565, the former Marian activist Thomas Harding, now a Louvain exile, adopted both the title and the distinctive literary form of the *Confutation* for his own *Confutation* of John Jewel's *Apologie for the Church of England*. Harding justified his adoption of the form in much the same terms as More: 'That I might seme to deale uprightly', he wrote, 'I would leave out nothing'.[55] Perhaps more surprisingly, Jewel responded in kind, once again using More's form to structure his own even vaster *Defence of the Apology*.[56] Archbishop Parker thought well enough of Jewel's book to order copies placed in every parish church in England, despite the misgivings of those like Bishop Parkhurst of Norwich, who thought that the form of the book gave hostages to fortune; Catholics too poor to buy Harding's books 'shall finde the same already provided for them'.[57] But the polemical advantages of More's novel form were evidently deemed to outweigh any such drawbacks.

And, in one way at least, Jewel outdid More. In Renaissance writing, *copia*, abundance or copiousness, was considered a species of merit, not a defect. Jewel's immense treatise weighed in at more than twice the length of More's *Confutation*. Yet though many have doubtless found Jewel's book tedious, no-one, so far as I am aware, has seen in the Elizabethan Protestant bishop's adoption of More's literary innovation a symptom of mounting hysteria, or evidence of a mind at the end of its tether.

University of Cambridge

---

[54] *The Workes of Sir Thomas More Knyght* (London, 1557); the *Confutation* occupies pages 614–832.

[55] Thomas Harding, A *confutation of a booke intituled An apologie of the Church of England* (Antwerp 1565); Alexandra Walsham, 'The Spider and the Bee: The Perils of Printing for Refutation in Tudor England', in John King, ed., *Tudor Books and Readers* (Cambridge, 2010), 163–90, quotation at 169. Surprisingly, Professor Walsham makes no allusion to More's responsibility for or use of the form.

[56] John Jewel, *A defence of the Apologie of the Churche of Englande conteininge an answeare to a certaine booke lately set foorthe by M. Hardinge, and entituled, A confutation of &c.* (London, 1567).

[57] Walsham, 'Spider and the Bee', 172, 174.

STAGING VICE AND ACTING EVIL: THEATRE AND ANTI-THEATRE IN EARLY MODERN ENGLAND*

by GEORGE OPPITZ-TROTMAN

This article revisits the relationship between dramatic production and religious change in the sixteenth century, specifically by examining the allegorical Vice figure – a dramatic embodiment of evil forces – that came to particular prominence during this period.[1] It suggests that the professional actor became increasingly associated with this figure of moral evil. I propose also that understanding the moral ambivalence of the actor's presence can inform our understanding of many plays in which no obviously coherent Vice figure is present, but in which possibilities of such an allegory are important. It would be impractical to present this argument across the range of dramatic examples it deserves, particularly since substantial contextual argument will be necessary if the article's conclusions are to have any weight. It is partly for this reason that an examination of Shakespeare's *Hamlet* concludes the paper, a play needing no introduction. It will be suggested that the play's issue of conscience was mediated in important ways by the actor's potentially Vice-like presence, defined as such by Tudor legislation as well as by a variety of anti-theatrical religious writings.

ORIGINS

The 'Vice' was the name given to the allegorical embodiment of various moral and social evils in medieval morality plays and later secular interludes, representing nihilism, ambition, pride, sedition and many other such attributes. The influential late antique allegory by Prudentius, the *Psychomachia*, described the pattern in which

* I would like to thank in particular John Kerrigan, as well as Richard Beadle, Catherine Belsey, David Hillman, Raphael Lyne, Subha Mukherji and Daniel Wakelin, who encountered this argument in a variety of earlier or expanded forms, and offered many helpful comments.

[1] Peter Happé dated the greatest influence of the Vice to the period 1547–79, in 'The Vice: A Checklist and an Annotated Bibliography', *Research Opportunities in Renaissance Drama* 22 (1979), 17–35, at 17.

the dramatic Vice may first have been conceived, with personified vices arrayed against the virtues in a titanic metaphysical battle for the human soul that borrowed heavily from Virgil's *Aeneid*.[2] Traditionally, vice had been distinguished from sin itself. Vice was, in the words of Peter Abelard (d.1142), the inclination; sin the realization or manifestation. Thomas Aquinas (d.1274), following Augustine, would write of vice as an unnatural disposition or habit (*habitus*), a mid-point between the capacity to do something and the doing of it.[3] Such theological foundations are useful for an initial understanding of the dramatic Vice, despite the distinctions we ought to make between conceptual and theatrically realized versions, for the dramatic Vice always addressed itself towards the construction of motivation and the organization of action, while its own motives remained entirely beyond the capacities of allegorical representation. In the play *The Triall of Treasure* (1567), the Vice is actually called 'Inclination'.

Indeed, the Vice's typological origins hint at the potential of the figures to occupy a powerful undetermined space on the margins of other play-elements. In his influential study *The Seven Deadly Sins*, Morton Bloomfield writes that the seven cardinal sins – the apparent conceptual ancestors of the Vice figure – '[were] the remnant of some Gnostic Soul Journey ... [of] the early Christian centuries'; that is, they were occasioned by sublime or metaphysical travel.[4] In the medieval English morality plays, the Vice figures, as well as the Virtues, were presented to the audience in a peculiar relation to the figure of Mankind or *Humanum Genus* at the heart of the performance, a performance which often figured the journey of the soul at the body's death. Elaine Scarry writes that the failure of belief is characterized often as the 'refusal or inability

---

[2]   See H. J. Thompson, ed., *Prudentius: Works, English and Latin*, LCL 387, 398, 2 vols (London, 1961–2), vol. 1.

[3]   Peter Abelard, *Ethics*, ed. and transl. D. E. Luscombe, OMT (Oxford, 1971), 2–5, esp. 4–5: 'vice is that by which we are made prone to sin, that is, are inclined to consent to what is not fitting so that we either do it or forsake it'; Thomas Aquinas, *Summa Theologica*, II–I q.71 a.2, ed. and transl. Fathers of the English Dominican Province (London, 1920–9), 1642: 'the vice of any thing consists in its being disposed in a manner not befitting its nature (*disposita contra id quod convenit naturae*)'.

[4]   Morton W. Bloomfield, *The Seven Deadly Sins: An Introduction to the History of a Religious Concept, with Special Reference to Medieval English Literature* (East Lansing, MI, 1967), 20.

to turn oneself inside-out'.[5] In the Prudentian *Psychomachia*, individual inner struggle was played out in external scenes organized by a multitude of bodies. The dramatization of such an allegory only emphasized this paradox. In late medieval drama the allegorical transformation of inner crisis into outward expression was crucial, indeed often constitutive of the dramatic scene itself. This pattern of representation would later be instrumental in the representation of what we like to think of as Shakespearean individuality.

In order to show how this occurred and why it might be important to our understanding of the Church's relationship to the literature of the time, it is necessary to delve a little into the history of the dramatic Vice figure. Although the Vice was incidental to the central representation of humankind, its presence did not offer an alternative certainty, but rather the opposite of all certainties. This basic function of reversal or undoing was reiterated in later uses of the Vice. A stage direction in the play *All for Money* (1578) simply ordered appropriate extemporization for the Vice: '*here the vyce shal turne the proclamation to some contrarie sence at euery time*'.[6] Little wonder, then, given the constitutive lack of fully realized nature in the Vice, that the critical history of its Tudor varieties is tinged with some controversy concerning its origins and significance. For reasons of brevity, it may help to review this critical history rather than make fresh arguments concerning the Vice figure's many and variable manifestations in a multitude of obscure sixteenth-century moral interludes.

Anglophone study of the Vice can be said to have begun in earnest with L. W. Cushman's book *The Devil and the Vice in English Dramatic Literature before Shakespeare*. Cushman established the tradition of seeing the Vice as derived from the morality play and distinguished the Vice from the Devil in dramatic terms, arguing that the Vice had its more specific origins in the seven deadly sins of earlier and larger-scale community drama.[7] Cushman also supposed that

5   Elaine Scarry, *The Body in Pain: The Making and Unmaking of the World* (Oxford, 1989), 202.
6   Thomas Lupton, *All for Money*, ed. Ernst Vogel, *Shakespeare Jahrbuch* 40 (1904), Act 2, lines 1008–9.
7   L. W. Cushman, *The Devil and the Vice in English Dramatic Literature before Shakespeare* (Halle an der Saale, 1900), 54–145. However, see also Adolphus William Ward, *History of English Dramatic Literature to the Death of Queen Anne*, 3 vols (London, 1899), 1: 109–12; Wilhelm Creizenach, *Geschichte des neueren Dramas*, 5 vols (Halle an der

the Vice barely survived the decline of the morality play and was remembered only in its buffoonish guise in the secular tragedies.

The prolific and influential scholar of English drama E. K. Chambers inaugurated a forceful contrary tradition. Chambers contended that the Vice's connection with pre-Tudor morality plays was much less certain, and preferred to locate the Vice as a distinct dramatic persona in the later fashion of Marian and Elizabethan interludes.[8] This assertion has generally been influential only among specialists in medieval and pre-Marlovian drama: in most Shakespearean scholarship, and to most others for whom the Vice is of perhaps incidental interest, the impression survives that the Vice bears with it the didactic scheme and tradition of the full-blown morality play of the late fifteenth and early sixteenth centuries, an impression lent a great deal of power by the assumed etymology of the word 'Vice' itself. However, the implications of Chambers's findings were taken up by some who found powerful evidence for the Vice's derivation from an ongoing folk tradition, seemingly distinguishable from the moralities.[9] These arguments offer other etymologies for the term 'Vice', with Frances Mares taking up Karl Friedrich Flögel's eighteenth-century proposition that, since the character nearly always wore a mask, or a blacked-out or reddened face in the manner of some folk fools, 'Vice' could just as easily derive from the word *vis*, meaning 'face' or 'visage' not only in Old French but also in fourteenth-century English vernacular.[10]

Saale, 1893–1916), 1: 463–70; 3: 504–48, esp. 504–6; Katherine Lee Bates, *The English Religious Drama* (London, 1893), 206–9.

   [8] E. K. Chambers, *The Mediaeval Stage*, 2 vols (London, 1903), 2: 204.

   [9] Peter Happé, 'The Vice and the Folk-Drama', *Folklore* 75 (1964), 161–93; Francis Hugh Mares, 'The Origin of the Figure Called "The Vice" in Tudor Drama', *Huntingdon Library Quarterly* 22 (1958), 11–29, based on idem, 'The Origin and Development of the Figure Called the "Vice" in Tudor Drama' (B.Litt. dissertation, University of Oxford, 1954); Robert Withington, 'The Ancestry of the "Vice"', *Speculum* 7 (1932), 525–9; Withington withdrew from this position slightly in 'Braggart, Devil, and "Vice"', *Speculum* 11 (1936), 124–9.

   [10] Mares, 'Origin', 28–9, based on a philological tradition dating from the end of the eighteenth century, for which see Karl Friedrich Flögel, *Geschichte der Hofnarren* (Leipzig and Liegniss, 1789), 57–8. Flögel's speculations as to the etymology of 'Vice' are not given in their entirety by Mares, but they are interesting, linking the Vice's name also to the *Vis d'ane* – the donkey mask or part-mask with which the fool has long been associated. Mares also considered the possible derivation from the Latin *vice*, meaning literally 'in the place of'.

With the exception of Robert Weimann's rich study of the Vice's language and role, Bernard Spivack's work on the subject remains perhaps the most extensive and consistently illuminating, open to the figure's ambiguity, and above all associating its emergence and mutability with changes in opportunities of dramaturgy – smaller companies, enclosed spaces – that prompted the allegorical *psychomachia* to develop from 'warfare to intrigue'.[11] The important studies of David Bevington and Robert Weimann take up this emphasis on the Vice's relation to circumstances of dramatic production. Weimann, in particular, situates the emergence of the figure within much broader contexts of dramatic and social reform. The Vice transcended its limited role in the traditional *psychomachia*, and emerged not only as an expert intriguer and theatrical deceiver, but as the main attraction of many Tudor plays. Indeed, the conventional distinction between theological or ecclesiastical origins and the figure's connection to the folk tradition of the fool or clown should not, perhaps, be maintained, as in the latter half of the sixteenth century Vice figures came increasingly to sustain allegorical performance of 'unnatural dispositions' by histrionic techniques of clownish or buffoonish subversion. Moreover, a conflation of social disapproval of the wandering folk player with theological definitions of vice as a disruption of natural identity underlay the crucial association of the figure with the professional actor of Shakespearean drama, as will now be suggested.

PERFORMANCE, LAW AND THE CHURCHES

During this evolution of the Vice from allegorical component to central theatrical attraction, the large-scale civic drama of York, Wakefield, Coventry and many other places came under attack by reformers for whom the representation of God or the saints by ordinary men was idolatrous. In 1569 the great York mystery cycle was performed for the last time; that at Wakefield was prohibited after 1575. Furthermore, whilst the sixteenth century saw the emer-

---

[11] Robert Weimann, *Shakespeare and the Popular Tradition in the Theater: Studies in the Social Dimension of Dramatic Form and Function*, ed. Robert Schwartz (Baltimore, MA, 1978), esp. 112–60; Bernard Spivack, *Shakespeare and the Allegory of Evil: The History of a Metaphor in Relation to his Major Villains* (New York, 1958), esp. 130–50, quotation at 135; see also Happé, 'The Vice: A Checklist'.

gence of a highly developed professional theatre, actors found their occupation subject to increasingly severe legal and cultural restrictions. London's commercial playing companies had their origins in a deep authoritarian distrust of public performance that manifested itself in legislative and bureaucratic records, particularly after 1572. At the start of that year, instructions were issued for more stringent application of early Tudor legislation which required the punishment of unlawful retainers and also of the illegal bestowal of livery by nobles to anyone but their 'menials' and 'lawyers'.[12] That summer, 'An Acte for the punishement of Vacabondes and for Releif of the Poore and Impotent' specified imprisonment and branding for

> all and everye persone and persones beynge whole and mightye in Body and able to labour, havinge not Land or Maister, nor using any lawfull Marchaundize Crafte or Mysterye whereby hee or shee might get his or her Lyvinge, and can gyve no reckninge howe he or shee dothe lawfully get his or her Lyvinge; & all Fencers Bearewardes Comon Players in Enterludes & Minstrels, not belonging to any Baron of this Realme or towardes any other honourable Personage of greater Degree ... shalbee taken adjudged and deemed Rogues Vacaboundes and Sturdy Beggars.[13]

This restatement and clarification of a fifteenth-century legal tendency was ratified and expanded in later legislation under Elizabeth, and by a Jacobean act of 1604 which made similar corporal provision for 'idle persons ... usinge any subtile Crafte or unlawfull Games or Playes', but which in a parenthesis excluded those 'Players of Enterludes belonginge to any Baron of this Realme ... authorized to play under the Hande and Seale of Armes of such Baron'. The Jacobean revision also forbade Barons or 'other

---

[12] 'Proclamation for the Execution of the Laws made against Unlawful Retainers', repr. in 'Two Early Player-lists', ed. E. K. Chambers, in *Collections 1/4 and 5*, Malone Society 29 (Oxford, 1911), 348–56, at 350, in reference to 3 Hen. VII (1487) c. 15, in *The Statutes of the Realm*, 12 vols (London, 1810–28), 2: 522.

[13] 14 Eliz. c. 5, sect. 5, in *Statutes* 4: 590. For later continuations and amendments under Elizabeth in 1576 and 1584–5, see 18 Eliz. c. 3, and 37 Eliz. c. 11, in *Statutes*, 4: 610, 718.

honourable Personage[s]' from intervening in the 'Paines and Punishmentes' of those arrested under the act.[14]

Some had it that the actor's profession was not an occupation at all, but rather an expression of an essential nature. Anthony Munday, a respected dramatist himself and a collaborator of Shakespeare's, asked rhetorically:

> Are [players] not as variable in heart, as they are in their parts? Are they not as good practicers of bawdry, as enactors? ... Doth not their talk on the stage declare the nature of their disposition? ... Are they not notoriously known to be those men in their life abroad as they are on the stage: roisters, brawlers, ill-dealers, boasters, lovers, loiterers, ruffians?[15]

Jean-Christophe Agnew suggests that the perception of the itinerant actor as 'virtually indistinguishable' from 'the casual labourer and the wandering rogue' underwrote the players' inclusion in the vagrancy laws of 1572.[16] The plethora of tracts which subsequently emerged to describe the Elizabethan underworld frequently characterized vagabonds and criminals with a language not dissimilar to that used to describe theatrical work.[17]

Such association went hand in hand with Reformation attacks on the 'outward show' imputed to the Roman Catholic faith. According to John Foxe, Bishop Ridley at his trial 'did vehemently inuey against the Romysh Byshyp and all that foolysh apparell, callyng hym Antichrist, and the apparell foolysh and abominable, yea to[o] fond for a Vice in a play'; elsewhere Foxe offers the marginal gloss of 'Here commeth in the vice in the play' to describe a 'counterfayted Bishop' seen by Stephen Gratwicke at his

---

[14]   1 Jac. I c. 7, 'An Acte for the Continuance and Explanation of the Statute made in the 39th yeere of the Raigne of our late Queene Elizabeth, intituled An Acte for Punishmente of Rogues, Vagabondes and Sturdie Beggars ...', in *Statutes*, 4: 1024.

[15]   Anthony Munday, *A Second and Third Blast of Retrait from Plaies and Theaters* (London, 1580), 112, 115.

[16]   Jean-Christophe Agnew, *Worlds Apart: The Market and the Theater in Anglo-American Thought, 1550–1770* (Cambridge, 1986), 66.

[17]   For example, Robert Greene, *A Disputation Between a He-Cony-Catcher and a She-Cony-Catcher* (London, 1592), in A. V. Judges, ed., *The Elizabethan Underworld: A Collection of Tudor and Early Stuart Tracts and Ballads* (London, 1930), 206–47, at 211: 'Tush, we dissemble in show, we go so neat in apparel, so orderly in outward appearance'.

trial.[18] Indeed, Foxe's collaborator, John Bale, in his didactic drama of reformation, appropriated the tradition of the Vice precisely in order to satirize the abuses of the Church: thus in Bale's *Three Laws* (1538; produced again in 1562), the Vices of Idolatry, Sodomy, Ambition, Covetousness, False Doctrine and Hypocrisy were dressed as 'an olde wytche', 'a monke of all sectes', 'a byshop', 'a spyrituall lawer', 'a popysh doctour' and 'a graye friar' respectively.[19] Bale explicitly reassociated the Vice with the papacy in *King Johan* (1538), via the self-descriptions of Sedicyon:

I am Sedycyon, that with the Pope wyll hold
So long as I have a hole with in my breche ...

Yet was I neither borne [in England], in Spayne, nor in Fraunce
But under the Pope in the holy cyte of Rome,
And there wyll I dwell on to the days of dome ...[20]

Thus Roman Catholic faith was associated by Reformation theatre with the depraved theatricality of the Vice. But this cut both ways, and the theatre became increasingly exposed to the charge of idolatrous behaviour even as it was revolutionized by the opening of permanent or semi-permanent theatre houses in London. A very prominent feature of the Vice was its tendency to make a lot of its assumption of a different identity. From the late 1570s onwards, the associations of the actor with vagrancy and disorder fed into fresh iterations of the stage Vice. The actor playing Vice became Vice playing actor. One of the first early modern anti-theatrical pamphleteers, John Northbrooke, worried that 'players ... will rather wear a vizard than a natural face'.[21]

William Prynne, possibly the most aggressive early modern anti-theatricalist, was very clear about the way in which 'vice' was transmitted by plays – by the action and movement of the players 'personating' vice. In his ferocious attack, the controversial *Histrio-mastix* (1633), he wrote:

---

[18] John Foxe, *Actes and Monuments* (London, 1583), 1767, 1977.
[19] John Bale, *Three Laws*, in *The Complete Plays of John Bale*, ed. Peter Happé, 2 vols (Cambridge, 1986), 2: 64–121, at 121 (Gɪᵛ).
[20] Bale, *King Johan*, in *Complete Plays*, ed. Happé, 1: 29–99, lines 90–1, 182–4.
[21] John Northbrooke, *A Treatise Against Dicing, Dancing, Plays, and Interludes*, Shakespeare Society 14 (London, 1843; first publ. 1577), 73; see esp. Jonas Barish, *The Anti-Theatrical Prejudice* (Berkeley, CA, 1981).

> Stage-playes are so farre from working an abhorring [of vice], *that they produce, not only a loue and liking, but also an imitation of those pernicious vices that are acted in them,* which are commonly set forth with such *flexanimous rhetoricall pleasing, (or rather poysoning) streines; with such patheticall, liuely and sublime expressions, with such insinuating gestures* ... This practise therefore of acting Vices, doth onely propagate them, not restraine them.[22]

Another anti-theatricalist, William Rankins, suggested that '[p]layers ... present before [the audience's] eyes, as well in life as continual exercise, such enchanting charms, and bewitched wiles, to alienate their minds from virtue'. 'Abandon their presence', he urged, 'then ceaseth their power'.[23] The exact nature of this identification of actor with Vice is not fully revealed by Stephen Gosson, the foremost anti-theatrical pamphleteer, quoting Lactantius (d.c.325), advisor to the Emperor Constantine I: 'The expressing of vice by imitation brings us by the shadow, to the substance of the same'.[24] Rather, for Prynne and others, it was precisely the substance of the actor and his action, his 'personation' of vice, which propagated moral failure.[25] Indeed, Philip Stubbes translates a different part of Lactantius which goes more directly to the salient idea: 'the shameless gestures of players ... move the flesh to lust and uncleanness'.[26] This powerful perspective on acting was not a uniquely puritan phenomenon, and emerged partly from within dramatic culture itself. Gosson, Munday and Northbrooke were playwrights or actors before or even during their anti-theatrical writing. Their fully-fledged animosity can be traced with some certainty through to Ben Jonson's more moderate distaste for

[22] William Prynne, *Histriomastix. The players scourge, or, actors tragœdie, divided into two parts* (London, 1633; repr. New York, 1974), 103; italics are Prynne's.

[23] William Rankins, *A Mirrour of Monsters* (London, 1587), 2^v, 13^v.

[24] Stephen Gosson, *Plays Confuted in Five Actions* (London, 1582), G4^v.

[25] Prynne's collocation of ends and means is noted by the apologist Richard Baker, writing quite soon after the publication of *Histriomastix*: 'the *evil* of *Hypocrisie* is not in the *Act*, but in the *End*: and though *Players* may be guilty of the *Act*; yet certainly of the *End* they are not': Richard Baker, *Theatrum Redivivum, or the Theatre Vindicated* (London, 1662), repr. in Arthur Freeman, ed., *The English Stage: Attack and Defence 1577–1730* (London, 1973), 21.

[26] Phillip Stubbes, *The Anatomie of abuses* (London, 1583; repr. New York, 1973), L6^v. For the context of the original, see Lactantius, *Divine Institutes* 6.20.29, ed. and transl. Anthony Bowen and Peter Garnsey, Translated Texts for Historians 40 (Liverpool, 2003), 376.

performance. These writings reflected a profound dependence of theatre upon anti-theatre in the sixteenth and seventeenth centuries: the Vice embodied this co-dependence.

Above all, it was the perceived triviality of the theatre which made it such an incongruous and suspicious activity. Imagining the vices of the mind, Bernard of Clairvaux (d.1153) had described what one of his modern translators renders wonderfully as vice's 'crazy labor' – a phrase hinting at the way in which human vice was understood as misspent time and work, energy wasted in self-defeating activity, occupying the space 'far from the path' described by St Augustine.[27] For the city authorities of London, who towards the end of the sixteenth century began introducing increasingly stringent economic and spatial control not only of the theatres but of the population in general, the theatre's potential to distract large numbers of apprentices and servants from their work during the day disturbed not only religious sensibility but also social policy that emphasized control of a subject economic population. The oligarchy's complaints to the Privy Council frequently emphasized the theatre's vicious capacity to draw the young away from proper work.[28]

DISCERNMENT OF THEATRICAL SPIRITS

Something of this movement by which the actor became deeply associated with the theatrical Vice itself can be gleaned from the *Newe Enterlude of Vice* (1567), better known as *Horestes*, the first extant play in which the Vice was named explicitly, as well as arguably the first 'revenge tragedy' ever to be produced in England and thus an important feature in *Hamlet*'s cultural hinterland.[29] Here, in

[27] Bernard of Clairvaux, 'On Conversion', in *Sermons on Conversion*, ed. and transl. Marie-Bernard Said, Cistercian Fathers 25 (Kalamazoo, MI, 1981), 31–79, at 50; Augustine, *Confessions* 7.21, ed. and transl. F. J. Sheed (London: Sheed and Ward, 1944, repr. 1978), 121, translation adapted. On Augustine's anti-theatricalism, see ibid. 3.2, which associates theatrical spectacle with the communication of disease.

[28] For example, note the allusion to a complaint of 1601 which had lamented 'the inordinate resort and concourse of dissolute and idle people daiele unto publique stage plaies': Minute of Letter from the Privy Council to the Lord Mayor and Aldermen of London, 31 December 1601, repr. in 'Dramatic Records of the City of London: The Remembrancia', ed. E. K. Chambers and W. W. Greg, in *Collections* 1/1, Malone Society 6 (Oxford, 1907), 43–100, at 83.

[29] All reference is to John Pykering, *A Newe Enterlude of Vice conteyninge the Historye of Horestes with the cruell revengment of his Fathers death upon his one naturall Mother* (London, 1567), in Marie Axton, ed., *Three Tudor Classical Interludes* (Cambridge, 1982).

a crisis of secular and familial authority appropriate to the play's probable performance at the court's Christmas revels, the Vice 'Revenge' presents himself as 'the messenger of godes', goading the protagonist Horestes to avenge the death of his father at the hands of his mother. Revenge is focused on the job of developing the disharmony of the court, and as such threatens the integrity of the kingdom in a more worrying and antagonistic way than the other group of Vices in the play, who indulge only in slapstick and trivial word-games. Despite this, Revenge's invisible orchestrations and rhetorical mind-games cannot disguise the perfunctory relation of this Vice to the main character, Horestes. While Revenge insists parenthetically that he is born of the protagonist's mind – 'And I as gyde with you shall go to gyde you on the way. | By me (thy mind) ther wrathful dome shalbe performd in dede' (lines 192–3) – the reference to a dramatic convention seems almost strategic on his part, another way of manipulating Horestes. His closing soliloquy admits as much: 'Well, syeth from them I am bannyshyd so, | I wyll seke a new master, yf I can him finde' (lines 1080–1). The threat is revealed as worryingly durable and independent: his banishment effectively indicates the continuation of his peripheral threat in a definite social sense, as vagrant and Vice-for-hire.

This strong reliance of earlier Vice characterization upon the effect of single allegorical embodiment gave way to a more complex distribution of recognizable Vice faculties and functions. Nowhere is this distribution more ambivalent or complex than in Shakespeare's *Hamlet*. The dramaturgical tradition of the Vice contributes to *Hamlet*'s construction of the ambiguities of revenge-taking and conscience, and therefore to the deferral of his revenge.[30] While the structural position of the Vice is up for grabs in the play, it is the Prince himself who seems to inherit the figure's monopoly on verbal invention.[31] Catherine Belsey suggests that the play pits the incentive to revenge against the 'conscience' of its protagonist, and that the phrase 'conscience doth make cowards' (III. i. 82) can be traced back to the manipulations of previous Vice figures – certainly it should be related to the figure of Revenge itself in

[30] William Shakespeare, *The Tragical History of Hamlet, Prince of Denmark*, ed. Ann Thompson and Neil Taylor (London, 2006). All further reference is to this edition, based on the second Quarto publication of the play.

[31] See Weimann, *Tradition*, esp. 120–33; Michael E. Mooney, *Shakespeare's Dramatic Transactions* (Durham, NC, 1990), 77–81.

Horestes.[32] In *Horestes*, this Vice is also referred to as 'Courage' – a Vice name to be found elsewhere, such as in *The Tide tarrieth no man* (1576). However, *Hamlet's* most famous direct reference to the Vice comes in the Prince's description of his uncle Claudius as a 'vice of kings':

>   A murderer and a villain
> A slave that is not twentieth part the kith
> Of your precedent lord, a vice of kings,
> A cutpurse of the empire and the rule,
> That from a shelf the precious diadem stole
> And put it in his pocket –

QUEEN   No more!

HAMLET   – a king of shreds and patches –

>   *Enter GHOST.*

> Save me and hover o'er me with your wings,
>   You heavenly guards! What would your gracious figure?

QUEEN   Alas, he's mad.

>   (III. iv. 94–102)

Hamlet's rant is interrupted directly by the entrance of Old Hamlet's ghost, come 'to whet [Hamlet's] almost blunted purpose' (lines 106–7), a seeming 'gracious figure' to dispel the image of a Vice-king. At the height, then, of Hamlet's description of his father as the very antithesis of Claudius's Vice role, Old Hamlet assumes the position of vicious prompter familiar from Pykering's Revenge. The scene is further complicated by the possibility that this appearance of the Ghost is itself a delusion of Hamlet, some kind of 'psychomachic' projection of his interior world: 'This is the very coinage of your brain', exclaims Gertrude; 'This bodiless creation ecstasy | Is very cunning in' (lines 136–7). Here, the condition of faith represented by allegorical externalization has been transformed into the possibility of madness.

Indeed, Stephen Greenblatt has noted that the identification of spirits in Shakespeare's plays often shades into misidentification of humans as spirits, producing the effect of 'a nebulous infection, a bleeding of the spectral into the secular and the secular into the

---

[32] Catherine Belsey, 'The Case of Hamlet's Conscience', *Studies in Philology* 76 (1979), 127–48.

spectral'.[33] But the actor's presence was caught up in this process of 'infection'. Many productions of *Hamlet* have exploited these ambiguities by having the same actor play Claudius and the Ghost, a form of conceptual doubling inspired by the Prince's reference to 'uncle-father' (II. ii. 313), as Ann Thompson and Neil Taylor note.[34] Similarly, despite the increasing fame and popularity of the Vice making doubling difficult in some plays in which he dominated the action (e.g. Nichol Newfangle in *Like wil to like quod the Deuel to the Colier*, c.1570), Ambidexter and Triall in Preston's *Cambises* (1569) had been played by a single actor, as had Revenge and Nature in *Horestes* (1567), and the demon-vice Titivillus and Mercy in the much older *Mankind* (1465–70). As Michael Camille suggests, 'evil was not an idea to medieval people [but] was real and had bodies'; likewise, the Vice's early modern threat had coincided traditionally with its non-representational dimension, that is, its apparently real presence on stage (an effect achieved by the close association of the figure with the processes of theatrical production itself).[35] The problem of the Ghost's ethereality in *Hamlet* – and the question of how to discern this 'spirit' – thus had implications linked to perceptions of the actor as Vice. The Vice was a custom 'to be quoted and recalled', as Robert Weimann writes.[36] In other words, recognition of the Vice was part of its growing appeal: this is indicated by Ben Jonson's sardonic references to the popularity of the figure in later plays.[37] Yet in *Hamlet*, recognition of the Vice was transformed into the possible misrecognition of Old Hamlet.

CONCLUSIONS

It has been suggested here that this tremendously productive period for English theatre relied on the power of a strain of anti-theatre in English religious culture. A suspicion of the theatre helped forge the rich traditions available to Shakespeare and his contemporaries. At the root of the Vice's power was its embodiment or incarnation

---

[33] Stephen Greenblatt, *Hamlet in Purgatory* (Princeton, NJ, 2001), esp. 180–95; quotation at 195.

[34] 'Appendix 5: Casting', in *Hamlet*, ed. Thompson and Taylor, 553–65, at 560.

[35] Michael Camille, *The Gothic Idol: Ideology and Image-Making in Medieval Art* (Cambridge, 1989), 63.

[36] Weimann, *Popular Tradition*, 150–1.

[37] See esp. Ben Jonson, *The Devil is an Ass*, ed. Peter Happé (Manchester, 1994), I. i. 40–6, in which the Vice 'Iniquity' is summoned ironically.

of moral weakness. I have argued that this anxiety around theatrical processes of embodiment was transferred from the Vice to the professional actor, thus allowing an ancient theological phenomenon to define a social reality and expand the scope of dramaturgical uncertainty in early modern England. The Vice figure in its familiar form vanished from the Tudor stage at around the same time that the professional player emerged: the ramifications of this transformation are yet to be properly described.

Corpus Christi College, Cambridge

WILLIAM PERKINS'S *THE ARTE OF PROPHECYING*: A LITERARY MANIFESTO

by W. B. PATTERSON

Illiam Perkins, the late sixteenth-century Cambridge theologian and one of the best-selling authors of his time, wrote the first major English book on preaching. During his ministry in Cambridge, as a fellow of Christ's College and lecturer at Great St Andrew's Church, he also preached a large number of sermons, which illustrated the art he taught.[1] Historians of preaching have generally seen him as the chief proponent of the puritan 'plain style', a way of preaching sometimes contrasted with the learned, elaborate, 'metaphysical' style of preaching fashionable in the Established Church during the early seventeenth century.[2] Recently it has been argued that preachers like Perkins

[1] The fullest account of Perkins as theologian, writer and preacher is that of Ian Breward, ed., *The Work of William Perkins*, Courtenay Library of Reformation Classics 3 (Abingdon, 1970), 1–131. For recent scholarship, see Paul R. Schaefer, 'Protestant "Scholasticism" at Elizabethan Cambridge: William Perkins and a Reformed Theology of the Heart', in Carl R. Trueman and R. Scott Clark, eds., *Protestant Scholasticism: Essays in Reassessment* (Carlisle, 1999), 147–64; Bryan D. Spinks, *Two Faces of Elizabethan Anglican Theology: Sacraments and Salvation in the Thought of William Perkins and Richard Hooker* (Lanham, MD, 1999), 1–92; Lori Anne Ferrell, 'Transfiguring Theology: William Perkins and Calvinist Aesthetics', in Christopher Highley and John N. King, eds, *John Foxe and His World* (Aldershot, 2002), 160–79; Karen Bruhn, 'Pastoral Polemic: William Perkins, the Godly Evangelicals, and the Shaping of a Protestant Community in Early Modern England', *Anglican and Episcopal History* 72 (2003), 102–27; W. B. Patterson, 'William Perkins as Apologist for the Church of England', *JEH* 57 (2006), 252–69. For the popularity of Perkins's books, see David McKitterick, *A History of Cambridge University Press*, 3 vols (Cambridge, 1992–2004), 1: 125–9, 133, 139, 231–3; Ian Green, *Print and Protestantism in Early Modern England* (Oxford, 2000), 8, 17–18, 106, 211, 215, 223, 241, 266, 308, 311, 479, 498, 556, 647–8. I am extremely grateful to David Parry of Cambridge University and William Engel of the University of the South for their advice on the subject of this essay.

[2] J. W. Blench, *Preaching in England in the Late Fifteenth and Sixteenth Centuries: A Study of English Sermons, 1450 – c. 1600* (Oxford, 1964), 58, 64, 101–2, 169; Horton Davies, *Worship and Theology in England*, 1: *From Cranmer to Hooker, 1534–1603* (Princeton, NJ, 1970), 72, 257, 272, 305, 308–10, 312–13, 320–3; Edward H. Davidson, '"God's Well-Trodden Foot-Paths": Puritan Preaching and Sermon Form', *Texas Studies in Literature and Language* 25 (1983), 503–27; Joseph A. Pipa, 'William Perkins and the Development of Puritan Preaching' (Ph.D. thesis, Westminster Theological Seminary, 1985); Horton Davies, *Like Angels from a Cloud: The English Metaphysical Preachers, 1588–1645* (San Marino, CA, 1986), 47; James Thomas Ford, 'Preaching in the Reformed Tradition',

were so insistent on the moral demands of the Scriptures, particularly those of the Old Testament, that they became increasingly unpopular in the English Church. According to Christopher Haigh, preaching of the kind favoured by Perkins and like-minded ministers – morally demanding, hortatory and focused on predestination – was deeply resented and strongly resisted by many English parishioners, who helped to fashion what he describes as a more relaxed, 'anglicised' Protestantism that they found more congenial.[3] Peter Iver Kaufman has written that Perkins, like other members of what he calls 'the Protestant opposition to Elizabethan religious reform', aimed to shame his hearers, and that 'at Cambridge, [he] taught the next generation of dissident preachers to shame and thus save their parishioners'.[4] Some parishioners were no doubt made uncomfortable by Perkins and preachers influenced by him. But these recent assessments of Perkins and his place in the history of preaching are misleading and inadequate. They underestimate the character and extent of his influence on preaching. Moreover, many commentators have failed to recognize the effect of Perkins's views on the development of English prose. This essay will show what Perkins taught in his treatise on preaching, and argue for its lasting significance for modern prose style.

Perkins's *The Arte of Prophecying* was published in Latin as *Prophetica* in 1592 and in an English translation by Thomas Tuke in 1607, five years after Perkins's death.[5] 'Prophecying', the word chosen by Perkins's translator for the title of the book, was scriptural. But it also reflected current usage. 'Prophesyings' were assemblies or conferences, chiefly of clergymen, which were held in

in Larissa Taylor, ed., *Preachers and People in the Reformations and Early Modern Period* (Leiden, 2001), 65–88, esp. 75–9.

3   Christopher Haigh, 'The Taming of Reformation: Preachers, Pastors and Parishioners in Elizabethan and Early Stuart England', *History* 85 (2000), 572–88; for Perkins, see 572–3, 577–8, 581, 583–4. See also idem, *The Plain Man's Pathways to Heaven: Kinds of Christianity in Post-Reformation England* (Oxford, 2007), 124, 130, 206–7.

4   Peter Iver Kaufman, 'The Protestant Opposition to Elizabethan Religious Reform', in Robert Tittler and Norman Jones, eds, *A Companion to Tudor Britain* (Oxford, 2004), 271–88; quotation at 280.

5   William Perkins, *Prophetica: sive, De sacra et vnica ratione concionandi tractatus* (Cambridge, 1592); *The Arte of Prophecying: or, A Treatise Concerning the Sacred and Only True Manner and Methode of Preaching*, transl. Thomas Tuke (London, 1607). Tuke was an undergraduate at Christ's College, Cambridge, during the time that Perkins taught there. After ordination, he served several parish churches in London: *ODNB, s.n.* 'Tuke, Thomas (1580/81–1657)'.

England in the 1560s and 1570s. At these gatherings, a minister delivered a sermon which was then discussed by those attending. The discussion focused on the sermon's form, content and contemporary relevance. The intention of the prophesyings was to improve the participants' understanding of the Scriptures and to provide an example of how a text could be treated in a sermon.[6] Since there was an acute shortage of clergy in the early years of Elizabeth I's reign, especially of those trained to preach, the prophesyings provided a means of clerical education. Archbishop Edmund Grindal, the primate of the English Church, favoured the prophesyings, as long as they were appropriately supervised. The queen saw them as potentially subversive and sectarian, and in 1576 she ordered the archbishop to suppress them. When Grindal refused to do so, she suspended him from his spiritual functions.[7] However, as Patrick Collinson has shown, the idea behind the prophesyings continued to attract the support of many clergy and laity, and it was sometimes realized in the form of conferences of clergy and municipally sponsored lectures or sermons.[8] Perkins's book seems clearly intended to promote the same educational purpose that the prophesyings had originally been organized to advance. Many historians have labelled the prophesyings, along with the conferences and lectures that succeeded them, as 'puritan'. But this is certainly not an accurate description of all such arrangements. There is no reason to think that effective preaching was exclusively a concern of members of the puritan movement. Other bishops beside Grindal, and many clergy and laity at all levels, were convinced, as Perkins was, that an educated preaching ministry was essential to the well-being of the Church of England.

---

6 Patrick Collinson, *The Elizabethan Puritan Movement* (London, 1967), 168–239; idem, *Archbishop Grindal, 1519–1583: The Struggle for a Reformed Church* (Berkeley, CA, 1979), 219–82. See also Peter Iver Kaufman, 'Prophesying Again', *ChH* 68 (1999), 337–58. Kaufman argues that the queen feared that substantial numbers of the laity would be attracted to the prophesyings, threatening the stability of church and state.

7 Collinson, *Grindal*, 233–52.

8 Patrick Collinson, 'Lectures by Combination: Structures and Characteristics of Church Life in 17th-Century England', in idem, *Godly People: Essays on English Protestantism and Puritanism* (London, 1983), 467–98; Patrick Collinson, John Craig and Brett Usher, eds, *Conferences and Combination Lectures in the Elizabethan Church: Dedham and Bury St Edmunds, 1582–1590* (London, 2003), xxi–cxvi. See also Paul S. Seaver, *The Puritan Lectureships: The Politics of Religious Dissent, 1560–1662* (Stanford, CA, 1970). Seaver's contention that lectureships were generally a source of religious and political dissent, however, is doubtful; see Collinson, 'Lectures by Combination', esp. 497.

When Perkins wrote *The Arte of Prophecying*, rhetoric, or the art of speaking and writing clearly and persuasively, was at the heart of the Cambridge undergraduate curriculum. Rhetoric had been a part of the curriculum at Cambridge since the university's founding in the thirteenth century, but in the late Middle Ages it had been largely superseded by dialectic and natural philosophy, which eventually became the natural sciences. A significant change occurred in the late fifteenth century, however, when, as Damien Riehl Leader has written, there was 'a gradual movement away from medieval logic as the primary study of the undergraduate, and a growing emphasis on classical literature that was codified by statute in 1488'.[9] The renewed interest in rhetoric came by way of the Renaissance stress on classical culture, and was partly a result of the rediscovery and appropriation of key ancient texts by Cicero and Quintilian. Humanist writers took as a model the orator, as described by Cicero, and strove to acquire and cultivate skills in written as well as oral compositions.[10]

At Cambridge, studies in rhetoric and dialectic were closely linked, as Lisa Jardine has shown. Basing her analysis on surviving book lists of members of Cambridge University who died between 1535 and 1590, she has written: 'we get a picture of the [undergraduate] course as one focused on the formal analysis of language in dialectic, supported by study of forensic oratory (particularly Cicero), Latin literature and historical background from the standard epitomes and some more sophisticated instruction in style and ornament'.[11] Quentin Skinner has shown that the study of rhetoric, based principally on texts by or attributed to Cicero, was central to the course of studies in English schools

---

[9]   Damian Riehl Leader, *A History of the University of Cambridge*, 1: *The University to 1546* (Cambridge, 1994), 32, 113–21, 236–42, 304–6, at 236–7. See also Wilbur Samuel Howell, *Logic and Rhetoric in England, 1500–1700* (Princeton, NJ, 1956), 64–145.

[10]   Hannah H. Gray, 'Renaissance Humanism: The Pursuit of Eloquence', *JHI* 24 (1963), 497–514; John Monfasani, 'Humanism and Rhetoric', in Albert Rabil Jr, ed., *Renaissance Humanism: Foundations, Forms, and Legacy*, 3: *Humanism and the Disciplines* (Philadelphia, PA, 1988), 171–235; Paul Oskar Kristeller, 'Rhetoric in Medieval and Renaissance Culture', in James J. Murphy, ed., *Renaissance Eloquence: Studies in the Theory and Practice of Renaissance Rhetoric* (Berkeley, CA, 1983), 1–19.

[11]   Lisa Jardine, 'Humanism and the Sixteenth Century Cambridge Arts Course', *History of Education* 4 (1975), 16–31, at 20; cf. eadem, 'The Place of Dialectic Teaching in Sixteenth-Century Cambridge', *Studies in the Renaissance* 21 (1974), 31–62.

and at both English universities in the late sixteenth century.[12] Aristotle's treatment of rhetoric was less influential, though John Rainolds lectured on Aristotle's *The Art of Rhetoric* at Oxford in the 1570s.[13] The undergraduate curriculum in Perkins's time at Cambridge was in large part aimed at developing facility in the use of the ancient languages in accordance with classical models and skill in constructing logical, coherent and persuasive arguments. This did not mean that the truth of the subject matter being discussed was unimportant. To Perkins, truth was all-important. His approach to teaching the art of preaching stressed the interpretation of Scripture as the source of the truths that ultimately mattered to the preacher and his hearers. Like other Protestant theologians in England and elsewhere, he stressed knowing the contents of the Bible, understanding its teachings, and communicating those teachings to men and women of all conditions of life and in all spiritual states.[14]

In *The Arte of Prophecying*, Perkins freely acknowledged his indebtedness to other writers whose books on preaching he had found particularly useful. They included the leading father of the Western Church, Augustine, who had once been a teacher of rhetoric, and the 'Prince of the Humanists', Erasmus of Rotterdam, whose treatise on preaching, *Ecclesiastes*, was the most comprehensive book on the subject during the European Renaissance.[15] They also included a succession of Lutheran scholars: Matthias Flacius Illyricus, Niels Hemmingsen, Johan Wigandus, and Andreas Gerardus of Ypres, from which city came his surname of Hyperius. Hemmingsen, also called Hemingius or Hemminge, was the author of a book translated into English as *The Preacher* in 1574.[16] Hyperius,

---

[12] Quentin Skinner, *Reason and Rhetoric in the Philosophy of Hobbes* (Cambridge, 1996, repr. 2004), 19–65. For the importance of rhetorical education for teaching and religious writing, see Peter Mack, *Elizabethan Rhetoric: Theory and Practice* (Cambridge, 2002), 253–92.

[13] Skinner, *Reason and Rhetoric*, 36; cf. Lawrence D. Green, ed., *John Rainolds's Oxford Lectures on Aristotle's Rhetoric* (Newark, DE, 1986).

[14] For the intellectual journey of one Renaissance humanist who became a Protestant theologian, see Serene Jones, *Calvin and the Rhetoric of Piety* (Louisville, KY, 1995), 1–46.

[15] For Perkins's list of the writers whom he found most useful, see *Prophetica*, 127; *The Arte of Prophecying*, 148. For Erasmus's *Ecclesiastes*, see John W. O'Malley, 'Erasmus and the History of Sacred Rhetoric: The "Ecclesiastes" of 1534', *Erasmus of Rotterdam Society Yearbook* 5 (1985), 1–29.

[16] Niels Hemmingsen [Nicholas Hemminge], *The Preacher or Method of Preachinge*,

whom Yngve Brilioth described as 'the first proper theoretician of the evangelical sermon', was the author of the influential work *De formandis concionibus sacris*, translated into English as *The Practise of Preaching* in 1577.[17] Perkins also cited the Reformed scholars Theodore Beza and Franciscus Junius. He did not cite Pierre de la Ramée (Ramus), but there is no doubt that the work of this French Huguenot philosopher and theologian profoundly influenced him.[18] As Donald McKim has shown, Perkins's stress on clear, straightforward definitions, his tendency to divide subjects into two parts and then to subdivide them further, his practice of moving from the general to the particular, and his search for practical uses suggested by biblical teachings are all features of the 'art' and 'method' that he shared with the French writer.[19]

Perkins emphasizes that the substance of preaching must be the word of God. He states that the word of God is the 'perfect and equall obiect of Preaching'; it is 'the wisdome of God concerning the trueth'.[20] The word of God is 'in the holy Scripture', which Perkins describes as having been 'written in a language fit for the Church by men immediately called to be the Clerks or Secretaries of the holy Ghost'.[21] The Scriptures are sufficient for the purpose for which they were written, pure in that they are 'voide of deceit

---

transl. I. H. (London, 1574). For Flacius Illyricus, Hemmingsen and Hyperius, see Debora K. Shuger, *Sacred Rhetoric: The Christian Grand Style in the English Renaissance* (Princeton, NJ, 1988), 64–76, 110–17, 160–73; Olivier Millet, 'La Réforme protestante et la rhétorique (circa 1520–1550)', in Marc Fumaroli, ed., *Histoire de la rhétorique dans l'Europe moderne, 1450–1950* (Paris, 1999), 259–312, esp. 274–5, 301–8; Jameela Lares, *Milton and the Preaching Arts* (Cambridge, 2001), 48–108. Lives of Hemmingsen, Hyperius, and Wigandus are included in Thomas Fuller, ed., *Abel Redevivus: or, The Dead Yet Speaking, the Lives and Deaths of the Moderne Divines* (London, 1651), 413–14, 264–70.

[17] Yngve Brilioth, *A Brief History of Preaching* (Philadelphia, PA, 1965), 125; Andreas Hyperius, *The Practise of Preaching, Otherwise Called the Pathway to the Pulpet Conteyning an Excellent Method How to Frame Diuine Sermons, & to Interpret the Holy Scriptures According to the Capacitie of the Vulgar People* (London, 1577).

[18] Howell, *Logic and Rhetoric*, 146–281; Walter Ong, *Ramus, Method, and the Decay of Dialogue: From the Art of Discourse to the Art of Reason* (Cambridge, MA, 1958); Frances A. Yates, *The Art of Memory* (London, 1966), 231–42. For Ramus's innovative revision of traditional Aristotelian logic, see Pierre de la Ramée, *Dialectiqve* (Paris, 1555).

[19] Donald K. McKim, 'The Functions of Ramism in William Perkins' Theology', *SCJ* 16 (1985), 503–17; idem, *Ramism in William Perkins' Theology* (New York, 1987), esp. 80–91. See also Brian Cummings, *The Literary Culture of the Reformation: Grammar and Grace* (Oxford, 2002), 256–63.

[20] Perkins, *Prophetica*, 4; *Arte of Prophecying*, 4.

[21] Perkins, *Prophetica*, 6; *Arte of Prophecying*, 6.

and error', and 'canonical' because they stand as 'a Rule or Line' for the determination of controversies in the Church.[22] To make clear which are the writings that make up the sacred Scriptures, Perkins lists and describes the books of the Old and New Testaments, distinguishing them from the books of the so-called Apocrypha.[23] By what criteria are the authentic books determined? There is, he says, one proof that is certain: 'the inward testimony of the holy Ghost speaking in the Scriptures, and not only telling a man within his heart, but also effectually perswading him that these bookes of the Scripture are the word of God'.[24] As for the Church's role in the process of determining the contents of the canon of Scripture, Perkins points to 'the perpetuall consent of the Church', witnessed to by the church fathers, the councils and the scholastic theologians.[25]

By what principles of interpretation are the Scriptures to be explained? Perkins's treatment of this subject constitutes a major portion of the book. He makes clear that any adequate attempt to interpret them from the pulpit must come after an extensive preparation, in effect suggesting a plan of study. Preparation should begin with a review of theology, with its 'definitions, diuisions, and explications'.[26] Perkins recommends that Scripture should then be read systematically, beginning with Paul's Epistle to the Romans and the Gospel according to John, and proceeding to the other New Testament books. The reading of the Old Testament should begin with the Psalms and then proceed to the prophets, especially Isaiah. The historical books of the Old Testament should come next, with special attention given to Genesis.[27] Perkins's order emphasized books of special importance to Protestants: it begins with the Epistle to the Romans, in which Paul treats divine grace in salvation in a way that was to shape the theology of the Reformers. Those embarked on this study are to use the 'arts', thereby employing 'a grammaticall, rhetoricall, and logicall analysis'

---

[22] Perkins, *Prophetica*, 4–6; *Arte of Prophecying*, 5–7.

[23] Perkins, *Prophetica*, 7–14, 20; *Arte of Prophecying*, 8–17, 24–5.

[24] Perkins, *Prophetica*, 14–15; *Arte of Prophecying*, 17.

[25] Perkins, *Prophetica*, 17–18; *Arte of Prophecying*, 20–1. For Perkins's approach to the church fathers, see Jean-Louis Quantin, *The Church of England and Christian Antiquity: The Construction of a Confessional Identity in the 17th Century* (Oxford, 2009), 64–6.

[26] Perkins, *Prophetica*, 21; *Arte of Prophecying*, 26.

[27] Perkins, *Prophetica*, 22; *Arte of Prophecying*, 26–7.

of the Scriptures.[28] Most important and preliminary to everything else is prayer: 'God must earnestly be sued vnto by prayer, that he would open the meaning of the Scriptures to vs.'[29]

Perkins proceeds from this plan of study to consider how to interpret a particular passage in order to open up 'the words and sentences of the Scripture', in such a way 'that one entire and naturall sense may appeare'.[30] He insists, despite the Roman Catholic teaching that recognized four senses in the Scriptures, that there is only one sense, namely the literal. As for the allegorical sense, Perkins asserts that the allegories in Scripture constitute 'a certaine manner of vttering the same sense'.[31] Both the tropological and the anagogical senses, the remaining two senses in the fourfold method of interpretation, are, in his view, applications rather than senses. The tropological is a moral application; the anagogical is a mystical application relating to the afterlife.[32] In the process of examining the text, the preacher should ask several questions. What is the relation of this passage or text to the overarching themes of Scripture as expressed in the Church's articles of belief? Under what circumstances was the text written, to whom, on what occasion and for what purpose? And what other passages in the Old Testament and the New Testament throw light on the text? It should not be assumed, he argues, that thematically related passages convey exactly the same meaning. Sometimes, for example, a passage in the New Testament elaborates on or circumscribes a passage in the Old Testament.[33] When assembling passages for comparison, he comments, 'the Greeke and Hebrew concordances serue very fitlie'.[34] Preaching ought to be biblical, doctrinal and practical, and not restricted to subjects that are narrowly spiritual.

Perkins writes perceptively of applying biblical teachings so as to fit the diverse needs of a congregation.[35] A preacher is most effective, he says, when he knows his people. In dealing with this subject Perkins describes a series of spiritual states. There are 'vnbeleeuers

[28] Perkins, *Prophetica*, 22; *Arte of Prophecying*, 26.
[29] Perkins, *Prophetica*, 23; *Arte of Prophecying*, 28.
[30] Perkins, *Prophetica*, 25; *Arte of Prophecying*, 30.
[31] Perkins, *Prophetica*, 25; *Arte of Prophecying*, 31.
[32] Perkins, *Prophetica*, 25; *Arte of Prophecying*, 30–1.
[33] Perkins, *Prophetica*, 26–38; *Arte of Prophecying*, 31–43.
[34] Perkins, *Prophetica*, 35; *Arte of Prophecying*, 41.
[35] Perkins, *Prophetica*, 85; *Arte of Prophecying*, 99.

who are both ignorant and vnteachable', those who are 'teachable, but yet ignorant', those who 'haue knowledge, but are not yet humbled', those who 'are humbled', those who 'beleeue', those who 'are fallen' into grievous sin, and, finally, 'a mingled people'.[36] None of the persons in these states is to be considered lost to God's love and mercy. Those in the first category, for example, though they seem to be unteachable, should be reasoned with and made ready 'to receiue the doctrine of the word'.[37] The most effective message is one that combines the law and the gospel. Perkins argues that faith, love and obedience to God's commands all have a place in the plan of salvation, which is an ongoing process in this life. Only in dealing with persons who 'haue knowledge, but are not yet humbled' does he specify an approach aimed at producing deep sorrow for sin and, consequently, 'the foundation of repentance'.[38] The preacher in this case is to attempt to evoke sorrow for sin, using some particularly relevant part of the scriptural law. Sorrow on the part of the person in this state must be for the sin itself, not just for 'outward calamities' or fear of punishment.[39] Repentance may then begin through the actions of the Holy Spirit, who 'reneweth men, that they begin to will and to worke those things that are pleasing to God'.[40] Perkins's advice in this chapter – entitled 'how to use and applie doctrines' – is that the minister is to do much more than preach sermons. The procedures Perkins describes involve disputing and reasoning, teaching and catechizing, hearing private confessions and offering pastoral counseling. Private or auricular confession, a practice central to Roman Catholic spiritual discipline, was advocated by Calvin in cases in which a Christian was 'afflicted with a sense of sins' and 'unable to free himself from them'. The penitent was advised by Calvin to confess in private to the pastor and receive consolation and gospel teaching.[41] If no one in the congregation is to be regarded as so spiritually impoverished as to be beyond the hope

---

[36] Perkins, *Prophetica*, 87, 90, 93, 96, 98, 99 [misnumbered 69], 103; *Arte of Prophecying*, 102, 105, 109, 112, 115, 116, 121.

[37] Perkins, *Prophetica*, 87–8; *Arte of Prophecying*, 102–3.

[38] Perkins, *Prophetica*, 93; *Arte of Prophecying*, 109.

[39] Perkins, *Prophetica*, 94; *Arte of Prophecying*, 110–11.

[40] Perkins, *Prophetica*, 95 [misnumbered 94]; *Arte of Prophecying*, 111.

[41] John Calvin, *Institutes of the Christian Religion*, 3.4.12, ed. John T. McNeill, 2 vols, LCC (Philadelphia, PA, 1960), 1: 637.

of redemption, so also no one is to be regarded as having been so completely renewed by the Holy Spirit as not to need further help and encouragement. The preacher is to remember that 'the assemblies of our Churches' are 'a mixt people'. The minister is to preach in the inclusive way that Jesus himself did at the Feast of the Tabernacles: 'Now in the last and great day of the Feast, Iesus stoode and cried, saying, If any man thirst let him come vnto mee and drinke.'[42]

Application also involves applying the text to the beliefs or behaviour of members of the congregation. From 2 Timothy 3: 16, Perkins draws four terms that he uses to describe the way the Scriptures are to be applied: 'The whole Scripture is giuen by God's inspiration, and is profitable for doctrine ... for Redargution or improouing, for correction ... and for instruction ... in righteousnesse.' The first two terms relate chiefly to belief or what Perkins calls 'Mentall' application; the last two to behaviour, or what he calls 'Practicall' application.[43] In dealing with belief, the preacher is to teach and inform his hearers about doctrine and to reprove them for errors.[44] Perkins says that in reproving, the minister should discuss matters that are 'thoroughly understood' in the congregation and which currently 'trouble the Church', rather than esoteric or archaic heresies.[45] In dealing with behaviour, the preacher is to give instruction about how to live well in the family, the commonwealth and the Church, and to correct actions that are not in keeping with scriptural teachings.[46] Concerning admonition, Perkins offers the following advice:

> This must be done, first generally, the circumstances of the persons being omitted ... Afterwards, if the former reproofe preuaile not, it must be vrged after a more speciall manner ... But alwaies, in the hatred of sinne, let the loue of the person appeare in the speeches; and let the Minister include himselfe (if he may) in his reprehension, that it may be more milde and gentle.[47]

42 Perkins, *Prophetica*, 103; *Arte of Prophecying*, 121.
43 Perkins, *Prophetica*, 104; *Arte of Prophecying*, 122.
44 Perkins, *Prophetica*, 104; *Arte of Prophecying*, 122–3.
45 Perkins, *Prophetica*, 104–5; *Arte of Prophecying*, 123.
46 Perkins, *Prophetica*, 105; *Arte of Prophecying*, 124.
47 Perkins, *Prophetica*, 105–6; *Arte of Prophecying*, 124–5.

Perkins cites in this connection 1 Corinthians 4: 6, where Paul points out that he too stands under judgement alongside those whom he exhorts to better actions.[48]

In the 'promulgation or vttering' of the sermon, two things are required: 'the hiding of human wisdome, and the demonstration (or shewing) of the spirit'. The first involves a paradox, since the preacher is expected to use all the arts and tools available in 'framing' the sermon, but he must not display this learning when he delivers the sermon, since this would be seen as trying to enhance the power of God's word. The word, which is the 'Testimonie of God, and the profession of the knowledge of Christ', needs no enhancement, but needs only to be clearly set forth. Perkins denies that this is to admit 'barbarisme', that is, ignorance or lack of education and skill, into the pulpit. It is the nature of art, he asserts, 'to conceale Art'. This is a classical adage, one version of which is found in Ovid's *The Art of Love*.[49] Such concealment, in the interest of doing nothing to detract from the power of God's word, applies to 'the matter of the sermon' as well as 'the setting forth of the words'.[50] The second requirement is to demonstrate the guidance of the Holy Spirit, which Perkins describes as follows: 'The Demonstration of the spirit is, when as the Minister of the word doth in the time of preaching so behaue himselfe, that all, euen ignorant persons & vnbeleeuers may iudge, that it is not so much hee that speaketh, as the Spirit of God in him and by him.'[51] He should, in other words, speak with conviction, boldness and passion. As Debora K. Shuger says of Perkins's rhetorical theory: 'The Holy Spirit does not simply pass through the speaker like light through glass but first transforms and arouses him, and his own inspired passion then enables him to stir others.'[52] The language used in the sermon should be 'both simple and perspicuous fit both for the peoples vnderstanding and to expresse the maiestie of the spirit'.[53]

Finally, what should be the form or general structure of the sermon? Perkins's description is remarkably simple and modest,

---

[48]   Perkins, *Prophetica*, 106; *Arte of Prophecying*, 125.

[49]   Ovid, *The Art of Love, and Other Poems*, transl. J. H. Mozley, LCL 232 (London, 1957), 86–7 (2.313).

[50]   Perkins, *Prophetica*, 112–13; *Arte of Prophecying*, 132–3.

[51]   Perkins, *Prophetica*, 113; *Arte of Prophecying*, 133.

[52]   Shuger, *Sacred Rhetoric*, 70.

[53]   Perkins, *Prophetica*, 114; *Arte of Prophecying*, 134–5.

consisting of four points. First, 'read the Text distinctly out of the Canonical Scriptures'. Second, 'giue the sense and vnderstanding of it, by the Scripture it selfe'. Third, 'collect a few and profitable points of doctrine out of the naturall sense'. And, fourth, 'applie (if he haue the gift) the doctrines rightly collected to the life and manners of men', presumably with reference to the congregation the preacher serves, expressed 'in a simple and plaine speech'.[54] Perkins sees the sermon as the climax to a thorough and deliberate process of coming to understand the scriptural text and of applying its contents to the needs of people whom the preacher knows well and to the experiences that both he and they encounter.

Perkins's book on preaching provides succinct advice to clergymen in the Church of England about one of their most important responsibilities. It offers clear reasons why preaching is important, namely for the education of their congregations in the message and meaning of the Scriptures, seen as containing the word of God for those in a variety of spiritual conditions. Sermons, Perkins argues, should respond to the needs of members of the congregation, ranging from those who are largely ignorant in matters of the faith to those who are committed and knowledgeable believers. Only in the case of those who 'haue knowledge, but are not yet humbled' does Perkins advocate the propounding of the law in such a way as to produce sorrow and thus an openness to the Holy Spirit, who can lead such persons to repentance and renewal. Since the preacher in a parish of the English Church typically addressed a 'mixt people', he would, if he followed Perkins's advice, use a mixture of teachings derived from a close reading of the text. These teachings, Perkins makes clear, are to be applied by the preacher to the circumstances in which he and his parishioners live.

In producing a Renaissance / Reformation rhetoric, in accordance with the Elizabethan religious settlement and in response to the needs of the English Church, Perkins did not want his university-trained students and colleagues to turn away from what they had learned in studying rhetoric but to use it in giving expression to what he and other English Protestants saw as their rich scriptural and theological heritage.

Perkins was one of the major English Protestant theologians in an era rich in religious thought. His theory of preaching was

---

54 Perkins, *Prophetica*, 126; *Arte of Prophecying*, 148.

significant beyond its specifically religious teaching. A familiar view of the development of English prose is that a modern way of writing and speaking emerged in the Restoration era, under the influence of the Royal Society and the rise of modern science. Thomas Sprat wrote in his *History of the Royal Society* (1667) that members were expected to submit reports on their experimental work in such a way as to avoid 'amplifications, disgressions, and swellings of style'. Sprat continued: 'They have exacted from all their members, a close, naked, natural way of speaking; positive expressions; clear senses; a native easiness; bringing all things as near the Mathematical plainness, as they can: and preferring the language of Artizans, Countrymen, and Merchants, before that, of Wits, or Scholars.'[55] Then, as this view holds, a new and simpler way of expressing oneself in English emerged. In place of the rich, complex, Latinate and metaphorical prose writing of many Elizabethan and early Stuart writers, writing came to be marked by other qualities. Brevity, clarity and concreteness came to be highly regarded. Ordinary language was preferred in public discourse. Persuasive arguments were considered likely to be those that stressed relevance and succinctness. Brian Vickers, however, has argued effectively that Sprat's formulation was intended to apply to scientific discourse and was not widely known in its time.[56] Vickers contends that the prose of the Restoration era was actually 'exuberant, inventive, imaginative, expressive, polemical, forceful, at times undisciplined, never "scientific"'.[57]

Nevertheless, there were persistent and forceful calls during the Restoration period for a plain style in religion and politics as well as in natural philosophy.[58] Plainness was stressed in the

---

[55] Thomas Sprat, *History of the Royal-Society of London, For the Improving of Natural Knowledge* (London, 1667), 113. For an influential commentary, see Richard Foster Jones, 'Science and English Prose Style in the Third Quarter of the Seventeenth Century', in idem, *The Seventeenth Century: Studies in English Thought and Literature from Bacon to Pope* (Stanford, CA, 1951), 75–110.

[56] Brian Vickers, 'The Royal Society and English Prose Style: A Reassessment', in idem and Nancy S. Struever, *Rhetoric and the Pursuit of Truth: Language Change in the Seventeenth and Eighteenth Centuries* (Los Angeles, CA, 1985), 1–76, esp. 6–9. See also the critical assessment of Sprat's programme in Robert Adolph, *The Rise of Modern Prose Style* (Cambridge, MA, 1968), 114–23.

[57] Vickers, 'The Royal Society and English Prose Style', 22.

[58] James Grantham Turner, 'From Revolution to Restoration in English Literary Culture', in David Loewenstein and Janel Mueller, eds, *The Cambridge History of Early Modern English Literature* (Cambridge, 2002), 824–8.

sermons and treatises of the Latitudinarians within the Established
Church and in the political pamphlets and speeches of both Whigs
and Tories. Roger Pooley has identified several characteristics put
forward by exponents of plainness, including decorum, or the use
of diction appropriate for teaching or popularizing; Englishness,
or the avoidance of 'inkhorn terms' and quotations in foreign
languages; honesty, communicated by the speaker or writer who
does not embellish the truth; and simplicity, or restraint in the
use of imagery, though the importance of parables and images in
the Gospels was acknowledged.[59] Plainness in the use of language
was thus variously understood. What seems important, however,
is that the reform of the English language, with the intention of
making it more effective as a vehicle of rational, critical, coherent
and persuasive thought, was a frequent theme among writers and
speakers during the latter part of the seventeenth century.

These rhetorical values did not, however, first appear in the 1660s.
The garrulous Polonius was, after all, admonished in *Hamlet* to
provide 'More matter, with less art.'[60] Francis Bacon challenged the
fashionable, overly elaborate English of his time. William Tyndale,
in the early sixteenth century, insisted on using clear, direct, vernacular English for his translation of the New Testament.[61] Perkins's
teaching in *The Arte of Prophecying* explicitly supports clarity, the
use of reason, close attention to understanding a biblical text as
fully as possible, and the need for adequate skills on the part of the
preacher as he prepared the sermon. Perkins also stresses a straightforward presentation of doctrines and moral applications, a diction
free from displays of learning, and a style adapted to the needs and
characteristics of members of the congregation. Many preachers
who were educated at Cambridge during Perkins's long career
there absorbed the principles of interpretation, logic, rhetoric and
style that he enunciated. Perkins enjoyed 'astonishing popularity as

[59] Roger Pooley, 'Language and Loyalty: Plain Style at the Restoration', *Literature & History* 6 (1980), 1–18, at 6; cf. idem, *English Prose of the Seventeenth Century,
1590–1700* (London, 1992), 3–4, 65, 115–16, 228–31.
[60] William Shakespeare, *Hamlet, Prince of Denmark*, II. ii. 95, ed. Constance Jordan,
2nd edn (New York, 2005), 43.
[61] For Bacon, see Morris W. Croll, *Style, Rhetoric, and Rhythm*, ed. J. Max Patrick
and Robert O. Evans, with John M. Wallace and R. J. Schoeck (Princeton, NJ, 1966),
188–202; for Tyndale, see Janel M. Mueller, *The Native Tongue and the Word: Developments in English Prose Style, 1380-1580* (Chicago, IL, 1984), 177–243.

preacher and writer in the 1590s', as Brian Cummings has noted.[62] Moreover, as Patrick Collinson points out, he remained 'a best-selling commodity for half a century' after his death in 1602.[63] Perkins's writings reached a large lay as well as clerical audience and the principles of expression he taught were influential long after his time, indeed to the era of the Restoration. *The Arte of Prophecying* was a literary manifesto in that it focused on principles of rhetoric that were relevant to the practice of preaching, the form of public discourse best known to most English men and women, and to speaking and writing generally.[64] He was certainly not the only writer to call for a simpler, more direct and more readily intelligible use of the English language, but he was one of the first and one of the most influential. Perkins and those influenced by his ideas helped to inaugurate a literary and cultural change in the seventeenth century that was of profound and lasting importance.

University of the South, Sewanee, Tennessee

---

[62] Cummings, *Literary Culture*, 258. See also Adolph, *Rise of Modern Prose Style*, 208–9; Ford, 'Preaching in the Reformed Tradition', 73–6.

[63] Patrick Collinson, 'Literature and the Church', in Loewenstein and Mueller, eds, *Cambridge History of Early Modern English Literature*, 374–98, at 395.

[64] See Lori Anne Ferrell and Peter McCullough, eds, *The English Sermon Revised: Religion, Literature and History, 1600–1750* (Manchester, 2000), Introduction, 2–21, for a perceptive analysis of 'the centrality of the sermon to the period': ibid. 10.

MILTON'S CHURCHES

by THOMAS N. CORNS

This essay considers both John Milton's relationship to the churches he attended and his developing attitude to the Church of England and to the wider Protestant faith community, nationally and internationally. The objective is better to place Milton within the divisive and shifting religious politics of seventeenth-century England. Only incidental reference is made to his poetry; this is primarily a study of life records and his prose publications.

It is relatively straightforward to track John Milton through the actual churches he attended, and, as for other Englishmen in his age and of his class, the surest, least ambiguous life records that chart his rites of passage relate to his membership of the Church of England.

He was baptized in All Hallows Church in Bread Street, London, his parish church, on 20 December 1608, a building somewhat past its prime since its steeple had been demolished after a lightning strike in 1559; nor was its rector, Thomas Edmonds, in better repair. Presumably because of the rector's physical indisposition, the baptism was performed by his curate and eventual successor, Richard Stock, a nimble churchman with a flair for attracting patronage. Stock's publishing career, which petered out shortly after Milton's birth, consisted of a cluster of fiercely anti-Catholic sermons and related items, and there is strong evidence of a pronounced streak of puritanism both in the company he kept and his role as one of the founding Feoffees for Impropriations, an organization established to secure lectureships for clergy of puritan inclination, which was to be abolished by William Laud in 1633. However, Stock's death in 1626 took him from the fray before the struggle started in earnest.

Stock was a keen catechizer, according to his funeral sermon, and in all probability catechized Milton. However, it should be stressed that John Milton senior, the poet's father, was living in the parish before Stock arrived; he did not move to live in a puritan's parish. Though Stock would almost certainly have lined up with many other London clergy against Laud's reforms and policies, his own inclinations constitute no evidence that Milton's own father shared them.[1]

Indeed, when (in or around 1625) Milton senior came to select a Cambridge college and a tutor for his sixteen-year-old son, his choices were far from puritanical. They were made in the context of the increasingly open controversy within the Church of England, particularly over aspects of liturgical practice and soteriology, a controversy that would deepen on the appointment of William Laud successively to the sees of London and Canterbury. Eschewing the Calvinist and anti-ceremonialist strongholds of Emmanuel and Sidney Sussex Colleges, the poet's father opted for William Chappell, a fellow of Christ's, a high-profile Arminian and future recipient of Laud's patronage, to be Milton's tutor. Thus, Milton's second church was Christ's College chapel. His youthful gift for neo-Latin funeral elegy shortly produced poems in commemoration of two Arminian luminaries, Nicholas Felton, the bishop of Ely, and Lancelot Andrewes, the bishop of Winchester and founding father of English ceremonial Arminianism, whose sermons were posthumously edited by Laud himself. At this time the Church of England was already manifesting, albeit incipiently, a dangerous disagreement over the doctrine of salvation. Some churchmen, probably a majority, remained committed to Calvinist predestination; others, particularly ceremonialists, were drawn to the views of the Dutch theologian Jacobus Arminius, who viewed grace as freely extended to all who would accept it. Although Milton left the tutorage of Chappell after some (currently unidentified) quarrel or misdemeanour and apparently a period of rustication, his new tutor, Nathaniel Tovey, marked no significant shift in religious predilection; twenty years later, he would be deprived of his Leicestershire living for his adherence to Laudian practices.[2]

Each stage of Milton's progression through Cambridge was marked by unqualified conformity with the practices of the Church of England. As he supplicated in 1629 for his B.A., he affirmed the three Articles of Religion required at that point. The second article accepted episcopalian church government and the

---

[1] Biographical information is drawn from Gordon Campbell and Thomas N. Corns, *John Milton: Life, Work, and Thought* (Oxford, 2008), 7–18; see also 386–92 for citation of the life-records and documents from which their narrative is drawn.

[2] Ibid. 26–47, 392–6nn.

Book of Common Prayer; the third endorsed the Thirty-Nine Articles. He duly repeated these affirmations as he proceeded to the degree of M.A. in 1632.[3]

Milton's third church was the chapel of ease in the village of Hammersmith, consecrated by Laud in 1631. Milton's mother and father had moved there as the chapel was nearing completion. The poet joined them on going down from Cambridge a year later. However, his parents developed a certain wanderlust in their old age, shifting the family home in 1636 to Horton, now adjacent to Heathrow Airport. His fourth church, St Michael, had as its rector Edward Goodall, who sided against the rise of Laudianism and who would serve actively in the Westminster Assembly of Divines, convened by the Long Parliament to reform further the Church of England. The Milton family evidently cut something of a dash in this community. Their pew was lofty enough to attract censure during a decanal visitation. Milton's mother died during their period at Horton, and was interred within the church in a prime spot near the altar; the orientation of her memorial stone attracted also adverse decanal comment, on the grounds that it faced in the wrong direction. Milton's incipient radicalization can probably be attributed to the Horton years, though it is difficult to determine which of several factors, both personal and on the national scale, weighed most heavily with him. However, both the decanal response to the family's over-exuberant profile and the influence of Goodall could have been components in that process.[4]

In all later major life events for which there is a clear record, we find Milton acting out the ceremonies and obligations of his national Church. Information is lacking for both his first marriage and the burial of his first wife, Mary Powell. As a loyal government employee he married his second wife, Katherine Woodcock, according to the terms of the 1653 Marriage Act in a civil ceremony, probably in the Guildhall. But her burial, less than five years later, was commemorated by an elaborate heraldic funeral with high ceremony in St Margaret's, Westminster, a church in reasonable proximity to their home in Petty France. Their child

---

3   Ibid. 63, 400n.

4   Ibid. 67–8, 400nn, 88–102, 404–6nn; Edward Jones, '"Church-outed by the Prelates": Milton and the 1637 Inspection of Horton Parish Church', *Journal of English and Germanic Philology* 102 (2003), 42–58.

was buried in the same church in the following month. Milton's sonnet 19, 'Methought I saw my late espoused saint', which almost certainly commemorates his grief for Katherine, perhaps discloses a nostalgia for at least one aspect of the old liturgy of the Church of England, by then displaced by the Directory devised by the Westminster Assembly of Divines. It alludes to the rite of churching women after childbirth, which was no longer conducted. His third and final marriage, to Elizabeth Minshull, was a church ceremony held in St Mary Aldermary in 1663. The venue, which was some distance from the place of abode of both bride and groom, was a splendid one, an impressive church in a rich parish and favoured by the City's mercantile elite. Its rector, Dr Robert Gell, was an old acquaintance and perhaps an old friend of Milton's. He had been a fellow of Christ's College in Milton's student days, and may perhaps have collaborated with him. As an angelologist and defender of astrologers, he was, moreover, an example of a principle which, I shall argue, Milton later expounded, that speculative notions can be entertained within the national Church. Indeed, Gell, though not evidently of puritan orientation, managed to keep his lucrative living while many were losing theirs through the expulsions of the 1640s and of the Restoration.

Milton's own funeral in 1674 was at St Giles Cripplegate, not far from his then home. His father was already interred near its altar, and the poet's coffin was placed alongside his father's, where it remained until unfortunate interference with the remains required that the body be relocated within the church. Accounts in the early lives stress the ceremonial nature of the burial. It was 'according to his Quality', and the funeral cortège included 'several Gentlemen then in Town, his principal wellwishers and admirers';[5] '[a]ll his learned and great Friends in London, not without a friendly concourse of the Vulgar, accompany'd his Body to the Church'.[6]

Cyriack Skinner, a former pupil, friend and early biographer, concluded, in a resonant phrase, that Milton 'had this Elogy in common with the Patriarchs and Kings of Israel that he was gath-

[5] Edward Philips, in *The Early Lives of Milton*, ed. Helen Darbishire (London, 1932), 76; Philips was Milton's elder nephew.
[6] John Toland, in ibid. 193; Toland did not know Milton personally, though had some access to those who did.

ered to his people'.[7] Indeed, he seemed finally and permanently, literally and metaphorically, lodged within the national Church in which he had lived, though possibly his conformity in later years may have shared the highly occasional character – births, marriages, and deaths – of some modern Anglicans. Skinner's sentiments are striking, but they seem to contradict two more frequently cited comments, by John Toland, a radical whig, and by Milton himself, though both remarks require some care in interpretation. Toland, speaking of Milton in the poet's Restoration seclusion, noted:

> In his early days he was a Favorer of those Protestants then opprobriously cal'd by the name of *Puritans:* In his middle years he was best pleas'd with the *Independents* and *Anabaptists*, as allowing of more Liberty than others, and coming nearest in his opinion to the primitive practice: but in the latter part of his Life, he was not a profest member of any Sect among Christians, he frequented none of their Assemblies, nor made use of their particular Rites in his Family.[8]

Toland was writing his biography to accompany an edition of Milton's prose writings,[9] and his account was shaped by his familiarity with that *oeuvre*, particularly over the 1640s. In those terms, it makes a kind of sense: Milton moves from alignment with the likes of Smectymnuus, to whom I shall shortly turn, to more radical thinkers: advocates of toleration, certainly independents, and perhaps, at least at the level of a broad agreement on certain issues, with people like Thomas Lambe, soap-boiler and preacher. However, the social gulf between Milton and such tub-preachers was a wide one.[10] As he reviews Milton's final years, Toland seems to exclude any suggestion that he attended the dangerous and shadowy world of Dissenter conventicles. Quite what Toland meant by 'Sect' remains somewhat uncertain, though the affirmation, by someone who did not know him personally, does not

---

7   Cyriack Skinner, in ibid. 34. Darbishire had attributed this anonymous manuscript account to Milton's younger nephew, John Philips, though the attribution to Skinner now seems proven beyond reasonable doubt.

8   Ibid. 195.

9   John Toland, ed., *A Complete Collection of the Historical, Political and Miscellaneous Work of John Milton … to which is prefix'd the life of the author* ('Amsterdam' [London], 1698).

10   Campbell and Corns, *John Milton*, 193–4.

seem to me to preclude a professed membership of the national Church. Indeed, the usual range and signification of the word applies primarily to groups like those Baptist and Quaker gatherings that risked – as Milton almost certainly did not – the rigour of Restoration legislation directed against Dissenters.

We must also consider a second passage, Milton's own observation in the biographical digression of his *Reason of Church-Government* (1642):

> ... it were sad for me if I should draw back, for me especially, now when all men offer their aid to help ease and lighten the difficult labours of the Church, to whose service by the intentions of my parents and freinds [*sic*] I was destin'd of a child and in mine own resolutions, till comming to some maturing of yeers and perceaving what tyranny had invaded the Church, that he who would take Order must subscribe slave, and take an oath withall, which unlesse he took with a conscience that would retch, he must either strait perjure, or split his faith, I thought it better to preferre a blamelesse silence before the sacred office of speaking bought, and begun with servitude and forswearing. Howsoever thus Church-outed by the Prelats, hence may appear the right I have to meddle in these matters, as before, the necessity and constraint appear'd.[11]

The word 'Church-outed', striking though the Miltonic neologism is, is somewhat unhelpful interpretatively. It cannot simply mean, as the *Oxford English Dictionary* asserts, 'put out of the church',[12] since Milton plainly was not. More likely, it holds a resonance of a possible meaning of 'Out', the verb 'oust from ... a[n] office' (sig. 1). Indeed, the passage is a ringing affirmation of Milton's intention, manifest throughout his anti-prelatical pamphlets of 1641–2, to engage energetically in the internal process of the continued reformation of the national Church. The passage offers a further puzzle for biographers, since Milton had twice in the 1630s taken in effect the same oath, of compliance with the Thirty-Nine Articles, which would have been required at his ordination. The Yale editor, Ralph Haug, somewhat ingeniously suggests that Milton alludes to the very similar oath

[11] John Milton, *Complete Prose Works of John Milton*, gen. ed. Don M. Wolfe, 8 vols (New Haven, CT, 1953–82), 1: 822–3 [hereafter: *CPW*].
[12] *OED, s.v.* 'church', n., C3, special combinations.

promulgated as part of the Canons of 1640, in which it was extended somewhat to require a positive defence of episcopal government,[13] although there is strong biographical evidence of Milton's waning interest in an ecclesiastical career before that date.[14] In the immediate context of the campaign against Laudianism, however, it marks a radical stance in favour of the role and rights of the laity in engaging in the regulation of the Church, in sharp conflict with Laud's insistence on the pre-eminence of the clergy. Milton is asserting that the Church of England, its doctrine and discipline, are of legitimate concern to its lay members.

Milton's first polemical engagement eschewed secular political issues, a decision that can be attributed in part to his personal contacts with the Smectymnuan group through his continuing friendship with Thomas Young, former tutor and future figure of some prominence in Presbyterian circles, combined with his lack of contacts among political activists. 'Smectymnuus' was the acronym for a doughty consortium of anti-Laudian and anti-ceremonialist churchmen, Stephen Marshall, Edmund Calamy, Thomas Young, Matthew Newcomen and William Spurstow, the initial of whose given name supplies the 'uu'. Of course such an association is itself indicative of a standing commitment; these were the men with whom Milton chose to align himself, all of them deeply loyal to the Church of England, which none of them chose to leave till the expulsions that followed the Act of Uniformity of 1662. Nor can the depth of Milton's engagement in the anti-prelatical cause be doubted in those first five fiery tracts, which constitute his anti-prelatical writings; reforming his mother Church, plainly, was for him the immediate priority of the early 1640s.

Yet Milton's view of the national Church, probably from the outset, stands outside the mainstream of moderate puritan opinion in both its populist and its scholarly manifestations. The broadside, *See heer, Malignants Foolerie* (Fig. 1),[15] nicely exemplifies some familiar emphases. The prelatical figure stands between a Protestant clergyman, who offers only Holy Writ, and 'A Ball'd-pate

---

[13] *CPW*, 1: 823 n. 161; the oath is sometimes known as the 'Et Cetera' oath.

[14] Campbell and Corns, *John Milton*, 101.

[15] I conjecture a date of publication between late 1641, when for the first time the term 'roundhead' entered currency (*OED*, *s.v.* 'roundhead') and approximately 1643, when popular interest in the anti-prelatical campaign was on the wane.

Fig. 1. Anon., *See, heer, Malignants Foolerie*

Fryer, a Round-head indeed', from whom he takes a crucifix as a
token of Romish innovation. The ecclesiastical architecture merits
a moment's consideration: on one side, a solid English Gothic
church, its tower sporting ancient crocketed pinnacles and the
whole manifesting a conspicuous lack of more recent adornment;
on the other, an Italianate structure replete with cross, sacring
bell and Marian icon. The enemy, however, is not simply Catholicism; rather the broadside targets Laudian innovation, additions to
English Protestant practice, under the influence of Catholicism.
Though the Smectymnuans were too committed to the academic
analysis of the records of the Early Church to stoop to such spirited if crude populism, they too were drawn to the argument that
the problems of the Church of England were substantially due to
relatively recent and somewhat Romish innovation, reflected in
the terminology of Laudian ceremonialism: 'The Church of God
hath alwayes been as diligent to resist novelties, of words, as her
adversaries are busie to invent them, for which cause shee will not

have us communicate with them, nor follow their fashions and phrase newly invented'.[16]

Innovation came as a package, and it came recently and ultimately from Rome: 'it comes to passe, that in England there is such increase of Popery, superstition, Arminianisme, and profanenesse more then in other reformed Churches'.[17] They spoke of a pressing, recent and accelerating process of damaging innovation under the malign influence of Rome, and for the Smectymnuans that innovation centred on a shift in the doctrine of salvation, away from the rigours of Calvinism to the new and dangerous Arminianism that had entered the Church in the days of Lancelot Andrewes and found its triumph in the ascendancy of Laud. The Smectymnuans and indeed the author of the broadside confirm quite precisely Nicholas Tyacke's influential thesis that the crisis within the Caroline Church originated in the breach of the previous unanimity primarily on matters of doctrine.[18]

Milton placed the emphases differently. For him, the failure of the Church of England was not recent (and not particularly connected with Arminianism, to the soteriology of which the poet had an early commitment). For him, the corruption extended back to the immediately post-apostolic Church, and he railed against the worldliness, the carnality, of 'the false Doctors of the Primitive Church'.[19] It reached its mature state under Constantine, whose Church, he observed, for good reason constituted an ideal for prelatical apologists:

> I do not see how it can be disputed what good this Emperour *Constantine* wrought to the Church, but rather whether ever any, though perhaps not wittingly, set open a dore to more mischiefe in Christendome. There is just cause therefore that when the *Prelates* cry out Let the Church be reform'd according to *Constantine*, it should sound to a judicious eare no otherwise, then if they should say Make us rich, make us

---

[16] 'Smectymnuus', *An Answer to a Booke Entituled, An Humble Remonstrance* (London, 1641), 92.

[17] Ibid. 90.

[18] See esp. Nicholas Tyacke, *Anti-Calvinists: The Rise of English Arminianism c. 1590–1640* (Oxford, 1997).

[19] John Milton, *An Apology against a Pamphlet Call'd A Modest Confutation* (*CPW*, I: 942).

lofty, make us lawlesse, for if any under him were not so, thanks to those ancient remains of integrity, which were not yet quite worne out, and not to his Government.[20]

He was scornful of the 'Primitive English Churches', which shared the petty fractiousness of other post-apostolic Churches. His contempt for the founding fathers of the Christian faith in England continued long past his first anti-prelatical exercises in Early Church history. His *History of Britain* (1670) playfully depicted as ludicrous the pivotal encounter between Ethelbert and Augustine, whose party approached the superstitious monarch like a modern papist procession 'singing thir solemn Litanies' and carrying cross and icon. The king's anxiety about the missionaries' casting a spell over him in Milton's account would have been reinforced by what he saw.[21]

Milton, like other anti-prelatical and anti-ceremonialist activists, exempted John Wyclif, the Oxford theologian who inspired the Lollard heresy, from any censure. Milton identified him and his followers as a source of 'that glimmering light' that anticipated the work currently in progress.[22] However, he differed from the Smectymnuans in his profound disappointment with the English Reformation, what he termed 'this forescore yeares vexation' of the Church,[23] and in his sustained and disparaging comparison of English ecclesiastical history with the experience of continental Reformed Churches. Milton had recently seen them at first hand, or at least two of them. He had travelled across France at a time when the Edict of Nantes still allowed Huguenots to worship pretty much as they pleased, and he returned from Italy via Geneva, where he stayed a little while, meeting daily with the Italian émigré Giovanni Diodati, the staunchly Calvinist uncle of his late friend Charles Diodati and a luminary within that staunchly Calvinist society.[24] In France and Italy he had seen, too, the characteristics of Catholic discipline and church government, what he termed 'the great darknesse of the Roman Church'.[25] To him it appeared evident that, in

[20] John Milton, *Of Reformation* (*CPW*, 1: 560).
[21] John Milton, *The History of Britain* (*CPW*, 5: 187–8).
[22] Milton, *Apology* (*CPW*, 1: 704).
[23] Ibid. 703.
[24] Campbell and Corns, *John Milton*, 125–7.
[25] Milton, *Church-Government* (*CPW*, 1: 850).

its liturgy, its ceremonialism, its vestments and its church government, the English Reformation was very incomplete. Throughout
his anti-prelatical tracts, with a distinctive earnestness, he invoked the
spirit of Protestant internationalism and the examples of continental
Churches. He praised their extinction of 'idolatrous and Gentilish
rites and ceremonies' still practised in the Church of England.[26]
English Protestants should strive for 'our *Uniforme Consent* to the
rest of the *Churches* abroad'.[27]

Turning the old prelatical charge that puritanism was schis-
matical against his adversaries, he developed, with a flamboyance
typical of the style of these early tracts, a protracted image:

> we must first of all begin roundly to cashier, and cut away
> from the publick body the noysom, and diseased tumor of
> Prelacie, and come from Schisme to *unity* with our neighbour
> Reformed sister Churches, which with the blessing of *peace*
> and *pure doctrine* have now long time flourish'd; and doubtles
> with all hearty *joy,* and *gratulation,* will meet, and welcome
> our Christian *union* with them, as they have bin all this while
> griev'd at our strangeness and little better then separation from
> them.[28]

As in his use of the term 'schism', smartly shifted from its usual
range of reference to allude to the gaps between the Church of
England and continental Protestantism, Milton was again playing
a linguistic game. 'Separation' had since the late sixteenth century
been used as a generic term for those more radical puritans, such
as the Brownists, who no longer maintained even a show of
communion with the Church of England.[29] Once more, Milton
suggested, the real dangers to unity across the Protestant nations, as
within English Protestantism, lay in ceremonialism and the practices maintained in the Church of England.

Milton's own radicalization certainly accelerated apace after
1643 and the sustained attack by what Ann Hughes has called
'the Presbyterian mobilisation'[30] on the first edition of his *Doctrine*

---

[26]   Ibid. 761.
[27]   Milton, *Of Reformation* (*CPW*, 1: 527).
[28]   Ibid.
[29]   *OED, s.v.* 'Separation', 4.
[30]   Ann Hughes, Gangraena *and the Struggle for the English Revolution* (Oxford,
2004); the term is used *passim* to denote the organized attempts by less radical puri-

and Discipline of Divorce. Very shortly, he understood at first hand that the kinds of heterodox theological speculation to which he had become drawn were incompatible with the version of church reform favoured by his former Smectymnuan allies, which would have resulted in a Calvinist orthodoxy on matters of salvation and probably a Presbyterian church government, both protected and confirmed by the power of civil magistrates.

Milton's currently most famous prose work, *Areopagitica* (1644), is still often regarded as an iconic text in the western liberal tradition, in its apparent assertion of the rights of a free press. It properly belongs in the debate that developed between, on the one hand, Presbyterians and, on the other hand, independent and more radical advocates of the toleration of a wide spectrum of Protestant belief. Viewed historically, it is a tolerationist, not a liberal, tract. Its particular concern with pre-publication licensing and press control reflected the importance of print dissemination to an activist like Milton, who had no access to parliamentary and pulpit platforms. Yet Milton's interest in tolerationism preceded his direct personal interest in resisting attempts to silence his advocacy of radical reform in the field of divorce legislation. Indeed, in his last two anti-prelatical tracts, *The Reason of Church-Government* and *An Apology*, he seemed at times more concerned with a limited defence of sects outside the Church of England than with the restructuring of its episcopalian model of church government. Moreover, with the power of hindsight, we may recognize in his *Reason of Church-Government* the origins of a radical perspective that would remain central to his thinking till his final tract of 1673. It found expression in an aggressive response to a familiar prelatical claim that, without the authority of bishops, sects would be rampant and disruptive of the national Church:

> What sects? What are their opinions? ... it will appeare both by your former prosecutions and your present instances, that they are only such to speak of as are offended with your lawless government, your ceremonies, your Liturgy, an extract of the Masse book translated. ... Noise it till ye be hoarse; that a rabble of Sects will come in, it will be answer'd ye, no rabble

tans to resist toleration, to oppose Independency and more radical sects, and to bring the Church of England to a settlement on the Scottish Presbyterian model, enforced by the civil magistrate.

sir Priest, but a unanimous multitude of good Protestants will then joyne to the Church, which now because of you stand separated.[31]

It could not be clearer. Milton's vision of the English national Church was so wide and inclusive that those who stood separated could re-enter – while prelates and ceremonialists were to make some sort of unspecified exit.

As a programme for reformation and indeed for the maintenance of a national Church this view is not without its problems. In step with Milton, John Goodwin was forming a broadly similar concept. Goodwin, though Milton's senior by some fourteen years, has been widely recognized as among the closest to him in terms of ideological development. Indeed, the tracking of their similarities is among the most useful aspects of Christopher Hill's biography of the poet,[32] though the point had been made by Don Wolfe[33] and has been eloquently confirmed in John Coffey's biography of Goodwin.[34] Indeed, if Milton had followed his once intended ecclesiastical career, it would perhaps broadly have resembled that of Goodwin, a man whose education, tolerationist values, scholarship and intellectual pugnacity broadly resembled his own. (G. E. Aylmer, in a telling phrase, brackets them as 'intellectual mandarins to their fingertips'.)[35] Goodwin's own problems in the mid 1640s illuminate some of the conflicting impulses present also in Milton's alternative vision for the Church of England. He had been ordained in 1620 and since 1633 had been vicar of St Stephen's, Coleman Street, London. As congregational Independency emerged as the leading alternative model to Presbyterianism and as Goodwin developed both as its advocate and as a leading defender of toleration, he faced an interesting problem. While retaining his parochial office and duties, he also became leader of a gathered church, a congregation closely aligned to those radical views that set him at odds with more conservatively inclined parishioners. The position proved untenable, as Tai Liu relates:

---

[31] Milton, *Church-Government* (*CPW*, 1: 787–8); quotation at 788.
[32] Christopher Hill, *Milton and the English Revolution* (London, 1977).
[33] Don M. Wolfe, *Milton in the Puritan Revolution* (New York, 1941).
[34] John Coffey, *John Goodwin and the Puritan Revolution* (Woodbridge, 2006).
[35] G. E. Aylmer, *The State's Servants: The Civil Service of the English Republic 1649–1660* (London, 1973), 279.

Some parishioners, therefore, brought charges against Goodwin to the committee for plundered ministers. Efforts were made to reconcile the differences but all failed. On 22 May 1645 Goodwin was sequestered. After his sequestration, he and his gathered church first met in some buildings in Coleman Street and afterwards at the parish church of St Mary Abchurch.[36]

Goodwin returned to his living and the gathered congregation migrated back to St Stephen's late in 1649, by which time he had emerged as among the foremost defenders of the regicidal regime, at least among its clerical supporters.

As a lay activist, Milton was never required to negotiate the potential conflicts for Independent ministers who wished to remain within the national Church. Independency had had a much simpler experience in New England, where the broad alignment between most Churches allowed the congregational model to develop. Goodwin, however, thereafter retained his parish and his living till he was deprived of both, and of holding any other office, at the Restoration of Charles II in 1660.

But through the late 1640s and the 1650s Milton was adding a broader anti-clericalism to his rejection first of ceremonial episcopacy and thereafter of Presbyterianism. The equation of Presbyterianism and prelacy had been made with sardonic wordplay, probably no later than 1646, in the assertion that 'New *Presbyter* is but old *Priest* writ large',[37] with its quibble that the word 'priest' is etymologically a contracted form of Latin 'presbyter'. 'On the New Forcers of Conscience under the Long Parliament', the poem that concludes thus, remained unpublished till 1673. Through the decade of his state employment initiated in 1649 Milton's publications remained scrupulously on message, declining involvement in theological debate and assiduously focusing on the political issues that fell to his responsibility. But in two other poems, both dating from 1652, which were to remain for some while in manuscript, we may discern his belief that Independent divines were as grasping as episcopalian and Presbyterian ones and that a beneficed clergy, supported by tithes and protected by magistrates, was unacceptable.

---

[36] *ODNB, s.n.* 'Goodwin, John (c.1594–1665)'.

[37] John Milton, 'On the New Forcers of Conscience under the Long Parliament', line 20, in *Complete Shorter Poems*, ed. John Carey, 2nd edn (London, 1997), 298 [hereafter: *CSP*].

Plainly it was to Independent clergy he alluded when he urged Oliver Cromwell, 'Help us to save free conscience from the paw | Of hireling wolves whose gospel is their maw'.[38] Again, Sir Henry Vane the Younger's achievements included the ability to distinguish 'spiritual power and civil, what each means, | What severs each'.[39] However, it was not until the end of Oliver's Protectorate in 1658 that Milton published two pamphlets in this vein.

In *Of Civil Power* and *Considerations touching the likeliest means to remove Hirelings out of the church* he gave vent to views long suppressed in the interest of the state he had served. A beneficed and educated clergy, supported by tithes, was to be rejected in favour of lay preachers moved by the Spirit, a concept plainly supported by some notion of the apostolic Church: 'They [who first taught the gospel] were otherwise unlearned men'.[40] Milton rehearsed, too, his sense that the core beliefs of Protestantism were easily understood and communicated: 'seeing then that Christian religion may be so easily attaind, and by meanest capacities, it cannot be much difficult to finde waies, both how the poore, yea all men may be soone taught what is to be known of Christianitie'.[41] An austere and militant vision of the Church emerged, in which the faith may be imparted by modestly recompensed and itinerant preachers and may be imparted anywhere: 'not withstanding the gaudy superstition of som devoted still ignorantly to temples, we may be well assur'd that he who disdaind not to be laid in manger, disdains not to be preachd in a barn'.[42]

So, the steeple-house and temple are redundant; universities are unnecessary to the training of preachers; the gospel may be disseminated most effectively by itinerants, and that role stands open to poor and uneducated men to take it on. Those views are wholly characteristic of the Quakerism of the late 1650s. Milton was no Quaker, disagreeing profoundly with several of their central tenets. But unsurprisingly in the decade following the Restoration, if not sooner, he found friendship and support among the Quaker community. Evidently, he liked their style.

---

[38] John Milton, 'To the Lord Generall Cromwell', lines 13–14 (*CSP*, 329).
[39] John Milton, 'To Sir Henry Vane the Younger', lines 10–11 (*CSP*, 331).
[40] John Milton, *Of Civil Power* and *Considerations touching the likeliest means to remove Hirelings out of the church* (*CPW*, rev. edn, 7: 302).
[41] Ibid. 303.
[42] Ibid. 304.

After 1660 Milton for long fell silent on issues of church reform. Although *Paradise Lost* is replete with lightly encoded critiques of kingship, it has little of an anti-clerical or anti-ceremonial nature to offer, beyond its endorsement of Adam and Eve's extempore style of worship. But in 1672, in *Paradise Regained*, he returned to some of the concerns and enthusiasms of his tracts of 1659 as he commemorated the humble home circumstances of the Son of God, 'low of birth, | A carpenter thy father known, thyself | Bred up in poverty and straits at home', while the apostolic Church in waiting were 'plain fishermen, no greater men them call, | Close in a cottage low together got'.[43] Taking the opportunity afforded by the confusions surrounding the Declaration of Indulgence (1672), he made one last sally into prose polemic, in his *Of True Religion, Haeresie, Schism, Toleration, And what best means may be us'd against the growth of Popery* (1673). Though it may seem somewhat of a paradox to modern readers, this was an implacably anti-Catholic tolerationist tract – though that formula could be applied as appropriately to *Areopagitica*. It exploited a growing climate of toleration towards Protestant Dissenters and an associated rise in hostility towards 'popery'. The work reprises many of the themes we have identified in his earlier writing. Once more, he took an internationalist perspective, reviewing possible errors that provoked divisions not only among English Protestants but between the Protestant faith communities of Europe. The core beliefs 'absolutely necessary to salvation' are few and simple. The differences between Lutherans, Calvinists, Anabaptists, Arians and Socinians, 'calmly and charitably enquir'd into', should not divide the Protestant community.[44] Such disagreements need not 'tend to the breaking of Communion; if they can agree in the right administration of that wherein they Communicate, keeping their other Opinions to themselves, not being destructive to Faith'.[45] Milton's ultimate vision for the Church of England was of a wide Protestant faith community in which people may worship together after their own inclination while subscribing – without contention – to a wide range of doctrinal positions, united by their commitment

---

[43] John Milton, *Paradise Regained*, bk 2, lines 413–15; ibid., lines 27–8 (*CSP*, 460, 445).

[44] John Milton, *Of True Religion, Haeresie, Schism, Toleration, And what best means may be us'd against the growth of Popery* (*CPW*, 8: 424–5).

[45] Ibid. 423.

to the foundation of religious belief on the revealed word of God. People can differ about soteriology, about the fate of the soul at death, about the nature of the marriage bond, about the doctrine of the Trinity, without breaking communion.

★ ★ ★

The study of Milton's churches offers an important perspective on puritanism and Dissent. Viewed from a post-1662 standpoint, once oppositional ministers had left the Church, radical Protestantism might appear to have been simply, eternally and inevitably at odds with and separate from the national Church. But Milton well exemplifies how many English Protestants who were fiercely critical of its ceremonialism and church government nevertheless regarded themselves for much of the 1640s and 1650s as members of the Church of England with a legitimate interest in its further reformation. At least for Milton, such possibilities remained even into the early 1670s.

What would Milton make of the twenty-first-century Church of England? No doubt on vestments and liturgy he would still have something to say. But tithes have gone, and civil magistrates rarely involve themselves in matters of religion. Its doctrinal inclusiveness and toleration of widely diverse opinion on doctrine and indeed on lifestyle meet late Miltonic criteria. It is home to creationists and Christian humanists alike. William Laud was paid like a prince; Rowan Williams is paid like a middle-ranking professor. Indeed, some Church of England clergy would probably argue that they are scarcely beneficed at all. Viewed from our own perspective, Milton's radicalism can sometimes be obscured by the success his ideas subsequently achieved. We take it for granted that our political masters may be held to account for their actions and that the law is above them, as he argued. There is a general assumption that, except in times of national emergency, the press should be free from pre-publication censorship, as he argued. Changes in divorce legislation have for decades permitted divorce on the grounds of incompatibility and straightforwardly allowed remarriage of both parties, as he argued. Perhaps the reformation of the national Church on Miltonic lines belongs, with some qualification, in that same set of Miltonic accomplishments.

Bangor University

ANTI-CATHOLICISM AND OBSCENE LITERATURE: *THE CASE OF MRS. MARY CATHARINE CADIERE* AND ITS CONTEXT

by COLIN HAYDON

As every historian knows, religious minorities and other 'out-groups' have repeatedly faced accusations of sexual misconduct and its consequences: seduction, the breaking of families, promiscuous fornication, participation in orgies, 'unnatural vice', incest, sadism and masochism. In the second or third century, Minucius Felix recorded such charges against the early Christians: they make 'love almost before they are acquainted; everywhere they introduce a kind of religion of lust, a promiscuous "brotherhood" and "sisterhood" by which ordinary fornication, under cover of a hallowed name, is converted to incest'.[1] The Cathars and other medieval heretics were accused of promiscuous, incestuous orgies.[2] Across early modern Europe, witches at their sabbats, it was learnedly pronounced, copulated with the Devil himself and, indiscriminately, with unknown members of both sexes, even parents, brothers and sisters.

In seventeenth-century England, the first Quakers were accused of fornication, sodomy and incest.[3] The following century, the early Methodists were targets. What occurred at their 'lovefeasts'? Did they, as was claimed, 'when they were assembled together ... put out the candles and ... [commit] lewdness'?[4] However, it was the Roman Catholics against whom sexual charges were most frequently brought in Stuart and Georgian Britain. Priests', monks' and nuns' vows of celibacy were deplored. Celibacy appeared unnatural and was, to Protestants, unscriptural. It seemed unhealthy too: did it not incubate dark, sick passions? Was feigned chastity

---

[1]   Minucius Felix, *Octavius* 9, in Tertullian, *Apology, De spectaculis*, Minucius Felix, *Octavius*, transl. T. R. Glover and Gerald H. Rendall, LCL 250 (Cambridge, MA, 1931), 336–7. I am grateful to Professor J. H. D. Scourfield for his advice about this passage.
[2]   Norman Cohn, *Europe's Inner Demons*, rev. edn (London, 1993), 73–4.
[3]   Barry Reay, *The Quakers and the English Revolution* (New York, 1985), 65, 93.
[4]   John Walsh, 'Methodism and the Mob in the Eighteenth Century', in G. J. Cuming and Derek Baker, eds, *Popular Belief and Practice*, SCH 8 (London, 1972), 213–27, at 224–5.

a mask for lust and debauchery? 'Their Church', one charitable publication proclaimed,

> consists of *vicious Popes*, the rest
> Are whoring *Nuns*, and bawdy *bugg'ring Priests*.

'*A noble Church!*', it continued,

> *daub'd with religious Paint*,
> Each Priest's a Stallion, every *Rogue's* a Saint.[5]

Such prejudices were amply confirmed by the alleged seduction between 1728 and 1730 at Toulon of Marie-Catherine Cadière, an aspirant novice, by Jean-Baptiste Girard, her confessor – and a hated Jesuit to boot: the cause célèbre that is the subject of this essay.

★ ★ ★

In 1775, a three-volume *British Chronologist* was published, '*Comprehending*', it extravagantly claimed, '*Every Material Occurrence, Ecclesiastical, Civil, or Military, Relative to England and Wales, From the Invasion of the Romans to the Present Time*'.[6] Worthy of inclusion, its compilers thought, was Cadière's story: 'The criminal conversation of father *Girard*, rector of the Jesuits at *Thoulon*, with Miss *Kitty Cadiere*, when she came to confession, was the general talk of all countries in *Europe*'.[7] Marie-Catherine Cadière, a beautiful young penitent, fervently hoped to become a nun and in 1728 she chose Jean-Baptiste Girard as her confessor. Lodged in Toulon and in a convent at Ollioules, she exhibited ecstatic behaviour and experienced visions, but then claimed that Girard had bewitched her, and was consequently exorcised. Thereafter, Cadière accused the Jesuit of seduction – by using Quietist arguments[8] and by means of sorcery – and rape and abortion; Girard retaliated by suing her for slander. If found guilty, he faced burning, she hanging. The cases were first heard at Toulon, but were transferred in January 1731 to the *parlement* of Aix-en-Provence, where formal hearings began in June. Over a hundred witnesses testified, and, in October, twelve

---

5 Anon., *Revolution Politicks*, 8 parts (London, 1733), 4: 60.
6 *The British Chronologist*, 3 vols (London, 1775), 1: title page.
7 Ibid. 2: 166.
8 See page 214 below.

judges voted to condemn Girard and release Cadière, while the other twelve voted to free the Jesuit. Following the *premier président's* vote for clemency for both, the *parlement* acquitted Girard and Cadière – illogically, since plainly either the former was guilty or the latter lying. Girard died two years afterwards, and Cadière faded from the record of history.[9]

★ ★ ★

The Cadière case soon became a publishing sensation in Britain, though the publications defy simple categorization. Julie Peakman categorizes them as pornographic/erotic,[10] but one can hardly ascertain how sexually arousing readers found them. Some, largely amusing, are part of rollicking English bawdry, best exemplified in the eighteenth century by Henry Fielding's *Tom Jones.* But in others, or parts of others, the sick, and sickening, passages are the most memorable.

There were earlier anti-Catholic erotic or bawdy works. Antonio Gavin's *A Master-Key to Popery* (1724) accused Catholic priests of sexual misconduct.[11] *The Case of Seduction* (1726) detailed the proceedings against the '*Reverend Abbée* [sic], *Claudius Nicholas des Rues, for Committing Rapes upon 133 Virgins*'.[12] But it was the extraordinary, intimate detail in the Cadière revelations, lacking in broad-brush accounts, which captured the public's interest. The scandal also erupted at a moment which ensured enormous coverage. Pornography's production was burgeoning during the first half of the eighteenth century in England.[13] Anti-Catholicism was ubiquitous in these years, and Gallophobia was intensifying following the Anglo-French alliance's collapse in 1731. London newspapers such as the *Daily Journal* and *Daily Post* reported the trial. When it ended, they advertised some of the numerous publications recounting the case, and printed the

9   B. Robert Kreiser, 'The Devils of Toulon: Demonic Possession and Religious Politics in Eighteenth-Century Provence', in Richard M. Golden, ed., *Church, State, and Society under the Bourbon Kings of France* (Lawrence, KS, 1982), 173–221; Jason T. Kuznicki, 'Sorcery and Publicity: The Cadière-Girard Scandal of 1730–1731', *French History* 21 (2007), 289–312.

10   Julie Peakman, *Mighty Lewd Books: The Development of Pornography in Eighteenth-Century England* (Basingstoke, 2003), 141–6.

11   Anthony Gavin, *A Master-Key to Popery* (Dublin, 1724; repr. London, 1725), 38, 39, 145.

12   Anon., *The Case of Seduction* (London, 1726), title page.

13   Peakman, *Mighty Lewd Books.*

spats of rival publishers. Some memoirs were largely translations of the French trial accounts. *The Case of Mrs. Mary Catharine Cadiere* astoundingly reached at least eleven editions by the end of 1732. *The Defence of F. John Baptist Girard* was printed in three parts, with part one having a fourth edition. These works were produced by James Roberts of London's Warwick Lane (a centre for erotica printing), but J. Millan, based near the Horse Guards, was a rival for the market, publishing two much lengthier works, *A Compleat Translation of the Whole Case of Mary Catherine Cadiere* and *A Compleat Translation of the Sequel of the Proceedings of Mary Catherine Cadiere*. The former reached at least six editions, the latter two, but they were perhaps unnecessarily demanding (respectively twice and nearly three times the length – ninety-six pages – of *The Case of Mrs. Mary Catharine Cadiere*). Many slighter pamphlets were produced: the 'Number of *Memoirs* published about the Affair of Father Girard and Mademoiselle Cadiere, increases so fast,' the *Daily Courant* exclaimed in October 1731, 'that there are already above 30 different Sorts of them'.[14] Roberts advertised that his books and pamphlets were sold 'by most Booksellers in Town and Country', and editions of *The Case of Mrs. Mary Catharine Cadiere* were produced in Dublin and Edinburgh.

That *The Case of Mrs. Mary Catharine Cadiere* was pre-eminently successful is explicable. Roberts clearly knew his market. He deliberately omitted details about French legal procedure and terminology (Millan snarled that a poor grasp of French explained it!).[15] He scorned feeble pamphlets (and Millan) in the newspapers, and adjusted *The Case's* price to outflank his competitors.[16] He flattered his readership: the sorcery charges, to rational Englishmen, 'may seem very incredible, though they are fully proved'.[17] *The Case* was 'entertaining', to be 'read with Pleasure'.[18] In short, it was what an English reader wanted – in today's vernacular, 'edited highlights'.

Verse treatments of the case proliferated too. There were *Miss*

[14]   *Daily Courant*, 5 October 1731.

[15]   Anon., *The Case of Mrs. Mary Catharine Cadiere* (London, 1732), ii; Anon., *A Compleat Translation of the Whole Case of Mary Catherine Cadiere*, 2nd edn (London, 1732), v.

[16]   *London Evening Post*, 14–16 October 1731; *Fog's Weekly Journal*, 23 October 1731.

[17]   Anon., *Case of Mrs. Cadiere*, vi. Roberts continued: the 'superstitious may attribute them [the unbelievable tales] to the operation of the Devil; but I cannot persuade my self they are any thing more than tricks of Legerdemain'.

[18]   *Fog's Weekly Journal*, 23 October 1731.

Cadiere's Case Very Handsomely Handled. In Metre. By a Gentleman Commoner (London, 1731), apparently '*proper to be read in all Christian families*'; *A Panegyrick on the Reverend Father John Baptist Girard, Jesuit* (Dublin, 1731), '[*a*]*ttempted in the nambypambaick strain*'; and Jeremy Jingle's *Spiritual Fornication. A Burlesque Poem* (London, 1732), '[*w*]*herein the case of Miss Cadiere and Father Girard are [sic] merrily display'd*'.[19] *The Star-Gazer*, published in 1739, included 'The Lamentable Ballad of the Rampant Jesuit and Deluded Virgin'.[20] As their titles indicate, the verse treatments were usually comic. It was easy to portray Girard as absurd and Cadière as positively idiotic in brisk rhyming couplets:

> *The goatish* Girard, Satan's *Imp*,
> *Uses* Religion, *as a Pimp*;
> *Under a Mask of* holy Grace,
> *Allures* Cadiere *to his embrace*;
> *Kisses each Part about her* gratis,
> *And often* Firks *her* Nunquam satis.[21]

Equally, a pithy rhyme served well when summarizing the scandal's events, as on the title page of *Spiritual Fornication*:

> *Priests, whether* Jesuits *or* Fryars,
> *Are Pious Cheats, Religious Lyars*;
> *Who use their Function as a Gin*,
> *To catch unwary* Maidens *in*.

Some poems were written to fit well-known tunes. '*Miss* Cadiere's Case' was a ribald song published in the *Gentleman's Magazine*. It had as its tune, unsurprisingly, 'A lovely Lass to a Fryer came'.[22]

Besides the written word, the Cadière case spawned prints, and plays were performed about it. One work's frontispiece shows Cadière seated before a large crucifix, and Girard, on his knees, stroking her breasts.[23] *Spiritual Fornication* has an illustration showing Girard whipping and kissing his penitent; the room contains a

[19] D. F. Foxon, *English Verse 1701–1750*, 2 vols (London, 1975), I: 465, 552, 749.
[20] Ibid. I: 755.
[21] Jeremy Jingle, *Spiritual Fornication* (London, 1732), 17.
[22] Anon., '*Miss* Cadiere's Case', *Gentleman's Magazine* I (1731), 446.
[23] Anon., *A Compleat Translation of the Memorial of … John Baptist Girard* (London, 1732), frontispiece.

Fig. 2. Girard and Cadière: kissing and flagellation

crucifix and a portrait of the pope (Fig. 2).[24] A third print shows the removal of the aborted foetus in a chamber pot, and Girard, holding a birch, with Cadière on a bed, kissing her naked, blood-spotted posterior (Fig. 3).[25] *A Compleat History of the Intrigues of Priests and Nuns*, which briefly examined the Cadière case, has, as its frontispiece, an illustration of the confessional, with a 'lascivious Priest'

[24] Jingle, *Spiritual Fornication*, between 16 and 17.
[25] Anon., *Compleat Translation of the Whole Case*, frontispiece.

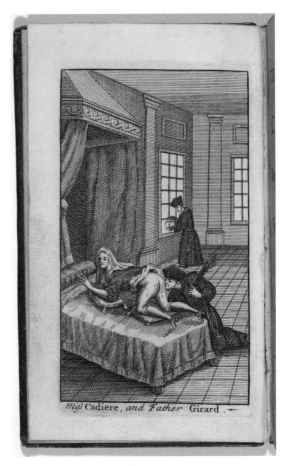

Miss Cadiere, and Father Girard.

Fig. 3. Girard and Cadière: kissing, flagellation and abortion

and an 'obedient Damsel' (Fig. 4).[26] Dramatists seized the day. The
theatre in Goodman's Fields in 1731 added 'an entertainment at the
close of ... [a] play relating to Father Girard and Miss Cadiere'.[27]
Henry Fielding's *The Old Debauchees* was performed the following
year at Drury Lane, with Theophilus Cibber as the lecherous Father
Martin, and was well received (it was revived as *The Debauchees: or,*

[26] Anon., *A Compleat History of the Intrigues of Priests and Nuns*, 4th edn (London,
1732), frontispiece.

[27] Jeremy Black, *London: A History* (Lancaster, 2009), 176.

Fig. 4. The confessional: a 'lascivious Priest' and an
'obedient Damsel'

The Jesuit Caught in 1745 as anti-Jacobite propaganda).[28] Its attack
on 'dirty Priests' was savage.[29] *The Wanton Jesuit*, a ballad-opera, was
performed at the New Theatre, Haymarket, and was a largely accurate rendering of the trial reports. Its text was published by Millan,
that of *The Old Debauchees* by Roberts.

[28] Martin C. Battestin with Ruthe R. Battestin, *Henry Fielding: A Life* (London,
1989), 134–5; *General Advertiser*, 16 October 1745.
[29] [Henry Fielding], *The Old Debauchees* (London, 1732), 2.

So, immensely quickly, memoirs of the Cadière scandal were 'almost in every body's Hands',[30] while it was depicted in verse, songs and prints, and on the stage. In June 1733, a horse named 'Miss Cadiere' ran at the Hounslow races – and won![31] What, then, were the principal themes in the case's various treatments?

★ ★ ★

The Cadière case spotlighted Protestants' enormous concerns about the confessional and the threat it supposedly posed to the patriarchal family. The preface to *The Case of Mrs. Mary Catharine Cadiere* maintained that the account conveyed 'a most excellent and necessary lesson' about 'cunning and wicked Confessors'; 'every virtuous Fair one, every tender Husband, Parent and Brother ... every *British* Subject and true Protestant' could profit from it.[32] Alone with a 'silly' woman in the confessional, and confident that what passed there was secret, a priest could direct the discussion to her unclean thoughts and conduct, or implant indecent notions in her mind (a technique used by Father Martin in *The Old Debauchees*).[33] Then he might embrace her:

> But if as my Life
> I lov'd Daughter or Wife,
> I'd be sure to keep off the Confessor;
> For by Bible or Book,
> Or by Hook or by Crook
> He'll find out some Way to caress her.[34]

From there, seduction might prove easy. 'What Libertine Lives do Priests and Friars lead!', Girard announces at the start of *The Wanton Jesuit*. 'They have the Privilege of Access to their Penitents at all Times in private, and under a Notion of infusing good Principles into them, they revel in forbidden Pleasures without Suspicion.'[35]

That *Auricular Chair*

---

30 *Fog's Weekly Journal*, 23 October 1731.
31 *Daily Journal*, 15 June 1733.
32 Anon., *Case of Mrs. Cadiere*, i.
33 [Fielding], *Old Debauchees*, 6, 18.
34 Anon., *Miss Cadiere's Case Very Handsomely Handled. In Metre* (London, 1731), 10.
35 Anon., *The Wanton Jesuit* (London, 1731), 13.

Is an excellent Snare,
A sweet Inlet to carnal Transgression,

sneered one piece of doggerel.[36] Moreover, whatever sins (however
heinous) were committed, absolution would follow; and thereby, in
Protestant eyes, further sin was encouraged.[37]

If the intimacy of the confessional excited sinister sexual fantasies
in the Protestant mind, so too did sequestered Catholic monasteries and nunneries. How many young women were immured in
convents? What were their relations with the priests who visited
them? *The Case of Mrs. Mary Catharine Cadiere* stressed Girard's
schemes to gain 'access to his dear disciple' at the convent at
Ollioules.[38] Permitted to speak to Cadière only through the parlour's
grate, he found 'a small wicket in ... [it], which he taught his disciple
to open', and, through this, 'put his head, or made his Mistress put
hers, sometimes to kiss her'.[39] Protestants deplored nuns' supposedly
wretched lives: one eighteenth-century English print shows a nun
at solitary prayer in a tiny, dreary room.[40] Cadière's story further
seemed to confirm suspicions that nunneries were often little better
than prisons. At Ollioules, Cadière 'was confined to a stinking room,
without any thing to lie upon but a little rotten straw in a corner
upon the ground'.[41] In *The Wanton Jesuit*, one scene is explicitly set
in a '*Prison in the Monastery of the* Ursuline *Nuns*'.[42] Did elderly nuns,
as disappointed embittered virgins, maltreat beautiful young novices?
Imaginations could luxuriate endlessly on occurrences in shuttered
rooms behind locked doors or high walls. One source for sexual
allegations about the early Methodists was the curiosity ignited by
their closed gatherings. 'The rabble', it was noted, 'wanted sadly to
know what they did at their private meetings.'[43] 'To how many
criminal liberties has ... [the] parlour [at Ollioules] been witness?',
asked *The Case of Mrs. Mary Catharine Cadiere*.[44]

---

[36] Anon., *Miss Cadiere's Case*, 10.

[37] 'How happy is a Priest, | Who can the blushing Maid's Resistance smother, |
With Sin in one Hand, Pardon in the other': [Fielding], *Old Debauchees*, 27.

[38] Anon., *Case of Mrs. Cadiere*, 18.

[39] Ibid. 24.

[40] Anon., *Compleat History*, between 96 and 97.

[41] Anon., *Case of Mrs. Cadiere*, 49.

[42] Anon., *Wanton Jesuit*, 44.

[43] Walsh, 'Methodism and the Mob', 224.

[44] Anon., *Case of Mrs. Cadiere*, 24.

Clerical celibacy was remorselessly condemned and derided. Girard was 'Goatish','the lustful Jesuit' with a 'bestial Appetite'.[45] In *The Wanton Jesuit*, his confidante, La Guiol, compares him to Jupiter and, Leporello-like, notes his 'Correspondents in all the Towns and Cities in *France*; especially with our Sex, to whom … [he is] very beneficial, whether they are married or single Women'.[46] He 'will soon have a Seraglio,' gasps another character, 'and out-do the Great *Turk* in Variety of Women'.[47] It is significant that Girard's age was very rarely mentioned in the various publications (he was 'an old Priest of fifty' when the events occurred).[48] Occasionally, Girard was depicted as just a libidinous Frenchman – 'as compleat a Rover as any Nobleman; always in Pursuit of fresh Game, and never tired'.[49] But, usually, Catholic vows of chastity were blamed for his alleged behaviour: vows which were unnatural, vows that engendered monstrous sexual frustration and desires that could only be satisfied sordidly and illegitimately.

> When a Man is deny'd
> The free Use of a Bride,
> It makes him as lewd as the Devil;
> So our Clergy to tame,
> We allow 'em that same
> In a Way that is lawful and Civil.[50]

The Book of Common Prayer proclaimed that marriage was 'instituted of God', and Protestants cited St Paul's precept that '[m]arriage is honourable in all, and the bed undefiled'.[51] The entry of young women into convents was consequently deplored too; for a male-dominated society, a woman's natural vocation was sexual fulfilment in marriage. The song published in the *Gentleman's Magazine* adopted Squire Western's tone when mocking nuns:

> MISS *Kitty*, by her Mamma bred,
> From her Childhood to Devotion:
> Tho' Fair, yet vow'd she ne'er wou'd wed,
> But wou'd slight each Lover's Motion,

---

45 Anon., *Wanton Jesuit*, 17, 27.
46 Ibid. 24–5.
47 Ibid. 17.
48 Anon., *Case of Mrs. Cadiere*, 54.
49 Anon., *Wanton Jesuit*, 17.
50 Anon., *Miss Cadiere's Case*, 10.
51 Heb. 13: 4.

Lack-a-day, Sirs! had ever charming Maid
So very odd a Notion?[52]

Celibacy, Protestants insisted, nurtured perversion too. Confession ritualized domination by the priest and the submission of the penitent: 'Father *Girard* was ... absolutely Master in his Disciple's Chamber'.[53] 'You must obey me in every Thing as my little Child', commands Girard in *The Wanton Jesuit*; 'I will submit myself entirely to you', Cadière bleats.[54] And penance was a cover for sadism (and sometimes masochism) too. In the next scene, Girard enters '*with a Scourge in his Hand*', recounting '[w]ith what Patience and Resignation did my dear *Cadiere* endure the Lash!'[55] The account in *The Case of Mrs. Mary Catharine Cadiere* stressed the Jesuit's deviant desires. He 'ordered her to get upon the Bed ... gave her a few Lashes with his Scourge, and then kissed the Part which he had whipped'.[56] Thereafter, 'he told her, God was not yet satisfied, and that she must necessarily strip naked before him. Frightened at such an Injunction she screamed out and fainted away; but as soon as she recovered he undrest her to her Shift'.[57] The author of *The Wanton Jesuit* emphasized that such flagellation was both sexually arousing and hatefully popish. 'Hereticks may condemn the Use of *Flogging*,' pronounces Girard, 'but we Catholicks have passed a Decree in its Favour, and esteem it to be a necessary Discipline ... [I]t irritates the Blood, and gives new Vigour to our flagging Spirits.'[58] Nevertheless, as Peakman has argued, anti-Catholic accounts of penance-whippings powerfully influenced the depictions of flagellation common in later eighteenth-century pornographic novels.[59] Ironically, a French cause célèbre was promoting *le vice anglais*.

In France, Jansenist zealots used the Girard-Cadière scandal to pillory the Society of Jesus,[60] and the trial records were therefore peppered with pungent anti-Jesuit propaganda and rhetoric.

---

[52] Anon., '*Miss* Cadiere's Case', 446.
[53] Anon., *Case of Mrs. Cadiere*, 14.
[54] Anon., *Wanton Jesuit*, 21.
[55] Ibid. 23.
[56] Anon., *Case of Mrs. Cadiere*, 14.
[57] Ibid.
[58] Anon., *Wanton Jesuit*, 23.
[59] Peakman, *Mighty Lewd Books*, 160.
[60] Kuznicki, 'Sorcery and Publicity'.

The Society had, it was maintained, employed 'cunning arts and powerful interests ... to stifle the truth'.[61] It had procured false witnesses, screened Girard and, intent on Cadière's retraction, imprisoned the young woman, during the trial's first phase, in the Toulon convent which it directed.[62] Such conduct was no 'different from ... [its] Maxims'.[63] There was much here for the English public to relish: were not the Jesuits, as history showed, the most wily, resourceful and dangerous emissaries of the popish Church? In *The Wanton Jesuit*, the evil Father Sabatier SJ even contemplates Cadière's murder.[64] Later, he remarks, '[i]f a Jesuit cannot compass his wicked Purposes, he ought to be expelled the Society'.[65] Jesuitical doctrines, it was held, facilitated Girard's seduction of Cadière. This was scarcely surprising. Could not the Society's casuistry make black appear white? The sexual charge was old: in the seduction scene of Molière's *Tartuffe* (1664/9), Tartuffe argues 'Jesuitically' to counter Elmire's ostensible concerns.[66] However, it was Girard's supposed Quietism that appeared even more alarming. With its emphasis on mystic passivity and submission to God's will, and hence the near-annihilation of individual responsibility, Quietist teaching risked the disregarding of temptation. Girard saw 'the greatest crimes as indifferent actions', his enemies asserted, and believed 'all pleasure of whatever nature to be lawful'.[67] He taught his penitent 'no other Principles of morality, but *to forget herself, to be entirely passive, and to banish all scruples*'.[68] Naturally, such theology was easily satirized. Fielding ridiculed it,[69] as did the song in the *Gentleman's Magazine*:

> This pious Lecture to the Fair
> He read, when he confest her;
> 'Henceforth Submission be your Care,
> 'All Piety doth rest there.

61 Anon., *Case of Mrs. Cadiere*, 2.
62 Ibid. 38, 40, 41, 45–6, 46–7, 48, 79, 82, 86.
63 Ibid. 87.
64 Anon., *Wanton Jesuit*, 40.
65 Ibid. 46–7.
66 Jean-Baptiste Poquelin Molière, *Tartuffe*, Act 4, Scene 5.
67 Anon., *Case of Mrs. Cadiere*, 72.
68 Ibid.
69 [Fielding], *Old Debauchees*, 18–20.

'Lack-a-day, Child! for Fasting and for prayer,
'They out of Fashion Jests are.

Grown bolder now when next he came,
A holy Trance procuring;
On Miss he satisfy'd his Flame,
Her Extasy enduring.
Lack-a-day, Sir! said the reviving Dame,
Your Doctrine is alluring.[70]

One further facet of the case disgusted English readers: Cadière's displays of enthusiasm. The Georgian Church of England prided itself on its rationality, its moderation, its staid and decorous worship. The antithesis was popish (and sometimes Methodist) enthusiasm and its manifestations: ecstatic visions, raptures, mortifications, wailing and convulsions. *The Case of Mrs. Mary Catharine Cadiere* contained many details of Cadière's religious experiences: her 'frequent Extasies and Visions'; trances; a vision of the Sacred Heart; and transfigurations with the appearance of stigmata on her side, hands and feet, and a 'bloody Crown' on her head.[71] *The Case*'s preface was brutally dismissive: 'Her visions were undoubtedly the effects of Enthusiasm joined to Father *Girard*'s conversation with her'.[72] John Henley, in one of his 'orations', denounced her '*High Fits of Zeal*'.[73] And popish enthusiasm and sexual misconduct were explicitly linked in *The Case*. The convulsions which Cadière experienced threw her into postures 'contrary to the rules of modesty'.[74] After the stigmata appeared, Girard examined 'her body from top to toe', and 'handled her Neck and Breast, and sucked the wound' in her side every day.[75] Further, 'he frequently handled her privy-parts, [so] that she found her self all wet, and sometimes swooned away'.[76] Generally, Cadière was depicted as Girard's victim: indeed, *The Wanton Jesuit*'s sub-title was *Innocence Seduced*. But her enthusi-

---

[70] Anon., '*Miss* Cadiere's Case', 446.

[71] Anon., *Case of Mrs. Cadiere*, 6, 10, 11.

[72] Ibid. vi.

[73] J. Henley, *A Lecture on High Fits of Zeal; or, Mrs. Cadiere's Raptures*, 3rd edn (London, [1732?]).

[74] Anon., *Case of Mrs. Cadiere*, 69.

[75] Ibid. 35, 70.

[76] Ibid. 36.

astic seizures, her 'Fits, and her Dreams' seemed bogus to the 'Gentleman Commoner':[77]

> But she went on so fast,
> Folks grew weary at last,
> And worshipping turn'd to Suspicion;
> Then soon did they smoke,
> Pretty Miss's fine Joke,
> And see through her Craft and Ambition.[78]

He thought Cadière a 'little Gipsy', a 'young Whore'.[79]

★ ★ ★

Anti-Catholic sexual slurs occur in different literary forms in the later eighteenth century, and much more might be said about these. Two famous examples must suffice as illustrations – one a history, the other a novel. In the *Decline and Fall*, the somewhat prurient Edward Gibbon showed himself fascinated by the early Christians who 'had devoted themselves to the profession of perpetual chastity'[80] – and their lapses besides their extraordinary efforts. The 'learned Origen', he sneered, 'judged it the most prudent to disarm the tempter', and added, in a note, '[a]s it was his general practice to allegorize scripture; it seems unfortunate that, in this instance only, he should have adopted the literal sense'.[81] Gibbon continued, chuckling unpleasantly:

> Disdaining an ignominious flight, the virgins of the warm climate of Africa encountered the enemy in the closest engagement; they permitted priests and deacons to share their bed, and gloried amidst the flames in their unsullied purity. But insulted Nature sometimes vindicated her rights, and this new species of martyrdom served only to introduce a new scandal into the church.[82]

---

77   Anon., *Miss Cadiere's Case*, 4.
78   Ibid.
79   Ibid. 3.
80   Edward Gibbon, *The History of the Decline and Fall of the Roman Empire*, 6 vols (London, 1776–88), 1: 485.
81   Ibid. 1: 485, lxxi n. 94. Gibbon's English text, despite his celebrated claim, was not always chaste.
82   Ibid. 1: 485.

Again, celibacy's demands seemingly spawned vice. The theme was central to M. G. Lewis's extraordinary Gothic novel, *The Monk* (1796), in which monstrous lust, once unchained, propels Ambrosio, superior of Madrid's Capuchins, to fornication, rape, incest, matricide and ultimately damnation. Ambrosio is introduced as 'so strict an observer of chastity, that he knows not in what consists the difference of man and woman'.[83] Later, his seductress, as she tempts him, declares, '[u]nnatural were your vows of celibacy; man was not created for such a state'.[84] Lastly, in the novel's concluding, horrific, chapter, Lucifer tells Ambrosio: 'your lust only needed an opportunity to break forth'.[85]

Pornography was a staple of popular 'No Popery' publications in the nineteenth century, as emphasized by G. F. A. Best long ago and Diana Peschier very recently.[86] Libidinous priests, sadistic and/or masochistic penances, sinister convents and the dangers of celibacy and the confessional continued to exert a sick fascination. *Maria Monk's Awful Disclosures of the Hotel Dieu Nunnery* was first published in 1836; by 1860, three hundred thousand copies had been sold in Britain and abroad.[87] Although the themes might appear subtly in sophisticated novels,[88] such trash could, naturally, be scorned in wholesome literature too. In *The Warden*, when Mr Harding visits the great lawyer Sir Abraham Haphazard in London, the latter's preoccupation is the Convent Custody Bill, whose 107th clause 'ordered the bodily searching of nuns for Jesuitical symbols by aged clergymen'. 'It was known that it would be insisted on with terrible vehemence by Protestant Irish members, and as vehemently denounced by the Roman Catholic'.[89] One doubts whether Mr Harding properly appreciated the sordid import of clause 107; or had read any anti-Catholic pornography (or, indeed, any pornography whatsoever). But, for vast numbers of

---

[83] M. G. Lewis, *The Monk*, 2nd edn, 3 vols (London, 1796), 1: 22.

[84] Ibid. 2: 181.

[85] Ibid. 3: 311.

[86] G. F. A. Best, 'Popular Protestantism in Victorian Britain', in Robert Robson, ed., *Ideas and Institutions of Victorian Britain* (London, 1967), 115–42, at 124–37; Diana Peschier, 'Religious Sexual Perversion in Nineteenth-Century Anti-Catholic Literature', in Julie Peakman, ed., *Sexual Perversions 1670–1890* (Basingstoke, 2009), 202–20.

[87] Peschier, 'Religious Sexual Perversion', 204 n. 3.

[88] Diana Peschier, *Nineteenth-Century Anti-Catholic Discourses: The Case of Charlotte Brontë* (Basingstoke, 2005).

[89] Anthony Trollope, *The Warden* (1855), ch. 16.

his countrymen, anti-popish bawdry and pornography were very important conduits, or sewers, for sustaining that popular Protestantism which Sir Geoffrey Elton, like Trollope an astute observer of the English, saw as 'one of ... [their] most marked characteristics' over centuries.[90]

It would be possible to multiply instances of such anti-Catholic literature if not *ad infinitum* then certainly *ad nauseam*. Yet how should one account for its enduring popularity? That comparable sexual charges were brought against different 'out-groups' in very different societies shows that the explanation should partly be sought by looking beyond the context of the Cadière publications and English Protestant armouries. The stories appealed to a range of human instincts. Besides fun or sexual titillation, *Schadenfreude* was plainly one ('*The Jesuit Caught*'). So was the brutal urge to unmask satisfyingly holier-than-thou hypocrites. Today, tabloid newspapers or satirical publications amply display such characteristics in their coverage of child-abuse scandals in the Catholic Church. The human psyche recoils at the violation of the family. But perhaps, too, Girard's alleged behaviour covertly represented readers' baser desires (decently repressed), feared temptations or perverse fantasies, which were therefore sublimated and unconsciously projected onto an alien figure, jocularly or darkly. If so, no society will lack its Girards and Cadières.

University of Winchester

---

[90] G. R. Elton, *England under the Tudors*, 2nd edn (London, 1974), 220. A comparison might be made with the corrosion of respect for the eighteenth-century French monarchy produced not only by respectable Enlightenment critiques but also by pornographic *libelles*: Robert Darnton, 'The High Enlightenment and the Low-Life of Literature in Pre-Revolutionary France', *P&P*, no. 51 (1971), 81–115; T. C. W. Blanning, *The Culture of Power and the Power of Culture* (Oxford, 2002), 390, 400–2, 411–13.

ENGLISH CONVENTS IN EIGHTEENTH-CENTURY TRAVEL LITERATURE*

by CAROLINE WATKINSON

'A Nun's dress is a very becoming one', wrote Cornelius Cayley in 1772.[1] Similarly, Philip Thicknesse, witnessing the clothing ceremony at the English Augustinian convent in Paris, observed that the nun's dress was 'quite white, and no ways unbecoming ... [it] did not render her in my eyes, a whit less proper for the affections of the world'.[2] This tendency to objectify nuns by focusing on the mysterious and sexualized aspects of conventual life was a key feature of eighteenth-century British culture.[3] Novels, poems and polemic dwelt on the theme of the forced vocation, culminating in the dramatic portrayals of immured nuns in the Gothic novels of the 1790s.[4] The convent was portrayed as inherently despotic, its unnatural hierarchy and silent culture directly opposed to the sociability which, in Enlightenment thought, defined a civilized society. This despotic climate was one aspect of a culture of tyranny and constraint, which rendered nuns either innocent and victimized or complicit and immoral. Historians have noted that these stereotypes were remarkably similar to those applied to the Orient and have thus extended Said's notion of 'otherness' – the self-affirmation of a dominant culture as a norm from which other cultures deviate – to apply not merely to oriental cultures but to those aspects of European culture deemed exotic.[5] In so doing, they have challenged the notion that travel

*   I am grateful to the Arts and Humanities Research Council for funding this research and to David Allan and Michael Questier for their comments.

[1]   Cornelius Cayley, *A Tour Through Holland, Flanders and Part of France in the year 1772* (Leeds, 1773), 56.

[2]   Philip Thicknesse, *Useful Hints to Those who make the tour of France in a Series of Letters Written from that Kingdom* (London, 1768), 48.

[3]   See, e.g., Anon., *The Cloisters Laid Open* (London, 1770).

[4]   E.g. Matthew Lewis, *The Monk* (London, 1790); Ann Radcliffe, *The Mysteries of Udolpho* (London, 1794).

[5]   Edward Said, *Orientalism* (London, 1978). For Said, Orientalism constituted a collection of false assumptions underlying Western attitudes towards the East. These assumptions were in direct contrast to the West's view of itself. For instance, the notion that the East was feminine, irrational and weak contrasted with the West's portrayal of itself as masculine, strong and rational. Chloe Chard, *Pleasure and Guilt on the Grand*

writing was an exact record of social experience and have initiated a more nuanced understanding of textual convention and authorial experience. For historians of eighteenth-century Britain this has led to an examination of the construction of anti-Catholicism within travel literature and its use as an ideology around which the Protestant nation could unite.[6] Thus, Jeremy Black has noted that anti-Catholicism remained the 'prime ideological stance in Britain' and has claimed that encounters with Catholicism by British travellers in France 'excited fear or unease ... and, at times, humour or ridicule'.[7] Likewise, Bryan Dolan and Christopher Hibbert have seen encounters with continental convents culminating in negative descriptions of rituals, relics and enclosed space.[8]

However, there are problems with this interpretation, especially with regard to exiled English convents.[9] Firstly, convents are portrayed as peripheral and passive: there is little sense of interaction with British travellers and no consideration of a shared culture. Secondly, there is limited analysis of the 'public sphere': notions of audience and issues affecting textual production are not discussed. Thirdly, both Protestantism and anti-Catholicism are defined monolithically: all travellers are identified as uniformly Protestant, while anti-monasticism is seen as merely another strand of anti-Catholicism. More recently, Tony Claydon has urged historians to avoid too rigid a 'polarisation' between Protestantism and Catholicism, pointing out that the latter was not viewed as an exotic 'other' in the same way as the non-Western world.[10] Claydon, despite considering travel literature a form of 'English confessional geography', notes that there were 'divergences of prejudice' reflecting 'a culture making a slow and uneven transition'.[11] Recent approaches

---

Tour (Manchester, 1998), has extended this idea to Protestant portrayals of Catholic countries as irrational, idolatrous and autocratic.

[6] Jeremy Black, *The Grand Tour in the Eighteenth Century* (Gloucester, 1992). This argument builds on that put forward by Linda Colley, *Britons: Forging the Nation, 1707–1837* (London, 1994).

[7] Jeremy Black, *France and the Grand Tour* (Basingstoke, 2003), 159–63.

[8] Brian Dolan, *Ladies of the Grand Tour* (London, 2001), 169–70; Christopher Hibbert, *The Grand Tour* (London, 1989), 121–32.

[9] English convents had been founded in exile on the Continent at the beginning of the seventeenth century. There were twenty-one in France and Flanders.

[10] Tony Claydon, *Europe and the Making of England, 1660–1760* (Cambridge, 2007), 62.

[11] Ibid. 18–20.

have employed the term 'transculturation' to refer to the process whereby travel writing results not in the imposition of one culture over another but in a process of cultural exchange.[12] In this paper I want to explore this sense of a cultural interaction in order to focus on travel literature's status as a contested text which, far from promoting stereotypical images of nuns and convents, could challenge perceived opinion. By so doing, I hope to show that the status of English convents as exiled institutions created a potentially productive environment for cultural interchange. Moreover, by examining the way representations of convents were shaped by professional considerations, I aim to show that travel literature resulted in a more complex portrayal than previous historiography has acknowledged. I aim to use convents as a case study to initiate a more nuanced understanding of encounters with Catholicism which will, I hope, render problematic any attempt to define national identity exclusively in terms of anti-Catholicism, not least because travel writers' own reactions were never uniform.

Travel writing is a hybrid form composed of other genres, but by the eighteenth century literary forms were dominant. Authors were increasingly sentimental in tone, prioritizing personal experience and adventure over the mere reporting of discoveries. The popularity of travel accounts, combined with critique of them in contemporary reviews, meant that the production of travel literature could aid the establishment of a literary reputation. Notable writers such as Samuel Johnson and Joseph Addison produced at least one travel book, and popular novels such as Jonathan Swift's *Gulliver's Travels* and Oliver Goldsmith's *The Citizen of the World* took the form of imaginary travelogues. The travel writers discussed in depth in this essay all published their accounts and wrote for a public audience. Philip Thicknesse was a professional travel writer and well known within political and literary circles.[13] Cornelius Cayley was a well-known author of poetry and theological tracts and initially intended his account for serialization in a local newspaper.[14] Joseph Shaw and Sacheverell Stephens were

---

[12] Mary Louise Pratt, *Imperial Eyes: Travel Writing and Transculturation* (New York, 1992); Karin M. Morin and Jeanne K. Gueske, 'Strategies of Representation, Relationship and Resistance: British Women Travellers and Mormon Plural Wives', *Annals of the Association of American Geographers* 88 (1998), 436–62.

[13] Thicknesse, *Useful Hints*, 2.

[14] Cayley, *Tour*, iii–iv.

notable polemicists aiming to shape public attitudes.[15] George Edward Ayscough was a soldier with literary aspirations. His letters were published and he aimed to write in an 'unvarnished stile, and … not prove … void of amusement'.[16] The anonymous author of *A Tour* wrote to provide a printed account of things 'never before published'.[17] Likewise, the author of *Letters to a Lady* published his personal account to a possibly fictional girlfriend and aimed 'to amuse' but to have 'all the merit truth can give'.[18]

In writing for a public audience authors were keen to present themselves as loyal Protestant subjects and used a degree of anti-Catholicism to express this identity. Despite marrying into a Catholic family and later sending his daughters to be educated in convents, Thicknesse decried the 'wickedness of [Catholic] clergy, the ignorant and idolatrous behaviour in which they encourage the common laity; [and] the use and abuse of auricular confession'.[19] His work was, in part, a response to 'the outcry we are so continually making in England against the increase of popery' and he aimed to show the 'superstition, the ignorance, the great number of holidays, and the poverty in consequence'.[20] As the son of Francis Ayscough, the Dean of Bristol and Preceptor to Prince George, George Edward Ayscough professed his Protestant heritage by revealing the 'superstitious idolatry of Roman Catholicism'.[21] The Methodist preacher Cornelius Cayley was a clerk in the Prince of Wales's treasury until 1752 and, despite extending the 'olive branch of peace' to Roman Catholicism, remained opposed to idolatry.[22] Sacheverell Stephens was even more polemical in tone: considering monastic institutions to have no 'foundation either in religion or Christianity', he asserted that Catholics were 'enemies

---

[15] Joseph Shaw, *Letters to a Nobleman from a Gentleman Travelling thro' Holland, Flanders and France* (London, 1709), xiii; Sacheverell Stephens, *Miscellaneous Remarks made on the Spot in a Late Seven Years Tour through France, Italy, Germany and Holland* (London, 1756).

[16] George Edward Ayscough, *Letters from an Officer in the Guards to his friend in England: Containing some Account of France and Italy* (London, 1778), 2.

[17] Anon., *A Tour Through Part of France and Flanders* (London, 1768), vii.

[18] A. R., *Travels into France and Italy in a series of Letters to a Lady* (London, 1771), 2.

[19] Thicknesse, *Useful Hints*, 73 (Letter VII).

[20] Ibid. 95 (Letter VIII).

[21] Ayscough, *Letters from an Officer*, 5–10.

[22] Cayley, *Tour*, 13.

to the mild religion and government of their native country'.[23]
The legal writer Joseph Shaw was also politically motivated, travelling in order to assess the state of France and Holland during
the interval of peace that followed the Treaty of Ryswick. He
made no attempt to hide his pro-Dutch sentiment and considered Catholicism 'manifestly destructive both to the Increase of
Trade, and of mankind it self'.[24] The anonymous author of *A Tour
Through Part of France and Flanders* also presented himself as a loyal
Protestant by decrying the 'fabulous history of Romish-miracles',
while the author of *Letters to a Lady* wrote to 'be of service to
[his] country'.[25]

Yet, despite professing anti-Catholicism, these authors offer a
remarkably sympathetic portrayal of convents. Where one might
expect to find discussions of the forced vocation a more complex
view emerges. Thicknesse initially expressed horror at the 'funeral-
like' rituals associated with the clothing ceremony but on a return
visit to the nuns he 'found them with their garlands still upon
their heads, and by their vivacity and conversation, they seemed
perfectly happy'.[26] They looked 'as merry as *Greeks*, and [he] could
scarcely believe they were the same grave, demure-looking damsels
[he] had seen the night before'.[27] Travel writers provide detailed
accounts of the stages potential recruits had to go through before
joining a convent, thereby rendering problematic any notion that
internment was sudden or forced. The author of *Letters to a Lady*
noted that it would take 'six months' before 'every votary thus
initiated may claim the second habit ... and one year after this
second period, [before] she may make a profession of her vows,
which is called the year of probation of noviceship ... [yet] ... even
at this time she may recede, as her inclination calls her'.[28] It helped
that many writers had personal knowledge of nuns returning to
England: they could tell that the 'charming young lady who left
the convent and came to England in 1756 ... Bab D[unsta]n [was]
now the amiable consort of Mr T[ildesle]y of Lancs'.[29] Cayley

---

[23] Stevens, *Miscellaneous Remarks*, 6.
[24] Shaw, *Letters to a Nobleman*, xiii.
[25] Anon., *Tour Through Part of France and Flanders*, 6–9; A. R., *Letters to a Lady*, 44–8.
[26] Thicknesse, *Useful Hints*, 52.
[27] Ibid.
[28] A. R., *Letters to a Lady*, 21.
[29] Anon., *Tour Through Part of France and Flanders*, 12–16.

knew schoolgirls who would 'return home again after some years, unless they chuse to become nuns', while Thicknesse told of a nun who 'left the pension at the age of seventeen, returned to England to her family and friends for four or five years, and then to Rouen, as the only place she could find happiness in!'[30]

Thus, far from being the victims of parental authority, nuns are portrayed as choosing to lead a cloistered life. During a profession ceremony at the English Benedictines, Ayscough noted that the nun 'performed the ceremony with great cheerfulness, when she quitted the habit of the world, the ornaments of which she flings from her with the greatest disdain'.[31] Cayley found he 'had an opportunity of seeing (what I did not expect) a number of healthful looking contented faces mixed with a great solemnity'.[32] Since nuns are shown to be cheerful on profession and in general free to leave, the notion of the convent as a centre of despotic constraint is challenged. Instead, an image of nuns as sociable and engaged emerges. The writer known only as A. R. found that the nuns' conversation was 'sprightly, witty, and entertaining and not full of that solemnity and gravity which their dull retreat prepares the visitor to expect'.[33] Stephens recorded conversing with a nun for 'almost two hours' and remembered this talk 'as one of the most agreeable of [his] whole life'.[34] Nuns are even shown to be engaged in conventual politics and active in the process of voting for new recruits:

> The nuns are seated at their proper seats, but not near the table, where they remain about a quarter of an hour in profound silence, in order to deliberate maturely whether they have any partiality for, or dislike to, the young lady, more than she deserves. When the time above mentioned is expired, the superior rises from her seat, and, going to the box, puts in a pea or bean: the nuns in their turns follow her example. This method of electing by ballot prevents the possibility of a discovery who are the young novice's friends or enemies.[35]

---

30 Cayley, *Tour*, 22; Thicknesse, *Useful Hints*, xxix.
31 Ayscough, *Letters from an Officer*, 39.
32 Cayley, *Tour*, 29.
33 A. R., *Letters to a Lady*, 125.
34 Stevens, *Miscellaneous Remarks*, 17–19.
35 Anon., *Tour Through Part of France and Flanders*, 32–9.

This image of convents as accountable to their inhabitants runs counter to the notion of nuns as the oppressed victims of tyrannical structures.

Admittedly, travel writers do not deny that life for English nuns was one of austerity and hardship. The English Poor Clares 'rise at midnight to prayer, sleep in their coffins, and eat but one meal a day, and then only one thing such as eggs, salt fish, salad, rice, and sometimes, by way of regale, potatoes!!'[36] The voices of the English Benedictines in Paris were 'so attenuated by fasting and mortification, they sounded like that of Lungs in the Achymist'.[37] Yet, in a reversal of Protestant polemic linking economic and social hardship to Catholic corruption and zeal, this aspect of constraint is marked out for approval rather than censure. Thicknesse noted that British society was 'apt to take a malicious delight in setting forth the dissolute manners and vices which we find therein, without thinking how grievously we offend, and justly too, those members who are truly good'.[38] Instead, he argued that convents 'produce many instances of shining virtues; there are few which do not contain some noble minds' and he challenged even 'the most established deist to see and converse with the English poor *Clares* at *Rouen,* and be insensible of their merit or without respecting them for their piety, and the hardships they endure throughout life'.[39] The more austere convents are frequently marked out for preference. Cayley preferred the harsh simplicity of the Poor Clares to the 'richer sort' of Benedictine or Augustinian convent in Dunkirk, which were not 'of the rigorous order that some are'.[40] He pointed out that 'worldly vanities creep into some of these places too much, and to the sorrow of many pious Roman Catholics, who are really crucified to the world with its lusts'.[41] Similarly, Stevens noted that 'affability accompanied poverty, as pride did riches'.[42] One even detects a note of pride in Ayscough's remark

---

[36] Thicknesse, *Useful Hints,* 118.
[37] Anon., *Tour Through Part of France and Flanders,* 38.
[38] Ibid. 121.
[39] Ibid. 122–8.
[40] Cayley, *Tour,* 51–4.
[41] Ibid. 54.
[42] Stevens, *Miscellaneous Remarks,* 321.

that 'wherever the English have convents they are distinguished', although 'it is a reputation I should never wish them to acquire'.[43]

Travel writing was not, then, simply a medium for the reproduction of popular stereotypes but a means of contesting them. Ayscough's acceptance of exiled convents as *English* institutions suggests that a shared national identity helped shape this portrayal. A. R. noted that 'convents are places I do not much frequent' but nonetheless paid a visit to the Poor Clares of Rouen since 'this being composed entirely of English, it was a compliment due to the nuns'.[44] Since exiled convents still saw themselves as comprised of English nationals, they limited recruitment to British-born subjects and maintained communication with friends and family remaining in the homeland.[45] They were thus easily identifiable as 'fellow countrywomen', many of whom were the daughters of well-known gentry families, and this encouraged a more considered approach to their portrayal than encounters with the anonymous nuns of continental convents.[46] Stereotypes emerge more frequently with regard to native French or Flemish convents than English ones. Thus, the French Ursulines are described as 'ugly, with dirty petticoats and solemn expressions' and the Montargis nuns as 'ugly (and) possessed with a zealous piety'.[47] However, nuns at English convents are clearly identified as 'Miss Canning, a former august beauty about London' or 'one of the daughters of the late Marquis of Powis'.[48] The writer of *A Tour* acknowledged that he knew a friend who 'resided in the Dominicans convent twelve years' and was thus 'perfectly acquainted with all their ceremonies, times of prayer, and all the different regulations of the convent'.[49] This sense of a shared social status linking the British elite with their exiled counterparts contributed to a more sympathetic portrayal of convents in travel literature.

---

[43] Ayscough, *Letters from an Officer*, 212.

[44] A. R., *Letters to a Lady*, 109.

[45] The English convents in exile referred to themselves as English subjects but their membership was composed of English, Welsh and Irish women. Scottish women seem to have joined French convents.

[46] Ibid. 110.

[47] Anon., *Tour Through Part of France and Flanders*, 32–3; Stevens, *Miscellaneous Remarks*, 318.

[48] Shaw, *Letters to a Nobleman*, vii, 75; Anon., *Tour Through Part of France and Flanders*, 102.

[49] Anon., *Tour Through Part of France and Flanders*, 21.

The ability of travel writers to identify the members of English convents suggests that they did not remain merely *observed* institutions but were central to the process of exchange and encounter. Since convents benefited financially from tourism, they were keen to encourage British travellers. The abbess of the English Benedictines at Ghent wrote frequently to Protestant families detailing convenient times for them to visit, and convents sold souvenirs to passing tourists.[50] Travel writers assert that one could purchase 'boxes of dressed figures representing all the different religious orders of the Romish church', 'purses, flowers and embroidered shoes' and 'many curiosities'.[51] Readers are even warned that convents might take advantage of the unsuspecting traveller. Ayscough noted that 'by these religious damsels (one) may be finely gulled and cheated (purchasing) at a much higher price than in the shops at Paris' and recorded that they 'publickly, as in a shop, offered all sorts of Poppets and Babies to be sold … at an unreasonable price'.[52] Travel writers were dependent on Catholic initiatives for access to relics and details of ceremonies. The author of *A Tour* recorded that he had been aided in his endeavours by 'some learned and worthy ecclesiastics of the Roman-Catholic persuasion' who were 'very complaisant and obliging in giving satisfactory answers to strangers of a different persuasion'.[53] It was only through the help of a Catholic friend that he was able to supply information on the vows taken at convent ceremonies since 'they [were] kept quite secret, and no body permitted to have a copy'.[54]

This process of interchange partly resulted from issues of readership and reception. In the first instance, travel writers aimed to ensure that their accounts were useful. There were travellers who 'for want of knowing the time of seeing the nuns … seldom see above one or two', so offering a 'full and circumstantial account of [the convents] could not fail to prove agreeable'.[55] Thus authors advised that they had only to choose 'the times specified in this work, [and] they would be sure of having an opportunity of

---

[50] Winchester, Hampshire Record Office, MS Banbury, 1M44/110/81: Letter of William Knollis to Mary Knollis, 20–23 January 1794.
[51] Ayscough, *Letters from an Officer*, 9; Thicknesse, *Useful Hints*, 49.
[52] Ayscough, *Letters from an Officer*, 9.
[53] Anon, *Tour Through Part of France and Flanders*, 7.
[54] Ibid. 21.
[55] Anon., *Tour Through Part of France and Flanders*, xvii.

gratifying their curiosity'.[56] Shaw assured his readers that 'a Traveller need only take this Book in his Hand without any other Guide'.[57] Travel literature had, therefore, to offer detailed accounts of convents, which often required 'long residence in the country' and 'repeated opportunities of considering attentively'.[58] Secondly, travel literature ought to be novel and entertaining since 'mere description was tedious'.[59] It was this consideration that led the author of *A Tour* to list the 'most minute ceremonies' in the hope of rendering his account original.[60] Thirdly, travel accounts had to reveal something of the author's character and personal experience, setting down in them 'all that happens to *me or mine*'.[61] This necessitated some degree of personal engagement with convent communities, leading Thicknesse to remark that 'like as at a play, I found myself often deeply interested for the parties'.[62]

However, if a notion of the 'public' conditioned what *should* be included, it also imposed constraints on what *could* be. The relationship between travel writers and their public was mediated by reviewers and patrons and governed by notions of what was appropriate within a professional context. The professionalization of travel writing during the eighteenth century increased the need to distinguish the 'writer by trade' from popularizers of cheap print media.[63] This distinction was harder to delineate at a time when the boundaries between travel literature and novels were increasingly blurred: Laurence Sterne's *A Sentimental Journey Through France and Italy* used a fictional narrator for a purportedly factual account, while Jonathan Swift's *Gulliver's Travels* satirized travel writers' fictional tendencies. Likewise the popularity of the epistolary model of travel writing – once the domain of philosophical reflection – led to the proliferation of printed 'letters home' in the press. Thicknesse stressed that when 'sailors or soldiers, men bred to arms and not to letters, publish their travels or remarks upon other nations, the readers may find entertainment by laughing at

---

56 Ibid.
57 Shaw, *Letters to a Nobleman*, xviii.
58 Anon., *Tour Through Part of France and Flanders*, 5; Thicknesse, *Useful Hints*, 17.
59 A. R., *Letters to a Lady*, 4.
60 Anon., *Tour Through Part of France and Flanders*, 16.
61 Ibid. 9–10.
62 Thicknesse, *Useful Hints*, 125.
63 Ibid. 31.

their folly' but from professionals 'every propriety [was] expected, every absurdity ... glaring'.[64] Despite the anonymity of A. R., he did not wish to repeat the 'sameness, or folly' found 'in every common journalist' and distinguished his account from 'those who write their travels at home'.[65]

As these authors suggested, distinguishing the professional account from that of popular print culture meant ensuring that certain standards were maintained. It necessitated 'purity of style, delicacy of sentiment and sterling judgement', for 'the public (would be) gulled and imposed upon if they do not meet with TRUTH'.[66] Shaw, despite his political incentive, aimed to be 'generally pretty near the Truth', since this was 'graceful and commendable in the Mouth of a Traveller'.[67] The establishment of the *Monthly Review* in 1749 and its rival the *Critical Review* in 1756 helped shape and define professional practice and set the standards for the establishment of an author's reputation. Authors of conduct manuals urged travel writers to promote 'national manners' and 'responsible ecumenicism'. In his 1778 work *On the Manner of Writing Voyages and Travels*, Vicesimus Knox stated that writers should 'interest the mind as much as a novel [but] instead of rendering it effeminate and debauched make it instructively inquisitive'.[68] Travel writers were widely criticized for producing accounts which seemed overly intolerant. Thus Tobias Smollett and Henry Fielding were both condemned by the *Critical Review* for unduly intolerant judgements and inappropriate subject matter. The cultivation of a 'tolerant' position was thus essential for professional credibility. Writers were aware that their audience was not exclusively Protestant: travel literature was reviewed by European journals and purchased by British Catholics. The characterization of Catholicism as a 'persecuting disposition, which is so unchristian and offensive', would only be convincing if Protestantism was proved the opposite, and writers could only 'abominate [the

---

[64] Ibid. 12.
[65] A. R., *Letters to a Lady*, 17–19.
[66] Thicknesse, *Useful Hints*, 18–22.
[67] Shaw, *Letters to a Nobleman*, xiv.
[68] Vicesimus Knox, *On the Manner of Writing Voyages and Travels* (London, 1778), 432–8.

Catholics'] uncharitable disposition towards all dissenters' if their own approach proved more ecumenical.[69]

Therefore, travel writing was less an aggressive assertion of a clearly defined belief than a process whereby the nature of Protestantism itself was defined and shaped. For many, travel literature had never quite lost its association with pilgrimage and acted as a personal exploration of faith. Cornelius Cayley may have been a little unusual in referring to himself as 'a Christian Catholic and a Protestant' but it is important to emphasize that within Protestantism there existed a wide spectrum of belief.[70] Defining their attitude to female monasticism offered a means for travel writers to assess this practice and to reflect on standards within their own faith. Throughout the eighteenth century the merit of female monasticism was much debated within British society. Nostalgic laments from Bishop Gilbert Burnet and Samuel Wesley contrasted with the vitriolic rebukes of pamphlet culture. Cayley's admiration for nuns' clothing resulted from his criticism of the 'foolish fantastic dresses of the modern taste'.[71] A. R. took a positive view of conventual life because it contrasted with the 'dissolute manners of our time'.[72] Travel writers reached both positive and negative conclusions as a result of their encounters with exiled convents. Sacheverell Stevens thought it 'worthy [of] the consideration of the legislature to prevent, as much as possible, the sending our young people, of both sexes, into foreign parts to receive their education'.[73] Yet Thicknesse felt it 'all conspired to operate very strongly upon [him] in their favour, though not in favour of their way of thinking'.[74]

The same contradictory attitudes to female monasticism would resurface when exiled convents attempted to refound themselves in Britain in the aftermath of the French Revolution. However, the notion that the unity of Christianity in response to the secular threat initiated a tolerant approach to monastic institutions, argued by Bernard Ward, David Matthew and Robert Ryan,[75] is prob-

69 Thicknesse, *Useful Hints*, 122; Shaw, *Letters to a Nobleman*, 229.
70 Cayley, *Tour*, 1–10.
71 Ibid. 99–100.
72 A. R., *Letters to a Lady*, 71–3.
73 Stevens, *Miscellaneous Remarks*, 6.
74 Thicknesse, *Useful Hints*, 161–2.
75 B. Ward, *The Dawn of the Catholic Revival in England 1781–1803*, 2 vols (London,

lematic particularly when we consider the process of interaction and sympathetic portrayals resulting from eighteenth-century travel literature. Far from being peripheral, exiled convents were key centres of interaction for British tourists: writers were able to identify individual nuns, and the process of recording ceremonies and conversations necessitated reciprocal involvement. This partly explains why an image of nuns as sociable and engaged, vastly different from the victimized nun of popular culture, emerges. However, issues of readership and professional credibility also shaped representations. The need to ensure that accounts were both novel and useful led authors to attempt more detailed and accurate descriptions. Moreover, a degree of toleration became an authorial obligation as writers sought to defend Protestantism's ecumenical tenets. Yet anti-Catholicism clearly surfaced in the travel literature discussed here. The fact that this did not result in the negative portrayal of convents suggests that authors were able to distinguish between alternate aspects of Catholicism.

This essay has presented a case study of attitudes to female monasticism, but a comparative approach to representations of monks, Jesuits and the papacy would help shape our understanding of anti-Catholicism as a diverse ideology. In addition, a consideration of private responses to convents, which surface in the correspondence and commonplace books of British travellers, would aid our understanding of the discourse of toleration within the public and private spheres. By getting back to this complexity, we challenge the idea that anti-Catholicism was a uniform ideology capable of uniting the British nation.

Queen Mary, University of London

1909), 2: 165; D. Matthew, *Catholicism in England 1535-1935: Portrait of a Minority; its Culture and Tradition* (London, 1936), 101–10; R. Ryan, *The Romantic Reformations: Religion and Politics in English Literature* (Cambridge, 1997), 23.

A NOVEL RESISTANCE: MISSION NARRATIVE AS THE ANTI-NOVEL IN THE EVANGELICAL ASSAULT ON BRITISH CULTURE

by BENJAMIN L. FISCHER

'Their annual increase is counted by thousands; and they form a distinct people in the empire, having their peculiar laws and manners, a hierarchy, a costume, and even a physiognomy of their own', wrote Robert Southey for the *Quarterly Review* in 1810, opening a balanced critique of what he called 'the Evangelical Sects'.[1] Leaders of the Evangelical Revival had taught in pulpit, pamphlet and periodical that to be truly Christian meant radical difference from others in society, even others professing faith; or, as Charles Simeon, the model and mentor for hundreds of Cambridge-educated evangelical ministers, stated it, 'Christians are either nominal or real'.[2] Following William Wilberforce's urging in his *Practical View of the Prevailing Religious System of Professed Christians ... Contrasted with Real Christianity*, Evangelicals strove in their separate spheres to accomplish a social revolution by which the mores, values and social practices received from the eighteenth century would be overturned by normalizing evangelical values in society. While working in their individual vocations, Evangelicals were also cooperating, 'linked in a single, if multiform, social and religious phenomenon'.[3] As Southey's comments indicate, even by 1810 their revolution was proving noticeably effective.

The purpose of this essay is to draw attention to a part of this hegemonic project, the part occupied by what we may call mission narratives, or extended accounts by missionaries of their experiences with foreign peoples. During the early decades of the nineteenth century, Evangelicals found themselves at odds with social and literary practices of the wider culture. Undoubtedly the most marked literary development of the period was the

---

[1] [Robert Southey], 'On the Evangelical Sects', *Quarterly Review* 4 (1810), 480–514, at 480.

[2] Charles Simeon, *Horae Homileticae*, 21 vols (London, 1832), 6: 351.

[3] Donald Lewis, *Lighten Their Darkness: The Evangelical Mission to Working-Class London, 1828–1860* (New York, 1986), 1.

experimentation with fictional prose narration, what came to be called the novel. Devoured by the middle class, novels were seen as inflaming a passion for social fantasy and for escape to the imagined spaces of new worlds beyond Europe, and as drawing thousands of readers away from their public duties or private concerns – including their spiritual condition. Even worse, novels might provide wicked models or justifications for unhelpful behaviour. As an antidote to this social epidemic, mission narratives did the cultural work of satisfying the evangelical appetite for story and imagined spaces without the danger of inattention to righteousness and the gospel. With this genre, Evangelicals had their answer to the secular novel. Operating in parallel to the novels of the circulating libraries, missionary writing formed the basis for evangelical conceptualization of the expanding Christian community around the world. Within evangelical culture these narratives became one of the most popular forms of extended text because they satisfied the theological standards expected of acceptable literature while also opening their readers' imaginations to exciting and unknown lands on the edge of empire.[4]

Furthermore, as a study of shared reading practices that helped Evangelicals craft ways of thinking about the place of Christians in the world, this essay contributes to the ongoing discussion of evangelical identity. Commended by the powerful organs of evangelical influence – the denominational and literary journals – mission narratives were among the texts that crossed the dividing lines of denomination and theological emphasis. My contention that Anglican Evangelicals, Methodists and Dissenters all turned to mission narratives for spiritually constructive light reading supports David Bebbington's argument that although particular theological stresses and church polity ultimately divided the British evangelical world, Evangelicals were nevertheless linked in a subculture based

---

[4] Susan Thorne, *Congregational Missions and the Making of an Imperial Culture in 19th-Century England* (Stanford, CA, 1999), and Anna Johnston, *Missionary Writing and Empire, 1800–1860* (Cambridge, 2003), explore the role of missionaries at the far outposts of the empire. Drawing on the recent work of anthropologists and historians, most notably Jean and John Comaroff, Catharine Hall, Brian Stanley and Andrew Porter, they turn attention to the texts produced by missionaries and to the rhetorical constructs of imperialist attitudes. Christopher Herbert, *Culture and Anomie: Ethnographic Imagination in the Nineteenth Century* (Chicago, IL, 1991), also considers 'missionary literature' as foundational for the development of ethnography.

on their worldview, their common heritage from the eighteenth-century revival movement, their practical relational ties and their shared emphasis on spreading the gospel.[5]

Historians and literary critics readily acknowledge the powerful influence of Evangelicalism on nineteenth-century Britain. By 1853, over a third of the Anglican clergy were evangelical, including the archbishop of Canterbury. According to the Religious Census of 1851, Congregationalists in England had more than quadrupled since 1800 and Methodists had tripled, while the population had only doubled in that time.[6] The obvious conclusion is that the evangelical movement proved exceedingly fruitful in the first half of the century. Likewise, within the realm of literature we also see the impact of evangelical effectiveness. The market share of religious books from 1801 to 1835 was roughly 22.2 per cent, but between 1836 and 1863 this rose to 33.5 per cent.[7] These figures suggest that the cultural and theological formulations that made them socially and politically effective had been developing in a specifically evangelical intellectual conversation.

In the face of caricature and disdain, as 'the public attention has been roused by their numbers, their zeal, and their activity, and alarm has been sounded against them from all quarters',[8] Evangelicals of all denominations felt the need to share an ongoing conversation and intelligent articulation of their mission in the world. They required some organ by which they might grasp a sense of their spread, their wider effectiveness as witnesses of the gospel in Britain, and – with the formation of the first missionary

---

5 See David Bebbington, *Evangelicalism in Modern Britain: A History from the 1730s to the 1980s* (London, 1989); Elisabeth Jay, *The Religion of the Heart: Anglican Evangelicalism and the Nineteenth-Century Novel* (Oxford, 1979); Boyd Hilton, *The Age of Atonement: the Influence of Evangelicalism on Social and Economic Thought, 1785–1865* (Oxford, 1988), 7–32; Ian Bradley, 'The Politics of Godliness: Evangelicals in Parliament, 1784–1832' (D.Phil. thesis, Oxford University, 1974); Doreen Rosman, *Evangelicals and Culture* (London, 1984), among others.

6 See Bebbington, *Evangelicalism*, 106–8. Lewis, *Lighten their Darkness*, 5, reports that by 1844, according to a never-published report prepared for the editor of *The Times*, the majority of the eighty-nine leading London clergy were Evangelicals. According to William Gladstone, 'The Evangelical Movement: Its Parentage, Progress, and Issue', *Gleanings of Past Years*, 7: *1843–79* (London, 1879), 201–40, at 213, before 1830 'not a single London parish, west of Temple Bar, was in the hands of the Evangelical party'.

7 Jay, *Religion of the Heart*, 7.

8 [Southey], 'Evangelical Sects', 481.

societies from 1793 onwards – their role as witnesses to foreign peoples. While sermons (both delivered and published) and hymns (for public and private use) inculcated a gospel focus and shaped Evangelicals' speech with a biblical cadence, private reading was also crafted to provide collective focus for the various societies and denominations. With this purpose in mind, the editors of the inaugural issue of the *Evangelical Magazine* in 1793 shared an expectation of a wide audience and circulation, as '[t]housands read a Magazine, who have neither money to purchase, nor leisure to peruse, large volumes.'[9] Church libraries, reading groups, or even the parlour of the minister's home could cheaply serve as the evangelical substitutes for the new circulating libraries that made available secular journals and novels.[10]

The Evangelicals' opponents certainly noted their tendency towards separation through reading media. 'No works in this country', wrote one critic (probably Southey) in the *Quarterly Review*, 'are so widely circulated, and studied by so many thousand readers, as the Evangelical and Methodist Magazines, and … we have no hesitation in saying … that they tend to narrow the judgment, debase the intellect, and harden the heart.'[11] The underlying complaint was that an evangelical subculture, while manifestly benefiting its members, also undermined the national spirit and weakened the total fabric of British society. In addition, they were doing their work at an alarming rate. To the extent that the evangelical journals achieved their object of nurturing a subculture with a distinct worldview, they were the more despised by the non-evangelical portions of society.

Eminently practical in their pursuit of righteousness, most Evangelicals welcomed guidance and discussion in determining boundaries of acceptable lifestyle and behaviour. The crafting of discrimination and taste for the evangelical subculture became largely the province of the evangelical journals: the *Evangelical Magazine, Baptist Magazine, Methodist Magazine, Eclectic Review, Christian Observer, Christian Guardian* and *The Record*. Recognizing

---

[9] Preface, *Evangelical Magazine* I (1793), I.
[10] Kathryn Sutherland mentions a group of working-class men in Gainsborough who made a joint subscription to the *Eclectic Review* through the 1820s: '"Events … have made us a world of readers": Reader Relations 1780–1830', in David Pirie, ed., *The Romantic Period* (New York, 1994), 1–48, at 14.
[11] [Southey], 'Evangelical Sects', 508.

that the secular journals of the day had increasing popularity and influence with middle-class readers, but at the same time finding their own worldview antagonistic to these popular periodicals, the emerging evangelical societies set up their own monthlies and quarterlies to counteract the influence of the secular journals and to provide reading that would fit easily within the bounds of 'innocent' entertainment. The preface of the *Eclectic Review* in 1807 shows their conscious purpose to rival their secular counterparts:

> To arouse the Christian world to a perception of the important influence which literature possesses, in obstructing, or accelerating, the progress of religious truth and human happiness, was the primary object, and to a very encouraging degree has been the result, of their disinterested efforts. It is, happily, no longer necessary to urge, that *the customary employment of such an engine against the interests of Religion and Morality, is the clearest of all arguments for adopting it in their defence.*[12]

Conceiving themselves on the side of righteousness against the pernicious influence of the *Edinburgh Review, Blackwood's Magazine* and the *Quarterly Review*, Evangelicals turned to their own periodicals for interpretations of current events, for news of movements in the Church, for reports of missionary labour at home and abroad, and for recommendations of other suitable reading matter.

The evangelical view of popular culture was particularly hostile in the early nineteenth century to the growing influence of novels, which were seen as 'so universally diffused, so easy of access, and of so insidious a nature, as nearly to preclude the possibility of safety'.[13] Shaped by the increasingly pervasive belief in an imminent premillennial return of Christ, the first quarter of the century saw a hardening attitude towards anything perceived as inseparable from the perishing order. Even among those who held a post-millennial view of Christ's return, novel-reading could be cast as distracting from the task of spreading the gospel to all nations and ushering in the return of Christ. In conformity with a strong belief in accountability on an impending day of judgement, the evangelical

---

[12] 'Preface', *Eclectic Review* 3 (1807), 555; italics mine.
[13] Edward Mangin, *An Essay on Light Reading, as it may be supposed to influence Moral Conduct and Literary Taste* (London, 1808), 12.

teachers of the day emphasized 'seriousness' of mind and the rejection of vain expenditure of time and energy.

Along with their concern for stewardship of time, Evangelicals believed novels to be dangerous to the spiritual health of a reader. Leading the flock of the 'serious' away from the vice-laden path of novel-reading was Hannah More. In *Strictures on the Modern System of Female Education*, she laboured to illustrate that 'the corruption occasioned by these books has spread so wide, and descended so low, as to have become one of the most universal as well as most pernicious sources of corruption among us'.[14] It seemed obvious that if Evangelicals chose their reading matter according to spiritual principles, then they would steer clear of secular novels.

In her own battle against the corrupting effects of novels, and in a truly evangelistic spirit, More went so far as to extend her hand into the lions' den by writing a 'decent' novel intended for readers in the circulating libraries. As with her later efforts for the Religious Tract Society, More decided that lost novel-readers needed the gospel message to come to them on their own terms. In a letter to William Pepys, she explains her approach with her first novel, *Coelebs in Search of a Wife*:

> I wrote it to amuse the languor of disease. I thought there were already good books enough in the world for good people; but there was a large class of readers whose wants had not been attended to; – the subscribers to the circulating library. A little to raise the tone of that mart of mischief, and to counteract its corruptions, I thought was an object worth attempting.[15]

As More suggests, *Coelebs* was not intended as a novel to slake an evangelical thirst; instead, it was a work of cross-cultural evangelism. Amusingly, the *Christian Observer* found that the anonymously published and moralistic *Coelebs* was 'apt to be vulgar' and discovered in it 'some want of taste and strict moral delicacy'.[16]

Consistent with More's concerns, evangelical periodicals were clear that their readers should not expect to find reviews of novels,

---

[14] Hannah More, *Strictures on the Modern System of Female Education*, 5th edn (Dublin, 1800), 131.

[15] William Roberts, *Memoirs of the Life and Correspondence of Mrs. Hannah More*, 2 vols (New York, 1836), 2: 168.

[16] A. G. Newell, 'Early Evangelical Fiction', *Evangelical Quarterly* 38 (1966), 3–21, at 9.

suggesting that such matter was not fit for evangelical Christians. Occasionally, when a popular novel gained repute for positive moral content – as in the case of *Coelebs* or R. W. Cunningham's *The Velvet Cushion* – reviewers felt pressed to explain their stance more explicitly, as in 1815 when the *Evangelical Magazine* stated: 'we will guard the Christian church against affording much countenance to novels; for though they may be multiplied by the religious to an indefinite extent ... yet they create so ravenous an appetite, that they will send our young people to the circulating library for trash poisonous to the soul'.[17] Again, silence towards secular works was typically enough to discourage potential evangelical readers, but under pressure from the success of Scott's Waverley novels, the *Christian Observer* became explicit in 1834:

> It was only in our last Number that we mentioned the displeasure we have incurred by our oft-expressed opinion respecting the Waverley Novels; and as for the publications of Mr. Bulwer, Theodore Hook, Leigh Hunt, and various other popular authors, so far as our pages are concerned, it would be a secret to the world that the writers had lived, or their works been written. ... [W]e are usually as unconscious of the last new popular work of fiction as of the last edict of the Grand Lama of Thibet. ... We do not, however, think that those who cannot find entertainment in argument should be deprived of a reasonable share of lighter matter; and there is always one resource in particular, which all classes of persons ... may in common avail themselves of – namely, interesting and useful narrative, especially religious biography – and we are therefore always happy to intersperse both our reviews and other papers with a large portion of this unexceptionable nutriment.[18]

In this suggestion the editors recognize the value of story and of a basic human tendency to delight in narrative. They were well aware that the works of Scott, Bulwer, Hook and Hunt were widely read – even by curious Evangelicals – but they suggest by their typical silence that Evangelicals should have no more to do with novels than with Buddhism.

---

[17] D. Mason, 'Religious Publications', *Evangelical Magazine* 23 (1815), 17–28, at 17.
[18] 'Remarks on Mr. Bulwer's "Pilgrims of the Rhine": An Editorial', *Christian Observer* 34 (1834), 731–2, at 731.

Popular novels had forced evangelical leaders to rethink their defensive posture against 'idle entertainment'. They understood that literary imagination was attractive to readers interested in the world beyond their immediate sphere. Nevertheless, the evangelical hermeneutic for reading Scripture supplied a model restricted to literal, linear truth through direct narrative and instruction. The beauty and didactic quality of story was admitted, but only insofar as any particular story reflected or participated in the one grand story, the gospel of God's incarnation, redemption and eternal reign. With their understanding of human nature as made to 'glorify God and enjoy him forever', it would be natural for all people to be interested in stories that reflect the plot of redemptive history.[19] Nevertheless, as articulated by Thomas Boston in *Human Nature in Its Fourfold State* (1720), which became a standard theological text for moderate Calvinist Evangelicals, 'natural man's affections are wretchedly misplaced … wholly disordered and distempered', with the corollary that the natural interest in story would be twisted so that unregenerate people would prefer corrupt and false stories rather than true and factual ones.[20] Believers, on the other hand, ought to prefer true stories, especially those that encourage imitation of Christian virtue. Although Evangelicals did begin to write novels in the mid nineteenth century in a competing market of ideas, early nineteenth-century evangelical orthodoxy would not permit either reading or writing about matters unconnected with God's *actual* work in the world, which was too great to be passed over for the fictional.

As seen above, the *Christian Observer* recommended an alternative to fiction: 'interesting and useful narrative, especially religious biography'.[21] These narratives, ranging from historical to contemporary, followed the lives of Evangelicals at home and abroad. Like medieval Catholic saints' lives in their sometimes hyperbolic attention to the achievements and personal holiness of the particular servant of God, they were intended to provide real models of piety and action while also fulfilling a desire for imaginative enter-

---

[19] Westminster Shorter Catechism, in Philip Schaff, ed., *Creeds of the Churches*, 3 vols (New York, 1889), 3: 676.
[20] Thomas Boston, *Human nature in its fourfold state, of primitive integrity, entire depravation, begun recovery, and consummate happiness or misery*, 25th edn (Edinburgh, 1779), 127.
[21] 'Remarks', 732.

tainment, with a focus on the kingdom of God. The writings of missionaries especially excelled in dramatic storyline while also satisfying evangelical standards of telling the truth and attention to the work of God. Missionaries attempted to settle in lands that few other Europeans might ever see, and they were often ahead of other imperial agents in making contact with foreign societies. By almost any measure, their lives were interesting, although unenviable. It should not be surprising that narratives of their settlement and their survival (or death) in distant lands would be captivating for segments of the British population who were learning, often for the first time, about the wonder, complexities and beauty of the wider world.

As evidenced by the attention given the popular genre of travel writing, even secular works were generally affirmed by evangelical journals. Without posing the moral danger of fiction, travel writing could imaginatively transport the reader to more exciting lands away from the difficulties of a changing Europe, but at the same time remain truthful. But missionary writing provided the added benefits of spiritual authority – with assumed better vision and attention to moments of real import – and religious instruction. In a review of six different mission narratives, the *Christian Observer* in 1836 explored the superiority of a missionary over a secular traveller:

> The Christian missionary stands on higher ground than either the popular or the scientific traveller. He may, with the former, observe what is most memorable [about] the places which he visits; and with the greater advantage, because his visit is often of long duration: while, with the latter, he may notice … the chief phenomena of natural history, botany, geology, meteorology, and so forth. But the staple of his observations will have reference to mankind in the most important of all relations: he goes out determined, like St. Paul, 'to know nothing but Jesus Christ and him crucified'.[22]

Non-Evangelicals might present interesting perspectives on foreign peoples, but their concerns lacked the explicit theological observations most intriguing to evangelical readers. At least

---

[22] Anon., 'Proceedings of Missionaries', *Christian Observer* 36 (1836), 186–8, at 186.

in their rhetoric, Evangelicals were interested in other peoples primarily because, 'in darkness and the shadow of death', foreign populations were in need of the 'glad tidings of salvation'.[23] Mission narratives encouraged evangelical readers that the kingdom of God was indeed spreading to the 'ends of the earth' (Acts 1: 8). In the eyes of their readers, mission narratives were as far above travel writing as the cause of the gospel was above sightseeing.

More precisely in competition with novels, though, mission narratives took their readers on an imaginative journey to faraway places and exciting adventures. The potential for such works was discovered almost by accident by the earliest missionaries of the movement. W. H. Medhurst, the third Protestant missionary to enter China, explains the genesis of his widely read *China: Its State and Prospects*:

> In the course of [the author's] tour through England ... *to plead the cause of missions*, he found it necessary to dilate more at large on the political, moral, and spiritual condition of the Chinese, and to relate in order the efforts that have been made for their evangelization. *These statements having been listened to with some interest, and awakened a sympathy on behalf of China,* the thought suggested itself that, possibly, *the feeling thus created might be extended and perpetuated by a publication.*[24]

Missionaries found on their very occasional returns to Britain – usually only one or two returns were made – that their stories were heard with eager fascination. In their brief time at home they became celebrities within their subculture, invited to speak at churches, society meetings and private home gatherings.[25] In addition to the awakened 'sympathy' on behalf of foreign nations mentioned by Medhurst, they also noticed the power of their stories to excite basic interest and imagination. It should not be surprising, then, that their longer narratives take on the structure of episodic accounts of adventure.

[23] George Burder, 'A Concise View of the Present State of Evangelical Religion Throughout the World', serialized in *Evangelical Magazine* 18–19 (1810–11), at 18: 385.
[24] W. H. Medhurst, *China: Its State and Prospects* (London, 1838), iii–iv (italics in original).
[25] On missionary celebrity, see Anna Johnston, 'British Missionary Publishing, Missionary Celebrity, and Empire', *Nineteenth-Century Prose* 32/2 (Fall 2005), 20–48.

In most cases of mission narrative, a voyage filled with surprise encounters and danger takes a prominent place in the recollections. John Williams's *Narrative of Missionary Enterprises in the South Sea Islands* (1837) is filled with voyages and 'first contacts' throughout the Tahitian islands.[26] For example, when Williams voyages to the island of Atiu, resulting in the conversion of a chieftain, he describes his first encounter with the island chief using rhetorical flourishes worthy of a Walter Scott novel:

> We had not been long near the island, when we perceived a large double canoe approaching us, in the centre of which, on an elevated stage, was seated the principal chief. His person was tall and slender, and his aspect commanding. He was clothed in a white shirt, having a piece of Indian print girt around his loins; his long and beautiful black hair hung gracefully over his shoulders, or waved in the passing breeze, as, with the motion of his body, he kept time to the rowers.[27]

With the slow unfolding of detail, and even the composition of the image, the prose uses the very descriptive methods mastered by secular novelists earlier in the century.[28] Likewise, Charles (Karl) Gützlaff's extremely popular *Journal of Three Voyages along the Coast of China* (1834) is a boys' adventure story of the missionary's voyages and clandestine journeys up coastal rivers, disguised as a Chinese merchant and 'filled with the Holy Spirit, imbued with humility, willing to suffer and to die for the great cause'.[29] Indeed, not unlike H. Rider Haggard's empire-inspiring late nineteenth-century African novels, Gützlaff's goal was to raise up Christian warriors willing to surmount any obstacles – ridicule, persecution and death – in the confidence that 'whatever may befall its champions, the final overthrow of the kingdom of darkness is sure, and the ultimate result will be glorious'.[30]

---

[26] John Williams, *Narrative of Missionary Enterprises in the South Sea Islands* (London, 1837).

[27] Ibid. 84.

[28] In Scott's *The Talisman*, consider the romantic description of Sir Kenneth's first contact with 'a mounted horseman, whom his turban, long spear, and green caftan floating in the wind, on his nearer approach, showed to be a Saracen cavalier' (who is actually Saladin): Walter Scott, *The Talisman: a Tale of the Crusades* (Edinburgh, 1868), 9.

[29] Charles [*sic*] Gützlaff, *Journal of Three Voyages along the Coast of China, 1831, 1832, and 1833* (London, 1834), 410.

[30] Ibid. 20.

As with most mission narratives, Gützlaff himself is presented as the model Christian champion who must overcome the obstacles of the kingdom of darkness. On several occasions, he must confront attempts on his life by the agents of evil – the opium smokers. He writes: 'Notwithstanding all this they formed a plot, principally on account of the riches which they supposed me to possess, to sink the junk, to seize the money, and then to flee in a small boat to the neighbouring shore'. But with the coming of a storm, '[i]t was most evident that these heroes in wickedness were cowards; they trembled, and their courage failed them, in the hour of approaching death.' As Gützlaff explains the foiling of the insidious plot, God himself intervenes with a storm to save his champion. The faith and courage of the missionary demonstrate a new kind of adventurer, willing to risk all for the gospel and expecting God to shape the course of the nations.

Gützlaff's self-depiction as a courageous protagonist in the cause of Christ reflects what some scholars have called the propagandist element of missionary writing. Susan Thorne's *Congregational Missions* and Anna Johnston's *Missionary Writing and Empire* both draw attention to the idealized representations of mission success crafted with the intention of stoking the financial fires of missionary support in Britain. Although the charge of exaggeration falls with justice on Gützlaff's narrative, his complete financial independence from any missionary society complicates the general characterization by Thorne and Johnston of missionary publication within a propaganda machine. Consistent with their arguments, however, Gützlaff's popularity as a visiting speaker and writer achieved his self-consciously propagandist goal of encouraging Christian readers' interest in foreign nations.[31] Even after Medhurst exposed his exaggerations to the public in 1838, his writing continued to find eager audiences.[32] At least some segment of the evangelical public was willing to overlook the foible that missionaries could be seduced into telling a good story rather than a strictly true one.

Such exciting works, which might better be titled 'missionary

---

[31] See Jesse Lutz, 'Karl F. A. Gützlaff: Missionary Entrepreneur', in Suzanne Barnett and John King Fairbank, eds, *Christianity and China: Early Protestant Missionary Writings* (Cambridge, MA, 1985), 61–87.

[32] Medhurst, *China*, 364–5.

adventures' than the conventional 'missionary enterprises', proved remarkably successful at doing just what Gützlaff hoped: inspiring future missionaries from the ranks of his evangelical readers. Among the most notable later missionaries who explicitly mentioned Gützlaff's work as an influence on their imagination and their initial thoughts towards missionary work were J. Hudson Taylor and David Livingstone.[33] By the time these influential missionaries came to write their own mission narratives, evangelical attitudes to novels had finally shifted to a more receptive posture. Nevertheless, mission narratives continued to be among the most widely read literary genres of the century, and David Livingstone's *Missionary Travels and Researches in South Africa* became one of the top-selling books of the nineteenth century in Britain.[34]

When the Christian community began to spread to the South Seas, China, Africa and India through the presence of evangelical missionaries, their brethren in Britain became eager to hear about their connections to new believers, partial realizations of the worldwide community of faith to which the Book of Revelation pointed. Through the overarching goal of illustrating the spread of the kingdom, mission narratives distinctly established the connection between the British evangelical genesis of the mission (along with the continuous support from those quarters) and the resulting emergence of an evangelical community overseas. Not only were missionaries doing their part to establish the evangelical community abroad, their works were influencing the evangelical community in Britain by filling up the place of imagination, adventure and excitement within the orbit of acceptable evangelical literature.

In the midst of analyses of mechanisms of raising support, of proselytizing from positions of power, and of imperial interventions, studies of mission and empire often overlook the primary concern of the missionary community and the larger group to which they belonged. Certainly missionaries needed support and used imperial resources, but their own focus was on the inclusion of new believers into a worldwide network of evangelical Christianity. Their offensiveness on the frontiers of the empire was due,

33 J. Hudson Taylor, *A Retrospect* (London, 1865), 7–16; David Livingstone, *Missionary Travels and Researches in South Africa* (London, 1857), 7–8.
34 For a discussion of texts influencing those interested in mission, see Terry Barringer, 'What Mrs. Jellyby Might Have Read; Missionary Periodicals: A Neglected Source', *Victorian Periodicals Review* 37/4 (Winter 2004), 46–74.

not to their making of converts, but to their brand of faith. Evangelical missionaries were so irritating around the empire because they spelled out in unequivocal terms their converts' separation from whatever world they had previously claimed. What is also frequently forgotten is that these same tenets made them equally irritating to the established social order at home.

This essay has suggested that Evangelicals, in forwarding their counter-cultural assault on rationalist hegemony, developed a new genre of literature unique to their own tastes and theological peculiarities. With the incipient missionary movement extending the worldwide presence of Evangelicals just as the novel form was becoming central to the reading practices of the wider British culture, distant lands became sites for the imaginative working out of the evangelical vision of the worldwide kingdom of God. Mission narratives, the extended testimonies of missionaries to the spread of the gospel abroad, filled the multiple roles of providing safe and edifying reading for conscientious evangelical readers, of encouraging reportage on God's work, and of provoking active response from British Christians on behalf of an emerging international Christian community.

Northwest Nazarene University, Nampa, Idaho

RESERVE AND PHYSICAL IMAGERY IN THE TRACTARIAN POETRY OF ISAAC WILLIAMS (1802–65)

by JOHN BONEHAM

T he Oxford, or Tractarian, Movement began as a conservative reaction to the reforming measures of the 1820s and 1830s and in particular to the Whig government's passing of the Irish Church Temporalities Bill in 1832. For the Tractarians, the cumulative effect of such legislation was that the authority of the Church was being seriously compromised by interference from the secular government, which could now include those who were not necessarily Anglicans or even Christians.[1] While it was these overtly political concerns that moved John Keble to preach his 'Assize Sermon' which has traditionally been seen as marking the beginning of the movement in July 1833,[2] the Oxford Movement was to develop into a spiritual revival whose concerns went far beyond politics. In rejecting the established relationship between Church and state the Tractarians came to emphasize the Church's innate spiritual autonomy and appealed increasingly to the authority of tradition as reflected in the writings of the church fathers of the third and fourth centuries.[3] In doing so their emphasis on certain beliefs and practices of the primitive Church, such as baptismal regeneration, the real presence and the apostolic succession, was seen as betraying sympathy for Roman Catholicism and disloyalty towards the Church of England.[4]

An important aspect of the Oxford Movement was the publication of the *Tracts for the Times* under John Henry Newman's editorship between 1833 and 1841, a series of treatises aimed at clergy which sought to propagate the main principles of the movement. Published volumes of sermons, including Newman's *Parochial and Plain Sermons* and Keble's *Sermons for the Christian Year*,

---

[1]   K. Hylson-Smith, *High Churchmanship in the Church of England* (Edinburgh, 1993), 123–30.
[2]   Cf. J. H. Newman, *Apologia Pro Vita Sua* (London, 1945), 23.
[3]   G. Herring, *What was the Oxford Movement?* (London, 2002), 29–34.
[4]   Ibid. 37–43.

were another important way in which the Tractarians expressed their teaching through prose. Equally important was their emphasis on poetry as a means of theological expression. John Keble was Professor of Poetry at the University of Oxford between 1831 and 1841 and was famous for his series of poems for each Sunday of the church year entitled *The Christian Year,* the popularity of which was such that it was produced in no less than ninety-five editions during his lifetime and even outsold the works of William Words-worth.[5] Newman also wrote much religious verse as an Anglican and was responsible for editing a collection of poems entitled *Lyra Apostolica* which was published in 1836 and included contributions from a number of the movement's leaders.[6]

The most prolific Tractarian poet, however, was Isaac Williams, Newman's curate at St Mary the Virgin, Oxford, between 1832 and 1842. Born in Aberystwyth and raised in London, Williams was educated at Harrow before entering Trinity College, Oxford, in 1822. During that year Williams became acquainted with John Keble, through whose influence he was drawn towards the Tractarian cause.[7] It is ironic that, although Williams wrote no less than eleven volumes of poetry for the movement, he has tended to be neglected by Tractarian historiography. His most recent biography (1971), by O. W. Jones, did attempt to remedy this, although the few pages dedicated to Williams's poetry do not seem proportionate to the contribution it made to the movement.[8] More recent studies have gone further in redressing this imbalance by examining Williams's poetic contribution to the movement in greater detail and from a literary and stylistic perspective.[9] G. B.

---

[5]   *ODNB, s.n.* 'Keble, John (1792–1866)'. For further biographical information on John Keble, see S. Prickett, 'Tractarian Poetry', in R. Cronin, A. Chapman and A. H. Harrison, eds, *A Companion to Victorian Poetry* (Oxford, 2002), 279–90, at 279; G. Battiscombe, *John Keble: A Study in Limitations* (London, 1963); B. W. Martin, *John Keble: Priest, Professor and Poet* (London, 1976); J. R. Griffin, *John Keble: The Saint of Anglicanism* (Macon, GA, 1987); K. Blair, ed., *John Keble in Context* (London, 2004).

[6]   Herring, *What was the Oxford Movement?*, 21–2.

[7]   *ODNB, s.n.* 'Williams, Isaac (1802–1865)'. For further biographical information on Isaac Williams, see *The Autobiography of Isaac Williams*, ed. G. Prevost (London, 1892), 1–186; O. W. Jones, *Isaac Williams and his Circle* (London, 1971); M. K. Williams, *The Doctrine of the Church in the Writings of Isaac Williams* (St Albans, 1983); R. W. Church, *The Oxford Movement: Twelve Years, 1833-1845* (London, 1891), 57–69.

[8]   Jones, *Isaac Williams*, 154–62.

[9]   G. B. Tennyson, *Victorian Devotional Poetry* (London, 1981); R. S. Edgecombe, 'Allegorical Topography and the Experience of Space in Isaac Williams' Cathedral',

Tennyson's *Victorian Devotional Poetry* was the first work to examine Williams's poetry in depth alongside that of Keble and Newman and to argue that, apart from making a significant contribution to the movement, Williams's verse rivalled Keble's in terms of its poetic quality.[10] More recently, Kirstie Blair has also demonstrated that Williams's poetic imagery was an important facet of the Tractarian emphasis on the sacramentality of the visible world through art and church architecture.[11]

This essay will focus primarily on the theological significance of Isaac Williams's verse, and will demonstrate that poetry was an important form of expression for him as it encouraged the use of imagery drawn from the physical world to explore theological themes in an indirect way. This was in line with the Tractarian emphasis on the doctrine of 'reserve', an important aspect of the movement on which Williams wrote two of the *Tracts for the Times*.[12] After considering the relationship between Williams's poetry and the principle of reserve, we will explore how he used physical imagery to deal with three important aspects of Tractarian belief in his poetry, namely the importance of the eucharist, the apostolic succession and the authority of tradition.

'RESERVE' IN THE POETRY OF ISAAC WILLIAMS

Isaac Williams's use of physical imagery to deal poetically with theological issues is central to his three most popular works of poetry, *The Cathedral* (1838), *The Baptistery* (1842) and *The Altar* (1847), each of which draws on imagery of ecclesiastical architecture. In *The Cathedral* this is linked to specific parts of a cathedral building, each of which is portrayed as possessing spiritual significance. *The Baptistery* makes use of allegorical images drawn from a seventeenth-century devotional manual, *Via Vitae Aeternae*,[13] in

---

English Studies 3 (1999), 224–38; Prickett, 'Tractarian Poetry', 279–90; K. Blair, 'Church Architecture, Tractarian Poetry and the Forms of Faith', in V. Morgan and C. Williams, eds, *Shaping Belief: Culture, Politics and Religion in Nineteenth-Century Writing* (Liverpool, 2008), 129–45.

[10] Tennyson, *Victorian Devotional Poetry*, 171.

[11] Blair, 'Church Architecture', 129–30, 133–41.

[12] See I. Williams, *Tract 80*, 'On Reserve in Communicating Religious Knowledge', *Tracts for the Times*, 4 (London, 1838), 1–83; idem, *Tract 87*, 'On Reserve in Communicating Religious Knowledge', *Tracts for the Times*, 5 (London, 1838–40), 1–144.

[13] This was written by the French Jesuit Anton Sucquet (1574–1627). The images

order to reflect on specific issues related to the Christian life of the baptized. In *The Altar*, images of a priest celebrating the holy communion service are linked to poetic meditation on Christ's passion, as a means of facilitating reflection on the mystery of the eucharist.

Central to Williams's approach to poetry was the principle of 'reserve', the belief, dear to the Tractarians, that religious doctrines ought not to be taught explicitly but revealed gradually and with reverence.[14] While the other Tractarian leaders also emphasized the importance of this principle,[15] Williams's *Tracts 80* and *87* provide its most comprehensive outline. Reserve could be seen at work in God's own means of revealing himself to humanity through the Scriptures and in the life of Jesus,[16] as well as in the *Disciplina Arcani* of the Early Church, the catechetical practice whereby catechumens were taught doctrines gradually as they progressed in faith and spiritual comprehension.[17]

Isaac Williams's emphasis on reserve helps to explain why he so valued poetry as a means of conveying religious truth. Whereas prose required an explicit outline of the most sacred doctrines of the faith, poetry allowed them to be expressed in veiled language that could only be fully comprehended by those who had the spiritual insight to grasp its meaning. For Williams, verse was a better method of conveying religious truth than prose, since it had been 'the divine mode of communicating with man' through the Psalms,[18] while the most skilled poets were often those who wrote in the most obscure style.[19] Poetry also provided a means whereby the poet could express his, or her, own inner thoughts and feelings in accord with the spirit of reserve, since 'many who are strongly moved by sentiments of a sacred, sublime, or tender nature beyond the reach and order of daily life, can find no way of giving vent to them so well as in poetic forms and expressions'.[20] It was, therefore,

---

in the volume were the work of the Flemish artist Boethius à Bolswert (1580–1633).

[14] Cf. Williams, *Tract 80*, 3.

[15] P. B. Nockles, *The Oxford Movement in Context: Anglican High Churchmanship 1760–1857* (Cambridge, 1994), 198–200.

[16] Williams, *Tract 80*, 3–5.

[17] Williams, *Tract 87*, 7.

[18] I. Williams, 'The Psalter, or Psalms of David in English Verse', *British Critic* 27 (1840), 1–23, at 2.

[19] Ibid. 23.

[20] Ibid. 15.

the most appropriate medium for expression of 'the more hidden feelings and principles of the heart'.[21]

The importance of reserve is reflected throughout Williams's poetry in his use of imagery drawn from nature to evoke reflection on spiritual themes in an indirect way. Imagery related to water, for example, including that of the sea, rivers, springs and human tears, was used to emphasize the importance of the sacrament of baptism, repentance and the human need to be cleansed from sin.[22] Williams saw a snowy landscape as foreshadowing the glory of heaven and also as suggesting the baptismal robe worn by the newly baptized in the Early Church.[23] He also interpreted a red autumnal sunset, said to precede a bright dawn, as an image of the inextricable link between Christ's passion, death and resurrection.[24]

At the heart of such imagery was a sacramental view of nature which saw the physical world as simultaneously pointing beyond itself to God, its creator, and as veiling his presence. Williams's poem on the *Disciplina Arcani* of the Early Church in *The Cathedral* aptly used nature as a metaphor for reserve. Just as the created world hid its greatest treasures in 'earth's deep mines or ocean's cells',[25] so the presence of God in creation was concealed beneath the physical world, and could be truly recognized by the 'pure in heart',[26] those who saw with the eye of faith as well as by sight. This was highlighted in the opening poem of *The Seven Days*, Williams's poetic reflection on the creation:

> For these Thy works that on our senses crowd
> Are syllables that speak the Eternal Mind,
> Could we but read aright; but such a cloud
> Our mortal vision dims, like men half blind
> We stretch our hands to Thee, and cannot find;
> Yet round Thy throne one chaunt of mystery

---

[21]   Ibid.

[22]   I. Williams, *The Seven Days, or the Old and New Creation* (Oxford, 1850), 63–4; I. Williams, *The Altar, or Meditations in verse on the Great Christian Sacrifice* (London, 1847), 31.

[23]   I. Williams, *Thoughts in Past Years* (London, 1848), 27; Williams, *The Seven Days*, 78.

[24]   I. Williams, *The Christian Seasons* (London, 1854), 85; Williams, *The Altar*, 87.

[25]   I. Williams, *The Cathedral, or the Church Catholic and Apostolic in England* (Oxford, 1838), 210–11.

[26]   Ibid. 211.

Sing all Thy works and answer sad mankind,
'The well of endless life is with Thee,
And in Thy Light divine man too the light shall see.'[27]

For Williams, since everything in the world has been created by God, it is fundamentally good and able to convey divine truth to those who are able to perceive it. Sin, however, threatens to 'cloud' and 'blind' the vision of faith and to prevent humanity from perceiving the presence of God in creation. This situation stands in contrast to that of the angels and saints in heaven who, free from the restrictions imposed by sin, are able to fully perceive and rejoice in the glory of the divine presence.

In *The Baptistery* Williams made it clear that it was not just imagery of nature which could be used to reflect on spiritual themes. Rather, since the Christian faith is based firmly on the doctrines of the creation and the incarnation, the physical world as a whole could be used to express divine truth and to give glory to God. Poetry, as well as the other arts, therefore had an essential contribution to make to the life of the Church and to the religious revival which Williams saw taking place in his own day:

The Church, 'tis thought, is wakening through the land,
And seeking vent for the o'erloaded hearts
Which she has kindled – pours her forth anew, –
Breathes life in ancient worship, – from their graves
Summons the slumbering Arts to wait on her,
Music and Architecture, varied forms
Of painting, Sculpture, and of Poetry;
These are allied to sense, but soul and sense
Must both alike find wing and rise to Heaven;
Both soul and body took the Son of Man,
Both soul and body must in Him serve God.[28]

Williams believed that poetry was directly linked to a spiritual revival in the life of the Church since it was able to help believers to lift their mind and heart to God. If, as the doctrine of reserve implied, the Christian faith was ultimately a mystery which could not be completely defined in words or fully comprehended by the

[27] Williams, *The Seven Days*, 3–4.
[28] I. Williams, *The Baptistery, or the Way of Eternal Life* (Oxford, 1844), x.

human mind, then poetry provided the most appropriate means by which the believer could approach this mystery in a spirit of reverence and awe.

Williams's emphasis on nature as both veiling and revealing the presence of God, while providing a means of reflection on theological truths, owed much to the influence of John Keble. In his poem for Septuagesima Sunday from *The Christian Year*, for example, Keble portrayed the created world as a book which could be read by those who possessed '[p]ure eyes and Christian hearts'[29] and he used the imagery of nature as metaphor for reserve.[30] Under Keble's influence, Williams also seems to have come to value the Romantic poetry of William Wordsworth, whose poem *The Excursion* was an important influence on his writing of *The Cathedral*.[31] Writing to his parents in 1825 he recommended Wordsworth's verse, claiming that it possessed an 'unrivalled sympathy of pathos' and that the poet was a favourite of Keble's.[32] Williams's verse, like that of Keble, was also influenced by George Herbert, whom he compared with the beloved disciple who reclined on Jesus's breast at the Last Supper (cf. John 13: 25).[33] Not only did Herbert's *The Temple*, in which the physical architecture of a church building evokes reflection on spiritual themes, help to provide him with the central idea behind *The Cathedral*,[34] but Williams's use of imagery echoes Herbert's in a number of places.[35] While Williams's style was very different to Herbert's, the two poets clearly shared a desire to use imagery drawn from the physical world to express theological ideas.

THE EUCHARIST

Isaac Williams's most extensive poetic reflection on the eucharist is to be found in *The Altar*. As the subtitle of the work, *Meditations on the Great Christian Sacrifice*, suggests, the purpose of this volume

[29] J. Keble, *The Christian Year* (London, 1887), 46.

[30] Ibid. 57–9.

[31] Williams, *The Cathedral*, v.

[32] London, LPL, MS 4476, fols 96–7: Isaac Williams to Isaac Lloyd Williams (no date); with permission of the Trustees of Lambeth Palace Library.

[33] Williams, *The Cathedral*, 192–3.

[34] Ibid. v.

[35] J. Boneham, 'Isaac Williams (1802–1865), the Oxford Movement and the High Churchmen: A Study of his Theological and Devotional Writings' (Ph.D. thesis, Bangor University, 2009), 73, 79, 83, 95, 97, 100.

was to reflect on the eucharist as a sacrifice. In line with the principle of reserve, however, Williams attempted to do this, not by explaining exactly how the sacrament related to Christ's sacrificial death on the cross, but by linking images of the Church of England's communion service to poetic meditations on different aspects of the passion. The priest processing towards the altar, for example, was linked in a poem to Christ's approach to the garden of Gethsemane; the broken bread on the altar to his death on the cross; and the covering of the consecrated elements to his body being wrapped in the linen shroud.[36] The structure of this work was clearly meant to highlight the Tractarian belief that the eucharist is not just a figure of Christ's death on the cross, but the means by which that sacrifice is made a living reality for the Christian in the present moment.[37] This was supported by a quotation from the writings of St Thomas à Kempis in the preface of *The Altar*, claiming that when the eucharist is celebrated it is 'as if on this same day Christ hanging on the cross did suffer and die for the salvation of mankind'.[38]

Williams used two prominent images in *The Altar* to invite reflection on the nature of the eucharist. The first of these was the image of the sepulchre in which the body of Christ was laid after the crucifixion, which Williams saw as a metaphor for the human heart. As the empty stone tomb was transformed by Christ so that it became a symbol of his resurrection, so the heart, though hardened by sin, could be renewed and invigorated by his presence, conveyed through the sacrament of holy communion:

> Make Thou my heart as this sepulchral hall,
> Though filled with recollections that appal;
> Till from a sepulchre, by Thee made clean,
> It shall become a Temple all serene.[39]

Another image employed by Williams was that of a cup. Alluding to Jesus's prayer in the garden of Gethsemane that his cup might pass away from him (cf. Mark 14: 36), this image was used to link

---

[36] Williams, *The Altar*, plates 1, 26, 29.
[37] Cf. A. Härdelin, *The Tractarian Understanding of the Eucharist* (Uppsala, 1965), 203–4.
[38] Williams, *The Altar*, v; cf. Thomas à Kempis, *The Imitation of Christ* (Oxford, 1849), 281.
[39] Williams, *The Altar*, 110.

Christ's sufferings to the act of receiving the sacrament. Although human sin was the cause of Christ's 'cup' of suffering, in the eucharist this was repaid by the gift of himself in holy communion:

> ... the cup that floweth o'er
> With these Thy sorrows is for evermore
> The cup wherein our health and gladness springs.
> The cup we give Thee is deadly wine,
> Made of the poisonous grapes our sins have borne;
> Thou givest in return the cup Divine,
> Full of Thy love.[40]

In Williams's poem 'Christ Bearing the Cross', the image of the cup was also used to teach that by partaking of the sacrament of holy communion the recipient did not just receive the benefits of Christ's sufferings, but was bound to bear life's sorrows in union with him, strengthened by the grace of the eucharist:

> Thus may we to that awful cup draw near
> Thou had'st to drink amid that multitude, –
> Draw near, and look into that cup of Blood,
> And see our very selves reflected there.
> We too must of a cup of sorrow drink;
> Our destined road is called 'the vale of tears,'
> Where we must bear our cross in human fears
> And sorrows, and to earth in silence sink.[41]

The use of such imagery in *The Altar* was a means by which Williams could portray the eucharist as a sacrifice which was inextricably linked to Christ's death on the cross, as an undeserved gift of love which could spiritually renew the human heart, and as the means by which the Christian was united to Christ in his sufferings for the salvation of the world.

THE APOSTOLIC SUCCESSION

Another important Tractarian belief which finds reference in Williams's poetry is the doctrine of the apostolic succession, the idea that the authority of the Church's bishops could be traced back

---

40 Ibid.,10.
41 Ibid. 71.

to the apostles themselves, via a line of successive ordinations.[42] In *The Cathedral*, the pillars of the nave upholding the building's roof were used as an image of the apostles whose ministry supported the Church as a spiritual institution.[43]

The doctrine of the apostolic succession itself forms the subject of the poem on the chapter house of the cathedral, the place where new bishops were traditionally elected by the cathedral's chapter. The image of the chapter house, which accompanies the poem, depicts it as having eight walls, corresponding to the eight verses of the poem. This octagonal room is supported by a single pillar, representing both Christ, from whom the apostles received their authority, and the bishop, who, as the successor of the apostles, was a focus of unity within his diocese.

Williams's poem on the chapter house took up the image of a harp to reflect on the importance of the apostolic succession. This idea was drawn from Ignatius of Antioch's *Epistle to the Ephesians*, which claimed that priests were 'united to the Bishop as the strings are to an harp'.[44] The poem took up this image by referring to the threefold apostolic ministry of bishop, priest and deacon as the '[m]ysterious harp of heaven-born harmony' which was essential to the maintenance of love, order and obedience in the Church.[45] Williams also emphasized the belief, common among the Tractarians, that the office of bishop was instituted personally by Christ through his commissioning of the apostles.[46] The apostolic succession therefore formed an integral link between the contemporary and the primitive church:

> ... Christ Himself, and His appointed few,
> Moulded the frame, and in the silvery bound
> Set all the glowing wires. Then potent grew ...

---

[42] S. W. Sykes and S. W. Gilley, '"No Bishop, No Church!": The Tractarian Impact on Anglicanism', in G. Rowell, ed., *Tradition Renewed: The Oxford Movement Conference Papers* (London, 1986), 120–39.

[43] Williams, *The Cathedral*, 257–69.

[44] Ibid. 43, quoting Ignatius of Antioch, *Epistle to the Ephesians* 4; cf. Ignatius, *Ephesians* 4, in W. Howley, ed., *The Genuine Epistles of the Apostolic Fathers* (London, 1833), 159.

[45] Williams, *The Cathedral*, 43.

[46] Cf. J. H. Newman, *Tract 1*, 'Thoughts on the Ministerial Commission', *Tracts for the Times*, 1 (London, 1834), 1–4, at 2; J. Keble, *Tract 4*, 'Adherence to the Apostolical Succession the Safest Course', *Tracts for the Times*, 1, 1–8, at 4.

The treasury of sweet sounds: deep aisle and fane
Prolong, from age to age, the harmonious strain.[47]

This use of the image of a harp to highlight the importance of
the apostolic succession is highly significant. Not only can the
strings of the instrument be seen to allude to the idea of a linear
succession of ordinations throughout the ages, but the fact that
each string must be tuned in order to work in harmony with the
others points to the belief that the authority of the successors of
the apostles was essential to the preservation of order and discipline in the Church. The idea of 'sweet sounds' filling a room as a
harp is played is also a valuable metaphor for the way in which the
apostolic succession allowed the 'harmonious strain' of orthodox
doctrine to be preserved and taught throughout the ages.

TRADITION

The importance of the appeal to the authority of tradition, a
fundamental aspect of Tractarian theology, also found a prominent
place in Isaac Williams's poetry. *The Cathedral* reflects the Oxford
Movement's veneration for the church fathers, whose writings were
highly valued as reflecting the teaching of the primitive Church.[48]
In his work, Williams associated them with the windows of the
cathedral building, and provided poems on many of the fathers.[49]
This association of the fathers with the cathedral windows suggests
that, just as the light shone through the windows and illuminated
the building, so their example of orthodoxy and fidelity helped
to reflect the light of Christ in the darkness of the heathen world.
This image was taken up in Williams's translation of the Latin
hymn *Vos succensa Deo splendida Lumina* from the Paris Breviary,
which portrays the fathers as 'glorious Lights, kindled at God's
own urn', whose faithfulness to Christ upheld the integrity of the
faith in the midst of the darkness of heresy and error.[50]

The image of the cathedral building itself was also a profound
symbol of the authority of tradition in Williams's poetry. It is
significant that his portrayal of the building owed much to the
influence of the Gothic revival, which was highly retrospective in

47 Williams, *The Cathedral*, 43–4.
48 See Nockles, *Oxford Movement*, 109–13.
49 Williams, *The Cathedral*, 274–97.
50 J. H. Newman, ed., *Lyra Apostolica* (Derby, 1843), 115

its appeal to medieval patterns of church design. In later editions of *The Cathedral*, Williams made it clear that the building's physical architecture was to be seen as alluding to the appeal to antiquity:

Beauty of holiness, still let me hold
Thy mantle skirts, and talk with thee awhile,
And let me read thy brow, which fairer seems when old;
Time's rude fingers, which other things defile,
Make thee more lovely.[51]

Williams's emphasis on church buildings as highlighting the value of Christian antiquity was also reflected in a poem about a pilgrimage which he made to St David's Cathedral in Pembrokeshire in 1841. This poem, which was included in *The Baptistery*, linked Williams's veneration for Christian tradition with the grandeur of the building:

It was St. David's ancient pile,
Chancel, nave, tower, and window'd aisle,
And skirting all the Western side,
A palace fair in ruin'd pride,
With storied range in order set,
And portal, arch and parapet.[52]

The majestic portrayal of this ancient cathedral in Williams's poem stands in contrast to the 'ruin'd pride' of the bishop's palace adjacent to it, which suggests the idea of a former glory which has passed away. While the cathedral building pointed to the Church of England's roots in tradition, the palace, which was built in the twelfth century and since 1633 had been allowed to fall into ruin,[53] was an image of the sacrilege which Williams saw taking place as its ancient authority was challenged by the political upheavals of the 1820s and 1830s. As he gazed on this sight, Williams claimed that:

Religion's venerable hold,
With wrecks and ruin manifold,
Burst full on the astonish'd eye,
Hoar in sublime antiquity.[54]

---

[51] Williams, *The Cathedral* (Oxford, 1848), 304.
[52] Williams, *The Baptistery*, 191.
[53] J. E. Hunt, *A History and Description of St. David's Cathedral* (Saffron Walden, 1966), 18–19, 36.
[54] Williams, *The Baptistery*, 191.

Such use of the image of the cathedral and bishop's palace at St David's illustrates how Williams was able to use imagery drawn from the visible world to evoke reflection on what he saw as the Erastianism and spiritual lethargy which threatened the Church of England in his own day.

CONCLUSION

Although Isaac Williams's role in the Oxford Movement has sometimes been undervalued, it is clear that his poetry can be seen as an invaluable expression of the theory of reserve which he expounded in his tracts. In line with this principle, Williams did not attempt to provide an explicit outline of theological themes in his poetry, but dealt with them analogically, using imagery drawn from the physical world. By providing a means of reflection on the most important principles which the Tractarians were attempting to propagate that was fully in line with the ideal of reserve, Williams's poetry made a significant contribution to the literature of the Oxford Movement and is worthy of further study.

Westminster Cathedral

W. E. HEYGATE: TRACTARIAN CLERICAL NOVELIST

by GEORGE HERRING

In the 1830s a small group of Anglican clerics, mainly resident tutors and fellows of Oxford University, initiated a campaign for the revitalization of their Church, which they perceived to be threatened by secular forces. The inspiration for this was derived from the pre-Reformation roots of Anglicanism, specifically from a study of the fathers of the Early Church, supplemented by the post-Reformation Caroline divines of the seventeenth century. One of the main vehicles for propagating these ideas was the series known as the *Tracts for the Times*, which ran to ninety titles issued between 1833 and 1841, and from which this growing Oxford Movement derived its more popular title of 'Tractarian'.

In the 1840s and 1850s a number of these Tractarian clerics turned to the novel as another potent vehicle for the propagation of the ideals of their movement. Yet until recently these novels have not received the attention from modern scholars that their importance merits.[1] S. A. Skinner has recently produced a detailed study of the social and political thought of the Oxford Movement using the novels of William Gresley and F. E. Paget.[2] Skinner's self-imposed limitations, both in terms of subject matter and chronology, have resulted in the almost complete absence of any discussion in his book of the works of William Edward Heygate. Born in 1816, Heygate graduated from St John's College, Oxford in 1839, at a time when the Tractarian movement was rapidly gaining notoriety in the university and beyond. He was ordained the following year, subsequently holding a series of curacies in

---

[1]   The only specific study, J. E. Baker, *The Novel and the Oxford Movement* (Princeton, NJ, 1932), is now very dated. More general studies such as Andrew Drummond, *The Churches in English Fiction: A Literary and Historical Study from the Regency to the Present Time, of British and American Fiction* (Leicester, 1950), or M. Maison, *Search Your Soul, Eustace: A Survey of the Religious Novel in the Victorian Age* (London, 1969), are either inaccurate or superficial. There is nothing for the Tractarians to compare in terms of scholarship with Elizabeth Jay, *The Religion of the Heart: Anglican Evangelicalism and the Nineteenth-Century Novel* (Oxford, 1979).

[2]   S. A. Skinner, *Tractarians and the 'Condition of England': The Social and Political Thought of the Oxford Movement* (Oxford, 2004).

a variety of rural parishes, until becoming an incumbent on the Isle of Wight in 1869. His first novel, *Godfrey Davenant: a Tale of School Life*, appeared in 1847, and in the following year he wrote one of the most significant Tractarian novels, *William Blake: or, the English Farmer.*[3] Heygate was also an important contributor to another genre, that of the manual or handbook for the practice of the clerical profession, at a time when formal pastoral training was still in its infancy. His most substantial work in this field was *Ember Hours* of 1857.[4]

This essay will restrict its focus to an interpretation of *William Blake* as a fictional realization of the advice proffered to Heygate's fellow clergy in *Ember Hours*. Using these works as exemplars of their respective genres, it will explore the idea that on one level Tractarian novelists had not only a rhetorical purpose common to much of their party's apologetic literature, but also a more narrowly didactic one in preparing the intending or recently ordained clergyman for his role as a model parson. Thus many of these novels had more than one specific target audience: not only literate Anglican parishioners who could be educated by them into the ideas of the movement, but also the clerical leaders who could be introduced to a range of pastoral techniques designed to make the movement a living parochial reality. Heygate himself hinted at something like this when he discussed the purposes of this type of fiction in the Preface to *William Blake*: among these was 'to give *advice* where it would otherwise not be possible'. In addition he asserted that the fiction 'pictures and makes vivid; it *realises*, and to all appearance renders possible … virtues which would generally seem difficult, and almost unobtainable'.[5]

In their fiction the Tractarian clerical novelists almost invariably selected one of two broad approaches to their subject matter: historical or contemporary. Their historical tales were usually set either in the Early Church, with a special fondness for heroic stories of martyrdom, or in the seventeenth century, and in the latter case the heroes were often set in the mould of Caroline divines and the

---

[3]   W. E. Heygate, *Godfrey Davenant: A Tale of School Life* (London, 1847); idem, *William Blake; or, The English Farmer* (London, 1848).

[4]   See Anthony Russell, *The Clerical Profession* (London, 1980); this is based on a study of about one hundred such handbooks published between 1750 and 1875.

[5]   Heygate, *William Blake*, viii (italics mine).

villains puritans, thus illuminating the sources of Tractarian inspiration. But, whatever the particular period, the 'moral message' was clear and comparisons with the nineteenth century sometimes crudely obvious. The alternative to this approach was the contemporary; and the setting for this was very often the nineteenth-century parish. This was the technique adopted by Heygate in *William Blake*. Set in the fictional village of Great Staunton with a population of six hundred souls, the narrative revolves around the efforts of the energetic new parson, Mr Lee – clearly a Tractarian, although never specifically identified as such – to influence one of the local farmers, William Blake, towards a higher consciousness of his spiritual and ecclesiastical duties, and consequently of his broader responsibilities to society.

To what extent, then, was the subject matter of the handbook echoed in fictional form in the novel? One of the hallmarks of the Tractarian clergy was a conviction that their movement was a necessary corrective to generations of neglect, manifest in the decayed state of much of the parochial life they observed in their Church. One of the radical changes required was thus in what Heygate termed the 'character' of the clergy.[6] By this he meant unremitting and heroic clerical sanctity. In *Ember Hours* he was at pains to contrast what he saw as the all too familiar concept of the parson derived from a discredited past model with the new type of cleric inspired by the ideals of the Oxford Movement. He implored his clerical readers to abandon the pursuits of the fashionable world: 'dancing and balls, and sporting, and all fashion in dress ... Do not all these things identify the parson more and more with the squirarchy?'[7] He used his first novel as a vehicle to portray this clergyman of the old type, more a squire than a parson, who thought more highly of his ancestral lands than of his priesthood, and then followed this with his first clerical handbook, *Probatio Clerica*, in which he argued that descent through saints and martyrs was better than any secular family tree.[8]

This theme of the lax parson at the heart of the decayed parish

---

[6] See W. E. Heygate, *Ember Hours* (London, 1857), 50.

[7] Ibid. 46–7.

[8] Heygate, *Godfrey Davenant*, 2, 72–3; W. E. Heygate, *Probatio Clerica, or, Aids in Self-Examination to Candidates for Holy Orders, or for those Clergy who may desire them* (London, 1845), 21–2.

then reappeared in the opening chapters of *William Blake*. Heygate described the incumbent, Mr Eccles, as a typical 'sporting' parson who could only attract thirty of his parishioners to his dreary Sunday services. In his unreformed parish the only true religion was to be found in the crowded meeting-house, attended by many out of ignorance rather than conviction; and in consequence the labouring classes in his parish turned to crime because of a neglected education, and the farmers saw nothing wrong in cheating one another provided they could avoid detection. Heygate made it clear that the reprehensible state of English society, of which this fictional parish was a microcosm, was due mainly to the failure of the parish church and its parson to fulfil their appointed roles.

Then Mr Lee arrived and the revolution began. The new incumbent was a man of a different order, revealed by the changes he made in the parsonage: all the sporting prints and luxurious furnishings were removed and replaced by a library as the most valuable commodity in the house, reflecting Heygate's view expressed in *Ember Hours* that the essence of a reformed clergy began with its education and a programme of spiritual reading. This was not undertaken for the sake of knowledge in itself but rather for what he called its 'moral effect'.[9] In the novel Heygate commented on the new parson's house: 'it contained nothing which would have excited the wonder of the poor, or made them afraid to sit down in their clergyman's house'.[10]

If the first evidence for this change in the tone of the parish was to be found in the parson and his house, the next would be announced by renovations in the church, its furnishings and its liturgy. Like all Tractarians Heygate regarded attention to these as fundamental, advising his clerical readers in *Ember Hours*:

> If our people see us indifferent to the treatment of the Church, to its decorations, and its music they must conclude either that we are slothful and careless, or else that we consider the outward service of GOD of no moment; which if they did believe they ought to think as lightly of us as we seem to do of GOD's honour.[11]

9   Heygate, *Ember Hours*, 5.
10 Heygate, *William Blake*, 60.
11 Heygate, *Ember Hours*, 41–2.

Heygate recommended personal clerical supervision of all aspects of the liturgy, a careful and systematic approach to the preaching of sermons conforming to the pattern of readings found in the lectionary prescribed by the Prayer Book, and the keeping of a parochial journal.[12]

In his fiction Heygate was to illustrate a number of these objectives. In *William Blake* it was significant that Lee's first real opportunity to transform his parish came when he initiated repairs to his neglected church. Lee had friends willing to pay for a total restoration, which convinced the miserly vestry meeting. The principal difficulty arose, however, when Lee proposed removing the rented box pews and replacing them with open and free seating. This gave the author the opportunity to put into the mouth of Lee what were emerging as the common Tractarian objections to rented pews:

> Now one of the great objects for which we come to church is, that we may learn to feel that we are *not* superior to others, that we are all equal in God's sight, who is no respecter of persons. But, if the more wealthy have their pews, and the poorer are crowded here and there, as it may be, the richer members of the congregation find the church itself a means of perpetuating and increasing that trust in riches, that feeling of inequality which they come here intending, I trust, to shake off.[13]

Despite Lee's eloquence it was only the offer of £150 from the priest himself which persuaded the vestry to accept the abolition of a pewed church. However, completion of the restoration, including removal of the hated pews, the following year gave Lee the setting he required for the introduction of another Tractarian objective, the Daily Service.[14] Heygate then described the growing impact of the restored church and renewed liturgy on the congregation:

> The church, too, was a changed building, and so were the services. All was very plain and simple still, but strictly correct

---

[12] Ibid. 42–4.
[13] Heygate, *William Blake*, 50.
[14] Ibid. 134.

and in harmony with sacred objects. The font stood at the entrance. The altar caught the eye in passing up the nave. The singing and chanting were very fair; and, what is more, quite natural, simple, and heartfelt. The majority of the congregation knelt and rose at the proper times. The responses were deep and musical, following the tone of the choir. The earnest sermon was listened to with great attention. The offertory was responded to cheerfully, and as much as £2 collected from that small flock; and when the service was over the people left the church very slowly, and quietly dispersed.[15]

This transformation of the parishioners of the fictional Great Staunton had not been achieved, however, by the restoration alone. Alongside that, Lee was portrayed as adopting a number of pastoral techniques which Heygate had recommended in his clerical handbooks. The vital component of pastoral work was, in his opinion, the individual parishioner, each a unique entity with a particular mixture of problems, needs and talents. It was precisely to this neglect of personal visiting and confidential intercourse between the priest and the souls entrusted to him in the preceding generations that Heygate ascribed the deplorable state of relations which he described in *Ember Hours*:

> Nothing is known of the private habits of the parishioner; how often he prays; whether he prays at all; whether he reads his Bible, or whether he does not; whether he communicates in guilt, and eats and drinks his own damnation, or whether he partakes unto life eternal; whether he holds the Catholic faith, or is a heretic; whether he indulges in private sins destructive to the soul, not knowing their enormity; whether he retains the sinful gain, or restores; whether he is at enmity, or in charity; whether he wars wisely with his sins, or through want of counsel fails, or does not war at all.[16]

For Heygate the Tractarian, one answer to this spiritual neglect was the practice of confession.[17] However, he was conscious that something less formal would need to be the standard practice, and that

[15] Ibid. 184.
[16] Heygate, *Ember Hours*, 25.
[17] Ibid. 25.

a clerical understanding of the spiritual lives of parishioners would commence in childhood, beginning at school and then progressing through confirmation preparation and night schools.[18] He was also aware that the system that he described was very much an ideal; in the majority of cases the neglect of the parochial system had resulted in 'persons who have grown up in ignorance and carelessness, and openly godless and evil livers'.[19] Once again individual attention was the answer; but in the absence of a progressive system in place from childhood the parson would have to wait for, or cultivate, specific opportunities which could be exploited to gain an opening into the soul, such as visiting after a family joy or sorrow. But above all he identified times of sickness as a unique pastoral opportunity: 'By sickness God singles a man out of the world,' he wrote in *Ember Hours*, 'separates him from his fellows, takes him into the wilderness, pleads with him, shows him to himself and Himself to him. Sickness is isolation for repentance'.[20] How, then, did he illustrate this in his fictional writing?

It is notable that in *William Blake* the occasion for the first individual and private exchanges between the young farmer and the rector occurred when the former's betrothed had to be removed from the village when she was feared to have consumption. Blake's heart and mind became unhinged, and gave Lee his opportunity for intervention and subsequent influence. The farmer was impressed by the parson's kindness, reinforced by the Sunday sermon on the topic of the relationship between the pastor and his people and imploring the latter to come to Lee at any time. Blake did so, coming to the rectory for the first time. And so one thing was enabled to lead to another; the farmer eventually became a regular communicant after lengthy and carefully organized preparation involving both personal instruction and a considerable list of reading material. Then the subsequent return of Blake's betrothed, Ellen, fully restored to health, gave the rector a further opportunity to proffer advice on a range of personal, household and charitable duties, accompanied by yet another extensive bibliography. But, however detailed the fictional account, the one thing missing was a description of formal confession. What might be acceptable in

---

[18] Ibid. 27–8.
[19] Ibid. 29.
[20] Ibid. 36.

a handbook written explicitly for fellow clergy was clearly not possible in a novel in 1848 designed for a wider audience at a time when Tractarians were under close scrutiny for any Jesuitical practices.

In his choice of William Blake's occupation, however, Heygate was on firmer ground. When this novel was written there were about a quarter of a million farmers in Britain, with several times that number engaged in agriculture, which remained the largest single source of employment, and almost half the population was still categorized as rural.[21] In selecting this form of employment for his eponymous hero Heygate had made a deliberate and informed choice. The statistical evidence further demonstrates that, like so many of their clerical colleagues, Tractarians had a strong tendency to gravitate to rural parishes in these decades. Of more than six hundred Tractarian incumbents active between 1840 and 1870 over half were in parishes of fewer than a thousand souls; Great Staunton might have been a fictional creation, but in that sense it was firmly anchored in reality.[22]

There were also other reasons beyond the demographic for Heygate to make William Blake a farmer. In the novel he asserted that 'this little fruit of rural parochial work' had been composed in the conviction that 'the farmers of England are an important class, and one hardly recognising its privileges, power, and consequent responsibility'. If each could be aroused to this consciousness he believed that individually he 'might be an anchor and a principle of *steadfastness*' to the country as a whole, and 'more useful by far, in his quiet circle, than many bustling men in larger spheres and of greater pretensions'.[23] Yet Heygate was equally aware that this ideal role was very far indeed from realization in 1848, and the picture of the agricultural community that Heygate painted in his novel was a far from flattering one. Nine years later, in *Ember Hours*, he was still lamenting the deplorable moral condition of society, with dishonesty rife among all sections of the community.[24]

---

21 See B. A. Holderness, 'The Victorian Farmer', in G. E. Mingay, ed., *The Victorian Countryside*, 2 vols (London, 1981), 1: 227–43. The statistics are derived from the 1851 census.

22 George Herring, *What Was the Oxford Movement?* (London, 2002), 76.

23 Heygate, *William Blake*, v, ix–x, 13.

24 Heygate, *Ember Hours*, 37–8.

Not surprisingly, then, one of the lengthy dialogues which took place between Blake and Lee in the novel dealt precisely with this problem. Labourers' wages were not rising enough to keep pace with the price of wheat and hence bread: what were the responsibilities of farmers in this situation? Lee asserted that 'no man has a right to make a time of scarcity and suffering a means of private advancement, by withholding that which he can afford to sell'.[25] The farmer thus had a moral duty to sell his produce at a fair price so that the poor, whether rural or urban, might be able to afford bread.

Thus in both *Ember Hours* and *William Blake* Heygate advocated and then illustrated broadly the same methodology for restoring the rural parochial system utilizing the existing social structure, and so to that extent the novel could indeed be seen as the fictional realization of the manual. Problems, whether moral or liturgical, could be rectified by what Tractarians such as Heygate referred to as the 'Church system', a coherent and interconnected set of ideas and practices originating from the objective authority of a visible Church in contrast to the more subjective opinions of individual Christians. This system could educate key groups such as farmers into a right conception of their duties to both God and their neighbours, resulting in better instruction and fairer wages for the labourers, and encouragement for all to attend a church no longer a half-empty preaching box but rather restored as a true house of prayer. Then the ills of English society that Heygate isolated and analysed in both books could begin to be removed, and the Established Church emerge in its role as the sanctifier of souls and the humanizer of minds and bodies.

What must also be noted, however, are the limitations, both artistic and historical, in the Tractarian novels and (to a lesser extent) in the manuals. The subject matter of the fictional works was invariably formulaic, and the precise plots often contrived and laboured. Heygate was hardly alone among Tractarian novelists in devising a fiction around the theme of a neglected parish rejuvenated by the arrival of an energetic Tractarian parson. In addition his creation, Mr Lee, on several occasions during the course of the

---

[25] Heygate, *William Blake*, 126.

tale conveniently discovered wealthy friends able and willing to pay for his various expensive schemes of improvement.

But whatever the creative weaknesses of the fictions, more important for the historian is the reality that lay behind them. Was the picture of the reformed young farmer, William Blake, an accurate one? Did the real Tractarian clergy succeed in any demonstrable way in convincing their local representatives of the Victorian rural middle classes of the truth of their religious ideals and persuade them to become good practising members of their particular parishes?

Sadly, the surviving evidence points in a negative direction. In the middle decades of the nineteenth century farmers 'were the active capitalists in English agriculture: they rented farms, conducted farming operations, employed labour, and received the profits. Having transformed the agricultural economy, and taken on the economic role of the middle class, they also acquired its distinctive social role, and transformed agrarian social relations as well'.[26] While it may be too sweeping to describe all farmers in the 1840s as middle class, what is true is that a growing number of them were aspiring to the same level of material comfort as their urban counterparts, and abandoning traditional practices such as housing unmarried agricultural labourers in the farmhouse with the immediate family, mirroring the Victorian concern for clearer class segregation. It was this expanding rural middle class, the farmers and their natural counterparts the village tradesmen, who in reality confronted the Tractarian clergy with a fundamental social and religious problem: how to persuade this newly enriched class to adopt more paternalistic social concepts, and at the same time to become practising Churchmen?

The Tractarians shared with other clergy a growing concern for the consequences of the hardening social divisions within English society. Heygate was himself a typical representative of these worried parsons and repeated many of their fears in his writings, whether fictional or otherwise, including a belief that if something was not done to lessen the growing separation of the classes then the only result would be the disintegration of society itself.[27]

[26] James Obelkevich, *Religion and Rural Society: South Lindsey 1825–1875* (Oxford, 1976), 46.
[27] See Frances Knight, *The Nineteenth-Century Church and English Society*

It was a particular concern of the Tractarians that this class system was having a deleterious effect on religious practice. In his novel *Charles Lever* William Gresley described the middle classes in the fictional town of Lexington as basically conservative, but then noted that 'conservatism without a higher principle is a feeble safeguard of virtue'.[28] In another novel he related the attitude of one of his characters, significantly a shopkeeper: 'he professed to be a member of the Church, and on the score of lounging into his pew about once a month when the service was half over, considered himself an excellent Churchman'.[29] W. J. E. Bennett, the Tractarian vicar of Frome, composed a fictional dialogue between a farmer and a tradesman, the latter claiming that he could not go to church on Ascension Day because he could not afford it, while the farmer argued that he must also absent himself in order to look after his crops.[30]

It was clear, then, that in devising a plot around a farmer's moral and religious progress, Heygate was reflecting widespread Tractarian clerical anxieties and hopes. Yet when in reality they attempted the kind of reforming programme portrayed in *William Blake*, itself derived from the clerical handbooks, what they almost invariably encountered was not compliance but rather hostility; it was the farmers and tradesmen who were often their most bitter opponents. William Butler, the vicar of Wantage from 1846, kept an almost daily record in his parish diaries of his struggle to turn hostile and suspicious farmers and tradesmen into good Churchmen and social paternalists. The results were almost universally discouraging. In 1850, after four years of labour, he noted 'the deadness of the tradesmen and farmers to all serious matters whether religious or secular'.[31] He regularly bemoaned the laxity of the local middle classes when it came to the observance of

(Cambridge, 1995), for a discussion of the similarities between all clerical parties with regard to these issues, and also my forthcoming book on the Tractarian parochial revival, provisionally entitled *Rebuilding the Ruined Shrines: The Tractarian Parochial Revival*.

[28] William Gresley, *Charles Lever: or, The Man of the Nineteenth Century* (London, 1841), 86.

[29] William Gresley, *Portrait of an English Churchman* (London, 1838), 285.

[30] W. J. E. Bennett, 'Ascension Day – A Dialogue between a Farmer and a Tradesman', *The Old Church Porch* 4/5 (1 May 1860), 74.

[31] Reading, Berkshire County Record Office, MS Wantage Parish Diaries, Add. MSS D/P, 143, 28/1: 3 February 1850.

holy days, and frequently criticized their parsimony where alms and church collections were concerned.[32] Butler made determined efforts to persuade the farmers and tradesmen to take responsibility for the machinery of local government. In this he was also far from successful, as he noted their reluctance to hold any public office for fear that their decisions would be unpopular and so damage their profits.[33] Finally, in 1855, after more than nine years of effort, he discovered that one of his most respectable tradesmen, a churchwarden, had committed adultery. In the privacy of his diary this occasioned a particularly fierce outburst of frustration:

> The real truth is, that our tradesmen, the representatives of that wonderful middle class, which newspapers and officials flatter and imagine to be the most capable of people to rule the country etc., etc., putting all local concerns into their hands, religion, education, sanitary reform, provision for the poor, are a thoroughly ignorant, ungodly set. There are no doubt, and thank God for it, bright exceptions, but the majority care for nothing except keeping up respectability and making money. They smile or sneer at every kind of sin which does not affect life or property. I do not hesitate to say all but entirely without God to the world, i.e. they refer nothing to His Presence, or their duty to Him, but only consider how far it affects their pocket, pleasure, or reputation.[34]

Thus a review of the evidence must inevitably lead to the conclusion that the portrait of William Blake remained at best aspirational, and equally that Tractarian fiction was in many respects highly idealized.

York University

---

[32] Ibid. 28/3: 12 May 1858; 28/2: 22 April 1855.
[33] Ibid. 28/3: 12 April 1858.
[34] Ibid. 28/2: 1 December 1855.

A WRITER OR A RELIGIOUS? LADY GEORGIANA FULLERTON'S DILEMMA

by KATHLEEN JAEGER

Discussing the conflict Gerard Manley Hopkins perceived between his two vocations of priest and poet, W. H. Gardner distinguished between 'character ... the stamp imposed upon the individual by tradition and moral training; which may also be desired and self-imposed, ... maintained by an effort of the will' and 'personality ... the free or comparatively untrammeled psychic individuality, that complex of native faculties ... which find their expression in art'.[1] Such a dichotomy can also be seen in a less familiar figure, Lady Georgiana Fullerton (1812–85), a novelist who for decades sought in vain to reconcile the demands of her religious aspirations with her drive for self-expression.

As a daughter of Granville Leveson Gower and Harriet Cavendish, Georgiana was part of a great network of notable families, including those of the Dukes of Devonshire, Sutherland, Westminster, Norfolk, Bedford and Leicester, and the Earls of Carlisle, Harrowby and Ellesmere, whose possessions, power and privilege had been secure since 1688. She, however, was to protest against their dominant characteristic – a wilful pragmatism bent on political and financial advancement – for in both her life and her art she attacked materialism, prejudice and the abuse of power in the family and in the state.

We have three nineteenth-century lives of Fullerton. All are useful, but none is truly satisfactory. *Lady Georgiana Fullerton: Sa vie et ses oeuvres* (1888), by her close friend Mrs Craven,[2] and the English version produced by Fullerton's literary executor, Father Henry Coleridge,[3] are over-reticent. Frances Taylor's *The Inner Life of Lady Georgiana Fullerton* (1899), written by a close associate in

---

[1] W. H. Gardner, *Gerard Manley Hopkins 1844–1889: A Study in Poetic Idiosyncracy in relation to Poetic Tradition*, 2 vols (London, 1948), 1: 2–3.

[2] Mme Augustus Craven, *Lady Georgiana Fullerton: Sa vie et ses oeuvres* (Paris, 1888).

[3] Henry James Coleridge, *Life of Lady Georgiana Fullerton, from the French of Mrs. Augustus Craven* (London, 1888). This is not a strict translation, for Coleridge omitted passages from the original and added material of his own.

her charitable work, verges on the hagiographic.[4] There is no later biography.[5]

Fullerton herself wrote an unfinished memoir that deals only with her early life.[6] Despite a privileged environment, as a small child in England and later as the British Ambassador's daughter in Paris, Georgiana was unhappy. From the age of four until she escaped the schoolroom to enter society at seventeen, her life was almost without a break controlled by Mademoiselle Eward, a rigid and unimaginative Swiss Protestant governess, who thought the elder daughter Susan a pattern of perfection, a view shared by the girls' mother. Misunderstood and underestimated, Georgiana was often openly rebellious, but also took refuge from her situation in daydreaming and reading, and later in writing. She was 'always scribbling something', and steeped as she was in Racine, Shakespeare and Metastasio, she produced a history play, part of an epic romance in verse and, at fourteen, a novel. This last achievement left her governess appalled that one so young could be so depraved. Worse was to follow, for at fifteen Georgiana fell in love first with Byron's poetry, then with the man himself, although he had been dead four years. This secret infatuation persisted until 1830, when she entered London society.

The succeeding decade saw her marriage to Alexander George Fullerton, the birth of their only child, and an increasing seriousness of mind. By 1840 she had moved from Evangelicalism through a dark period of absolute doubt, and had become a close observer of the Oxford Movement and French Ultramontanism. In 1841 we find her expressing to her sister the fear that 'in the position we are in there is great danger of our wasting our lives in trifles ... [rather than doing] the best one can where one is. It is that that I am afraid

4   Frances M. Taylor, *The Inner Life of Lady Georgiana Fullerton, with Notes of Retreats and Diary* (London, 1899).

5   For a brief account with a useful sampling of references, see *ODNB*, *s.n.* 'Fullerton, Lady Georgiana Charlotte (1812–1885)', online edn, <http://www. oxforddnb.com/view/article 102242>, accessed 9 November 2010. For a more extensive, critical account, see Kathleen Jaeger, 'Lady Georgiana Fullerton (1812–1885): A Reassessment' (Ph.D. dissertation, Dalhousie University, 1986), 18–176.

6   The memoir was written for Maria Giberne, in exchange for an account of Giberne's role in the Achilli affair, and so cannot date earlier than 1852. Extensive passages from it (the whereabouts of the original are currently unknown) appear in Coleridge, *Life*, 3–42.

of not doing'.[7] This fear of not living up to perceived obligations is a persistent feature of Fullerton's nature that came in time to dominate her religious experience. At this point, however, it led her to try to make money for good works by writing. Bentley paid her twelve guineas for a translated poem, but advised her to turn to fiction as being more lucrative. For Fullerton, writing fiction was not a matter of 'wasting our time in trifles'; moreover, by the 1840s the earlier evangelical distrust of the novel as at best ephemeral and at worst dangerous to morals and the Utilitarian contempt for imaginative literature as useless to society were giving way to the great popularity of works provided by authors and publishers fully alert to their public's sensitivities.[8] With Queen Victoria and William Gladstone reading novels, and such diverse worthies as Eliot, Gaskell, Kingsley, Martineau and Newman all writing them, Fullerton began her career when fiction was not only 'respectable' but an accepted vehicle for the serious themes she was to explore.

Fullerton had started a novel in 1839, but began concentrated work on it in 1841. At twenty-nine, she was entering a period that seemed likely to be devoted to travel and happy family life.[9] She could have written an insider's story of fashionable life in London, Paris or Rome, frothy or minatory, but instead she produced *Ellen Middleton* (1844), a novel about deep human needs and fears. Its youthful heroine is at once guilt-ridden and rebellious; its most striking male figure, the anti-hero, shares her characteristics. In such passionate company, the novel's attempts to portray the corrosiveness of secrecy in family relations and the healing powers of charity are overwhelmed. It was a very considerable success, read far beyond fashionable circles. Tractarians saw the work as propaganda for auricular confession,[10] but the general reader was simply struck by its power. Harriet Martineau found herself 'carried away by a torrent of passion'.[11] Edgar Allan Poe classed it amongst 'the most passionate of fictions', so severe in style, so luminous and

---

[7]   Coleridge, *Life*, 115.

[8]   See Richard Altick, *The English Common Reader: A Social History of the Mass Reading Public 1800–1901* (Chicago, IL, 1957), 81–140; John Sutherland, *Victorian Novelists and Publishers* (London, 1976), 9–40.

[9]   Lord Granville had retired in 1841, and on leaving Paris the Granvilles and the Fullertons travelled in France and Italy for some months.

[10]   For examples, see Coleridge, *Life*, 157–63.

[11]   Ibid. 184–5.

thorough that he found it hard to believe a woman had written it.[12] The absorption of such readers in the book mirrors Fullerton's state when writing it: 'she was absorbed in it. She wrote … in a room full of people, … in the garden, … even in the carriage. Nothing … distracted her.'[13]

In *Ellen Middleton* we find the most extreme expression of themes that persist in Fullerton's major works: the longing for a Christian ideal and the desire to expose the destructive workings of egoism. Principal characters are often tormented by their sense of the Pauline divided self: 'The good that I would I do not; but the evil which I would not do, that I do' (Romans 7: 19). Such was Fullerton's judgement also on herself, as revealed in her verses 'Unstable as water, I shall ne'er excel'.[14] For Coleridge, however, Fullerton had been 'a truly noble and simple soul',[15] and when reviewing the biographies by Craven and Coleridge, Fullerton's close friend Emily Bowles protested at their inadequate accounts of a woman she had seen as 'ardent', with 'a nature that had within it the most powerful elements of good and evil'.[16]

After her reception into the Roman Catholic Church in 1846, Fullerton, surely a complicated convert, came under the moderate direction of the Jesuit James Brownbill, whose advice was simple, with no stress on any kind of extreme. He remained her confessor until he left the Jesuit headquarters at Farm Street, London, in 1854. As early as 1850, however, both the Fullertons had met the Oratorian Frederick Faber, and had come to share his enthusiasm for Italianate styles of devotion. Faber was a man of great personal charm, close to Fullerton in age, also a convert, and (like her) optimistic and efficient in practical matters. By 1854, when he became her director, the bond between them was already very close. The interaction of Faber and Fullerton had its dangers, since both were what Michael Hill has called 'religious virtuosi', whose extremism

---

[12] Edmund Clarence Stedman and George Edward Woodberry, eds, *Complete Works of Edgar Allan Poe*, 10 vols (New York, 1914), 7: 306–7.

[13] Coleridge, *Life*, 140.

[14] Lady Georgiana Fullerton, *The Gold Digger and Other Verses* (London, 1872), 24; cf. Gen. 49: 4a.

[15] Coleridge, *Life*, ix.

[16] Emily Bowles, review of Craven and Coleridge, *Dublin Review* 103 (1885), 311–31, at 313.

can take the form of seeking a monastic ideal of perfection.[17] In the grief that followed the sudden death at twenty of her only child, Granville, in 1855, Faber was Fullerton's chief support, and probably the influence that led her to the very sorts of excesses in devotion and in bodily mortification Father Brownbill had discouraged. Both the Fullertons were devastated by their loss, but after a brief period resumed their active and influential roles among the laity. They also made a vow to live, as far as possible in the world, the life of a religious, confirming this when they were accepted into the Third Order of St Francis in 1857.

In her *Inner Life of Lady Georgiana Fullerton*, Frances Taylor gives us all of 'the secret outpourings of a soul to its God' that she found in Fullerton's papers,[18] thus shedding light on her subject's inner religious life; but Fullerton had had since childhood another inner life, that of the creative imagination. The conflict between these two inner lives, the spiritual and the artistic, is reflected in her 'Spiritual Diary' and 'Notes on Retreats'. The diary consists of brief daily entries; the notes made during month-long retreats follow the pattern imposed by Ignatius Loyola's *Spiritual Exercises*, a series of ascetical activities pursued in isolation designed to help the retreatant arrive at some important decision.[19] Both diary and notes show the same concerns: efforts at physical mortification; a growing anxiety as to what God's purpose in creating her was; and a particular doubt as to the place of writing in her life.

This last had been an issue between her and Faber for years. Faber had faced the question himself. At Harrow he had had ambitions to be a poet and, according to one biographer, an Evangelical's fear that 'nothing was valuable unless it was of positive use to religion'.[20] From 1837, by then an Anglican priest and a published poet, he was a close friend of Wordsworth, who encouraged his writing. Faber then consulted Keble, admitting that 'I have very sinfully permitted the man of letters to overlay the priest', and Keble also advised that he continue to write.[21] Later, after

[17] Michael Hill, *The Religious Orders: A Study of Virtuoso Religion and its Legitimization in the Nineteenth-Century Church of England* (London, 1973), 2.

[18] Taylor, *Inner Life*, v.

[19] For a discussion of the particular appeal of the *Exercises* to Victorian Catholics, see Walter J. Ong, *Hopkins, the Self and God* (Toronto, ON, 1986), 4–6, 54–65.

[20] Ronald Chapman, *Father Faber* (London, 1961), 15.

[21] Ibid. 71.

wading through a thousand lines of Faber's *Sir Lancelot*, Words-worth changed his mind, but Faber turned out verse to the end of his days.

In an undated letter Faber gave Fullerton twelve points of direction, the first being: 'I would give up literature altogether, both composition and light reading.'[22] This letter is surely earlier than one dated 6 October 1856, in which he wrote:

> I wonder if I shall not make you misunderstand me – ... I do not understand you, and I think I made a mistake about you at first. There are many ways of being all for God. I took it into my head you wanted to be all for God in a particular way. Thus I counseled desisting from all writing and literary pursuits. I wanted to lead you in the 3rd mystical life, the prac-tice of abandonment and to a special devotion to the Third Person of the Eternal Father. Well! You did not understand me. You were not prepared to abandon literature wholly. The utmost you thought of was to add to it gravity and direct religious influence. Even this you doubted ...[23]

He attributed his mistake to having seen little of her, and opined that, when travelling, as she had been, 'interior life, in 999 cases out of 1000, is impossible. I was all in the dark as to where you were in matters spiritual. You wrote. Your letters were quite *partial* disclosures of yourself ... I was, or am, without a view about you.'[24] By 28 August 1858, he had modified his position. Apparently in response to her questions, he now warned her about charitable work. Her life as a religious did not, he thought, preclude 'active work; yet it does not easily comport with satisfaction of natural activity, or any intense interest in outward work'. As for writing, 'I cannot see that you need be afraid of writing tales, so long as it is not an employment that gets down deep enough into you to touch your prayers.'[25] Reasonable enough, perhaps, but hardly the most imaginative message to send a woman who did have an 'intense interest' in her charitable work, especially direct work among the Irish poor in London, and who took her writing seriously.

---

[22] Kew, TNA, Granville Papers, 30/29.
[23] Ibid.
[24] Ibid.; italics in the original.
[25] Ibid.

In 1859 Fullerton wrote:

> My God, I pray Thee to show me what Thou will have me do … I wish to bring myself to think of nothing but the present, and of my God, and of my dear child, for whom I work, and who awaits me. I ask to suffer for him.
>
> If I am called to be a Saint, I must sacrifice everything to attain that end; but am I so called? If God intends me to be a Saint, and I do not answer that end, will my salvation be endangered?
>
> Give me someone to obey … I will refuse nothing … I want only one thing, which is to love Thee more, and I do not care what it costs me.[26]

Nonetheless, she did care, and remained anxious about the proper direction of her life. She resolved that 'I must never for a single moment go on doing something which I cannot fairly say is God's work', and continued to ask the same question: 'having my soul and its mortification in view … If literature is or is not to be followed up.'[27]

Bodily mortification, whether in a simple mode of life or even her regular use of the discipline, presented Fullerton with little difficulty, for, as we recall, she sought to suffer for her son. It is clear though that denying herself the exercise of her creative gifts was very hard indeed, but, she believed, essential, since she had come to see writing as the base of her egoism, the pride that separated her from God and negated all her other efforts. By 1860 she had reached this point: 'I have struggled with other sins; but I have spared my pride – that dreadful sin which makes my heart a cold grave for my God. It is my vanity, it is all the shapes of the terrible passion which makes my God enter into my soul and find there Herod's likeness.'[28]

This was how Fullerton saw herself when she came under the direction of the Jesuit Peter Gallwey, who remained her confessor until her death in 1885. Shrewd, kind and energetic, he was convinced that progress in spiritual life resulted not from introspection but from experiments. He too had a vision for Lady

---

[26] Taylor, *Inner Life*, 285.
[27] Coleridge, *Life*, 306–7.
[28] Ibid. 389.

Georgiana Fullerton, and it was a startling departure from Faber's instructions. Gallwey believed that for someone of her age and position, the ideal apostolate was as a proselytizer amongst persons of rank and fortune, for, he told her, '[o]ne person that you gained for God in the higher classes of society, is of more importance than ten in the worst courts of London, because their influence would extend far beyond what you can personally effect by yourself going among the poor.'[29]

She pledged obedience, though she observed that she had hitherto been singularly unsuccessful in that line. Understandably she was at a loss to know '[h]ow to combine this new idea of duty with the kind of life that for the last few years I have been aiming at'.[30] For years bidden to live as a religious and urged to give up writing, she was now to sally forth into fashionable society, and not only was novel-writing not proscribed, but both *Constance Sherwood* (1865) and *A Stormy Life* (1867) were commissioned for *The Month*, a Jesuit-owned review instigated by Gallwey.[31]

Lest we imagine that when not writing novels Fullerton spent her time reclining on a sofa bemoaning her shortcomings, it is important to recognize that all these years she was, as Gillow put it, 'succouring the poor in charities too numerous to name', setting up schools and clubs, personally tending the old and sick.[32] In 1859 she exerted her political influence to enable the establishment in London of some Sisters of St Vincent de Paul from Paris; in 1860 she organized a vast charity bazaar at the request of Gallwey, and around the same time aided him in establishing the Charity of the Immaculate Conception.

In the isolation of her annual retreats, however, she had to face her increasing anxiety, resulting in part from the contradictory influences of Faber and Gallwey, but also from her own divided self. In her daily examinations of conscience she lists recurring

---

29 Taylor, *Inner Life*, 286.

30 Ibid. 287.

31 *The Month* was a Catholic review of literature, science and the arts, which ran from 1864 to 2001. Originally owned and edited by Frances Taylor, it was bought by the English Jesuit Fathers in 1865. Taylor always said that Gallwey was its actual founder: see Francis Charles Devas, *Mother Mary Magdalene of the Sacred Heart* (London, 1927), 320–1.

32 Joseph Gillow, *Bibliographical Dictionary of the English Catholics from the Break with Rome in 1534 to the Present Time*, 5 vols (London, 1885–1902), 2: 336.

faults stemming from her consciousness of herself as an author. She upbraids herself for 'wishing to remind others of my writings', resolves to read only unfavourable reviews of her books, and confesses that she still wants them to succeed.[33] One day she describes as 'pretty well ... did not notice any particular fault ... except as usual setting about too eagerly the new book I have in view. Too much natural eagerness.'[34]

Between 1858 and 1869 Fullerton published six novels, all save the last, *Mrs Gerald's Niece* (1869), set in the past. Both *Laurentia* (1861) and *Constance Sherwood* (1865) sought to stimulate lay interest in Catholic martyrs, and so can be seen as part of her apostolate in the world. The same may be true of *A Stormy Life* (1867), but this work has a different interest in our context, for it depicts the spiritual journey of Margaret of Anjou, who displays the characteristics Emily Bowles saw in Fullerton herself. Her highly idiosyncratic version of Margaret is revealing. All considerations of historical accuracy give way to the author's purpose: to show the archetypal self-assertive, intelligent and passionate woman, daughter of one weak king and wife of one even weaker, who fights to achieve her ambitions and control her world, only ultimately to debase herself in an extreme penitence. In the final chapter, when Margaret's will is broken, she comes to believe that her battle had been not against her enemies, but against God. Her confidante tells us that 'the force of ... character was ... turned entirely against herself', and that '[s]he thirsted for penance as she had once for greatness'.[35] In her portrait of this medieval queen, Fullerton releases her most vigorous attack on pride and the drive for self-expression. Margaret's repudiation of everything – beauty, talent and power – that enabled her to impose her ambitions upon her world, presents in highly charged fictional terms the guilt Fullerton felt over her delight in the free power of artistic creation. As a novelist, she created worlds, controlled them and imposed them on her readers.

In 1868 Fullerton made a private retreat at Roehampton, where her son was buried. Depressed and ill, she found she could respond to little, but near the end she records that she had made 'the best and happiest meditation' she had ever had, adding '[i]f all medita-

33 Taylor, *Inner Life*, 389.
34 Ibid. 346.
35 Lady Georgiana Fullerton, *A Stormy Life* (London, 1867), 535.

tion could be like that there would not be a greater pleasure … I must ask to what degree it is well to use the imagination.'[36] The subject of the meditation had been 'The Hidden Life at Nazareth', surely a most fertile topic for the free range of the creative imagination.

These retreats might have offered this active woman her best opportunity to resolve her conflict, but even the rigorous techniques for making decisions that the *Exercises* provided repeatedly failed her. By 1868 she was so deeply distressed that her physician, her director and her husband united in forbidding her to write further fiction. No other change in her way of life was imposed, and the edict seems to have resulted in peace of mind. In an intimate and charming letter to Mrs Craven, however, Fullerton ruefully described the impact this ban would have on her work with the poor. She had long ago sold all her jewels; her husband, though generous, grew impatient when she overspent, and until now, if down to her last penny, she had always counted on raising fresh funds by writing another novel. Pious tales and saints' lives brought in nothing at all. The best she could see in her new situation was that it would be good for her soul to be denied so much satisfaction from helping others.[37]

By this time, as we have seen, Fullerton had been in conflict about the legitimacy of her literary work for many years, and had come to see it as a pursuit grounded in self and a stumbling block to spiritual progress. While the letter to Mrs Craven does not sound like one from a woman who had suffered a grave trauma from the prohibition against fiction, we need not accept Susan Oldfield's claim that Fullerton had never enjoyed writing novels but had looked on it as an irksome task pursued for a worthy end.[38] We have seen her absorption in the composition of *Ellen Middleton*, her diary entries noting her eagerness in setting about a new novel and chiding herself for taking an extreme interest in criticism and reviews, and above all the depth of the anxiety she had developed when she contemplated giving up her creative life. All these suggest that this rejection of the novel was a comforting rationalization, arrived at after her acceptance of the edict against

---

36 Taylor, *Inner Life*, 375.
37 Craven, *Lady Georgiana Fullerton*, 456–7.
38 Ibid. 457. Susan Oldfield was Fullerton's niece.

fiction. Yet by 1872 her attitude had hardened: she tells Mrs Craven that the previous year she had understood a priest to say that all her novels were edifying, but that she herself was not of that opinion.[39]

Her final novel, *Mrs Gerald's Niece*, was addressed to men and women in religious conflict, and indeed the Marquis of Ripon claimed to have been converted by reading it. It shows no sign of failing powers and impresses with its even-handed presentation of various religious positions. Restrained in style and material when set against her earlier works, it received a patronizing stamp of approval from a Catholic reviewer. Having acknowledged 'the great mental powers of the authoress', he judged that Fullerton's novels 'for the most part are products of merit ... Their great fault has been too much intensity of passion, a quality that has been subdued ... in the present novel ... it is safe and sound enough to satisfy the most fastidious confessor.'[40]

Such a confessor would undoubtedly have approved of 'Ad Majorem Dei Gloriam', Fullerton's recantation, in which she expresses her concerns about the moral dangers of fiction. An uneasy mixture of thinly-veiled autobiography and pious didactic, this short story has Madame N., a famous author of edifying works, recall how the sermons of a missioner had made her question the worth of her first work, a novel said by her worldly mentors to be marked by 'passionate feeling' and 'delicacy of expression': in short, an *Ellen Middleton*.[41] Initially, she tells herself that 'there is much good in it', and that publishing it would pave the way for her projected edifying works, but her fears that it would be 'fatally successful' are confirmed when she visits a girl dying 'in shame and disgrace' brought on by reading 'a story that confused her ideas of right and wrong and weakened her horror of sin'. Madame N. burns the manuscript 'as a sacrifice ... for Him that died for me',[42] and henceforth devotes herself to pious tales and good works.

Set against the moving passages we see in her diary and notes, this confessional story seems a disappointingly crude simplifica-

---

[39] Ibid. 413–14.

[40] 'Mrs. Gerald's Niece, by Lady Georgiana Fullerton', *Catholic World* 10 (1869–70), 264.

[41] Lady Georgiana Fullerton, *Seven Stories* (London, 1873), 121–90, at 159.

[42] Ibid. 179. Fullerton opposed the republication of *Ellen Middleton*, and sought to prevent a French translation of her other 'passionate' work, *Lady Bird* (1853).

tion of Fullerton's own experience. For nearly twenty years she had struggled with the two conflicting inner lives that had grown from her 'personality' as an artist and her 'character' as a religious, and had come to believe that writing fiction endangered her own salvation. She had found her dilemma intractable, and its resolution came in the end not through prayer or the exercise of reason, but only through the direct intervention of authority.

University of King's College, Halifax, Nova Scotia

WRITING THE SABBATH: THE LITERATURE OF THE NINETEENTH-CENTURY SUNDAY OBSERVANCE DEBATE

by MARTIN SPENCE

'It was a Sunday evening in London, gloomy, close and stale.' This line from Charles Dickens's *Little Dorrit* encapsulates the common view that the nineteenth-century Sabbath was a tedious, gloomy and tiresome institution that embodied the full weight of Victorian Britain's old-fashioned, sombre and somewhat hypocritical evangelical piety.[1] Taking such contemporary portrayals at face value, historian John Wigley, whose thirty-year-old monograph remains the only full treatment of the subject, depicted the Victorian Sabbath as 'a day which had a funereal character, notorious for its symbols – the hushed voice, the half-drawn blind and the best clothes'.[2] Sabbatarianism, he argued, 'appeared to consist of a perverse reluctance to enjoy oneself on Sundays and a determination to stop other people enjoying themselves too'.[3]

For Wigley, Sabbatarianism was about the enforcement and prohibition of certain behaviours. Other historians have nuanced this picture by reminding us that people could also enjoy Sundays.[4] However, the framework of these counter-arguments is often the same as that within which those painting a pessimistic image of Sunday operate; it is concerned with what happened on an average Victorian Sunday, and what people thought about it. The 'Victo-

---

[1]   J. F. C. Harrison, *Late Victorian Britain, 1875–1901* (Abingdon, 2000), esp. 113–14.

[2]   John Wigley, *The Rise and Fall of the Victorian Sunday* (Manchester, 1980), 185. For other aspects of the Victorian Sabbath debates, see Brian Harrison, 'The Sunday Trading Riots of 1855', *HistJ* 8 (1965), 219–45; idem, 'Religion and Recreation in Nineteenth-Century England', *P&P*, no. 38 (1967), 98–125; George M. Ellis, 'The Evangelicals and the Sunday Question' (Ph.D. thesis, Harvard University, 1952); Ian Rennie, 'Evangelicalism and English Public Life, 1823–50' (Ph.D. thesis, University of Toronto, 1962), 211–34.

[3]   Wigley, *Rise and Fall*, 2–3.

[4]   Doreen Rosman, *Evangelicals and Culture* (London, 1984), 111; Andrew Atherstone, 'The Undergraduate Diary of Francis Chavasse', in Mark Smith and Stephen Taylor, eds, *Evangelicalism in the Church of England, c.1790 – c.1900* (Woodbridge, 2004), 109–282, at 135–6.

rian Sabbath' has thus been studied as a social, rather than as a religious or theological, phenomenon.

The place to begin looking for the realities of religious belief, however, is not only in ritual social actions, but also in the words, symbols and thought-world of popular religious literature. While there is not 'nothing but the text', there is, nonetheless, the text – a large and still surprisingly under-explored text, replete with the symbolic language of the popular Victorian religious imagination. All too often historians assume they know what a particular form of religious belief is about and simply move on to use their imagined definition to explain the behaviours of their protagonists, without stopping to explore whether the religious texts themselves really justify their presuppositions. In the words of Susan S. Sizer: 'Scholars treat religion as composed of belief systems – systems which the scholars have constructed – rather than as it appears in the forms which are its vehicles.'[5]

The brief exploration of the literature of the Victorian Sabbath question in this essay attempts to take the 'forms which are the vehicles' of religious ideology seriously. While not wishing to deny the important issue of Victorian Sabbath customs, it will argue that there was a Victorian Sabbath beyond social protocols. This was the Sabbath of literary imagination, forged with symbols, rhetoric and poetry in the copious literature produced on the topic of Sunday. Firstly, we shall explore the context for the creation of this literature before, secondly, turning to examine some of its literary themes.

Rewriting the Sabbath

The Sabbath was reconceptualized significantly in the middle decades of the nineteenth century. A new discourse emerged that sought to refute the image of Sabbatarians as 'canting hypocrites' who unjustly sought to stifle the Sunday pleasures of the poor.[6] Discussions of what should or should not be done on the Lord's day were supplemented by a more abstract poetical depiction of the essence of the institution. This idealized, superlativized Sabbath lived most pristinely in literary form.

This rewriting of the Sabbath occurred naturally in numerous

---

[5] Susan S. Sizer, *Gospel Hymns and Social Religion* (Philadelphia, PA, 1978), 129.
[6] *Hansard's Parliamentary Debates* (ser. 3), vol. 113, col. 588 (31 July 1850).

established popular formats, such as the journal, the tract, the essay collection and the printed sermon.[7] The representation of the Sabbath in mid Victorian Britain also had a self-consciously creative dimension in the numerous prize essay competitions organized to create a new body of Sabbath literature. A central figure in the promotion of this new genre was the Glaswegian Evangelical John Henderson (1782–1867), one of the co-founders of the Evangelical Alliance. Henderson was an evangelical literary impresario. 'Mr. Henderson was a great believer in the power of books', wrote the nineteenth-century Glasgow publisher James MacLehose (1811–85). 'He would advance a cause ... which had not then produced a literature, he would employ the ablest men he could find to write on the subject, publish their essays, and scatter them broadcast over the country.'[8]

In 1847 Henderson published a collection of essays on the Sabbath that he had commissioned from notable Christian leaders.[9] 'Mr. Henderson had enjoyed so much success in this series of tracts', explained John Jordan (vicar of Enstone and one of the contributors), 'that the idea occurred to him, – and a noble as well as original one it was, – Might not the labouring classes themselves be engaged in the discussion and defence of the principles of the Sabbath?'[10] In 1847 Henderson offered three prizes for the best essays on the Sabbath by working men; 1,045 entries were submitted.[11] John Allan Quinton (b.1817), a printer's compositor from Ipswich, won first prize with 'a composition that would not discredit any student in either of our chief Universities of Cambridge or Oxford'.[12]

7   For a contemporary bibliography of Sabbath literature, see Robert Cox, *The Literature of the Sabbath Question*, 2 vols (Edinburgh, 1865).

8   James MacLehose, *Memoirs and Portraits of One Hundred Glasgow Men* (Glasgow, 1886), 159–60, online at <http://gdl.cdlr.strath.ac.uk/mlemen/index.html>, accessed 8 June 2010.

9   John Henderson, ed., *The Christian Sabbath, Considered in its Various Aspects, by Ministers of Different Denominations* (Edinburgh, 1850).

10   John Jordan, 'Sabbath Essays by British Workmen', *Evangelical Christendom* 4 (1850), 281–7, at 282.

11   Ibid. This article also contained a list of the occupations of 700 of the essayists. It found the best represented profession to be 'that of joiners, carpenters, and cabinet-makers'. Of those that stated a denominational allegiance, English Independents were best represented (111 essays), followed by the Church of England (76 essays) and the Scottish United Presbyterians (74 essays).

12   Jordan, 'Sabbath Essays', 285. Birth and death dates for the prize essayists are

Henderson wanted to create a literary corpus demonstrating that, far from opposing Sabbatarian campaigns, the labouring classes in fact valued and enjoyed the Sabbath. Moreover, the competition seemed to prove that Sabbath-honouring men were also exactly the kind of industrious individuals who had developed the skills needed to produce a substantial piece of written work. The essays, reported John Jordan, showed both 'the literary powers' and 'the extent of spiritual knowledge and depth of piety amongst our labouring classes'.[13] He also reported with satisfaction that some men had formed impromptu literary societies to discuss drafts of their essays, a clear indication of their moral and mental seriousness.[14]

The essayists hoped that their readers would respect the craftsmanship and hard work that they had invested in the exercise. 'No one knows but myself and my wife the difficulty I experienced in procuring the materials for writing the Essay', asserted David Calvert.[15] George Bryan requested that his essay be sent back to him for revision after adjudication, suggesting that failure to honour this request would be an insult to his status as a serious writer:

> You would not deprive the sculptor of the final stroke from his chisel, or the painter from the last touch by his fine-haired brush, much less would you say to the poor man, who produced his Essay after ten or twelve hours' hard labour, with his body and mind borne down with fatigue, 'You shall not enjoy the same privileges as the well-educated, learned, and accomplished author'.[16]

The essayists also hoped that the broader significance of their work would be recognized. 'Here is a new thing on earth, from which a new era in the course of human affairs may be destined to take its data', enthused essayist John Younger, 'in all past ages when were working classes ever before invited to write?'[17]

The organizers encouraged this high view of the texts. 'Your

provided in this article where available.
13 Ibid.
14 Ibid.
15 *Working Man's Charter* [hereafter: *WMC*], August 1848, 35.
16 Ibid. 38.
17 John Younger, 'The Light of the Week', in [John Allan Quinton, John Younger

essays are a very remarkable, and a very honourable event, in the history of our nation', said John Henderson.[18] The essayists' endeavours were celebrated with the paraphernalia of Victorian religious festivity: prize-giving breakfasts at Exeter Hall, letters from the queen, and a tea party sponsored by the popular Congregationalist minister John Angell James (1785–1859).[19] Copies of the essays were sent to every Member of Parliament.[20] Henderson had created a great Victorian religious-literary event.

Henderson's enterprise spawned other Sabbath literary initiatives. In 1848 John Jordan began a short-lived journal, *The Working Man's Charter*, to publicize working-class Sabbatarianism. The Evangelical Alliance and the Religious Tract Society ran essay competitions in the following years, and over one hundred other sponsors gave further prizes.[21] These popular essays meshed with, and were often derivative of, works published in the 1840s and 1850s by more established Christian writers. To avoid the charge of trying to force people to become 'godly by legislation', both established and novice authors often studiously avoided premising their arguments for Sabbath observance upon an appeal to the fourth commandment. Freed from the necessity of grounding an argument in the unassailable command of Scripture, the canvas was wiped clean for Sunday to be painted with the myriad colours of literary inventiveness and lyrical persuasion. The remainder of this essay briefly introduces two pervasive themes of this new Sabbath literature: the Romantic Sabbath and the democratic Sabbath.

THE ROMANTIC SABBATH

Many eighteenth- and nineteenth-century pastoral and Romantic poets eulogized the beauty of the Sabbath. ' 'Tis sweet to hear a brook, 'tis sweet | To hear the Sabbath-bell | 'Tis sweet to hear them both at once | Deep in a woody dell', mused Samuel Taylor Coleridge (1772–1834).[22] His son (David) Hartley Coleridge

---

and David Farquhar], *The Workman's Testimony to the Sabbath* (London, 1851), 77–116, at 88.

[18] *WMC*, August 1848, 9.

[19] *WMC*, October 1848, 69; Jordan, 'Sabbath Essays', 284.

[20] Ibid.

[21] A list of all published essays appears in Jordan, 'Sabbath Essays', 285–7.

[22] Coleridge, 'The Three Graves', in *The Poems of S. T. Coleridge*, 3 vols (London, 1848), 1: 284.

(1796–1849) described the Sabbath as 'a calm slip of intervening heaven'.[23] The poet Bernard Barton (1784–1849), a close friend of Robert Southey (1774–1843) and Charles Lamb (1775–1834), modernized a stanza written by the metaphysical poet Henry Vaughan (1621–95), and thereby created several lines frequently quoted by Victorian Sabbatarians, which described Sabbaths as 'eternity in time – the steps by which | We climb to future ages | … Foretastes of heaven on earth'.[24]

As writing about the Sabbath became democratized in the 1840s and 1850s, this Romanticism was absorbed into popular Sabbatarian prose. Firstly, the prize essayists were influenced by the Romantic vision in general. 'Of some of Byron's works I was passionately fond', recalled prize essayist John Allan Quinton of his youth.

> From reading, I soon began to write poetry. I lived in a land of dreams and ideal enchantments. The poetic afflatus or inspiration has oftentimes … filled me with trembling … I felt inarticulate longings for something above the actual. The state of feeling and emotion breathed itself out in innumerable fragmentary effusions.[25]

Another essayist, John Greet, narrated his spiritual history solely in terms of his expanding Romantic vision: 'I read poetry with unmingled gratification, and afterwards invoked the Muse for a transmission of the divine afflatus.'[26] The prize essays were peppered with quotations from the popular Romantic and pastoral poets of the day, including Edward Young (d. 1765), James Thomson (1700–78), Robert Montgomery (1807–55), William Cowper (1731–1800), James Beattie (1735–1803) and Robert Burns (1759–96).

Secondly, Romantic sensibility manifested itself more specifi-

---

[23] *Poems by Hartley Coleridge*, 2 vols (London, 1851), 2: 340.

[24] Bernard Barton, 'Sabbath Days', in Joseph Cundell, ed., *Sabbath Bells Chimed by the Poets* (London, 1856), 43–4.

[25] John Jordan, 'Introduction', to [Quinton, Younger and Farquhar], *Workman's Testimony*, 9–18, at 15–16.

[26] John Greet, 'The Pilgrim's Arbour on His Way to Glory', in *WMC*, Supplemental Series, 245–60, at 249. The monthly supplements to *The Working Man's Charter* (1848–9) provided a forum for the publication of the prize essays. The supplements were issued without a volume number, but with consecutive page numbers. In the British Library, the supplements and the journals are bound together and catalogued as *The Working Man's Charter*.

cally in the depiction of the Sabbath as a place of tranquil repose within a busy world. This was part of a Romantic interest in attaining a timeless state of existence, a mountain-top vista from which one could survey the world rather than being caught up in its frantic mutability.[27] The essays presented the Sabbath as the means by which to hold back the rush of time: 'During the week-days all is attention, bustle and confusion', noted John Browning, 'but the Sabbath changes all this.'[28] Florence Gittins, an entrant in an essay competition held in Leicester, said that she delighted in the Sabbath because it provided 'refreshment from the over-charging weight of the things of time and sense', and a way of escaping 'from the emptiness, vanity, and fleeting character of things sublunary, to the fullness, sufficiency, and satisfying possession of things heavenly and eternal'.[29] Other depictions of Sunday used the imagery of industrial pollution to speak about the Sabbath's otherness. David Maxwell thought that 'the recurring Sabbath is a great antidote to the moral poison, amidst the pestiferous fumes of which we, for the six days, live and breathe. It is a powerful moral medicine, – purging off the week's impurities, which else would sink themselves deep into the soul, festering and rotting.'[30]

Although some of this language about finding release 'from time and sense' sounded Neoplatonic, the nineteenth-century Romantic tradition was characterized not only by a desire to escape from the temporal realm but also by its quest for an *integration* of time and eternity.[31] Unity and wholeness were more authentically Romantic themes than separation and other-worldliness. In the prize essays, Sunday was depicted not only as an escape from the temporal realm but also as an institution that sacramentally fused earth with

---

[27] George Poulet, 'Timelessness and Romanticism', *JHI* 15 (1954), 3–22. Sabbath literature exemplified the time-hauntedness, prevalent in much nineteenth-century literature, caused by the speed of Victorian social and industrial change: see Jerome H. Buckley, *The Triumph of Time* (Cambridge, MA, 1966), viii, 5–13.

[28] John Browning, 'The Universal Treasure', *WMC*, Supplemental Series, 119–38, at 122.

[29] Florence Gittins, 'God's Holy Day, Not Man's Holiday', in *Leicester Prize Essays on Sunday Amusements* (Leicester, 1857), 11. Each essay in this volume is paginated separately.

[30] David Maxwell, 'Labour's Great Charter', *WMC*, Supplemental Series, 67–84, at 72.

[31] Keith Cunliffe, 'Recollection and Recovery: Coleridge's Platonism', in Anna Baldwin and Sarah Hutton, eds, *Platonism and the English Imagination* (Cambridge, 1994), 207–16, at 214–15.

heaven. John Allan Quinton, echoing Hartley Coleridge, thought that 'it is that strip of our time, which especially links Earth with Eternity'.[32] John Younger said that it was 'a silken cord, flung out from the eternal sanctuary of Divine love amidst the rolling tides of the world's time, to ... gradually draw the sanctity of earth into the glorious circle of the eternal Sabbath'.[33] David Farquhar claimed that 'every Sabbath is a step in the ladder which [God] is constructing between earth and heaven'.[34] The Sabbath was thus portrayed as a Wordsworthian 'spot of time' through which it was possible to find spiritual vision and emotional exhilaration. As one anonymous essayist mused:

> How many for the first time have [by keeping the Sabbath] felt their minds expand, their faculties enlarged, their energies braced, and their hopes brightened, until they have exclaimed in a kindred spirit to that of the penniless poet,[35] when he stood upon the mountain top, 'Creation's heir! the world, the world is mine!'[36]

THE DEMOCRATIC SABBATH

'Hail, SABBATH! thee I hail, the poor man's day.' So wrote the Scottish poet James Graham (1765–1811) in his popular poem *The Sabbath* (1804), a work lauded by Sir Walter Scott.[37] The vision of the Sabbath as the 'poor man's day' grew in potency during the 1840s and 1850s. Indeed, by the mid 1850s the notion that the Sabbath was the 'Lord's day' had been quietly displaced by presenting Sunday as 'the People's day', a charter of equality and freedom bestowed upon all humanity. This argument was put forward most forcefully by the Irish Methodist William Arthur (1819–1901). Arthur rebranded the Sabbath from a divine command to an English custom, speaking of it as 'that hallowed shade, under which the English working man now rests'. He warned that

---

[32] John Allan Quinton, 'Heaven's Antidote to the Curse of Labour', in *Workman's Testimony*, 19–78, at 74.

[33] Younger, 'Light of the Week', 91.

[34] David Farquhar, 'The Torch of Time', in *Workman's Testimony*, 125–76, at 154.

[35] Oliver Goldsmith (1730–74).

[36] 'Essay I – By a Porter, Formerly a Gardener', in *Prize Essays on the Temporal Advantages of the Sabbath to the Labouring Classes* (London, 1849), 3–30, at 30.

[37] *ODNB*, *s.n.* 'Graham, James (1765–1811)', online edn, <http://www.oxforddnb.com/view/article/11229>, accessed 25 November 2010.

proposals to open the 'People's Palace' at Sydenham on a Sunday would make 'the PEOPLE'S DAY ... a bitter day, when men worked, remembering that their fathers rested'.[38]

This theme of Sunday as the people's day was central to the prize essays. Indeed, Henderson stipulated that the contributors to the essay competition should focus on its 'temporal advantages' to the labourer, and not discuss its religious obligations.[39] In particular, the prize essay competition was conceived in response to the Chartist movement and borrowed its language. 'Of all the Charters now agitating mankind, none have the same amount of tangible benefit, because none adapt themselves so vitally to the whole being of the working men as the Sabbath Charter', wrote one contributor, a mechanic, to the *Working Man's Charter*.[40] God, it was claimed, had created the Sabbath to protect the poor against avarice and exploitation.

One essayist spoke of the Sabbath as 'a barrier between the tyranny of gold and the helplessness of want'.[41] Similarly, John Allan Quinton eulogized at length:

> Oh! precious day! the workman's jubilee – the slave's release – the shield of servitude – the antidote to weariness – the suspension of the curse! How it smoothes the brow of Care! How it brightens the countenance of Gloom! ... It ... is designed to protect the poor from the bribes of wealth, and the weak from the encroachments of power.[42]

There was a radical tinge to such imagery. The prize essayists adduced the Sabbath as testament to the belief that hard, grinding labour was not part of the divine order. Prize essayist Thomas Davies explained: 'The Sabbath may be regarded as a recurring guarantee, that the physical condition of the labourer shall be ameliorated'.[43] Indeed, Davies used his Sabbath essay to condemn abuses of power and greed, and to remind employers that the

---

[38] William Arthur, *The People's Day* (London, 1855), 8.

[39] Jordan, 'Sabbath Essays', 282.

[40] *WMC*, August 1848, 18.

[41] 'Essay I – By a Porter, Formerly a Gardener', in *Prize Essays on the Temporal Advantages*, 14.

[42] Quinton, 'Heaven's Antidote', 16–18.

[43] Thomas Davies, 'The Lever in Possession, and How to Use It', *WMC*, Supplemental Series, 27–46, at 30.

Old Testament prophets tended to condemn injustice.[44] Davies was particularly strident, but his utilization of the Sabbath to challenge the notion of submission to the social order was not unique. Indeed, the Religious Tract Society was compelled to issue a disclaimer to its volume of essays, warning: 'coming from the working classes, there is very occasionally a freedom of remark respecting their position in society, which must not be considered as our sentiments'.[45] The way in which some essayists appealed to Sunday as the divine basis for ending social inequalities must complicate any simplistic suggestion that Victorian Sabbatarianism was simply a matter of the evangelical middle classes enforcing a stern code of ethics on society.[46]

Sabbath as the working man's privilege also resonated with the mid Victorian emphasis on self-improvement. 'The Savings' Bank of human existence is the weekly Sabbath-day', noted the *North British Review*, a journal of the Free Church of Scotland, in an article that publicized the prize essay competition.[47] Barbara Farquhar (who was disqualified from the competition for being a 'labourer's daughter', not a working *man*, but who nevertheless published her essay, dedicated it to Queen Victoria, and sold thirty thousand copies within the first few months)[48] noted that 'its rest refreshes and invigorates the physical constitution, and affords time to apply the mind to the attainment of useful knowledge'.[49] Sabbath 'rest', she said, was not a time for 'listless, motionless silence' but rather for 'strenuous exertion for the improvement of ourselves and others in holiness, virtue, and intelligence'.[50] The Sabbath was presented as an opportunity for cultural and literary, as well as religious, progress. 'The Sabbath is productive of personal elevation', agreed prize essayist Thomas Brown. A man 'obtains, in the ministrations of the Sabbath, material to occupy and engage

44 Ibid. 38.
45 *Prize Essays on the Temporal Advantages*, x.
46 Wigley, *Rise and Fall*, 183.
47 'Sabbath Observance', *North British Review*, May 1868, 66–76, at 67.
48 Jordan, 'Sabbath Essays by British Workmen', 284; Barbara H. Farquhar, *The Pearl of Days* (London, 1850), xiii.
49 Ibid. 28.
50 Ibid. 74.

his thoughts, and to carry on a refining and elevating process in his mind during the week'.[51]

In respect of this theme, it is important to consider how the media reinforced the message. The prize essayists wanted to portray themselves as the archetypes of Sabbath-keeping working-class respectability. At the request of the judges, several authors prefixed their essays with a short biographical sketch that narrated their own spiritual and intellectual progress, sometimes with Pooterish bathos.

> Thirty-three years ago [began John Browning, a shoemaker from London], the 12th of October last, in a little village, 228 miles from London, by name Pencara, near the town of Camelford, in the county of Cornwall, was it said, 'a man-child is born;' – his name, at once, was decided to be John. That was the present writer.[52]

These sketches were miniature versions of the popular genre of Victorian religious autobiographical literature. The nineteenth-century penchant for narrating stories of the self was shaped by the distinctive narrative cadences of the evangelical conversion account, as well as by the broader Romantic interest in self-analysis that nurtured the Victorian fascination with the biographical genre.[53] There was a democratization of the autobiographical genre in the mid nineteenth century as stories of 'moral "improvement" became synonymous with Christian "salvation"' in numerous 'improving magazines' and cheap tracts.[54] In particular, observes Linda H. Peterson, conversion was often narrated as 'a series of encounters with written texts'.[55]

This conflation of literary and spiritual progress is evident in some of the prize essayists' autobiographies. John Browning, for

---

[51] Thomas Brown, 'The Sabbath, Britain's Best Bulwark', in *WMC*, Supplemental Series, 101–18, at 105.

[52] John Browning, 'Universal Treasure', 118.

[53] For an exploration of the evangelical conversion narrative, see Bruce Hindmarsh, *The Evangelical Conversion Narrative* (Oxford, 2005). For a description of Victorian interest in autobiography in general, see Jerome H. Buckley, *The Turning Key: Autobiography and the Subjective Impulse since 1800* (Cambridge, MA, 1984).

[54] Callum G. Brown, *The Death of Christian Britain: Understanding Secularisation 1800–2000* (London, 2001), 70.

[55] Linda H. Peterson, *Victorian Autobiography: The Tradition of Self-Interpretation* (New Haven, CT, 1986), 16.

example, narrated two conversion experiences in his sketch: the first was the occasion 'when it pleased God … to reveal his Son in my heart', and the second came when his 'mental life was awakened by having my attention especially called to Cobbett's *Grammar*'.[56] Similarly, David Farquhar attributed his spiritual well-being to the power of reading, rather than to God. By absorbing himself in books as a young man, he explained, 'I was saved from the temptations to which but too many of my class became willing and easy victims.'[57] No doubt this parading of literary and intellectual accomplishment was in part intended to win favour with the judges and other readers; yet it also demonstrated the power of the written text in popular Victorian religion and culture, a power of which the organizers of the prize essay competitions were well aware and which they hoped to harness in order to both popularize and dramatize Sunday observance. In the words of Wordsworth, as quoted by prize essayist George Smith: 'Books we know, | Are a substantial world, both pure and good.'[58]

CONCLUSION

John Coffey and Alister Chapman have argued that the religious historian's 'principal obligation is to do everything possible to see things their way – to understand past agents on their own terms in their own contexts'.[59] By attending to the patterns of language and symbolism in the literature of those Christians who self-consciously promoted the value of Sunday observance, and by thinking about the textual media in which these descriptions were embodied, this article has attempted to recover 'their way' of viewing the Sabbath. For these individuals, the Sabbath was no mere religious obligation, but a divine gift that held back the monotonous, overwrought commotion and pollution of industrial society; integrated time and eternity; offered protection for the

---

[56] Browning, 'Universal Treasure', 119.

[57] Farquhar, 'Torch of Time', 124.

[58] George Smith, 'The Weekly Springtime', in *WMC*, Supplemental Series, 309–24, at 311. He was quoting William Wordsworth, 'Personal Talk' (1807).

[59] John Coffey and Alister Chapman, 'Introduction: Intellectual History and the Return of Religion', in Alister Chapman, John Coffey and Brad S. Gregory, eds, *Seeing Things Their Way: Intellectual History and the Return of Religion* (Notre Dame, IN, 2009), 1–23, at 16.

labourer against exploitation and greed; and spoke of intellectual progress and freedom.

This potent, sacramental and useful Victorian Sabbath was never realized within the social structures of nineteenth-century Britain, but the Sabbath literature, and the story of how some of it was created, was as much an authentic part of the 'Victorian Sunday' as the experiences of those individuals who detested wearisome and hypocritical Sunday rituals. Richard R. John's summary of American Sabbatarian debate in this era ought to be heeded by historians of British society and religion: 'For Sabbatarians and anti-Sabbatarians alike, the Sabbath had a rich symbolic meaning that it has subsequently lost.'[60] This insight pushes historians to analyse the 'texts' of Sunday, for it was in these multi-layered idealizations of the Sabbath that Sunday was both defined and then subtly redefined during the course of the nineteenth century. The Victorian Sabbath was a once-a-week socio-religious reality, but it was also a richly textured religio-literary construction.

International Christian College, Glasgow

---

[60] Richard R. John, 'Taking Sabbatarianism Seriously: The Postal System, the Sabbath, and the Transformation of American Political Culture', *Journal of the Early Republic* 10 (1990), 517–67, at 518.

THE PASTOR CHIEF AND OTHER STORIES: WALDENSIAN HISTORICAL FICTION IN THE NINETEENTH CENTURY

by MARK SMITH

[The Pastor spoke.] The whole audience listened to this brief but emphatic address as if spell-bound. Curiosity had moved them to listen; amazement at the supernatural calmness of the speaker held them attentive; and as he uttered the last words and turned his eyes from the human throng beneath him, to the clear, blue vault of heaven, his countenance became so radiant with hope and joy, so indicative of a soul already severed from the things of time, and sharing – ere yet stripped of its clay tabernacle – in 'the blessedness of the just made perfect,' that every eye became riveted upon it, with the rapture of admiring awe; and it was the breathless silence of the spectators which at length roused Jacomel from the oblivion to which alone all were indebted for the unwonted mercy of such a pause.

'Fire the faggots!' he exclaimed, fiercely, 'what are you waiting for? Coward hearts, do your work!' and ere his sentence was finished, the match had been applied to the pile; but the fresh timber did not readily ignite; and before the fire was well kindled, a cloud of blue smoke enveloped the body of the martyr. It seemed to stupify him, for his head was seen to decline from its upright position; then the flames rose red and high. There was a brief writhing of the fettered frame, and again the column of blue smoke concealed the horrid spectacle. But it is time to draw the veil over a scene which humanity shudders to contemplate. Let faith ascend to that which humanity cannot reach, and remember the white-robed and palm-bearing multitude which no man can number.[1]

---

[1] E. J. Standish, *The Pastor's Family; or Faith and Fanaticism: A Vaudois Tale of the Sixteenth Century* (London, 1851), 192–3.

Thus, in *The Pastor's Family; or Faith and Fanaticism* by E. J. Standish, passed into glory the saintly Waldensian pastor Samuel Raymond at the hands of the chief inquisitor in the valleys. Jacomel, a stony-eyed, cold-hearted fanatic, wreaks further destruction on the pastor's family and friends; subsequent chapters see an infant impaled on a pike, its mother driven insane by the murder of her child, and a helpless invalid bound and thrown over a precipice.[2] Such scenes were only too well attested in the successive assaults to which the Waldensian churches of Piedmont were subjected in the sixteenth and seventeenth centuries, and provided a ready source of material for the small rash of historical novels set in the world of Alpine Protestantism that appeared before the English reading public in the middle decades of the nineteenth century.

At first sight, then, these novels might be classified along with the general anti-Catholic literature of an era that saw a growth of concern about the advance of Catholicism within as well as beyond the Established Church. They thus would sit alongside the mid century reprints of Foxe's *Book of Martyrs* and the strand of popular fiction that focused on the incarceration of reluctant teenage girls in convents together with attempts to rescue them.[3] However, given the plethora of British and Irish examples on which to draw, the close interest displayed by these writers in an apparently obscure corner of continental Protestantism requires a more specific explanation.

Descended almost certainly from the preaching movement established, according to Catholic sources, by Peter Waldo of Lyons in the late twelfth century, the Waldensians of the Cottian Alps survived for some four hundred years as a semi-clandestine dissenting group, sometimes ignored and sometimes persecuted by the Catholic authorities.[4] In the middle decades of the sixteenth century, the Alpine Waldensians came into contact with the mainstream Reformation, especially in its Genevan Calvinist form, and emerged openly and with considerable rapidity as a Reformed

---

[2] Ibid. 208–13.

[3] See G. F. A. Best, 'Popular Protestantism', in R. Robson, ed., *Ideas and Institutions of Victorian Britain* (London, 1967), 115–42.

[4] M. Lambert, *Medieval Heresy*, 3rd edn (Oxford, 2002), 70–96, 158–89; E. Cameron, *Waldenses* (Oxford, 2000), 11–206.

community with churches and a settled pastorate.[5] They then went on to make a disproportionately significant contribution to the whole Reformed world – not so much as a living Church but rather as an argument. As is well known, early Catholic controversialists charged sixteenth-century Protestants with simply reviving the heresy of the Hussites and the Waldensians, and the Protestants ultimately responded by turning the argument on its head and asserting the Reformed orthodoxy of these earlier groups. They thus established a pedigree for their own theology reaching back beyond the corruptions of popery, and the continuous existence of a faithful witness to the truth through all the ages of darkness and error down to their own day. It was certainly as such an argument that the Waldensians first achieved prominence in the sphere of English-speaking Protestantism – in Foxe, who saw medieval Waldensians as preservers of the true gospel of Christ, and more systematically in Archbishop Ussher's *Historical exposition of the unbroken Succession and State of the Christian Church* (1613).[6] By the nineteenth century the argument had been elaborated and repackaged for a new readership by Joseph Milner, who devoted four chapters of his *History of the Church of Christ* to the Waldensians. Summing up their place in the history of the Church, Milner concluded:

> The Waldenses are the middle link, which connects the primitive Christians and Fathers with the reformed; and, by their means, the proof is completely established, that salvation, by the grace of Christ, felt in the heart, and expressed in the life, by the power of the Holy Ghost, has ever existed from the time of the Apostles till this day.[7]

The further popularization of this argument was certainly one object of Waldensian historical fiction. Mrs Burrows, author of *The Martyr Land; or Tales of the Vaudois*, described her subjects as 'the earliest protestants' and attributed their origins to the eighth-century bishop Claude. Crona Temple, in *The Glorious Return*,

---

[5] Ibid. 232–84.

[6] For a discussion of this historical tradition, see E. Cameron, *The Reformation of the Heretics* (Oxford, 1984), 230–52.

[7] J. Milner (revised by I. Milner), *The History of the Church of Christ*, 4th edn (London, 1812), 437–511.

298

shared a similar view although she traced the Waldensians to a flight from persecution by early Christians from Rome. The anonymous author of the most ambitious of the Waldensian novels, *The Pastor Chief; or The Escape of the Vaudois*, a three-decker romance published in 1843, also produced the most ambitious account of Waldensian origins, attributing their doctrines to preaching by the apostles themselves – quite possibly by St Paul, who would have preached in Piedmont en route from Italy to Spain.[8] Moreover, these authors also circulated a corollary to this argument, as important as it was imaginary – that the British in particular owed a debt to the Waldensians of Piedmont. Mrs Webb, author of what was probably the first of the Waldensian novels, was clear on this point:

> In times of severe persecution, they have been hunted as prey by their cruel enemies, and frequently been forced to take refuge in 'caves and dens of the earth[']; and sometimes at length to flee into other countries. Some of them wandered so far as into Provence and Languedoc; and their descendants were the famous Albigenses, or 'heretics of Albi,' as they were called by the Papists. From Guienne, then in possession of the English their pure doctrine spread into our own country; and to those heroic, but much injured people, we may consider ourselves indebted for the first dawning of the Reformation, when Wicliff preached the doctrines which had for centuries before been taught in the valleys of Piedmont.[9]

The idea of an English Protestant debt owed to the 'Reformed' of Piedmont was pervasive, but Anglophone engagement with Waldensianism always carried with it the potential to render the notion of debt purely theoretical. Indeed, the existence of a contemporary Waldensian community was entirely superfluous to the Waldensians' role as a middle link between the fathers and the Reformers. Nonetheless, twice in the seventeenth century the actual condition of the Alpine Waldensians did strike a chord in the English consciousness. Firstly, in the 1650s news of the

---

[8]   E. Burrows, *The Martyr Land; or Tales of the Vaudois* (London, 1856), 7–8; C. Temple, *The Glorious Return: A Story of the Vaudois in 1689* (London, 1889), 23; Anon., *The Pastor Chief; or The Escape of the Vaudois: A Tale of the Seventeen Century*, 3 vols (London, 1843), 1: viii–ix.

[9]   Mrs J. B. Webb, *A Tale of the Vaudois Designed for Young Persons* (London, 1842), 12–13; Burrows, *Martyr Land*, 244–5.

slaughter of Protestants in the valleys, which seemed to the inter-
regnum government all too reminiscent of the late massacres in
Ireland, produced a reaction of international Protestant solidarity.
Cromwell put diplomatic pressure on both the French and Savoyard governments in favour of the Waldensians; a public subscription raised a relief fund of over £38,000, around two-thirds of
which eventually reached the valleys; and Milton's famous sonnet
might stand for the general tenor of informed opinion in Britain:[10]

> Avenge, O Lord, thy slaughter'd Saints, whose bones
> Lie scatter'd on the Alpine mountains cold,
> Ev'n them who kept thy truth so pure of old
> When all our Fathers worship't Stocks and Stones ...

Again, in the 1680s, when an even more brutal attempt to extirpate
the Waldensians was launched by the Duke of Savoy at the urging
of his French ally, the Piedmontese Waldensians benefitted from
financial, diplomatic and ultimately even limited military assistance
from William III. He sponsored support for the Waldensians as a
means of opening a back door into what remained of Huguenot
southern France, and his success in detaching Savoy from Louis
XIV and attaching it to the Grand Alliance ultimately ensured the
success of the Vaudois attempt to repossess their valleys.[11] Although
appeals to international Protestant solidarity still resonated in the
eighteenth century and Savoyard state pressure continued to be
brought to bear on the Waldensians, there was no repeat of the
violent assaults of the 1680s. Consequently, consciousness of the
Waldensians as a living community tended to fade after 1700. The
British Crown still continued to provide some small financial assistance to Waldensian pastors and schoolmasters and a church brief
was issued in their favour in 1768, but their affairs were largely
eclipsed by the glamour of more recent assaults on Protestantism
in the Palatinate and Salzburg which brought refugees directly to
the shores of England.[12]

---

[10] For a brief account of the assault of the 1650s known as 'The Piedmontese
Easter', see G. Audisio, *The Waldensian Dissent* (Cambridge, 1999), 204–7.
[11] Ibid. 207–11; C. Storr, 'Thomas Coxe and the Lindau Project', in A. De Lange,
ed., *Dall'Europa alle valli valdesi* (Torino, 1989), 199–214.
[12] T. Claydon, *Europe and the Making of England 1660–1760* (Cambridge, 2007); S.
Nishikawa, 'English Attitudes toward Continental Protestants with Particular Reference to Church Briefs c.1680–1740' (Ph.D. thesis, University of London, 1998), 15–130.

It was not until the end of the war with Napoleon and the opening up of the traditional Grand Tour routes into Italy that renewed interest began to stir, and the most significant figure in that renewal was William Stephen Gilly. An Anglican clergyman and later canon of Durham, with close links to Bishop Shute Barrington, Gilly visited the Waldensian valleys in 1823 and was moved by what he found there. In the following year he published *Narrative of an Excursion to the Mountains of Piedmont, and Researches among the Vaudois, or Waldenses*, a work which created considerable interest and reached a third edition in 1826. His footsteps were rapidly followed by others, including Hugh Dyke Acland and Bewick Bridge.[13] Largely through the influence of Gilly, a Waldensian committee was launched in London in 1825 with a wide range of membership, including both evangelical and High Church clergy and laymen.[14] Thus began a remarkable philanthropic enterprise aimed at improving the conditions of the Waldensians, which ultimately produced funds for the assistance of the pastorate and the maintenance of schoolteachers, for the construction of a college and upkeep of a hospital at Torre Pellice, for the repair of churches, and for the building and support of over a hundred schools in the Waldensian valleys.[15] Rarely can an imaginary debt have been repaid with such energy and enthusiasm, and most often it was to the maintenance of this charitable impulse that the historical novels aimed to contribute.[16] It is primarily in the context, then, of international Protestantism rather than English anti-Catholicism that these novels should be read; but how did they represent their subjects and what might this reveal about the preoccupations of the English supporters of the Waldensians?

[13] W. S. Gilly, *Narrative of an Excursion to the Mountains of Piedmont, and Researches among the Vaudois, or Waldenses*, 3rd edn (London, 1826); H. D. Acland, *A Brief Sketch of the History and Present Situation of the Valdenses in Piemont, Commonly Called Vaudois* (London, 1825); B. Bridge, *A Brief Narrative of a Visit to the Valleys of Piedmont, Inhabited by the Vaudois* (London, 1825).

[14] There was parallel interest among English Dissenters and the Church of Scotland. For the latter, see R. D. Kernohan, *An Alliance across the Alps* (Exeter, 2005).

[15] Minute Book of the Vaudois Fund Committee 1825–1858, in the possession of Peter Meadows of Cambridge (consulted by permission); J. P. Meille, *General Beckwith: His Life and Labours among the Waldenses of Piedmont*, transl. W. Arnot (London, 1873).

[16] 'Aunt Annie', *The Mountain Refuge; or, Sure Help in Time of Need: A Tale of the Vaudois in the Sixteenth Century* (London, 1862), 231–2; Webb, *Tale*, 3–4.

For this genre of campaigning novel to function, it was essential to convey the impression that they represented the Alpine Waldensians with accuracy. Mrs Webb, whose tale was set in the eighteenth century, declared as her aim to let British children become 'acquainted with the manners and mode of life of the people from whom we have reason to believe the doctrines of our reformed church first spread into England'.[17] 'Aunt Annie' declared in a postscript to *The Mountain Refuge* that '[t]he Authoress wishes it to be distinctly understood, that all the most striking and interesting incidents in this tale are *facts*', and acknowledged her indebtedness to a number of authorities, including Gilly.[18] Most remarkably, *The Pastor Chief*, a novel which took considerable liberties with the lives of major historical figures, nonetheless took care to support its general picture of the Waldensians and their seventeenth-century context with no fewer than ninety-eight pages of notes citing a range of historical sources.[19] If the stories were fictions, the audience was to understand, the descriptions of the valleys, their inhabitants and the Waldensian Church were all authentic and called for action on the part of the reader.

As Protestant islanders in a sea of popery, it was clearly important that the Waldensians should display key Protestant characteristics, and they duly did so. Descriptions of the Waldensian agricultural system abound in the novels, and the industriousness of the local peasantry in the unpromising environment of the Alpine valleys is a common theme. The equation between prosperity and Protestantism was a more problematic issue, however, because the conspicuous absence of the former in the valleys was the point of the relief effort. The novelists were anxious to explain, therefore, that poverty was entirely a consequence of environmental factors rather than a failure on the part of the local population. The Waldensian poor were deserving poor whose homes were kept clean and tidy despite their poverty.[20] Moreover, the environmental factors with which they had to contend were not limited to steep slopes and thin soils but also included religion and politics. According to Mrs Webb, for example:

17 Webb, *Tale*, 4.
18 'Aunt Annie', *Mountain Refuge*, 231–2.
19 Anon., *Pastor Chief*, 3: 206–303.
20 For an exception, see Burrows, *Martyr Land*, 205.

Protestant inhabitants are obliged to observe all the festivals of their Roman Catholic fellow-subjects, and therefore to pass two or three days almost every week in idleness; the wages of the labourers are very low, seldom exceeding 15 sous a day, and they are compelled to pay a much higher rate of taxes than the Papists.[21]

The association of Protestantism with a love of liberty was plain for all to see, especially given the sixteenth- or seventeenth-century setting of most of the novels which invited concentration on the theme of persecution endured or resisted. However, this too raised a problem, especially for an Anglican readership which had not yet learnt to be entirely comfortable with Cromwell and the puritans. What should they make of a group of peasants who had taken up arms, ultimately successfully, against their lawful sovereign on at least three occasions between 1560 and 1690, and in the name of their religion too? This problem was addressed by a constant emphasis in the novels on the natural and deep loyalty of the Waldensians, their readiness to submit to all the lawful demands of the Duke of Savoy, their reluctance to take up arms, the extremity of the provocations that forced them to it, and finally their anxiety to come to terms at the first possible opportunity. In *The Pastor Chief*, for example, Henri Arnaud, the pastor of Angrogna and future leader of the 'glorious return', commends submission to all of the Duke's decrees with the exception of a requirement that all Waldensian children should be subjected to Catholic baptism, and only resorts to resistance when his community is expelled from their homes at three days' notice in the depths of winter.[22] Subsequently, in an interview with Victor Emmanuel,

> the venerable pastor rose, and, with the impressive calmness of truth addressed the Duke. He spoke respectfully, of the allegiance and fidelity his flock had ever maintained to the house of Savoy, and declared how they had preserved the purity of their Christian religion, without any mixture of human traditions, since first they received the doctrines of the gospel from the apostles themselves ... He adduced in proof of the truth of that religion, the patience with which they had borne the

[21] Webb, *Tale*, 60.
[22] Anon., *Pastor Chief*, 1: 38, 176–7.

extremity of suffering; the obedient resignation with which they had submitted to their oppressor's will; the uniform sanctity of their lives – fruits which sprung from its holy seed alone.[23]

All these essentially Protestant characteristics could readily be displayed in sharper relief by contrasting them with the surrounding Catholics. Julio Arnouf, the hero of Mrs Webb's novel,

> was much struck, as they travelled through Savoy, with the wretched appearance of the inhabitants of the little hamlets they passed. Their houses were miserable, their clothing scanty, and their persons dirty and unhealthy; while the frequent appearance of the goitre, a large swelling on the throat; and the number of idiots whom they remarked in idleness and beggary, made him think of his own fellow-countrymen with satisfaction and gratitude; for though poor and often oppressed, they had never sunk into such an abject state as the Savoyards had been reduced, and an air of freedom and cheerfulness still reigned among the high-spirited Vaudois.[24]

It is important to note, however, that this kind of contrast was used relatively sparingly and that almost all the novels feature sympathetic Roman Catholic characters. Mrs Webb's Julio for example is kidnapped as a youngster and taken ultimately to a monastery in Turin for forcible re-education. His eventual escape, however, is facilitated by a fellow native of the valleys, Frederic, who was taken as a baby and brought up as a Catholic and by Frederic's adoptive parents, the delightful Monsieur and Madam D'Aubigny. They subsequently protect Julio against various attempts by sinister monks to recapture him, facilitate his education as a Waldensian pastor in Geneva and finally fund rebuilding work at Angrogna in the aftermath of a devastating avalanche. As Julio tells his mother, 'their piety, generosity and zeal for the good of their fellow-creatures would do honour to any religion'.[25]

The piety of the Waldensians, too, is exemplary. All the novels emphasize their devotion to the Scriptures, and '[i]t is rare indeed

---

[23] Ibid. 1: 251–2.
[24] Webb, *Tale*, 137.
[25] Ibid. 128.

to meet a Vaudois peasant who cannot read and write, and is not also well versed in the Bible'.[26] Their devotions are plain, centred on psalms, hymns, Scripture repetition and prayer.[27] The Waldensians have developed an instinctive orientation to faithful worship, whether in moments of crisis or as part of the regular round of family and communal life.[28] The practice of worship was of course a contested issue in mid nineteenth-century England, and might have been expected to cause some difficulty for the cross-bench coalition that had been mobilized to support the Waldensians. In practice, however, the authors seem to have found common ground in the spirituality of Waldensian devotion, and only in *The Pastor Chief* do we find reservations about the destruction of Catholic images that had been intruded into Waldensian churches in the 1680s.[29] If the Waldensian laity is exemplary in religion, then their pastorate is heroic. The life of a pastor, noted 'Aunt Annie':

> was rendered one of almost incessant toil and hardship by the long and fatiguing journeys undertaken in all weathers between the widely scattered hamlets, perched, as many of them were, in almost inaccessible situations, upon the brow of the mountains; he was necessarily obliged, from the nature of the country, to travel on foot.[30]

The pastors' income was small and so they necessarily farmed like the rest of their flock in order to support their families. Julio's pastor 'was a man of exemplary piety and much learning; and contented to bury his talents among his native mountains, and devote his life to the good of his humble countrymen, rather than accept the preferment offered to him in Switzerland'.[31] The ordinary Anglican ministry, not to mention its own 'mountain clergy' memorably depicted by W. J. Conybeare, was bound to suffer by comparison with such paragons,[32] and the moral was clear enough for most of the writers to leave readers to draw their own conclusions. Only Mrs Burrows made the

[26] Ibid. 61.
[27] 'Aunt Annie', *Mountain Refuge*, 31.
[28] See, e.g., Webb, *Tale*, 10; Anon., *Pastor Chief*, 1: 34, 215.
[29] Ibid. 2: 86.
[30] 'Aunt Annie', *Mountain Refuge*, 11.
[31] Webb, *Tale*, 65–6.
[32] W. J. Conybeare, 'The Church of England in the Mountains', *Edinburgh Review* 97 (1853), 342–79.

point explicit, noting after her description of the spartan conditions in an Alpine pastor's cottage that it 'should put to shame the luxurious lives led by many professed servants of God among ourselves.[33] There was, however, more going on in the picture presented by the novelists than a rehearsal of traditional heroic Protestant tropes applied to the Waldensians on the basis of the research of Gilly and his friends. The novels engaged in a process of remaking their subjects, displaying them romantically recast in a mode calculated to garner the sympathy of a Victorian readership. The setting was of course irresistible – a sort of lost world of aboriginal Protestantism protected and even inspired by the sublime landscape of the Alps. None of the authors could resist making the link and luxuriating in the opportunities it presented for vivid, not to say highly coloured, description. Interestingly, though, it was in the most consciously evangelical of the novels, *The Pastor's Family*, published in 1851, that this Romantic mood was most powerfully expressed. There Alpine sublimities even begin to penetrate the hardened carapace of a Roman missionary:

> When standing amid the magnificent amphitheatre of hills which gird the valley of Lucerna, the lofty thoughts inspired by solitude, and by the grandeur of the scenery that surrounded him, flowed into the stream of his deepest feelings, and made the strong current rush with impetuous fury. The beautiful, however marred and mixed, has in it always of the nature of the heavenly, and the instinct which recognizes and responds to its appeal, is not of the earth ... The silent sky, the solemn wood, the snow clad mountain, had a language for his soul, which, enthralled though it was in the bondage of ignorance and superstition, it never heard in vain; for beauty spoke to him of truth.[34]

But what of the people who inhabit this landscape? We have seen they are industrious but poor, lovers of liberty and instinctively loyal, a people of determined devotion and living faith. But they are also

---

[33] Burrows, *Martyrland*, 197.

[34] Standish, *Pastor's Family*, 51. For the influence of this Romantic mood on mid nineteenth-century Evangelicalism, see D. W. Bebbington, *Evangelicalism in Modern Britain: A History from the 1730s to the 1980s* (London, 1989), 81–171; M. Smith, 'The Mountain and the Flower: The Power and Potential of Nature in the World of Victorian Evangelicalism', in Peter Clarke and Tony Claydon, eds, *God's Bounty? The Churches and the Natural World*, SCH 46 (Woodbridge, 2010), 307–18.

natural mountaineers: hardy, vigorous, and brave; they are honest and straightforward, their word is their bond. They are an open and generous people, hospitable even to their enemies, charitable to a fault – no Waldensian home is complete in this genre until it has taken in at least one orphan. They resemble nothing so much as Sir Walter Scott's newly refurbished Highlanders let loose in the Cottian Alps with the additional allure of primitive Protestantism.[35] No image could have been better calculated to win the developing Victorian novel-reading public to the cause of Waldensian relief.

Beginning in a period that, in the judgement of John Sutherland, probably represents 'the nadir of nineteenth century historical fiction',[36] the Waldensian novels are a mixed bag, to say the least, in quality as well as in perspective. The audience to which they were directed was varied. Some of the novels were aimed at children and in one case published by the Religious Tract Society and doubtless frequently given as a Sunday school prize;[37] others, such as *The Pastor Chief*, were clearly addressed to an adult audience. The campaign to support the Waldensian churches was a broad one in the mid nineteenth century, encompassing English Nonconformists and members of the Church of Scotland as well as both High Church and evangelical Anglicans. This too is reflected in the novels, which only occasionally bear marks of a distinctive theological position[38] and thus bear witness to the continued possibility of a cross-bench appeal to a common Protestantism, even within a Church of England disturbed by controversies over Ritualism and baptismal regeneration. In consequence, the Waldensian novels share strong commonalities as a genre. They are imaginative fictions building on and circulating a pious fiction. They intend entertainment, education and edification, all at the same time; but they are campaigning novels too, and thus made a distinctive contribution to one of the more remarkable, if little known, charitable efforts mounted by British Christianity in the nineteenth century.

University of Oxford

---

[35] See, e.g., W. Scott, *Waverley* (Edinburgh, 1814), ch. 24.
[36] J. Sutherland, *The Longman Companion to Victorian Fiction*, 2nd edn (London, 2009), 299.
[37] For the Religious Tract Society, see Temple, *Glorious Return*. Mrs Burrows and Mrs Webb also wrote avowedly for a juvenile audience.
[38] Standish's work stands out as unusual in this respect.

THE JESUIT AS VILLAIN IN NINETEENTH-CENTURY BRITISH FICTION

by JOHN WOLFFE

In *The Jesuit*, an early work by the popular novelist John Frederick Smith, three young English officers pass through Lisbon during the Peninsular War. While exploring a church they meet a mysterious Jesuit, who engages them in conversation about hostile British attitudes to his order. He tells them that 'You paint a devil of your own creation, give it horns and attributes, then shudder at the phantom you have raised'.[1] However, in the context of the novel, the threat from Jesuits is all too real. The villain of the story, the order's General in Spain, has no scruples about engaging in a sustained career of deception, manipulation, theft, abduction, rape and murder behind a façade of outward respectability and high religious office. He also exercises considerable power behind the vacant Spanish throne and even attempts unsuccessfully to make the future Duke of Wellington the unwitting agent of his nefarious purposes. The 'devil' Smith himself created was indeed a formidable one.[2]

Nineteenth-century British anti-Jesuitism has yet to receive focused scholarly attention. There has indeed been extensive research on nineteenth-century anti-Catholicism in its popular, political, cultural and literary manifestations.[3] However, important monographs discussing anti-Jesuitism in France, Germany and the United States suggest that there is in fact a significant distinction to be made between a broader anti-Catholicism and a more specific anti-Jesuitism, not least because the latter was also widespread among Catholics themselves.[4] Accordingly this paper

[1] [J. F. Smith], *The Jesuit*, 3 vols (London, 1832), 2: 164.
[2] It was also entirely fictional, as the Jesuits had been dissolved in 1773, and were not restored in Spain until 1815 and in Portugal until 1829.
[3] See, e.g., John Wolffe, *The Protestant Crusade in Great Britain, 1829–1860* (Oxford, 1991); D. G. Paz, *Popular Anti-Catholicism in Mid-Victorian England* (Stanford, CA, 1992); Susan M. Griffin, *Anti-Catholicism and Victorian Fiction* (Cambridge, 2004); Michael Wheeler, *The Old Enemies: Catholic and Protestant in Nineteenth Century English Culture* (Cambridge, 2006).
[4] Geoffrey Cubitt, *The Jesuit Myth: Conspiracy Theory and Politics in Nineteenth-Century France* (Oxford, 1993); Róisín Healy, *The Jesuit Specter in Imperial Germany*

explores negative British portrayals of Jesuits in the medium of the novel, showing how, paradoxically, they could often be associated with implicitly more positive views of Catholicism in general.

Jesuits had a substantial presence in nineteenth-century British fiction. Online searches[5] have identified a dozen titles of novels first published in London or Edinburgh, containing the word 'Jesuit(s)', and ranging in date from Isaac D'Israeli's *Despotism: or the Fall of the Jesuits* (1811) to the anonymous *John Drummond Fraser: A Story of Jesuit Intrigue in the Church of England* (1893). These books were obviously the tip of a larger iceberg of other works in which Jesuits were central characters, but which cannot be systematically identified from the titles alone. The literature was further augmented from abroad: Eugène Sue's *Le juif errant*, a seminal French anti-Jesuit novel first serialized in *Le Constitutionnel* between June 1844 and June 1845, had appeared in three different English translations before the end of 1845; and *Stanhope Burleigh: The Jesuits in Our Homes* was reprinted by Blackwood's London Library in the same year, 1855, that it was first published in New York.[6]

Occasionally Jesuits, especially in Catholic hands, could be fictional heroes. For example, in *Father Oswald: A Genuine Catholic Story*[7] the eponymous character is introduced as a man of 'great piety and sanctity; … a professed Father of the Society of Jesus, … of a fine majestic exterior, and open engaging countenance'.[8] He is instrumental in eventually reconciling an estranged married couple in shared commitment to Roman Catholicism. In M. Bourchier Sandford's *The Romance of a Jesuit Mission*,[9] a seventeenth-century Jesuit struggles with his very human attraction to a young woman. However he remains faithful to his vows, while heroically assisting her in braving the perils of early colonial North America. Eventually she marries another man, and he dies a martyr's death. Simi-

(Boston, MA, 2003), 4; Timothy Verhoeven, *Transatlantic Anti-Catholicism: France and the United States in the Nineteenth Century* (New York, 2010), 103–27.

⁵ Principally of the BL catalogue, <http://www.catalogue.bl.uk>, and the Internet Archive, <http://www.archive.org>.

⁶ Cubitt, *Jesuit Myth*, 121; BL catalogue. 'Helen Dhu', the named author of *Stanhope Burleigh*, was almost certainly a pseudonym.

⁷ Anon., *Father Oswald: A Genuine Catholic Story* (London, 1842).

⁸ Ibid. 9; R. L. Wolff, *Gains and Losses: Novels of Faith and Doubt in Victorian England* (New York, 1977), 34–8.

⁹ M. Bourchier Sandford, *The Romance of a Jesuit Mission* (New York, 1897).

larly in the anonymous *Bride of Ramcuttah*,[10] set in the East Indies in the sixteenth century, the hero is a Jesuit associate of Francis Xavier, who dies trapped in a burning church by hostile locals. The Anglican author was, though, careful to distinguish the Jesuits of that period from their successors:

> Those were the early days, when the Society of Jesus was still in the pristine purity of its first love, ere the duplicity and love of power which afterwards made it so hated and dreaded, and which finally caused its suppression of a while, had crept in. … [I]n most points, I think we should agree with them far better than modern Romans would.[11]

Normally, however, Protestant authors did not attempt such distinctions and saw Jesuits in any era as natural villains. Although no straightforwardly anti-Jesuit novel has secured an enduring place in the literary canon, many such works were penned by authors well-known in their time, such as Wilkie Collins, Isaac D'Israeli, Charles Kingsley, Catherine Sinclair, John Frederick Smith and Frances Trollope. The genre has received some attention from literary scholars,[12] but has hitherto been neglected by historians of religion, for whom they offer significant insights into attitudes towards Roman Catholicism across a spectrum of elite and more popular culture.

The English tradition of anti-Jesuitism had its roots in the 'black legend' focused on the attempts of Robert Parsons to bring about the deposition of Elizabeth I and restore Catholicism. Such memories were revived in 1690 by Edward Gee's publication of Parsons's *Memorial for the Reformation of England* (that is, its restoration to Catholicism), which Gee presented as indicative of the intentions of the recently deposed Catholic James II. Extracts from Gee's pamphlet were republished in 1825.[13] Alongside fears of Jesuit political intrigue, a sexual current of anti-Jesuitism was

---

10 Anon., *Bride of Ramcuttah* (London, 1860).
11 Ibid. 51–2.
12 Wolff, *Gains and Losses*; Griffin, *Anti-Catholicism*; Wheeler, *Old Enemies*.
13 *The Jesuits' Memorial for the Intended Reformation of England, under their first Popish Prince* (London, 1825); ODNB, *s.nn* 'Persons [Parsons], Robert (1546–1610)', 'Gee, Edward (bap.1657 d.1730)', online edn, <http://www.oxforddnb.com/view/article/21474>, <http://www.oxforddnb.com/view/article/10498>, accessed 22 February 2011.

stirred in the early 1730s by Father Jean-Baptiste Girard's trial in Aix-en-Provence for the alleged rape of Marie-Catherine Cadière, which was widely reported in Britain.[14]

Where Jesuits were concerned, the boundary between fact and fiction was a very porous one. Some works professing to provide factual narratives by or about former Jesuits, or objective accounts of malign Jesuit influence in public and private affairs, contained so many implausibilities and unsustainable inferences that they have to be regarded as at best the work of paranoid and conspiratorial minds and at worst as deliberate fabrications. For example, in *The Jesuit Conspiracy*, a translation of a French original appearing in English in 1848, Jacopo Leone claimed by chance to have stepped into a closet in his superior's study, come across hidden secret books there, and then from this unintended concealment to have over-heard a lengthy conversation of senior Jesuits regarding the order's secret plans for world domination.[15] In *The Female Jesuit* (1851), Jemima Luke prefaced her narrative with the acknowledgement that it was 'stranger than fiction', but claimed that it was nevertheless 'literally true'. However the subsequent narrative of elaborate deceptions practised on well-meaning Protestants by an escaped nun suggests that the underlying reality was much more likely to have been one of a disturbed and manipulative young woman than of a concealed Jesuit agent.[16] The anonymous compiler of the 1872 edition of a collection of documents relating to the Jesuits cited rumours that they had instigated the Franco-Prussian War, exercising their influence over the pious Empress Eugénie and through her on the French government, with a view to enforcing German submission to the papacy. However, he smugly continued, it was 'fortunate ... that these subtle plans against freedom had been turned to the discomfiture of their originators'.[17]

Meanwhile even when authors acknowledged their narratives to be fictional, they still sometimes included real or contemporary

[14]   See, in this volume, Colin Haydon, 'Anti-Catholicism and Obscene Literature: *The Case of Mrs. Mary Catharine Cadiere* and its Context', 202–18.

[15]   Jacopo Leone, *The Jesuit Conspiracy: The Secret Plan of the Order* (London, 1848), 14–28.

[16]   [Jemima Luke], *The Female Jesuit; or The Spy in the Family* (London, 1851); Diana Peschier, *Nineteenth Century Anti-Catholic Discourses: The Case of Charlotte Brontë* (Basingstoke, 2002), 48–50.

[17]   Anon, *A Glimpse of the Great Secret Society*, 3rd edn (London, 1872), xiv–xvi.

historical figures, and were often accompanied with claims that art reflected rather than exaggerated reality. Thus the 312 pages of Isaac D'Israeli's *Despotism*, concerned with events leading up to the Marquis de Pombal's banishing of the Jesuits from Portugal in 1759, were followed by a further 162 pages of notes intended to offer historical evidence of the overweening Jesuit ambition and elaborate intrigue that was dramatized in the plot of the novel itself. The preface to the American edition of William Sewell's *Hawkstone* acknowledged the criticism that the novel presented 'a very much exaggerated impersonation of the spirit and principles of Jesuitism', but defended it as an ideal type that logically followed from 'the Constitutions and Rules of the *soi-disant* Society of Jesus'.[18] The prominent Scottish cleric and writer George Gilfillan contributed a preface to the popular edition of *Nightshade*, giving it as his opinion that 'Mr Johnston, so far from exaggerating, has rather understated the "owre true tale" which it has been his mission to tell.'[19] Even Wilkie Collins seemed partially at least to believe in the malignity of his own Jesuit creation in *The Black Robe* when he wrote shortly after the publication of the novel that '[t]he French Government has acted most wisely … in getting rid of the Jesuit enemies of the Republic.'[20]

Some of the variants and recurrent characteristics of anti-Jesuit fiction can be explored by considering a sample of five novels: Isaac D'Israeli's *Despotism*,[21] John Frederick Smith's *The Jesuit*, Charles Kingsley's *Westward Ho!*,[22] William Johnston's *Nightshade*[23] and Wilkie Collins's *The Black Robe*.[24] Between them these works span much of the nineteenth century, and their authors represent a variety of religious viewpoints: D'Israeli was Jewish; Smith was probably a lapsed Catholic; Kingsley a Broad Church Anglican;

---

[18] [William Sewell], *Hawkstone: A Tale of and for England in 184_*, 4th American edn, 2 vols (New York, 1848), v.

[19] William Johnston, *Nightshade*, new edn (London, 1858), Preface.

[20] William Baker and William W. Clarke, eds, *The Letters of Wilkie Collins*, 2: *1866–1889* (Basingstoke, 1999), 435.

[21] Isaac D'Israeli, *Despotism*, 2 vols (London, 1811).

[22] Charles Kingsley, *Westward Ho!*, 3 vols (Cambridge, 1855).

[23] The BL copy of the 1857 first edn has been destroyed, so references are to the 1858 edn.

[24] Wilkie Collins, *The Black Robe*, 3 vols (London, 1881).

Johnston an evangelical Anglican and Collins an agnostic rebel against his parents' devout High Anglicanism.[25]

The central character of *Despotism* is Ribadeneira, a fictional Jesuit General active during the pontificate of Benedict XIV.[26] Ribadeneira accepts his high office with apparent humility, but in reality 'he grasped the terrific code of universal despotism'.[27] For a while, Ribadeneira, possessed of a genius for intrigue and working through the unquestioning obedience of his subordinates, overcomes the Jansenists, infiltrates the courts of Europe and seems to be fulfilling his ambition to become the effective ruler of the world. Eventually, however, he is outwitted by Pombal, whose own intrigues undermine Jesuit influence in Portugal, driving a desperate Ribadeneira to countenance a bungled attempt to assassinate King Joseph I (based on the real-life Tavora plot of September 1758).[28] Pombal thus has the perfect pretext for suppressing the Jesuits, dispatching a gloating letter to Ribadeneira, who on receiving it drinks poison, but with his dying words warns: 'Let the Kings of the Earth scatter my people over the Universe; they fear not Exile, not the Dungeon, not the Scaffold! Be the Order abolished, still shall the Order triumph; and be more terrible in its dispersion than in its union.'[29]

Despotism, tellingly described by one reviewer as lacking 'a well constructed story',[30] fails as a novel, but is compelling as a critique of politicized religion and authoritarian government. There was obviously a strong implicit parallel with the contemporary despotism of Napoleon, but D'Israeli also perceived the hidden hand of the Jesuits themselves in events since their suppression, including the

[25] For background on the authors, see, respectively, James Ogden, *Isaac Disraeli* (Oxford, 1969); *ODNB, s.n.* 'Smith, John Frederick (1806–1890)', online edn, <http://www.oxforddnb.com/view/article/37982>, accessed 22 February 2011; Susan Chitty, *The Beast and the Monk: A Life of Charles Kingsley* (London, 1973); *ODNB, s.n.* 'Johnston, William (1829–1902)', online edn, <http://www.oxforddnb.com/view/article/34214>, accessed 22 February 2011; Catherine Peters, *The King of Inventors: A Life of Wilkie Collins* (London, 1991).

[26] His real life namesake Pedro de Ribadeneira (1526–1611) was a leading early Jesuit and biographer of Ignatius Loyola: *The Catholic Encyclopedia*, 'Pedro de Ribadeneira', online edn, <http://www.newadvent.org/cathen/13029a.htm>, accessed 8 July 2010.

[27] D'Israeli, *Despotism*, 1: 21.

[28] Ibid. 2: 289–301.

[29] Ibid. 2: 306–10.

[30] *Critical Review* ser. 3, 24 (1811), 31–42, quoted by Ogden, *D'Israeli*, 69.

French Revolution.[31] However D'Israeli avoids tarring the Roman Catholic Church as a whole with the Jesuit brush: some of the strongest charges against them are put into the mouth of Benedict XIV himself as he nervously confronts Ribadeneira:

> Your Order ... stands accused of being a political people, governed by a secret code; which cannot become Law, with the extinction of other Laws. To establish the oppressive grandeur of the Order, even your own subjects must become its Victims. With you it is said to be a maxim, that the State is every thing, and the Individual nothing![32]

D'Israeli portrays the pope as a weak man, but gives him credit for good intentions. This ability to discriminate rather than engage in blanket polemic against Roman Catholicism was also, as his son Benjamin observed, a characteristic of his historical as well as his fictional writing.[33]

In *The Jesuit* Smith sets the personal history of Sir Henry Arden and his family against the backdrop of major historical events, especially the French Revolution and the Peninsular War. The Jesuit, Juan de Hernard, swears revenge on Sir Henry after the baronet saves the beautiful Marie de Fleurie from his unwanted attentions. Sir Henry and Marie marry, but de Hernard has the young bride and her infant son abducted, and then years later tries to bring about an incestuous union between the boy, Henri, and Sir Henry's daughter by his second marriage, Julia. Once again Sir Henry intervenes to avert sexual transgression, but Julia subsequently dies of despair. The action now moves to the Iberian peninsula, where Sir Henry's son Frederick is serving with his regiment, de Hernard is Jesuit General in Madrid, and a disconsolate Henri is living in his household. De Hernard attempts to engineer a fatricidal confrontation between Frederick and Henri, who remain unaware that they are half-brothers, but when Henri discovers the plot the Jesuit poisons him. As Henri dies, he and

---

[31] D'Israeli, *Despotism*, 2: 462–3.

[32] Ibid. 1: 180–1.

[33] Isaac Disraeli, *Curiosities of Literature with a View of the Life and Writings of the Author by his Son*, 3 vols (London, 1849), 1: lv. Note that at some point both father and son dropped the apostrophe from their surname.

Frederick are reconciled, and Sir Henry arrives on the scene to kill de Hernard.

This story well illustrates the usefulness of a Jesuit villain to a novelist, quite independent of any polemical religious agenda. Smith maintains suspense through the gradual disclosure of de Hernard's sinister purposes, and speculation as to whether his plans will be discovered and thwarted. However, he also directly attacks the Jesuits:

> these defenders of the church are, to its welfare, what the janizaries are to the turks, destroyers, not protectors. ... No project is too vast for their ambition; no degradation too severe to attain the slightest point. The feelings of kindred, country, friends, are lost in the passion for personal aggrandizement; nature is dead within their breasts or made subservient to the worst of passions.[34]

However these words are themselves spoken by a Catholic, and other Catholic characters in the novel are also presented in a positive light. They are as much victims of the Jesuit's intrigues as are the Protestant characters.

The distinction between Jesuit villains and 'good' Catholics also runs through Charles Kingsley's *Westward Ho!* Amyas Leigh, the central character, is a Devonian Elizabethan adventurer in the mould of Drake and Grenville, the latter featuring in the novel as the hero's godfather. However Amyas's uncle is a Catholic recusant, whose son Eustace has been educated by Jesuits, with whom he continues to consort. Like Juan de Hernard in *The Jesuit*, Eustace is in sexual competition with the hero, making a botched attempt to woo the local beauty, Rose Salterne. He also assists the Jesuits Parsons and Campion when they visit Devon. Later Eustace helps the Spaniard Don Guzman to elope with Rose, and then warns the Spanish that Amyas is planning a rescue. Eustace's ultimate perfidy is to betray both Rose herself and Amyas's brother Frank to the Inquisition, leading to them both being tortured and burnt at the stake as heretics. Eustace then vows to join the Jesuits himself, at which point Kingsley writes him out of the rest of the story because:

---

[34] Smith, *The Jesuit*, 1: 63–4.

> This book is a history of men ... and Eustace is a man no
> longer; he is become a thing, a tool, a Jesuit; which goes only
> where it is sent, and does good or evil indifferently as it is bid;
> which by an act of moral suicide, has lost its soul, in the hope
> of saving it ...[35]

Kingsley's dislike of the Jesuits was deep-seated: he believed that
by rooting up 'every element of faith in ... the daily duties and
relations of human life' they had unwittingly created the social
climate that brought about the Terror of 1793 in France.[36] It is,
however, misleading to regard *Westward Ho!* as a straightforwardly
anti-Catholic novel.[37] Other Catholic characters are presented in
a more sympathetic light. Don Guzman is a noble enemy who
treats Rose honourably and allows her to retain her Protestant
faith, until their relationship is destabilized by Eustace's attempts
to convert her. Mr Leigh, Eustace's father, has stayed faithful to the
old religion, but he also sees himself as a loyal subject of Queen
Elizabeth, and is embarrassed and distressed by his son's activities.

One other incident in the book shows Kingsley significantly
qualifying his anti-Catholicism. At a lonely inn on Dartmoor
Amyas and his men are attacked by Catholic thieves who are in
league with Eustace and the Jesuits, and the leader of the ruffians
is mortally wounded in the fight. When Father Parsons, the Jesuit,
starts to minister to the dying man, the Anabaptist Salvation Yeo
wants to intervene 'to speak a word in season'. Amyas, however,
restrains him:

> Silence! ... he knows them and he don't know you; they are
> the first who ever spoke to him as if he had a soul to be saved,
> and first come first served; you can do no good. ... How do
> you know his words will not go to the right person after all,
> though he may not send them there? [38]

For Kingsley, the Broad Churchman, it seemed possible that *in
extremis* even Catholics could be saved. Moreover the pastoral

---

[35] Kingsley, *Westward Ho!*, 3: 34.
[36] F. Kingsley, ed., *Charles Kingsley: His Letters and Memories of His Life*, 2 vols (London, 1877), 1: 429–30.
[37] *Pace* Wheeler, *Old Enemies*, 105–10.
[38] Kingsley, *Westward Ho!*, 2: 182.

concern of the otherwise despised Jesuit pointed up the deficiencies of the Protestant clergy.

Such shades of grey are, however, lacking in another popular Protestant novel of the 1850s, *Nightshade*, by William Johnston, a leading Ulster evangelical layman, passionately opposed to Roman Catholicism on both theological and political grounds.[39] The central strand in the plot is the attempt of the Jesuits to defraud two orphaned sisters of their liberty and property by impersonating their late father's step-brother. As the novel unfolds, a wider web of deception and manipulation becomes apparent. For example, a Jesuit, Mr Prynne (namesake of a prominent real-life Ritualist), masquerades as an Anglican clergyman and plots to have the hero, Charles Annandale, lured over to Ireland so he can be murdered there by Catholic insurgents.[40] Other Catholic characters, such as the authorities in the Paris convent where one of the sisters is confined, are portrayed unsympathetically and as being in alliance with the Jesuits. Johnston's construction of a deep-seated and wide-ranging Catholic conspiracy spearheaded by the Jesuits engenders mounting suspense and excitement.

Westward Ho! and *Nightshade* were both products of the intense Protestant excitement that followed the restoration of the Roman Catholic episcopal hierarchy in 1850. By the time Wilkie Collins wrote his Jesuit novel, *The Black Robe*, in 1880 and 1881, attitudes were somewhat less sharply polarized. Nevertheless there was still a ready market for his scheming Jesuit, Father Benwell. The plot of *The Black Robe*, like that of *Nightshade*, revolves around Jesuit attempts to acquire Protestant landed property, in this case through securing the conversion to Catholicism of Lewis Romayne, the owner of Vange Abbey, and then convincing him that lands seized from monks at the Dissolution should rightfully be returned to the Church. The morality of the situation is ambivalent: at times there is a sense that Benwell and the Catholic Church have natural justice on their side, and Benwell's ingenuity inspires a perverse admiration from the reader. Moreover, a second Jesuit, Arthur Penrose, represents a more positive and heroic image of the order.

---

[39] P. Sutherland, 'The Role of Evangelicalism in the Formation of Nineteenth-Century Ulster Protestant Cultural Identity (1859–1885)' (Ph.D. thesis, Open University, 2010), 29–109.

[40] Collins, *Nightshade*, 258.

Longing for Romayne's conversion, but reluctant to assist Benwell in deceiving him and destroying his marriage, Penrose ends up being dispatched as a missionary to New Mexico, where he narrowly escapes martyrdom. Benwell, like Ribadeneira, appears to triumph for a time, but when Romayne, who has deserted his wife for the priesthood, is told that he now has a son, he is reconciled to her on his deathbed and incites the child to burn the will that would have given his inheritance to the Jesuit. As in the other novels considered, the Jesuits succeed in doing a lot of damage, but they cannot be allowed to win in the end.

Thus in all the texts discussed, apart from *Nightshade*, the authors discriminate between Jesuits and other Catholics, and sometimes between different kinds of Jesuits. Ambivalent rather than uniformly hostile attitudes are even more apparent in two works by major novelists that feature Jesuit characters, Thackeray's *History of Henry Esmond* (1852) and Charlotte Brontë's *Villette* (1853). Both were written at the height of the anti-Catholic hysteria of the early 1850s, but on a careful reading it is clear that while they reflected this cultural climate they did not endorse it. Father Holt, the Jesuit character in *Henry Esmond*, is ultimately an inconsequential rather than dangerous figure, who 'was the most unlucky of men, he never played a game but he lost it; or engaged in a conspiracy but 'twas certain to end in defeat'.[41] In *Villette* there is surely an intentional irony in the fact that the two characters with allegedly 'Jesuitical' tendencies, Madame Beck and Monsieur Paul, are not really Jesuits, whereas the one actual Jesuit in the novel, Père Silas, is a harmless well-meaning old man.[42]

Reviews of *Nightshade* further illustrate highbrow literary culture's bemused detachment from the more sensational kind of Jesuit fiction. The *Saturday Review* gave a lengthy account of the implausibilities of the plot,[43] while the *Athenaeum* complained of a style liable to 'offend a fastidious taste past all forgiveness'.[44] On the other hand its potential popular appeal was recognized: there were fears for its impact on 'elderly ladies of strong Protestant principle', who would be led to believe themselves to be

---

[41] W. M. Thackeray, *The History of Henry Esmond, Esq*, 3 vols (London, 1852), 3: 320.
[42] Cf. Peschier, *Anti-Catholic Discourses*, 153–8.
[43] *Saturday Review*, 18 July 1857, 66–7.
[44] *The Athenaeum*, 13 June 1857, 757–8.

surrounded by conspiring Jesuits, and it was acknowledged to have 'a dramatic interest kept up throughout, which will carry a reader to the end'. There had been a similar response to Smith's *The Jesuit,* seen as a promising work for a new author, 'full of incidents and character', and owing something to Mrs Radcliffe and the Gothic novelists.[45] *Westward Ho!* enjoyed extensive and enduring success. Kingsley had written it with a conscious eye to its popular appeal, to which he saw Jesuits as a desirable contributory ingredient, and the book indeed proved much the most successful of his novels, having reached its eleventh edition by the time of his death in 1875.[46] The new resort village of Westward Ho! was named after it in the 1860s. *The Black Robe* in its initial serial form appeared in numerous magazines and newspapers on both sides of the Atlantic and was judged 'the best thing' Collins had written for some time.[47]

Scheming Jesuits continued to have a place in early twentieth-century fiction, notably in the popular novels of the Methodist Joseph Hocking,[48] and, in a very different literary milieu, in the person of Father Rothschild in Evelyn Waugh's *Vile Bodies* (1930). However, the more contemporary fictional parallels to the nineteenth-century Jesuit lie not only in specifically religiously motivated conspiracies in novels such as *The Da Vinci Code*[49] and *The Afghan*,[50] but also in the webs of cosmopolitan secular intrigue evoked in later twentieth-century spy-thrillers.[51] Moreover, in similar fashion to a James Bond novel or film, anti-Jesuit novels were liable to evoke an exciting range of exotic locations. One did not have to believe in the reality of an elaborate Jesuit conspiracy any more than that of the more lurid fantasies regarding Soviet, Islamist or Templar plots to enjoy a good story.

Nevertheless the fluidity of the boundary between fact and fiction enhanced the capacity of these works to reinforce a wide-

---

[45] *Gentleman's Magazine* 102 (1832), 239; *The Athenaeum*, 7 April 1832, 220.

[46] London, BL, MS Add. 54911, fols 31–2: Kingsley to Macmillan, 1 June 1854; BL catalogue.

[47] Baker and Clarke, eds, *Letters of Wilkie Collins*, 431–2, 437.

[48] For example *The Woman of Babylon* (London, 1906) and *The Jesuit* (London, 1911). See also, in this volume, Martin Wellings, '"Pulp Methodism" revisited: The Literature and Significance of Silas and Joseph Hocking', 361–72.

[49] Dan Brown, *The Da Vinci Code: A Novel* (London, 2003).

[50] Frederick Forsyth, *The Afghan* (London, 2007).

[51] Cf. Tony Bennett and Janet Woollacott, *Bond and Beyond: The Political Career of a Popular Hero* (Basingstoke, 1987), 25–8, 82–7.

spread climate of suspicion of Jesuits. It was a context in which fiction could influence interpretation of reality, as in a widely circulated attack on Gladstone, which interpreted his utterances and actions as evidence that he was a crypto-Jesuit.[52] Jesuits were presented as subversive at all levels of society, from the intimate ties of marriage and the family to high politics and international relations. Above all, they were presented as un-English, scheming to undermine the security and stability of a free and Protestant nation from their sinister headquarters in Rome and Madrid. However, the very portrayal of Jesuit villainy highlighted the development of a more tolerant attitude to other Roman Catholics.

Open University

---

[52] J. Luther Scott, *The Jesuit Premier* (Leamington, 1881). The pamphlet had reached its seventh edition by the time of Gladstone's retirement in 1894.

CHRISTIAN DICKENS

by ANDREW SANDERS

In September 1844 Charles Dickens had a vivid dream while he was staying at the Villa Peschiere in Genoa. He dreamed that he was 'in an indistinct place, which was quite sublime in its indistinctness' and he was visited by a spirit which wore blue drapery, 'as the Madonna might in a picture by Raphael', but which bore no resemblance to anyone he had known. He recognized a voice, however, and concluded that this was the spirit of his much loved sister-in-law, Mary Hogarth. The seventeen-year-old Mary had died in his arms on 7 May 1837, six years before she conjured herself up in Dickens's dream. At the time he had been distraught. For months after her death he had dreamed of her 'sometimes as a spirit, sometimes as a living creature, never with any of the bitterness of my real sorrow, but always with a kind of quiet happiness'. Those dreams had long ceased, but the new manifestation of Mary in Genoa was evidently of a different kind. He beheld this visionary Mary 'in a great delight, so that I wept very much, and stretching out my arms to it called it "Dear."' He then entered into a dialogue with the spirit. 'Oh! give me some token that you have really visited me!', he pleaded. 'Form a wish', the spirit replied. Dickens then asked that Mary's mother might be released from 'great distresses' and he was told that this would be so. He then posed a new question: 'What is the True religion?' The spirit seems to have hesitated, and Dickens blurted out: 'Good God ... You think, as I do that the Form of religion does not so greatly matter, if we try to do good? – or' (the ghost still hesitated) 'perhaps the Roman Catholic is the best? Perhaps it makes one think of God oftener, and believe in him more steadily?' '"For you," said the spirit, full of such heavenly tenderness for me, that I felt as if my heart would break; "For you, it is the best!"' Dickens then woke up, with tears running down his cheeks.[1]

We could offer rational enough explanations for this dream, as Dickens himself did in the letter that described his vision. Dickens,

[1]   *The Letters of Charles Dickens*, 4: *1844–1846*, ed. Kathleen Tillotson, Pilgrim edn (Oxford, 1977), 196: Dickens to John Forster, 30 September 1844.

newly arrived in Genoa, was tense after the near-drowning of his brother in the bay. The city was beset with thunderstorms and Dickens had already experienced a series of vivid dreams. There was an altar in the grand bedroom at the Villa Peschiere 'at which some family who had once inhabited this palace had mass performed in old time'. Above the altar was the mark where a picture had once hung and Dickens tells us that he speculated as to what the picture might have been and, if it had shown a face, 'what the face was like'. Moreover, the bells of neighbouring convents had been ringing for the night offices. The Catholic atmosphere of Genoa had doubtless permeated Dickens's otherwise resolutely no-nonsense Protestant soul, and had disturbed it. But the dream ended; the vision dissipated and the no-nonsense Protestant side of Dickens returned him to equanimity. There was to be no conversion, though it may be an ironic comment on the dream that, thanks to the marriage of Dickens's youngest son, Henry, to a French Catholic woman after the author's death, many of his descendents have been born Catholic.

None of us needs to be told that Charles Dickens had a vivid imagination, and even the most ill-read does not need to be reminded that it was Dickens who, a year before this extraordinary Genoan dream, had published his 'Ghost Story of Christmas', *A Christmas Carol*. Unlike Dickens in Genoa, Ebenezer Scrooge responds immediately and positively to the monitory nature of the spirits in his dream. What essentially links *A Christmas Carol* with Dickens's Genoan dream is not necessarily the issue of conversion, but the insistent riposte that the novelist records in his letter: 'You think, as I do that the Form of religion does not so greatly matter, if we try to do good.' Many commentators have argued that *A Christmas Carol* is a singularly secular work with only a minimal degree of religious or doctrinal reference. Of course, the essential message of Dickens's Christmas story is one about 'trying to do good'. Scrooge's conversion is to good works and not to any defined faith. Nevertheless, to see *A Christmas Carol* in exclusively secular or social terms seems to miss the true essence of the story. It is, for example, a celebration of a distinctively Christian feast which rejoices both in human community and in acts of feasting and giving. It offers, moreover, a strong warning against closed minds and closed hearts. Very early on in the narrative, the ghost of Jacob Marley tells Scrooge of the ever-present need for a responsive openness to conversion:

> ... this earth must pass into eternity before the good of which it is susceptible is all developed ... any Christian spirit working kindly in its little sphere, whatever it may be, will find its moral life too short for its vast means of usefulness ... no space of regret can make amends for one life's opportunity misused![2]

Marley is insisting both on faith and works, and he is placing a particular stress on a change of life. This might not represent a statement of specifically Roman Catholic doctrine, but it is unequivocally Christian. Equally, in Stave Three of the story, when the Ghost of Christmas Present opens to doors of the Cratchit household, Bob Cratchit describes Tiny Tim's behaviour in church:

> Somehow he gets thoughtful sitting by himself so much, and thinks the strangest things you ever heard. He told me, coming home, that he hoped the people saw him in the church, because he was a cripple, and it might be pleasant to them to remember upon Christmas Day, who made lame beggars walk and blind men see.

Sentimental? Yes, of course, but this is also a strikingly Christian reminder of the earthly mission of Jesus, in the midst of the animated and detailed account of the Cratchits' Christmas feasting.

The themes of repentance, rebirth and the consequent importance of living out a new life return powerfully when Scrooge is faced with a vision of his own unvisited grave. The terrified Scrooge in the deserted and rank graveyard is suddenly desperately aware of the damnable nature of his unreformed life. He is not able to articulate to the guiding spirit his need for penitence:

> 'Men's courses will foreshadow certain ends, to which, if persevered in, they must lead,' said Scrooge. 'But if the courses be departed from, the ends will change. Say it is thus with what you show me!'
>
> The Spirit was as immovable as ever ...
>
> 'Spirit!' he cried, tight clutching at its robe, 'hear me! I am not the man I was. I will not be the man I must have been but

---

[2]   Dickens, *A Christmas Carol*, Stave One.

for this intercourse. Why show me this, if I am past all hope?'
...

'Good Spirit,' he pursued, as down upon the ground he
fell before it: 'Your nature intercedes for me, and pities me.
Assure me that I may yet change these shadows you have
shown me, by an altered life!'

The kind hand trembled.

'I will honour Christmas in my heart, and try to keep it
all the year. I will live in the Past, Present, and the Future. The
Spirits of all Three shall strive within me. I will not shut out
the lessons that they teach. Oh, tell me I may sponge away the
writing on this stone!'[3]

Dickens, of course, knows that Scrooge cannot undo the fact
of his future death, but he emphatically can change the nature of
his life. He can, therefore, lay claim to a fuller life and to the life
of the Resurrection. Scrooge insists that he will free himself of
time itself – turning away from his past by learning lessons for the
present which will in turn dictate the nature of the opening future.
This declaration of a turning away from sin and depravity does not
strike me as peculiarly 'secular'.

Some twenty-three years after the publication of *A Christmas
Carol*, on the very morning of his own untimely death – 8
June 1870 – Dickens addressed a letter to one John Makeham
concerning what Makeham had supposed was an over-casual, and
therefore slighting, reference to Scripture in *The Mystery of Edwin
Drood*. In the novel Dickens had referred to 'the highly popular
lamb who has so long and unresistingly been led to the slaughter'.
His reply makes it quite clear not only that there was no hint of
blasphemy in his turn of phrase, but that he held the Christian
Scriptures in the highest regard:

> I have always striven in my writings to express veneration
> for the life and lessons of Our Saviour; because I feel it; and
> because I re-wrote that history for my children – every one of
> whom knew it from having it repeated to them, long before
> they could read, and almost as soon as they could speak.

[3]   Ibid., Stave Four.

But I have never made proclamation of this from the house-tops.[4]

Dickens is referring here to his children's text of 1846 which was published in 1934 as *The Life of Our Lord*. He is also being emphatic that, as a writer, the Christian religion had always been implicit in his work but that he had consistently been unwilling to pose as a proselytizer. Not for him, therefore, novels that expounded any explicit doctrinal lessons. Everything was to be implied, to be shadowed out, to be suggested. It is extraordinary therefore to find him on the same 8 June 1870 writing the following paragraph in the last completed chapter of the *Edwin Drood* that he would never finish. We are offered a ravishing description of Dickens's fictional cathedral city – Cloisterham – on an early summer morning. It was doubtless a reflection of the view that Dickens himself had from the windows of his Kentish chalet, some three miles from Rochester, where he wrote these memorable words:

> A brilliant morning shines on the old city. Its antiquities and ruins are surpassingly beautiful, with the lusty ivy gleaming in the sun, and the rich trees waving in the balmy air. Changes of glorious light from moving boughs, songs of birds, scents from gardens, woods, and fields – or, rather, from the one garden of the whole cultivated island in its yielding time – penetrate into the Cathedral, subdue its earthly odour, and preach the Resurrection and the Life. The cold stone tombs of centuries grow warm; and flecks of brightness dart into the sternest marble of the building, fluttering there like wings.[5]

Dickens does not normally 'do' natural description, but here he is 'doing' religion as well.

Dickens had consistently found himself the object of unhappy conjecture on the part of many of his more narrowly devout readers. In May 1843 one David Dickson (whom the editors of the Pilgrim edition of the novelist's letters conjecture was the minister of St Cuthbert's, Edinburgh) wrote complaining about a supposedly flippant reference to Scripture in the *Pickwick Papers*.

---

4   *The Letters of Charles Dickens*, 12: *1868–1870*, ed. Graham Storey, Pilgrim edn (Oxford, 2002), 548: Dickens to John Makeham, 8 June 1870.
5   Charles Dickens, *The Mystery of Edwin Drood*, ch. 23.

Dickson was offended by what he assumed was Mr Weller's over-casual references to the Revd Mr. Stiggins as 'the Shepherd' and to his doctrine of 'the new birth'.[6] In reply Dickens insisted that he was attempting to show 'how sacred things are degraded, vulgar-ised, and rendered absurd when persons who are utterly incom-petent to teach the commonest things take upon themselves to expound such mysteries, and how, in making mere cant phrases of divine words, these persons miss the spirit in which they had their origin'. There was clearly a sting in what Dickens was implying to Dickson. This was no mere self-justification, let alone an apology: it was an expression of polite vexation with a humourless bigot. Dickens went on:

> Whether the great Creator of the world and the creature of his hands, moulded in his own image, be quite so opposite in character as you believe, is a question which it would profit us little to discuss. I like the frankness and candour of your letter, and thank you for it. That every man who seeks heaven must be born again, in good thoughts of his Maker, I sincerely believe. That it is expedient for every hound to say so in a certain snuffling form of words, to which he attaches no good meaning, I do not believe. I take it there is no difference between us.[7]

There was, of course, a good deal of difference between the two men. That Dickens remained vexed by complaints like David Dick-son's is evident from a section of the Preface he added to the cheap edition of *Pickwick Papers* in 1847, a preface which was reprinted in the collected editions of Dickens's novels that appeared in 1858 and 1867. In this Preface he insisted to his readers that he felt that there was a real distinction between 'religion' and 'the cant of religion' and between 'piety' and 'the pretence of piety'. This was exem-plified by what he saw as a clear distinction between a 'humble reverence for the great truths of scripture' and 'an audacious and offensive obtrusion of its letter and not its spirit'. Furthermore, an 'extraordinary confusion of ignorant minds' existed, which he

---

[6]   Charles Dickens, *Pickwick Papers*, ch. 22.
[7]   *The Letters of Charles Dickens*, 3: *1842–1843*, ed. Madeline House, Graham Storey and Kathleen Tillotson, Pilgrim edn (Oxford, 1974), 484–5: Dickens to David Dickson, 10 May 1843.

saw as fostering 'one of the most evil and mischievous falsehoods existent in society', and this 'extraordinary confusion' was evident in the pronouncements of Exeter Hall (for many Evangelicals the most important London venue for public meetings) and an Ebenezer Chapel alike:

> It may appear unnecessary to offer a word of observation on so plain a head. But it is never out of season to protest against that coarse familiarity with sacred things which is busy on the lip, and idle in the heart: or against the confounding of Christianity with any class of persons who, in the words of SWIFT, have just enough religion to make them hate, and not enough to make them love, one another.[8]

Despite the fact that it seems to have been Dickens's earlier writings which attracted the adverse criticism of the evangelically minded, which in turn provoked this kind of response from Dickens, some religious commentators did grudgingly admit that the novelist had his merits as a *moral* rather than a *doctrinal* teacher. Take, for example, the unnamed reviewer of *The Haunted Man* in *Macphail's Edinburgh Ecclesiastical Journal* in January 1849:

> Mr Dickens commenced his career as a novelist, by aiming chiefly, if not entirely, at the *amusement* of the public … and for some time back, he has sought to be the solemn teacher, as well as the light-hearted jester, of the age … the creator of *Pickwick* sets himself up as the regenerator of the human race! His Christmas books are grand moral lessons. The pretty and innocent tales are precious allegories, containing, in his opinion, individual and social ethics of transcendent value. We cannot say that we have a profound respect for his teaching. Though he surrounds himself with *ghosts* to make himself look very earnest …[9]

This is indeed damnation by means of the very faintest praise. For a certain class of religious reader in the 1840s, therefore, Dickens offended by sins of omission and commission. His reverence for

---

[8] Charles Dickens, *The Pickwick Papers*, ed. James Kinsley, The Clarendon Dickens (Oxford, 1986), Appendix B, 887.
[9] *Macphail's Edinburgh Ecclesiastical Journal*, January 1849, 23–31; repr. in Philip Collins, ed., *Dickens: The Critical Heritage* (London, 1971), 179–80.

Scripture was self-evidently deficient, while his attempts at moral allegory were more likely to be propped up by sentimentality than they were to be supported by sound ethical argument.

But what can one say about the true nature of Dickens's religion? He was born into the Church of England and for the most part of his life appears to have been content with its doctrine and worship. He quotes the Authorized Version of the Bible regularly and accurately, with a decided preference for the New Testament. He is also clearly well versed in the phraseology and rhythms of the Book of Common Prayer. He strikingly uses one of the 'bidding sentences' from the order for Evening Prayer ('When the wicked man …') in the opening chapter of *Edwin Drood* as Jasper rushes into Cloisterham Cathedral in his dirty surplice, and, yet more weightily, quotes the verse from St John's Gospel ('I am the Resurrection and the Life') from the Burial Service in *A Tale of Two Cities*. The gloomier aspects of the Burial Service are also echoed and re-echoed throughout Chapter 11 of *Bleak House*. David Copperfield confesses to inserting the name of his beloved Miss Shepherd into the 'Prayer for the Royal Family'. Significantly too, citations of the Psalms are generally from the Prayer Book version.

On Christmas Eve 1856, Dickens wrote to the Revd R. H. Davies, a Dublin graduate and incumbent of Chelsea Old Church. Davies had written to him complaining of the novelist's lack of proper reverence and evangelical urgency:

> There cannot be many men, I believe, who have a more humble veneration for the New Testament or a more profound conviction of its all-sufficiency than I have. If I am ever (as you tell me I am) mistaken on this subject, it is because I discountenance all obtrusive professions of, and tradings in, Religion, as one of the main causes of real Christianity's having been retarded in this world; and, because my observation of life induces me to hold in unspeakable dread and horror, those unseemly squabbles about the Letter, which drive the Spirit out of hundreds of thousands.[10]

---

[10]   *The Letters of Charles Dickens*, 8: *1856–1858*, ed. Graham Storey and Kathleen Tillotson, Pilgrim edn (Oxford, 1995), 244–5: Dickens to R. H. Davies, 24 December 1856.

This letter gives emphasis to something most readers of Dickens would readily recognize as figuring vividly in his novels: he disliked scriptural literalism, firmly holding that 'the letter killeth', and possessing a strong distaste for inter-religious quibbling. In the 1850s, for example, he was particularly exercised about the rise of the Oxford Movement and its seemingly divisive insistence on tradition. Tractarians, as he rudely caricatured them in *Bleak House*, were little more than 'religious' dandies intent on 'turning the clock back'.

Retrospects, fond or wilful, were never likely to appeal to Dickens's innate progressiveness and the Tractarian mission to rewrite aspects of English church history left him at best antipathetic and at worst angry. The debates about theology, tradition and worship within the Church of England in the 1830s and 1840s seem to have turned Dickens against the Established Church *tout court*. His visit to the United States in 1842 marked a turning point, for, in the republic, which constitutionally barred any established church, Dickens found common religious currency with American Unitarians. He seems to have admired their doctrinal openness and their concomitant lack of 'obtrusive professions' and 'tradings in' religion. He also warmed to their active libertarianism and to their resolute opposition to slavery. For a year or two (or possibly five) after his return to Britain, Dickens worshipped as a Unitarian, taking a pew at the Little Portland Street Chapel in London and maintaining a close friendship with its minister, the Revd Edward Tagart. Dickens's intimate friend and biographer, John Forster, himself a Unitarian, was insistent, however, that this was a mere temporary flirtation on Dickens's part:

> That he did cease [to be a member of Tagart's congregation], after two or three years, I can distinctly state: and of the frequent agitation of his mind and thoughts in connection with this all-important theme, there will be other occasions to speak. But upon essential points he had never any sympathy so strong as with the leading doctrines of the Church of England; to these, as time went on, he found himself able to accommodate all minor differences; and the unswerving faith in Christianity itself, apart from sects and schisms, which had never

failed him at any period of his life, found expression at its close in the language of his will ...[11]

Forster went on to quote the lines from that will:

> I commit my soul to the mercy of God, through our Lord and Saviour Jesus Christ; and I exhort my dear children humbly to try to guide themselves by the teaching of the New Testament in its broad spirit, and to put no faith in any man's narrow construction of its letter here or there.

Traces of Dickens's sympathy for Unitarian beliefs may well be evident in *The Life of Our Lord*, written for domestic consumption and not made public until 1934 when a family member sold the manuscript to the proprietor of the *Daily Mail*. Certainly the Jesus who emerges from this text is cast more as a universal teacher than as a redeemer, but it should be remembered that the work was written by a storyteller for impressionable children and intended to be a first instructor rather than a definer of doctrinal niceties. Dickens ends this text with another insistence on living the good life:

> REMEMBER! – It is Christianity TO DO GOOD always – even to those who do evil to us. It is Christianity to love our neighbour as ourself, and to do to all men as we would have them Do to us. It is Christianity to be gentle, merciful, and, and to keep those qualities quiet in our own hearts, and never make a boast of them, or of our prayers or of our love of God, but always to shew that we love Him by humbly trying to do right in everything. If we do this, and remember the life and lessons of Our Lord Jesus Christ, and try to act up to them, we may confidently hope that God will forgive us our sins and mistakes, and enable us to live and die in Peace.[12]

This is certainly more like Mrs Cecil Frances Alexander than John Henry Newman, but we have to recall that *The Life of Our Lord* reveals a devout father offering his own children religious and moral instruction at a level that they might appreciate. He is not pleading a special doctrinal case. His stress here, as in the roughly

---

[11] John Forster, *The Life of Charles Dickens*, ed. J. W. T. Ley (London, 1928), 298–9.
[12] Charles Dickens, *The Life of Our Lord* (London, 1934), 128.

contemporary *A Christmas Carol,* is on the propriety of living the Christ-filled life and on being able to approach death with a clear and faithful mind. The Christian is bidden to receive Christ as a little child, and to believe in a Saviour who had taken little children into his arms. It is interesting, however, to note that Dickens adds to the notion of God forgiving sin the idea that he is also a ready pardoner of 'mistakes'.

A parallel to *The Life of Our Lord,* the religious instruction given to his children, is the clearly deeply felt letter Dickens sent to his son, Edward Bulwer Lytton Dickens ('Plorn') when the latter was about to leave for a career in Australia in September 1868:

> I write this note to-day because your going away is much upon my mind, and because I want you to have a few parting words from me, to think of now and then at quiet times ...
>
> Try to do to others, as you would have them do to you, and do not be discouraged if they fail sometimes. It is much better for you that they should fail in obeying the greatest rule laid down by our Saviour than that you should.
>
> I put a New Testament among your books for the very same reasons, and with the very same hopes, that made me write an easy account of it for you, when you were a little child; because it is the best book that ever was or will be known to the world, and because it teaches you the best lessons by which any human creature who tries be truthful and faithful to duty can possibly be guided. As your brothers have gone away, one by one, I have written such words as I am now writing to you, and have entreated them all to guide themselves by this book, putting aside the interpretations and inventions of man.
>
> You will remember that you have never at home been wearied about religious observances, mere formalities. I have always been anxious not to weary my children with such things, before they are old enough to form opinions respecting them. You will therefore understand the better that I now most solemnly impress upon you the truth and beauty of the Christian Religion, as it came from Christ Himself, and the impossibility of your going far wrong if you humbly but heartily respect it ... Never abandon the wholesome practice

of saying your own private prayers, night and morning. I have never abandoned it myself, and know the comfort of it.[13]

Dickens often seems to have found it difficult to be truly intimate with his children. Perhaps he seemed aloof because he was so busy, so very public, so much in demand. He was so often called away by his writing, his readings and the demands of his public. Like many Victorian men he left household concerns and domestic necessities to his wife and, in his case, to his ever competent sister-in-law, Georgina, who acted as housekeeper. The slow decline in his marriage also undoubtedly damaged his relations with his children. Yet he was, from their own testimony, a loving, responsive, inventive and hugely amusing father, when he gave himself the opportunity to be one. All of the children had affectionate nicknames and when he was in a party mood the children's father made the family the envy of all their friends. Both *The Life of Our Lord* and *A Child's History of England* (a volume which he *was* prepared to publish in his lifetime) suggest that he was particularly attentive to his children's education. Nevertheless, the boys in particular seem to have been more than a little in awe of Dickens's energy and his drive, and to have been the victims of his essential selfishness as an artist. What his letter reveals, however, is how in his attempts to be intimate he also becomes intensely pious. Love seems to dictate moral lessons, and morality and fatherliness, as in his novels (think particularly of *Dombey and Son*), are equated with divine lessons and with Bible teaching.

More accurately speaking, this is New Testament teaching. Both his present of the New Testament to Plorn, and the insistence in his will that the children guide themselves by the same book, indicate a profound and unquestioning response to the figure of Jesus and to central Christian teaching. Despite an active enough interest in modern science and an informed interest in pre-Darwinian geology and biology, Dickens appears to have been untroubled by the post-*Origin of Species* controversies which seem to have left other Christians disturbed and even bereft of faith. What Dickens seems to have most disliked was sectarian readings of Scripture. He seems to have been equally repelled by the expression of narrow Evangeli-

---

[13] *Letters*, 12: *1868–1870*, ed. Storey, 187–8: Dickens to Edward Bulwer Lytton Dickens, 26 September 1868.

calism in the Church of England and by Nonconformity in general. His Evangelicals, such as the Murdstones or Miss Barbary in *Bleak House*, seem to be defined by a lack of charity and by a drastic misreading of what Dickens regarded as essential New Testament teaching. Miss Barbary, with her firm belief in sin and in the child Esther's inherited and unpardonable taint of bastardy, emerges as particularly unpleasant and unbending. Though the forgiving Esther recounts the story without any noticeable smugness or bitterness, it is wonderfully ironic that Miss Barbary should have a seizure as she reads aloud the story of the woman taken in adultery. She who has so condemned Esther's errant mother seems to be struck down by a divine stone. Mrs Clennam in *Little Dorrit* is equally attached to the kind of Old Testament texts which speak of divine vengeance, the smiting of foes and an awesome and unforgiving God.

Dickens's Dissenters are far less middle class, but equally narrow in their reading of Scripture. He was particularly offended by their ardent Sabbatarianism, being greatly attached to the principle of opening of museums and art galleries on Sundays in order to offer the working classes some relief from the dreariness of their workaday lives. Most Dickensian Dissenters are, however, more comic than they are sinister. Mr Stiggins is habitually drunk; the ranting Revd Melchisedek Howler in *Dombey and Son* is so attached to a precise, but pragmatic, millenarianism that he announces 'the destruction of the world for that day two years hence, at ten in morning, and opened a front-parlour for the reception of ladies and gentlemen of the Ranting persuasion'.[14] Howler's imminent millennium, we realize, proves to be a conveniently movable feast. Less immediately comic is Mr Chadband in *Bleak House*, a preacher so unctuous in his manner that he is described as 'a large yellow man, with a fat smile, and a general appearance of having a good deal of train oil in his system'. The nature of Chadband's religion is revealed to us not so much by his extraordinary, and always inappropriate, use of biblical language and imagery as by his inability to pronounce the word 'truth' (it distortedly emerges as 'Terewth'). It is he who patronizes poor Jo rather than offering either practical religion or practical support, and it is he who is condemned for his failure to embody the gospel. No Anglican clergyman (and there are relatively few in Dickens's novels) is ever so tainted by the same kind of hypocrisy.

---

[14] Charles Dickens, *Dombey and Son*, ch. 60.

So where does this leave us with Dickens's Christianity? Is the faith he professes in his letters, and insists on to his children, evident in his fiction? One great Christian novelist, Fyodor Dostoevsky, was insistent that Dickens was decidedly a great religious teacher and, moreover, that Mr Pickwick was a prime example of an exemplary Christian.[15] Tolstoy too seems to have found deep spiritual nourishment in Dickens. When asked to list the literary works that had most influenced him, Tolstoy defined them as an extraordinary trinity: Rousseau's *Confessions*, St Matthew's Gospel and Dickens's *David Copperfield*.[16] As we have seen, this acceptance of Dickens as an implicitly Christian moralist is precisely what the novelist himself aspired to. What Dostoevsky and Tolstoy seem to have sensed, even through the medium of the sometimes clumsy translations in which they read his work, was that Dickens was at one with their own variety of spirituality.

Dickens's work, it seems to me, completely transcends any narrow emphasis we might want to put on 'good works' and on merely secular conversions to charity and decency. Central to much of his very best writing is the idea of something far more profound than Scroogian conversion. Dickens believes in a resurrection which is both here and now, and to come. This is something I wrote about at length in my study *Charles Dickens: Resurrectionist* in 1982.[17] Let me here merely summarize what I see as a reiterated exploration of the theme of spiritual regeneration in Dickens's fiction. Most obviously, we have the play on coming back to life in *A Tale of Two Cities*. The play is both verbal and factual. Dr Manette, released from sixteen years in the Bastille, is described as having been 'recalled to life'; Jerry Cruncher parodies the idea by pursuing a nefarious career, his night job, as a 'Resurrection man' providing freshly buried corpses for the medical trade. Most significant, however, is the career of Sydney Carton, the alcoholic barrister, stirred into new life by human love (albeit an unrequited love for Lucie Manette), who finally lays down

[15] For Dickens and Dostoevsky, see Angus Wilson, 'Dickens and Dostoevsky', in idem, *Diversity and Depth in Fiction: Selected Critical Writings of Angus Wilson*, ed. Kerry McSweeney (London, 1983), 64–87. Wilson is cited in the entry on Dostoevsky in Paul Schlicke, ed., *The Oxford Readers' Companion to Dickens* (Oxford, 1999), 191.

[16] For Tolstoy and Dickens, see Henry Gifford, 'Dickens in Russia: The Initial Stage', *Forum for Modern Language Studies*, January 1968, 42–52; repr. in Stephen Wall, ed., *Charles Dickens: A Critical Anthology* (Harmondsworth, 1970), 509–17.

[17] Andrew Sanders, *Charles Dickens: Resurrectionist* (London, 1982).

his life for his friend (and rival in love). At the end of the novel he stands on the scaffold, and inwardly expresses his faith:

> 'I am the Resurrection and the Life, saith the Lord: he that believeth in me, though he were dead, yet shall he live: and whosoever liveth and believeth in me shall never die.'
>
> The murmuring of many voices, the upturning of many faces, the pressing on of many footsteps in the outskirts of the crowd, so that it swells forward in a mass, like one great heave of water, all flashes away. Twenty-Three.
>
> ...
>
> They said of him, about the city that night, that it was the peacefullest man's face ever beheld there. Many added that he looked sublime and prophetic.

This prophetic sublimity is not the consequence of a ghostly visitation, but of something essentially religious. It comes from something deeply internalized, not from an external prompting. *A Tale of Two Cities* has long been regarded by those critics who decline to admire it as grossly sentimental, contrived, or simply un-Dickensian. It seems to me that this sublimity is part and parcel of a theme that runs through all of Dickens's late works. Major characters in all of these late novels need to find themselves, and they are obliged to do so by exploring complex disguises, alter egos, tricks, tests, sacrifices and discoveries. Dickens's last completed novel, *Our Mutual Friend*, is, for example, quite as dependent on the mystery of spiritual and physical resurrection as is *A Tale of Two Cities*, but the idea is more veiled, more complex, more essentially mysterious. It does not seem to me idle that Dickens chose the name 'Nicodemus' for Mr Boffin (though Boffin is generally known as 'Noddy'). I am happy with the argument that the whole novel can be seen as a meditation on Jesus's words to Nicodemus in John 3, and that the strange series of disguises, confusions, adoptions of false personalities, and slow unveilings of truth, are akin to the ideas that Nicodemus is obliged to puzzle over in his night-time encounter with Jesus. I would also suggest that *The Mystery of Edwin Drood* might also have turned out to be a story hinged on the idea of coming back to life – but as Dickens never got round to presenting us with the fullness of the mystery, we shall never properly know what he finally intended.

I hope that this essay has adequately suggested a Christian reading both of Dickens the man and of Dickens the novelist. It is necessary to end, however, with a return to Dickens's Genoan dream of 1844: would the Roman Catholic Church have been Dickens's 'true' spiritual home? Probably not, given the way that the Roman Church sought to define itself and those outside its pale in the nineteenth century. Dickens's general antipathy to Catholicism was based on its political pretensions as much as on its unequivocal insistence on its own 'truth' and the schismatic or heretical nature of all those who dissented from it. Dickens generally distrusted all establishments and institutions and those that pretended to infallibility particularly stuck in his gorge. As *A Child's History of England* reveals, he had no love for popes or for the pre-Reformation Church, and no pronounced admiration for post-Reformation adherents to the old religion. But, equally, he had no love for the founders of the English Reformation, famously dismissing Henry VIII as 'a most intolerable ruffian, a disgrace to human nature, and a blot of blood and grease upon the History of England' and Elizabeth as having 'a great deal too much of her father in her, to please me'.[18] Dickens, like Macaulay, seems to have taken it for granted that the Reformation marked a break with the superstitious faith of the Middle Ages and with the tyranny of an overweening Church. Progress and Protestantism were integrally linked. What Dickens seems to have responded to in Italy was the theatricality of Catholicism, but this was not enough to tempt him to abandon his deep-seated liberal Protestantism. For him, Catholics were little more than picturesque and the modern Catholic Church little more than a buttress to tyrannical princes and narrow patterns of thought. Dickens was no Newman, and his spiritual search was never to be concerned with niceties of doctrine or with a restless demand for definition. He was equally no Pugin, and, for him, the Middle Ages were best left both unsentimentalized and unrevived. For Dickens it was always the Spirit that gave life and always the letter that killed. The spirit that spoke to him in Genoa was too much of a phantom in a dream to persuade him to start a series of redefinitions of his faith, but Dickens's own account of his dream certainly suggests that he was briefly open to the awkward and inconvenient promptings of something deep inside him.

Durham University

---

[18] Charles Dickens, *A Child's History of England* (London, 1914; first publ. 1851), 210, 246.

DISRAELI'S NOVELS: RELIGION AND IDENTITY

by DAVID BROOKS

'**D**izzy's attachment to moderate Oxfordism is something like Bonaparte's to moderate Mahomedanism',
observed George Smythe in 1842. 'Could I only satisfy
myself', wrote his fellow Young Englander, Lord John Manners, a
year later, 'that d'Israeli believed all that he said, I should be more
happy: his historical views are quite mine, but does he believe
them?'[1] As a politician, Disraeli was and remains a man of mystery,
an identity which he took some care to cultivate. His protean
career in public life found a counterpart in his literary works, in
which likewise over the years he appeared to assume a range of
different positions. His religious allegiance is similarly elusive. He
had attended a Unitarian school, and his theological position, with
little sense of the divinity of Jesus, reflected that branch of Christianity most akin to Judaism. On the other hand, he was fascinated
by the rituals of Roman Catholicism and the cult of the Virgin
Mary, and it was perhaps natural that he should find his spiritual
home in the Church of England, that house of many mansions
which to his mind reflected the rich diversity of national life. How
far there was an underlying principle in Disraeli's life and art is a
question that has intrigued numerous historians, and it will be the
chief concern also of this essay in respect of two key issues: religion
and national identity.

Disraeli of course does not lack distinguished biographers,
beginning with the monumental work by Monypenny and Buckle,
published nearly a century ago.[2] More recent studies, for instance
those by John Vincent, Stanley Weintraub, Paul Smith and Jane
Ridley,[3] have focused more particularly upon his literary works

---

[1]   Sarah Bradford, *Disraeli* (London, 1982), 131 and 17 respectively.
[2]   William Monypenny and George Buckle, *The Life of Benjamin Disraeli Earl of
Beaconsfield*, 6 vols (London, 1910–20).
[3]   John Vincent, *Disraeli* (Oxford, 1990); Stanley Weintraub, *Disraeli* (London, 1993);
Paul Smith, *Disraeli: A Brief Life* (Cambridge, 1996); Jane Ridley, *The Young Disraeli,
1804–46* (London, 1995). Other recent biographical works include Richard Aldous, *The
Lion and the Unicorn: Gladstone vs. Disraeli* (London, 2007); Ian Machin, *Profiles in Power:
Disraeli* (London, 1995); Charles Richmond and Paul Smith, eds, *The Self-Fashioning
of Disraeli, 1818–51* (Cambridge, 1998); John Walton, *Disraeli* (London, 1990). Disraeli's

and ethnic background. Naturally, a key point of reference remains Robert Blake's classic biography published in 1966, which considers Disraeli's novels especially in terms of their literary qualities and the way in which they rate alongside those of other Victorian writers.[4] Blake's eminently sympathetic study of Disraeli portrays him as at heart an opportunist. Lately this view has been amended somewhat in an article by Jonathan Parry which emphasizes the coherence and consistency in Disraeli's thinking, and not least his concern with English identity.[5] What follows here will endeavour to carry the examination a stage further.

Why indeed did Disraeli eventually choose to make politics rather than literature his career? In one sense, of course, he never did. Each essential aspect of his life infused the other. The success of the parliamentary onslaught on Peel can be attributed in considerable part to Disraeli's theatricality, to his ability to personalize opponents almost as if they were characters in a play or novel. Conversely, it is the political element in his works of literature which brings them most to life. Disraeli's novels have drawn criticism in terms of characterization and plot, but debate gives them dynamism. In *Sybil* the reader's attention becomes thoroughly engaged in the scene set amidst the imposing ruins of Marney Abbey, today's Fountains, where Lord Egremont and Walter Gerard debate the dissolution of the monasteries. Key arguments are deployed, not least concerning welfare, community and the growing division between rich and poor, the 'two nations' which provide the novel's subtitle. Only one thing can interrupt their eager verbal contest, as 'from the Lady's chapel there rose the evening hymn to the Virgin: a single voice, but tones of almost supernatural sweetness'. Walter Gerard's daughter, Sybil, makes her first appearance. Disraeli is deeply susceptible to the mood and symbolism of the old religion.

Ultimately Disraeli's choice of career was a matter of circumstance and opportunity. Like his great rival, Gladstone, Disraeli

---

literary works are considered in Thom Braun, *Disraeli the Novelist* (London, 1981); Daniel Schwarz, *Disraeli's Fiction* (London, 1979); Robert Stewart, *Disraeli's Novels Reviewed, 1826–1968* (Metuchen, NJ, 1975). Also relevant here are Richard Faber, *Young England* (London, 1987); Alan Warren, 'Disraeli, The Conservatives and the National Church', *Parliamentary History* 19 (2000), 96–117.

4   Robert Blake, *Disraeli* (London, 1966).
5   Jonathan Parry, 'Disraeli and England', *HistJ* 43 (2000), 699–728.

effectively came of age at a time of almost unprecedented political upheaval, associated with the bitter constitutional conflicts of the late 1820s and early 1830s. Both men sensed serious danger in the air, perhaps even revolution of the kind that returned to France in 1830, although Disraeli, as a sort of latter-day Mirabeau, also saw his chance as an outsider to break into the traditional elite. Gladstone, having warned the Oxford Union against the perils of reform, graduated in late 1831 and became a Conservative Member of Parliament a year later. Disraeli also finished his (less formal) education in 1831, when he returned from an extended tour of the Mediterranean and the Middle East. Undertaken partly to recover from a protracted nervous illness, this left him with a lifelong affection for the Ottoman Empire, which he admired for its essential conservatism and for its ability to rule over a diversity of peoples and religions without experiencing the revolutionary upheavals increasingly to be found in western Europe. Disraeli would return to this theme in his novel, *Tancred*, published in 1847. Back in England, Disraeli's political ambitions were not immediately realized. He failed twice in seeking election to Parliament in 1832, and for the next five years pursued intermittently a literary career. His writings from this period are not much remembered nowadays, but in 1837 he was at last successful in becoming a Member of Parliament, for Maidstone. For the time being he put down his pen, only to take it up again with the publication of *Coningsby*, the first of the Young England trilogy, in 1844.[6]

The three Young England novels, especially *Sybil* (1845)[7] and *Tancred* (1847), provide the main focus of this essay. Why did Disraeli take up writing again in 1843–4 after such a long intermission? For one thing, he now had matters which he very much wanted to impart. Disraeli's marriage in 1839 had given him financial as well as emotional stability. He no longer felt under pressure to write in haste for money. Also, his wife insisted that he throw over his former debauched acquaintances, such as D'Orsay and Bulwer Lytton. Disraeli's new circle of friends consisted of youthful aristocrats, in particular George Smythe and Lord John Manners, who formed the nucleus of what became known as the Young England

---

[6]   Benjamin Disraeli, *Coningsby or The New Generation* (London, 1927).

[7]   Benjamin Disraeli, *Sybil or The Two Nations* (Oxford, 1981); idem, *Tancred or The New Crusade* (London, 1927).

group inside the Conservative party. Despite its name, its values were very much those of an older, pre-industrial society, still dominated by traditional influences such as the monarchy, the aristocracy and the Church of England. All of this appealed to Disraeli, whose instincts, although he had flirted briefly with radicalism in the early 1830s, were essentially conservative. In any case, he now had another axe to grind, in the shape of frustrated political ambition. Disraeli's party leader, Sir Robert Peel, had refused to give him office when the Conservatives returned to power in 1841, and Disraeli saw this as proof of Peel's apostasy, his abandonment of true Toryism in favour of the accursed principles of Whiggery.

Disraeli's politics, it is suggested, cannot be considered independently of his works of literature, nor vice versa. A good instance of this is provided by a speech made by Disraeli in the House of Commons in April 1845, a month before the publication of his most famous novel, *Sybil*. The occasion was the debate on the Maynooth grant, the most important trial of strength on ecclesiastical and religious policy during the decade. Peel's proposal to increase the state's grant to a Catholic seminary near Dublin sent shock waves through the ranks of the Conservative party, which saw it as evidence of collusion with English Whiggery and Irish separatism. Disraeli, with no liking for Peel, yet had a difficult path to tread. He wanted Toryism to be inclusive and national, and not exclusively identified with ultra-Protestantism. His solution was to argue against the subservience of religion to the state, in a way which would have found favour with the Oxford Movement. 'I deny', he declared, 'that the Church of England is the creature of the state. The alliance between them has been one formed and maintained upon equal terms.' Peel was guilty of perpetuating the state intervention, utilitarianism and centralization practised by the Whig governments of the 1830s.

> Will you [Disraeli asked pointedly] apply the principle of endowment to sectarians and schismatics of every class? Will you adopt a pantheistic principle [whereby] any body of sectarians that can prove a certain population to Downing Street will be considered to have a claim to an emolument? For my own part, I confess that I have no great confidence in the cure

of souls in that quarter ... From that quarter has proceeded the assault on the parochial constitution of the kingdom.[8]

This last was, of course, a hit against the New Poor Law of 1834, established by a Whig government but maintained by Peel's, which had replaced welfare provision at the parish level by a new administrative superstructure involving union workhouses and a centralized commission. The idea that religion could serve the material as well as the spiritual needs of society better than the state is at the heart of *Sybil*. But which religion, the reader will be moved to ask. Disraeli felt his way carefully, and sought inspiration in England's past, in an apparent golden age before the political upheavals attending in particular the Stuart kings. Actually, as we have seen, in *Sybil* the rot really started with the dissolution of the monasteries. 'Never', declared Sybil's father, Walter Gerard, 'was such a plunder ... it was worse than the Norman conquest; nor has England ever lost this character of ravage.'[9] Disraeli was careful not to call for an outright return to pre-Reformation days. The preservation of the monasteries arguably would have been consistent with the new order in Church and state. 'You might', continued Gerard, 'have changed the religion of the abbots as you changed the religion of the bishops: but you had no right to deprive men of their property, and property moreover which, under their administration, so mainly contributed to the welfare of the community.'[10] In discussing the fate of Charles I a century later, Disraeli also addressed the themes of social cohesion and national unity, in what some may consider a somewhat fanciful reading of English history.

> Thanks to parliamentary patriotism [he rather tendentiously observed] the people of England were saved from ship-money, which money the wealthy paid, and only got in its stead the customs and excise, which the poor mainly supply. Rightly was King Charles surnamed the Martyr; for he was the holocaust of direct taxation. Never yet did man lay down his heroic life for so great a cause: the cause of the Church and the cause of the Poor.[11]

[8] *Hansard's Parliamentary Debates* (ser. 3), vol. 79, cols 555–69 (11 April 1845).
[9] Disraeli, *Sybil*, 63.
[10] Ibid. 64.
[11] Ibid. 230.

Throughout his life Disraeli professed a nostalgia for the lost world of the Stuarts. With that dynasty's effective demise in 1714 had been forfeited the chance of a historic compromise between Anglicanism and Catholicism, and not least of a reconciliation between Ireland and Great Britain. As always, he guarded himself against accusations of Ultramontanism, describing 'the English nation' as 'at all times a religious and Catholic people, but who even in the days of the Plantagenets were anti-papal'. Their loyalty was to 'the Catholic and Apostolic Church, independent of any foreign dictation'.[12] The opportunity for a great national rapprochement of religions might yet recur, but not, he felt certain, under Peel's direction. Like the rest of Young England, Disraeli looked to a revival of traditional Toryism, of 'the party that ruled Ireland by a scheme which reconciled both churches … a party that has prevented the Church from being the salaried agent of the state, and has supported through many struggles the parochial polity of the country which secured to every labourer a home'.[13] To Disraeli, traditional Toryism took on a strongly religious dimension.

> It sympathises with the lowly, it looks up to the Most High; it can count its heroes and its martyrs. [Indeed] … toryism will yet rise from the tomb over which Bolingbroke shed his last tear, to bring back strength to the Crown, liberty to the Subject, and to announce that power has only one duty: to secure the social welfare of the PEOPLE …[14]

The search for national religious reconciliation had wider implications still for Disraeli. It was addressed in a key scene in *Sybil*, in which Egremont, in the kind of debate which Disraeli so much enjoys, confronted the Tractarian vicar, St Lys, over ritualistic tendencies within the Church of England. 'The people of this country', asserted Egremont, 'associate them with an enthralling superstition and a foreign dominion.' But, countered St Lys:

> … forms and ceremonies existed before Rome … Rome did not invent them: upon their practice we cannot consent to her

12   Ibid. 21.
13   Ibid. 272–3.
14   Ibid. 273.

founding a claim to supremacy. For would you maintain then that the church did not exist in the time of the prophets? Was Moses then not a churchman? And Aaron, was he not a high priest? Ay! Greater than any pope or prelate, whether he be at Rome or at Lambeth.[15]

This takes us into an area of religious discourse that Disraeli was to make particularly his own, his insistence on Christianity's profound indebtedness to Judaism. This, he felt, put the long-standing rivalries between the various Christian churches into due perspective.

In all these church discussions [observes Disraeli's effective *alter ego*, St Lys], we are apt to forget that the second Testament is only a supplement. Christianity is completed Judaism, or it is nothing. What has Rome to do with its completion? ... I do not bow to the necessity of a visible head in a defined locality. When Omnipotence deigned to be incarnate, the Ineffable Word did not select a Roman frame. The prophets were not Romans; the apostles were not Romans; she who was blessed above all women, I never heard she was a Roman maiden. No, I should look to a land more distant than Italy, to a city more sacred even than Rome.[16]

Disraeli had been captivated by his visit to Jerusalem in 1831. The experience had quickened his sense of ethnic identity, whereas his religious identity (formally at least) remained Anglican following his baptism at the age of twelve. Disraeli always retained an ambiguity about his Jewishness, but in the 1840s he came to view it in a more positive light, perhaps in compensation for his rejection by Peel in 1841. His reinvention of Jewish identity found expression in *Coningsby*, in the character of Sidonia, one of 'the aristocracy of Nature',[17] proud of his race, omniscient, a powerful if usually unseen influence in European affairs, probably modelled on a member of the Rothschild dynasty. In 1847, Disraeli took the brave decision to speak out in favour of Jewish emancipation in the House of Commons,[18] but his argument that Christianity

---

[15] Ibid. 111–12.
[16] Ibid. 112.
[17] Disraeli, *Coningsby*, 232.
[18] *Hansard's Parliamentary Debates* (ser. 3), vol. 95, cols 1321–30 (16 December 1847).

owed everything to Judaism found little favour among Tory back-benchers. The whole theme was explored much more fully in his novel *Tancred*, published in the same year. This is an intriguing and strange tale about a young English aristocrat, a quintessentially Disraelian creation, who journeys to Palestine in search of truth, as 'the Creator of the world speaks with men only in this land'.[19] Like *Sybil*, *Tancred* was concerned with national decline. England in the 1840s was portrayed as given over to materialism and railway mania, comfort instead of civilization, while beneath the surface lurked dark social forces such as Chartism or even revolution on the European model. 'The people of this country have ceased to be a nation, they are a crowd', lamented Tancred.[20] They had been let down by time-serving political and religious leaders. 'The English are really neither Jews nor Christians, but follow a sort of religion of their own, which is made every year by the bishops, in what they call a parliament, a college of muftis.'[21] What a contrast with the lands of the East, the cradle of so many religions, where spiritual values still prevailed over that graven image, progress. As in *Sybil*, a key scene in *Tancred* consisted of a debate in a signifi-cant location, in this case between the two principal characters in a garden at Bethany near Jerusalem. 'Are you', asked Eva, the nobly born Jewish lady, of Tancred, 'of those Franks who worship a Jewess; or of those who revile her, break her images, and blaspheme her pictures?'[22] The intolerance and divisions within Christendom were contrasted with the tolerance and inclusiveness of the East. And here Eva moved on to an argument of particular significance for Disraeli.

> Now tell me [she asked], suppose the Jews had not prevailed upon the Romans to crucify Jesus, what would have become of the Atonement? The holy race supplied the victims and the immolators. What other race could have been entrusted with such a consummation? ... We have saved the human race, and you persecute us for it.[23]

---

[19] Disraeli, *Tancred*, 268.
[20] Ibid. 52.
[21] Ibid. 215.
[22] Disraeli, *Tancred*, 194; again, note the Virgin Mary's significance for Disraeli. The term 'Franks' harks back to European crusaders in medieval times.
[23] Ibid. 199.

One historian, Jane Ridley, has noted another element possibly at work here. *Tancred* was mostly written in the aftermath of Peel's removal from office in mid 1846, and, as she observes:

> Disraeli was too keenly attuned to the political mood not to realize the symbolic religious dimension to Peel's fall … Disraeli's Judaeo-Christian interpretation of the atonement mirrored, or rather justified, his role in crucifying Peel, the mediator, redeeming the sins of politics through his crucifixion. Without the agency of Disraeli, what would have become of Peel's atonement?[24]

'I observe', remarked Eva, 'that Jesus was as fond of asking questions as of performing miracles.'[25] As we have seen, Disraeli was also keen on posing questions on religious matters in his novels, but he offered very few answers. In *Tancred* the hero had a vision on Mount Sinai, where an angel instructed him to 'announce the sublime and solacing doctrine of theocratic equality'.[26] The reader is not enlightened further, and one is reminded that Disraeli was always more adept in discovering political rather than spiritual solutions. The Ottoman Empire impressed him not least as it seemed to have found an answer to the problem of religious diversity. 'I aspire', declared the emir Fakredeen in *Tancred*, 'to a dominion where I have to govern the Maronites who are Christian, the Metoulis who are Mahomedans, the Anzareys who are Pagan, and the Druses who are nothing'.[27] Perhaps the inspiration of the East could have provided an answer to what Disraeli perceived as the problem of Britain's national decline.

> It is finished with England [asserted Fakredeen]; Louis-Philippe can take Windsor Castle when he pleases. [But] … let the Queen of England … transfer the seat of her empire from London to Delhi … We will acknowledge the Empress of India as our suzerain, and secure for her the Levantine coast. If she likes, she shall have Alexandria as she now has Malta.[28]

24 Ridley, *Young Disraeli*, 331.
25 Disraeli, *Tancred*, 196.
26 Ibid. 300.
27 Ibid. 208.
28 Ibid. 270–1.

Whatever else this be, it is certainly prophetic, and it does have subtle religious implications. The word 'imperialism' would not enter the English language until the 1870s, yet in *Tancred* Disraeli sketched forth much of what would be accomplished by his own and other British governments in the course of the half-century before the end of World War I. Queen Victoria would indeed become Empress of India, and later the capital of the Raj would indeed be moved to Delhi. Similarly Alexandria would be seized, though by Gladstone, not Disraeli; and, far from capturing Windsor, Louis-Philippe's successors would be manoeuvred out of large areas of the Middle East by British soldiers and politicians. During this period there developed a distinct sense of what might be termed manifest destiny, a still stronger perception of the British as a chosen people. It is not too much to say that by the start of the twentieth century the defence of Britain's imperial mission had replaced defence of the Church of England at the heart of Conservative party ideology.

In one other quasi-religious sense *Tancred* was also prescient. 'All the great things', it stated boldly at one point, 'have been done by the little nations.'[29] This must rate as one of Disraeli's less sincere utterances, and later as Prime Minister he would become notorious for his lack of sympathy with small nationalities. But in *Tancred* he lent expression to what had only recently become a subject of popular interest, the return of English Jews of the diaspora to the Promised Land. Here at least was a little nation worthy of Disraeli's solicitude. During the 1840s, the main advocate in Britain of what would later become known as Zionism was the MP Lord Ashley, later to become the seventh Earl of Shaftesbury. A prominent Evangelical, he considered that the conversion and restoration of the Jews to their ancient homeland would be a fulfilment of biblical prophecy and bring about the second coming and the millennium.[30] This was not quite Disraeli's agenda, but already in the 1840s the fate of Palestine was becoming an issue in European diplomacy, in a way that would portend developments in the early twentieth century. Palmerston, for whom Disraeli professed admiration in *Tancred*, was anxious to check French ambitions

---

[29] Ibid. 236.
[30] Victoria Clark, *Allies for Armageddon: The Rise of Christian Zionism* (New Haven, CT, 2007), 66.

in Syria by securing British interests in the Holy Land; and in 1841, he cooperated with Lord Ashley in establishing an Anglican-Lutheran bishopric of Jerusalem. As mentioned in *Tancred*, the first incumbent was a convert from Judaism.[31] This use of religion for avowedly secular purposes caused further crisis within the Oxford Movement, and helped to speed Newman's conversion to Roman Catholicism. But Palmerston's priority, just like Balfour's in 1917, was to turn the Jews into an unofficial British garrison in Palestine, as the French were already doing with the Maronites in Syria.

Disraeli's attitude to proto-Zionism, it must be said, remained ambiguous. Only once does he seem to have expressed fervent support for a Jewish recolonization of Palestine. This was in 1851, in a conversation with Lord Stanley, son and heir to Disraeli's political boss, the fourteenth Earl of Derby. Stanley was impressed. Like Smythe and Manners, he had at times found himself wondering how far Disraeli believed in anything at all.[32] In 1851 Disraeli and his party were out of office, but when later he became Prime Minister he did nothing for the Jews in Palestine, and instead chose to establish a British protectorate in Cyprus, a possibility also hinted at in *Tancred*.[33] There are several possible reasons for this. He considered that exile made a race more virile, and where Judaism (and indeed most things) was concerned, Disraeli's emphasis was invariably on race rather than on religion. In *Tancred* he even bracketed the Jews with their traditional enemies, the Armenians, declaring that 'if you want to make a race endure, rely upon it you should expatriate them'.[34] Also, like those well-assimilated Jews who later opposed the Balfour Declaration, Disraeli may have feared that the establishment of a Jewish homeland might call into question the loyalty of British Jews to throne and empire. Finally, he probably considered that the Jewish community would flourish better not as an independent nation but as a powerful influence behind the scenes (whether in Britain or abroad), as personified by the all-pervading character Sidonia in *Coningsby*. Disraeli was always fascinated by intrigue, but his hint at what would later in

[31] Disraeli, *Tancred*, 194.
[32] Bradford, *Disraeli*, 186.
[33] Disraeli, *Tancred*, 244.
[34] Ibid. 198.

some quarters be termed a Jewish world conspiracy would leave a sinister echo in the twentieth century.

This essay has focused mainly on the 1840s. The decade's middle years were Disraeli's most productive as a novelist, and the three volumes of the Young England trilogy have all stood the test of time. They reveal the author's intense engagement with questions of religion and identity, and in particular his sense that the Church of England, working in parallel with government, could provide a potent force for national renewal and reconciliation, as well as a vital barrier against the twin perils of revolution and bureaucratic despotism. Disraeli was confident that the instincts of the English people were basically Anglican as well as Tory, and that a reinvigorated, more inclusive, national Church could override even such inveterate divisions as those between Stuart and Hanoverian, Britain and Ireland, and indeed Gentile and Jew.

Queen Mary, University of London

BREADTH FROM DISSENT: ADA ELLEN BAYLY ('EDNA LYALL') AND HER FICTION

by CLYDE BINFIELD

Attitudes change. They broaden as well as contract. They reflect the permeation of dissenting ideas in apparently settled communities and the assimilation of conventionally accepted ideas by dissenters. The process is transformative. Literature is a prime medium for the transmission of ideas. It shapes attitudes. What, then, of the role of popular literature, especially fiction, in shaping the attitudes, especially the religious attitudes, of a rapidly growing, clearly intelligent and significantly female reading public? This paper considers an Anglican writer, formed in part by Dissent, whose work particularly appealed to Nonconformists exercising their citizenship in a complex but now promisingly open society. This Broad Churchwoman enlarged the minds of her readers in liberal directions without diminishing their Dissenting formation. She is now quite forgotten, but her apparently modest achievement was in fact considerable.

'Edna Lyall' was a late Victorian novelist with a particular vogue among intelligent young women from the liberally minded middle and lower-middle classes. The scope of her novels ranged widely, from seventeenth-century romance to contemporary doubt. Her style was clear. Her plots were well made. They were shapely, designed to be unexpected at the right place. Their impact was gently but insistently page-turning. The research for them was carefully done but it was seldom obvious. Her authorial voice was a pleasant accompaniment. Its balance engaged most readers, intrigued many, and worried some. She was manifestly a woman of liberal, even radical, views. Her sympathy lay with those who had lost their faith or whose dissent was born of slow conviction rather than instinct. She was a pacificist who found Quakers attractive. Her pride in a naval forebear was balanced by her belief that most wars were unnecessary and that the South African War was especially so; she died before war with Germany could test her growing conviction that all war was wrong. She favoured Home Rule for Ireland, prison reform and a proper role for women in politics and society. She enjoyed music, the theatre and art; here her tastes were intelligently conventional. All this is clear from her books. Those who saw her as a freethinking republican had some foundation for their views, although in fact she was a woman of firm moral compass, quietly but consistently Anglican. That, too, is apparent from her books.

Ada Ellen Bayly (1857–1903), who wrote under the name of Edna Lyall, was quite as interesting as her nom de plume.[1] Her intellect was acute, her health was frail, her friendships long-lasting and her company good. Her extended family circle was affectionate, blessed with the assurance provided by several generations of lawyers, parsons and medical men. It included bankers and some had entries in *Walford's County Families*. It was London and provincial. Her people, in short, belonged to the political nation of unreformed England, county voters to a man, and they justified that nation's nineteenth-century reform and enlargement. Her own politics were at once inherited and distinctive. Her paternal grandfather had been a founder of the Reform Club; Free Trade was an article of the family creed; Henry Fawcett, the young local MP, was a family hero;[2] and W. E. Gladstone became a fixed point in their firmament. Nonetheless she also found room for Charles Bradlaugh, or at least for his principled stand on the parliamentary oath; she admired the Peace Society; overboiled at the Armenian atrocities; and was sharply critical of the Boer War and British treatment of Boer civilians. So much for her immediate politics.

There was a further strand, however, which derived more from her mother's side. Here her heroes belonged to the seventeenth century: Milton, Bunyan, Hampden, Cromwell, Algernon Sydney, Richard Baxter, she knew them all. She had read whatever they had written and all that had been written about them.[3] Her

---

[1]   To simplify matters this paper will refer to her as Edna Lyall, a name using nine letters from Ada Ellen Bayly. General information about her is drawn chiefly from four sources: George A. Payne, *Edna Lyall: An Appreciation* (Manchester, [1903]), J[esse]. M[aria]. Escreet, *The Life of Edna Lyall (Ada Ellen Bayly)* (London, 1904); *DNB, Supplement 1901–1911, s.n.* 'Bayly, Ada Ellen (1857–1903)'; *ODNB, s.n.* 'Bayly, Ada Ellen (1857–1903)'. I am grateful to David Wykes and the late Jonathan Morgan of Dr Williams's Library, London, for help in the preparation of this paper.

[2]   In the 1850s and 1860s the Baylys lived in Brighton; Henry Fawcett was Liberal MP for Brighton 1865–74: *ODNB, s.n.* 'Fawcett, Henry (1833–1884)'.

[3]   The extent of her reading and the depth of her research are indicated by her biographers, Payne and Escreet, and are apparent from her books. Thus, for the purposes of the present essay, *In the Golden Days* (1885) demonstrates her knowledge

literary heroes complemented her political and ancestral ones. She added Shakespeare to Milton and Bunyan; G. H. Lewes, Thomas Carlyle, F. W. H. Myers and the Brownings provided epigraphs for her chapters. It follows that her Anglicanism, although not the most logical conclusion of her politico-literary formation, was broad. It was also active. Her brother and two brothers-in-law were Anglican clergymen. She made her home with her married sisters, participated in parish life, for nineteen years conducted a Bible class for Eastbourne shop assistants, gave three bells to the church where one brother-in-law was curate and seating and a stained glass window to the church of which he became vicar. Her ashes (cremation was a radical last request) were placed at the foot of the cross in her brother's country churchyard and her biographer concluded her *Life* with appreciative letters from the bishops of Hereford and Ripon, Archdeacon Wilberforce of Westminster and Canon Rawnsley.[4]

The publication of two biographies within two years of her death, the inclusion in one of them of such warm clerical commendation, and her appearance in the first of the *Dictionary of National Biography*'s twentieth-century supplements, indicate her contemporary standing as a novelist.[5] There can be no doubt as to her material success: she left £25,966.[6] After a slow yet early, almost precocious, start her novels were published by reputable houses: Hurst and Blackett, Longmans Green, and Methuen. Their sales, again after a slow start, were more than reputable. To select five of the best known: *Donovan* (1882) was only a *succès d'estime* when its sequel, *We Two* (1884; 'refused by half a dozen publishers'), made her name and returned *Donovan* to public notice; *We Two* reached its tenth edition in 1888; *In the Golden Days* (1885) achieved three editions and twenty-one reprints by January 1903, the month before her death; *Knight Errant* (1887) reached its fifteenth edition

---

of Algernon Sydney, Hampden and Baxter; and *The Burges Letters* (1902) engagingly notes on page 43 her childhood memory of *Pilgrim's Progress* as an example of allegorical Sunday reading that was neither dull nor sad.

4   Escreet, *Lyall*, 257–63.

5   Payne, *Edna Lyall*; Escreet, *Lyall*; DNB, *Supplement 1901–1911*, s.n. 'Bayly, Ada Ellen'.

6   ODNB, *s.n.* 'Bayly, Ada Ellen (1857–1903)'.

in 1894; *Derrick Vaughan, Novelist* (1889) marked its eleventh thousand in its first year of publication.[7]

Her association with a fourth publishing firm introduces a further dimension of success. It also helps to explain the particular nature and direction of her influence. James Clarke (d. 1888) and his eldest son, James Greville Clarke (1854–1901), owned the *Christian World*, an influential weekly heading a stable of religious journals.[8] Clarke pioneered serial fiction as a proper component of his publications; moreover, Emma Jane Worboise and Mary Ann Hearn (Marianne Farningham), women who were unfailingly popular with the Sunday school teaching classes, were on his payroll.[9] Edna Lyall fitted perfectly into his brand of accessibly serious popular religious journalism. It helped that there was a family connection. James Clarke's younger son, Percy, was married to a first cousin of Edna Lyall's. There was both family and commercial sense in their relationship. There was also a meeting of minds.

The *Christian World* was primarily a Congregational publication. The Clarkes might be described as Broad Church Congregationalists. They were as judiciously radical in their views as Edna Lyall was in hers; they too had readerships to maintain. James Clarke had a weakness for lapsed ministers and for more or less persecuted heretics.[10] In 1885 his principal leader writer was James Allanson Picton (1832–1910), the recently elected Liberal MP for Leicester.[11] Picton had been a Congregational minister, he wrote a life of Oliver Cromwell and, having developed a horror of all dogmatism, he moved well beyond the verges of agnosticism.[12] He was tailor-made for an Edna Lyall hero.

These Congregational links were not wholly fortuitous. The Clarkes were successful publishers with useful Fleet Street contacts. They had settled in Surrey, moving to Caterham, then an up-and-

7   This information is drawn from the title pages of *We Two*, new edn (London, 1888); *In the Golden Days*, new edn (London, 1899, repr. 1903); *Knight Errant*, 15th edn (London, 1894); *Derrick Vaughan, Novelist* (London, 1889). For *Donovan: A Modern Englishman* and *We Two*, see Payne, *Edna Lyall*, 23, 25.

8   For James Clarke, founder of James Clarke and Co., see Harry Jeffs, *Press, Preachers and Politicians. Reminiscences: 1874–1932* (London, 1933), 44–6; for James Greville Clarke (1854–1901), see *Who Was Who: 1897–1916* (London, 1920), 140.

9   Jeffs, *Reminiscences*, 47, 50–1.

10   Ibid. 57.

11   For Picton, see *ODNB*, s.n. 'Picton, James Allanson (1832–1910)'.

12   Jeffs, *Reminiscences*, 55.

coming, spaciously villa-ed, hillside and valley resort. Caterham was where Edna Lyall's nearest family on her mother's side, the Winters, also lived. Like the Clarkes, the Winters were Congregationalists and, like the Clarkes, the Winters had substantial Suffolk connections. This was how traditions were mediated, mindsets evolved, and the constituent parts of a plural society gained the confidence necessary for successful and assured coexistence.

Since the Winters and their kinsmen featured in Edna Lyall's fiction, her background calls for further exploration. The Anglicanism was recent. On her father's side there was Unitarianism, on her mother's side there was Congregationalism, on both sides there had been Baptists. Her grandfather Bayly, Bencher and Treasurer of Grays Inn, supposedly of Huguenot stock and certainly with Flemish connections, was a Unitarian; her father, barrister of the Inner Temple, had been reared a Unitarian.[13] Hampden Gurney Jameson, the clerical brother-in-law with whose family she lived longest, was of mixed Baptist and Congregational stock. His Gurneys were the parliamentary shorthand-writing and legal Gurneys. Their given names – Hampden, Russell, Sydney – testified to pride in an unmistakable political tradition.[14]

Gurney Jameson's brother, Kingsbury Jameson, also an Anglican clergyman, and a successor of F. D. Maurice as vicar of St Edward's, Cambridge, extended the mix.[15] He married a daughter of George Macdonald, Congregational minister turned Broad Churchman, poet, novelist and creator of dreamworlds.[16] Such connections were natural in large families of this sort, and the customary picture which they might suggest of Dissenters turning into Anglicans with the advent of propriety and improved education needs some modification: extended families encompassed and accommodated a wide denominational variety. There was nothing *nouveau* or fly-by-night about the Bayly circle. Their ancestry was easily traced to the seventeenth century and Ada Ellen Bayly brought much of it into the fiction of Edna Lyall.

There is another point to be made about this background. It

[13] Payne, *Edna Lyall*, 18.
[14] An extensive family tree is to be found in W. B. Gurney, *Some Particulars of the Gurney Family* (London, 1902).
[15] Greville Macdonald, *Reminiscences of a Specialist* (London, 1932), 270.
[16] Ibid. 270, 310. For George Macdonald (1824–1905), see *ODNB*.

did not reflect what sociologists might call a deviant subculture. It reflected an alternative culture, an alternative establishment indeed, such as might have prevailed had politics turned out differently. Edna Lyall's ancestors, Anglican and Dissenting, were equal heirs of an English Church. This conviction fuelled her Victorian pride in country. Its exegesis may have been Whig history of purest essence but, woven into her present commitment and mediated through her writing, it was powerfully persuasive. Here was Broad Church radicalism for the Free Church world of Christian Endeavour, Mutual Improvement and Sunday School Institutes.

Its mediation can be shown in three books – *In the Golden Days* (1885), *The Burges Letters* (1902) and *Derrick Vaughan, Novelist* (1889) – covering, in this order, successive generations of the Wharncliffe family. Edna Lyall wrote more obviously relevant fictions for future historians: *We Two*, for example, was admired by Bradlaugh's supporters; *Doreen* (1894, first serialized in the *Christian World*) promoted Home Rule and introduced a land reformer who was a thinly disguised Michael Davitt; *The Autobiography of a Truth* (1896) was pro-Armenian and anti-Turk; *The Hinderers* (1902) was pro-Boer or at least anti-Boer War. The Wharncliffe books, however, traced the evolution of a mindset and placed it where it belonged – in the mainstream of contemporary life.

According to J. M. Escreet, Edna Lyall's friend and biographer, the Winters 'descended from the family of that name, who, at the time of the Gunpowder Plot, were sturdy Romanists and suffered for the cause'.[17] More immediately the Winters were Protestant Dissenters. Their most celebrated connection was 'Bold Bradbury', Thomas Bradbury (1676/7–1759), Edna Lyall's direct ancestor five genera-tions back, 'a man of war from his youth' and minister at two famous London meeting-houses, Fetter Lane and New Court.[18] It was 'Bold Bradbury' whose sudden prayer for King George during Sunday worship announced to the Dissenting world that Queen Anne was dead and that the Schism Bill awaiting her signature could not now become an Act.[19] 'Thomas Bradbury' became favourite names for

[17] Escreet, *Lyall*, 3.
[18] Ibid. 3–4; Arthur Pye-Smith, *Memorials of Fetter Lane Congregational Church, London* (London, 1900), 14–18; *ODNB, s.n.* 'Bradbury, Thomas (1676/7–1759)'. Brad-bury ministered at the Congregational Fetter Lane from 1707 to 1728, and at the Presbyterian New Court (it became statedly Congregational on his settlement) from 1728 to 1759.
[19] Pye-Smith, *Memorials*, 16–17.

Winters and Clarkes. Thus Edna Lyall's favourite Caterham uncle was Thomas Bradbury Winter. T. B. Winter's sister, the piquantly named Henrietta Martha, had married another Congregationalist, Nathaniel Warner-Bromley (1823–96), of Badmondisfield Hall, Suffolk, lord of the manor of Badmondisfield and lay rector of Wickhambrook, Justice of the Peace and barrister (non-practising).[20] His family were Edna Lyall's Wharncliffes. His house (pronounced 'Bansfield') was their Mondisfield Park.

Badmondisfield was a moated hall set in a small park. Its manorial history stretched back to the reign of Henry I, its architectural history to the reign of Elizabeth.[21] It had been a puritan house since the early seventeenth century and it was a Dissenting house well into the twentieth century. It passed by inheritance from Warners to Barretts, Bromleys, Warner-Bromleys and Barrett Warner Bromleys. Although they were evangelical Dissenters, Nathaniel and his father, Joseph (d.1860), belonged to the circle of the Unitarian Henry Crabb Robinson (1775–1867) and handled some of his Suffolk affairs.[22] In Nathaniel's day the estate included a secondary house, The Gesyns, where Samuel Cradock had conducted a Dissenting academy and which served from time to time as the Congregational manse.[23] There were several Congregational ministers in the family circle and there was an illuminating family link with the Evangelical Revival and its part in the abolition of the slave trade: Nathaniel's uncle, the Revd Henry Bromley (1798–1878), was first married to Joanna Vassa (1795–1857), the only surviving child of Gustavus Vassa, the freed slave now better known as Olaudah Equiano (1745–97).[24] Edna Lyall seems not to have latched on to this exciting connection.

There was, however, much else to latch on to. Mondisfield and the Wharncliffes figure significantly but in different ways in each of the books. Mondisfield, large, three-storied and 'washed a sort

[20] *Walford's County Families of the United Kingdom*, 38th edn (London, 1898), 126.

[21] E. Sandon, *Suffolk Homes: A Study of Domestic Architecture* (Woodbridge, 1977), 216, 219.

[22] The Henry Crabb Robinson correspondence (London, DWL), contains letters from Joseph (HCR 1856, 7a, 8a, 11b, 36a; 1857, 14a) and Nathaniel Warner Bromley (HCR 1862, 63a; 1864, 1a, 7b).

[23] T. J. Hosken, *History of Congregationalism and Memorials of the Churches of our Order in Suffolk* (Ipswich, 1920), 289–90.

[24] For Henry Bromley, see *Congregational Year Book*, 1879, 703–5; for Olaudah Equiano (*c.*1745–97), see *ODNB*.

of salmon colour', stands for an ordered, welcoming tradition.[25] 'There it stood, and there it had stood since the reign of Edward III, though how far the original house resembled the present it was hard to say, since there had been many restorations'.[26] The Wharncliffes themselves are centre-stage for *In the Golden Days*, they are hospitable cousins in *The Burges Letters*, and they provide the narrator of *Derrick Vaughan, Novelist*. That narrator, Sydney Wharncliffe, was the eponymous hero of the novel in progress when Edna Lyall died.[27] Its title would have intrigued readers of *In the Golden Days*.

That novel (dedicated 'With my love to the kinsfolk at "Mondis-field"') is set in the reign of Charles II. It is a romance about a divided family in which the hero, thwarted by a calculating and much older brother, eventually marries his true love who is a distant kinswoman; their marriage keeps Mondisfield in the family. At that level it is almost an inverted Carolean *Mansfield Park* (should Mondisfield be pronounced 'Mansfield'?). In fact the Rye House Plot becomes the story's pivot; Suffolk, London and Amsterdam provide its settings. There are heroes outside the family. 'Francis Bampfield, Saint', former prebendary and present Seventh-day Baptist, is one; his death is described with a moving economy.[28] Algernon Sydney, patriot and republican, is a compelling presence; the account of his execution is powerfully handled.[29] Even though the style inevitably comes too close too often to the 'fain, prithee, and methinks' school of writing, its hallmarks are clarity, structure and a passionate good sense, and these allow the author to insert her late Victorian voice into what she writes with a wholly acceptable authority.

The Burges Letters was written for children. It provides young Edwardians with a 'Record of Child Life in the Sixties'.[30] The young Burgeses live comfortably in Helmstone. They are regular church-goers. Their father is a barrister of Liberal political views. They go to a day school – although boarding school looms for at least one

25 Edna Lyall, *In the Golden Days*, new edn (London, 1899, repr. 1903), 17.
26 Ibid.
27 Escreet, *Lyall*, 244–6, 248.
28 Lyall, *In the Golden Days*, 306–12. For the original Francis Bampfield (1614–84), see *ODNB*.
29 Lyall, *In the Golden Days*, 287–90.
30 Edna Lyall, *The Burges Letters: A Record of Child Life in the Sixties* (London, 1902).

of them – and have visiting tutors. Their holidays tend to be in or near country towns, save for a leisurely visit of unalloyed delight to Mondisfield, where the chief letter-writer is especially conscious of a child's portrait, rescued from the Great Fire of London; it is the portrait of a Wharncliffe ancestor, Hugo, the hero of *In the Golden Days*. The style is engagingly simple. It is never condescending. It depicts the broad good sense of a happy and well-integrated cousinhood, accommodating an evolving variety of views. The Burgeses are the Baylys; Helmstone is Brighton – the disguises are modest. Burges was a Bayly name and Captain Burges RN, killed at Camperdown and with a memorial in St Paul's Cathedral, was a Bayly hero.[31] The Caterham Winters and the Warner-Bromleys of Badmondisfield duly appear. Here is the moral bedrock of the traditional but still lively political nation, in which children and women are now playing their due part, with more in view.

Derrick Vaughan, Novelist is in all respects a contrast. For a start it is very short. Its narrator is a young Oxford-educated barrister, its hero is to be a novelist; that is his vocation. The hero is doggedly Anglican, sustained by the Prayer Book. The action takes place between the mid 1870s and the late 1880s. It is set chiefly in London, Bath and Ben Rhydding (near Ilkley), but a yachting holiday from Southampton to Tresco plays its due part and there is a menacing imperial backcloth which is partly Indian and possibly South African. The authorial voice is male; it essays a young man's diction, colloquial but never slangy.

The novel is to be read at several levels. It is a love story; the path of true love, confirmed in the gardens of Tresco Abbey and resumed there years later, is convincingly thwarted. It is, no less convincingly, a temperance tract; alcoholism and temperance are fundamental to the plot. It is also autobiographical. Derrick Vaughan's shaping as a novelist, his sense of vocation, his dealings with publishers and his emergence to popular and critical acclaim, echo the experience of Edna Lyall.

There are other congruences. The friendship between Derrick Vaughan and Sydney Wharncliffe, the narrator, is cemented in their boyhood – at some point in the 1860s – driving in the Wharncliffe carriage from Newmarket station to Mondisfield. As the carriage

---

31 Payne, *Edna Lyall*, 26.

passes Silvery Steeple, Sydney's father comments: 'That is a ruined church; it was destroyed by Cromwell in the Civil Wars'. At once young Vaughan is alert. 'Was Cromwell really once there?' 'So they say … are you an admirer of the Lord Protector?' '"He is my greatest hero of all", said Derrick fervently'.[32]

With the Wharncliffe tradition thus announced and embraced, we are ready for its translation to contemporary issues. In *Derrick Vaughan* this is heralded by an epigraph from Arnold Toynbee: 'Sympathy is feeling related to an object, whilst sentiment is the same feeling seeking itself alone'.[33] Toynbee reappears later in the novel when Vaughan, a literary success at last, 'used to spend two evenings a week at Whitechapel, where he taught one of the classes in connection with Toynbee Hall, and where he gained that knowledge of East end life which is conspicuous in his third book – "Dick Carew"'.[34]

Sympathy is central to Edna Lyall's creed. It reconciles faith and doubt, issues of war and peace, questions of retribution. It allows for insight and reason. It is impatient of ecclesiology but not of due order. Derrick Vaughan, for example, is braced by the sympathetic discipline of regular worship at Bath Abbey.[35] The most interesting insights, however, come from the balance of worship in the other two books. Hugo Wharncliffe, the hero of *In the Golden Days*, worships at Mondisfield parish church and finds himself vulnerable to liturgy and setting: 'here and there sentences flashed forth with new meaning in the old words – words which, true at the time to human nature, must be true throughout the ages'.[36] Meanwhile, 'through the pointed windows the sunshine streamed brightly, glorifying the simple gothic arches and pillars. The village church was plain enough and bare enough to please a Puritan; there was not a vestige of colour in it … it seemed … cold and even ugly. And yet …'[37]

That same morning Hugo is forced to interrupt worship in

---

[32] Edna Lyall, *Derrick Vaughan, Novelist* (London, 1889), 4–5.
[33] No source for the quotation is given. For Toynbee (1852–83), see *ODNB*.
[34] Lyall, *Derrick Vaughan*, 136. Toynbee Hall, the pioneer university settlement, was conceived in November 1883 and opened in Whitechapel, in memory of Arnold Toynbee, in December 1884.
[35] Lyall, *Derrick Vaughan*, 99–100.
[36] Lyall, *In the Golden Days*, 37.
[37] Ibid.

the hall barn where about forty men and women are gathered
with his Wharncliffe cousins from the big house. Again he finds
himself vulnerable. The setting – a wooden desk, rough benches,
corn stacked at one end – attracts him, and so does a word from
the preacher, 'a little, insignificant man': 'You *must* rise above the
circumstances in which you are placed; if you don't your circumstances will swallow you up, will drag you lower and lower'.[38]

Nearly two hundred years later, in rather more settled times,
Elfie Burges is at Mondisfield. On Sunday afternoon she worships
with her uncle and aunt in the parish church, sitting importantly
with them in the squire's pew (Uncle Wharncliffe, it should be
remembered, is the lay rector), with ample opportunity to watch
the vicar's daughter in the opposite pew 'raise' the hymn tunes on
a pitchpipe, and the beadle 'who carries a stick and walks about in
the sermon, shaking his stick in a threatening way at any baby who
cries or any child who fidgets'.[39] But that morning she had already
worshipped with her uncle and aunt at the meeting-house, which
is 'really an ordinary square red brick house outside but inside has
got galleries and a delightful old square pew in the corner with
very high hassocks'. Though 'rather long and hot', the Meeting has
two advantages. One is that its beadle 'not only shakes his stick at
the children, but he raps the boys on the head when they behave
badly. Then the girls score, for they wear hats'. The other is 'that in
the faded green baize which lines the family pew you can watch
the moths stealing in and out. When the time goes slowly a child
is very glad to have an interesting thing like moths to watch.'[40]

It is the balance that counts. This is more than a literary device,
for each of these aspects of English village life reflects – in perfect
parity – the Church. The family pew in the meeting-house is
invaded by moths; the silver cake basket at the vicarage croquet
party is invaded by ants.[41] And in this village all unite for the Bible
Society meeting, with its long, dry speeches and the singing of the
'Old Hundredth', 'a tune that makes your heart stir just as the roll
of a drum stirs it'. That meeting is held in the hall barn, decorated
with evergreens, uniting an apparently divided community.[42]

---

[38] Ibid. 38, 39.
[39] Lyall, *Burges Letters*, 133.
[40] Ibid. 134.
[41] Ibid. 134–5. Croquet became the rage in the 1860s.
[42] Ibid. 137.

The fourth Wharncliffe book, *Sydney Wharncliffe*, unfinished at the time of its author's death, remained unpublished. Its hero, who may or may not have been a latter-day Algernon Sydney, was a man of Edna Lyall's age. It was, perhaps, as well that the book was unfinished because the last male Warner-Bromley to be squire of Wickhambrook was certainly material for a novel.[43] He was Edna Lyall's first cousin, Nathaniel Barrett Warner-Bromley (1869–1936), Cambridge to Sydney Wharncliffe's Oxford, a solicitor to Wharncliffe's barrister, and at least a dozen years younger; so he could not have been Sydney's model. His life was nonetheless a parable for his age: prefect at The Leys, the Wesleyan boarding school opened at Cambridge in his boyhood; undergraduate at Emmanuel College, where he rowed, or rather coxed, joined its exclusive Mildmay Essay Club (reading essays on 'Civilization' and 'Thrift'), contemned the current system of Poor Relief at its Debating Society, and read Law.[44] He owned, or so it was recalled much later, half Wickhambrook. He let his estate to tenant farmers and was regarded as a good landlord. He married the daughter of a Congregational minister. He was treasurer of Wickhambrook Congregational Church and also of a local benefit society. That, it seems, proved his downfall. Caught in the wash of the Clarence Hatry scandal,[45] he was imprisoned for the misappropriation of funds. It was 1931; he resigned his church offices, the hall was sold, and his unmarried sisters, Alice, Evelyn and Clara Mary Henrietta, retreated to The Poplars, a house in the village.

The sisters effectively ran Wickhambrook's Congregational Church. Evelyn ran its Women's Bible Class; Mary (1863–1942), who wrote poetry and published some of it, ran its Men's Bible Class, fifty strong, as well as its Young Men's Brotherhood. She was also the Sunday School superintendent, the church organist and – for fifty years – the church secretary, and was duly elected life deacon.[46] Mary was one of the Wharncliffe toddlers visited at

[43] I am indebted for much of what follows to information provided by the late Jessie Ridge, a niece of the last Mrs Warner-Bromley of Badmondisfield.
[44] *Handbook and Directory with War Record of The Leys School, Cambridge*, 9th edn (Cambridge, 1920), Part II, 28. I am indebted also to Amanda Goode, Emmanuel College Archivist.
[45] For Clarence Hatry (1888–1965), company promoter and financier, sentenced to fourteen years' penal servitude for fraud in January 1930, see *ODNB*.
[46] There is a mural tablet to her memory in Wickhambrook Congregational (now United Reformed) Church.

Mondisfield years before by cousin Elfie Burges;[47] so was Amelia, the only sister to marry. Her husband bought Badmondisfield Hall after the crash. His family too were Suffolk Congregationalists but from a lower drawer: it was a descent which rankled.[48]

The fallen Warner-Bromley had two sons, also at The Leys, also distinguished by their given names – Robarts Nathaniel Warner and Frederick Fairfax Warner. They became automobile engineers in Coventry; Frederick called his house in Baginton Road 'Mondisfield'.[49]

What would Edna Lyall have made of that? George A. Payne, the first of her two immediately posthumous biographers, was a Unitarian minister in Knutsford.[50] He readily admitted that she was no Eliot, Brontë or Gaskell – he could hardly do otherwise – but he saw in her 'one of the teachers of our day, who has done a great deal in softening bitterness and prejudice, and in broadening the minds of narrow and small-souled people'.[51] That is an accurate judgement. It sounds modest but it masks a considerable achievement. Today she is forgotten but the present writer's Congregational mother and grandmother and his Anglican aunt were devotees of her books, and it might be noted that a founder member and past president of the Ecclesiastical History Society also admitted to having read Edna Lyall in his boyhood.[52] He was Geoffrey Nuttall (1911–2007).[53] *In the Golden Days* played its part in the formation of a leading twentieth-century historian of seventeenth-century Dissent and, by extension, in the formation of this society.

University of Sheffield

---

[47] Lyall, *Burges Letters*, 117–18, 128–9.

[48] According to Jessie Ridge.

[49] *Handbook and Directory of The Leys School*, 14th edn (Cambridge, 1948), 37.

[50] For George A. Payne (1865–1950), minister at Knutsford 1890–1930 and Gaskell enthusiast, see *The Inquirer*, 4 March 1950, 78.

[51] Payne, *Edna Lyall*, 8.

[52] Geoffrey F. Nuttall to Clyde Binfield, 20 October 1988.

[53] Colin Richards, ed., *Geoffrey Fillingham Nuttall 1911–2007* (Prestatyn, 2008).

'PULP METHODISM' REVISITED: THE LITERATURE AND SIGNIFICANCE OF SILAS AND JOSEPH HOCKING

by MARTIN WELLINGS

Writing pseudonymously in the *New Age* in February 1909, Arnold Bennett, acerbic chronicler of Edwardian chapel culture, deplored the lack of proper bookshops in English provincial towns. A substantial manufacturing community, he claimed, might be served only by a stationer's shop, offering 'Tennyson in gilt. Volumes of the Temple Classics or Everyman. Hymn books, Bibles. The latest cheap Shakespeare. Of new books no example, except the brothers Hocking.'[1] Bennett's lament was an unintended compliment to the ubiquity of the novels of Silas and Joseph Hocking, brothers whose literary careers spanned more than half a century, generating almost two hundred novels and innumerable serials and short stories.[2] Silas Hocking (1850–1935), whose first book was published in 1878 and last in 1934, has been described as the most popular novelist of the late nineteenth century.[3] By 1900 his sales already exceeded one million volumes.[4] The career of Joseph Hocking (1860–1937) was slightly shorter, stretching from 1887 to 1936, but his output was equally impressive. The Hockings' works have attracted interest principally among scholars of Cornish life and culture.[5] It will be argued here, however, that they have significance for the history of

---

[1] Arnold Bennett, 'The Potential Public', in idem, *Books and Persons: Being Comments on a Past Epoch, 1908–1911* (London, 1917), 101–8, at 103. The article first appeared on 18 February 1909, signed 'Jacob Tonson'.

[2] *ODNB, s.n.* 'Hocking, Silas Kitto (1850–1935)', online at <http://oxforddnb. com/view/article/33912>, accessed 18 August 2009. This article seriously underestimates the output of the brothers, for which see Alan M. Kent, *Pulp Methodism: The Lives and Literature of Silas, Joseph and Salome Hocking. Three Cornish Novelists* (St Austell, 2002), 221–6. There are brief biographical articles in John Sutherland, *The Longman Companion to Victorian Fiction* (Harlow, 1988), 301.

[3] D. W. Bebbington, *Evangelicalism in Modern Britain: A History from the 1730s to the 1980s* (London, 1989), 131.

[4] Indicated in endpaper advertisements in, e.g., S. K. Hocking, *The Strange Adventures of Israel Pendray* (London, 1899). Some sources (e.g. *ODNB*) suggest that a single title sold a million copies, but this is not supported by the contemporary catalogues.

[5] Kent, *Pulp Methodism*, 11–25; Charles Thomas, 'Methodism in Cornish Litera-

late Victorian and Edwardian Nonconformity, both reflecting and reinforcing the attitudes, beliefs and prejudices of their large and appreciative readership.

The Hockings were born in Cornwall, and both entered the ministry of the United Methodist Free Churches (UMFC), one of the products of the mid nineteenth-century convulsions in the Wesleyan Methodist Connexion.[6] Silas became a UMFC minister in 1869, serving in a succession of appointments in major northern towns. Like a number of his fictional heroes, Silas began writing stories for newspapers and magazines before producing his first novel, *Alec Green: A Tale of Sea Life*, in 1878. This story, serialized in the *Burnley Advertiser* and taken up by the publisher Frederick Warne, was only a modest success. The following year, however, *Her Benny*, a tale of a Liverpool street arab, published first in the *UMFC Magazine* and then by Warne, became a best-seller.[7] *Her Benny* made Silas's name, and thereafter he produced one or two novels almost every year for the next four decades. Silas gained increasing celebrity, and was in much demand as a guest preacher and lecturer. In 1896 he resigned from the ministry, although he continued to preach regularly. A staunch opponent of the Boer War, he stood unsuccessfully for Parliament in 1906 and 1910.[8] By the time of his death in September 1935 Silas had written some ninety-six novels and earned over £60,000 from his literary endeavours.[9]

Joseph Hocking, ten years younger than his brother, followed him into the ministry of the UMFC, training at Victoria Park College, Manchester, from 1881 and serving circuits in Leicestershire, London and Lancashire.[10] Like Silas, Joseph began with short stories and serials, and his first novels, *Harry Penhale: The Trial of His Faith* and *Gideon Strong: Plebeian*, were published by the UMFC Bookroom in 1887 and 1888 respectively. A travel book,

ture', in Sarah Foot, ed., *Methodist Celebration: A Cornish Contribution* (Redruth, 1988), 52–6.

[6] Oliver A. Beckerlegge, *The United Methodist Free Churches: A Study in Freedom* (London, 1957), remains the only history of the UMFC.

[7] Kent, *Pulp Methodism*, 66–8; Silas K. Hocking, *My Book of Memory* (London, 1923), 69–70, 78–83.

[8] Kent, *Pulp Methodism*, 72, 77–80; Hocking, *Book of Memory*, 163–90.

[9] Kent, *Pulp Methodism*, 87.

[10] Ibid. 99–103.

From London to Damascus, followed in 1889, and this enabled Joseph to begin a fruitful relationship with Ward, Lock and Company. *Jabez Easterbrook: A Religious Novel*, published in 1890, brought Joseph popular and commercial success. He matched his brother's output, writing ninety-four novels between 1887 and 1936. Like Silas, Joseph retired from the ministry in middle age; unlike his brother, Joseph adopted a strong pro-war stance during the 1914–18 conflict.[11]

In seeking to explain the phenomenal success of the Hocking brothers, several points need to be borne in mind. First, they took up the writing of popular fiction at a time when the British reading public was expanding, when the novel reigned supreme as a literary vehicle, and when the publishing industry was geared to the mass production of cheap fiction. During the second half of the nineteenth century the population increased considerably, with England and Wales alone growing from 17.9 million people in 1851 to 36 million in 1911.[12] This expansion was matched by a drive to improve levels of literacy, first by voluntary societies, then by the pressure of government grants and inspection, and finally (from 1870) by legislation to facilitate the building of schools and gradually to encourage and then to compel attendance.[13] In 1870 adult literacy stood at an estimated 80% of men and 70% of women; by 1913 less than 1% of the population was functionally illiterate.[14] Adding the burgeoning American and colonial markets, it has been suggested that between 1830 and 1890 the reading public for books published in English mushroomed from 50,000 to 120 million people.[15] This growing readership was eager for novels. Anthony Trollope, a beneficiary of this trend, observed in 1870: 'We have become a novel-reading people.'[16] More than 40,000 novels were published during Queen Victoria's reign,[17] and, with expanding markets and developments in printing technology, the price of

---

[11] Ibid. 109, 170.
[12] P. J. Waller, *Town, City and Nation: England 1850–1914* (Oxford, 1983), 7.
[13] E. J. Feuchtwanger, *Democracy and Empire: Britain 1865–1914* (London, 1989), 14–15.
[14] Waller, *Town, City and Nation*, 268–9; David Vincent, *Literacy and Popular Culture: England 1750–1914* (Cambridge, 1989), 4.
[15] J. A. Sutherland, *Victorian Novelists and Publishers* (Chicago, IL, 1976), 64.
[16] Philip Davis, *The Victorians* (Oxford, 2002), 226.
[17] Ibid. 223.

books fell dramatically. In the 1840s a penny would purchase a 250-word broadside. By the 1880s the same sum would buy a 20,000-word novelette, and through the 1890s and early 1900s enterprising publishers established Penny Libraries to supply cheap editions of classic works.[18] The hitherto dominant form of the three-decker thirty-one-shilling novel fell into disfavour in the last decade of the century: finally embargoed by the powerful circulating libraries in 1894, it was replaced by single-volume works priced at six shillings.[19] Hocking titles typically retailed at a more modest three shillings and sixpence in book form, but they were also accessible even more cheaply as serial publications in newspapers and magazines.

Secondly, the rise in the general reading public was matched by a growing constituency of literate Nonconformists. All the major Nonconformist denominations increased in membership in the last third of the nineteenth century, with about a million members in the Baptist, Congregational, Wesleyan and Primitive Methodist Churches by 1901.[20] Bearing in mind that chapel communities typically represented four times the official membership, clearly Nonconformists comprised a significant segment of the British reading public. As important for the success of the Hockings as the numerical growth of Nonconformity, however, was its evolving attitude to novels and novel-reading.

In *Methodism Divided* Robert Currie argues that the second half of the nineteenth century witnessed a gradual process of cultural accommodation, as behaviour and practices previously regarded as 'worldly' by Methodists were permitted or even endorsed. Currie cites novel-reading as an example of this process, finding evidence of changing attitudes particularly in the 1870s, as Silas Hocking began writing fiction.[21] A similar case is made for Nonconformity in general by Richard Helmstadter, who dates the erosion of a distinctive Nonconformist culture to the mid 1880s and cites the reading and writing of novels by ministers as an indication of

---

[18] Vincent, *Literacy and Popular Culture*, 211; Jonathan Rose, *The Intellectual Life of the British Working Classes* (New Haven, CT, 2002), 132–6.

[19] Sutherland, *Longman Companion*, 2.

[20] James Munson, *The Nonconformists: In Search of a Lost Culture* (London, 1991), 10–11.

[21] Robert Currie, *Methodism Divided: A Study in the Sociology of Ecumenicalism* (London, 1968), 133–6.

'assimilation into the mainstream of English society'.[22] At first sight, the Hockings and United Methodism may stand as an example of this trend. Salome Hocking, sister of Silas and Joseph, recalled a local preacher denouncing novel-reading 'as a special sin to be shunned', while her father James was dismayed when Silas published a novel.[23] After the serialization of *Alec Green* Silas found his congregation in Burnley divided over his new-found fame, and one member of the church was so unused to fiction that he assumed Alec Green must be a real person, and suggested inviting this interesting character to give a public lecture on his adventures.[24] Against this anxiety, antagonism and plain incomprehension may be set the publication of stories, serials and reviews in the *UMFC Magazine* through the 1880s, and the issuing of Joseph Hocking's first novels from the denominational press. By the 1890s the *Magazine* had been redesigned, with fiction as a significant element of its contents and with full-page advertisements for novels, penny stories, fiction-based 'reward books' for Sunday schools, and even a 'service of song' built around *Her Benny*.[25]

The picture of Nonconformity's slide into cultural accommodation through the acceptance of novels, however, needs to be qualified. Silas Hocking wryly reminded the anxious editor of the *UMFC Magazine* that even denominational obituary notices often employed the skills of creative writing; less provocatively, E. E. Kellett recalled 'a large and fascinating literature' of historical and missionary biographies, rivalling adventure stories in their narrative appeal. Allegory was familiar through the works of Bunyan, and there was an extensive subculture of edifying tracts and moral stories for children which were acceptable even to the most strait-laced among the devout.[26] Moreover, Methodists and Noncon-

---

[22] R. J. Helmstadter, 'The Nonconformist Conscience', in Gerald Parsons, ed., *Religion in Victorian Britain*, 4: *Interpretations* (Manchester, 1988), 61–95, at 87.

[23] Salome Hocking, *Some Old Cornish Folk* (London, 1903), 175–6; Kent, *Pulp Methodism*, 67.

[24] Hocking, *Book of Memory*, 71–2.

[25] The *Magazine* was renamed *The Methodist Monthly* in 1892; see April 1894 endpapers for an advertisement for the 'service of song', a sequence of songs and readings designed for an informal or midweek service.

[26] Hocking, *Book of Memory*, 81; E. E. Kellett, *As I Remember* (London, 1936), 117–18. On missionary biographies, see, in this volume, Benjamin Fischer, 'A Novel Resistance: Mission Narrative as the Anti-Novel in the Evangelical Assault on British Culture', 232–45. On children's literature, see Margaret Nancy Cutt, *Ministering Angels:*

formists were reading fiction proper well before the 1870s.[27] Wesleyan Methodist masters at Woodhouse Grove School read Dickens's *Pickwick Papers* as the serial parts were issued; Benjamin Gregory found his circuit steward in Ilkeston in 1841 to be 'the literary oracle' of the town, an avid reader of Scott and 'a devotee of modern English literature'; and Gregory's precocious son Alfred owed his spiritual development in the early 1860s to the inspiring example of Esther Sommerson in *Bleak House*.[28] While some Nonconformists had little time to read and little taste for fiction, others read widely, bringing theological reflection to their engagement with contemporary literature.

In 1872 the respected UMFC minister Joseph Kirsop published an article 'Concerning Works of Fiction' in the denominational *Magazine*.[29] Acknowledging that older Methodists would be surprised to see novelettes in the religious serials, Kirsop argued that the basic principles of Methodism had not changed. It was legitimate, he asserted, to use fiction for instruction and for recreation, but novels should be chosen carefully and read sparingly. It was 'incessant and indiscriminate novel-reading' that should be avoided.[30]

Rather than a model of cultural capitulation, or perhaps of emancipation from the restrictions of a world-denying piety, Kirsop's case for a discriminating approach to fiction reflects the position of many Nonconformists in the late nineteenth century. It is possible to analyse the appeal of the Hockings in terms of Kirsop's categories, and to consider their fiction as didactic, recreational and wholesome. Thus they met the needs of a market eager to read novels, but novels of the right sort.

In justifying their turn to fiction, Silas and Joseph Hocking

A Study of Nineteenth-Century Evangelical Writing for Children (Wormley, 1979); J. S. Bratton, *The Impact of Victorian Children's Fiction* (London, 1981).

[27] Valentine Cunningham, *Everywhere Spoken Against: Dissent in the Victorian Novel* (Oxford, 1975), 56–61.

[28] Benjamin Gregory, *Autobiographical Recollections* (London, 1903), 235, 272, 280; Benjamin Gregory, *Consecrated Culture: Memorials of Benjamin Alfred Gregory* (London, 1885), 17.

[29] O. A. B[eckerlegge]., 'Kirsop, Joseph (1825–1911)', in John A. Vickers, ed., *A Dictionary of Methodism in Britain and Ireland* (Peterborough, 2000), 194. Kirsop was elected President of the UMFC Annual Assembly in 1875.

[30] Joseph Kirsop, 'Concerning Works of Fiction', *UMFC Magazine* 15 (1872), 103–12, quotation at 104.

made much of the potential of the novel as a vehicle for religious teaching. Writing in the *Methodist Monthly* in October 1894, Joseph described the novel as 'one of the best means for communicating knowledge to the popular mind'. Contrasting the readership of *Robert Elsmere* with that of A. M. Fairbairn's *The Place of Christ in Modern Theology*, Joseph claimed that '[t]he work of the story-teller, rightly understood, is more effective to teach than that of the teacher at his desk, and not less sacred than that of the divine in the pulpit.'[31]

Hocking fiction certainly contained a strong didactic element, captured by John Sutherland as 'a tendency towards preachiness'.[32] *Jabez Easterbrook*, Joseph's answer to *Robert Elsmere*, was summarized by a hostile reviewer thus: 'a sturdy young Wesleyan minister encounters a fascinating young lady of agnostic tendencies. They argue throughout the tedious length of the novel.'[33] Theological debate, signalled by representative stereotypical characters and carried on through ponderous dialogue, was a Hocking staple, whether in the battle between traditional orthodoxy and 'modern thought' in Silas Hocking's *Where Duty Lies* (1895) or in controversy between Protestants and Catholics in Joseph's *The Scarlet Woman* (1899), *The Purple Robe* (1900), *The Woman of Babylon* (1906) and *The Soul of Dominic Wildthorne* (1908). Setting some of his scenes in Rome allowed Joseph to recycle descriptive material about the Eternal City published elsewhere, while placing Protestant polemic into the mouths of his characters.[34]

The Roman Catholic Church as an institution seldom fared well in the Hocking corpus, with Joseph in particular attacking its theology and spirituality; the sinister Jesuit Father Anthony Ritzoom was one of Joseph's most memorable villains.[35] Although the brothers were nurtured in Methodism, the Free Churches were not immune from criticism: witness, for example, the callous leaders of the Trevisco chapel in *Where Duty Lies*, who seek to

---

[31] Joseph Hocking, 'Novels and Novel Writers', *Methodist Monthly*, October 1894, 304–5.

[32] Sutherland, *Longman Companion*, 301.

[33] Ibid.

[34] Compare the descriptive passages in *The Purple Robe* with Joseph's articles: 'A Protestant Pilgrimage to Rome', *The Puritan*, April 1899, 183–6; May 1899, 312–15.

[35] On the portrayal of Jesuits as villains, see, in this volume, John Wolffe, 'The Jesuit as Villain in Nineteenth-Century British Fiction', 308–20.

exploit the death of three young fishermen to foment a revival. In their fiction as in their careers in ministry, both Silas and Joseph Hocking increasingly turned away from conservative dogmatism, and sought to promote practical charity over ecclesiastical order.

Fiction could only be educationally effective if it was also entertaining and therefore appealing to an audience. Judging by the notices in the press, their longevity and their remarkable sales figures, the Hockings succeeded in reaching a large readership in search of respectable recreational fiction. Reviewing *The Day of Recompense* in August 1899, *The Puritan* commented of Silas Hocking: 'Mr Hocking understands the taste of his vast public to a nicety'. Six months earlier, the same journal noted of the brothers that 'each has a distinct style of his own, and there is little in their books to denote the relationship the authors bear to one another'.[36] It may be agreed that their *oeuvre* had some variety: Silas's early novels included examples of waif fiction, for instance, whereas Joseph wrote more historical novels than his brother; Silas tackled the moral issues of the Boer War from an anti-war stand-point in works which struggled to find a publisher, while Joseph wrote popular patriotic fiction during the Great War; Silas gradually moved away from the explicit Methodism of his early works, while Joseph set one of his last novels (somewhat improbably) against the background of the Methodist reunion of 1932.[37] There were some experimental works, such as *The Strange Adventures of Israel Pendray*, in which Silas touched on Gothic themes of ghosts and witches. More typical of both brothers, however, was a contempo-rary setting, often in Cornwall, the industrial North or the Home Counties, with characters close to the life experience, aspirations or fantasies of a lower-middle-class readership: the dutiful son of a widowed mother, struggling to run a small shop while writing his first novel and simultaneously wooing the squire's daughter, was a standard Hocking hero, reflecting familiar experiences of financial hardship, untimely bereavement and limited opportuni-ties, leavened by dreams of romance, fame and fortune. Whatever

---

[36] 'Books and Their Writers', *The Puritan*, August 1899, 586; Howard Cameron, 'Free Church Links with Literature', *The Puritan*, February 1899, 13.

[37] Joseph Hocking, *Not One in Ten* (1933), for which see Kent, *Pulp Methodism*, 174–5. The cover design showed the heroine watching the celebration of Methodist Union at the Royal Albert Hall.

the setting, whether contemporary or historical, there was a strong element of adventure, with the marks of the serial story's end-of-episode cliff-hanger still visible in most chapters. Every novel had clearly identifiable heroes, heroines and villains, a couple of romantic plots and a satisfactorily tidy and comprehensive denouement, in which innocence was vindicated, virtue rewarded and vice exposed and duly punished.

Contemporary opinions varied on the quality of the Hockings' fiction. The *Free Methodist* called Silas 'a prince of story-tellers' and the *Bristol Mercury* described him as 'a master of his craft'.[38] Reviewing Joseph's *Ishmael Pengelly* in April 1894 the *Methodist Monthly* enthused that 'without any perceptible effort, Mr Hocking rises superior to the mere story-teller, and gives evidence of the novel-writer of remarkable power'. The reviewer was anxious, however, that there was a risk of overwork: in order to produce a great book, Joseph should 'curb his labour by patience' and resist the temptation to write too much. As if in rebuke to this warning, two months later two more of Joseph's novels were reviewed – favourably – in the same journal.[39] Silas, too, drew critical reviews for over-production. An anonymous reviewer in *The Puritan* for July 1900 described *When Life is Young* as 'the kind of thing Mr Hocking has accustomed his readers to expect – even more so', counselling Silas 'against the results of a more rapid production of books than the author's creative ability warrants'. 'Life must be very young indeed,' concluded the review tartly, 'to find anything stimulating or satisfying in the book entitled *When Life is Young*.'[40]

Even those who were reluctant to praise the Hockings for their creativity or literary merit agreed that their novels were respectable. 'Wholesome' was the adjective most frequently deployed to describe their works, and it was reported that only Campbell-Bannerman's death deprived Silas of an honour in recognition of his services in 'providing healthy fiction for the young people of this country'.[41] James Britten, the Roman Catholic controversialist who lambasted Joseph for the inaccuracies in his polemical Protes-

[38] Endpapers of *The Quenchless Fire* (1911) and *The Strange Adventures of Israel Pendray* (1899).

[39] *Methodist Monthly*, April 1894, 128; June 1894, 191.

[40] 'Books I have been Reading', *The Puritan*, July 1900, 588.

[41] 'Mr Silas K. Hocking: Moral Purpose in Fiction', *The Times*, 16 September 1935, 14.

tant novels, conceded that he avoided the 'filthy fictions' of popular anti-Catholicism.[42] Hocking plots involved manly heroes, chaste heroines, decorous romantic encounters, exemplary characters able to resist the temptation to behave meanly or dishonourably, and an inevitably satisfactory moral resolution at the end of the book. There was perhaps some development over time, from an explicit, often Methodist, piety to an ethic of practical Christianity without denominationalism, but the tone of the books was always thoroughly respectable. The Hockings touched on contemporary issues, including crime and punishment (*Gripped*), slum housing (*Smoking Flax*), intemperance (*Alec Green*) and loveless marriage (*The Quenchless Fire*), but without adopting the approach of the 'problem novel', with its exploration or exploitation of the grey areas of morality. This made Hocking fiction less profound and more predictable, and also commercially more successful.

Although three of Joseph's novels were still in print in the late 1950s as part of Ward, Lock's 'master novelist' series, the Hockings had passed their heyday twenty or thirty years earlier. Their obituaries in 1935 and 1937 spoke of 'novels of the simple old-fashioned type' and suggested that *Her Benny* was Silas's greatest success.[43] To recognize, as James Munson does, that Hocking novels 'are now mainly collected for their colourful bindings',[44] however, is not to underestimate their influence and representative significance in the world of late Victorian and Edwardian Nonconformity, as evidenced by their commercial success. Three concluding observations may be offered.

Firstly, the Hockings may be located in a wider group of Nonconformist and Methodist writers of novels and popular fiction. Preceded by Mark Guy Pearse and James Jackson Wray, whose first novels appeared in the early 1870s, the brothers were followed by Ellen Thorneycroft Fowler and W. H. Fitchett, as well as by the lesser literary figures who supplied serial stories for the denominational newspapers and magazines. When Howard Cameron reviewed 'Free Church Links with Literature' in *The*

---

[42] James Britten, 'The Scarlet Woman', in J[oseph]. Keating, ed., *A Brace of Bigots (Dr Horton and Mr Hocking)* (London, 1909), 7. This volume is a collection of pamphlets with separate pagination, consisting mainly of articles reprinted from *The Month*.

[43] *The Times*, 16 September 1935, 14.

[44] Munson, *Nonconformists*, 230.

Puritan for February 1899, he concluded that the popular authors with Free Church antecedents were 'too numerous' to list.[45]

Secondly, the Hockings reflected the outlook and concerns of their faithful Nonconformist readership. Their contemporary stories were largely set in the world of the upwardly mobile or aspiring classes, well represented in the chapels of the period. If some protagonists achieved a higher social class, this was usually the result of hard work, professional success or an unexpected legacy. Miners and fishermen, small shopkeepers and journalists and even provincial solicitors might be Hocking heroes, but not the landed gentry and their admirers, nor usually prosperous farmers. Free Church ministers were generally well regarded, and so were some of the clergy of the Church of England, provided they were open-minded, generous and manly, and free from sacerdotal pretensions. The ideal of Englishness expressed in such characters was echoed too in Joseph's Protestant and historical novels. The underlying ethic endorsed by the Hockings was one of earnest endeavour, honour and honesty, thrift and generosity, courage and sobriety, with a respect for the Sabbath, a horror of alcohol and a preference for practical Christian charity over dogma.

Thirdly, the novels supplied some evidence of the changing place and outlook of Nonconformity across two or three generations. There were strictures against narrow or judgemental theologies and against Christians reluctant to assimilate 'modern thought'. Even if the prosperous lifestyle of the Hockings' protagonists was only an aspiration for their readers, the fiction implicitly endorsed such ambitions. The constituency reflected in the novels became less of a 'peculiar people', identified by its own subculture and shibboleths, and it may be asked whether this indicated a broadening of Nonconformity or an attempt by the brothers to reach a new readership.

Historians are familiar with the often hostile portrayal of Nonconformity in the classical fiction of the nineteenth century. The work of the 'brothers Hocking', among others, shows that there is more to be made of this relationship than might be deduced from a concentration on Dickens, Trollope and Hardy, or even on Mrs Gaskell, George Eliot and Mark Rutherford. Nonconformists were not only consumers of fiction, but also producers; not only

---

[45] Cameron, 'Free Church Links with Literature', 12.

targets of popular culture, but also discriminating critics, able to deploy the print media to serve their own purposes. In so doing, of course, Nonconformity was itself shaped, influenced and changed by its ventures into popular fiction.

Oxford

SOME POPES IN ENGLISH LITERATURE
c.1850–1950

by BERNARD HAMILTON

In 1850 the Roman Catholic hierarchy was re-established in England. Although this caused widespread resentment, one consequence was, as its critics had feared, that the pope once again became a part of English social and religious life. This change was reflected in English creative writing during the next hundred years. Here and throughout this essay I use the term English rather than British advisedly, because different conditions obtained in other parts of the United Kingdom. This essay will examine how five writers with widely different viewpoints represented the pope, and will consider how their work may reflect attitudes to the papacy among the reading public.

The first work to be considered is Robert Browning's poem *The Ring and the Book*, published in 1868–9.[1] It is based on a historical event, the trial of Count Guido Franceschini and four accomplices in 1698 for the murder of his wife Pompilia and her adoptive parents. Guido and his accomplices were apprehended and sentenced to death, but Guido entered a plea of *crime passionnelle*, claiming that his wife had been unfaithful and that in killing her he was avenging his honour. An English court would not have accepted this defence, but it was sometimes, until quite recently, used successfully in Italian law. This was the story told in the book of the poem's title, a collection of printed documents relating to the trial, which Browning had found on a Florentine second-hand bookstall. The ring of the title is the art by which the poet transmuted those historical facts into a living drama. The poem is written in blank verse, it is divided into twelve books, and Book Ten, which is more than two thousand lines long, is entitled 'The Pope'.[2] The pope in question is Innocent XII (1691–1700). As temporal ruler of the Papal States he is the final court of appeal

---

[1]   It was first published in four volumes, one a month between November 1868 and February 1869.

[2]   'The Ring and the Book', in *The Poetical Works of Robert Browning*, 2 vols (London, 1896), 2: 1–291.

in matters of justice. He is very conscious of the responsibility this confers on him, for he is eighty-six years old and is aware that at any time he might be called before the tribunal of God. Each day he reads part of the official history of the papacy, and when we are introduced to him he is pondering what is probably the most discreditable episode in papal history, the trial in 897 of the dead Pope Formosus (891–6), whose corpse was arraigned in the Lateran basilica by Stephen VI (896–7).[3] Cardinal Baronius, in his magisterial history of the Western Church, described this event and its sequel – when six popes held power in as many years, some of whom condoned Stephen VI's action while others condemned it, and most of whom met violent deaths – as the time when Christ was asleep in the ship of Peter.[4] Browning did not choose this example of the exercise of papal authority at random, but used it as a critique of the high view obtaining in his own day in the Roman Church of the powers of the pope as Vicar of Christ. His pope, Innocent XII, is led to ask about the popes who had given diametrically opposed rulings in the Formosan controversy: 'which of my predecessors spoke for God?'[5]

The portrait of Innocent XII which Browning gives is far from polemical. The pope is concerned that justice should be done, but Browning uses a very striking image when describing Count Guido kneeling before him asking for mercy. He is

> just at the edge, over the awful dark,
> With nothing to arrest him but my feet ...[6]

Innocent reviews the people involved in the case, including the hired assassins, and weighs their moral motivation. He concludes that Guido's wife Pompilia, despite appearances, had not committed adultery, and that Guido had been inspired not (as he claimed) by anger at her unfaithfulness, but by avarice: his central concern had been to secure her dowry for himself. But Innocent also hears in

---

[3] Browning would probably have known about this from F. Gregorovius, *Geschichte der Stadt Rom im Mittelalter bis zum XV Jahrhundert*, 8 vols (Stuttgart, 1859–73); ET Annie Hamilton, *The City of Rome in the Middle Ages*, 8 vols in 13 parts (London, 1895), 3: 224–38.

[4] C. Baronius, *Annales Ecclesiastici*, ed. J. D. Mansi and D. Georgius, 38 vols (Lucca, 1738–59), 15: 571.

[5] Browning, 'The Ring and the Book', bk 10, line 152.

[6] Ibid., lines 175–6.

his mind the very different voice of Roman public opinion, saying that because Guido is a nobleman he should not be treated like a common criminal; and arguing that if Innocent ordered the execution of a man whose only crime had been to kill his adulterous wife, he would be undermining family values, because other wives might think that they could be unfaithful with impunity. The pope is not swayed by these appeals to human respect. He concludes:

Enough, for I may die this very night;
And how should I dare die, this man let live.[7]

He therefore sends to the prison governor and orders Guido's execution.

When Browning wrote this poem he was not simply describing an antiquarian situation. In 1869 Pius IX was still a temporal ruler with sovereign powers, just as Innocent XII had been. This was undoubtedly a matter of concern to some of Browning's English readers. That situation changed in 1870 when the Papal States were forcibly united to the rest of Italy. No violence was offered to the pope, but he was stripped of his temporal sovereignty. Pius IX and his immediate successors did not, however, renounce their claims to that sovereignty, but shut themselves in the Vatican Palace and refused to acknowledge the legitimacy of Italian rule in the city of Rome and the former States of the Church. Pius IX had excommunicated all those who in whatever way cooperated with the new government, and that, of course, included those who took part in elections.[8] This had political and diplomatic consequences which the popes did not, perhaps, fully anticipate. *Whitaker's Almanack* for that period, when giving information about foreign countries, lists Italy and then appends an afternote (I cite the 1900 edition): 'Rome: Sovereign Pontiff Leo XIII, elected 20 February 1878, Secretary of State to His Holiness, the Cardinal Rampallo del Tindaro, appointed 1887.'[9] Nothing more is recorded. The papacy had ceased to be a sovereign world power.

This loss of diplomatic status was seen by some liberal humanist thinkers as evidence that the Roman Catholic Church as a whole was fading. Among them was Richard Garnett, superintendent of

7   Ibid., lines 2133–5.
8   *Pii Noni Papae Acta*, 9 vols (Rome, 1854–78), 3: 137–47.
9   *An Almanack for the Year of Our Lord 1900* (London, 1899), 567.

the British Museum Reading Room from 1875 to 1884, and chief editor of the British Museum Library's first printed catalogue.[10] In 1888 he published a collection of short stories entitled *The Twilight of the Gods.* Two of them are about the papacy, and their inclusion in this collection, along with stories about the Greco-Roman pantheon, though no doubt showing some element of wishful thinking, suggests that in Garnett's view the contemporary papacy also had fallen into decline. One of them, entitled *Alexander the Ratcatcher,* relates to the brief pontificate of Alexander VIII (1689–91).[11] It begins by describing how Rome is suffering from a plague of rats who are immune to any normal treatment such as poison. The pope pronounces a liturgical curse against them, but it has no effect, and he appoints Cardinal Barbadico to take charge of the city and to deal with the practical problems which the rats are causing there. While carrying out these duties the cardinal meets an old man dressed in rat skins, who has a remarkably educated voice. He says that he can rid the city of rats, but that he will only do so if the pope agrees to meet him alone, at midnight, in the Borgia apartments of the Vatican Palace. In desperation, the pope accepts those conditions, and when they meet the Ratcatcher reveals that he is Alexander VI, the Borgia pope. He is now a member of Lucifer's kingdom, he tells Alexander VIII, and has been appointed Ratcatcher by his Satanic Majesty, something which his Holiness should know about already because Rabelais has recorded it in his *Pantagruel.*[12] The rats infesting Rome were infernal rats, and that was why Alexander VIII's curse had had no effect on them. But Alexander VI is bored with hell, and he strikes an agreement with a reluctant Alexander VIII that he will send the rats back to Lucifer's kingdom if the pope will hold a public procession during which prayers will be offered that God will allow Alexander Borgia to enter heaven. This is done, and during the procession a great hole gapes open in the Borgo S. Pietro and the rats return to their infernal home. Richard Garnett concludes: 'It is not probable that Alexander passed, like Dante's sigh, "beyond

---

[10]   *ODNB, s.n.* 'Garnett, Richard (1835–1906)'.

[11]   R. Garnett, *The Twilight of the Gods and other Tales,* new edn (London, 1903), 156–76.

[12]   F. Rabelais, *Gargantua and Pantagruel, Pantagruel,* bk 1, ch. 30, ET with intro. by D. B. Wyndham Lewis, 2 vols (London, 1929), 2: 236.

the sphere that doth all spheres enfold", but, as he was never again seen on earth, it is not doubted that he attained at least as far as the Moon.'[13] So Garnett pokes gentle fun at the papacy, an institution which, in his view, was fading into the twilight like the other mythologies of earlier ages.

The reaction of the English Roman Catholic community to the retirement of the popes into the Vatican Palace was rather different. Whereas under the leadership of Cardinal Vaughan the Roman Catholic Church in England was flourishing, a success symbolized by the building of Westminster Cathedral, the head of that Church remained in diplomatic limbo.[14] The sense of frustration which this produced is reflected in Frederick William Rolfe's novel, *Hadrian VII*, published in 1904.[15] Rolfe, who styled himself Frederick Baron Corvo, was an adult convert to the Roman Church who had begun to train for the priesthood but had been rejected as unsuitable by his religious superiors. He considered that their decision had been unjust, but he was unable to obtain redress and suffered from symptoms of advanced paranoia, which made him very difficult to befriend.[16] His novel begins as a thinly disguised autobiography. His hero, George Arthur Rose, is a very devout young man who is refused ordination by his superiors, but, unlike Rolfe's own superiors, Rose's admit after some years that they have done him a dreadful injustice. He is not only ordained priest, but is present as a chaplain in the English delegation which attends a papal conclave. The cardinals are deadlocked about the choice of a new pope and, improbably, decide to elect George Arthur Rose as pontiff. As he is the first Englishman since Nicholas Breakspear, Hadrian IV (1154–9), to become pope, he takes the name Hadrian VII. As might be expected in a story by a man with Rolfe's temperament, the new pope uses his authority to settle old scores: he radically reforms the seminary system, for example, explaining in detail to the rectors of colleges why this is necessary, and he gives a severe and specific reprimand to the General of the Jesuit Order. But some of Hadrian's acts are directed to improving the public image of the papacy. At the beginning of his reign he opens

13 Garnett, *Twilight*, 176.
14 P. Rogers, *Westminster Cathedral: From Darkness to Light* (London, 2003).
15 Fr.[*sic*] Rolfe, *Hadrian VII, a Romance* (London, 1904).
16 A. J. A. Symons, *The Quest for Corvo* (London, 1934).

negotiations with the government of Italy, offering to renounce his claims to temporal jurisdiction if the king will allow him to move freely around the city of Rome of which he is bishop. This permission is readily granted, and Hadrian spends much of his time going through Rome in procession and celebrating mass in its many churches. He also arranges that the treasures of the Vatican should be sold and the proceeds given to the poor of the world. The book ends when, during one of his progresses through Rome, Hadrian is shot by a maverick socialist, which makes him appear a martyr for the faith. *Hadrian VII* was published a year after the conclave which elected Pius X:[17] in part it is a work of personal wish-fulfilment, but in part it is an expression of the exasperation felt by some lay Roman Catholics in England that yet another pontificate had begun without any attempt having been made to reach an agreement with the Italian state so that the pope could once again take a proactive part in world affairs.

This had still not happened over twenty years later when Ronald Firbank wrote about the pope. Firbank had been received into the Roman Catholic Church while an undergraduate at Cambridge in 1907.[18] His novels did not receive much praise in his lifetime except from the Sitwells, but as Margaret Drabble has commented: 'His use of dialogue, his highly coloured fantasies and his intense concentration of language and image are now seen as truly innovative'.[19] This opinion is cited because his work appears to have influenced Muriel Spark: his portrait of the pope bears a strong resemblance to her characterization of the Abbess of Crewe.[20]

This pope appears in Firbank's last novel, *Concerning the Eccentricities of Cardinal Pirelli*, which was published in 1926, shortly after the author's death.[21] Cardinal Pirelli is archbishop of Clemenza, a fictional city in Andalusia. His life is scandalous, but what most distresses his critics is that he has baptized a puppy belonging to

---

[17] Pius X, elected 4 August 1903, consecrated 9 August 1903, died 29 August 1914.

[18] I. K. Fletcher, *Ronald Firbank, a Memoir* (London, 1930).

[19] M. Drabble, ed., *The Oxford Companion to English Literature,* 5th edn (Oxford, 1985), 351.

[20] M. Spark, *The Abbess of Crewe* (London, 1974).

[21] *Concerning the Eccentricities of Cardinal Pirelli,* in *The Complete Ronald Firbank* (London, 1961), 645–98. Firbank died in 1926, a few weeks before the novel was published.

a strong-minded Andalusian duchess; because of this act of sacrilege and heresy he is denounced to Rome. The pope, Tertius II, is an elderly man with an abundance of white curly hair. He is a Neapolitan by birth and loves the open air, but because, when Firbank was writing, no agreement had yet been reached with the Italian government, the only open air readily available to him was to be found in the Vatican gardens. These are quite extensive, but rise very steeply on the side of the Vatican hill behind St Peter's Basilica. Consequently, members of the curia, whose offices were all in the Vatican Palace, were forced to climb up the hill to the gardens when they wished to consult the pope. Tertius is shown walking in the gardens reading his breviary, accompanied by his pet squirrel, who jumps from bough to bough. We meet him at the point when a cardinal makes his way up the hill to tell him about the proceedings of a curial committee which has just met, and which has recommended that Cardinal Pirelli should be removed from office and degraded from holy orders. While the cardinal is haranguing him about this, Tertius's attention wanders: he reflects that the cardinal is inclined to gesture, and thinks 'how many miles his hands must have moved in the course of the sermons he has preached'. The pope will not give his assent to the cardinal's request that Pirelli should be disciplined. Instead, when the cardinal has finished speaking, the pope walks him to the top of a long flight of steps which leads to a courtyard in the Vatican Palace. Giving the prelate a blessing to signify that the audience is at an end, he adds, as the cardinal begins the long descent: 'It's a bore there being no lift'. Then, as he goes back into the gardens, he says to his squirrel: 'I often laugh when I'm alone.'[22]

The last work to be considered was written by Charles Williams. In his youth he had been influenced by the Golden Dawn, an esoteric movement which had W. B. Yeats among its members.[23] Williams later left this group and became an Anglo-Catholic and subsequently a friend of Tolkien and of C. S. Lewis, but his esoteric background continued to colour most of his creative writing. One of his central literary interests was the Matter of Britain, the Arthurian legends, and in particular those relating to the Holy

---

[22] Pope Tertius appears only in ch. 4 (pages 656–9 in this edition).
[23] James Webb, *The Flight from Reason* (London, 1971), 155–88.

Grail.[24] He published two collections of poems on this theme: *Taliessin through Logres* came out in 1938, and its sequel, *The Region of the Summer Stars*, in 1944, the year before the author's death.[25] The bard Taliessin, who is the voice of many of these poems, is named in a work incorporated in some manuscripts of the *Historia Britonum*, and is said to have lived in the late sixth century.[26] He therefore cannot have been a contemporary of Arthur, if Arthur existed, since according to the *Annales Cambriae* Arthur lived in the first half of the sixth century, but Williams was a poet, not a historian.[27]

Williams wrote about an imaginary world of late antiquity which bore some relation to the historical facts, and he set his very idiosyncratic interpretation of the Arthurian legends in that context. He described a Christian Roman Empire of the sixth century, ruled from Byzantium, which extended south to Jerusalem and the Holy Land, and west to Rome and Italy, and whose rulers were acknowledged as suzerains by the Christian kings of Francia and in Britain by the Celtic ruler Arthur, who had succeeded for a time in stemming the Anglo-Saxon advances. This empire was seen by Williams as an embodiment of right Christian secular order, and Logres, the kingdom of Arthur in Britain, had a crucial role to play because it was there that the Holy Grail, which Williams understood as a manifestation of God's presence among men, was preserved.[28] But because of human frailty this empire could not be sustained. In Logres, Launcelot, the king's closest friend and vassal, betrayed his trust by seducing the queen, while the king's nephew Mordred, driven by ambition, initiated a civil war in which Arthur died. In the following years the Grail was removed to the mystical city of Sarras, and the empire crumbled as

---

[24] G. Cavaliero, *Charles Williams: Poet of Theology* (London, 1983), 97–125.

[25] Charles Williams, *Taliessin Through Logres* and *The Region of the Summer Stars*, one-volume edn (London, 1952).

[26] Nennius, *Historia Britonum*, ch. 62. Chs 57–66 of this work are found only in two BL manuscripts: Harleian 3859 and Cotton Vespasian D.xxi: F. Lot, *Nennius et l'Historia Britonum: Étude critique suivi d'une édition des diverses versions de ce texte* (Paris, 1934), 74–5, 201.

[27] K. H. Jackson, 'The Arthur of History', in R. S. Loomis, ed., *Arthurian Literature in the Middle Ages* (Oxford, 1959), 1–11.

[28] Logres derives from Loegria, a term used by Geoffrey of Monmouth to signify the whole of England in pre-Roman times: *Historia Regum Britanniae*, bk 2, ch. 1.

it was attacked by pagan Saxons from the east and Saracens from the south.

The Region of the Southern Stars ends with a poem called 'The Prayers of the Pope',[29] whom Williams describes as 'the young pope ... Deodatus, Egyptian born'. This is a reference to Pope Adeodatus I (615–19), who came from Egypt, although nothing is known about his age at the time of his election.[30] William shows him praying in the church of St John Lateran before celebrating the Midnight Mass of Christmas. He is reflecting on the collapse of the Christian empire. Williams tells us: 'The Pope saw himself as a ruin of empire'.[31] The pope reflects not only on the political decline of the empire, but also on the revival of paganism and sorcery which this collapse has facilitated. But he goes on to reflect that when Christ harrowed hell he defeated evil for ever, and he comes to understand that the Mass of Christmas, which he then celebrates, is an expression of the true empire of God on earth, and is not subject to mutability as earthly empires are.

By the time Williams was writing this, the papacy had resolved its long dispute with the Italian government. In 1929, by the Lateran Treaty, Pope Pius XI recognized the Italian state and accepted that Rome was its capital. In return, the Italian state recognized not only the sovereign jurisdiction of the popes over the Vatican City but also, which was equally important, 'the sovereign independence of the Holy See in the international field'.[32] The papacy had become once again an independent power, though with minimal secular jurisdiction. The young Egyptian pope Deodatus about whom Williams wrote was a very different figure from Pius XII, in whose pontificate he was writing 'The Prayers of the Pope', but the Taliessin poems are not only a study of the place of Britain in sixth-century Europe, but also a meditation about the place of Christianity in a world at war. That the pope could be used as a symbol of the Church by an Anglican is an indication of changing religious perceptions, but it is arguable that the pope could not

29 Williams, *Region*, 50–61.
30 L. Duchesne and C. Vögel, eds, *Le Liber Pontificalis de l'Église romaine*, 3 vols (Paris, 1955–7), I: 324.
31 Williams, *Region*, 54.
32 *Acta Apostolicae Sedis* 21 (1929), 209–74.

have been used as a symbol in this way unless the Vatican City had been seen to be an independent sovereign state.

The changes of fortune in the history of the papacy during the century which followed the restoration of the English hierarchy were mirrored in the writings of English poets and novelists. Although some of the works discussed here describe the papacy in critical, satirical or (in the case of Firbank) frivolous terms, none of them is polemical. This is surprising, since Pius IX, by publishing the *Syllabus of Errors* in 1864 and promulgating the doctrine of papal infallibility in 1870, challenged the values of contemporary society and accentuated the doctrinal division between the Roman Catholic and Protestant Churches; while this intransigence was maintained by his successor, Leo XIII, who in his bull *Apostolicae Curae* of 1896 declared that Anglican orders were totally invalid. These measures certainly produced a good deal of anti-papal theological polemic in England in the period under discussion, but this did not seem to affect the way in which poets and novelists wrote about the popes or the way in which most of their readers reacted to their work: they did not view popes with hostility, but rather with indifference. Henrietta Darwin, Charles Darwin's daughter, when discussing Roman Catholicism with her niece, Gwen Raverat, said: 'I could swallow the Pope of Rome, but what I cannot swallow is the celibacy of the clergy.'[33] I suspect that this attitude was not uncommon among lay people and that it reflected the way in which they experienced Roman Catholicism. As a result of Catholic emancipation in 1829 and the restoration of the hierarchy in 1850, Roman Catholics in England had increased in numbers and had a far higher social profile than at any time since the seventeenth century, while for much of the time with which this paper is dealing the popes had withdrawn into the Vatican Palace and had ceased to be an overt force in world politics.

This situation changed in two ways after the First World War. First, High Church Anglicans became aware that Roman Catholic opinion was more diverse than official Vatican pronouncements suggested. At the Malines conversations between Anglicans and Roman Catholics held under the patronage of Cardinal Mercier for several years from 1921, the possibility of union between the

---

33   Gwen Raverat, *Period Piece: A Cambridge Childhood* (London, 1952), 133–4.

two communions was considered and the role of the papacy in a united Church was openly discussed.[34] Charles Williams's attitude was certainly influenced by those discussions. On the other hand, the Lateran Treaty of 1929 which restored the Holy See to an active role in world affairs also led to its becoming identified with the ultra-conservative and fascist powers in Europe by many British people who held left-wing and even centre-left political views. Nevertheless, the theologically aware and the politically committed only formed part of the general readership of the works which I have been discussing, for many of whom the local Roman Catholic community was a familiar presence while the pope remained a distant figure.

University of Nottingham

---

[34] J. de Bivort de la Saudée, *Anglicans et Catholiques*, 2 vols (Brussels, 1949).

JESUIT PULP FICTION: THE SERIAL NOVELS OF ANTONIO BRESCIANI IN *LA CIVILTÀ CATTOLICA*

by OLIVER LOGAN

The successful and highly authoritative Jesuit opinion-journal *La Civiltà Cattolica* was founded in 1850 to assert Catholic values in the face of 'the Revolution', an allegedly nefarious process that had begun with the Revolution of 1789 and was seen by the Jesuit writers as continuing with the 1848 revolution in Italy and the ongoing Risorgimento movement; this called the temporal power of the papacy into question and also entailed wider issues of secularization. For these writers, the periodical press was a dangerous new force and the only way to combat it effectively was on its own ground.[1] The serial novels which ran in the fortnightly journal from 1850 until 1927 were evidently written in the belief that the devil should not be left with all the most gripping yarns. The dangers to morality posed by romantic novels were constantly emphasized in the journal's own fiction.[2] The dominant tone of this fiction was polemical. The villains represented the forces of Jacobinism, the secret societies of the early Risorgimento, and Freemasonry. Conspiracy was a constant theme. Indeed, the leitmotifs of anti-Jesuit polemic depicting the Society of Jesus as an occult conspiratorial organization[3] were in turn deployed by the Jesuit writers against Freemasonry. In the present study, however,

[1] *La Civiltà Cattolica* [hereafter: *CC*] was published fortnightly, normally in 4 volumes a year in 18 series from April 1850 until 1903, but designated simply by year thereafter. Until 1933 articles and instalments of novels in the journal were anonymous. However, most novels and many collections of thematically connected articles were eventually published in book form under the author's name. On the periodical generally, see Oliver Logan, 'A Journal: *La Civiltà Cattolica* from Pius IX to Pius XII', in R. N. Swanson, ed., *The Church and the Book*, SCH 38 (Woodbridge, 2004), 375–85.
[2] On similar dangers posed by the theatre, see Anon., 'Del teatro italiano', *CC* ser. 2, 5 (1854), 257–77.
[3] Cf. Geoffrey Cubitt, *The Jesuit Myth: Conspiracy Theory and Politics in Nineteenth Century France* (Oxford, 1983), 182–96, 295–314; Peter Burke, 'The Black Legend of the Jesuits: An Essay in the History of Social Stereotypes', in *Christianity and Community in the West: Essays for John Bossy*, ed. Simon Ditchfield (Aldershot, 2001), 165–82; in this volume, John Wolffe, 'The Jesuit as Villain in Nineteenth-Century British Fiction', 307–19.

the emphasis will be primarily on what the works of Antonio Bresciani (1798–1862), the pioneer Jesuit novelist between 1850 and 1861, had to say about Christian life and values. This, in fact, has most relevance to the genre of the romantic novel.

La Civiltà Cattolica was addressed to laity as well as clergy and above all to a young audience.[4] The main development of a Catholic lay activist movement (Catholic Action *avant la lettre*), with both male and female wings, which was strongly supported by the Jesuit journalists, only came from the late 1860s, after Bresciani's death, in response to the forcible annexation of the former papal domain to the new Italy, and to the secularizing policies of the liberal state.[5] However, the Jesuits, almost from their inception, had sought to nurture an elite of committed Catholic men capable of exercising influence in the Church's interests.

Of the earlier authors who influenced *La Civiltà Cattolica*, the great counter-Revolutionary figure of François René de Chateaubriand (1768–1848) is of particular relevance here. 'Christian civilization' was a major theme in Chateaubriand's work, primarily with *Génie du christianisme* (1802), as it was for the Jesuit journalists, albeit the French writer's concerns were primarily literary, while these Jesuits, however much they were concerned with the arts, defined 'civilization' first and foremost in ethical terms. Moreover Chateaubriand was a pioneer of the Christian novel of sentiment, with *Atala* (1801) and above all *Les Martyrs* (1809).

Antonio Bresciani's intellectual formation was in the Restoration era. When he joined the founders of *La Civiltà Cattolica* he had ended a teaching career in his order as rector of the Collegio di Propaganda Fide which trained missionaries,[6] and he already had a large literary production.[7] In a treatise on Romanticism (1839), he asserted: 'Romanticism is not natural in itself ... is not natural to Italian taste ... [and] is harmful to the Christian religion, to good political regimen and to morality'. In point of fact, Bresciani's objections, issues of compositional order apart, were to the treat-

---

4   Logan, 'A Journal', 376, 378–9.
5   Gabriele De Rosa, *Il movimento cattolico in Italia. Dalla Restaurazione all'età giolittiana*, 5th edn (Rome, 1979), 7–85.
6   *DBI, s.n.* 'Bresciani Borsa, Antonio'.
7   Antonio Bresciani, *Opere*, 17 vols (Turin, 1865–9). On Bresciani's writings, mainly from a sociologizing Gramscian perspective, see Alessandra di Ricco, 'Padre Bresciani: populismo e reazione', *Studi storici* 22 (1981), 832–58.

ment of Catholicism in 'Gothic' novels and to Byronic amorality.[8] Bresciani, indeed, was the exponent of a sanitized Romanticism. The mutual love of young people, with all its dangers, was a central concern for him and he claimed to be defending the true love of refined sentiments against the ultimately cold and calculating erotic passions portrayed in many novels.[9] Moreover, there is a link between his descriptions of landscape and his value-system, which again brings him within the framework of Romanticism.

THE PLOTS

The main figures of Bresciani's novels, young persons in fact, follow courses to faith or to a more intense religious life, on the one hand, or, on the other hand, to total moral and psychological degradation. Even the more closely delineated evil characters have much innate goodness, but by rejecting repeated opportunities for repentance, they become increasingly hardened in sin. Thus most of Bresciani's novels belong to the genre of the conversion narrative. Examples of this genre are Alessandro Manzoni's *I promessi sposi* (*The Betrothed*, published in different versions in 1827 and 1840), containing accounts both of the dramatic conversion of a robber baron and of the religious maturation of the hero; John Henry Newman's two novels *Loss and Gain: The Story of a Convert* (1848) and *Callista* (1855); and the cosmopolitan Cardinal Nicholas Wiseman's *Fabiola or the Church of the Catacombs* (1854, Italian translation 1856 and subsequent editions). The conversion narrative may be regarded as a Christian response to the *Bildungsroman* (novel of formation) of which the archetype was Goethe's *Wilhelm Meister*. A constant theme structuring Bresciani's narratives is that of the effects of good or bad *educazione* (upbringing, nurture), also a major concern of the Jesuit journal in general.[10]

Bresciani's first full novel, *L'Ebreo di Verona* (*The Jew of Verona*) (1850–1) had some international success in book form. It is set during the revolution of 1848. The hero, the Jew Aser, a noble, sensitive, colourful and indeed exotic figure, reminiscent of Sidonia

---

[8]   Antonio Bresciani, 'Del Romanticismo italiano rispetto alle lettere, alla religione, alla politica e alla morale', *Opere*, 2: 331–82.

[9]   Bresciani, 'Lorenzo' [see n. 15 below], *CC* ser. 3, 3 (1856), 148–58.

[10]   Especially relevant here is [Giuseppe Calvetti], 'Dell'educazione dell'uomo e della donna', *CC* ser. 2, 7 (1854), 491–505; ser. 2, 8 (1854), 25–35.

in Disraeli's *Coningsby*, is a member of the Mazzinian patriotic movement Young Italy, depicted here as a sinister conspiratorial society. The heroine, Alisa, is a pious, proper maiden, but over-prone to romanticism. Aser comes to realize the infamy of Young Italy. He is converted to Catholicism, partly through love of Alisa, who has given him a miraculous medal, partly through admiration of the simple piety of a Swiss peasant family. He is murdered by conspirators. Alisa's hot-headed cousins Lando and Mimo have been seduced into joining the campaign against Austria by the rhetoric of demagogues. In the war, they learn hard lessons.[11] *Della Repubblica Romana* (1851–2), a sequel to *L'Ebreo di Verona*, recounts Alisa's difficulties in coming to terms with Aser's death and Lando's vocation as a Carthusian.[12] Encapsulated within this work is the novelette *Lionello*, an account of the ill effects of bad upbringing. Lionello has many good qualities, but his parents have let him be pampered by servants; he is allowed to read romantic novels; a 'trendy' priest-tutor introduces him to Enlightenment philosophies; and he is exposed to evil influences at university. His rake's progress moves through indebtedness, membership of a secret society and of Freemasonry, crime, piracy and madness to eventual suicide.[13]

The effects of good and bad upbringing are further developed in *Ubaldo ed Irene* (1853–5), set around the time of the invasion of Italy by the armies of Revolutionary France. The twins of the title have been left to the influence of their pious mother, the Countess Virginia, who ensures that they have good tutors. They accordingly grow up pious and moral. Their elder sister Lauretta, however, has been indulged by their Voltairean father, the Count Almavilla. She reads the worst possible sort of novels imported from France. She grows up petulant and lazy and contracts a clandestine marriage with a bogus French count who is in fact a one-time butcher and a Jacobin terrorist to boot. After being dragged by him through a career of piracy and then abandoned, Lauretta becomes insane.

---

[11]   Antonio Bresciani, 'L'Ebreo di Verona' [hereafter: 'L'Ebreo'], serialized in *CC* 1–6 (1850–1); also *Opere*, vols 6–7.

[12]   Antonio Bresciani, 'Della Repubblica Romana: Appendice all'Ebreo di Verona' [hereafter: 'Repubblica'], serialized in *CC* 6–11 (1851–2), including parts entitled 'Il giubileo della Repubblica Romana', *CC* 7 (1851), 559–79, and 'Don Alessandro il mansionario', *CC* 8 (1852), 50–71; also *Opere*, vols 8–9.

[13]   Antonio Bresciani, 'Lionello', serialized in *CC* 8–10 (1852).

The Count Almavilla seeks to thwart Ubaldo's religious vocation by forcibly enrolling him in a French military academy. Ubaldo is coarsened by the experience and becomes casual in his attitude to religion, but still retains his innate moral fibre and a spark of religious sense, originally fostered by his mother's care. After a distinguished military career in the Napoleonic army, he finally becomes a Camaldolese hermit. The gentle Irene becomes a tough Sister of Charity.[14] *Lorenzo o il Coscritto* (1856) is set in the period of the Napoleonic regime in Italy. The hero avoids conscription into the imperial army for the excellent motive of sparing his mother and sister pain. A freethinking but otherwise admirable young man, he is weaned to Catholicism by his lady love.[15] The theme of winning back errants runs through *Don Giovanni o il benefattore occulto* (*Don Giovanni the Secret Benefactor*) (1856), set *circa* 1848. While continuing the anti-Risorgimento polemic, it holds up the model of a charitable, understanding parish priest.[16]

La Contessa Matilda di Canossa e Iolanda di Groningen (1857), set in the eleventh century, tells of a high-born damsel pursued by an over-passionate German count. She is protected by the Countess Matilda, the ally of Pope Gregory VII against the tyrannical Emperor Henry IV. The latter is yet another example of bad upbringing. Matilda was, for Bresciani, a pioneer in the process of civilizing high medieval Italy, of which the castle of Canossa stands as a permanent testimony. This plot allows the author to make comparisons between Gregory and Pius IX, both doughty defenders of the Church against invasive secular forces.[17]

Edmondo o dei costumi del popolo romano (*Edmund: The Mores and Customs of the Roman People*) (1859) tells of a priggish English gentleman who accuses contemporary Romans of a combination of superstition and religious indifference. But Edmund is one of those mad northern Romantics. Endowed with a febrile imagination, he conceives an insane passion for the fantasy figure of

[14] Idem, 'Ubaldo ed Irene', serialized in *CC* ser. 2, 1–8 (1853–4).

[15] Idem, 'Lorenzo o il coscritto', serialized in *CC* ser. 3, 1–3 (1856); also in *Opere*, vol. 12.

[16] Idem, 'Don Giovanni o il benefattore occulto', serialized in *CC* ser. 3, 3–4 (1856); also in *Opere*, vol. 12.

[17] Idem, 'La Contessa Matilda di Canossa e Iolanda di Groningen', serialized in *CC* ser. 3, 7–11 (1857–8); also in *Opere*, vol. 13. On Henry's upbringing, see *CC* ser. 3, 10 (1858), 31–6.

a girl of the people of whom he has simply heard and whose portrait he has seen. He is *furioso*, like Ariosto's Orlando. His wits are restored by conversion to Catholicism. Here Bresciani examines the picturesque but rumbustious aspects of Catholicism and Roman life that were most rebarbative to the Anglo-Saxon Protestant mentality.[18] Bresciani's colourful account of Roman festivals is linked to the contemporaneous efforts of *La Civiltà Cattolica* to depict the Roman populace as fun-loving yet well behaved, happy under the benign rule of Pius IX.[19]

La casa di ghiaccio (*The Igloo*) (1860) is the only novel of the former rector of the Collegio di Propaganda set in a mission field. The theme of Catholic Christian civilization which Bresciani had opened up in *Matilda di Canossa* is now developed in a different context. The novel, which ranges from the frozen wastes of the Arctic to the Canadian forests, tells of Martin, a French soldier turned mariner, who is sheltered by an 'Eskimo' family. The 'Eskimos' are portrayed as noble savages of coarse and unappealing habits but generous hearts. Martin civilizes and educates the girl Ermine and commences her conversion, together with that of her less educable brother Heron, to Catholicism. Just as the malodorous whale oil with which she insulates herself is washed off and coarse animal skins, symbolic of the old self, are replaced by more graceful attire, so, through *educazione*, is revealed the inner God-given innate grace which opens the way to Ermine's full conversion.[20] It is in this novel that Bresciani's theological concept of man and his soteriology are most developed.

In 1860 the Papal States were invaded by both Garibaldian irregulars and the Piedmontese royal army. An international volunteer force, the papal Zouaves, was formed, essentially with French organization, as new crusaders to defend the Papal States.[21] The ailing Bresciani truncated *La casa di ghiaccio* to compose his final and most disorganized work, *Olderico ovvero il Zuavo Pontificio* (1861).

---

[18] Idem, 'Edmondo o dei costumi del popolo romano', serialized in *CC* ser. 4, 1–4 (1859); also in *Opere*, vol. 14.

[19] 'Cronaca 12–26 febbraio', 'Cronaca 26 febbraio – 12 marzo', *CC* ser. 4, 1 (1859), 587–8, 741–2.

[20] Antonio Bresciani, 'La casa di ghiaccio o il cacciatore di Vincennes', serialized in *CC* ser. 4, 5–8 (1860); also in *Opere*, vol. 14.

[21] Charles A. Coulombe, *The Pope's Legion: The Multinational Fighting Force that Defended the Vatican* (Basingstoke, 2008).

This is mainly a regurgitation of reports in the French Catholic press and of family papers, but running through it is the fictional account of the noble Olderic and his equally noble fiancée Jacqueline.[22] This is but one example of a large, mostly French, 'Zouave literature', but is the first actual novel of the genre. In common with this literature as a whole, Bresciani held up the Zouaves as authentic martyrs and extolled the heroic sacrifice of their womenfolk. In the more or less authentic narrative accounts belonging to the genre, this sacrifice was simply that of mothers; only in fiction were wives and fiancées considered.[23] Here Bresciani recounts the travails of a fiancée. The theme of martyrdom was an important one in the French and Italian ultramontane piety of this time, fed by the major excavations of the catacombs from the beginning of the century.[24] *La Civiltà Cattolica* had recently published a digest version of Wiseman's *Fabiola*, which featured the martyrs Sebastian, Agnes and (most notably) the boy saint Pancras, whose parents, in the novel, support his sacrifice.[25] Bresciani held up similar examples of parental conduct in his Zouave saga.[26]

BRESCIANI'S VALUE-SYSTEM

In Catholic thought generally, from the seventeenth century, the 'passions' were the blameworthy emotions, out of control and closely linked to egotism; the 'affects' (Italian *affetti*) were the emotions that could bring men closer to God and to other human beings, although in a human context they needed moderation.[27] This dichotomy is central to Bresciani's novels, although he may occasionally refer to the most intense emotions, even benign ones, as 'passions'.[28] These novels portray the base passions as the root

[22] Antonio Bresciani, 'Olderico ovvero il Zuavo pontificio. Racconto del 1860', serialized in *CC* ser. 4, 9–12 (1861); also in *Opere*, vol. 16.
[23] Carol E. Harrison, 'Zouave Stories: Gender, Catholic Spirituality, and French Responses to the Roman Question', *JMH* 79 (2007), 274–305.
[24] Vincent Viaene, 'Gladiators of Expiation: The Cult of the Martyrs in the Catholic Revival of the Nineteenth Century', in Kate Cooper and Jeremy Gregory, eds, *Retribution, Repentance and Reconciliation*, SCH 40 (Woodbridge, 2004), 301–16.
[25] Anon., 'Un romanzo storico di genere nuovo', serialized in *CC* ser. 3, 1–3 (1856). Note also the journal's sympathetic review of Newman's *Callista*: *CC* ser. 3, 3 (1856), 675–82.
[26] Bresciani, 'Olderico', *CC* ser. 4, 9 (1861), 413.
[27] A classic statement of the distinction is St François de Sales, *Traité de l'amour de Dieu*, bk 1, ch. 5.
[28] For condensed statements, see Bresciani, 'Ubaldo', *CC* ser. 2, 8 (1854), 402–3;

cause of the revolutionary process from 1789 onwards. Thus both
the sinister, cold-souled instigators of the upheavals of 1848 and
the often idealistic and courageous young men who were their
dupes were in differing degrees animated by *furor* (madness, rage).
Furor was cold, it was the outer manifestation of a terrible inner
void. By contrast, the good Catholics and those who eventually
saw the error of their ways were people of delicate sentiments.[29]
However, the affects, if unregulated, could easily deteriorate into
passions. Love, even where it was initially inspired by the virtue
and piety of its object, could get out of control. Young girls, just
like poor Edmund, were proverbially prone to *fantasia*, the imagination that spins much out of little.[30] Bresciani reserved the high
drama of the emotions for the religious sphere, whether in the
rapture of prayer or in crises of conversion.[31] His attitude to music
can be seen in this context. It is an expression of sensitive souls,
it can raise hearts and minds to God,[32] but it has its dangers. A
would-be seducer may exploit it; the balance of even a pious and
good person may be swayed by it.[33] Dolour (*dolore*) at one's own
sins or those of others or indeed at the sufferings of others is
valuable. However, extreme dolour at bereavement or separation
from loved ones is really a form of human weakness; a restrained
grief (*mestizia*) is the appropriate emotion.[34] Alisa, whose dolour is
exacerbated by *fantasia*, is haunted by the image of the murdered
Aser;[35] the still immature Jacqueline is similarly obsessed when
she believes that Olderic is dead.[36] It is here that the potential
morbidity of amorous passion becomes evident. However, 'tears'
in a theologically loaded sense deriving from baroque piety, as
signifying compunction, commiseration, sorrow at the spiritual

---

CC ser. 2, 12 (1855), 643–8.

[29] Notably in 'L'Ebreo' and 'Repubblica'.

[30] Bresciani, 'L'Ebreo', *CC* 3 (1850), 310.

[31] Idem, 'L'Ebreo', *CC* 6 (1851), 59–60, 282–97; 'Repubblica', *CC* 11 (1852), 623–5,
630–4, 639–41; 'Ubaldo', *CC* ser. 2, 6 (1854), 54–64, 276–7, 607; 'Lorenzo', *CC* ser. 3,
2 (1856), 427–8, 503–11, 634–6; 'Matilda', *CC* ser. 3, 9 (1858), 62–4.

[32] Idem, 'L'Ebreo', *CC* 7 (1851), 178–80; 'Repubblica', *CC* 11, 620–1; 'Matilda', *CC*
ser. 3, 7 (1857), 305–6, 534–6.

[33] Idem, 'Matilda', *CC* ser. 3, 8 (1857), 179–81; 'Ubaldo', *CC* ser 2, 7 (1854), 372–93,
516–25, 639–50.

[34] Idem, 'Ubaldo', *CC* ser. 2, 11 (1855), 617–26.

[35] Idem, 'Repubblica', *CC* 7, 178–80; 'Lionello', *CC* 8 (1852), 292–5.

[36] Idem, 'Olderico', *CC* ser. 4, 11 (1861), 437–46.

predicament of others, or gratitude to God, are meritorious and even potent, especially those of saints and mothers.[37]

In a world in which fathers of the affluent classes are often free-thinkers or are casual in their religious commitment, and in which women tend to have been more carefully nurtured than men,[38] mothers have great powers of religious and moral influence;[39] so indeed may sisters.[40] Again, sweethearts whose outer beauty is a mirror of beauty of soul have great powers to win freethinking men to religious values.[41] Bresciani seems positively to have a concept of feminine charisma. Women, moreover, have great capacities for tact.[42] Here there is an interesting parallel between the role of women and that of pastors in the process of conversion. In the Jesuit tradition, Bresciani is an apologist for a tactful and supple approach towards penitents and those in spiritual turmoil. *Soave* (mild, gentle) is an epithet he constantly applies to the methods of his ideal pastors.[43] A wise priest may actually entrust the opening moves in reclaiming or converting a man to Catholicism to a mother or other mature lady.[44]

Bresciani's young heroines are mostly *care fanciulle, care damigelle* (sweet girls, sweet damsels). His mothers, too, are conventionally feminine. But there are also the *donne forti* (strong women) or viragos in his novels. One fanciful variety is that of the warrior maiden on the model of Ariosto's Bradamante: Olga the Croat in *L'Ebreo di Verona*, who has managed to join the Austrian army,[45] and the historical figure of Countess Matilda, a 'bronze-breasted' lady with a gentle heart.[46] However, another model is provided by

---

37 Idem, 'L'Ebreo', *CC* 6, 298; 'Ubaldo', *CC* ser. 2, 6, 57–8, 168–9, 276; ser. 2, 12, 555, 566–7; 'Matilda', *CC* ser. 3, 9, 449–50.

38 Idem, 'Lionello', *CC* 8, 428, 'Repubblica', *CC* 11, 510–12, 521–4.

39 Notably in idem, 'Ubaldo'.

40 Idem, 'Lionello', *CC* 8, 432–4; 'Ubaldo', *CC* ser. 2, 12, 564–8, 'Lorenzo', *CC* ser. 3, 1 (1856), 31.

41 This is the major theme of 'L'Ebreo' and of 'Lorenzo', explicitly stated in the conclusion to the latter: *CC* ser. 3, 3 (1856), 158–62. Note also idem, 'Lionello', *CC* 9 (1852), 648–51.

42 Idem, 'Lorenzo', *CC* ser. 3, 2, 163; 'Edmondo', *CC* ser. 4, 3 (1859), 183–94.

43 Idem, 'Ubaldo', *CC* ser. 2, 7, 38–45; 'Lorenzo', *CC* ser. 3, 2, 635–6; ser. 3, 3, 34–5; 'Don Giovanni', *CC* ser. 3, 4 (1856), 421–34, 670–2.

44 Idem, 'Lorenzo', ibid. 511–28; 'Edmondo', *CC* ser. 4, 4 (1859), 572–7.

45 Idem, 'L'Ebreo', *CC* 3 (1850), 25–40, 126–7.

46 Idem, 'Matilda', *CC* ser. 3, 7, 51–66; ser. 3, 9, 552–3; ser. 3, 10 (1858), 691–5; ser. 3, 11 (1858), 43.

Sisters of Charity, who combine great tenderness of heart with immense toughness. Thus Irene evolves from *cara damigella* to *donna forte*.[47] Ermine the Eskimo maiden, sensitive and compassionate, who can gut a bear and fell a maddened bison with a single pistol-shot, is a related figure.

Journeys of the soul are usually bound up with physical journeys through a variety of landscapes. Highly crafted landscape descriptions form a significant part of Bresciani's novels and have a closer relationship to his message than, say, with Chateaubriand or Manzoni. Bresciani's vision of Italy is a positively Goethian one. It is a land where the lemon-tree blooms, but also one of rugged and terrifying vistas. The two kinds of landscape express different sides to the Italian character. The religious and cultural history of Italy is interwoven with its landscapes. These are the settings of its great abbeys and also of its castles. The latter are testimony to the past grandeurs of its aristocracies. The harsh but sublime mountain landscapes are both the context and the symbol of the most ascetic monastic traditions.[48] But there are also the truly sinister natural features: Vesuvius and the caves of the ancient pagan oracles which symbolize the subterranean forces of anarchy.[49] A population may derive its virtues in part from an austere environment, *vide* the much maligned Croats[50] and the inhabitants of Alpine Switzerland,[51] both patriarchal societies. Finally, the mountains are a place where an urban bourgeois can reinvigorate his soul and take stock of his life.[52] Bresciani was in some measure in line with

[47] Idem, 'L'Ebreo', *CC* 6, 163–7; 'Ubaldo', *CC* ser. 2, 11, 626–31; ser. 2, 12, 402–4.

[48] Idem, 'Ubaldo', *CC* ser. 2, 7, 506–12 (on a Camaldolese hermitage in the Valle di Lanzo, Piedmont); 'Don Giovanni', *CC* ser. 3, 4, 658–68 (on St Benedict's cave); 'Matilda', *CC* ser. 3, 7, 164–9 (on the rock of Canossa and its castle), and *CC* ser. 3, 8, 434–40, 447, 451–2 (on the mountains of the Trentino where Iolanda encounters a hermit); 'Edmondo', *CC* ser. 4, 4, 36–9 (on the rock and nuns' school at Tor de' Specchi outside Rome, as a symbol of ancient barbarism and the civilizing effects of Christianity).

[49] For Vesuvius, see idem, 'L'Ebreo', *CC* 1 (1850), 75–8; 2 (1850), 157–60; for the volcanic oracle-cave by Lake Nemi, see 'Lionello', *CC* 10 (1852), 493–5; for the oracle-cave in Val Pantena near Verona, see 'Ubaldo', *CC* ser. 2, 7, 23–9.

[50] Idem, 'L'Ebreo', *CC* 3, 25–7; *CC* 5 (1851), 530–3.

[51] Idem, 'L'Ebreo', *CC* 6, 42–59. This was very similar to English Protestant idealization of the Waldensians; see, in this volume, Mark Smith, '*The Pastor Chief* and other Stories: Waldensian Historical Fiction in the Nineteenth Century', 296-307.

[52] Bresciani, 'L'Ebreo', *CC* 5 (1851), 662–77.

that Romantic tradition which saw an affinity between landscape and national character.

CONCLUSION

Sensitivity and sensibility are key themes in Bresciani's work. For all the absurdity of his plots and the naïveté of his psychology in many respects, he was the heir of a sophisticated tradition of spiritual and moral counselling and he was out to defend the sensitive, psychologically canny pastoral approach of the Jesuits which had been a bone of contention with so-called 'Jansenists'. Of particular interest is the complementarity between the supple pastoral approach on the part of clergy which he advocated and the contribution to the salvation of others of feminine tact and sensitivity, whether those of matrons or of sweet young ladies. His notion of a female religious mission was compatible with a highly romantic image of woman. Bresciani's roots in Baroque piety led him to attribute positive value to the emotions in a religious context. Moreover, his concern with emotional equipoise is partly an inheritance from Baroque secular literature. This concern was combined with a Romantic preoccupation with sensibility. Faced by the challenge of romantic literature with a small 'r', he embraced a sort of Neoplatonic attitude towards the loves of young people. This professed anti-Romantic, albeit with greater caution than Chateaubriand, sought to claim sensibility as Catholicism's own. This concern is less evident with the Jesuit novelists who followed him and who had fewer literary pretensions.

In the long term, the development of a Catholic lay activist movement was to have an impact on Italian Jesuit fiction, and in particular on the notion of acceptable models of womanhood, the female characters (it should be said) generally being more strongly drawn than the male ones in the novels. A woman, if not called to be a nun, fulfilled her natural role as a domestic angel, but the very domestic hearth needed to be defended in society at large. The writers of *La Civiltà Cattolica* sought to define a specifically feminine role in lay Catholic action, clearly distinguished from that of men, one in which women's maternal instincts were deployed in 'social maternity', that is, in organized charity, in the protection of female virtue among the lower orders, and in agitation against proposed legislation on marriage which was seen as a threat to the integrity of the family. As the challenge of militant secularism developed in the post-Risorgimento era, the type of the Catholic hero or heroine needed to be defined in relation to the Church's opponents, as the Jesuits caricatured them. A 'true' femininity was to be delineated in contrast to such monsters as female political activists, women-Freemasons and secularist feminists; but it could be a tough femininity, capable of doing battle in a hostile world.

Bresciani's literary successors were to emancipate themselves from his astonishingly aristocratic perspective as they looked for a wider range of models of active Catholic life than those provided by fashionable gentlefolk and trusty peasants.[53] They began to take account of the employment of educated women in office work. Thus *Donna antica e donna nuova* (*Woman as of Old and Woman of Today*) (1906) by Giovanni Giuseppe Franco (1824–1908), the most prolific of *La Civiltà Cattolica's* novelists, producing novels from 1863 onwards,[54] now held up the image of two Catholic lay female activists, talented organizers at different levels, an aristocratic widow exercising a 'social maternity' at national level and her energetic and methodical aide, a telegraphist, both of them ladies who combined the innocence of doves with the wisdom of serpents.[55] The image of the *donna forte*, which had been so fanciful with Bresciani, had now come down to earth, while investigations of a complex balance between the movements of the heart and self-control had given way to a more rigid emphasis on self-mastery, perhaps more typical of Jesuit tradition. This was appropriate to militants in an embattled Church.

University of East Anglia

---

[53] There was still a marked contrast with the status-mobile heroes in the Methodist fiction described, in this volume, by Martin Wellings, '"Pulp Methodism" Revisited: The Literature and Significance of Silas and Joseph Hocking', 361-72.

[54] Anon., 'Giovanni Giuseppe Franco S.I.', *CC*, anno 59.4 (1908), 350-4.

[55] G. G. Franco, 'Donna antica e donna nuova: Scene di domani', serialized in *CC*, anno 56.12 – anno 59.1 (1906–8).

CANON PATRICK AUGUSTINE SHEEHAN: PRIEST AND NOVELIST*

by SHERIDAN GILLEY

‘The primary object of a novelist is to please’,[1] said Anthony Trollope, but he also wanted to show vice punished and virtue rewarded. More roundly, Somerset Maugham declared that pleasing is the sole purpose of art in general and of the novel in particular, although he granted that novels have been written for other reasons.[2] Indeed, good novels usually embody a worldview, even if only an anarchic or atheist one, and the religious novel is not the only kind to have a dogma at its heart. There is the further issue of literary merit, which certain modern Catholic novelists such as Evelyn Waugh and Graham Greene have achieved, giving the lie to Newman's assertion that in an English Protestant culture, a Catholic literature is impossible.[3] But Newman[4] and his fellow cardinal Wiseman both wrote novels; Wiseman's novel, *Fabiola*,[5] with its many translations, had an enthusiastic readership in the College of Cardinals, and was described by the archbishop of Milan as ‘a good book with the success of a bad one’.[6] Victorian Ireland was a predominantly anglophone Catholic country, and despite poor literacy rates into the modern era, the three thousand novels in 1940 in the Dublin Central Cath-

---

* This essay is dedicated to the memory of the recently deceased W. R. Ward, FBA, President of the Ecclesiastical History Society forty years ago, in 1970, when I became a member.

[1] Anthony Trollope, *An Autobiography* (London, 1946), 221.

[2] W. Somerset Maugham, *Ten Novels and their Authors* (London, 1954), 6–7.

[3] Ian Ker, *The Catholic Revival in English Literature, 1845–1961: Newman, Hopkins, Belloc, Chesterton, Greene, Waugh* (Leominster, 2000), 1.

[4] J. H. Newman, *Loss and Gain: or, the Story of a Convert* (London, 1848); idem, *Callista: A Sketch of the Third Century* (London, 1855); Robert Lee Wolff, *Gains and Losses: Novels of Faith and Doubt in Victorian England* (London, 1977), 41–72; Sheridan Gilley, ‘Newman as Novelist’, *Chesterton Review* 33/1-2 (Spring/Summer 2007), 139–58.

[5] N. Wiseman, *Fabiola or, The Church of the Catacombs* (London, 1854); Wolff, *Gains and Losses*, 161–5; Andrew Sanders, *The Victorian Historical Novel 1840–1880* (London, 1978), 132–7.

[6] Wilfrid Ward, *The Life and Times of Cardinal Wiseman*, 2 vols (London, 1897), 2: 107.

olic Library indicate a sizeable literary culture,[7] comparable to the cultures of other Churches.[8] The 'literary canons' who contributed to this literature around 1900 included the Irishman Canon Patrick Augustine Sheehan, the subject of this essay;[9] another Irishman, Canon Joseph Guinan, who wrote eight novels on Irish rural life;[10] Canon William Barry, the son of Irish immigrants in London, whose masterpiece was the best-selling feminist novel, *The New Antigone*;[11] Henry E. Dennehy, commended by Margaret Maison in her classic study of the Victorian religious novel;[12] and the prolific Monsignor Robert Hugh Benson, the convert son of an archbishop of Canterbury.[13] Catholic writers were often ignored by the makers of the contemporary Irish literary revival, non-Catholics anxious to separate nationalism from Catholicism (sometimes by appealing to the nation's pre-Christian past), but this Catholic subculture is now being studied. Despite the dismissive entries about Sheehan in various reference works,[14] a reflection of

---

7 Stephen J. Brown, *Novels and Tales by Catholic Writers: A Catalogue* (Dublin, 1940).

8 Margaret M. Maison, *Search your Soul, Eustace: A Survey of the Religious Novel in the Victorian Age* (London, 1961); Wolff, *Gains and Losses*; Andrew Sanders, 'Christianity and Literature in English', in Sheridan Gilley and Brian Stanley, eds, *CHC*, 9: *World Christianities c.1815 – c.1914* (Cambridge, 2006), 136–41.

9 There is a good standard biography using original material by Sheehan's American friend and patron Fr Herman J. Heuser, *Canon Sheehan of Doneraile: The Story of an Irish Parish Priest as told chiefly by himself in Books, Personal Memoirs and Letters* (London, 1918). The centenary edition of Sheehan's works was published in 1952, as was Michael P. Linehan, *Canon Sheehan of Doneraile* (Dublin, 1952).

10 Catherine Candy, *Priestly Fictions: Popular Irish Novels of the Early Twentieth Century* (Dublin, 1995), 94–113.

11 William Francis Barry, *The New Antigone: A Romance* (London, 1887); idem, *Memories and Opinions* (London, 1926); Sheridan Gilley, 'Father William Barry, Priest and Novelist', *Recusant History* 20 (1999), 523–51.

12 Maison, *Search Your Soul*, 153. The two listed novels by Dennehy are *Alethea, at the Parting of the Ways* (London, 1906); *A Flower of Asia: An Indian Story* (London, 1901).

13 C. C. Martindale, *The Life of Monsignor Robert Hugh Benson*, 2 vols (London, 1917); Janet Grayson, *Robert Hugh Benson: Life and Works* (Lanham, MD, 1998).

14 Thus Robert Hogan, ed., *The Macmillan Dictionary of Irish Literature* (London, 1980), 601: 'he had the conventional opinions one would expect in a Roman Catholic cleric of his day', though the writer thinks this a strength as well as a weakness. See also Patrick Maume, 'Sheehan, Canon Patrick Augustine', in Brian Lalor, ed., *The Encyclopaedia of Ireland* (Dublin, 2003), 984, though for Maume's considered view, see n. 15 below. Sheehan gets brief entries in works such as Henry Boylan, ed., *A Dictionary of Irish Biography* (Dublin, 1998), 396; Louis McRedmond, ed., *Modern Irish Lives: Dictionary of 20th-Century Irish Biography* (Dublin, 1996), 291.

the new Irish anti-clerical mood, Sheehan himself is the subject of recent articles,[15] a lengthy study[16] and an excellent monograph.[17]

Like many historians, a novelist states and explores his themes by taking his characters through a plot or narrative: hence the attention to plot in this essay. Sheehan's stories declare his views on the strengths and weaknesses of Irish clerical training and of the Irish Catholic clergy, on the Church's role in Irish life, on the central role of women, on the Irish nationalist tradition in both its constitutional and revolutionary forms, on Irish poverty, capitalism, strikes and emigration to America, on the need for the regeneration of Irish culture through a Catholic literature, and on English landlordism and colonialism and their effects on Irish life. It is the aim of this essay to show how as a storyteller he is a many-sided commentator on his faith and fatherland.

Patrick Augustine Sheehan was born in 1852, at Mallow in County Cork. Of his two brothers, one died in childhood. His two sisters, to whom he was devoted, joined the Sisters of Mercy and died when young. Sheehan and his siblings had been orphaned as children, and as the ward of their parish priest, Dr John McCarthy, later bishop of Cloyne, Sheehan was trained for the priesthood first at St Colman's College, Fermoy, and then at the national seminary of St Patrick's College, Maynooth. He thought that his Maynooth education had rested too much on fear and not on idealistic faith, a fear which was an inadequate safeguard against a later lapse into selfish worldliness.[18] He described the philosophical and theolog-

---

[15] Catherine Candy, 'Canon Sheehan: The Conflicts of the Priest-Author', in R. V. Comerford et al., eds, *Religion, Conflict and Coexistence in Ireland: Essays Presented to Monsignor Patrick J. Corish* (Dublin, 1990), 252–77; Lawrence W. McBride, 'A Literary Life of a Socially and Politically Engaged Priest: Canon Patrick Augustine Sheehan (1852–1913)', in Gerard Moran, ed., *Radical Irish Priests 1660–1970* (Dublin, 1998), 131–48. There is no *DNB* entry on Sheehan as he died in 1913; the volume for that decade appeared in 1927 after partition. The recent sympathetic entry in *ODNB* is by Lawrence McBride. See also Patrick Maume, 'Sheehan, (Canon) Patrick Augustine', in James McGuire and James Quinn, eds, *Dictionary of Irish Biography*, 9 vols (Cambridge, 2009), 8: 882–4.

[16] Candy, *Priestly Fictions*, esp. 21–93; on the reception of Sheehan's works, ibid. 129–54.

[17] Ruth Fleischmann, *Catholic Nationalism in the Irish Revival: A Study of Canon Sheehan, 1852–1913* (Basingstoke, 1997). Her work, though very critical, seems to me the best in its field, and its bibliography is the most complete that I have seen about Sheehan.

[18] Heuser, *Canon Sheehan*, 39.

ical teaching as dry. 'Relentless logic, with its formidable *chevaux-de-frise* of syllogisms, propositions, scholia; metaphysics, sublime, but hardened into slabs of theories, congealed in mediaeval Latin ... The Graces were nowhere!'[19] He found solace in the literature class, in Carlyle, Wordsworth, Shelley, Keats, Tennyson, Browning and George Eliot,[20] sometimes hidden inside a theological tome, and in reading in foreign languages. One comfort was Shakespeare, whom he called, with reference to that 'terrible "Timon of Athens," [and] that still more terrible "Lear"', 'the greatest interpreter of humanity the world has ever seen'.[21] His youthful enthusiasm for Carlyle[22] led him into a love of Germany — there are only good Germans in his novels — and a highly critical interest in the German philosophies of Kant, Fichte and Schelling, 'that most poetical of German philosophers',[23] who is prominent in his learned musings in *Under the Cedars and the Stars* on his 'two constant, never varying loves — my philosophers and my poets'.[24] This went, however, with a passionate revulsion against the secular modern mind and its terrible power against religious faith:

> Literature has usurped the place of religion, as the guide and teacher of mankind; and religious persons have not been wise enough to retaliate and carry the war in to the enemy's country ... Goethe had a gospel; so had George Eliot; so had Carlyle; so had Tennyson; so had Browning.[25]

His early essays, according to Chesterton, 'constitute a consistent and incessant appeal to Ireland, his country, to stand up as the champion of the things which the modern world so largely mocks, positive virginity, abstract chivalry, and, above all, the firm feet of humility that are planted on the ancient earth and take hold of

---

[19] Cited in Fleischmann, *Catholic Nationalism*, 20–1. However Sheehan, in *Under the Cedars & the Stars* (Dublin, 1940; first publ. 1903), 33, states: 'In our own colleges, there can be no great change from the rigid, logical method, because such method is preparatory and fundamental'.

[20] All are discussed in Sheehan, *Under the Cedars*.

[21] P. A. Sheehan, *Lisheen: or, The Test of the Spirits* (London, 1914; first publ. 1907), 132.

[22] Heuser, *Canon Sheehan*, 30–1.

[23] Sheehan, *Under the Cedars*, 10.

[24] Ibid. 119; on Kant and Fichte, see ibid. 104–5; on Hegelianism, ibid. 197–8; on Hegel and Schelling, ibid. 56–7, 77–9; on Schelling, ibid. 240.

[25] Ibid. 223.

it'.[26] His novels discuss philosophy and metaphysics, but he thought
that access to the popular imagination lay in the literary presentation of philosophical ideas, and that the German philosophers
who so fascinated him could be answered by the practical experience of ordinary people. As one of his young intellectuals puts it,
contemplating the happiness of a family redeemed from disorder
and drink, 'Schopenhauer takes a back seat here.'[27]

There was a positive side to his view of Maynooth. He admired
as pastors the priests who had succeeded their more timid conti-
nentally trained successors: 'the strongest, fiercest, most fearless army
of priests that ever fought for the spiritual and temporal interests
of the people – men of large physique and iron constitutions,
who spent ten hours a day on horseback, despised French claret,
loved their people and chastised them like fathers',[28] and then, the
new generation of 'clean-cut, small of stature, keen-faced, bicycle-
riding, coffee-drinking, encyclopaedic young fellows', regarded by
their elders with 'tolerant contempt'.[29] He was of another type, as
one of nature's ascetics, who disliked the prosperity of many of the
clergy, and looked on the material success of his own Church with
a distrustful eye, as one fearful for its future.

On his first pastorate, in the English diocese of Plymouth, his
mind was sharpened by the contrast between Ireland and England,
where he claimed to have learned more theology than in his whole
Irish training, but after a disastrous disarrangement of the bishop's
cappa magna he suspected that the 'English people, clergy, Bishop
and all' were 'conceited and formal as well as individualistic',[30]
preoccupied with respectability and better versed in rule keeping
and rubrics than in religion. Yet on his return to Ireland, first as
a curate to Mallow, and then to the cathedral at Queenstown
(now Cobh), with something of an English accent, he tried to
introduce his flocks to English standards of punctuality, cleanli-

[26] G. K. Chesterton, 'The Variety of Essays' [review of P. A. Sheehan, *Early Essays
and Lectures* (London, 1906)], *Daily News*, 31 October 1906; I owe this reference to Dr
Julia Stapleton. See Heuser, *Canon Sheehan*, 88–95.

[27] P. A. Sheehan, *The Triumph of Failure: A Sequel to Geoffrey Austin, Student* (London,
1904; first publ. 1899), 263.

[28] P. A. Sheehan, *My New Curate: A Story Gathered from the Stray Leaves of an Old
Diary* (London, 1928; first publ. 1899), 165.

[29] Ibid. 166.

[30] Heuser, *Canon Sheehan*, 61.

ness and efficiency, and to inspire Irish education with a literary idealism which would raise Ireland in the intellectual world while confirming the country's religious and national character. In this he rejected English materialism, yet his view of Ireland was critical and remained so. 'It is an unhappy and distracted country', he wrote in 1911 to his friend, the American jurist Oliver Wendell Holmes, of his own attempt at a cross-denominational debate, *The Intellectuals*,[31] 'and the one thing which hitherto saved it – a certain kind of Celtic idealism – has now given way before the advance of materialism.'[32] Progress was necessary, but progress could mean materialism, and the loss of a precious and heroic history.

As an educational reformer, writing in the *Irish Ecclesiastical Record*, he deplored the worldly values of the new system of success by public examinations, especially for the civil service, which he regarded as an enemy to the faith, and which Patrick Pearse was to denounce as a 'murder machine'.[33] The lack of positive reaction helped make him a novelist. Here he could also voice his feelings about the paganism of literary culture and the shortcomings of the Catholic Church in Ireland, its failure to rise to the intellectual and spiritual challenges of the society around it, especially as presented by the literary movements of the time. He saw the novel as the best contemporary way of teaching science and history as well as morality. His larger aim was '"to create our own civilization" … founded on simplicity, self-surrender; and as alien as possible to all our modern ideas of progress'.[34] The difficulty was that of diminishing poverty without collapsing into materialism, chiefly represented by the 'American fever'[35] of the mass emigration by the young to the New World, on which he wrote a deterrent comic

---

[31] P. A. Sheehan, *The Intellectuals: An Experiment in Irish Club-Life* (London, 1911).

[32] Heuser, *Canon Sheehan*, 237. This correspondence has been published: David H. Burton, ed., *The Letters of Justice Oliver Wendell Holmes and Canon Sheehan* (Washington, DC, 1976).

[33] See Ruth Dudley Edwards, *Patrick Pearse: The Triumph of Failure* (London, 1977), 206: 'What Pearse was railing against … was the repressive spirit of Irish education, which squeezed out pupils' individuality and made them slaves to examinations and unsympathetic teachers, who had themselves been rendered impotent by the rigid imposition of narrow curricula.'

[34] Heuser, *Canon Sheehan*, 178.

[35] P. A. Sheehan, *Glenanaar: A Story of Irish Life* (London, 1918; first publ. 1905), 274.

song.[36] Two of the characters in his novel *Miriam Lucas*[37] become prostitutes in New York and represent his view of its moral danger. He feared the loss of native virtue in the decline of traditional folklore and local superstition, in which he took a scholar's delight. He vainly upheld the cleanliness and culture of the German Catholic peasantry, even to the extent of advocating the removal of the middens from near Irish cabin doors. His Ireland was a tragic country, of falling population and material decay, which he largely attributed to the landlord system of increasing the rent for any improvement that a tenant might make. His heart was in the revolutionary tradition, though his head opposed it.

As parish priest of Doneraile, in County Cork, he was kept out of controversy by his personal mildness and good relations with local landowners, especially by his friendship with Lord Castletown of Doneraile Court, a Gaelic League enthusiast, whom Sheehan advised on the setting up of the Irish National University. Sheehan secured for Doneraile a water supply, electric lighting and street paving. He gave lectures and formed literary societies, though in his novel *The Blindness of Dr Gray* the performance of *Hamlet*, brought to the village by its cultivated curate, is greeted by the audience when the ghost appears with choruses of 'Finigan's Wake', their apology being that 'The timtation was too great!'[38] Sheehan assiduously supervised the seven schools of his parish, and more controversially negotiated the local arrangements under George Wyndham's Land Act of 1903 by which the Catholic tenantry became peasant proprietors, though he later voiced the fear that some had 'degenerated into public house loafers'.[39] In his communal role, Sheehan was like many other Irish clergy, but he was estranged from the mainstream Home Rule movement, supporting in 1910 the Cork-based All-for-Ireland League of his childhood friend, the Nationalist MP William O'Brien, who (like Sheehan) had been born in Mallow in 1852 and who had been in gaol for his politics.[40] A few days before his death, Sheehan destroyed the manuscript of his memoirs lest they should cause

---

[36] Heuser, *Canon Sheehan*, 355–9.
[37] P. A. Sheehan, *Miriam Lucas* (London, 1912).
[38] P. A. Sheehan, *The Blindness of Dr Gray: or, The Final Law* (London, 1909), 246.
[39] Sheehan, *The Intellectuals*, 61. This may be only the speaker's view.
[40] Joseph V. O'Brien, *William O'Brien and the Course of Irish Politics 1881–1918* (Berkeley, CA, 1976), 185–212.

offence. His people were proud of him, and gave him a royal funeral. He had already passed his literary income to the diocese for the benefit of sick and aged clergy. He was buried under a Celtic cross with the inscription, '"Where dwellest thou, Rabbi?" And Jesus said "Come and see."'[41]

Sheehan's ten completed novels[42] are written with pace and excitement, but have the disadvantage for the modern reader of indulging in the Victorian taste for detailed description, an elaborate narrative and an intricate plot spun over five hundred closely printed pages or more, for the enjoyment of long winter evenings.[43] They are relieved from tedium by their author's agreeable vice of letting social realism succumb to sensationalism, a combination recommended by Trollope himself.[44] Their humour is largely reportage of the rug-pulling wit of the Irish peasantry.

Sheehan's first novel, *Geoffrey Austin: Student*, anonymously published in 1895 and affectionately dedicated to the Catholic youth of Ireland, fell stillborn from the press. Its hero, the orphaned ward of a kindly priest, like Sheehan himself, attends Mayfield, a 'Grinding School', in order to pass a civil service exam for the Control Department in the Army. The name refers to Gayfield School, founded to cram Irish Catholic boys for the civil service exams and attended by Sheehan's brother. There is a blight on Mayfield from its more brutish students and its presiding pedagogue 'the Grinder', Hugh Bellamy, with his harshly utilitarian view of education as a way of getting on, his abuse of his brother and sister, and his mysterious past disgrace. The more virtuous

---

[41]   Heuser, *Canon Sheehan*, 391.

[42]   Sheehan left incomplete *Tristram Lloyd: The Romance of a Journalist*, about an embittered young man brought to better spirits by faith. His anger at the plight of the poor is contrasted with the rage of an anti-Semitic Russian revolutionary who marries and then murders Lloyd's sister. The work was finished by his literary executor Henry Gaffney OP (Dublin, 1928). Sheehan also wrote stories for children (Heuser, *Canon Sheehan*, 99), and a melodrama, '*Lost Angel of a Ruined Paradise': A Drama of Modern Life* (London, 1904), for the benefit of a convalescent home for sick children, about three girls whose future is foretold as a wife, a nurse and a nun. It was not performed. The sensationalist plot involves a malicious suitor, the bankruptcy of the father of one girl by the father of another, and the death of one girl. I have not studied Sheehan's poetry.

[43]   For the full critical bibliography of his fictional works, see Rolf Loeber and Magda Loeber, *A Guide to Irish Fiction 1650–1900* (Dublin, 2006), 1185–9.

[44]   On being realistic and sensational: 'A good novel should be both, and both in the highest degree': Trollope, *Autobiography*, 204.

boys include Austin's friend Charlie Travers, who has crushed the school bully but is now sick from overstudying. Austin blocks the flue to a stove, filling the school hall with smoke and so inadvertently spoiling the social evening at which Bellamy tries to butter up some men of influence. The tale is broken by the storytelling among the boys around the winter fire, including a bizarre fantasy about a leper prince in the Pacific whose riches cannot cure him, and a young Frenchman's anecdote of escaping a firing squad after the Paris Commune when he crosses himself and so proves that he is not a Communard. This points, in a self-interested manner, to the need to show one's faith, and condemns Irish Catholics for not doing so. Austin and the Frenchman establish their valour when they save the sickly Travers from the resurgent bully. There is a rural interlude with the tragic story of a young man who has gone to an Irish Queen's College, loses his faith, shoots at his saintly parish priest and dies impenitent. The Grinder's character is softened; his secrets are exposed: another marriage after deserting his first wife, the madness of his second, and a secret son at the school. The school closes, but Bellamy is reconciled to his abused siblings.

The teachers interest Austin in classics and foreign languages but not in mathematics, the examination that Austin fails. His friend Travers also fails, but in a religious experience, Travers condemns their classical literary education as more pagan than Christian. With its epigraph from Newman, on the tragic necessity of 'unlearning the world's poetry, and attaining to its prose', and its chapter headings from non-Catholics (George Eliot, Schiller, Ruskin, William Blake and Coleridge), Sheehan exalts the authors and philosophers with the saints above any more practical or worldly form of educational training or success, while condemning a pagan philosophy based on literature alone.

Sheehan resumed Austin's history in *The Triumph of Failure*, published in 1899. His hero's semi-pagan education has damaged his faith, and he lives in abject poverty and increasing mental distress in his quest for a truth to live by. His suffering is partly relieved by his friendships with the few Catholics who have the serenity he lacks, such as the Bellamy household of Hugh's brother and sister and his old German tutor, Herr Messing, whose idealism is contrasted with the materialism of much of the Dublin Catholic middle class, its half-apologetic shame for being Catholic, the formalism of its religious practice, its indifference to the disease, poverty and suffering around it and its casual attitude (especially among young men) to religion. Typical is the determination of a Catholic mother to marry her daughter to a rich, depraved, alcoholic Protestant. The Grinder, Hugh Bellamy, dies a penitent Catholic. The message of the work is profoundly other-worldly, though this is lightened by portraits of a group of good if care-free and careless medical students. Sheehan's own hope for a lay Catholic revival is voiced in the passionate preaching of humility and holy poverty by Austin's old friend from Mayfield, Charlie Travers. Travers is committed to gaol, the victim of a plot by publicans and others hurt by his crusades to convert the poor and to establish a Magdalen asylum, and dies after his release, while Austin, after years of intellectual struggle, becomes a Carmelite friar. Even while rehearsing the Church's cultural achievements, Sheehan hardly thinks them the point, for the heart of Christianity lies not in any such cultural triumph but in the triumph of failure on Calvary. *The Triumph of Failure* is the subtitle of Ruth Dudley Edwards's biography of Patrick Pearse,[45] the leader of the 1916 Rising, whose personality looks like an attempt to embody the character of Geoffrey Austin. The precise nature of Travers's crusade to create a devout and effective laity is unclear, and Austin in his quest for holiness ends up not as a layman but a friar.

The literary historian John Wilson Foster has described *The Triumph of Failure* as 'essential reading for anyone who seeks the entire picture of Irish fiction in the 1890s',[46] and as sharing with Yeats 'the *fin-de-siècle* theme of spiritual brinkmanship', of fascination with 'debauchery, dreams, and dark nights of the soul as necessary preludes to salvation'.[47] Its author had little sympathy from his fellow clergy, apart from the Jesuit Matthew Russell. But *Geoffrey Austin* attracted the attention and encouragement of Fr Herman Heuser, the Jesuit editor of the *American Ecclesiastical Review*, which published Sheehan's next book, *My New Curate*. This appeared as a separate work in 1900.[48] Its background is

---

[45] Dudley Edwards, *Patrick Pearse*.
[46] John Wilson Foster, *Fictions of the Irish Literary Revival: A Changeling Art* (Syracuse, NY, 1987), xiii–xiv.
[47] Ibid. 179.
[48] Loeber and Loeber, *A Guide*, lists a Boston edition of 1899.

rural Ireland, which Sheehan knew better than Geoffrey Austin's Dublin. Fr Daniel Hanrahan, known as Daddy Dan, has annoyed his bishop, who decides to send him a curate who will break his heart in six weeks. After thirty years in the impoverished seaside village of Kilronan, Fr Dan has settled into comfortable old age, having lost his ambitions to express his classical learning in print or to improve the living conditions of the parish with a new fishing station and factory, defeated by the remoteness of the landlord, the indifference of his agent and the government, and the stubborn conservatism of his people. 'Nothing on earth can cure the inertia of Ireland. It weighs down like the weeping clouds on the damp heavy earth'.[49] The new curate, Fr Letheby, a vigorous young man with years of service in Manchester, shares a love of the classics with the parish priest, whose Latinity was part of presbytery culture, but Letheby is appalled by the inconsistencies of his devout but rough-hewn flock, with their admirable 'fervid Celtic imagination'[50] and a character which he cannot pierce, and by their 'ancient Irish customs'[51] of fairy folklore. Sheehan describes the Celtic temperament: generous, open-hearted and witty, but superstitious, irascible, irresponsible and irrational, with a hair-trigger temper unless restrained by the clergy, to whom the peasants are devoted. This is what three hundred years of English landlord oppression have made them.

Fr Letheby exposes the local revolutionary organizer as a British spy – there is only contempt here for the Fenians and their rising in Ireland in 1867 – and the priest quells the rabble by alleging the hidden influence among them of Jews and Freemasons, who even manufacture Catholic articles of devotion; Fr Dan later suggests that they are financing pornography. The reader is not prepared to meet in Ireland these demons of the nineteenth-century clerical mind, which were then dividing France,[52] though Irish anti-Semitism was not uncommon,[53] and there was to be a persecution

---

[49] Sheehan, *My New Curate*, 13.

[50] Ibid. 152.

[51] Ibid. 155.

[52] Ruth Harris, *The Man on Devil's Ireland: Alfred Dreyfus and the Affair that Divided France* (London, 2010).

[53] R. F. Foster, *Paddy and Mr Punch: Connections in Irish and English History* (London, 1993), 32. There is a good Jew, Levi, in *Tristram Lloyd*, and some favourable comparison with Jews, but these may be the work of Sheehan's continuator, Fr Gaffney.

in 1904 of the Jews in Limerick. Letheby converts the violent and
faithless Catholic landlord to better ways by showing his courage
on the landlord's yacht in a storm, and more importantly he helps
to convert the young gentleman Protestant who is engaged to
the landlord's daughter; but the prime agents of religious conversion are (as elsewhere in Sheehan's work) the holy women, both
the young lady herself and the village saint (the former village
belle), who is apparently dying of a dreadful skin disease but then
recovers, though by natural means. Irish Catholicism is shown as a
conspiracy between the womenfolk and the clergy. Letheby greatly
improves the ardour and musical quality of the new order of religious observance produced by the Irish 'Devotional Revolution',[54]
with confraternities and sodalities. He establishes a shirt-making
factory, and commissions a new fishing boat. But the factory closes
with debts because of the wayward behaviour of its girl workers,
whom public opinion exiles to America, and the boat is sunk, it
seems at first without proper insurance. Letheby is only saved by
the generosity of a fellow priest who has a nice nest-egg from
his mission in Australia, and whom the curate has rescued from
the heresies of Modernist biblical scholarship. Letheby becomes
administrator of the cathedral, while Daddy Dan declines a canonry,
leaving the proffered rochet, mozzetta and biretta of a canon at
his death to his departed protégé. The book begins with an act of
episcopal tyranny and concludes with one of episcopal generosity,
which seems to show that all is right in the Church at the end.

The book is pervaded by the priest's respect for the suffering
and poverty of the poor, which gives them an inherent spiritual
power. But the priest is, if benevolent, also all-powerful over
them. To lighten the message, there are many excellent touches of
conversational wit and of description, as of an old curate's cart on
exit from his parish, with

> three loads of black turf, carefully piled and roped; then two
> loads of hay; a cow with a yearling calf; and lastly, the house
> furniture, mostly of rough deal ... hardly good enough for one
> of our new labourers' cottages, ... a kitchen table, its four legs
> pointing steadily to the firmament, like an untrussed fowl's,

---

54 Emmet Larkin, 'The Devotional Revolution in Ireland, 1850–75', *AHR* 77
(1972), 625–52.

and ... the plague and the pet of the village, Nanny the goat, with her little kid beside her ...[55]

The traditional Irish marriage, usually the result of hard-headed haggling and barter, is sentimentally observed, and contrasted with the wickedness of foreign customs and with the incoming rage among the young for romantic attachments. Another omission is of the notorious 'gombeen' men, the shopkeeper moneylenders of Irish life, who preyed upon the hard-pressed farmers. In short, though partly inspired by the Fenian Charles Kickham's novel *Knocknagow*,[56] *My New Curate* has some of the characteristics of the contemporary 'Kailyard School' of J. M. Barrie and 'Ian Maclaren' in their delightful but sentimental depictions of Scottish village life. *My New Curate* was Sheehan's most popular work, was translated into many languages (including Italian), and won him a doctorate from Rome.

Intended for inclusion in the work was the story 'The Monks of Trabolgan', to figure as a tale by Fr Letheby, in which an Irish abbey is seized by the government after a young monk makes enemies for the community with a political pamphlet defending the Church against the secular power – a warning against rash publication, however justified – and then brings disaster when in innocence he guides a German warship into a nearby harbour.[57] The tale foreshadows the expulsion of the religious orders from France, the tension between the Church and the Irish MPs, and the British fear of a German invasion of Ireland. Sheehan's other short stories include 'A Spoiled Priest' (a phrase which he strongly deprecates), about a Maynooth seminarian mysteriously denied ordination who discovers his vocation as a Carthusian in a kindly word from a younger priest who had hero-worshipped him.[58] In 'Rita, the Street-Singer', a variant on 'Hansel and Gretel', a Neapolitan girl with a beautiful voice loses through death her beloved sister and her hostile stepmother, and is reunited by song with the father who had abandoned her.[59] The bloodcurdling supernatural tale, 'Remanded', is based on the Doneraile story of Thomas Duan,

[55] Sheehan, *My New Curate*, 2.
[56] Charles P. Kickham, *Knocknagow: or, the Cabins of Tipperary* (London, 1879).
[57] P. A. Sheehan, *A Spoiled Priest and other Stories* (London, 1905), 43–85.
[58] Ibid. 1–26.
[59] Ibid. 86–135.

a priest charged with a political crime by a woman who then commits suicide. The priest overrules his parishioners to give her a Christian burial, and her corrupting corpse returns to frighten to suicide the magistrate who had bribed her for her testimony.[60] 'How the Angel became Happy' is a gruesome vignette, like one of Monsignor Benson's,[61] of an angel who pleads for the death of a child to ensure her salvation.[62] 'Frank Forrest's Mince-Pie' is a Dickensian Christmas yarn of a boy who gives food, including his mince pie, to a poor woman with two children who come to the door on a snowbound Christmas Eve. Frank is rewarded with dreams warning him of the dangers awaiting him in later life.[63]

In *Luke Delmege*, first serialized in the *American Ecclesiastical Review* and separately published in 1901, Sheehan retold his experience of England. A young priest, the hero of the title, returns to his native place in Ireland full of academic honours from Maynooth, to find them ignored by everyone, even his bishop, who sends him on the English mission. Before departing Luke dines with some of the homely native priests and then, in an appalling social ordeal, with his own parish priest, a canon who has a noble history of improving his people's lot but is proudly aloof, conservative and respectable. Luke is humiliated by the supercilious young nephew of the canon, and the canon is mortified when Luke shatters the stuffiness of the drawing room by singing a revolutionary ballad. In London and then in an English cathedral city, Luke is seduced by English gentility to substitute a gospel of spiritual and material progress and human perfectibility for Christianity through the worship of the God in man, though he is horrified by the barbarism of an English execution, disagreeing with both his superior and his intellectual English circle about capital punishment. But on his return home to celebrate his sister's wedding, he is also repelled by the vulgar merriment of the occasion and by Irish backwardness and begging. The canon's young nephew, a doctor in London, has become a drug addict, and has to be rescued from an opium den by his saintly sister. The brother dies, and the sister quixotically

---

[60] Ibid. 136–67; the outcome is a little unclear.

[61] Benson's story is especially distressing, as the protective angel pushes the boy beneath a cart: R. H. Benson, 'The Bridge over the Stream', in idem, *The Light Invisible* (London, 1911), 97–106.

[62] Sheehan, *A Spoiled Priest*, 168–90.

[63] Ibid. 191–203.

expiates his sin incognito, affecting to be a repentant prostitute, in a convent of the Good Shepherd order. Luke is disgraced in England as the unwitting agent of the lapse from the faith of an English intellectual convert. Luke returns to Ireland, calling it 'Siberia',[64] 'a land of death and ruin',[65] 'of cast-iron conservatism'.[66] He rages at the landlord class, contrasting them with the down-bent, wind-burnt farmers who toil

> for the agent, that he might have his brandy and cigars; and for two old ladies in a Dublin Square, that they might give steaks to their lap-dogs; and for a solicitor again above them, that he might pay for his son in Trinity; and, on the highest pinnacle of the infamous system, for the lord, that he might have a racer at the Derby and St Cloud, and a set of brilliants for Sadie at the *Opéra Comique*.[67]

But Luke estranges his Irish parishioners by his English manner and his English attempts to improve them, and he outrages them by damning the unpunctuality, inconvenience and drink of an Irish funeral. Yet it is the poor, who insist on interment in a distant skull-and-bone-strewn ruined abbey graveyard, who are preserving the native tradition. On visiting England, Luke finds that it is the poor Irish and Italians at his old mission who welcome him. He has to be reconverted doubly, to Irish ways and to a life of absolute material renunciation. The agents of the change are his mother's funeral, attended in pouring rain by a vast congress of peasants and clergy, and the old soldiers at All Souls' Tide paying for masses for their fallen comrades. He wins his congregation with a sermon on the gallantry of the Irish Brigade at the battle of Cremona, and he is overcome by the holiness of the Good Shepherd penitent and the order's saintly chaplain, in a vignette which, in its high Victorian sentimentality, is not saved by Sheehan's usual redeeming touch of astringency. Then there is violence: the landlord demands back rent from his tenants for the increased profitability of the local farms effected by the worthy canon; Luke's aged father is evicted; and Luke is gaoled for snapping the sword of the evicting officer.

[64] P. A. Sheehan, *Luke Delmege* (London, 1932; first publ. 1901), 332.
[65] Ibid. 333.
[66] Ibid. 380.
[67] Ibid. 344.

He dies in his humble mission as the servant of God and his people, having become again an Irishman. Sheehan recalls in Luke some of his English experiences, as in picking out 'of reviews and pamphlets more theological information than he had acquired in his four years' divinity course';[68] in being told to burn a sermon of which he had been proud; and in smothering the bishop in his *cappa magna*. His moral is that Irish prosperity must be found in an Irish way congruent with the gospel, and not in the manner of England.

Sheehan's examination of the pathos of the sacerdotal life earned him the dislike of Monsignor John Hogan of Maynooth, who in the *Irish Ecclesiastical Record* described the book as full of 'stilted nonsense' while still being 'a clever, an instructive and a good one'.[69] Some priests feared that the demonstration of their humanity exposed the vulnerability of their calling. Sheehan therefore turned from the subject of the priesthood back to rural Ireland in *Glenanaar*, published in 1905; the story is recorded in his own persona as parish priest of Doneraile as he hears it from a 'Yank', a mysterious returned émigré from America who has intervened to great effect and injury to himself in a local hurling match. Sheehan had read up the court reports on the Doneraile informers, who in 1829, in the war to enforce the payment of Church of Ireland tithes, had falsely denounced twenty-one local men for conspiring to murder three brutal and unpopular land-lords. Some of the 'conspirators' were defended at their trial by the Irish Liberator, Daniel O'Connell, but there could be no public forgiveness for the informers or their families, who were henceforth outcasts shunned by all. In Sheehan's story, one of their victims, a decent local farmer, at great risk to himself, takes into his house on a snowy Christmas Eve an informer's abandoned child, who is called Nodlag, the Irish word for Christmas. When she grows up she incurs the jealousy of the new wife of the household, her disgraceful origins become known, and she is turned out onto the roads, only to return nearly dead of starvation during the Famine. She is saved again by the local blacksmith, who has loved her and marries her. A growing delicacy about her tragedy protects her children from the knowledge of their informer grandfather, but a

---

[68] Ibid. 191.
[69] Candy, *Priestly Fictions*, 34. Hogan disliked Sheehan's fear of the pagan classics.

son who has become a passionate Fenian and a champion hurler has his tainted ancestry thrown in his face as an insult when he smashes a boy's teeth during a hurling match. In his agony of hurt pride and shame over his unclean ancestry, he insults his mother, abandons his fiancée, goes to America, makes his fortune and returns as the 'Yank' twenty-five years later, hoping to marry his old flame, now a widow. Out of a pride as great as his, she refuses him, and instead he marries her daughter who resembles her as she was in her youth, in what Sheehan must have thought the best of outcomes. The book is the most neatly plotted of Sheehan's novels, and was written out of his experience of his negotiation of tenant purchase, urging the necessity to let the old agonizing hatreds die. He was to query this later on.

Sheehan was always fascinated by an idealism not his own. He opens *Lisheen*, published in 1907, by summarizing the well-to-do young men of Trinity College in three broad categories: those who work for their own advancement and end up defending the 'things that are'; the sowers of wild oats, who become equally defensive of the 'things that are'; and the wild young dreamers who are dangerous, with a vision of things 'as "they ought to be"'.[70] His hero, a young Irish landlord, Robert Maxwell, is in the third category. He reads Tolstoy, and abandons his class to work incognito as a farm labourer among the Irish peasantry, who are shown as suffering, kindly, devout and hardy, if occasionally idiotic as well as hotheaded, and greatly oppressed by landlord callousness. The village of Lisheen is in Kerry, one of the poorest counties of Ireland. The family which gives Maxwell refuge is evicted and their children are gaoled for resisting the bailiffs, but he ultimately saves the situation with the aid of a cynical, atheistic and socially enlightened English industrialist, who brings prosperity to his neighbourhood and is the foil to his friend, the simple unworldly priest who believes in the possibility of human virtue. Maxwell marries the Englishman's daughter and all ends happily, with the somewhat paradoxical implication that Ireland can be saved from landlordism by English wealth and industry, without reference to religion. There is a parallel tale of a tragic marriage between a society beauty and a dissipated ex-Indian army officer, who is pursued by his Indian mistress, turns out to be a leper

[70]   Sheehan, *Lisheen*, 4.

and drowns. The depiction of the poor parallels the scenes set in fashionable Dublin, but though the Irish virtues, such as their hospitality to strangers, are bound up with their poverty, Sheehan's narrative oddly implies that English-sponsored social and material improvement could be the salvation of Ireland.

Sheehan returned to the clergy with his third clerical failure in *The Blindness of Dr Gray*, published in 1909. Dr Gray is a savage old parish priest, whose blindness is not just his failing sight but his 'hard, proud, domineering disposition' hardened by 'a rigorous theological system, that approached as closely to Jansenism as orthodoxy might'. Intellectually, Dr Gray was bound five times over by the law: the 'Law of Nature, so unfeeling, so despotic, so revengeful; the Natural Law ...; the Law of the Realm ...; Canon Law ...; Ecclesiastical Law, national, provincial, diocesan', received as the perfect expression of the divine mind.[71] Dr Gray's people respect him for his learning and generosity to the poor and his rule by righteousness, but fear him for his lack of pity. His redemption from the religion of law begins with his niece, the daughter of a sister whom he has banished to America for a minor youthful frivolity. Here as elsewhere, America is the Botany Bay of the Irish sinner. Luckily the niece, taught by nuns, can read him his Latin authors. Dr Gray also has the help of a more humane curate, although he withers the lad for daring to play the piano and to love the works of Goethe, Heine and the gentle Lutheran Jean-Paul Richter. The old priest, for all his erudition, is a veritable Tertullian; he has never read a novel, and hates and despises worldly literature, which his curate wants to sanctify for Christianity. The curate agonizes over whether to burn his books, and denounces his superior's medievalism: '"The body – an open sewer; women – so many devils; poetry – the wine of demons; art – the handmaid of iniquity"; that kind of thing won't do now, sir!'[72] Dr Gray has the cunning to give Latin lessons to the sons of the Protestant doctor's family, warmly depicted, to spite his parishioners by showing his respect for good Protestants, but he

---

[71]   Sheehan, *Dr Gray*, 8.

[72]   Ibid. 288. This was Sheehan's view: 'I never could understand that mediaeval idea of the worthlessness and contemptibility of the body ... it seems almost a denial of that ineffable mystery [of the Incarnation] to speak of the body as a "sewer of filth"': *Under the Cedars*, 90–1. 'It seems incredible ...', he wrote, 'that the ordinary people ... do not know ... how their bodies are constructed': Heuser, *Canon Sheehan*, 336.

denounces his niece, who has been repelled by the attentions of one of the doctor's sons and goes to Dublin to train as a nurse, when she gives scandal by accompanying another of these sons (who is dying of consumption) to South Africa. The girl marries yet another brother in Africa, converts him, and ultimately returns to receive her chastened uncle's blessing. There is a lively story about a so-called 'grabber', the purchaser of a farm whose tenants have been evicted, and who is saved from drunken ruin by the good offices of the curate; but the grabber's good fortune, especially in his marriage, provokes the jealousy of the neighbouring farmer and of a gypsy family who have occupied an old castle and have become involved with the doctor's eldest son in smuggling. The jealous farmer grumbles against the authority of the priest, who throws him bodily from the presbytery but then saves him from the gallows by his testimony when the man is charged with the murder of the 'grabber', a crime committed by one of the gypsies, which too neatly shifts the blame from the village to an outsider and non-believer. It is only in Dr Gray's final state, as he resigns his parish, blind and isolated, and is humiliated in court by confessing his violence towards his enemy, that he learns of the love of his people and that love is the whole law. The work reads as a tract for Sheehan's fellow clergy, insisting that spiritual despotism is not Christianity.

Here, as elsewhere in Sheehan's works, the heroine, the nursing niece from America, is the ultimate repository of Irish Catholic character and virtue, who marries and converts the doctor's surviving heir. The village saint is its washerwoman, who spends her time in work and prayer. The curate's sister becomes a contemplative nun, to the initial disgust of her friend, the more practically minded American heroine. The curate, under his sister's otherworldly influence, enters a monastery.

The same theme of female virtue triumphant occurs in *Miriam Lucas*, published in 1912, about a young woman who lives in isolation in an Irish seaside village in County Cork. Miriam's father is an infirm recluse, living in the large and desolate Glendarragh House, which is haunted by a legend of a family curse. Miriam's only friends are the local kindly and unworldly Church of Ireland rector and his benevolent but strong-minded wife, who has an aristocratic self-confidence impervious to convention. Miriam herself is worshipped by the humble Catholic villagers for her gentleness and good works. There is a mystery about Miriam's lost mother which exposes Miriam herself to insult and disgrace when she enters fashionable Dublin society, ruthlessly depicted as snobbish and heartless. Miriam's weak-minded father, before his disappearance somewhat sensationally in a Gothic thunderstorm, leaves her and her property in the power of a corrupt and wealthy railway director and lawyer, Holthsworth, who wants to marry her. He forces Miriam to live with him in Dublin, where in her social isolation she embraces Marxist socialism and becomes the inspiration of a strike with revolutionary intent among the city's railwaymen, a strike which is being secretly financed by a rival English company. The strikers' leader is an idealistic consumptive student at Trinity College, Ian Albrecht, a friend of a medical student, Hugh Ireton, who loves Miriam but because of her murky origins is forbidden by his mother to have anything to do with her. Albrecht, a figure described with great sympathy, dies after his confrontation with a foreign friar, Father Hugo, whose Confraternity of the Holy Family is disputing with the revolutionary movement the leadership of the Dublin workers, by teaching the value of suffering and self-sacrifice. Such confraternities with their massive memberships were the great popular institutions in late Victorian Dublin[73] – the novel is set in the 1880s – and Sheehan has anticipated the industrial unrest led by Jim Larkin in the city in 1913. The strikers' plans are betrayed to Holthsworth, who plans a police ambush to shoot them down, a plot which Miriam averts, though not before Father Hugo is accidentally killed.

The arch-villain here is the capitalist, and Sheehan puts the revolutionary case with all his sympathy for the poor and for secular utopian idealism even while denouncing it as the enemy of the faith. Miriam flees to New York and finds her mother, who is dying after years as a prostitute and gaolbird, having been thrown out of the family for becoming a Catholic, the faith in which she has baptized Miriam. She leaves a will and the deeds which reveal Miriam's ownership of the Glendarragh property, restored to her in a melodrama climaxing in the violent death of Holthsworth, which lifts the local curse. Miriam returns to the village as the

---

[73] Though their high point was between the World Wars; see Maurice Hartigan, 'The Religious Life of the Catholic Laity of Dublin, 1920–40', in James Kelly and Dáire Keogh, eds, *History of the Catholic Diocese of Dublin* (Dublin, 2000), 331–48.

idol of the villagers, having wed Ireton, now the local doctor, and embraced the faith of her baptism. Sheehan makes a positive point of this religiously mixed marriage, and his religious portraits vary: Holthsworth is a hypocrite though outwardly a strict Calvinist Nonconformist; Ireton's mother is a bigoted anti-Catholic; and Albrecht's mother is a still more bigoted member of the Plymouth Brethren, intoxicated with the Book of Revelation and bitterly hating Catholics and socialists. On the other hand, the Church of Ireland rector and his wife are admirable people, and the rector, in his charming, learned and affectionate other-worldliness, and his common-sense spouse, who is his perfect complement and foil, suggest a model of holiness lightly drawn from life.

The theme of insurrection also occurs in *The Queen's Fillet*, published in 1911, in which Sheehan tried his hand at a narrative of the French Revolution, probably inspired by Carlyle's history, within the framework of the conventional view: the people of France were starving and oppressed by a mostly dissolute and unbelieving aristocracy, who in their pride were contemptuous of the monarchy itself and who reaped the whirlwind at the hands of the equally depraved Parisian mob. The hero, Maurice de Brignon,[74] disowned by his father and forced into the Church, is a participant in events in Paris, while some of the scenes take place in the Catholic revolution in the Vendée, depicted as the home of a virtuous and united Catholic aristocracy and peasantry. Sheehan's preference here is for a traditional feudal society over both monarchical despotism and modern democracy. There are two fine portraits, of the renegade bishop Talleyrand, the very embodiment of sardonic brilliance, with a strand of benevolence – he employs de Brignon as a secretary – and of the revolutionary poet André Chénier, the essence of everything finest and most fearless in the revolutionary spirit, whom Sheehan loves for his wild freedom from calculation and self-interest. The heroine of the work is Marie Antoinette, converted through suffering from a coquette to a Catholic mother martyr. The fillet of the title is the headband which she wore at her execution, and which de Brignon acquires. The final chapters, set at the Restoration, are the story of de Brignon's daughter Adèle, who has been reared

---

74   The name Sheehan uses elsewhere for a royalist: *Geoffrey Austin: Student* (Dublin, 1895), 10.

by her revolutionary maternal grandfather. She becomes involved in a plot to restore Napoleon and has to be rescued from the police by the intercession of her father, who has now renounced the world and is a Carthusian abbot. This endpiece is interesting for Sheehan's enthusiasm for the Bonapartist General Ney and his loathing of the legitimist cause and of the restored Bourbons, who in their cruelty have forgotten nothing and learned nothing from the Revolution and are riding for another fall. The author avoids the difficult subject of their championship of the Church, indeed of its immersion in the *Ancien Régime*. The work is a tract against the resort to violence, however justified by tyranny, as a judgement on the revolutionary tradition in Ireland.

Sheehan's own ecumenical endeavour was *The Intellectuals*, a work published in 1911, in which a young priest brings together some middle-class Irish people calling themselves the '*Sunetoi*' ('The Select' in Greek) to read essays and poetry to one another and to discuss religion and literature. The author hopes that 'the barriers of racial and sectarian prejudices may be broken down, and the higher humanities accepted as an integral portion of social and domestic life'.[75] His characters represent the three nations, Ireland, England and Scotland, and the three churches, Catholic, Anglican and Presbyterian. There is some gentle humour. The snobbish musical wife of the Catholic doctor declares that '[t]here *must* be class-distinctions'[76] of a very refined type, extending even to the quality of the china; that 'Protestants are quite as nice, and sometimes much superior';[77] and that '[n]o lady or gentleman nowadays laughs'.[78] The young Catholic bluestocking graduate 'looks charming in her hood and gown',[79] and a young Church of England naval engineer falls in love with her. His Anglo-Saxonist sister insists that the Celtic imagination is a barrier to modern progress, encouraging the Irish in 'nursing with a kind of petulance your wrongs and rights, your impossible dreams and hopeless aspirations'.[80] She is nonetheless attracted to an elderly poet, who reads his verse and disputes the authorship of Shakespeare's plays.

---

[75] Sheehan, *The Intellectuals*, v.
[76] Ibid. 2.
[77] Ibid. 8.
[78] Ibid. 109.
[79] Ibid. 8.
[80] Ibid. 345.

He may have proposed to the lady, but dies, having inherited an earldom. A young Presbyterian lady insists on the supreme value of heroism. A Catholic banker quotes Nietzsche on the worship of Mammon, and excuses the enormities of Napoleon until he is told that the great man had robbed a bank.[81] A Protestant professor of philology defends the classics as necessary to the refinement of a gentleman, who thereby becomes 'an idealist in daily life; in politics, a conservative; in philosophy, a subjectivist; in religion, a theist and a Christian',[82] while he damns the natural scientist as 'in philosophy a materialist; in politics, a socialist; in religion, an atheist'.[83] Closer to his subject, he derives the Welsh and Irish languages from their Aryan root. When the Catholic young lady comments on the mystic character of ancient Irish poetry, the young priest, in a hit at nationalist illusions, assures her that it is as 'as erotic and sensual as Catullus or Sappho'.[84] There is chat about the shape of the earth and about Sheehan's own scientific interest, astronomy. The text only really catches fire when the Catholic doctor distresses the young priest by letting down the side in Protestant company, in denouncing the immaturity of the Irish electorate and the emptiness of Irish politicians. The doctor declares, 'Orators! … Why, there is the curse and bane of our race. We are all orators – stump orators, platform orators, hustings orators, Parliamentary orators',[85] windbags who, whenever they rise to speak, clear the Commons in 'a general stampede to the library, to the tea-room, to the terrace'.[86]

The last of the thirty-seven gatherings is a picnic, where the young priest, kneeling awkwardly on the grass, insists that the point of their proceedings is not their views but that they are talking to one another at all. Having rather sententiously declared that '[s]ome of the most beautiful souls I have ever seen do not belong to the religion I profess', he hopes that:

> broader views and more generous and kindly thoughts may
> be spread abroad amongst our fellow country-men under the

---

[81] Ibid. 242.
[82] Ibid. 238.
[83] Ibid. 237.
[84] Ibid. 355.
[85] Ibid. 225.
[86] Ibid. 254.

benign influence of education; and that the more we read, and thus grow in sympathy with the master-minds of the world, the more we may grow in mental and moral stature, expanding our ideas until they become comprehensive enough to embrace a Universe, and our principles until they touch the widest human limits of gentle and comprehensive charity.[87]

The priest, the doctor and the banker then play a game on the beach, abandoning their solemn professional characters by throwing pebbles at a row of bottles. In retrospect, this seems a forlorn hope in a world about to plunge into half a century of bloody revolution and war.

The Irish difficulty was the sheer appeal of the violence of the nationalist tradition. In *The Blindness of Dr Gray*, the old priest remembers the tradesmen transfigured into glory as the revolutionary Fenians, and the loss of their spirit to contemporary commercialism. Sheehan here recalled his own burning memory of a dinner at St Colman's, when bishop, priests and students 'clapped and thundered' as a famous Fenian entered to receive the bishop's blessing.[88] Here Sheehan's view of revolution has changed since *My New Curate*: the Fenians, however mistaken, are the heroic enemies of modern materialism. *The Graves at Kilmorna*, published posthumously in 1915, was in this prophetic of the future. It opens with a picture of the drunkenness, debauchery and corruption of an Irish election, driven by fake nationalism and self-interested politicians, which Sheehan saw as a child in Mallow, and its hero, Myles Cogan, the well-to-do Catholic son of a self-made merchant, embraces the hopeless cause of the revolution of 1867 out of a combination of Irish patriotism and zeal for moral renewal which ends in his brutalization in prison, an incident inspired by Sheehan's own visit to Dartmoor as a curate in Plymouth, when he saw the land reformer Michael Davitt in chains attending mass in the prison chapel. After his release, Cogan is (unlike Davitt) repelled by the Land League, with its promise to free Irish tenant farmers, while the general growth in Irish prosperity seems to him a kind of gross materialism, 'the commercial immorality that we supposed belonged to clever Yankees or perfidious Englishmen',[89] and a

---

[87] Ibid. 377.
[88] Sheehan, *Dr Gray*, 234.
[89] P. A. Sheehan, *The Graves at Kilmorna: A Story of '67* (London, 1915), 337.

betrayal of the patriotic spirit. Even the growth of the Church, in its splendid new churches and cathedrals and institutions and its multitude of devotional confraternities and sodalities, is for Cogan evidence of decline. Only the past, of the legendary Ireland of missionary saints and heroes and political martyrs, of learning and chivalry and self-sacrifice, is safe from this commercial contagion. Cogan contemplates becoming a Cistercian at Mount Melleray, while his fine-spirited sister becomes a nun. As elsewhere, the final refuge of holiness is a contemplative order. The novel is notable for its picture of the tightly drawn snobberies and class distinctions of Catholics in a small Irish town where 'twopence half-penny did not know twopence!',[90] which separate Cogan from the woman he loves. As the novel opens with a drunken election riot, so it concludes with one, in which Cogan is killed, a reluctant martyr to the grossness of Irish public life, from which he has withdrawn for forty years and which he thinks is 'wholly corrupted'[91] with no hope for the future. This, of course, is Cogan's view rather than the author's, but it reflects Sheehan's distaste for democracy as mob rule, and as a last word on Ireland it is singularly depressing.

This strikes at the heart of the ambiguity of Sheehan, which was also that of Patrick Pearse, who was to lead his revolt out of a passionate desire for a spiritually pure and Gaelic Catholic country rather than from the wish to see Ireland prosperous as well as free. Pearse, like Cogan, wanted not military victory over the British but the triumph of failure, of self-cleansing and salvation from selfishness through martyrdom at the oppressor's hands. Like Patrick Pearse and his Catholic socialist compatriot James Connolly, Cogan thinks that only blood sacrifice will save Ireland. This belief in blood sacrifice was a much wider sentiment during the First World War, exemplified by Rupert Brooke's warriors, 'as swimmers into cleanness leaping',[92] but it was to have a terrible legacy in 1916 in the eager spilling of Irish blood. This ambiguity haunted Ireland for much of the twentieth century, a holy Catholic country which laid claim to spiritual superiority amidst economic decline, and could only sustain that superiority by late marriages, emigration and a falling population which remains

90 Ibid. 53.
91 Ibid. 338.
92 Rupert Brooke, 'Peace', *Collected Poems of Rupert Brooke* (London, 1930), 144.

smaller than it was before the Famine. The novel also depicts the clergy's ambiguity over the revolutionary tradition: its opposition to rebellion to the point of excommunication, as if the rebellious Young Irelanders and Fenians were one with the Young Italian enemies of the pope, and an equally passionate and wholly contradictory clerical sympathy with the same revolutionaries as saints and heroes, converting the Church to the cause of the 1916 Easter Rising, which at first it had condemned.

In this, Sheehan's very contradictions are an image of the contradictions around him. He is a complex explorer of the condition of contemporary Ireland, intellectual, social and political, but he did not merely wish to ensure the cultural triumph of Catholic nationalism, though that was one of his aims, but of a world-renouncing Christianity. As a young Protestant says to an Irish Catholic missionary in Africa: 'Father, by all means, make Christians of these poor heathens; but, for God's sake, *don't civilize them.*'[93] Modern civilization was corruption. This meant Ireland also renouncing the world, creating the country's cultural isolation that prevailed for much of the twentieth century, an isolation which has only disappeared quite recently. Sheehan was in the difficult position of a critic in an institution and culture which felt that it was fighting for its life. When it was triumphant after 1916, he would no doubt have found his new holy Catholic nation too this-worldly and lacking his lofty literary ideal. His suspicion of capitalism, his hatred of landlordism, his sympathy with revolution, his fascination with and rejection of the avant-garde, even his love of English and foreign literature, belonged, nonetheless, to the mindset of one whose hope was not here but hereafter. In this, his critics ignore the central fact about him, that he was a quintessentially religious man. His were not merely the Victorian values of respectability or of contemporary Irish Catholic nationalism, as he tried to show, with realism, humour and sentiment, the role of religion in the sufferings and aspirations of a place, a period and a people.

Durham University

---

[93] Sheehan, *Dr Gray*, 452.

'OH DEAR, IF ONLY THE REFORMATION HAD HAPPENED DIFFERENTLY': ANGLICANISM, THE REFORMATION AND DAME ROSE MACAULAY (1881–1958)

by JUDITH MALTBY

'Take my camel, dear', said my aunt Dot, as she climbed down from this animal on her return from High Mass.

Thus begins, with one of the most memorable opening sentences in twentieth-century Anglophone fiction, Dame Rose Macaulay's novel *The Towers of Trebizond*.[1] It is now largely seen as a somewhat quirky 'niche novel' for Anglican aunts or a perfect present for the diminishing number of ordinands with historical and literary interests. In fact, *Trebizond* was a transatlantic literary sensation, a best-seller as well as a critical success.[2] It won Macaulay the prestigious James Tait Black Memorial Prize for fiction and was no doubt partly responsible for her being made a Dame Commander of the British Empire in 1958, the year of her death.

The Towers of Trebizond was not a breakthrough moment but represented the climax of Macaulay's long and distinguished career as a novelist, poet, travel writer and frequent contributor to a range of publications of the English intelligentsia – the *Times Literary Supplement*, *The Spectator*, *The Listener*, *Time and Tide* – as well as a regular broadcaster on the BBC Home Service.[3] Macaulay was, we would say now, a 'public intellectual'. Her reputation was such that she features in Noel Annan's classic essay, 'The Intellectual Aristocracy' (1955), as a living example of an English intellectual descending from a legion of brainy ancestors.[4]

---

[1] Rose Macaulay, *The Towers of Trebizond* (London, 1995; first publ. 1956), 3. I am grateful to Diarmaid MacCulloch, Gillian Sutherland and William Whyte for their comments on this essay.

[2] Jane Emery, *Rose Macaulay: A Writer's Life* (London, 1991), 317–18; Alice R. Bensen, *Rose Macaulay* (New York, 1969), 154–5, 158–9.

[3] Philip Waller, *Writers, Readers and Reputations: Literary Life in Britain 1870–1918* (Oxford, 2006), 673.

[4] Noel Annan, 'The Intellectual Aristocracy', in *Studies in Social History: A Tribute to G. M. Trevelyan*, ed. J. H. Plumb (London, 1955), 254–60. For an assessment of Annan,

What is striking, given such critical and popular regard in her lifetime, is how Macaulay's reputation has not so much declined as faded away. Since the 1980s, her work has enjoyed a small committed readership, in part made possible by the publishing enterprise of Virago, which brought back into print many neglected women novelists. But the scholarly output on her work has been small for someone whose standing was so significant in the first half of the twentieth century. This seems of a piece, however, with a generally under-studied aspect of British literary and intellectual life in the twentieth century: the Anglican novelist and intellectual. One need only reflect briefly on the contrast with the volume of secondary scholarship on 'Catholic novelists' and 'Catholic intellectuals', such as Greene, Waugh and Chesterton. Why do we not speak of 'Anglican novelists' and 'Anglican intellectuals' in the same way?

Despite being Annan's prime example of a living intellectual in 1955, Macaulay is completely absent, for example, from Stefan Collini's important study of British intellectuals, *Absent Minds*. Strikingly, the religious faith of the most significant Anglican in his study, T. S. Eliot, is treated as a displacement activity keeping Eliot from more serious intellectual pursuits. Collini's implication is that 'intellectuals' should not be interested in religion and if they are, their credentials as intellectuals are compromised.[5] But Anglicans are also partly to blame. Inexplicably, the author of '"Take my camel, dear"' is not to be found in anthologies of Anglican writings.[6] She is absent, for example, from *Love's Redeeming Work: The Anglican Quest for Holiness* – a striking omission, as the 'Anglican quest for holiness' would be an excellent way to describe central themes in *Trebizond*.[7] Why is the 'Graham Greene of Anglicanism' ignored in this way?[8]

Like Graham Greene, Macaulay had a complicated personal

---

see William Whyte, 'The Intellectual Aristocracy Revisited', *Journal of Victorian Studies* 10 (2005), 15–18. See also the fuller genealogy provided in Constance Babington Smith, *Rose Macaulay* (London, 1972), 237.

[5]   Stefan Collini, *Absent Minds: Intellectuals in Britain* (Oxford, 2006), 140–5, 311–16. I am grateful to William Whyte for making this point to me. Women, not simply Macaulay are greatly under-represented in *Absent Minds*.

[6]   Macaulay, *Trebizond*, 3.

[7]   Geoffrey Rowell, Kenneth Stevenson and Rowan Williams, eds, *Love's Redeeming Work: The Anglican Quest for Holiness* (Oxford, 2001).

[8]   There are a few examples of engagement with the significance of Macaulay's Anglicanism in her fiction and non-fiction: Douglas Stewart, *The Ark of God: Studies*

life. In 1918, in her mid thirties, Rose met and fell in love with a married man, the novelist Gerald O'Donovan, when they were both working in the Italian Department of the War Office. O'Donovan had been a Roman Catholic priest in Ireland and had become increasingly disillusioned and at odds with the hierarchy of the Irish Church. He left the priesthood in 1908 and married in 1910.[9] The relationship between Macaulay and O'Donovan continued until his death in 1942, Rose occupying the public role of a family friend; indeed, she was godmother to one of his grand-children.[10] Readers will recognize similarities with the protagonist Laurie in *Trebizond*, who is also involved in a long relationship with a married man.[11] Macaulay withdrew herself from the sacra-mental life of the Church during these years. Laurie, in her guilt and grief, never made it back to the fellowship of the Church at the close of *Trebizond*.

> I live now in two hells, for I have lost God and live also without love, or without the love I want, and I cannot get used to that either. Though people say that in the end one does. To the other, perhaps never … Still the towers of Trebizond, the fabled city, shimmer on a far horizon, gated and walled and

---

in *Five Modern Novelists* (London, 1961); David Hein, 'Faith and Doubt in Rose Macaulay's *The Towers of Trebizond*', *AThR* 88 (2006), 47–68.

[9]   O'Donovan's most successful novel was his first, *Father Ralph* (1913), a critique of the state of the Irish Church in the late nineteenth and early twentieth centuries. For O'Donovan's literary career, see Catherine Candy, *Priestly Fictions: Popular Irish Novelists of the Early Twentieth Century* (Dublin, 1995). Candy is oddly coy about the nature of the relationship between Macaulay and O'Donovan: ibid. 64 (I am grateful to Sheridan Gilley for this reference). See also *ODNB, s.n.* 'O'Donovan, Gerald (1871–1942)', online edn, <http://www.oxforddnb.com/view/article/62954>, accessed 18 July 2010.

[10]   Babington Smith, *Macaulay*, 105; Emery, *Macaulay*, 184, 190–3, 269–70. For Macaulay's relationship with her goddaughter, see *Letters to a Friend, 1950–1952*, ed. Constance Babington Smith (London, 1961), 143, 149, 297; Rose Macaulay, *Last Letters to a Friend, 1952–1958*, ed. Constance Babington Smith (London, 1963), 22, 118–19, 126–7, 129, 130, 132, 137, 199, 205, 208–9; Babington Smith, *Macaulay*, 159, 201–2, 209.

[11]   Laurie's lover is killed in a car accident while she is at the wheel; O'Donovan was severely injured in a car accident in which Macaulay was driving in 1939. He never fully recovered, though in the end he died of cancer in 1942. In an earlier novel, *Told by an Idiot* (1923), the autobiographical protagonist Rome is also involved with a married man: A. N. Wilson, 'Introduction' to Rose Macaulay, *Told by an Idiot* (London, 1983), x; Emery, *Macaulay*, 256–7; *ODNB, s.n.* 'O'Donovan, Gerald'. Macaulay was apparently a notoriously bad driver: William Plomer, 'The Pleasures of Knowing Rose Macaulay', in Babington Smith, *Macaulay*, 234–5.

held in a luminous enchantment. It seems for me, and however much I must stand outside them, this must for ever be. But at the city's heart lie the pattern and the hard core, and these I can never make my own: they are too far outside my range. The pattern should perhaps be easier, the core less hard. This seems, indeed, the eternal dilemma.[12]

Rose, unlike Laurie, did return to the communion of the Church. Indeed, it was eucharistic devotion and practice which was the key for her in the early 1950s – not the quelling of 'doubts' or a grasping onto a tidy set of beliefs. '"I value the contact with God through the Sacrament more than anything in the world"', she reflected to Father Hamilton Johnson in the early 1950s.[13]

It was in the last decade of her life that Macaulay entered into correspondence with Johnson, an English priest based in Cambridge, Massachusetts, at the house of the Society of St John the Evangelist, known informally as the Cowley Fathers. Johnson initiated the correspondence in 1950, having re-read her novel about poetry and religion in the English Civil War, *They Were Defeated*. Johnson reminded Rose that he had been her confessor thirty-five years before and that she had attended a retreat he had conducted.[14]

It was late in life for both of them. Her letters to Johnson (his do not survive) are engaging, humorous, learned and humane.[15] Their publication by Collins in 1961 and 1963, however, caused a furore in the British broadsheets and across the Atlantic. The episode tells us something of Macaulay's post-war reputation as extracts from *Letters to a Friend* were published in *The Observer*, underlining its significance as a publishing 'event'. *The Observer* was keen to highlight her sharper comments on literary contemporaries such as E. M. Forster and Graham Greene.[16] But the real matter of concern for many was that Macaulay had instructed the priest to destroy her letters. Both Johnson and Rose's cousin

---

[12] Macaulay, *Trebizond*, 276–7.
[13] Cited in Babington Smith, *Macaulay*, 195–6.
[14] Ibid. 194–5.
[15] *ODNB*, *s.n.* 'Macaulay, Rose (1881–1958)', online edn, <http://www.oxforddnb.com/view/article/34668>, accessed 15 July 2010. For her relationship with Johnson, see Emery, *Macaulay*, 298–305.
[16] 'Rose Macaulay: Letters to a Priest', *The Observer*, 15 October 1961.

Constance Babington Smith took the remark to be light-hearted and Johnson handed over the letters to Babington Smith to edit. She also published the first biography of Macaulay in 1972.[17]

This did not stop the critics of publication. 'Did this priest betray this woman?' thundered Rhona Churchill in the *Daily Mail*.[18] E. M. Forster deeply disapproved.[19] Publication did have its high-powered supporters, such as Harold Nicolson in the *Observer*, William Plomer in *The Listener* and Stevie Smith in *The Spectator*.[20] Constance had the support too of the Cambridge Cowley Fathers (Johnson had died in 1961), and Archbishop Michael Ramsey wrote to her to express his pleasure in reading the letters and added the observation (not for the first or last time by an archbishop of Canterbury) that 'some very stupid things have been said in the controversy in some of the papers'.[21]

In retrospect, we can be grateful for their publication. The letters convey much insight into English intellectual and literary life in the grim post-war years, of which Macaulay was a key figure, and contain charming details such as 'I went to drink[s] with G[raham] Greene last week; not a single priest there! Can they have dropped him, or he them?'[22] They also provide real insight into her intellectual priorities in matters of faith and especially in terms of her understanding of Anglicanism's place on that larger canvas and in her own life. Because Macaulay was a fine novelist, and the novel by its nature has a number of voices, faith questions are treated suggestively in her fiction. In her letters and other non-fiction writings, the nature of her Anglicanism can be, at times, more directly observed.

Johnson is sometimes presented as Rose's mentor during the 1950s. Although he was clearly important in her return to the life

---

[17] See Babington Smith's letter to the *New York Times* explaining her motives in publishing the letters (29 January 1962): Cambridge, Trinity College Archives [hereafter TCC], ERM 13/195. Babington Smith undertook extensive consultation with individuals mentioned in Macaulay's letters before publication: TCC, ERM 13, 14.

[18] 'Did this Priest Betray this Woman?', *Daily Mail*, 12 October 1961.

[19] TCC, ERM 13/96, 97, Letters to Babington Smith from E. M. Forster, 11, 14 October 1961.

[20] 'The Joyous Faith of Rose Macaulay', *The Observer*, 22 October 1961; 'The Way Back', *The Listener*, 26 October 1961; 'Soul of Gossip', *The Spectator*, 27 October 1961.

[21] TCC, ERM 13/116, 24 October 1961. For a discussion of the controversy over publication of the letters, see Sarah LeFanu, *Rose Macaulay* (London, 2003), 279–96.

[22] 20 August 1952: Macaulay, *Letters to a Friend*, 345.

of the Church, he was in many ways more her friendly foil than her guide, especially as the years progressed. With the success of *Trebizond*, Johnson urged her to write to the *Times Literary Supplement* to make it clear that in contrast to Laurie, Rose did not believe the path to heaven was too difficult – illustrating nicely how ill-suited good fiction is to the promotion of an 'argument'. Rose did not write the letter and commented to her sister Jean that the Cowley Father was so 'so unquestioningly devout and single-minded, and who I don't think has ever been troubled by doubts'. She added, 'He is so old and has been so kind to me'; Johnson was in fact only four years older than Macaulay.[23] She was not the type of woman given to the adoration of the male clergy, as the creation of Father Hugh Chantry-Pigg in *Trebizond* or the Victorian clerical patriarch of *Told by an Idiot* reveals. Her letters are warm but could not be described as in any sense deferential, and one suspects that Father Johnson, with his great certainties, was in part the inspiration for Father Chantry-Pigg.

A recurring topic in her letters to Johnson concerns the historical and theological nature of Anglicanism, especially in terms of the impact of the Reformation on its formation, and it is to that topic that we now turn. Less than six months into their remarkable eight-year epistolary relationship, Macaulay expressed her ambivalent feelings towards the English Reformation:

> Oh dear, if only the Ref[ormation] had happened differently, under the leadership of More, Colet, Erasmus, if only Somerset hadn't been as he was, if only they hadn't had that orgy of smashing and spoiling, if only the Marian persecutions hadn't sent Protestants fleeing to Amsterdam to be infected with Calvinism, or if only they hadn't come back.

The result of all these 'ifs' would have been an Anglican Church 'from the first more lovely, fine and learned, without puritanism, sabbatarianism, or fundamentalism', though she was compelled to add 'still, we could scarcely have had a better prayerbook and liturgy'. She speculated in the same letter whether Roman Catholics experienced the same unease about the Counter-Reformation. 'In some ways, one could; and obviously (as we think of our

---

[23] Rose Macaulay, *Letters to a Sister*, ed. Constance Babington Smith (London, 1964), 202–3 (probable date 24 September 1956); Emery, *Macaulay*, 317.

own [Reformation]) ... [the Counter-Reformation] could have done much better.'[24] The Roman Catholic historian John Bossy expresses a not dissimilar view concerning the impact of the European Reformations on his own tradition in his classic work *Christianity in the West 1400–1700*.[25]

Near the beginning of *The Towers of Trebizond*, the narrator Laurie lays out for the reader a particular interpretation of the history of the Church of England. It is worth quoting at length:

> Perhaps I had better explain why we are so firmly Church, since part of this story stems from our somewhat unusual attitude, or rather from my aunt Dot's. We belong to an old Anglican family, which suffered under the penal laws of Henry VIII, Mary I and Oliver P. Under Henry VIII we did indeed acquire and domesticate a dissolved abbey in Sussex, but were burned, some of us, for refusing to accept the Six Points; under Mary we were again burned, naturally, for heresy; under Elizabeth we dug ourselves firmly into Anglican life, compelling our Puritan tenants to dance around maypoles and revel at Christmas, and informing the magistrates that Jesuit priests had concealed themselves in the chimney-pieces of our Popish neighbours. Under Charles I we looked with disapprobation on the damned crop-eared Puritans whom Archbishop Laud so rightly stood in the pillory, and, until the great Interregnum, approved of the Laudian embellishments of churches and services, the altar crosses, candles and pictures ... During the suppression, we privately kept outed vicars as chaplains and attended secret Anglican services, at which we were interrupted each Christmas Day by the military, who, speaking very spitefully of Our Lord's Nativity, dragged us before the Major-Generals. After the Glorious Restoration, we got back our impoverished estates, and, until the Glorious Revolution, there followed palmier days, when we persecuted Papists, conventiclers and Quakers with great impartiality, and, as the clerical status rose, began placing our younger sons in fat livings, of which, in 1690, they were deprived as Non-Jurors, and for the next half century or so carried on an

[24] Macaulay, *Letters to a Friend*, 40 (15 December 1950); see also 169–70.
[25] John Bossy, *Christianity in the West 1400–1700* (Oxford, 1985), 153–71.

independent ecclesiastical existence, very devout, high-flying, schismatic, and eccentrically ordained, directing the devotions and hearing the confession of pious ladies and gentlemen, and advising them as to the furnishings of their private oratories, conducting services with ritualistic ceremony and schismatic prayer-books, absorbing the teachings of William Law on the sacramental devotional life, and forming part of the stream of High Church piety that has flowed through the centuries down the broad Anglican river, quietly preparing the way for the vociferous Tractarians.[26]

Macaulay's gently ironic characterization of a certain Anglo-Catholic reading of the Church of the sixteenth and seventeenth centuries is beautifully drawn.

In addition, two things are striking about the passage from the perspective of more recent scholarship of the English Reformation. Firstly, Macaulay presented the process of the formation of the Church of England as progressing into the eighteenth century and did so decades before the term 'Long Reformation' had come into widespread use among historians. This is the currently dominant historiographical view, that the process of reformation in England cannot be seen as culminating with the Elizabethan Settlement in 1559 but needs to be understood as embracing the Civil War and Restoration. It has even been suggested that the Long Reformation continued to 1833 – just in time for the Church of England to be rescued from it by the Oxford Movement. Secondly, as Diarmaid MacCulloch has shown, the narrative framework, skilfully satirized by Macaulay, in which a 'broad Anglican river' can be clearly delineated from 'damned crop-eared Puritans', has been a remarkably potent one. This 'Puritan versus Anglican' polarity owes much to the rewriting of the history of the early modern Church at the heart of Oxford Movement ecclesiology and has influenced historians far beyond the confessional boundaries of Anglicanism.[27]

---

[26] Macaulay, *Trebizond*, 4–5.

[27] On the 'Long Reformation', see, e.g., Nicholas Tyacke, 'Introduction' to idem, ed., *England's Long Reformation 1500–1800* (London, 1998), 1–32; Diarmaid MacCulloch, 'The Myth of the English Reformation', *JBS* 30 (1991), 1–19, at 3–5 (repr. in A. Pettegree, ed., *The Reformation: Critical Concepts in Historical Studies*, 4 vols (London, 2004), vol. 2). I explore these issues more fully in '"Neither too mean / nor yet too gay"? The Historians, Anglicanism and George Herbert's Church', in Christopher Hodgkins,

As the correspondence with Johnson unfolds over eight years, it becomes clear that, although 'high', Macaulay did not share the extreme Anglo-Catholicism or 'Anglican Papalism' of her friend.[28] She increasingly found herself defending the Church of England, and Anglicanism more broadly, against Johnson's criticisms and gently chided what she saw as his excessive deference to the truth claims of the Roman Catholic Church. It is important to remember that this is a correspondence between two Anglicans, though one could be forgiven for forgetting that at times. In December 1953 she wrote to Johnson: 'What you say sometimes about our Church saddens me a little; it sounds almost as if you disliked and despised what to me is a beautiful treasury of riches and mystery, and a source of spiritual life and strength'. Macaulay maintained that the 'Anglican Church [is] more Christian [than Roman Catholicism] and more what I want [from] religion'. Perceptively, but kindly, she suggested that Johnson's real spiritual home was the Church of Rome and 'sometimes I feel a little sad for fear *you* are sad about being in the wrong Church'.[29] This is a recurrent theme in their later letters, Macaulay having taken Johnson to task six months earlier for comparing the Church of England to the prodigal son. We do not have Johnson's side of the correspondence but it is safe to assume that he had been promoting the Anglo-Catholic trope that all was doom and gloom in the English Church from the Reformation until the Oxford Movement. Macaulay could not countenance such a view and countered:

> One thinks of George Herbert, of Bp Andrewes, of Hooker, Jeremy Taylor, the non-Jurors, the quiet Anglican rectors who did their duty (your ancestors and mine), who never felt they served a Church which was no good; and the millions of faithful people who belonged to it. But no more![30]

Individuals such as Andrewes and Taylor appear here more in their capacity as authors than as bishops, as it is the appeal to the literary achievements of the Church of England which was a key idea in

---

ed., *George Herbert's Travels: International Print and Cultural Legacies* (Newark, DE, 2011), 27–55.

[28] For a view of this eccentric mindset, see Michael Yelton, *Anglican Papalism: A History 1900–1960* (Norwich, 2005), 1–19.

[29] Macaulay, *Last Letters*, 128 (5 December 1953).

[30] Ibid. 107 (30 July 1953).

Macaulay's thinking about Anglicanism over a long period, both before and after her return to the communion of the Church. She put it even more directly over twenty years before, deep in her period of self-imposed sacramental exile, in her Hogarth lectures of 1931:

> Anglicanism, fortified by its Authorized Version and its Book of Common Prayer, was settling into its dignified and leisurely stride ... A Church which, within the space of a century, produced Colet [charmingly but fancifully described by Macaulay as 'the first liberal High Churchman'], Latimer, Hooker, Donne, Burton, the Fletcher brothers, George Herbert, Lancelot Andrewes, Henry Vaughan, Robert Herrick, and Thomas Traherne ... has reason to give itself literary credit, and to feel that, whatever may be said for or against the somewhat peculiar position it has been held by some critics to occupy in Christendom, the experiment has, on the whole, pretty well suited the English genius.

And this Church was in Macaulay's mind, for all its imperfections, one which avoided 'some of the negations, the doctrinal acceptances, the austerities, and the excesses' of both Roman Catholicism and Dissenting Protestantism, which in her mind were 'oddly in some respects alike in the puritanic fundamentalism of their otherworldly doctrine and in a certain excessiveness of sentiment in its expression'.[31] Sentimentality, as we shall see below, was about the worst thing, in Macaulay's mind, that could happen to Christianity.

Macaulay is not, therefore, rightly remembered as an Anglo-Catholic and certainly had no sympathy for Anglican papalism. Her friend and fellow novelist, William Plomer, remarked in his review of the *Letters to a Friend*:

> Nothing could have been more catholic, less provincial, than her Anglo-catholicism; she would have liked to have revised the lectionary to include Philo, the Neo-platonists, Jakob Boehme and 'a lot of wisdom from the east'; and would rather, she said,

---

[31] Rose Macaulay, *Some Religious Elements in English Literature* (London, 1931), 66, 84–5, 85 respectively. I discuss some of these themes more fully in relation to Macaulay's views on George Herbert in '"Neither too mean/nor yet too gay"?'.

commemorate at Mass the births of Cicero and Erasmus 'than some of these rather obscure, not to say potty, saints'.[32]

Rose was simply too independently minded to buy into Anglican papalism's deference to the Roman Catholic Church. She moves between affectionate bemusement and real irritation with Johnson on that matter in their correspondence. The poet Stevie Smith picked up on this in her review of the *Letters*:

> What is entirely enjoyable in these letters is Miss Macaulay's affection for the Anglican Church and the shrewdness of her thrusts against Rome. She points out that there has been too much of a fashionable swing to Rome on the part of our intellectuals and that the time has come to look again at Rome's opposition to truth and falsification of history.[33]

Macaulay clearly possessed a strong sense that Anglican Christianity, however 'peculiar [a] position it has been held by some critics to occupy', could hold its head up and did not need the validation of the Church of Rome for its authenticity.

Not everyone liked what they found in Macaulay's letters to Johnson. Illtud Evans, a Dominican reviewer of *Letters to a Friend*, was somewhat shaken to find that Macaulay did not *expect* the church to provide certainties. He quoted from one of her letters disapprovingly: '"Validity", no, the word has no meaning to me'.[34] Indeed it did not, and Evans inadvertently put his finger on something central to Macaulay's faith.

It is at this point we turn to what might be one of the last pieces of formal prose written by Macaulay. In an unpublished lecture, 'Image and Sacrament', to be given in Cambridge in 1958 (the year of her death), she reflected that it was a pity that Christianity, unlike Judaism and Islam, did not forbid the pictorial representation of the divine. 'How much have our ideas been dominated and demeaned by the

---

[32] Plomer, 'The Way Back'. Macaulay and Plomer often appeared together on the BBC radio programme 'The Critics'. Plomer, a poet and novelist who is best remembered for the four librettos he produced in collaboration with Benjamin Britten, also returned to the communion of the Church of England in later life: *ODNB*, *s.n.* 'Plomer, William (1903–1973)', online edn, <http://www.oxforddnb.com/view/article/31556>, accessed 19 July 2010.

[33] Smith, 'Soul of Gossip'.

[34] Illtud Evans, review of *Letters to a Friend*, *New Blackfriars*, no. 499 (January 1962), 41–2.

figures of Christ, and sometimes of God, in even great pictures?' More surprisingly, she went on to comment that 'the puritans, the Albigenses, the ikonoclasts [*sic*] of the Reformation, had got something'. Fanaticism and 'a sheer love of destruction' clearly motivated many acts of iconoclasm, but 'there seems to have been in the higher minds among their leaders, a glimmering of the idea that idolatry was backward and misleading'. Macaulay's views were conventional enough in terms of the regret of the cost of the Reformation to Europe's material culture. But her critique takes a surprising turn: 'However much one may for many reasons regret the Reformation in Europe – and it is difficult not to – one must allow it something even aesthetically.' A defence of the Reformation on aesthetic grounds might well appear surprising in terms of current scholarship on the cultural impact of the Reformation. Eamon Duffy, for example, has influentially described the Edwardian Reformation and its impoverishing effect on parish religion as the 'locust years'.[35] But Macaulay had little time for the material culture of the late Middle Ages, the Counter-Reformation or Ultramontanism. In the churches of Italy (where she had spent part of her childhood), France, Spain, and even in English Roman Catholic and Anglican churches, she felt distaste 'set about as they are with what one must, I fear, call simpering saints, sentimental modonnas [*sic*], even sentimental Christs'.[36]

Macaulay's distaste is less unexpected if we recall that her spiritual and intellectual life was most fed and shaped by the literary culture of English Christianity – not its visual or material culture. The keystone of her apology for Anglican Christianity to Father Johnson was the richness of its literary accomplishments – a tradition she was unabashed to trace back to the Anglo-Saxons in her Hogarth lectures of 1931.[37] Her catalogue of tradition-defining figures – Hooker, Donne, Herbert, the Fletcher brothers, Vaughan,

---

[35] Eamon Duffy, *The Stripping of the Altars: Traditional Religion in England 1400–1580* (New Haven, CT, 1992, 2nd edn 2005), 503; MacCulloch, 'Myth of the English Reformation', 12–14. For recent assessments of the historiography of the impact of the Reformation, see Peter Marshall, '(Re)defining the English Reformation', *JBS* 48 (2009), 564–86; Alec Ryrie, *The Age of Reformation: The Tudor and Stewart Realms 1485–1603* (London, 2009), 147–204; Maltby, '"Neither too mean/nor yet too gay"?'.

[36] TCC, ERM 8/10, Rose Macaulay, 'Image and Sacrament: Final Version of talk to be given in Cambridge Nov. 1958', 3. It is not clear whether this unpublished talk was delivered or not and it appears never to have been published. Macaulay died suddenly the following month.

[37] Macaulay, *Some Religious Elements*.

Herrick and so forth – forms her chief argument against the charges of Anglicanism's spiritual, cultural, theological and intellectual poverty, not a list of members of the ecclesiastical hierarchy, or even of particularly saintly individuals per se. Her hostility, therefore, towards the visual, or rather (to put it better) her ambivalence towards the representational, should not surprise us.[38]

Nearly forty years after Macaulay's death, Rowan Williams suggested that it was precisely this kind of symbolic overload that helped to cause the Reformation:

> Late medieval culture was heavily weighted with symbolism: its world was one in which virtually anything could speak of or point to virtually anything else ... It is not surprising, then, that the devotional and artistic practice of the late Middle Ages tended to more and more complex levels of elaboration.[39]

Religious sensibilities collapsing under the weight of endless embellishments, which Williams understands both in theological and visual terms, Macaulay saw chiefly in terms of the representational. She speculated:

> Perhaps the image of the concealed God should be indirect. Turning from the sacred wood to, say, the convent parlour, with the saccharine forms of saints and the crucified God, one is driven back with revulsion on oneself and one's own strainings after the knowledge of the unportrayable, almost unimaginable God ...[40]

It is here, as observed at the beginning of this essay, that we see the centrality of the eucharist in Macaulay's intellectual and spiritual life. 'It has always seemed to me that the power and rightness of the chief Christian secret, the bread and wine which are to Christians the reception of God within themselves, lies largely in their developed and remote symbolism [and] the lack of any attempts to portray'. Bread and wine are 'the poetic image' according to Macaulay. As with pictorial representations of the

---

[38] Macaulay's appreciation of rural English church architecture, however, is shown in her charming essay, 'A Church I Should Like', *St Paul's Review*, May 1929, 12–14.

[39] Rowan Williams, 'Religious Experience in the Era of Reform', in Peter Byrne and Leslie Houlden, eds, *Companion Encyclopedia of Theology* (London, 1995), 576–93, at 576.

[40] Macaulay, 'Image and Sacrament', 5.

divine, she thought 'the Roman doctrine of transubstantiation tries to materialize it'. This, she concluded, quoting Article 28 of the Thirty-Nine Articles, '"overthroweth the very nature of a sacrament"', adding 'and it is one of the very few intelligent things the Articles do say'.[41] In her critique of the defects of transubstantiation, one detects the influence of Macaulay's most 'Anglican' of poets, George Herbert:

> ffirst I am sure, whether bread stay
> Or whether Bread doe fly away
> Concerneth bread not mee ...
> I could beleeue an Impanation
> At the rate of an Incarnation
> If thou hadst dyde for Bread ...[42]

Leave the eucharist, she wrote, as 'a poetic image, and it becomes the indwelling God. I should myself prefer all religious imagery to be remote, several times removed from attempted realism'.[43] Realism in religious matters will always be for Macaulay 'attempted' – and always a failure.

Macaulay embodied the High Anglican intellectual's ambivalence towards the Reformation: while refusing to see it as wasteland, it would have been better if it had 'happened differently'. Writing at the end of her life, Macaulay found the historical claims of Roman Catholicism unconvincing but her real problem lay in its 'attempted realism', either in material or doctrinal terms. Her Dominican reviewer, Illtud Evans, noted an absence from her letters and chided her: 'she [Macaulay] never says it is a good fortune to belong to a Church that claims to teach the truth about God and man'.[44] But that was precisely her point, profoundly and dynamically sacramental: 'leave it as a poetic image, and it becomes the indwelling God'.[45]

Corpus Christi College, Oxford

---

[41] Ibid. For Macaulay's superb treatment of the Thirty-Nine Articles, see *Trebizond*, 227–34. I am grateful to Gregory Seach for reminding me of the importance of this passage.

[42] George Herbert, 'The H. Communion', in Helen Wilcox, ed., *The English Poems of George Herbert* (Cambridge, 2007), 8–9; see also ibid. 10–12. For Macaulay, Herbert was the first fully 'Anglican' poet: *Some Religious Elements*, 97–8.

[43] Macaulay, 'Image and Sacrament', 5.

[44] Evans, review of *Letters to a Friend*, 41–2.

[45] Macaulay, 'Image and Sacrament', 5.

THE ARCHBISHOP OF CANTERBURY, THE LORD CHAMBERLAIN AND THE CENSORSHIP OF THE THEATRE, 1909–49

by PETER WEBSTER

It was ever the lot of the archbishops of Canterbury to be involved in seemingly incongruous affairs. The position of the archbishop at the heart of the Establishment engendered requests to be patron, advocate or opponent of almost every conceivable development in national life. One such entanglement was his role as unofficial advisor to the Lord Chamberlain in the matter of the licensing of stage plays.

Under the Theatres Act of 1843, the Lord Chamberlain, in addition to his duties in ordering the royal household, was responsible for the review and licensing of all plays intended for commercial production in an area of London which covered the main theatrical district in the West End; a system limited in theory but in fact observed nationwide. According to the report of the 1909 Joint Select Committee on the system, he was able to refuse a licence to any play that was likely 'to do violence to the sentiment of religious reverence', to be indecent, or 'to be calculated to conduce to crime or vice'.[1] It was on matters such as these that from time to time the Lord Chamberlain's office would consult the archbishop.

Despite the apparent oddity of a senior churchman's being asked to adjudicate on artistic matters such as this, the matter has hitherto received little attention from religious historians to match that given to the censorship of the cinema and to the Lady Chatterley trial of 1960.[2] It has also received scant attention from successive archiepiscopal biographers, due perhaps to its apparently

---

[1] Dominic Shellard and Steve Nicholson, with Miriam Handley, *The Lord Chamberlain Regrets ... A History of British Theatre Censorship* (London, 2004), 61–3, at 63.

[2] G. I. T. Machin, 'British Churches and the Cinema in the 1930s', in Diana Wood, ed., *The Church and the Arts*, SCH 28 (Oxford, 1992), 477–88; on *Chatterley*, see Mark Roodhouse, 'Lady Chatterley and the Monk: Anglican Radicals and the Lady Chatterley Trial of 1960', *JEH* 59 (2008), 475–500; in the present volume, Stuart Mews, 'The Trials of *Lady Chatterley*, the Modernist Bishop and the Victorian Archbishop: Clashes of Class, Culture and Generations', 448–63.

epiphenomenal nature.[3] The role of the archbishops is treated in passing in general accounts of the censorship, but by its very nature this scholarship has not treated the theme directly.[4]

The present essay does not attempt to review wider Christian reactions to perceived irreverence or obscenity on the stage. Discussion of the religious and moral views of the successive Lord Chamberlains and their officers when applied to stage plays is also beyond its scope. Taking as its period the forty years from the Joint Select Committee report in 1909 to the unsuccessful attempt in Parliament to reform the system in 1949, it details the curious unofficial position of the archbishops within the system of censorship. The various grounds on which Archbishops Randall Davidson (1903–28) and Cosmo Gordon Lang (1928–42) in particular offered their advice to the Lord Chamberlain are then examined.[5] The essay thus provides a case study of the singular and often anomalous position of the archbishop at the heart of the Establishment in Britain, and the extent to which the secular and ecclesiastical powers combined in the regulation of the life of the nation, both moral and aesthetic. In addition, it examines a unique nodal point in the interaction between the Church and the arts.

★ ★ ★

One of the chief criticisms made of the censorship was of its secretive and unaccountable operation. The Lord Chamberlain needed neither to make public nor to justify privately his decisions, and there was no right of appeal. Within this already opaque system, the archbishop had a yet more shadowy position, being nowhere named as an advisor. His role was therefore not publicized, and on more than one occasion his office took action to disassociate the

---

[3] George Bell included a handful of letters in his *Randall Davidson: Archbishop of Canterbury*, 3rd edn, 2 vols (London, 1952), 2: 1211–15. There is still less in J. G. Lockhart, *Cosmo Gordon Lang* (London, 1949).

[4] General accounts include Shellard and Nicholson, *The Lord Chamberlain Regrets*; Anthony Aldgate and James C. Robertson, *Censorship in Theatre and Cinema* (Edinburgh, 2005); Steve Nicholson, *The Censorship of British Drama 1900–68*, 3 vols (Exeter, 2003–9); John Johnston, *The Lord Chamberlain's Blue Pencil* (London, 1990).

[5] The holders of the office of Lord Chamberlain during this period were Lord William Sandhurst (1912–21); John, 8th Duke of Atholl (1921–2); Rowland, 2nd Earl of Cromer (1922–38); George, 6th Earl of Clarendon (1938–52).

archbishop from any such function.[6] Despite this, his involvement was apparently enough of an open secret by 1949 to be mentioned in Parliament.[7]

The archbishops had also to reckon with lobbying with regard to decisions that had already been made, from both within and outside the Church. In 1912 Davidson was invited to a private production of *The Secret Woman* by Eden Phillpotts, a performance intended to garner influential support for the reversal of some changes ordered by the censor.[8] In addition, the Public Morality Council, under the guidance of the bishop of London, frequently addressed the Lord Chamberlain directly on the overall direction of plays already licensed. The Council kept Lambeth Palace informed of its activities, and was on at least one occasion supported privately by the archbishop.[9]

The other Christian Churches were of course concerned with the state of the theatre. The decision to license *Family Portrait* in 1939, a play which depicted the life of Christ's siblings, was vigorously opposed by Roman Catholic representatives of the highest standing.[10] It was also the case that representatives of other denominations were from time to time drawn into the informal consultations before a play was licensed.[11] By and large, however, the privilege of being consulted about new plays as a matter of course remained reserved to the archbishop alone.

★ ★ ★

[6]   This action extended to correcting reports in the press, as in the case of the play *Public Saviour No. 1* in 1935: London, LPL, Lang Papers, vol. 137, fols 20–4. The Lang, Davidson, Fisher and Ramsey Papers are cited by kind permission of the Librarian of Lambeth Palace.

[7]   *Hansard House of Commons* (ser. 5), vol. 463, col. 742 (25 March 1949).

[8]   London, LPL, Davidson Papers, vol. 180, fol. 39, Maggie Ponsonby to Davidson [hereafter: RTD], 29 February 1912. On the affair, see Nicholson, *Censorship*, 1: 88.

[9]   The London Council for the Promotion of Public Morality awaits its historian. On its impact in relation to the theatre, see Nicholson, *Censorship*, 1: 158–9, 300. See the 'Memorial' on the depiction of sexual scenes, sent to the Prime Minister in August 1925: Davidson Papers, vol. 205, fols 250–1. Davidson wrote in support of a 1927 memorial on the use of bad language: ibid., vol. 215, fol. 288, RTD to Cromer, 8 October 1927.

[10]   London, BL, Lord Chamberlain's Correspondence [hereafter: LCP, CORR] 1939/2844 *Family Portrait*, Cromer to Lady Winifred Elwes (Catholic Women's League), 6 June 1940; Nicholson, *Censorship*, 2: 145–6.

[11]   See the correspondence concerning a proposed English production of the Oberammergau passion play: Lang Papers, vol. 102, fols 200–23, October–December 1930.

Amongst the many and various matters on which Davidson and Lang were consulted, some were easier to adjudicate than others. The one rule that was applied consistently throughout the whole period was the ban on any impersonation of the three persons of the Trinity: a clear rule, easily and thus frequently applied. In some cases, the decision was made easy by the manner of the play itself, as with one which not only showed Christ (as a child), but was a 'travesty of the method of mystical interpretation' and presented a Christ fundamentally different to that portrayed by the Church.[12] Davidson also advised, however, against the licensing of a Irish nativity play, translated by Lady Gregory, a work free from doctrinal difficulty and indeed 'conceived in a reverent spirit'.[13] Were it licensed, Davidson feared that it would become much more difficult, if not impossible, to rule against a less reverent treatment of an equally central event. The rule, for Davidson, was clear and easily understood by public and playwrights alike: 'Its value lies in its definiteness.'[14]

It has been this inflexibility which has attracted greatest censure in the general literature on the censorship, particularly since playwrights of the standing of John Masefield and George Moore were to be caught by it.[15] The most famous case was that of *The Green Pastures* by Marc Connelly, for which a licence was refused several times between 1930 and 1961. One commentator has described the treatment of the play as 'a blot on the record of stage censorship' and 'a monument to bureaucratic rigidity'.[16] However, it was on this ground (representation of one of the persons of the Trinity) that Michael Ramsey (1961–74) was to give what may have been the last such advice, in 1961. It remained a rule that could be easily applied, even as most of the others became less and less tenable as time went on.[17]

The persistence of successive archbishops in upholding this rule was connected, at least in part, with the Church's adoption of a

---

[12] Davidson Papers, vol. 205, fol. 237, RTD to Cromer, 17 June 1924.

[13] Ibid., vol. 173, fols 26–7, RTD to Douglas Dawson, 19 June 1911.

[14] Ibid., vol. 213, fols 98–100, RTD to Cromer, 10 March 1926.

[15] On Masefield's *The Trial of Jesus* (1926), see Davidson's letter reproduced in Bell, *Davidson*, 1: 1213–15; Nicholson, *Censorship*, 1: 191–2. On Moore's *The Passing of the Essenes* (1930), see Nicholson, *Censorship*, 1: 167–8; Lang Papers, vol. 102, fols 190–1, Lang to Cromer, 27 October 1930.

[16] Aldgate and Robertson, *Censorship*, 161

[17] See the file at LCP, CORR, LR (1930), *Green Pastures*.

self-denying ordinance in relation to religious drama staged in churches. The Act of 1843 exempted plays written before the passage of its predecessor of 1737, and as such the growing number of performances of the medieval mystery and morality plays could proceed without the need to obtain a licence.[18] However, the period from the late 1920s saw an efflorescence of newly written religious drama, most prominently in the plays associated with Canterbury Cathedral, which included work by John Masefield (*The Coming of Christ*, 1928), Dorothy L. Sayers (*The Zeal of Thy House*, 1937; *The Devil to Pay*, 1939), and T. S. Eliot (*Murder in the Cathedral*, 1935).[19] After some confusion, and the securing of repeated legal opinions, the Church of England had by the end of the period reassured itself that plays staged in churches as part of an act of worship did not fall within the remit of the Lord Chamberlain.[20] However, whilst plays written for church use were seldom irreverent or conducive to crime or vice, steps were taken to ensure that they should also not impersonate the persons of the Trinity. In 1930 Lang urged George Bell, bishop of Chichester and president of the Religious Drama Society, 'to use all his influence to see that even Dramas of this kind produced in Church or under expressly religious influence and guidance should conform to [the Lord Chamberlain's] rule'.[21] The policy was confirmed by a meeting of the bishops in 1938 and persisted well into the 1950s since, as Archbishop Geoffrey Fisher (1945–61) put it, as soon as the Church relaxed the rule itself 'there will be nothing to aid the Lord Chamberlain and the Film Censor in their very difficult task'.[22] As with many other issues, the bishops were reluctant to take any unilateral action that might create gaps in the united front of state and Established Church.

[18]   The plays had been edited by A. W. Pollard, *English Miracle Plays, Moralities and Interludes* (Oxford, 1890). This had reached its seventh edition by 1923.

[19]   Kenneth Pickering, *Drama in the Cathedral: The Canterbury Festival Plays 1928–1948* (Worthing, 1985).

[20]   The question was considered in 1932, 1946 and 1950, with a policy document being privately circulated in 1952: copy at London, LPL, Fisher Papers, vol. 106, fols 239–42.

[21]   Lang Papers, vol. 102, fols 216–19, Lang to Cromer, 28 December 1930, at fol. 219.

[22]   Fisher Papers, vol. 204, fol. 85, Fisher to Leslie Hunter, bishop of Sheffield, 31 May 1958. This was in connection with a proposed production of Dorothy L. Sayers's *The Man Born to be King*.

There were other areas in which the archbishops tended to react conservatively, one of which was apparently disparaging portrayals of the Churches and other contemporary religious movements. In 1925 Davidson acted to reinforce the opinion of the Earl of Cromer (Lord Chamberlain 1922–38), of *The Last Judgment*, incongruously described as a 'theological farce'. Written by Robert King, the play ridiculed the historical record and current modes of discourse of each of the main Churches, as well as reflecting more obliquely on doctrines of heaven, the last judgement and Scripture. Davidson found 'a great deal that is rather gratuitously irreverent and would certainly cause indignation on the part of ordinary religious people, especially those of the conventional kind'.[23] A similar decision was taken in 1940 in relation to a play set during a house party of the Oxford Group, in which the attendees convince themselves that one member possesses miraculous powers. Alan Campbell Don, Lang's chaplain writing on his behalf, conceded that whilst some aspects of the movement might well attract criticism, it nonetheless did some good and as such deserved the 'sympathy and toleration of right-minded people … I do not think that the stage is the proper place for the voicing of such criticisms.'[24] Here was the archbishop acting as a defender of Christian organizations in general, and not of the Church of England alone.

As has been observed by several of the historians of the censorship, there was a strong sense that action presented on stage retained a peculiarly powerful ability to influence the behaviour of the observer, such that matters which were uncontroversial in literature were wholly inappropriate on the stage.[25] As such, if any morally ambiguous matter was to be presented, the play would need to treat it in such a way that it could in no way be conducive to vice. Steve Nicholson has examined the differing treatment of two plays by Eugène Brieux (*Damaged Goods* and *Maternity*, the former being licensed but the latter not), showing that whilst the former

23 Davidson Papers, vol. 205, fol. 252, RTD to Cromer, 14 October 1925; Robert King, *The Last Judgment: A Theological Farce* (Tynemouth, 1929).
24 Lang Papers, vol. 178, fols 334–6, Don to Colin Gordon, 26 February 1940. The play was *Our Brother Oliver*. On the ambivalence of the Established Church towards the movement, see David Bebbington, *Evangelicalism in Modern Britain: A History from the 1730s to the 1980s* (London, 1989), 235–40. On Lang's own attitude, see Adrian Hastings, *A History of English Christianity 1920–1990*, 3rd edn (London, 1991), 288.
25 Shellard and Nicholson, *The Lord Chamberlain Regrets*, ix.

was licensed as effective propaganda against venereal disease, the latter was not licensed because it did not make a comparably clear moral statement.[26] Davidson admired the tone of *Maternity* and its avoidance of coarseness. However, whereas the moral of *Damaged Goods* had been 'clearly and effectively drawn', the main motive force of *Maternity* appeared to Davidson to be something other than as a corrective to seduction, desertion and abortion: as such 'I fail to see what good purpose, social or moral or intellectual or educational its production in England at present would promote.'[27] A similar view was later taken in regard to *The Hand of the Potter* by Theodore Dreiser, which portrayed the psychological disintegration and suicide of a young man after the rape and murder of a young girl. Don advised that whilst the matter concerned was unsavoury, the play was one of serious purpose and was not obviously indecent. As such, Don thought it difficult to justify the refusal of a licence.[28] Permitting the depiction of issues of sexual morality on stage, whether unsavoury or not, was contingent on the overarching moral stance of the play.

If the rule on the representation of God was clear and easily understood, greater difficulties were attendant on scriptural subjects not involving the persons of the Trinity. In 1899 George Bernard Shaw had claimed that there was a complete prohibition of the portrayal of biblical stories.[29] However, as early as 1913, this particular rule was softening in the case of *Joseph and his Brethren* by Louis Parker. Sir Douglas Dawson, Comptroller of the Lord Chamberlain's Office, thought the play so 'glorious, so reverently & beautifully written, it could surely only work for good', an opinion shared by Lord Chamberlain Sandhurst himself.[30] Dawson suggested that faced with a choice between a rigid prohibition

---

[26] Nicholson, *Censorship*, 1: 109–14, 131; Shellard and Nicholson, *The Lord Chamberlain Regrets*, 73–6.

[27] Quoted in full in Nicholson and Shellard, *The Lord Chamberlain Regrets*, 76.

[28] Lang Papers, vol. 164, fol. 162, Don to Norman Gwatkin, 27 May 1938. Theodore Dreiser's *The Hand of the Potter: A Tragedy in Four Acts* was first published in New York in 1918. It was subsequently published in London in his *Plays, Natural and Supernatural* (1930). See also Keith Newlin, *A Theodore Dreiser Encyclopedia* (Westport, CT, 2003), 177–9, 305.

[29] In an essay in the *North American Review*, quoted at length in Nicholson, *Censorship*, 1: 24–5.

[30] Davidson Papers, vol. 188, fols 106–7, Dawson to RTD, 1 February 1913; vol. 188, fols 104–5, Sandhurst to RTD, 31 January 1913.

and judging each play on its merits, '[a]ccording to modern ideas I think we incline to the latter course'. Davidson declared himself open to such movement, but not without some reservations. Whilst not advising against a licence, he nonetheless reflected that a clumsy rule was still easier to apply than no rule at all. The play contained, he agreed, nothing irreverent or indecorous, and the main pitfall of Potiphar's wife had been avoided. However, he was keen not to be seen as encouraging such plays, and particularly ones that might tread closer to the 'inner and sacred shrine of religious truth'.[31] Davidson later advised the king against attending a performance of the same play, though it was 'all quite reverent and innocent', since the king's attendance might encourage further attempts to dramatize biblical stories 'which it wd. be difficult to condemn, but mischievous to encourage'.[32]

Once any rigid rule was abandoned with regard to biblical subjects, the archbishops were exposed to the need to adjudicate play by play. They occasionally suggested amendments to scripts, to remove minor but contentious details from an otherwise unobjectionable whole. In one case, Don advocated the renaming of a character to remove any suggestion of identification with the real Matthias of Tyre, the disciple chosen to succeed Judas Iscariot, since the play suggested some sexual relation between the character and Mary Magdalene.[33] On other occasions the faults in a script were more fundamental. Had *The Chastening* by Charles Rann Kennedy not fallen foul of the rule of representing Christ, then Davidson would likely have recommended a ban in any case since '[s]o far as it catches public imagination at all it would be by replacing the Gospel picture with something fundamentally different'; the playwright had been 'aiming after an imitation of medieval mysticism without having in the least caught its spirit'.[34]

The archbishops were well placed to give authoritative advice on orthodoxy. Of Davidson and Lang, it was Davidson, not himself a regular frequenter of the theatre, who was most often prepared to take issue with plays on apparently artistic grounds: an area

[31] Ibid., vol. 188, fols 109–11, RTD to Sandhurst, 3 February 1913.

[32] Ibid., vol. 189, fol. 140, RTD to Lord Arthur John Bigge Stamfordham [private secretary to the king], 4 November 1913.

[33] Lang Papers, vol. 164, fols 158–60, Don to Gwatkin, 9 February 1938. See also LCP, CORR 1938/1159, *The Love of Judas* [by Teresa Hooley and Cedric Wallis].

[34] Davidson Papers, vol. 205, fols 237–8.

in which the authority of the archbishops was less obvious. One play failed nearly all of the tests that were to be applied. Not only did it introduce the figure of Christ, but it was also 'a travesty of the Gospel story' in which the story was handled with a 'reckless disregard of the fact as narrated in Scripture'. It was also 'a commonplace, vulgar and illiterate production', with its 'shipwreck' of grammatical and spelling errors an indication of its general manner.[35] Davidson advised the king that *Joseph and his Brethren*, whilst not harmful, offensive or profane, was nonetheless 'poor stuff', the biblical story marred by 'second rate additions & third rate dialogue'.[36]

However, the period either side of the First World War was one during which larger questions were beginning to be asked, that went beyond grammar and dialogue, as to both the desirability and characteristics of a new religious drama, produced by Christians but for the use of all. The period was also marked by increased experimentation with drama on religious subjects in churches, not least (from 1925) in Davidson's own cathedral of Canterbury under its energetic new dean, George Bell.[37] With this experimentation arose the question of the artistic standard appropriate for sacred subjects, and of the relation between orthodoxy and artistic freedom.[38] In his reactions, Davidson often articulated the widely held conviction that sacred subjects somehow required a particular and higher standard of treatment. 'I wish they did not write these Plays' was his reaction to a 1924 play on the life of Judas Iscariot, 'for the men who write them are not men qualified to handle these great subjects greatly'.[39] A later play on the same subject was 'commonplace and dull' and as such 'I should greatly prefer that it were not

---

[35] Ibid., vol. 200, fols 8–10, RTD to Dawson, 24 October 1921, concerning an unidentified play.

[36] Ibid., vol. 189, fol. 140, RTD to Stamfordham, 4 November 1913.

[37] Ibid., vol. 180, fols 1–10. On Bell's early experimentation at Canterbury, and other work nationally, see Peter Webster, 'George Bell, John Masefield and "The Coming of Christ": Context and Significance', *Humanitas: The Journal of the George Bell Institute* 10 (2009), 111–24, at 112–14.

[38] Peter Webster, 'The "Revival" of the Visual Arts in the Church of England, c.1935 – c.1956", in Kate Cooper and Jeremy Gregory, eds, *Revival and Resurgence in Christian History*, SCH 44 (Woodbridge, 2008), 297–306.

[39] Davidson Papers, vol. 213, fol. 93, RTD to Cromer, 13 November 1924. This letter is given in full in Bell, *Randall Davidson*, 2: 1213.

put on the stage for I think it will vulgarise things which ought to stand upon a totally different level.'[40]

Yet religious plays by serious playwrights held their own risks for the Church. The archbishops were occasionally faced with challenging scripts from prominent playwrights, far from the commonplace or dull. Davidson thought *Adam the Creator* by Karel Čapek a remarkable play of serious purpose, which raised 'not unwholesomely the profound question of the world's existence … by satirising contemporary life'. Was it, however, 'justifiable to present what is really an Aristophanic comedy in a Christian State? I doubt whether it is, for it does practically make God a party to a farce.' However, Davidson's sense of the limits of the censorship was acute. The play would probably scandalize those who had not thought through the profound religious issues involved, and those who had engaged with the issues might well disagree with the play's treatment of them, Davidson included. However, the archbishop nonetheless advised that a ban could not be justified. 'What you have to prevent is indecency or gross profanity, and flippant though this is I do not think that its general purport can be said to be either really profane or indecent.'[41] One apparently throwaway remark from Davidson to Cromer further witnesses to the archbishop's unease: 'I am rather glad that Bernard Shaw does not take a Play of that sort in hand for he might raise for us much more perilous issues.'[42]

★ ★ ★

In 1940 Colin Gordon of the Lord Chamberlain's office solicited Lang's opinion on the play *Family Portrait* by the American playwrights Lenore and William Joyce Cowen. Don accepted the 'obvious reverence and restraint' of the script but raised some fundamental concerns. The first issue, as has already been noted, was the portrayal of the brothers and sisters of Christ, the very non-existence of whom was a matter of some importance to Roman Catholics and to some within the Church of England.

---

[40] Davidson Papers, vol. 215, fol. 294, RTD to Cromer, 19 November 1927.

[41] LCP, CORR 1928/8304, *Adam the Creator*, Davidson to Cromer, 21 April 1928.

[42] Webster, 'Bell and Masefield', 117; Paul Foster, 'The Goring Judgement: Is it still Valid?', *Theology* 102 (1999), 253–61. Davidson had seen Shaw's *St Joan* in 1924, and evidently appreciated it: Bell, *Randall Davidson*, 2: 1212.

The second was the downplaying of the incarnation to the extent that Christ appeared as solely an ethical teacher, although a great one. Don concluded that the play ought not to be licensed in the usual way.[43]

Here was the archbishop's representative advising in accustomed fashion. When called upon, Davidson and Lang had advised on the licensing of plays on a number of different grounds: the likelihood of incitement to vice or gratuitous offence to religious people; and theological or artistic defect. They helped shape the formulation of guiding principles, and advised in cases where there was doubt.

It is, however, an indication of the degree to which the situation had changed by 1940 that *Family Portrait* had in fact already been licensed the previous year, without reference to Lambeth at all. The query was in fact occasioned by a letter, after the licence had been issued, to the Lord Chamberlain from Canon J. K. Mozley of St Paul's. Gordon nonetheless concluded that Don's objections were not sufficient to revoke a licence already issued.[44]

The exchange was one of the last of its kind. After a peak in the 1920s and early 1930s, there had been a marked decline in the number of plays referred to Lambeth. The reasons for this are too complex to treat at length here, although it may partly be explained by the involvement of Geoffrey Dearmer, poet and Anglican, and son of Percy Dearmer, as Reader of Plays for the Lord Chamberlain from 1936.[45] Lang's successors William Temple (1942–4) and Geoffrey Fisher were seldom consulted, although Fisher was kept informed of major changes in policy, such as the relaxation of restrictions on the portrayal of homosexuality in 1958. One of Fisher's few interventions was to reinforce the ban on *The Green Pastures* in 1951, a decision confirmed by Michael Ramsey ten years later.[46] So it was that the single stipulation relating to the impersonation of the persons of the Trinity was by 1949 the only remaining matter on which the archbishops advised the Lord Chamberlain.

---

[43] Lang Papers, vol. 178, fols 339–43, Don to Gordon, 2 April 1940.

[44] Ibid., vol. 178, fol. 344, Gordon to Don, 15 April 1940; LCP, CORR 1939/2844 *Family Portrait*, J. K. Mozley to the Lord Chamberlain, 14 March 1940.

[45] Nicholson, *Censorship*, 2: 142–4.

[46] Fisher Papers, vol.86, fols 210–12, Fisher to the Earl of Clarendon, 30 April 1951; London, LPL, Ramsey Papers, vol. 8, fol. 17, Ramsey to the Earl of Scarborough, 29 October 1961.

I hope elsewhere to continue the story beyond 1949, and to treat of the attitude of Anglicans to the final abolition of theatre censorship in 1968. Anglican support for abolition was in part fostered by the manifest anachronism of the remaining rule and its stultifying effect on religious drama within the Church. That aside, the operation of the system to 1949 is demonstrative of some governing assumptions concerning the joint operation of Church and state in the regulation of morals; of understandings of the appropriate modes of representing the national faith; and of some of the tensions in the relationship between the Church and the arts.

Institute of Historical Research

THE TRIALS OF *LADY CHATTERLEY*, THE MODERNIST BISHOP AND THE VICTORIAN ARCHBISHOP: CLASHES OF CLASS, CULTURE AND GENERATIONS

by STUART MEWS

'Now firmly established as a modernist novelist',[1] D. H. Lawrence (1885-1930) remains a controversial writer, especially for the ambiguity of his attitudes to fascism and feminism. This essay considers the role played by the then forty-one-year-old bishop of Woolwich, John Robinson, in offering evidence for the defence in the Old Bailey trial in 1960 which acquitted Penguin Books of obscenity in publishing Lawrence's novel *Lady Chatterley's Lover*. In taking part in the trial Robinson acquired notoriety (or credit). His public admiration for Lawrence's writing placed him at odds with the two post-war archbishops, Geoffrey Fisher (Canterbury) and Cyril Garbett (York). In the words of Mark Roodhouse in a pioneering article, 'for ecclesiastical historians the Lady Chatterley trial not only reveals changing social attitudes but also growing division within the Church of England between "two Christianities" over the way to respond to these changes'.[2] Robinson did not receive further advancement in the Church.

The storm over Bishop Robinson can be compared to the generally favourable responses evoked by the monk Father Martin Jarrett-Kerr (who had entered the Community of the Resurrection at Mirfield in 1940), when he sought advice after being also asked to give evidence. The different reactions might be partly explained by the weight given to the views of a bishop in contrast to those of a mere monk at a time when there was considerable uncertainty both within the Church and on the part of the British public about the role of a bishop,[3] but there was also the provoca-

---

[1] Linda R. Williams, ed., *Bloomsbury Guide to English Literature: The Twentieth Century* (London, 1992), 218.

[2] Mark Roodhouse, 'Lady Chatterley and the Monk', *JEH* 59 (2008), 475–500.

[3] Kenneth Thompson, 'Church of England Bishops as an Elite', in Philip Stanworth and Anthony Giddens, eds, *Elites and Power in British Society* (Cambridge, 1974),

tive, even flippant, tone of the bishop's evidence. In 1961 the view was expressed that in the workshops of the Steel Company of Wales the appointment of Archbishop Michael Ramsey to Canterbury was welcomed 'on the ground of his venerable appearance' but the trial evidence of Robinson 'was equally generally disapproved of on the grounds that this was not the sort of book a Bishop should have supported'.[4]

★ ★ ★

D. H. Lawrence 'became really famous only after his death in 1930'.[5] A Nottinghamshire miner's son, steeped in the values of Eastwood Congregational Chapel which he formally renounced at the age of twenty-two but never entirely forgot,[6] his publishing career lasted from 1911 to 1928. *Lady Chatterley's Lover*, which was completed in 1926, had to wait until 1960 for publication in Britain because of the likelihood of prosecution for its salacious accounts of extramarital intercourse between Sir Clifford Chatterley's refined wife and the rough-spoken gamekeeper. Crossing the divide between body and soul, the sacred and the profane, had been a feature of the Edwardian literary imagination, in which 'sacramentalized sexuality' could find expression in physical fulfilment outside marriage and which for autonomous women did not inevitably lead, as had been common in Victorian fiction, to death or disgrace.[7]

Lawrence was an obvious target for the interdenominational Council for Public Morals, chaired by the then bishop of London, Arthur Winnington-Ingram. In 1915 the Council succeeded in securing the banning of an early novel, *The Rainbow*, now regarded as a masterpiece. A police raid on an exhibition of Lawrence's paintings in 1929, which he believed had resulted from a complaint by the Council, led to an outburst of indignant fury:

198–207; Glyn Simon, ed., *Bishops* (London, 1961), includes a visionary essay by John Robinson, 'The New Model Episcopacy': ibid. 125–38.

4   Simon, ed., *Bishops*, 2.

5   *ODNB*, *s.n.* 'Lawrence, David Herbert (1885–1930)'.

6   Margaret J. Masson, 'D. H. Lawrence's Congregational Inheritance', *D. H. Lawrence Review* 22 (1990), 53–68. For the wider influence of the former Church of England priest Edward Carpenter, see Emile Delavenay, *D. H. Lawrence and Edward Carpenter: A Study in Edwardian Transition* (London, 1971).

7   G. R. Searle, *A New England? Peace and War 1886–1918* (Oxford, 2004), 583.

The greatest of all lies in the modern world [Lawrence wrote] is the lie of purity and the dirty little secret ... The grey ones left over from the nineteenth century are the embodiment of the lie. They dominate in society, in the press, in literature, everywhere, and naturally they lead the vast mob of the general public along with them.[8]

This was his mood when he started to write *Lady Chatterley's Lover*, the first version of which was completed in 1926. Four years later Lawrence died; he never saw the novel in print.

In 1932, F. R. Leavis of Downing College, Cambridge, became editor of *Scrutiny*, a literary review. Leavis was crucial in promoting Lawrence as the supreme exponent of modernism. 'Modernists wanted to shock and to outrage; and through the outrage awake people into seeing the world about them in a new way', explained Noel Annan, Provost of King's College, Cambridge, and witness for the defence at the Lady Chatterley trial. He believed that Lawrence was 'the most vocal of all the writers before the Great War in celebrating "life"'.[9]

The Second World War had been a people's war, and was followed by a people's peace. In this climate, what novelist Alan Sillitoe (best known for *Saturday Night and Sunday Morning*) has called 'the proletarian novelist' flourished.[10] In the opinion of the Sussex academic Alan Sinfield, 'D. H. Lawrence suddenly became very important': he could be celebrated for his working-class origins and his portrayal of the alienation of working-class life, but he also featured in the Leavisite crusade to render high culture earnest, appeared progressive on sexual relations and had been persecuted by 'the establishment'. He seemed to bridge the gap between the New Left and the working class.[11] In January 1960 *The Times* seemed to be reading the runes correctly when it forecast: 'If anyone is making a list of authors who will come into their own in 1960, then D. H. Lawrence claims to be the

---

8   D. H. Lawrence, *Sex, Literature and Censorship* (1955), quoted in E. J. Bristow, *Vice and Vigilance: Purity Movements in Britain since 1700* (Dublin, 1977), 222.

9   Noel Annan, *Our Age: Portrait of a Generation* (London), 53, 62.

10   Alan Sillitoe, 'Proletarian Novelists', *Books and Bookmen*, August 1959, 13.

11   Alan Sinfield, *Literature, Politics and Culture in Postwar Britain* (Berkeley, CA, 1989), 259.

favourite'.[12] By 1965 the historian A. J. P. Taylor, himself, like Lawrence, from a provincial Nonconformist background, could describe Lawrence as 'the greatest English novelist of the twentieth century'.[13] The *Times* prediction would have rejoiced the heart of at least one Church of England priest, Father Martin Jarrett-Kerr. He had encountered the writings of Lawrence while studying English at Oxford, and in 1951 published *D. H. Lawrence and Human Existence* under the pseudonym William Tiverton, a book which was dismissed by Leavis for its application of ethical and theological judgements. These led Jarrett-Kerr to conclude that 'Lawrence seems to me much closer to the Christian view of sex, properly understood, than were many of his opponents'.[14] In Anglican official circles in the 1950s this was very much a minority opinion. A more authoritative and representative judgement was probably that of the archbishop of York, Cyril Garbett. In 1956 Penguin Books published a revised paperback edition of his *In an Age of Revolution*. The chapter on 'Moral Chaos' listed the three authors who, in the opinion of this octogenarian bachelor, had had the greatest influence on the popular mind in the previous half-century: Shaw, Lawrence and Wells. Incredibly in 1956, Garbett could write of 'Mr. D. H. Lawrence, whose popularity will puzzle future generations, if indeed his writings are still read by them'.[15] The archbishop continued: 'In language which is almost hysterical, [Lawrence] writes of the dark sensual underworld which lies beyond the boundaries of man's conscious mind, and from which surges up impulses and wants which must be gratified if true life is to be experienced.'[16]

Having perused the Cambridge edition of the *Letters of D. H. Lawrence*, Archbishop Garbett concluded that it was difficult 'to give any other interpretation to this doctrine except as the assertion that the true end of life ... can be found only through the complete gratification of sex'.[17] Only four years later another Anglican bishop, John Robinson, was to provide a rather more

12 *The Times*, 2 January 1960.
13 A. J. P. Taylor, *English History 1914–1945* (Harmondsworth, 1965), 325.
14 Roodhouse, 'Lady Chatterley', 478–80.
15 Cyril Garbett, *In an Age of Revolution* (Harmondsworth, 1956), 75.
16 Ibid. 76.
17 Ibid. 77.

positive interpretation of the insights of the Nottinghamshire proletarian novelist.

To mark the thirtieth anniversary of Lawrence's death in 1960, Penguin Books decided to republish all his novels in paperback, including an unexpurgated version of *Lady Chatterley's Lover*. This led to the celebrated court case which has often been cited as ushering in the 'swinging Sixties'.[18] What had changed were the more open post-war intellectual climate and the passing of the Obscene Publications Act in 1959, long championed by A. P. Herbert and Roy Jenkins. This allowed publication of works where it could be proved that this was 'for the public good' in the opinion of experts. The Director of Public Prosecutions, Theobald Matthew, a practising Roman Catholic, was initially reluctant to take action regarding *Lady Chatterley's Lover* so soon after the passing of the act. However, what seems to have alarmed him was the news that Penguin intended to publish a paperback for three shillings and sixpence. Penguin's solicitor, Michael Rubinstein, busied himself asking over three hundred 'experts' if they would testify on behalf of publication.[19] John Robinson, who had left Cambridge only the year before to become bishop suffragan of Woolwich, was anxious to help, 'if you can arrange for a copy to be sent to me', adding: 'I find the prosecution of this book very difficult to understand'.[20] Robinson had spent most of his adult life in Cambridge as an undergraduate and postgraduate student before becoming Dean of Clare College from 1951 to 1959. He was typical of the 1950s dissident intellectuals who were frustrated by the complacency of the Macmillan government and of Fisher's Church of England. But John Robinson had deeper intellectual foundations. His Ph.D. dissertation had involved in-depth study of Martin Buber's *I and Thou*, and intense relationships were especially important to him.

There were others eager for their day in court. Ernest Raymond was a minor English writer whose first novel, *Tell England*, was the

[18] Arthur Marwick, *The Sixties* (Oxford, 1999) 3–16; Hugh McLeod, *The Religious Crisis of the 1960s* (Oxford, 2007), 68.

[19] Paul Ferris, *Sex and the British: A Twentieth Century History* (London, 1993), 176. Ferris was the first to use the relevant file from the Directorate of Public Prosecutions.

[20] Bristol, University Library, Penguin Book Archive, DM 1679/4, John Robinson to M. Rubinstein, 21 August 1960. I am grateful to Rachel Hassall for help with this archive.

literary sensation of 1922. It was based on his experiences as a First World War Church of England army chaplain, and its success had led him to resign his orders and devote himself to full-time authorship. 'Certainly I am willing – indeed eager to take some part in the defence of Penguin Books', he wrote to Rubinstein. His written statement was uncompromising: 'Lawrence was a man of genius; ... it is imperative, not only "for the public good" but for a public need, to have the canon of his writings complete.'[21] Raymond had a special reason for supporting a more open attitude to sexual matters. Although in *Who's Who* he listed his father as William Bell Raymond, in his 1968 autobiography he explained how he found out that he was really the illegitimate son of Major-General G. F. Blake and that the 'aunt' who lived with the family and brought him up was really his mother.[22] Raymond's testimony was not, however required in the Old Bailey trial, which opened on 20 October 1960.

Four Anglican clergymen gave evidence in favour of publication: John Robinson, bishop of Woolwich; Stephen Hopkinson of the Industrial Christian Fellowship; T. R. Milford, Master of the Temple; and Donald Tytler, Director of Religious Education for the Birmingham diocese. The first to take the stand was Robinson. 'What do you say are the ethical merits of the book?' asked Gerald Gardiner for the defence. 'What I think is clear', replied the bishop. 'It is that what Laurence is trying to do is to describe the sex relationship as something essentially sacred. Archbishop William Temple ...' 'Before you talk about Archbishop William Temple,' interrupted Mr Justice Byrne, the trial judge, 'he was trying to portray what?' – 'The sex relation as essentially something sacred', responded the bishop. 'I think Lawrence tried to portray this relation as in a real sense something sacred, as in a real sense an act of holy communion. For him flesh was completely sacramental of spirit. Neither in intention nor in effect is this book depraving'. 'As you read this book', interposed the judge,' does it portray the life of an immoral woman?' 'It portrays the life of a woman in an immoral relationship ... I would not say it was intended in any way to exalt immorality.' Gardiner concluded his examination by asking: 'Is it a book which in your view Christians ought to read?'

[21] Ibid., DM 1979/6, Ernest Raymond to M. Rubinstein, 21 August 1960.
[22] Ernest Raymond, *The Story of My Days* (London, 1968), 59–60.

'Yes I think it is. Because I think what Lawrence was trying to do
…' Yet again the prosecuting barrister Mervyn Griffith-Jones was
on his feet, but the bishop had said enough to provide headlines
for the evening papers: 'A BOOK ALL CHRISTIANS SHOULD
READ'.[23]

On 2 November 1960 the jury, after a three-hour deliberation,
returned a verdict of 'Not guilty'. There had been no certainty
about the outcome. Compton Mackenzie, by now an elderly
writer, who had converted to Roman Catholicism as a young
man, had first met D. H. Lawrence at the end of August 1914,
but had got to know him better when Lawrence stayed with him
in Capri after the war. Mackenzie took a keen interest in the
trial and observed it from the public gallery. On the day after the
verdict, by chance he bumped into the defence barrister Gerald
Gardiner in a London restaurant. 'The best I hoped for was the
jury's disagreement, and I was very doubtful even of that', he was
told.[24] Mackenzie had been asked to testify for the defence but
he had explained that 'compared with Lawrence's best novels, it
was contemptible'. His comment on the trial was that 'some of
the 35 witnesses for the defence talked portentous humbug and
canting balderdash in the witness box'. He was scathing of John
Robinson: 'We may wonder if Dr. Robinson will find *Lady Chatterley's Lover* of verbal use if he be called upon to translate the
Song of Solomon for the New English Bible. Why not? Under the
Bishop's eloquence,' he continued, 'the four-letter words took on
a kind of liturgical meekness'.[25] If Mackenzie, as a fellow author,
had been willing to offer his assessment of the book to the jury, it
might have offset some of the humbug and balderdash of which
he complained.

Things might also have gone differently if, instead of one bishop
appearing in the witness box, there had been two: moreover,
bishops singing from different hymn sheets. John Robinson had
not been the only bishop asked to give evidence. The bishop of
Llandaff, Glyn Simon, later to be archbishop of Wales, had also

[23] C. H. Rolph, *The Trial of Lady Chatterley: Regina v. Penguin Books Ltd* (Harmondsworth, 1961), 70–3.
[24] Compton Mackenzie, *My Life and Times: Octave Ten 1953–1963* (London, 1971),
152.
[25] Compton Mackenzie, *On Moral Courage* (London, 1962), 125–6.

been approached. He was senior to Robinson, a diocesan not a suffragan, and had had a notable ministry in the pit villages and steel works of South Wales. He has been described by one of his successors, Rowan Williams, as 'the greatest ornament of the Welsh bench since disestablishment'.[26] Simon's reaction to Robinson's appearance for the defence had been one of regret. He told Archbishop Fisher: 'I know that many simple Church folk have been greatly perplexed.' He had himself read *Lady Chatterley* years before in the expurgated version 'but thought it dull, but then I have a "blind spot" about Lawrence and cannot share the rapture which people go on about'.[27] In his response to Michael Rubinstein, Simon wrote that in his opinion publication 'would not be for the public good and I could not support it'. His reasons were:

> a) that Lawrence's aim of getting rid of the 'dirty little secret' attitude to sex is today beside the point; the whole thing is wide open to discussion and experiment, even its clinical aspects are topics of the breakfast table;
> b) Making even the widest allowance ... I have no doubt that for 75% of people under 35 this book would be what Confessors call 'an occasion of sin.'
> The general merits, literary and otherwise, are in my opinion insufficient. The literary merits as a whole do not seem to me to place it among Lawrence's better works.[28]

Bishop Simon was not alone amongst church leaders in refusing to support publication. Dr Leslie Weatherhead was a Methodist minister, ex-President of the Conference, who had drawn huge congregations to the City Temple in London. He had been an early pioneer in the use of psychology in pastoral ministry. In 1931 he had produced a controversial best-seller, *The Mastery of Sex through Psychology and Religion*, which had eventually been published by the SCM Press following its rejection after much agonizing by the Methodist Epworth Press. The book was still selling in the 1950s and 1960s, and through it Weatherhead had gained a reputation

---

[26] *ODNB, s.n.* 'Simon, (William) Glyn Hughes (1903–1972)'; Owen W. Jones, *Glyn Simon: His Life and Opinions* (Llandysul, 1981).

[27] London, LPL, Fisher Papers, vol. 246, fol. 173, Glyn Simon to G. F. Fisher, 7 November 1960.

[28] Ibid.

as a 'liberal' in his attitude to sexual morals and behaviour. He agreed to read *Lady Chatterley's Lover*, and then burned the book. He told Michael Rubinstein that 'in spite of the literary merits of the book, it would get into the wrong hands, sell in millions and do immense harm both to young people and to many frustrated older people also'. He was opposed to publication 'in our country where already sexual immorality is at a danger level'.[29]

The Office of the Director of Public Prosecutions tried to enlist the help of Noel Annan and Helen Gardner as prosecution witnesses, but they were already committed to the other side, and efforts to secure T. S. Eliot and Lord David Cecil came to naught. Academics might have found *Lady Chatterley's Lover* insubstantial compared to *Sons and Lovers* but few were willing to stand up in court and advocate the banning of a book, although it is said that Evelyn Waugh had offered his services. Outside academe, Malcolm Muggeridge was at the height of his fame as a regular presenter for the BBC flagship programme *Panorama* and had a loathing for Lawrence but kept his head down when the search was on for prosecution witnesses. In Oxford Basil Blackwell sought 'to keep unworthy books out of unworthy hands'. He interpreted *Lady Chatterley* as the vicarious revenge of the 'gutter born' Lawrence on an aristocratic society.[30]

Once the trial was over and the verdict announced, Archbishop Fisher moved quickly to take control of the situation. In the words of Eric James in his admirable biography of John Robinson, 'the trial of Lady *Chatterley* was over. The trial of the Bishop of Wool-wich was about to begin.'[31] Edward Carpenter, in his life of Geof-frey Fisher, reported that 'Lambeth was overwhelmed with letters and telephone calls protesting against the bishop.'[32] However, it is perhaps significant that Carpenter devoted only one page out of over eight hundred to the incident. As a canon of Westminster, Carpenter had himself encouraged Robinson to get involved in

[29] John Travell, *Doctor of Souls: Leslie Weatherhead 1893–1976* (Cambridge, 1999), 69.

[30] Ferris, *Sex and the British*, 176–7; Malcolm Muggeridge, *Chronicles of Wasted Time* (London, 1972), 65; Bernard Bergonzi, *Wartime and Aftermath: English Literature and its Background 1939–1960* (Oxford, 1993), 210; Rita Ricketts, comp., *Adventurers All: Tales of Blackwellians, of Books, Bookmen, Reading and Writing Folk* (Oxford, 2002), 250.

[31] Eric James, *A Life of John A. T. Robinson, Bishop, Pastor, Prophet* (London, 1987), 96.

[32] Edward Carpenter, *Archbishop Fisher: His Life and Times* (Norwich, 1991), 304.

the trial and at the height of the storm had published a short newspaper article in his support.[33] The day after the verdict, Fisher wrote a stern letter to Robinson, beginning with a reminder that 'a short while ago I gave you a private hint which you did not welcome'. As a result, 'I am now in the very embarrassing position' of having to respond to the avalanche of complaints.'I cannot defend you of course at all. The distress you have caused to many Christian people is so great'.[34] The archbishop was in no doubt that a public reprimand was called for and he used his address to the Canterbury diocesan conference on 5 November 1960 to issue this, although to his credit he did send an advance copy to Robinson. The archbishop was clear: 'In my judgement, the Bishop was mistaken to think that he could take part in the trial without becoming a stumbling block and a cause of offence to many ordinary Christians, and I think I ought to say so here.'[35]

Robinson replied politely but in turn enclosed a copy of an article 'Why I gave evidence', which with some additions designed to placate the archbishop was published in *The Observer* on 13 November. In it he quoted a former archbishop of Canterbury, Cosmo Gordon Lang, who had said on 4 April 1930 (in words hunted out by Michael Rubinstein): 'We want to liberate the sex impulse from the impression that it is always to be surrounded by negative warnings and restraints, and to place it in its rightful place among the great creative and formative things'. Robinson justified his actions to Fisher by insisting that he saw his own role as prophetic as well as pastoral: 'Where the prophetic witness of the Church is concerned, I imagine there will always be honest and sincere divisions of opinion between Christians at every level'.[36]

The archbishop's statement and Robinson's *Observer* article polarized opinion in Church and nation. An examination of the papers of both the principal actors in the ecclesiastical drama reveals that those who wrote to the bishop overwhelmingly supported his stand, whilst those who opposed him overwhelmingly preferred to vent their dismay and disgust on the archbishop

[33] James, *Robinson*, 89.
[34] Fisher Papers, vol. 246, fol. 168, G. F. Fisher to J. A. T. Robinson, 3 November 1960.
[35] Ibid., fol. 162, Archbishop's Canterbury statement; James, *Robinson*, 98.
[36] Ibid., fol. 177, J. A. T. Robinson to G. F. Fisher, 8 November 1960.

of Canterbury. Both Fisher and Robinson could claim popular support for their positions but neither was able to see the whole picture. Robinson was encouraged by a letter from E. M. Forster: 'I admire you for coming to give evidence'.[37] The archbishop could claim the support of Enid Blyton, who had also been approached about appearing for the defence: 'though how anyone who cares genuinely for children as I do, could do so I do not know ... I would deserve to have my own book burned if I stood up in court and declared the book to be holy or puritanical. No parent would trust me after that'.[38] What probably counted for more with Fisher was a letter addressed to Colonel Hornby, his recently appointed press secretary, and forwarded to the archbishop. It came from an ordinary layman of the church in a Wimbledon parish, who had been taking part in a Christian Stewardship campaign. He had been told time and again that the Church had drifted and its leaders lacked the guts to face up to the challenge of the modern cult of materialism and immorality. The congregation were going to ask their parish priest to give them guidance from the pulpit.[39]

In Cambridge Alec Vidler, Dean of King's, organized a letter to *The Times* regretting that 'when a bishop has caught the ear of the nation in a manner befitting a spokesman of the national Church he should have been publicly rebuked by the Archbishop of Canterbury'.[40] The Dean of Trinity, Harry Williams, had already put his head above the parapets by writing independently to Fisher 'very humbly about something which is worrying a number of devout Church people'. It was that the authorities of the Church 'never seem to present Christian morality in a positive, let alone a dynamic form. All we get from the newspapers is a series of prohibitions.'[41] On his return from a visit to Africa, Fisher took up the challenge, pointing out to Williams:

> it is a fact of some significance that practically the only people of any consequence who have criticised my statement have

[37] London, LPL, Robinson Papers, vol. 3539, fol. 67, E. M. Forster to J. A. T. Robinson, 2 November 1960.

[38] Fisher Papers, vol. 347, fol. 168, Enid Blyton to G. F. Fisher, 6 November 1960.

[39] Ibid., vol. 246, fol. 158, A. H. Cuckney to Col. Hornby, 2 November 1960.

[40] Robinson Papers, vol. 3539, fol. 133, A. R. Vidler to J. A. T. Robinson, 9 November 1960; James, *Robinson*, 104. The letter was signed by Geoffrey Lampe, Donald M. MacKinnon, Hugh Montefiore, Alec Vidler and Harry Williams.

[41] Fisher Papers, vol. 258, fol. 199, Harry Williams to G. F. Fisher, 7 November 1960.

been university teachers. … You are thinking about teaching. John Robinson was thinking about being a teacher or a prophet, but the circumstances of a trial were such as not even the Archangel Gabriel could teach or prophesy.[42]

The archbishop went on to complain that if he ever mentioned sex it was bound to be reported but if he talked about the work of the Church's Moral Welfare Council, it fell on deaf ears.

I still think it is good from time to time to tell the world that adultery is a sin, and to tell you the truth I think it is very dangerous merely to say that sex is sacred. Sex is one of God's gifts and everything depends on how we use it.[43]

For Fisher, 'sex is always to be regarded in the context of the family. That is really positive teaching, but John Robinson did not even refer to it'.[44]

The Church press appeared to know where it stood, but to take this at face value would not give a true picture. The *Church Times* on 11 November had a resolute leading article under the headline, THOU SHALT NOT. 'We have received protests from responsible readers, in many parts of the country, who declare themselves horrified by this evidence [given by clergy] and in particular by certain statements by the Suffragan Bishop of Woolwich.' But on this occasion the Anglo-Catholic brick wall was built on shallow foundations. Bishop Robinson must have been surprised to receive a letter from Portugal Street, where the *Church Times* had its office, signed by Jane Dart (reporter) and Felicity Babington (editor's secretary): 'We would like to dissociate ourselves from the editorial policy of the *Church Times* and expressed in the leader last week … We are also sorry that the selection of letters published during the last two weeks suggest an overwhelming support for the leader-writers and critical of you.'[45]

The somewhat fusty *Church Times* was not alone in not being able to keep its entire staff on board. Archbishop Fisher kept his beady eye on all possible sources of dissent. John Robinson's natural

---

[42] Ibid., fol. 201, G. F. Fisher to H. Williams, 23 November 1960.
[43] Ibid.
[44] Ibid.
[45] Robinson Papers, vol. 3539, fol. 85, Jane Dart and Felicity Babington to J. A. T. Robinson, 18 November 1960.

supporters included the young radicals who gathered round *Prism*, a new magazine, originally financed by Nicholas Moseley but taken over by the wealthy young liberal priest Timothy Beaumont. A fortnight after the revolt on the right came signs of faltering on the left. On 1 December Fisher wrote to Beaumont complaining about the coverage in *Prism* of the now notorious trial. 'In *Prism* you conjoin the motion on world hunger and the Bishop of Woolwich's appearance in a book trial as signs that the Church is looking outwards. You suggest that the second sign was hastily obliterated by his Grace of Canterbury'. He also challenged Nicholas Moseley's comments elsewhere in the same issue of the magazine:

> I have not expressed any judgement of any sort on the book itself [complained Fisher]. I have not criticised the Bishop's evidence, though you must know, it is open to a good deal of criticism. I criticised the Bishop not for his views but for giving evidence *at all* in circumstances in which he would inevitably cause confusion to many people and grave embarrassment to many others charged as he is with pastoral responsibilities. The Bishop thought himself, I think, as a teacher, and a prophet. But a pastor cannot effectively teach or prophecy in a witness box on a point of law. And when he is not allowed to discuss the pastoral problem involved. As a pastor, a Bishop has to take into account so much that is quite irrelevant to the point of law.[46]

The archbishop was sure that 'as chief pastor, I have to think not only of university students or dons, or of wholesome and unwholesome literature, still less now'. He pointed out:

> The Bishop of Woolwich has the same liberty that you or I have to form his own judgement on a book and as you know many well-read and scholarly Christians do consider that ... one has to take account of D. H. Lawrence who was a sincere person and try to see what he was after. I rebuked the Bishop of Woolwich not for his literary judgement about a book but

46 Fisher Papers, vol. 261, fol. 116, G. F. Fisher to Timothy Beaumont, 1 December 1960.

for his gross lack of pastoral wisdom in appearing in the trial at all and saying that – all Christians should read the book.[47]

In response to this broadside Beaumont conceded certain points: 'I agree with you in feeling that the Bishop of Woolwich should not have given evidence (although I think that his evidence, as given was absolutely right.)'. Beaumont went on to state that he thought *Lady Chatterley* should have been published, and although he did not consider it a Christian book, 'I do think it has many insights into truth far deeper than seems to be the general attitude of the church. I agree with (I think) everything the Bishop of Woolwich said in the witness box.' He went on to argue that although Robinson's evidence might have done harm in certain circles it definitely did good in others. Beaumont also questioned the right of the archbishop to rebuke publicly the suffragan of another diocesan, adding the stinging flourish: 'I wonder if you would have felt called upon to utter a rebuke so firmly and so publicly if the Bishop of Woolwich's evidence had been on the other side in this case?'[48]

Despite the difference in their respective positions in the Church, Fisher clearly relished a challenge and replied with a point by point response:

> I have not read the book and for that reason have never expressed an opinion about it. The real disaster I should say was not the book but the trial. Furthermore I should say that now the trial is over the less said the better about the book. In sheer amount there is far too much talk about sex nowadays; and the best way to help people to be healthy on the subject is to stop them dwelling on it more than they need.

That was the Victorian headmaster, born in 1887, speaking. 'I rebuked the Bishop not for what he said in the witness box but for being there', Fisher continued. 'I certainly should not feel able, as you do, to agree with everything he said there ... without more explanation'. The archbishop queried one of Robinson's most quoted lines, and countered: 'Sex is not sacred. It is a possession of the person and it is the personality which is sacred'. He went on:

---

47 Ibid.
48 Ibid., fol. 121, Timothy Beaumont to G. F. Fisher, 3 January 1961.

'If the good teacher had to use the phrase "Holy Communion" in this connexion, he would have to safeguard it in every kind of way from shocking his hearers.' But what particularly rankled was Robinson's insubordination: 'He is very junior. He took on himself to be the spokesman for the Church. Any other bishop would have consulted me or some other senior bishop before doing such a thing. He consulted no one'.[49]

It is not true that Robinson 'consulted no one', but he had not asked the archbishop's permission, possibly because he did not see the need, probably because he knew that the answer would be negative. Eric James reported that Robinson had told his own bishop, Mervyn Stockwood, who had been in post at South-wark for only one year. James also relates that before agreeing to give evidence Robinson consulted the group convened by T. R. Milford (Master of the Temple) to discuss sexual ethics, which included George Appleton and Edward Carpenter. 'They encouraged him to take the stand'.[50]

The spat between Beaumont and the archbishop was but one instance of differences which ran through all levels of the Church. Eric Abbott's article in the *Daily Mail* gave rise to two obscene letters a day and he reported that Eric James, after supporting Robinson in *Time and Tide*, 'rang me up in a great deal of distress as George Reindorp [then Provost of Southwark] attacked him rather violently on the telephone ... If what Eric has written causes the Archbishop of Canterbury to write to him and summon him to his study, I have urged him to consult Mervyn first before seeing the archbishop'.[51]

The use of literature in the service of religion was not however, universally approved. Valerie Pitt, a teacher of literature at Woolwich Polytechnic and radical Anglican (she wrote the note of dissent to the Chadwick Report on Church and State), in a private letter had lambasted Fisher for what she considered the anti-intellectualism of his synodal rebuke of Robinson, and asked him whether she should avoid including in her course any books with characters who had committed adultery. But while supporting freedom of

---

[49] Ibid., fol. 119, G. F. Fisher to Timothy Beaumont, 19 January 1961.

[50] James, *Robinson*, 89.

[51] Robinson Papers, vol. 3539, fol. 46, Eric Abbott to J. A. T. Robinson, 14 November 1960.

speech, she was not impressed by what the bishop had said. 'What nobody noticed in the theological furore was that Dr. Robinson was talking nonsense about Lawrence', she later wrote.

> The one thing Lawrence does not say about physical love is that it is sacramental: the relationship between Connie Chatterley and Mellors is itself, not the outward and visible sign of an inward and spiritual something or other. This is the trouble in this making use of literature: none of the theological critics will open his mind and enter into a willing suspension both of belief and unbelief, and really receive the writer's vision.

Earlier in the same chapter, she had written: 'It seems to be almost an iron law that the theologian who turns to literature does not so much turn into a first-rate heretic as second-rate literary critic'.[52]

The trial of *Lady Chatterley* was a turning point in Church and society. It encouraged the Young Turks in the Church of England to feel that they should use every opportunity to address the intellectual and moral needs of the nation. It was a clash of cultures, between the arts of literary criticism and traditional Christian ethical principles. It was a clash between the values of elite Victorian Anglicanism and those of the trendy modernist bishop. It was a clash of generations. Thirty years later Fisher's successor but one, Robert Runcie, could write of him that 'in some matters, his opinions now seem echoes from a world long gone … his comments on the *Lady Chatterley's Lover* case were vulnerable to accusations of philistine narrow-mindedness'.[53] It can now be seen that in 1960 it was not only a book and its publisher which were on trial, but also a modernist bishop and a Victorian archbishop.

Grantchester

---

[52] Valerie Pitt, *The Writer and the Modern World: A Study in Literature and Dogma* (London, 1966), 78.

[53] Robert Runcie, Foreword to Carpenter, *Fisher*, vii.

THE CLOISTER AND THE CRIME: MEDIEVAL MONKS IN MODERN MURDER-MYSTERIES

by SARAH FOOT

The monastic day continued at its steady, unhurried, unvarying pace. Vespers was sung in church, followed by a light supper of bread and fruit, washed down with a glass of ale.

Kenelm and Elaf were absent from the table, however. Hungry by the time of Vespers, they were famished when the bell for Compline summoned the monks to the last service of the day. As they shuffled off to the dormitory with the other novices, they were feeling the pangs with great intensity.

Escaping the dormitory to look for something to eat as soon as their peers were asleep, the novices are disturbed and take refuge in the bell tower. There Elaf falls across an obstruction and lets out a yell of sheer terror: he is lying across the stiff, stinking body of a man. 'The missing Brother Nicholas had at last been found'.[1]

Here in the opening of *The Owls of Gloucester* by the Welsh novelist, Edward Marston, we encounter all the classic features of the modern monastic murder-mystery. The murder of one of its holy brothers shatters the ordered peace of the cloister – here the Benedictine Abbey of St Peter at Gloucester. The monks' spiritual refuge is despoiled and, for a while, the whole cloister is poisoned: Gloucester appears to have become a charnel house.[2]

A closed environment, with a static and clearly defined population, the monastery makes an ideal location for a murder-mystery: its separate space limits the number of potential suspects, while intensifying the antipathies born of enforced intimacy. Murder disturbs the monastic peace of the Gloucester community, but only superficially. After the arrest of Brother Nicholas's (secular) killer, when the underlying cause of his death is revealed to arise from his own involvement in the selling of novices for the slave-trade in Ireland, the immutable rhythms of the monastic day can continue uninterrupted.

---

[1]   Edward Marston, *The Owls of Gloucester* (London, 2000), 4, 8.
[2]   Ibid. 27, 272.

Since 1977 when the English writer Ellis Peters (a pseudonym of Edith Pargeter) published her first story about the Benedictine monk of Shrewsbury Abbey, Brother Cadfael, medieval monastic mysteries have burgeoned on both sides of the Atlantic. Historical mysteries represent a particular type of crime novel, relatively recently invented but increasingly popular; among these, medieval mysteries abound, reflecting a wider public interest in medievalism of substantially longer duration.[3] Within this type, monastic mysteries (often unthinkingly categorized with mysteries set in modern clerical environments such as Agatha Christie's *Murder at the Vicarage*, first published in 1930) in fact constitute a discrete sub-genre deserving of separate treatment.[4] What in contemporary culture might have made the medieval monastery so attractive an environment for locating murder-mysteries?

In an essay published in 1948, well before the emergence of this genre, W. H. Auden argued for the impossibility of setting crime fiction in a monastic milieu. He identified as the ideal setting for detective stories the closed and inward-looking society of the college, where all the members (bound together by their pursuit of knowledge and commitment to truth) become potential suspects. He observed parenthetically:

> The even more ideal contradiction of a murder in a monastery is excluded by the fact that monks go regularly to confession and, while the murderer might not confess his crimes, the suspects who are innocent of murder but guilty of lesser sins cannot be supposed to conceal them without making the monastery absurd. Incidentally, is it an accident that the detective story has flourished most in predominantly Protestant countries?[5]

3   T. J. Binyon, *'Murder will out': The Detective in Fiction* (Oxford, 1989), 125; Catherine E. Hoyser, 'Historical Mystery', in Rosemary Herbert, ed., *The Oxford Companion to Crime and Mystery Writing* (Oxford, 1999), 209–10.

4   Susan Oleksiw, 'The British Clerical Milieu', in Herbert, ed., *Oxford Companion*, 74–5; Catherine Aird, 'Clerical Sleuth', ibid. 75–6, who gives examples of sleuths in other religious traditions, including the Methodist Revd C. P. 'Con' Randolph and various detecting rabbis, plus a Tibetan Buddhist monk. See also Binyon, *'Murder will out'*, 64–6; Mike Ashley, 'Mistress of the Medieval Mystery', *Million: the Magazine of Popular Fiction*, no. 4 (July–August 1991), 6–11.

5   W. H. Auden, 'The Guilty Vicarage' (1948), repr. in Robin W. Winks, ed., *Detective Fiction: A Collection of Critical Essays* (Englewood Cliffs, NJ, 1980), 15–24, at 18.

We shall look here at monastic mysteries written in Anglo-Saxon Protestant countries; I deliberately ignore Umberto Eco's great novel, *The Name of the Rose*, set in a Benedictine abbey in 1327, partly because of its literary merits and references to serious philosophical and theological debates, but also because its contemporary resonances should be heard in a specifically Italian (and arguably an anti-clerical) context, which differs sharply from the cultural environment from which the English and American versions derive. In all of the novels discussed here the Church is understood to mean the universal Western Catholic Church of the Middle Ages, led by the pope in Rome; what readers experience, however, is a narrower vision of local churches, closely bound into the lay societies they served and of course, given the particular focus of this essay, one in which the monastic life played a central role.

ENCLOSURE AND TRANSGRESSION

As already suggested, the cloister functions (as did the country house for writers of the golden age of detective fiction in the 1920s and 1930s) as the central closed space, to which a restricted number of potential murderers had access and where final resolution was achieved. Its physical location, isolated from lay society, often in a rural environment, made it an ideal site for detection, equipped with physical barriers to keep the world out, and so potential suspects within. Monasteries represented places of safety – of sanctuary, indeed[6] – in medieval culture; the quiet calm of their cloisters was unsullied by the noise and commercialism of urban life, and safe from the danger and lawlessness rampant outside. The cloister still represents idealized perfection in crime fiction set in the modern era, of course; P. D. James set *Devices and Desires* (1989) on a remote Norfolk headland where a ruined Benedictine abbey stands for lost eternal verities, and a nuclear power station represents the brutality of modernity. Yet, location of detective stories in the medieval past potentially brings more vividly to life the religious faith which ruined buildings can only symbolize.

Internally the monastery also recreates perfection, its society apparently mirroring the sort of inter-war, upper-middle-class British society portrayed in the country settings of golden-age

---

[6] Ellis Peters, *The Sanctuary Sparrow* (London, 1982).

crime fiction.[7] Cloistered monks and nuns of medieval murder-mysteries belong to one social class and educational background; the monastic *horarium* structures their day, making individual suspects' activities (and whereabouts) as predictable as in the regular timetable around which a country-house weekend revolved. Some monastics may have undertaken various undemanding forms of manual labour (including the cultivation of monastic herb-gardens), but heavy agricultural obligations intrude rarely into the routine of the monastic day. Once in *The Devil's Novice*, all hands joined forces – 'choir monks and servants, and all the novices except the schoolboys' – to gather an orchard full of ripe apples.[8] More typically, at St Frideswide's monastery in Oxfordshire in the first of the American novelist Margaret Frazer's Dame Frevisse stories, *The Novice's Tale*:

> ... there was awareness of the harvest but none of its haste or noise; only, as nearly always a settled quiet. A sway of skirts along stone floors, the muted scuff of soft leather soles on the stair; ... the rule of silence held here, except for the hour of recreation and the proper, bell-regulated hours of prayer sung and chanted in the church.[9]

Generally, rigid social stratification kept nobly born monks and high-status visitors to their cloisters, carefully segregated from skilled artisans, peasants and unfree serfs without, and from lay people serving within. In *Death comes as Epiphany*, by the American writer Sharan Newman, the wilful Sister Catherine gets too close to a young stonemason at Saint-Denis – a 'common workman' – mourning the sudden death of the master mason Garnulf.[10] Brand, the errant bondservant calling himself Hyacinth in *The Hermit of*

---

7   Stephen Knight, 'The Golden Age', in Martin Priestman, ed., *The Cambridge Companion to Crime Fiction* (Cambridge, 2003), 77–94; John L. Breen, 'Golden Age Traditions', in Herbert, ed., *Oxford Companion*, 186–8. For a survey locating golden-age fiction in the context of contemporary historical writing, see Charles J. Rzepka, *Detective Fiction* (London, 2005), 151–75. For a wider discussion of the formula of the classic detective story, see John G. Cawelti, *Adventure, Mystery and Romance: Formula Stories as Art and Popular Culture* (Chicago, IL, 1976), 80–105.

8   Ellis Peters, *The Devil's Novice* (London, 1983; paperback edn 1985), 23.

9   Margaret Frazer, *The Novice's Tale* (New York, 1992; Berkley Prime Crime edn 1993), 1.

10   Sharan Newman, *Death Comes as Epiphany* (New York, 1993; paperback edn 1995), 59.

Eyton Forest, befriends the ten-year-old lord, Richard Ludel, but both parties remain aware of the social limits constraining their relationship.[11] A servant, Ælfric, becomes a suspect in *Monk's-Hood*, but even he, it transpires, had once been free and was made a villein unjustly by the murdered man; he regains his freedom as part of the general resolution at the end of the novel.[12] More than social hierarchy preserved the convenient separation of a monastic environment from secular society, however: monastic vows set nuns and monks apart from the world, secluded within their calm, ordered and entirely predictable environment, timeless and unchanging.

Murder represents a transgression of monastic peace. Narrative tension comes from the needless destruction of the idyll created by the author's successful evocation of monastic perfection, so that we lament the violation of the sacred. Greed motivates the poisoning of Lady Ermentrude in the guest house of St Frideswide, temporarily disrupting the calm and order of nunnery life.[13] Although the Dominican Brother Athelstan encountered his first murders outside the walls of his abbey among the crowded streets of late fourteenth-century London in the English writer Paul Harding's *The Nightingale Gallery* (1991) and *The House of the Red Slayer* (1992), in *Murder Most Holy* (1992) death occurs at the Great Chapter of Dominicans meeting at Blackfriars. A greater potential shock arises from the three murders in *Absolution by Murder* (1994) by Peter Tremayne (the pseudonym of the English historian, Peter Berresford Ellis); these intrude directly into the heart of the abbey at Whitby where the synod of 664 is in session. Yet our anticipated horror at the uncovering of the perpetrator (a nun, thwarted by her unrequited passion for a visiting abbess of the Columban party) is muted by the portrayal of the double house at Whitby as conforming to a quite different sort of monastic ideal.

Often in these novels, the deaths around which the story revolves occur, in fact, outside the cloister.[14] Brother Cadfael, Dame Frevisse and Susanna Gregory's Brother Matthew Bartholomew all

---

[11] Ellis Peters, *The Hermit of Eyton Forest* (London, 1987; paperback edn 1988).
[12] Ellis Peters, *Monk's-Hood* (London, 1980; paperback edn 1984), 37, 222.
[13] Frazer, *Novice's Tale*, 228.
[14] For example Ellis Peters, *One Corpse too Many* (London, 1979); *The Leper of St Giles* (London, 1981).

move readily into the world to investigate crime because of their knowledge of medicine and plants.[15] Similarly, in Ariana Franklin's *Mistress of the Art of Death* (2007), Adelia Aguilar, the likeable if rather implausible Salerno-trained doctor with an Arab assistant, enters the nunnery of St Radegund in Cambridge to treat the sisters suffering with cholera and from within that cloistered environment investigates a series of child-abductions and murders outside.[16] Paul Harding's sleuth, Brother Athelstan, has parochial responsibilities for a congregation around St Erconwald's, which regularly take him out into a violent, secular community, although *The Field of Blood* (1991) opens with his discovery of three mutilated corpses on the steps of his church. Like the golden-age novels on which they are modelled, few monastic murder-mysteries focus closely on the realities of murder, neither describing the pains and indignities of death nor dwelling much on the state of the bodies when discovered. Insofar as horror is evoked at all in these stories, it derives from shock at the sudden and unpredicted cessation of human life, particularly a death unshriven. Hyper-realism plays no part in this genre.

Auden argued that the satisfaction of detective novels, that which makes them 'escape literature and not works of art, is the illusion for the reader of being dissociated from the murder'. For him, detective stories represented a 'fantasy of being restored to the Garden of Eden, to a state of innocence'.[17] As noted earlier, Auden rejected the possibility of locating detective stories inside the cloister, yet since his time monastic and cathedral settings have proved surprisingly common locations for crime fiction.[18] What about medieval monasticism makes it so attractive a location for crime fiction beyond its representation of the archetypal closed environment? Auden's argument that the nature of the milieu in detective stories should reflect the Great Good Place, that the

---

[15] Susanna Gregory is the pseudonym of Elizabeth Cruwys, a Cambridge academic who was previously a coroner's officer.

[16] Ariana Franklin, *Mistress of the Art of Death* (London, 2007; paperback edn 2008). Ariana Franklin was the pen-name of Diana Norman, a British former journalist turned novelist.

[17] Auden, 'Guilty Vicarage', 24.

[18] Examples set in contemporary eras include P. D. James, *The Black Tower* (London, 1975); *Death in Holy Orders* (London, 2001); Sara Paretsky, *Killing Orders* (New York, 1985); see David G. Hawkins, 'Whodunit Theology', *AThR* 71 (1989), 273–80, at 278–80.

more Eden-like it can be shown to be, the greater the contradiction of murder, warrants further exploration.[19]

(IM)PURITY AND DANGER

The evocation of the medieval past as an aesthetic to be admired and imitated is scarcely, of course, a novel idea. Most directly we can trace the roots of contemporary medievalism back to the nineteenth century and the growth of interest in all aspects of medieval culture from chivalry to castles. We see its evocation in historical novels, the Gothic Revival in architecture, the Pre-Raphaelites, and the Arts and Crafts movement.[20] Intellectual and academic interest in the Middle Ages has a longer pedigree extending into the immediate post-Reformation era, when divines and laymen could still admire the intrinsic aesthetic beauty of the medieval world and lament the sacrilegious destruction born of puritan excess.[21] We sense the prevalence of ruins in Shakespeare's evocative likening of an avenue of winter trees to the roofless choirs and chancels of abandoned abbeys in the phrase which gave David Knowles his title for the abridged edition of the third volume of his *Religious Orders in England* on the dissolution of the monasteries: *Bare Ruined Choirs* (1976).

Yet conventionally, while regret for the despoiling and defiling of the physical spaces of medieval religion found clear expression in post-Reformation England, such laments seldom extended to the way of life such places represented. The cloister might have been beautiful, but it inspired melancholy, not delight: it was never Eden. While the medieval and Gothic could give access to history, to cathedral, abbey and castle ruins and a reminder of the days of faith, the period also symbolized slavery and the transience of earlier forms of domination.[22] Protestant distaste for conventual

[19] Auden, 'Guilty Vicarage', 19.
[20] Mark Girouard, *The Return to Camelot: Chivalry and the English Gentleman* (London, 1981); Alice Chandler, *A Dream of Order: The Medieval Ideal in Nineteenth-Century English Literature* (London, 1981).
[21] Judith Maltby, 'Sacrilege and the Sacred in Revolutionary England', unpublished paper read at a conference at King's College, University of Aberdeen, 20–22 July 2006: 'Icons and Iconoclasts: The Long Seventeenth Century, 1603 to 1714'.
[22] David Punter, *The Literature of Terror I: The Gothic Tradition*, 2nd edn (London, 1996), 94. Cardinal Gasquet, of course, thought otherwise: David Knowles, *Cardinal Gasquet as an Historian* (London, 1957); Hugh Trevor-Roper, 'The Twilight of the Monks', in idem, *Historical Essays* (London, 1958), 67–73.

religion appears in the earliest English novels, perhaps most obviously in the Gothic novel, in which the monastery or convent always functions, as David Punter has argued, 'as a site of hypocrisy and violent incarceration'.[23] Matthew Lewis's *The Monk* (1795) best typifies the perspective of Gothic horror and tyranny, but the same themes appear in Scott's epic poem *Marmion* (1808), and in the anti-Catholic rhetoric of the Church of Ireland cleric Charles Robert Maturin's *Melmoth the Wanderer* (1820). Walter Scott's two novels of 1820, *The Monastery* and *The Abbot*, are set in the fictional abbey of Kennaquhair (based on Melrose Abbey in the Scottish borders) on the cusp of the Reformation in Scotland. Both ultimately reject Roman Catholicism as primitive, superstitious and divisive. Yet the picturesque and aesthetic sides of Catholicism appealed to Scott; he retained some reverence for its liturgy and admired also its lightness, even humour, which he contrasted favourably with the dour stiffness of Protestantism.[24]

If we turn to the evocation of medieval monasticism in the modern whodunit, we may locate C. J. Sansom's first Matthew Shardlake murder-mystery, *Dissolution* (2003), within the same tradition, for it presents what is fundamentally a reforming, Protestant view of the corruption of the monastic Church. As Sansom has Thomas Cromwell say near the start of the novel: 'That is what monasticism is. Deceit, idolatry, greed and secret loyalty to the bishops of Rome. The monasteries are a canker in the heart of the realm and I will have it ripped out.'[25] Antonia Fraser's novel, *Quiet as a Nun* (1977), set in the present day, puts a similar, almost unthinking, anti-Catholic prejudice into the mouth of Jemima Shore's lover, Tom. He comments disparagingly on a recent scandal in St Eleanor's Convent, reflecting an antipathy to papists that he locates (when challenged) in his childhood upbringing.[26] Yet in the murder-mysteries which have been the focus of this essay something quite different is portrayed: there the Catholic monastic

[23]   David Punter, 'Scottish and Irish Gothic', in Jerrold E. Hogle, ed., *The Cambridge Companion to Gothic Fiction* (Cambridge, 2002), 105–23, at 118.

[24]   Anthony Hull, 'Walter Scott and Medievalism', in idem, *English Romanticism* (London, 2000), 109–22, at 115–19; Michael Alexander, *Medievalism: The Middle Ages in Modern England* (New Haven, CT, 2007), 50–64, esp. 58–9 for critique of Scott's sectarianism in *Marmion*.

[25]   C. J. Sansom, *Dissolution* (London, 2003), 13. Sansom is a British writer.

[26]   Antonia Fraser, *Quiet as a Nun* (London, 1977), 9.

cloister has become an idyllic place, a utopia, the Eden which Auden saw as the perfect crime milieu.

UTOPIA

For this to happen, Catholic society needs to have been made to appear desirable, no longer automatically dismissed as dangerous, corrupting or superstitious. The Catholic revival of the 1920s may have played some role here, even though it finds no reflection in detective fiction of the golden age.[27] Social changes in the 1960s may have been more significant, specifically that decade's sense of social breakdown, its belief it had lost a secure, shared set of common moral values, and the growing perception of increased crime and violence.

Shifts in the historiography of monasticism also brought a re-evaluation of the medieval Church. David Knowles's four-volume study of the religious orders in England offered a more subtle and sympathetic picture of medieval monasticism than did G. G. Coulton, whose *Five Centuries of Religion* provided an important spur to Knowles's history.[28] Richard Southern *made* the Middle Ages from beginnings in Gerbert's cloister at Rheims.[29] Reforms in contemporary Catholicism after Vatican II may further have led Catholics and non-Catholics to think differently about the pre-Reformation past. After the abandonment of the Latin mass, it may have seemed easier to idealize a medieval Church now become more remote, particularly the Church of the High Middle Ages, unsullied by the ills that made the Reformation necessary. That Church became increasingly familiar to a readership accustomed to visit the ruins of England's monastic heritage.[30] Although part of our explanation may lie in the growth of the heritage industry, this alone does not answer our question, for antiquarian interest in ruins goes back much farther in England without leading to this sort of literature. One might compare modern New Age and

[27] Ian Ker, *The Catholic Revival in English Literature, 1845–1961: Newman, Hopkins, Belloc, Chesterton, Greene, Waugh* (Notre Dame, IN, 2003).

[28] Letter of Knowles to Adrian Morey, October 1929, quoted in Morey, *David Knowles: A Memoir* (London, 1979), 120.

[29] Richard Southern, *The Making of the Middle Ages* (London, 1953).

[30] Membership of the National Trust expanded sharply during the 1960s and 1970s: 'National Trust Timeline', <http://www.nationaltrust.org.uk/main/w-trust/w-thecharity/w-history_trust-timeline.htm>, accessed 19 July 2010.

romantic perceptions of the 'Celtic Church' as a peaceful, wise and gentle institution, close to nature and beauty, free from the materialism of contemporary society. Such views represent an alternative, romanticized nostalgia for a golden age, conveniently ignoring the extremes to which its ascetic rejection of material possessions could extend as well as the rigours of the early Irish Church's penitential discipline. Yet they also draw on a more informed understanding of the role of medieval monasticism in agriculture and the part monasteries played in shaping the landscape, so may inherit some of the ideas about the return to nature that characterized Romanticism.[31]

Monastic mysteries do more than imagine solid buildings where now only ruins survive; they treat the monastic way of life as a positive ideal, albeit one imperfectly described. Although the rhythms of the monastic day underpin all these narratives, most say little about the nature of monastic worship, offering a neutered, sanitized impression of a liturgy in which the office most resembles a Latin version of Anglican cathedral evensong. Beyond the office, monastic spirituality remains obscure; individual contemplation and the sacraments barely feature. Auden's problem about confession disappears when that rite occurs so seldom (and then only in the process of resolution, rarely during the mystery). Mindful of the interests (and education) of their readers, few of our authors make much attempt to discuss medieval theology – another reason for omitting *The Name of the Rose* from our survey – yet this further diminishes any sense of the faith underpinning medieval monasticism. Paradoxically Sharan Newman's *Death Comes as Epiphany* reveals more about Jews in twelfth-century Paris than about the worship of Suger's Saint-Denis. Similarly, one gets a vivid and powerful sense of what the religious life of nuns was like in sixteenth-century Italy through the English novelist Sarah Dunant's two books – *The Birth of Venus* and *Sacred Hearts* – even though both offer critical readings of monasticism as a way of life, portraying the cloister as prison, not paradise.[32] Those Ellis Peters stories that attempt to engage with twelfth-century theology or

---

[31] V. Ortenberg, *In Search of the Holy Grail: The Quest for the Middle Ages* (London, 2006), 191.

[32] Helen Cam noted how sympathetically medieval nunneries were portrayed in Sylvia Townsend Warner, *The Corner that Held Them* (London, 1948), concerning a fourteenth-century Norfolk nunnery, and H. F. M. Prescott, *The Man on a Donkey*

religion stand out sharply from the rest of her output; indeed in some of her mysteries the monastery barely features, offering the sketchiest of backdrops to action outside the cloister.[33]

An unequivocal morality underpins all medieval monastic mysteries. Ellis Peters claimed to have one sacred rule in writing her thrillers: 'It is, it ought to be, it must be, a morality. If it strays from the side of the angels, provokes total despair, wilfully destroys —without pressing need in the plot — the innocent and the good, takes pleasure in evil, that is unforgiveable sin.'[34] If the criminal represents the general, sinful nature of humanity — 'for all have sinned and come short of the glory of God' (Romans 3: 23) — detectives act as God's representative on earth, discovering the truth, stamping out evil, ensuring redress is made for wrongs committed, and restoring equilibrium. Although some of the guilty escape the full force of the law, natural justice prevails.[35] A contemporary sense that the guilty often evade justice, their sins going unpunished, may help explain the popularity of the genre in the modern world; the fictional detective, acting in the place of God, can uncover the guilty and find redress for the innocent. Since the classical detective story represents the most effective fictional mode in which to create the illusion of rational control over life's mysteries,[36] clerical or religious sleuths add an extra dimension to the genre, for their pastoral and theological understanding equips them well to act as the vicars of God. Chesterton's Father Brown fits this mould well, but Cadfael conforms ideally to this image of detective as the hand of God.[37] No other

(London, 1952), which portrays the nunnery of Marrick on the eve of the Dissolution: *Historical Novels* (London, 1961).

33 Edwin Ernest Christian and Blake Lindsay, 'The Habit of Detection: The Medieval Monk as Detective in the Novels of Ellis Peters', *Studies in Medievalism* 4 (1992), 276–89, at 284–5. Most revealing of theological themes among Ellis Peters's Cadfael books are *The Confession of Brother Haluin* (1988), *The Heretic's Apprentice* (1989), *The Potter's Field* (1989) and *Brother Cadfael's Penance* (1994).

34 Quoted in Lesley Henderson, ed., *Twentieth-Century Crime and Mystery Writers*, 3rd edn (Chicago, IL, 1991), 848. On the morality of Peters's writing, see John F. X. Harriott, 'Detective Extraordinary', *The Tablet* 240, no. 7631 (11 October 1986), 1066.

35 Hawkins, 'Whodunit Theology', 276–7.

36 Cawelti, *Adventure, Mystery and Romance*, 137.

37 Christian and Lindsay, 'Habit of Detection', 286. Among contemporary monastic sleuths Sister Mary Helen, a nun at Mount St Francis College for Women in San Francisco, stands out, created by Sister Carol Anne O'Marie, a Sister of St Joseph of Carondelet who lives in Oakland, California; Sister Mary Helen appeared first in *A Novena for Murder* (London, 2006).

monastic sleuth quite achieves the same wholly modern and scientific rationality expressed within the outward forms of a medieval
monastic; at times, indeed, the reader can become uneasy when,
as happens in several of the novels, Cadfael's personal sense of
what is right wins out over the justice of the law. Cadfael is, in
fact, quintessentially Anglican in his worldview; the trappings of
his medieval monasticism rarely extend deeper than his habit. Ellis
Peters's novels make the medieval cloister part of the history of the
Church of England, colonizing that past space as part of Anglican
history, so making it familiar, no longer alien or other.

One further factor may underlie the popularity of the medieval monastic mystery: the growing secularization of contemporary western society. The statistics for participation in organized
religion during the twentieth century demonstrate clearly how far
attendance both at regular and occasional services has declined.[38]
Yet David Martin has contrasted those figures with the evidence
of polls asking about religious belief among the general population
which present a completely different picture. People may not go to
church any more, yet the vast majority of the English population
will still, if asked, define itself as 'Christian'.[39] Martin has explained
this by arguing that 'what lurks behind the word "Christian" is not
secularity, but pre-Christian religion and (what is partly the same
thing) the superstitious periphery of Catholicism'. He argues:

> For instance it may be that very large segments of our popula-
> tion believe at one and the same time in an impersonal fate
> possessed by a malicious sense of symmetry (such as that all
> disasters occur in threes) and a personal providence which
> balances up moral account-sheets over reasonable periods of
> time.

Thus he concludes that the English have 'little religion but much
morality'.[40] And that morality they find affirmed in these medieval
murder-mysteries, a form of fiction which presents a similar view
of Christianity to the one Martin defines in our own society, much

[38] Callum G. Brown, *The Death of Christian Britain: Understanding Secularisation
1800–2000* (London, 2001); Steve Bruce, *God is Dead: Secularization in the West* (Oxford,
2002).
[39] David Martin, *The Religious and the Secular: Studies in Secularization* (London,
1969), 106.
[40] Ibid. 107–8.

more a pre-Christian folk religion than an advanced theological worldview, still less a developed Christological soteriology.

The monastic cloister works as an idyllic milieu for detection by creating an idealized, utopian society whose loss we can readily lament without having to engage too closely with the specificities of its religious culture. Monasticism in these pages becomes a way of life devoted to the service of an almighty but essentially beneficent Creator. His hand visibly governs the ordering of the natural world, but he sometimes requires help in determining the fates of individual men and women. The recurring rhythms of the agricultural seasons underpin these narratives, revolving in gentle harmony with the cycle of the Christian year, albeit a year in which Christmas recurs more frequently than does Good Friday. This is a society close to the land, in touch with nature, pure and uncorrupted by modernity. Outside the peace of the cloister lies a violent and dangerous world, but one that never proves uncontrollable, where wrongs will ultimately always be righted. In the monastery above all other places, detective addicts may find themselves restored to the innocence of the Garden of Eden, and thus escape the horrors of modern reality.

Christ Church, Oxford

PIETY AND POLEMIC IN EVANGELICAL PROPHECY FICTION, 1995–2000

by CRAWFORD GRIBBEN

No one studying the impact of Evangelicalism's most successful cultural products could doubt their mass-market appeal both within and beyond the 'conservative revolution' of contemporary America.[1] With concerns to fashion the spirituality of their readers, the Left Behind novels (1995–2007) represent the 'first outlines of a fully commercialised, fully mediatised Christian blockbuster culture'.[2] The series dramatizes the end-time expectations of a popular evangelical system of eschatological thinking, known as dispensational pre-millennialism. This system maintains that Christ could return imminently to 'rapture' true believers to heaven; that this rapture will be followed by a catastrophic seven-year period known as the 'Great Tribulation', in which the Antichrist will rise to power to persecute those who, despite being 'left behind', have converted to evangelical faith; and that the tribulation will end with the 'glorious appearing' of Christ, the last judgement and the inauguration of a thousand-year reign of peace known as the millennium.[3] Despite the complexity of its theology, the series has sold over sixty-five million copies since the publication of their eponymous debut novel in 1995, and has been identified as the best-selling fiction series in American literary history.[4] After 1998, successive instalments in the series topped the *New York Times* best-seller lists. The seventh novel in the series, *The Indwelling* (2000), topped the best-seller lists of the *New York Times*, *Publishers Weekly*, *Wall Street Journal* and *USA Today*. Sales soared after 9/11, and *Desecration*, published one month after the terror

---

[1]   Klaus J. Milich, 'Fundamentalism Hot and Cold: George W. Bush and the "return of the sacred"', *Cultural Critique* 62 (2006), 92–125, at 92.

[2]   Christian Thorne, 'The Revolutionary Energy of the Outmoded', *October* 104 (2003), 97–114, at 99. On the history of this particular evangelical prophecy genre, see Crawford Gribben, *Writing the Rapture: Prophecy Fiction in Evangelical America* (Oxford, 2009).

[3]   For a description of Dispensationalism, see Mark Sweetnam, 'Defining Dispensationalism: A Cultural Studies Perspective', *JRH* 34 (2010), 191–212.

[4]   Tristan Sturm, 'Prophetic Eyes: The Theatricality of Mark Hitchcock's Premillennial Geopolitics', *Geopolitics* 11 (2006), 231–55, at 250 n. 14.

attacks on the World Trade Centre and the Pentagon, pushed John Grisham from the top rank in *Publishers Weekly* by becoming the best-selling work of adult hardback fiction in the world.[5] Since then, Left Behind has been developed into a variety of successful franchises by its authors, Jerry B. Jenkins and Tim LaHaye, by their original evangelical publisher, Tyndale House, and more recently by mainstream publishers such as Bantam and Hodder & Stoughton.[6] These franchises have taken the Left Behind brand into clothing, board games, music, the internet, several movies and a controversial video game.[7] The series dominates the 'growing conservative culture industry'.[8] At the same time, it has attracted a wide range of critical comment. Some of that comment has come from intellectuals concerned by the commitment of the series to social and political conservatism, some of it from theologians appalled by the project's lack of scholarly gravitas, and some of it from Evangelicals concerned by its deviation from traditional patterns of orthodoxy and its preference for social and political inaction.[9] A number of

---

[5]   Gribben, *Writing the Rapture*, 129–30.

[6]   Hodder & Stoughton began as Christian publishers, and in fact published two volumes of autobiography by the author of the first series of novels in the rapture fiction genre, Sydney Watson: *Life's Look-out: An Autobiography of Sydney Watson* (London, 1897) and *Brighter Years: The Second Part of the Autobiography of Sydney Watson* (London, 1898). Watson's rapture novels were published as *Scarlet and Purple* (London, 1913), *The Mark of the Beast* (London, 1915) and *In the Twinkling of an Eye* (London, 1916). For a survey of Watson's importance in the genre, see Crawford Gribben, 'Rapture Fictions and the Changing Evangelical Condition', *Literature and Theology* 18 (2004), 77–94. On trends in publishing, see Richard Bartholomew, 'Religious Mission and Business Reality: Trends in the Contemporary British Christian Book Industry', *Journal of Contemporary Religion* 20 (2005), 41–2; Paul C. Gutjahr, 'No Longer Left Behind: Amazon.com, Reader-Response, and the Changing Fortunes of the Christian Novel in America', *Book History* 5 (2002), 209–36.

[7]   Recent literature on the Left Behind novels includes Gribben, 'Rapture Fictions'; Bruce David Forbes and Jeanne Halgren Kilde, eds, *Rapture, Revelation and the End Times: Exploring the Left Behind Series* (New York, 2004); Amy Johnson Frykholm, *Rapture Culture: Left Behind in Evangelical America* (Oxford, 2004); Sherryll Mleynek, 'The Rhetoric of the "Jewish Problem" in the *Left Behind* Novels', *Literature and Theology* 19 (2005), 367–83; Glenn W. Shuck, *Marks of the Beast: The Left Behind Novels and the Struggle for Evangelical Identity* (New York, 2005); Milich, 'Fundamentalism Hot and Cold', 108–13. The wider genre context is surveyed in Gribben, *Writing the Rapture*.

[8]   Milich, 'Fundamentalism Hot and Cold', 108.

[9]   See, respectively, Melani McAlister, 'Prophecy, Politics, and the Popular: The *Left Behind* Series and Christian Fundamentalism's New World Order', *South Atlantic Quarterly* 102 (2003), 773–98; Darryl Jones, 'The Liberal Antichrist: *Left Behind* in America', in Kenneth G. C. Newport and Crawford Gribben, eds, *Expecting the End: Millennialism*

these evangelical critiques of the series have returned to issues of spirituality. Some of that concern is related to general patterns of spirituality within Dispensationalism, especially its retreatist individualism, but other critiques, including some from within the dispensational camp, are related to specific patterns of spirituality developed in Left Behind, especially its political assumptions.

These criticisms have led evangelical writers to produce alternatives to the piety and polemic of the Left Behind series. So, from the rapture fiction genre, which dates back to the 1870s, a wider variety of evangelical prophecy fiction has emerged.[10] These novels regularly interrogate the presuppositions of Left Behind. Some have reminded readers of the importance of the prophetic culture that pre-dated the Left Behind phenomenon: Hal Lindsey's *Blood Moon* (1996) drew attention on a number of occasions to its author's long-standing interest in prophetic 'non-fiction', reasserting Lindsey's status as the premier prophetic teacher of the pop dispensational theology which his blockbuster *The Late Great Planet Earth* (1970) essentially defined. Other novels have provided a more foundational challenge to the exegetical basis of Left Behind. Hank Hanegraaff and Sigmund Brouwer published a fictional critique in their novels *The Last Disciple* (2004) and *The Last Sacrifice* (2006), which argued that the contents of Revelation referred primarily to events in the first century and not, as Left Behind assumed, to events at the end of the age. Some novels have challenged the cultural inadequacies of the series or its lack of contemporary political engagement: Kim Young's *The Last Hour* (1997) provided a searing critique of an America in the grip of Bill and Hilary, thinly disguised as Bob and Emily, while The

---

in Social and Historical Context (Baylor, TX, 2006), 97–112; Ian S. Markham, 'Engaging with the Theology that Really Sells', *Conversations in Religion and Theology* 1 (2003), 115–18; and Crawford Gribben, *Rapture Fiction and the Evangelical Crisis* (Webster, NY, 2006); idem, 'After *Left Behind*: The Paradox of Evangelical Pessimism', in Newport and Gribben, eds, *Expecting the End*, 113–30; Peter Althouse, '"Left Behind" – Fact or Fiction: Ecumenical Dilemmas of the Fundamentalist Millenarian Tensions within Pentecostalism', *Journal of Pentecostal Theology* 13 (2005), 188–91.

10   Gutjahr subsumes rapture and prophecy fiction within the category of 'spiritual warfare novels', a genre he believes emerged within evangelical publishing during the 1980s: 'No Longer Left Behind', 215. Most critics who comment on the phenomenon argue that rapture fiction emerged as a genre in the 1990s: e.g. Thorne, 'Revolutionary Energy', 98. Rapture fictions developed a genre consciousness shortly after their first appearance in the 1870s: Crawford Gribben, 'Rethinking the Rise of Prophecy Fiction: H. R. K.'s *Life in the Future* (?1879)', *Brethren Historical Review* 7(2011), 68–80.

Christ Clone Trilogy (1997, 1998, 2004) by James BeauSeigneur
was invested with a political and scientific sophistication that had
not previously been seen in evangelical fiction writing, even as
it warned readers of dangerous New Age spiritualities that were
exercising immense influence throughout mainstream culture.
Other novels have challenged Left Behind's preference for cultural
retreat: Michael Hyatt and George Grant's account of *Y2K: The
Day the World Shut Down* (1998) warned that dispensational disen-
gagement from the mainstream could develop into a self-fulfilling
expectation of marginalization and called upon readers to embrace
an activist faith that could prepare for and even survive the crisis
in finance and social infrastructure that its authors believed to be
imminent. Whatever their other differences, these prophecy novels
shared a concern to provide an alternative to the spirituality developed in Left Behind. In doing so, they identified narrative fiction
as the forum for debate about the basis and development of an
authentic evangelical spirituality.

This essay will focus on the Left Behind novels and the most
significant of their alternatives, which, though they have sold many
fewer copies, represent trends that are re-contouring evangelical
political expectations. It will contrast the piety and polemic of
Left Behind and its alternatives to argue that recent prophecy
novels present a substantial contrast between dispensational and
non-dispensational spiritualities. Nevertheless, this essay concludes,
the substantial differences that exist between these novels cannot
obscure the trope in which their spiritualities are rooted: a profound
alarm at the prospects of the American evangelical future.

★ ★ ★

The Left Behind novels, like the rapture fiction genre from which
they emerge, are a species of occasional fiction: they do not attempt
to outline a complete systematic theology, nor do they claim to
present a rounded, polished discussion of evangelical faith. This is
in keeping with their relatively minor status in the wider literary
culture of Evangelicalism. In a report published in 2000, when the
Left Behind phenomenon was at its height, evangelical bookshops
in the UK indicated that fiction accounted for only 13% of their

sales.[11] Figures from the USA – were they available – would probably indicate a greater percentage of fiction sales within evangelical
bookshops, but would probably confirm the point that Evangelicals
consume fiction only as a minor part of a larger literary culture.
The prominence of Left Behind novels on secular best-seller lists
should not obscure this point, for American best-seller lists do
not include sales data from Christian bookshops and cannot be
used as indicators of the textual preferences of evangelical culture.
The Left Behind novels are not the only influence on evangelical
spirituality. The factors shaping evangelical spirituality are much
broader than the movement's most successful fictional series.

All the same, readers are clearly being influenced by these
novels. Rapture novels offer a clear example of conversionist
writing. Novels frequently include exhortations for characters
(and, implicitly, readers) to embrace salvation, and there is evidence
that the series has been successful in seeing these goals achieved.
In 2002, the publishers of Left Behind had received letters from
some three thousand readers testifying that the books had enabled
them to 'receive Christ'.[12] That same year, a survey of readers'
reviews on Amazon.com discovered that a number of respondents
were linking their conversions to the experience of having read
the novels, while a further thirty percent were claiming that the
novels had 'caused them to reflect on their own spiritual convictions'.[13] The authors have made similar claims for their formative
influence. The fourth novel in the series, *Soul Harvest* (1998), was
dedicated to 'our brand-new brothers and sisters' – evidently those
who had become Evangelicals as a consequence of reading books
in the series. Five years later, Jenkins and LaHaye published an
anthology of readers' conversion narratives entitled *These Will not
be Left Behind: True Stories of Changed Lives* (2003). The conversionist ambitions of the series were confirmed in *The Authorized
Left Behind Handbook* (2005), which argued that 'the success of the
books has driven the opportunity for an unprecedented harvest
of souls'.[14] The authors of the series, the *Handbook* continued,

---

[11] Bartholomew, 'Religious Mission and Business Reality', 50.
[12] Ken Walker, 'Left Behind: Stronger than Fiction', *Today's Christian* 40/6
(November/December 2002), 14.
[13] Gutjahr, 'No Longer Left Behind', 226.
[14] Tim LaHaye et al., *The Authorized Left Behind Handbook* (Wheaton, IL, 2005), 4.

'get many letters every day from readers who have had their relationships with Christ strengthened through reading the books'.[15]
In fact, Jenkins added in an interview, LaHaye had insisted that
every book in the series should contain 'a believable, reproduc-
ible conversion experience ... We hear from people all the time
who say they prayed the prayer of salvation right along with the
character.'[16] LaHaye himself has agreed: 'The letters that pour into
our offices daily relate instance after instance of spiritual bless-
ings resulting from the reading of these books.'[17] The authors and
original publisher of Left Behind have therefore invited readers
to consider the novels as spiritually forming texts, as texts which
encourage the development of specified options of response.
Throughout the genre, several possible varieties of that response
have been illustrated in characters coming to faith for the first
time, in other characters moving from non-evangelical Christianities to embrace the evangelical faith, and in other evangelical characters moving towards the dispensational pre-millennialism that
contours the genre's plots. In the Left Behind project, more than
any other rapture fiction project before it, the novels' theology and
spirituality are made credible by the results they appear to have in
the lives of thousands of their consumers. These published details
of 'changed lives' highlight the novels' status as spiritual texts with
a deliberate and influential formative influence.

These reports of conversions, however, have not elevated the
Left Behind novels above scrutiny. Liberal critics are consistently
concerned by the books' identification of evangelical spirituality
with the gun-toting machismo of Southern conservatism. Even
conservative Evangelicals, who might be expected to applaud the
novels' impact on the ungodly, have expressed concerns about the
ideals expressed in the series. A number of commentators have
described the ways in which the series deviates from the dispensational theology of earlier decades, particularly in offering a second
chance of salvation to those who had rejected Jesus Christ before
the rapture; the ways in which the series homogenizes evangelical
spirituality into a particular portfolio of (often neo-conservative)

---

[15] Ibid. 4.
[16] Ibid. 20.
[17] Tim LaHaye, 'Introduction', in Mark Hitchcock and Thomas Ice, *The Truth
Behind Left Behind: A Biblical View of the End Times* (Sisters, OR, 2004), 6.

political and social agendas; and the ways in which the series encodes some of the weaknesses, as well as some of the strengths, of North American Evangelicalism at the start of the twenty-first century.[18] The series may indeed be winning converts to the fold, but some Evangelicals are still concerned by their procedure and the results it is believed to generate.

That concern has been voiced in different ways. Hal Lindsey's rapture novel *Blood Moon* (1996) was published shortly after *Left Behind* (1995). Like Lindsey's other writing, it focuses on the prophetic significance of political events. It is more critical of Israeli government policy than any other rapture novel, using both Jewish and Muslim characters to condemn the 'land for peace' deals. In many ways, the novel can be seen as an attempt to rehabilitate Lindsey's reputation. On a number of occasions, characters in *Blood Moon* remember that they had been exposed to Lindsey's prophetic teaching long before their conversion. As the world plunges into chaos, Jeremy Armstrong grows 'curious about lessons his Mom had tried to teach him … She kept sending him books by some nut named Hal Lindsey.'[19] After his conversion, Armstrong is no longer prepared to dismiss the 'frayed old book … *The Late Great Planet Earth*'. Lindsey no longer sounded like a 'total nut case' – especially as Armstrong began to realize that 'most of what he interpreted from the Hebrew prophets is now coming true'.[20] *Blood Moon* emphasized that the spirituality advocated by the best-selling author of dispensational 'non-fiction' already recognized that 'not everything of significance that occurs in our world happens in the visible, natural realm'.[21] But, in the novel, Lindsey's purpose was strictly limited. His focus was more political than spiritual: 'I want this book to be a blessing for all who read it. I hope it opens your eyes to the amazing truth of biblical prophecy and how it is being fulfilled all around us.'[22] Above all else, *Blood Moon* wanted its readers to recognize that 'we are the generation' that would

---

[18] See, for example, comments by Stephen Spencer, a dispensationalist theologian and former Dallas Theological Seminary professor, quoted in Mark Reasoner, 'What does the Bible say about the End Times?', in Forbes and Kilde, eds, *Rapture, Revelation and the End Times*, 71–98, at 90; Gribben, *Rapture Fiction and the Evangelical Crisis.*

[19] Hal Lindsey, *Blood Moon* (Palos Verdes, CA, 1996), 67.

[20] Ibid. 252.

[21] Ibid. 5.

[22] Ibid. 7.

witness the second coming.[23] A purpose of transformation was being eclipsed by a purpose of information, and dispensational piety by dispensational politics. *Blood Moon* was an implicit critique of the political apathy of Left Behind.

Yet Lindsey's critique was ironic. Most criticisms of the Left Behind novels focus on their very social and political activism. There is little contemplation in the Left Behind novels; instead, the novels advance from a very basic emphasis upon conversion to depict the Christian life as one of almost constant activity. The piety that does exist is focused on the 'Sinner's Prayer', a mechanistic and relatively recent innovation in evangelistic method, in which those who wish to repent express that repentance in a formulaic prayer which downplays the necessity of conviction of sin and the prolonged struggle for assurance assumed by many earlier generations of Evangelicals. As a character in LaHaye's latest series puts it, '[y]ou just have to say a prayer and ask Him in.'[24] The Sinner's Prayer evangelistic technique is certainly not a universal feature of the genre: it is not used in *Blood Moon* or *The Christ Clone Trilogy*, for example, though it is possible that its absence signals that these novels actually assume an existing faith commitment among their readers. In the Left Behind novels, the Sinner's Prayer telescopes the experience of conversion into the recitation of a set form of words followed by an axiomatic promise of salvation: its terms guarantee that God cannot fail to respond. The Sinner's Prayer offers a species of instant salvation that is entirely at odds with the struggles for salvation experienced by earlier generations of Evangelicals. David Bebbington has identified a new rapidity in the experience of gaining assurance as one of the features distinguishing eighteenth-century Evangelicalism from earlier varieties of popular Protestantism.[25] Despite his claims, extended and difficult conversions continued to be common within the evangelical movement he describes, especially within the Reformed communities whose theology did so much to pattern earlier varieties of Dispensationalism.[26] It is ironic that

[23]   Ibid. 6–7.

[24]   Tim LaHaye and Bob Philips, *The Secret on Ararat* (New York, 2004), 202.

[25]   David Bebbington, *Evangelicalism in Modern Britain: A History from the 1730s to the 1980s* (London, 1989), 7–8.

[26]   D. Bruce Hindmarsh, *The Evangelical Conversion Narrative: Spiritual Autobiography in Early Modern England* (Oxford, 2005).

contemporary Evangelicalism, which elsewhere appears so fascinated by experience, should produce and consume texts whose
descriptions of conversion appeal to the basic, rationalist formula
offered by the Sinner's Prayer.

This bare and rather spartan piety is the bedrock of the novels'
spirituality. As the model of the Sinner's Prayer suggests, the Left
Behind novels are relentlessly individualistic. While the Tribulation Force, those who come to faith after the rapture, gather into
informal fellowships, readers are offered no extended descriptions
of their modes of worship. These new believers are not baptized
and are not invited to participate in the Lord's Supper: in line with
traditional Dispensationalism, they are not part of the Church, the
body of Christ, and so are not in a position to benefit from the
sacraments.[27] The 'tribulation saints' (i.e. those converted after the
rapture) therefore develop a piety which is focused solely on the
word. Even then, while the novels recount numerous passages of
individual exhortation, readers find very few descriptions of characters preaching to a gathered audience. The word, more often than
not, is communicated through the internet – and the website of
the Tribulation Force is described as the most popular internet site
in history – but the choice of that medium promotes this incipient
individualism.[28] It is also an entirely voluntary medium: and, as in
the website, so in the gatherings of believers. The fellowships of
tribulation saints are not provided with any kind of government
or properly constituted pastoral authority. Earlier prophetic fiction
had lamented this drive towards individualism within the evangelical community; Dayton Manker's *They That Remain* (1941) had,
for example, berated the 'self-appointed leaders' who sprang up to
steal church members away from ordained clergy.[29] Five decades
later, this anti-clerical individualism had become an assumed
norm. Through much of the series, the Tribulation Force operates

---

[27] This position changes in the original novels' spin-off series, Mel Odom's *Apocalypse Dawn* and Neesa Hart's *End of State*. There are no sacraments in *Left Behind*;
believer's baptism is introduced in *Apocalypse Dawn*; and communion is introduced
alongside baptism in *End of State*. Dispensational theologians have repeatedly rejected
the idea that tribulation saints have a right to the sacraments. But the wider Left
Behind project, which increasingly fails to control the theological coherence of its
various elements, appears to offer no consensus about the relationship between spirituality and the sacraments.

[28] Tim LaHaye and Jerry B. Jenkins, *Desecration* (Wheaton, IL, 2001), 100.

[29] Dayton A. Manker, *They that Remain* (Cincinnati, OH, 1941), 28.

under the informal leadership of Rayford Steele. He is not a pastor or an elder, nevertheless, and his leadership can be challenged or denied. The tribulation saints are expected to develop a spirituality divorced from the structures or discipline of the Church.

This relentless individualism contributes to characters' ahistorical and contextless Bible reading. Again, in contemporary prophecy fiction, this interpretative approach is grounded in distrust of specialist clergy. One character in *Blood Moon* 'found the ministers were preaching messages in direct contradiction to what he was reading in the Bible. So he just kept secretly searching on his own.'[30] Similarly, in Left Behind, the reading and exposition of Scripture take place outside the controls of exegetical history. Of course, historical perspectives are occasionally brought to bear on this material. Bruce Barnes, for example, defends his eschatological convictions by arguing that the 'doctrine of the end times' was 'much, much older' than its apparently recent recovery (or origin) might suggest.[31] Significantly, the age of the pre-tribulation rapture doctrine is something of a 'hot potato' in evangelical scholarship, and this moment in the narrative provides the authors with an opportunity to comment on that debate. They fail to do so, however, and the question of the historicity of Dispensationalism is invoked only to be dismissed. Readers are provided with no evidence for the antiquity of its method or conclusions, and are left to accept Barnes's assertion on its own merits. In the Left Behind novels, piety is based on the word, but the word is interpreted largely at a personal level and comes without the interpretative dimension of the Church. This produces a spirituality divorced from the wider community or history of the Church. It is, nevertheless, a spirituality confirmed by the returning Jesus Christ. Even at the moment of eschatological consummation – when the believers who survive the tribulation finally meet their Saviour – Jesus speaks to them and names them, simultaneously, as individuals. As one critic has noted, the 'knowledge that the same thing is happening to everyone around them in no way mitigates the pleasure of hearing Christ say their names'.[32] Thus begins the consummation of the believer's 'personal relationship' with Jesus.

[30] Lindsey, *Blood Moon*, 73.
[31] Tim LaHaye and Jerry B. Jenkins, *Tribulation Force* (Wheaton, IL, 1996), 67.
[32] A. Diana Forster, 'The Paradox of Paradise Regained in the *Left Behind* Series',

Perhaps this reiterated individualism explains why the novels offer little emphasis on prayer. Earlier rapture novels had prioritized prayer as the believer's first recourse in difficult times. In *They That Remain* (1941), for example, Rev. and Mrs Clarence Saunders's first response to news of rising taxes – which they understand as evidence of a Communist takeover of America – is prayer:

> When a crisis comes in a Christian life, prayer is the answer. Rhetoric, elegance, fine phrasing, eloquent language – these find little place in the simple plea of truly distressed hearts … How relaxed and restful the nerves and mind of one who has passed through a crisis and found strength at the feet of the Lord. When, after long, earnest prayer the minister and his wife arose to retire for the night, they slept well, comforted by the Divine Presence.[33]

By contrast, in Left Behind, prayer is a last resort: a preference for activism charges the enthusiasm of the series for technology and professional skills. The Tribulation Force – a group of survivalists which never numbers more than about a dozen – includes several pilots, a renowned economist and a Pulitzer Prize-winning journalist. These above-average Joes become a gung-ho band of brigands who take on the Antichrist in his traditional territory, invasive technology. While earlier rapture fictions had depicted the Antichrist's power as being based on unchallengeable technological prowess, the Left Behind novels show this isolated band of believers making greater technological strides than the world's most advanced regime. There is little need for prayer when believers exercise so much power over their enemies. One character, Chang, recognizes the practice of prayer as a last resort when his equipment fails him: 'with all the technology God had allowed them to adapt for the cause of Christ around the world, he was suddenly left with nothing to do to help, except old-fashioned praying'.[34] Of course, the demands of characterization qualify the critic's temptation to attribute Chang's point of view to the authors. Jenkins and LaHaye are unlikely to be dismissing the value of prayer: else-

---

Chrestomathy: Annual Review of Undergraduate Research, School of Humanities and Social Sciences, College of Charleston 4 (2005), 65–79, at 76.

[33] Manker, *They that Remain*, 25.

[34] Tim LaHaye and Jerry B. Jenkins, *The Remnant* (Wheaton, IL, 2002), 210.

where they assert its importance, and the wider evangelical culture from which they emerged has similarly refused to identify prayer with passivity.[35] Nevertheless, his response illustrates the dilemma of encoding evangelical spirituality in a fast-moving thriller. It is true that the conventions of the thriller genre require the relentless activity of an autonomous protagonist and tend to militate against the careful psychological exploration of characters. Ironically, Chang's equating prayer with a frustrating passivity – or at least his identification of prayer as something Christians do only when their technology fails – makes it possible for readers to adopt the same perspective. Furthermore, in the Left Behind novels, the passivity of prayer is occasionally celebrated. Tsion Ben Judah, the spiritual leader of the Tribulation Force, is identified as a model 'prayer warrior'. His successes in prayer were due to the fact that he had

> studied the discipline of intercession, largely a Protestant tradition from the fundamentalist and Pentecostal cultures. Those steeped in it went beyond mere praying for someone as an act of interceding for them; they believed true intercession involved deep empathy and that a person thus praying must not enter into the practice unless willing to literally trade places with the needy person.[36]

At this point, Tsion is the literal embodiment of one important

---

[35] See, for example, Tim LaHaye, *How to Study the Bible for Yourself* (Eugene, OR, 1998). One reviewer on Amazon.com criticized the lack of emphasis on prayer in this text: 'towards the end of the book LaHaye says, "Personally I think it is more important to read, memorize, and study the Bible than to pray, for it is more important for God to talk to us than for us to talk to Him. We certainly are not going to tell Him anything He does not know, but he has much in His Word that He wants us to learn." The book then goes into a page explantation [*sic*] citing that it is important to pray and gives an example of how to pray. Out of all the other criticisms of the book – the condescending tone and the shameless selfpromotion [*sic*] – the lack of emphasis of prayer is the most disturbing. Prayer and study of the Bible go hand in hand; you really cannot have one without the other; they are like the two feet we stand upon, cut one away and we loose [*sic*] our balance and fall. One of the biggest differences that separates Christianity from all other religions is that Christianity isn't about a set of rules to follow, it's about relationship; our relationship to God and in turn how that relationship affects our relationships with all other people. Prayer is one of the most vital parts of that relationship ("Pray without ceasing") and to barely mention it in a book on studying the Bible is a major mistake': <http://www.amazon.com/How-Study-Bible-Yourself-LaHaye/dp/1565076311>, accessed 7 March 2007.

[36] Tim LaHaye and Jerry B. Jenkins, *Indwelling* (Wheaton, IL, 2000), 77.

element of the evangelical tradition. Therefore, when his intercession generates unusual out-of-body experiences, readers are primed to regard them as normative, especially when the context of these passages fails to highlight their abnormality.[37] A reader tuned into biblical archetypes will recognize parallels with the experiences of the anonymous individual described in 2 Corinthians 12. But there is a difficulty in the failure of the novels to balance the unusual with the less exciting experiences of traditional evangelical spirituality. Hal Lindsey's *Blood Moon* seems much more prosaic in its description of its protagonist's discovery of prayer, despite its rather wobbly trinitarian theology: 'He hadn't seen any bright lights or writing in the sky or heard any voices, but he did feel a certain level of comfort in communing with the God described in the Bible, especially the one called Jesus Christ.'[38] It is fair to say, however, that *Blood Moon's* descriptions of divine voices in telephone calls and angelic encounters are somewhat out of the evangelical mainstream.[39] Dispensational rapture novels present a theology of prayer that is far removed from that of their tradition.

Left Behind's emphasis on activity might also explain its failure to develop a theology of fasting. If Chang considers prayer to be unusually passive, fasting seems to be the antithesis of the Tribulation Force's macho culture. This omission of bodily weakness relates to the failure of the series to develop a wider theology of suffering. In the world of Left Behind, an activist spirituality has more to do with survivalist politics than self-giving suffering. In a sense, therefore, one of the most significant things that can be said about these evangelical novels is that they fail to develop a theology of the cross. Of course, as in any authentically evangelical text, a great deal of attention is paid to the death of Jesus Christ. Characters, nevertheless, evidence little sense of what it means to live under the cross, a way of life so important to Martin Luther that he identified life under the cross as an essential mark of the true Church.[40] The Left Behind novels concentrate on activist strength, rather than redemptive weakness, and, in contrast to the Pauline

---

[37] Ibid. 76–79, 87, 232.
[38] Lindsey, *Blood Moon*, 73.
[39] Ibid. 76, 250–1.
[40] See Graham Tomlin, *The Power of the Cross: Theology and the Death of Christ in Paul, Luther and Pascal*, Paternoster Biblical and Theological Monographs (Carlisle, 1999), 111–95.

epistles, they fail to develop any notion that that the servants of Jesus Christ are called to follow him into suffering, that in fact this quality of suffering authenticates the true servants of Jesus Christ, and that this suffering weakness is the means by which the grace and power of God is made glorious in the lives of his people.[41]

Perhaps that is also why the novels say so little about the humble service of one's neighbour. The novels reiterate again and again the need to love and be loved by God. There is little attention paid to the need to combine the first great commandment with the second, to love one's neighbour as oneself. Instead, the novels encourage a spirituality of retreat, encouraging the idea that faith can best survive when least engaged with a hostile world. The Evangelicals in the Left Behind novels point to the importance of the cross while themselves failing to live under it.

These believers also have little to say about the Christian's ultimate destination, the new heavens and new earth. In evangelical culture more generally, the hope for eschatological vindication in a world of righteousness is grounded on the assumption that there is a contrast between the experience of Christians in this age and the next. Believers hope for restorative justice, in one sense: this is what the future coming of Christ is believed to involve. But, in Left Behind, the Tribulation Force want to be in a position in which they have as little need as possible for divine redress. Ironically, the very militancy of these believers – their can-do 'muscular Christianity' – dulls the appeal of the ultimate divine intervention. Their eschatological myopia has an obvious impact on the development of an evangelical spirituality within the series. In contrast to earlier generations of Dispensationalists, the authors of the Left Behind novels seem to communicate little in the way of heavenly hope. In the first ten volumes of the first series, at least, the millennium is rarely mentioned, and believers evidence little anticipation of what lies beyond it. In this sense, the Left Behind novels represent the ultimate nadir of the long decline of the earlier dispensational emphasis on heavenly union with Jesus Christ. This 'bridal piety', so typical of early generations of dispensational writers, was eclipsed within Dispensationalism as the movement entered its

---

[41] Thomas R. Schreiner, *Paul: Apostle of God's Glory in Christ* (Leicester, 2001), 87–102.

scholastic period in the earlier twentieth century.[42] In Left Behind, that heaven-directed piety has entirely disappeared. The novels let concerns about earthly conflict overcome the expectation of heavenly glory, and their explication of spirituality is stunted as a result. It provides for an ironic conclusion: by allowing the events of the tribulation to eclipse a millennial or heavenly hope, the most defining rapture fictions of the genre provide its best example of eschatological short-sightedness.

★ ★ ★

James BeauSeigneur first published The Christ Clone Trilogy as sales of Left Behind were beginning to soar. BeauSeigneur was a military consultant and former Republican Congressional candidate who had written two books related to the defence industry, Military Avionics (1985) and Strategic Defense (1986), and was keen to combine those various interests to improve fictional and non-fictional prophetic writing. He had found Hal Lindsey's books to 'strain reality and common sense' but had been 'impressed' by Salem Kirban's work – until, that is, he read his rapture novel, 666 (1970), which BeauSeigneur dismissed as 'dreadful, just plain silly'. The failures of Lindsey and Kirban convinced BeauSeigneur of the need for 'well-conceived and well-written' prophetic fiction, and he began work on The Christ Clone Trilogy in 1987.[43] The trilogy, like Left Behind and the fictional work of Lindsey and Kirban, is part of a wider publishing project. A footnote in the closing pages of the third novel advertises a study guide to go along with the Christ Clone Trilogy, which does not yet appear to have been published.[44] BeauSeigneur's aim was clearly to succeed where other writers had failed. The trilogy worked very hard to appear scientific and politically astute, and provided itself with a solid foundation as science fiction.[45] The success anticipated by BeauSeigneur

[42] See Gary L. Nebeker, '"The ecstasy of perfected love": The Eschatological Mysticism of J. N. Darby,' in Crawford Gribben and Timothy C. F. Stunt, eds, Prisoners of Hope? Aspects of Evangelical Millennialism in Britain and Ireland, 1800–1880, Studies in Evangelical History and Thought (Milton Keynes, 2004), 69–94.

[43] 'Interview with James BeauSeigneur', <http://www.christian-fandom.com/oli-jbs.html>, accessed 13 March 2011.

[44] James BeauSeigneur, Acts of God, The Christ Clone Trilogy (1997; reissued New York, 2003), 505.

[45] See, for example, James BeauSeigneur, Birth of an Age, The Christ Clone Trilogy (1997; reissued New York, 2003), 51–64, 83–113.

was a long time coming. The trilogy – *In His Image* (1997), *Birth of an Age* (1997) and *Acts of God* (1998) – first appeared under the imprint of a minor evangelical press. BeauSeigneur explained that this firm, Selective House, was 'a small publishing company whose focus is books and videos which bring the Gospel to a secular audience'.[46] Five years later, he had much less need for modesty when the novels were re-released by Warner into the market for rapture fiction that had been created by the success of Left Behind.

There is little doubt that BeauSeigneur's work is among the most accomplished in the genre, from a literary point of view, at least, largely because it breaks the traditional narrative pattern in finding its main focus on Decker Hawthorne and the circle of friends that gather around Christopher Goodman, who, as his name ironically suggests, is eventually revealed to be Antichrist. From a theological point of view, however, the trilogy draws some surprising conclusions, including a doctrine of soul sleep, based on the medieval heresy of mortalism, and the idea that the bodies of Christians would be left behind in the rapture. In the 'Important note from the author' reprinted at the beginning of each novel, BeauSeigneur emphasized that his work would be more concerned with voice and characterization, and much less overtly didactic, than many earlier examples in the genre: 'Never assume that the characters – any of the characters – speak for the author.'[47] It was a point he reiterated in footnotes when the going got theologically rough.[48] Selective House may have aimed to 'bring the Gospel to a secular audience', but The Christ Clone Trilogy's evangelistic component was much less overt and much more confusing than that of the Left Behind series with which it competed.

The Trilogy's didactic intentions are clearly underplayed. The exhortations to Christians are irregular, though impressive enough when they appear: 'your wife was certainly not the first Christian to make the mistake of thinking she had plenty of time to get around to sharing her faith with those she cared about. But then the Rapture came, and there *was* no more time.'[49] This downplaying of didactic intent appears to be related to BeauSeigneur's

---

[46] 'Interview with James BeauSeigneur'.

[47] James BeauSeigneur, *In His Image*, The Christ Clone Trilogy (1997; reissued New York, 2003), 'Important note from the author', n.p.

[48] Ibid. 217 n. 31, 462 n. 64; BeauSeigneur, *Birth of an Age*, 246.

[49] BeauSeigneur, *Acts of God*, 140.

narrative focus. The Christ Clone Trilogy clearly assumes the basic premises of the Dispensationalism that had informed earlier rapture novels, but it differs from other examples of the genre in that it does not focus on a small group of tribulation saints surviving under the Antichrist's regime. The series does refer to tribulation saints – they are the troublesome members of 'a few fundamentalist Christian churches'[50] – but it does not describe how they come to faith after the rapture. The tribulation saints are incidental characters in this series, and there are no Sinner's Prayer conversions. An evangelistic component still exists, however: one character in the first novel exhorts another to remember that 'the one way God offers is entirely unrestricted, completely free, and totally accessible to each and every person on the planet. God is no farther from any of us than our willingness to call upon him.'[51] However, it takes a long time for these stray references to come together into a coherent evangelistic or exhortatory thrust. In fact, the first example of extended evangelistic exhortation in the trilogy occurs midway through the final novel.[52] Similarly, Decker's extremely low-key 'conversion' – which is only ever hinted at until his arrival by resurrection in the millennial kingdom – occurs in the few seconds of life that remain after his decapitation at the end of the third novel. The continual postponing of his conversion reshapes the traditional narrative pattern of rapture fiction. In Left Behind, and in most examples of the genre, the most significant conversions occur in the first instalment of the series, and subsequent novels narrate the dangers of their endurance: the story is one of survival and derring-do. In The Christ Clone Trilogy, by contrast, Decker's conversion occurs when he is an old man, in the final pages of the series, and so the story is one of quest and suspense. Necessarily, therefore, the two series narrate spirituality in markedly differing ways.

The Christ Clone Trilogy seems more concerned to narrate the dangers of New Age spirituality than to emphasize the development of an evangelical alternative. As in Frank Peretti's blockbusters *This Present Darkness* (1986) and *Piercing the Darkness* (1989), and in Irene Martin's rapture-romance novel *Emerald Thorn* (1991), the New Age

---

[50]   Ibid. 76–7.
[51]   BeauSeigneur, *In His Image*, 308.
[52]   BeauSeigneur, *Acts of God*, 149–83.

movement is presented as 'a tangled web of death'[53] masquerading as 'a bunch of clergymen, business leaders, and positive-thinking normal people trying to get the world to stop fighting, end war, and save the environment'.[54] The sinister web is ubiquitous. Beau-Seigneur lists individuals, organizations and cultural products that have expounded New Age beliefs, a list which includes Christian Science, familiar in earlier rapture fiction as an enemy of true faith, as well as *Star Wars* and *Star Trek*.[55] Adherents of New Age belief include 'heads of state, members of the World Court, celebrities from television and movies, sports figures, labor leaders, the entire board of the World Council of Churches, several Roman Catholic and Orthodox hierarchs, some high-profile Protestant ministers, and numerous other religious leaders'.[56] Even the 'best known preacher since Billy Graham' appears to have 'lost all faith in Yahweh' in favour of the new spirituality – although, admittedly, he had 'served for years on the World Council of Churches' and was, therefore, already theologically suspect.[57] The openness of these clergy to the unusual explains their capitulation to Christopher Goodman's claim to have been cloned from cells from the body of Jesus Christ that had been preserved on the Turin Shroud. Their credulity also enables him to become the focus of world faiths:

> For the Jews, he is Messiah; for the Christians, the returning Christ; for the Buddists he is the Fifth Buddha; for the Muslims, the Thirteenth Heir to Mohammed or Immam Mahdi; the Hindus call him Krishna; the Eckankar call him Mahanta; the Bahá'í look to the coming Most Great Peace; to the Zorastrians he is Shah-Bahram; to others he is Lord Maitreya, or Hadhisattva, or Krishnamurti, or Mithras, or Deva, or Hermes and Cush, or Janus, or Osiris.[58]

Nevertheless, Christopher's agenda is clear. If the evangelical char-

---

53 Irene Martin, *Emerald Thorn* (Oklahoma City, OK, 1991), 59.

54 Ibid. 175.

55 BeauSeigneur, *Birth of an Age*, 271.

56 BeauSeigneur, *Acts of God*, 46.

57 Ibid. 268.

58 BeauSeigneur, *Birth of an Age*, 309–10.

acters do not emphasize spirituality, he certainly does:'it is not my own godhood that I have come here to proclaim ... it is yours!'[59]

Christopher's proclamation of the divinity of humanity is intended as an assault on Yahweh. Christopher explains a complex alternative theology that has Yahweh as an extra-terrestrial being who is resisting the evolutionary development of humankind.[60] 'God is not at all what we have perceived him to be!'[61] 'Even when the writers of the Bible put the best face on his actions, ultimately they could not disguise the sadistic, twisted being that Yahweh truly is ... an arrogant, self-serving, maniacal despot!'[62] Instead of working for humanity's betterment, therefore, Yahweh had been frustrating the evolutionary leap in self-consciousness that would alert humans to a realization of their status and power as spiritual beings. That leap in human self-consciousness would demarcate history 'just as the coming of Christ had divided time between B.C. and A.D.'[63]

Not everyone is persuaded by Christopher's claims. The tribulation saints attempt to frustrate Christopher's plans by turning violently active. Their violence begins on the first day of the distribution of 'the communion', the small medicinal samples of Christopher's blood that accompany the mark of the beast: 'In scenes reminiscent of the sit-ins of the 1960s or the fundamentalist blockades of women's clinics in the 1990s, fundamentalists started the day in dozens of cities from Sydney to Beijing by attempting to block the entrance to communion clinics as they opened this morning.'[64] As violence spreads, communion clinics are firebombed, and although Fundamentalists deny responsibility, they are regularly described as 'terrorists'.[65] Other Fundamentalists engage in violent hijackings and in 'bombing and drive-by shootings at communion clinics'.[66] The sequence is an implicit warning against evangelical political activism. In the series, tribulation saints explain that initial Christian protests were up-ended

59 Ibid. 311.
60 Ibid. 246–75.
61 Ibid. 245–6.
62 Ibid. 260.
63 BeauSeigneur, *In His Image*, 483.
64 BeauSeigneur, *Acts of God*, 99–100.
65 Ibid. 102.
66 Ibid. 103, 105.

by the violence that had been stage-managed to discredit them.[67] Christopher later admits this, though he also points to the unpredictable element of the evangelical 'lunatic fringe'.[68] His strategy of smearing Evangelicals was clearly successful: 'the news media … make it sound like they're subhuman … It's a regular witch-hunt out there'.[69]

The emerging conspiracy theory warns evangelical readers of the dangers of getting involved in events they cannot ultimately control. Although BeauSeigneur has been politically active – he stood as a Republican Congressional candidate against a youthful Al Gore – his writing warns against uncalculating political activism. His novels are not denying that political interventions have a place in an authentic spirituality. Neither is the trilogy ambivalent about the ethical potential of sacred violence. Decker's friend, Tom Donafin, assassinates Christopher, but his violence is justified as that of the 'Avenger of Blood' (Numbers 35: 9), the last blood relative of Jesus Christ taking revenge for his murder.[70] The assassination is rationalized: 'When Tom shot Christopher, he was acting as Jesus's Avenger of Blood, striking the head of Satan in accordance with the prophecy in Genesis.'[71] The contrast with other rapture fiction is striking: in *Blood Moon*, the Antichrist is assassinated by an Islamic terrorist; in *Left Behind*, Rayford agonizes over his ambition to murder the Antichrist; in The Christ Clone Trilogy, Tom Donafin knows he is doing the right thing. Murder is a key component of sacred violence that evangelical rapture novels could once only attribute to the agents of Islamic terror.

---

[67] Ibid. 209.

[68] Ibid. 372.

[69] Ibid. 209. Compare this statement with the words of Wendell Bell, Professor Emeritus of Sociology at Yale University, who asserts that Evangelicals and other Fundamentalists 'disturb me. They arrogantly assume an attitude of religious superiority, including beliefs that their religion is the only true religion and that their God is the only true God … They are a threat to the kind of future I'm talking about. They are extremist and intolerant. In the United States, for example, some evangelical Christians have religious beliefs that include "fanaticism, superstition and obscurantism." Many such people believe "in personal (and self-serving) miracles," are ignorant "of basic science and history," demonize popular culture, try to censor textbooks, and display their separatist leanings by home-schooling their children': Wendell Bell, 'On Becoming and Being a Futurist: An Interview with Wendell Bell', *Journal of Futures Studies* 10 (2005), 113–24, at 119–20.

[70] BeauSeigneur, *Acts of God*, 195.

[71] Ibid. 199.

While The Christ Clone Trilogy rewrites the traditional codes of evangelical ethics, it also undermines some of what has made the trilogy distinctive. The Holy Spirit is not a major player in the series, for example. In earlier rapture novels, Scripture is obscure to unbelievers. In one of the earliest examples, Satan is depicted as being unable to understand the Bible: 'I fail to comprehend prophetic words, that men believe and thus increase their faith in God. I cast a shadow on the page when I stand before the prophet's words.'[72] In The Christ Clone Trilogy, however, readers are encouraged to believe that Scripture can be properly understood by anyone – irrespective of the enlightening work of the Holy Spirit. The unconverted Decker is informed that:

> Of all the religious documents in the world, the Bible is the only one that deals with events of the future with the same certainty that it deals with the events of the past and present. No other book, religious or otherwise, includes the minute details and the grand scale of prophecies as does the Bible; whether discussing the rise and fall of empires and king-doms that had not even been created when the prophecy was written, or prophecies of individuals who would not be born for hundreds of years afterward.[73]

The conversation goes on to include a long defence of messianic prophecies that Decker is clearly meant to understand.[74] A character gives him a Bible with 'a list of the key prophecies ... so you can look them up'.[75] Decker appears to do so, and later in the series, while still unconverted, uses that knowledge of Bible prophecy to anticipate events and make plans for contingencies.[76] The necessity of the illumination of the Holy Spirit is downplayed at the same time as the potential of the occult is exaggerated. Christopher is determined to exterminate the Jewish remnant and the tribulation saints, and, in the dramatic denouement of the series, sixty million of his troops march on Petra to battle the remnant using only their newly discovered occult powers.[77] Of course, they are defeated, but

72 Joseph Birkbeck Burroughs, *Titan, Son of Satan* (Oberlin, OH, 1905), 79.
73 BeauSeigneur, *Acts of God*, 158.
74 Ibid. 158–60.
75 Ibid. 163.
76 Ibid. 282.
77 Ibid. 428, 438.

not before they have identified spirituality as the battleground of the faithful. As so often in the genre, the novels imagine a handful of individuals pitted against the collective might of their spiritually empowered enemies.

★ ★ ★

The conflict between a godly minority and their spiritually empowered enemies was also foundational to the argument of *Y2K: The Day the World Shut Down* (1998). *Y2K* was a prophecy novel, in that it was concerned with apocalyptic events in the near future, but an anti-rapture novel, in that it disputed the foundational assumptions of Dispensationalism and argued that Christians should direct their energies into the long-term reconstruction of a Christian civilization. Written by Michael Hyatt and George Grant, *Y2K* was designed to popularize an alternative eschatology and piety within the American evangelical community. As the book was being published, Hyatt was coming to the end of a six-year career as a literary agent, and was joining Thomas Nelson Publishers, of which he has since become President and Chief Executive Officer.[78] George Grant was, and remains, a Presbyterian pastor and widely published author whose ecclesiastical and educational innovations paralleled his broad vision for the reformation of Evangelicalism. *Y2K* combined its authors' interests to combat dispensational hysteria within the evangelical community by positing an alternative to its pre-millennial concern.[79]

The novel displays its authors' acute consciousness of the prophetic anxiety that had taken hold of large parts of the evangelical world, an anxiety that seemed both the cause and consequence of the culture that produced Left Behind. In *Y2K*, the character most closely identified with the authorial voice is

---

[78] 'My Biography', <http://www.michaelhyatt.com/ about.htm>, accessed 13 March 2011.

[79] Surveys of evangelical responses to the Y2K phenomenon can be found in Lisa McMinn, 'Y2K, the Apocalypse, and Evangelical Christianity: The Role of Eschatological Belief in Church Responses', *Sociology of Religion* 62 (2001), 205–20; Andrea Hoplight Tapia, 'Techno-Armageddon: The Millennial Christian Response to Y2K', *Review of Religious Research* 43 (2002), 266–86; Nancy A. Schaefer, 'Y2K as an Endtime Sign: Apocalypticism in America at the *fin-de-millennium*', *Journal of Popular Culture* 38 (2004), 82–105.

not at all surprised that the year 2000 would attract the attentions of conspiracy theorists, prophetic doomsayers, eschatological seers, eternal pessimists, and various other worry-warts. The Y2K computer crisis had obviously become the latest Armageddon option: a convenient catastrophe for those who had alternately looked to killer bees, Beast-coded Social Security checks, hitch-hiking angels, conflict in the Middle East, secret federal cover-ups, biological warfare, Area 51 alien invasions, botched genetic engineering, and black helicopter deployments to usher in the last days of this, the terminal generation.[80]

This statement juxtaposes a list of the wacky, the weird and the wonderful with an allusion to Hal Lindsey's prophetic 'non-fiction', *The Terminal Generation* (1981). It is a telling dismissal of the most influential of the pre-millennial writers. Equally striking, however, is the novel's attack on the conspiratorial culture of a large and panicking section of popular Evangelicalism.[81] The impending crisis called for preparation, not panic, the novel claims, as it defends its authors from the charge of inactivity in an age in which 'the speculations of men ran to the frantic and the frenetic. Ecstatic eschatological significance was read into every change of any consequence – be it of the weather or of the government. Apocalyptic reticence was chided as faithlessness, while practical intransigence was enshrined as faithfulness.'[82]

The novel's authors were emphasizing an imminent danger – perhaps even a danger more imminent than the end-times scenario anticipated in Left Behind – but their emphasis was on long-term, not short-term, survival. In fact, their goal appeared to include reorientating Evangelicals into embracing a long-term vision for the renewal of Western culture. Consequently their novel begins and concludes with a cautionary tale: the description of a scene in St Peter's, Rome, on the last day of 999, when, 'weeping and wailing', Christians 'gathered there to await the end of the world'.[83]

---

[80] Mike Hyatt and George Grant, *Y2K: The Day the World Shut Down* (Nashville, TN, 1998), 84.

[81] The prophetic culture that provided several of these myths has been described in Paul Boyer, *When Time Shall Be No More: Prophecy Belief in Modern American Culture* (Cambridge, MA, 1992).

[82] Hyatt and Grant, *Y2K*, 264.

[83] Ibid. 1.

As their expectations were unfulfilled, the congregants left St Peter's to rebuild the world they imagined they would never see. *Y2K* calls on its evangelical readers to go and do likewise.

This reorientation towards the contemporary world would require a redefinition of piety. *Y2K* refined the quality of Christian 'faithfulness' to include 'apocalyptic reticence'. Spirituality was no longer about the construction of a conspiratorial worldview or a longing for an escapist rapture, but was now an activist and programmed lifestyle that made virtues of prudence and caution. Strangely, however, *Y2K* contains very little reference to spiritual development or the pastoral issues this reorientation would involve. The novel's concerns are certainly not evangelistic. Its protagonist, Bob Priam, is, like his counterpart in Left Behind, largely indifferent to spirituality, but unlike Rayford Steele or Jeremy Armstrong, he does not pass through any conversion experience. He appears as a lukewarm believer, who gets to grips with his faith after he loses his job. *Y2K* appears, therefore, to have been written for readers within the evangelical camp. The spirituality which is developed is that of a cautiously activist faith. Nevertheless, the novel's exhortatory dialogue – so common in the prophecy fiction genre – is here restricted to making points about family life and educational ethics, as well as business and technical solutions to the much-vaunted millennium bug.[84] At times the novel's emphases appear surprising. Priam's wife insisted that 'the younger women needed to fully comprehend the importance of the domestic arts that so many made light of. The word *faith*, she loved to point out, is used less than 300 times in the Bible. The verb *to eat* is used more than 800 times.'[85] *Y2K* does not make the obvious application – that, in the development of an evangelical spirituality, eating might be more important than believing – but the comment does underscore the different set of priorities at play in the novel. This is a robustly, if rationally, activist spirituality.

The rationalism of that activist spirituality becomes evident in the novel's concern to encourage its readers to prepare for life after a potential doomsday on 1 January 2000, when, as was widely expected in the late 1990s, the technological infrastructure of the West could suddenly collapse. Hyatt and Grant used the novel to

[84]   Ibid. 151.
[85]   Ibid. 140.

propose a traditional approach to life, a method of preparation they described as the 'grandma strategy':

> for many Americans the grandma strategy may seem a little radical – get out of debt, keep a productive garden, have some food on hand in case of a storm, learn how to tend sickness at home, be able to defend yourself, have some basic tools around and the skills to use them, have a good contingency plan if times get tough, save up for a rainy day, and simplify your needs.[86]

Radical or not, the 'grandma strategy' was deemed sufficiently important for the novel to provide in its exhortatory dialogue an extended description of what it might involve. In Left Behind, by contrast, exhortatory dialogue focused instead on issues of faith, ethics and Christian living.[87]

It is hardly surprising, therefore, that the conclusion to Y2K lacks any kind of evangelistic zeal, or even any kind of significant Christian reference. Y2K ends by explaining that the 'the great lesson of each *fin de siècle* ... not just those of the tenth and twentieth centuries' is that survival could not be solitary. It was a startling alternative to the relentless individualism of the dispensational texts. Y2K hammers home the point: 'ordinary people gathered together in community are ultimately the ones who determine the outcome of human events – not kings and princes, not masters and tyrants, not even clocks and calendars ... plain folks, simple people, can literally change the course of history'.[88] And Hyatt was certainly attempting to do so. The novel's endpaper provided an advert for his *New York Times* bestseller, *The Millennium Bug: How to Survive the Coming Chaos* (1998), which was, in turn, part of his wider interest in disaster preparation: his e-business was selling a year's supply of food for $3,395 plus shipping.[89] However, as the novel noted elsewhere, 'preparing for the end, though perhaps dispiriting, is not nearly so difficult as preparing for what comes after the end' – especially if events disconfirm your direst predictions.[90] In fact, there was to be no 'coming crisis', for the world did not

86 Ibid. 191.
87 Ibid. 227–32.
88 Ibid. 267.
89 Schaefer, 'Y2K as an Endtime Sign', 88.
90 Hyatt and Grant, Y2K, 3.

'shut down'. But at least the disappointed did not have to face it on their own.

★ ★ ★

Rapture and prophecy novels are directly engaged in debate about the possibility and character of evangelical spirituality. Left Behind, *Blood Moon* and The Christ Clone Trilogy maintain the popular dispensational assumption that godliness is linked to the development of an acutely sensitive conspiratorial worldview, while *Y2K* refutes this position, and argues instead that a practical this-worldliness should characterize the faithful. The dispensational novels emphasize the importance of events in the Middle East, while *Y2K* assumes that American issues are the only ones that count. The novels also divide over their preference for a dispensational individualism or collective alternative. These differences are to some extent predictable. What is surprising is that each of these novels – both those which advance and those which undermine Dispensationalism – point to the need for short-term alarm. The dispensational novels assume the possibility of an imminent rapture, while *Y2K* assumes the possibility of a worldwide technological collapse. Perhaps, ultimately, it is this agreement that is the most striking characteristic of the debate. In the late 1990s, Evangelicals were debating prophecy, theology, exegesis, ethics and their position in political culture. Their interventions, represented by Left Behind, had gained unprecedented market success. But if these novels are anything to go by, believers agreed that their safety in the present might not long endure. Their piety and polemic insisted on the point: a truly evangelical spirituality – in Dispensationalism and also far beyond it – could never escape from a pervasive sense of alarm.

Trinity College Dublin